THE HOMERIC HYMN
TO DEMETER

THE
HOMERIC HYMN
TO DEMETER

EDITED BY

N. J. RICHARDSON
Fellow of Merton College
Oxford

OXFORD
AT THE CLARENDON PRESS

Oxford University Press, Walton Street, Oxford OX2 6DP

OXFORD LONDON GLASGOW
NEW YORK TORONTO MELBOURNE WELLINGTON
KUALA LUMPUR SINGAPORE JAKARTA HONG KONG TOKYO
DELHI BOMBAY CALCUTTA MADRAS KARACHI
NAIROBI DAR ES SALAAM CAPE TOWN

First published 1974
Reprinted 1979

Printed in Great Britain
at the University Press, Oxford
by Eric Buckley
Printer to the University

TO

COLIN HARDIE

PREFACE

THE *Homeric Hymn to Demeter* has not previously been the subject of a separate commentary in English. The edition of Allen and Sikes (Macmillan, 1904), and the revision of this by Allen and Halliday (Oxford, 1936), cover all the Hymns, and although both of these (particularly the first) contain much useful material, they remain selective and uneven. The *Hymn to Demeter*, by the nature of its subject, repays study at more than one level. It is not only a fine example of post-Homeric epic poetry, but also the earliest literary work which sheds light on the Eleusinian Mysteries, whose foundation it celebrates. I have tried to take account of both these aspects, by considering its place in relation to other early epic poetry, and also its religious significance. I hope that the length of the commentary will not detract from appreciation of the poem's intrinsic beauty, but will help to place it more clearly in its literary and religious context.

A mechanical aid to the assessment of the poetic technique is provided by the list of formulaic parallels which accompanies the text. An account of the system used for these is given in the Introduction (p. 30), together with some general discussion. Parallels from later Greek poetry which I have noted as possibly significant are also given with the text. The *apparatus criticus* makes no attempt to list all past emendations in full, and I have little of my own to add in the way of improved textual readings. In quite a number of cases, however, I have found the readings of earlier editions preferable to those of the Oxford editors. As there is only one surviving manuscript of the *Hymn*, and this contains several lacunae, the possibility of future improvement of the text, by emendation or discovery of new papyri, is still open.

This book owes its beginnings in large measure to the late Professor Eduard Fraenkel, whom I consulted at the outset, and who suggested that I should work on the *Hymn to Demeter*. Later also he took an interest in its progress for which I was very grateful.

Before beginning work on the commentary itself I had the benefit of a term spent at Cologne University, where I was able to take advantage of the wide knowledge of Greek religion and early epic poetry of Professor R. Merkelbach. I am grateful to him for giving me a most interesting insight into the background to the myths of Persephone and Demeter.

At all stages I have received much encouragement from Professor H. Lloyd-Jones. He and Professor G. S. Kirk examined this work when it was submitted as a doctoral thesis in 1970, and I am very grateful to them both for many helpful suggestions and criticisms.

I should also like to thank Professor Anna Davies, Professor M. H. Jameson, Mr. D. M. Lewis, Mr. O. Taplin, and Mr. N. G. Wilson, for their assistance on various points, and Mr. P. W. Martin for some valuable discussions.

My greatest debt of gratitude is due to my supervisor, Dr. M. L. West. How much I have profited from his published work will, I hope, become apparent in the course of what follows. I also owe more than I can express to his patient and painstaking scrutiny of the various stages of the commentary, and to the numerous observations, corrections, and additions which he has made. It should hardly be necessary to add that any defects of scholarship or presentation are entirely my own responsibility.

The manuscript of this work was given to the Press before the appearance of Professor W. Burkert's book *Homo Necans* (Berlin, 1972), and I regret that I have been unable to take account of his treatment of the Eleusinian Mysteries (pp. 274 ff.). Although I am not convinced by his argument for the central importance of sacrificial ritual in the Mysteries, I have found his discussion of the evidence useful and stimulating.

Dr. Fritz Graf, of Zürich University, very kindly allowed me to read his dissertation on the Eleusinian Mysteries and the Orphic poetry of Athens, and again I regret that when I did so it was too late for me to take account of it in this commentary. His work, which will be published shortly, will be essential reading for any student of this difficult subject, and it corrects a number of misconceptions of earlier scholars which have coloured my own brief discussion of the topic (pp. 79 ff.). He also read a draft of this commentary, and made a number of valuable suggestions for which I am most grateful.

Finally, I wish to express my thanks to the Clarendon Press for their patient assistance in bringing a refractory manuscript to the light of day, and to my wife for her constant support and interest. The book is dedicated to my tutor, in gratitude for his teaching, friendship, and encouragement.

N. J. R.

Merton College
Oxford
June 1973

NOTE TO THE SECOND IMPRESSION

In detecting misprints and minor errors I have been assisted by Dr. A. W. James, Mr. R. Janko, and Professor M. L. West. I regret that it has not been possible to make any more substantial changes in the light of recent publications, but I should like to draw attention in particular to the valuable criticisms and suggestions made by the following reviewers:

W. Burkert, *Gnomon* 49 (1977), 440 ff.
A. W. James, *JHS* 96 (1976), 165 ff. (on the text)
M. H. Jameson, *Athenaeum* 54 (1976), 441 ff. (mainly on religious aspects)
H. Metzger, *RÉG* 89 (1976), 408 ff. (on the artistic background to the myths)

A select list of recent books and articles is also added here as a supplement to my earlier Bibliography:

A. EDITIONS AND TRANSLATIONS

CÀSSOLA, F., *Inni Omerici*, Milan, 1975. A useful new edition, with introduction, text, translation, and commentary.
ATHANASSAKIS, A., *The Homeric Hymns*, Baltimore and London, 1976. Introduction, translation, and notes.

B. BOOKS AND ARTICLES

1. *Text, Epic Technique, etc.*

FORDERER, M., *Anfang und Ende der abendländischen Lyrik. Untersuchungen zum homerischen Apollonhymnus und zu A. Koltz*, Amsterdam, 1971.
GAISSER, J. H., 'Noun-epithet Combinations in the Homeric Hymn to Demeter', *TAPA* 104 (1974), 113 ff.

LENZ, L. H., *Der homerische Aphroditehymnus und die Aristie des Aineias in der Ilias*, Diss. Frankfurt, Bonn, 1975.

LORD, M. L., 'Withdrawal and Return: An Epic Story Pattern in the *Homeric Hymn to Demeter* and in the Homeric Poems', *CJ* 62 (1967), 241 ff.

PODBIELSKI, H., *La structure de l'hymne homérique à Aphrodite*, Wrocław, 1971.

PAVESE, C. O., *Tradizioni e Generi Poetici della Grecia arcaica*, Roma, 1972.

—— *Studi sulla Tradizione epica rapsodica*, Roma, 1974.

WEST, M. L., *Hesiod, Works and Days*, Oxford, 1978.

2. Cult, Religion, and Ethics

BÉRARD, C., *Anodoi, Essai sur l'imagerie des passages chthoniens*, Neuchatel, 1974.

BURKERT, W., *Griechische Religion der archaischen und klassischen Epoche*, Stuttgart, 1977.

CLINTON, K., *The Sacred Officials of the Eleusinian Mysteries*, Philadelphia, 1974.

GRAF, F., *Eleusis und die orphische Dichtung Athens in vorhellenistischer Zeit*, Berlin, 1974.

MEULI, K., *Gesammelte Schriften*, Basel, 1975.

PRICE, T. HADZISTELIOU, *Kourotrophos. Cults and Representations of the Greek Nursing Deities*, Leiden, 1978.

Merton College   N. J. R.
Oxford
September 1978

CONTENTS

ABBREVIATIONS

THE four major *Homeric Hymns* are referred to as follows:—

Ap.	*Hymn to Apollo* (*Hy.* 3)
Aph.	*Hymn to Aphrodite* (*Hy.* 5)
Dem.	*Hymn to Demeter* (*Hy.* 2)
Herm.	*Hymn to Hermes* (*Hy.* 4)

The remainder are referred to by their number in Allen's Oxford text, as '*Hy.* 1' etc.

The first edition of the Oxford commentary on the *Hymns* (1904) is referred to as 'Allen and Sikes', the second (1936) as 'Allen and Halliday'. For other editions see Introduction, Section XII.

Quotations from Hesiod's *Theogony* are from M. L. West's edition (Oxford, 1966). Hesiodic fragments are cited from the edition of R. Merkelbach and M. L. West (Oxford, 1967), the *Works and Days* ('Hes. *Op.*') and *Shield of Heracles* ('Hes. *Sc.*') from Rzach's Teubner edition (Leipzig, 1902).

The following abbreviations may also be noted:

Beazley, *ABV*	J. D. Beazley, *Attic Black-Figure Vase-Painters* (Oxford, 1956).
Beazley, *ARV*	J. D. Beazley, *Attic Red-Figure Vase-Painters*, 1st ed. (Oxford, 1942).
Beazley, *ARV*²	The same, 2nd ed. (Oxford, 1963).
Chantraine, *GH*	P. Chantraine, *Grammaire Homérique* (Paris, 2 vols., 1942–53).
Denniston, *GP*	J. D. Denniston, *Greek Particles*, 2nd ed. (Oxford, 1954).
Deubner, *AF*	L. Deubner, *Attische Feste*, 2nd ed. (Hildesheim, 1966).
Ebeling	H. Ebeling, *Lexicon Homericum* (Leipzig, 1885).
Frazer, *GB*³	J. G. Frazer, *The Golden Bough*, 3rd ed., 12 vols., (London, 1911–18).
Frisk	H. Frisk, *Griechisches etymologisches Wörterbuch* (Heidelberg, 1954–70).
Hoffmann, *Gr. Dial.*	O. Hoffmann, *Die griechischen Dialekte*, 3 vols. (Göttingen, 1891–8).
K–B	R. Kühner, *Ausführliche Grammatik der griechischen Sprache*, 1. Teil, besorgt von F. Blass (Hannover, 1890–2).

K–G   The same, 2. Teil, besorgt von B. Gerth
                       (Hannover, 1898–1904).
Kretschmer,   P. Kretschmer, *Die griechischen Vaseninschriften*
  Vaseninsch.   (Gütersloh, 1894).
La Roche, *HU*   J. La Roche, *Homerische Untersuchungen* (Leipzig,
                       1869).
Lehrs, *QE*   K. Lehrs, *Quaestiones Epicae* (Königsberg, 1837).
LSJ   Liddell–Scott–Jones, *A Greek–English Lexicon*
                       (Oxford, 1925–40).
LSJ, *Supplement*   The same. *A Supplement*, ed. E. A. Barber, P.
                       Maas, M. Scheller, and M. L. West (Oxford,
                       1968).
Monro, *HG*²   D. B. Monro, *A Grammar of the Homeric Dialect*,
                       2nd ed. (Oxford, 1891).
Nilsson, *Gesch.* i³   M. P. Nilsson, *Geschichte der griechischen Religion*,
                       Bd. I, 3rd ed. (Munich, 1967).
Nilsson, *Gesch.* ii² The same, Bd. II, 2nd ed. (Munich, 1961).
PMG   D. L. Page, *Poetae Melici Graeci* (Oxford, 1962).
Preller–Robert   L. Preller, *Griechische Mythologie*, 4. Aufl.
                       bearbeitet von C. Robert (Berlin, 1894–1926).
Pritchard, *ANET*²   *Ancient Near Eastern Texts*, ed. J. B. Pritchard,
                       2nd ed. (Princeton, 1955).
RE   Pauly–Wissowa, *Real-Encyclopädie der classischen
                       Altertumswissenschaft* (Stuttgart, 1894–   ).
Roscher   *Ausführliches Lexikon der griechischen und römischen
                       Mythologie*, hrsg. von W. H. Roscher (Leipzig–
                       Berlin, 1884–1937).
Schulze, *QE*   W. Schulze, *Quaestiones Epicae* (Gütersloh, 1892).
Schwyzer, *Gr. Gr.*   E. Schwyzer, *Griechische Grammatik* (Munich,
                       1939–50).
Ziehen, *LGS*   L. Ziehen, *Leges Graecorum Sacrae*, Pars altera
                       (Leipzig, 1906).

INTRODUCTION

I. SUMMARY OF THE HYMN

1–90. *The Rape, and Demeter's Search*

1–32. After stating his subject (Demeter and the Rape of Persephone), the poet at once goes on to describe how Persephone was carried off by Hades, with the consent of Zeus. She was gathering flowers with the nymphs on the plain of Nysa when the earth gaped and Hades sprang forth and carried her away on his chariot. Her cries for help were heard by no one except Hecate and Helios, and Zeus was far away.

33–90. At last Demeter heard her, and was stricken with grief. For nine days she wandered in search of her, with burning torches, fasting, and without washing herself. On the tenth Hecate met her, and announced that she had heard Persephone's cry, and together they went to Helios. Demeter asked him for information, and he told her that it was Hades who had carried off her daughter, and attempted to console her.

91–304. *Demeter at the House of Celeus*

91–117. In her anger, Demeter leaves the gods and wanders on earth, disguised as an old woman. She comes to Eleusis, where she sits beside the well Parthenion. Here she is met by the four daughters of Celeus, king of Eleusis, who ask her who she is.

118–68. She replies with a false story, that she has been captured by pirates from Crete and brought to Thoricos in Attica, from where she has escaped, and come to Eleusis. She asks to be allowed to act as a nurse or housekeeper to a family in Eleusis. The girls tell her the names of the rulers of the town, and offer her a position as nurse to Celeus' baby son, Demophon.

169–211. They run to the palace, to get the consent of their mother Metaneira, and then return, and lead Demeter to the palace. As she enters, she takes her divine form again for a moment. She is offered a chair, but refuses, until the maid Iambe gives her a stool. She sits down in silent sorrow, until Iambe makes her laugh. She refuses to drink wine, but accepts a simple mixture of barley and water.

212–55. Metaneira welcomes her, and asks her to nurse the child. She promises to keep him from all harm, and taking him anoints him secretly with ambrosia, breathes on him, and holds him in her arms. At night she places him in the fire, to make him immortal. His parents are amazed at his growth, and Metaneira watches and detects her. She cries out, and Demeter is angry and snatches Demophon from the fire.

256–74. She condemns mankind for their folly, and says that Demophon cannot be immortal, but will have an annual ceremony in his honour. She reveals herself, orders a temple and altar to be built outside the city wall, and promises to teach the Eleusinians her rites.

275–304. Once more the goddess resumes her true form, and leaves the palace. Metaneira is speechless with terror. Her daughters jump from their beds and come to the rescue, trying to comfort the baby Demophon. All night they attempt to propitiate the goddess, and next day Celeus is told what has happened. He summons the people, and they build the temple and altar. Demeter sits in it, grieving for her daughter.

305–489. *The Famine, Return of Persephone, and Institution of the Mysteries*

305–45. Demeter causes a dreadful famine, which threatens the existence of mankind and the sacrifices and honours of the gods. Zeus sends Iris, and then all the gods in turn, to ask her to relent, but she refuses. At last he sends Hermes to bring back Persephone.

346–74. Hermes asks Hades to let her go. He consents, and tells her to return, promising that she will have great honours as his wife, both in heaven and below the earth. He gives her a pomegranate-seed to eat, secretly, which binds her to return to him.

375–433. Hermes takes her back to earth, and she is reunited with her mother, who asks if she has eaten in the underworld, and how she was carried off. She tells her what has happened.

434–58. They spend the day in happy reunion, and are joined by Hecate, who becomes an attendant of Persephone. Zeus sends Rhea to ask them to come to Olympus, promising that Persephone will live there for two-thirds of the year. The rest she must spend in the underworld.

459–82. Rhea gives her message, and Demeter consents. She makes life return to the fields, and teaches her solemn rites to the princes of Eleusis, rites whose secrecy is absolute, and which guarantee to the initiate alone a happy fate after death.

483–9. The goddesses go up to Olympus. Happy is the man on earth whom they favour, and to whom they send the blessing of Prosperity!

490–5. *Final Invocation*

The *Hymn* closes with the customary invocation and a prayer for divine favour.

II. THE NATURE OF THE *HOMERIC HYMNS*

The collection called Ὁμήρου Ὕμνοι consists of hymns in praise of Greek deities, of widely differing lengths and of various periods. The *Hymn to Demeter* is one of the four longest, the others being the *Hymn to Apollo* (which appears to be two poems joined together), and those to Hermes and Aphrodite. The *Hymn to Dionysus* which is placed first in the collection is fragmentary, and was perhaps also quite long, and the second, complete *Hymn to Dionysus* (No. 7) is of 59 lines. The others vary in length from three lines (No. 13) to forty-nine (No. 19).

It is generally (but not universally) accepted that all the four longer hymns belong to the archaic period, i.e. approximately the seventh and sixth centuries. Many of the shorter ones are impossible to date, but the *Hymn to Pan* is probably not earlier than the fifth century, those to the Sun and Moon (Nos. 31 and 32) can hardly antedate the Alexandrian period, and the *Hymn to Ares* (No. 8) seems by its content and style to belong rather to the hymns of Proclus, the Neo-Platonist philosopher of late antiquity, which are found together with the Homeric and Orphic hymns in some manuscripts (cf. M. L. West, *CQ* 20 (1970), 300 ff.).

The earliest reference to a *Homeric Hymn* describes it as a προοίμιον, i.e. prelude (Thuc. 3. 104, of the *Hymn to Apollo*) and it is fairly clear that in origin at least they were intended as preludes to epic recitation. They show in general the characteristics of traditional epic poetry, and were evidently originally composed for recitation. Some actually close with an appeal to the deity for victory in the poetic contest (cf. 6. 19–20, and similarly 10. 5, 24. 5, 25. 6, which ask the deity to give the song honour and favour). Other closing formulae show that the poet is now going on to another song, and in the case of the later hymns to the Sun and Moon he explicitly states that the subject-matter of these songs will be the deeds of the heroes, i.e. epic narrative of the type of the *Iliad* or *Odyssey* (cf. on *Dem.* 495 and also on *Dem.* 1–3). In the *Odyssey* itself we find that it was customary for a singer to begin with an invocation to a deity (*Od.* 8. 499, and Schol. ad loc.). The *Iliad* and *Odyssey* invoke the Muse at the outset, and one may note the alternative opening line of the *Iliad*, Μούcαc ἀείδω καὶ Ἀπόλλωνα κλυτότοξον. More relevant are the hymns at the beginning of Hesiod's *Theogony* and *Works and Days* (cf. West on *Th.* 1–115).

We are told by Pindar (*Nem.* 2. 1–3) that the Homeridae used to begin Διὸc ἐκ προοιμίου. It is thus reasonable to conclude that it was customary at a poetic recitation, and perhaps especially in a contest, for the poet to preface his epic narrative with a hymn to whichever deity was appropriate to the place and circumstances of composition. It is sometimes assumed that such invocations were originally quite brief, and later were expanded into an epic narrative. But the contrary may equally well have been the case (cf. West on *Th.* 94–7). Expansion is a characteristic tendency of all epic traditions (and story-telling in general), but abbreviation is equally an epic technique (seen, for example, in the recapitulation of myths from earlier generations in the *Iliad* and *Odyssey*).

The length of the major hymns has led some scholars to question whether they could have been intended as preludes to further recitation (cf. Allen and Halliday, xciv f.). This would seem to show neglect of the character of early epic, and the powers of endurance of its audience. The *Hymn to Demeter*, at least, gives no grounds for supposing that it was not composed by a poet using the same techniques of traditional oral poetry as Homer and Hesiod. One might therefore assume that the circumstances of composition were also traditional, although by this stage the exact sense of the closing formula (*Dem.* 495) was probably forgotten (cf. note ad loc.). In the hymns composed at a later period, and certainly those of post-classical date, the use of such formulae was probably only a literary device. But in the archaic period there is no reason to assume this.

III. THE *HYMN TO DEMETER*:
DATE AND CIRCUMSTANCES OF COMPOSITION

This leads us to a consideration of when and where this *Hymn* was composed, and for what purpose. The style and language, as will be shown below, are not essentially different from those of the Homeric and Hesiodic poems. To a large extent the formulaic language agrees with that of Homer, but there are also a noticeably large number of words and phrases which are paralleled first in Hesiod. In some cases the parallels actually suggest direct awareness of Hesiod's poetry, and although this cannot be proved, the cumulative effect is striking. There are also a few passages where it is possible that the poet has in mind a particular passage in the *Iliad* or *Odyssey*. The *Hymn to Aphrodite* shares with the *Hymn to Demeter* certain phrases and words not found elsewhere in early epic. Here it is impossible to establish a definite precedence, but in the case of Homer and Hesiod the weight of evidence tends to suggest that the *Hymn to Demeter* was composed later than, and with an awareness of, at least the *Theogony*, and perhaps also the *Iliad* and *Odyssey*.[1]

The dating of these poems is a matter for debate. Recent scholarship, at least in England, has favoured the late eighth century for the *Iliad* and *Odyssey*.[2] West has also argued for a date in the late eighth century for the *Theogony*, and would place the *Works and Days* not long afterwards (*Theogony*, pp. 40 ff.), although he regards Hesiod as prior to Homer.[3] These dates are useful as rough estimates only: obviously one is dealing here with a balance of probabilities.

More important perhaps is the occurrence of literary and artistic references to Homeric themes. The verses on the Ischia scyphos referring to 'the cup of Nestor' unfortunately do not prove anything about knowledge of our *Iliad*.[4] The sudden popularity of the Polyphemus episode after *c.* 680 (two proto-

---

[1] For an attempt to state a case against any dependence of this kind see J. A. Notopoulos, *AJP* 83 (1962), 337 ff. He is criticized by Kirk, *YCS* 20 (1966), 155 ff.

[2] e.g. Kirk, *Songs*, 282 ff., D. H. F. Gray, *Fifty Years (and Twelve) of Classical Scholarship* (Oxford, 1968), 29 f.

[3] For some recent criticism of this cf. Edwards, *Language of Hesiod*, 203 ff.

[4] Cf. Dihle, *Hermes* 97 (1969), 257 ff. For the view that they do see most recently K. Rüter, *Zeitschr. für Pap. u. Epigr.* 2 (1968), 231 ff., esp. 249 ff.

Attic examples, one proto-Argive, and one from Caere)[1] might be more significant, as it could suggest a recent literary version with wide appeal. But artistic fashion or other unknown factors may equally well be responsible. Trojan themes in general appear with certainty in art from *c.* 700 B.C., but no definite representation of a scene described in the *Iliad* appears before *c.* 625 B.C., and in Attica not before the second quarter of the sixth century. Such representations are not common in Attica until *c.* 550, and until *c.* 520 they are largely taken from the last part of the poem and continue to be relatively infrequent (cf. Johansen, *The Iliad in Early Greek Art,* 25 ff., 46 ff., 85 ff., 223 ff.). Johansen concluded that the *Iliad* did not become well known and popular at Athens until the end of the sixth century, and that this was to be connected with the tradition about Hipparchus (Ps. Plat. *Hipparch.* 228 b; Johansen, 231 ff.). It seems clear that the poet of our *Hymn,* if not of necessity himself from Attica (cf. Introduction, 52 ff.: Atticisms), was at least intimately acquainted with Eleusis, its topography and ritual, and was probably composing for recitation to an Attic audience. If the vase-paintings could be treated as at all relevant, they might be thought to point towards the sixth rather than the seventh century for composition by a poet working in Attica.[2] But it is dangerous to argue from art to literature, and we must also remember that a professional bard's knowledge of Homeric and Hesiodic poetry must have been wider than that of other people. Probably, therefore, no definite conclusion as to *terminus post quem* can be drawn, although a date before the second quarter of the seventh century seems unlikely.

A *terminus ante quem* is also hard to establish with certainty. The *Hymn* does not mention Athens, and this has often been held to point to a date before Athens began to take control of the Mysteries.[3] According to tradition the incorporation of Eleusis into the Attic state belonged to the prehistoric period, but

---

[1] Cf. K. F. Johansen, *The Iliad in Early Greek Art* (Copenhagen, 1967), 34 f.; Kirk, o.c. 285.

[2] One might also note that Solon seems 'not to have made much use of Homer', as opposed to epic tradition in general, although he evidently knew the poems. Cf. Bowra, *Early Greek Elegists* (Cambridge, 1935), 78.

[3] Walton, however, argued that the silence was deliberate, the *Hymn* being an Eleusinian polemic against Athens soon after the Athenian take-over. Cf. *Harv. Theol. Rev.* 45 (1952), 114, and my notes on *Dem.* 126.

Eleusis was allowed to retain control of the Mysteries.[1] Modern scholars have a tendency to believe that Eleusis was not in fact incorporated until the end of the seventh century, or that it seceded and was then reconquered (cf. Allen and Halliday, 112 n. 1, Mylonas, *Eleusis*, 63). There is no real evidence of this.[2] Equally, the fact that the Archon Basileus at Athens was in charge of administration of the Mysteries does not indicate that Athenian control antedates the creation of this office at the beginning of the seventh century. There is, however, some evidence that Athenian interest in the Mysteries first becomes significant and noticeable in the mid sixth century (see below).

Noack (*Eleusis*, 45 ff.) wished to date the *Hymn* before 600 B.C., on the grounds that it refers to a temple (270) but not a hall of initiation, and that such a hall was not built until the end of the seventh century. The *Hymn*'s silence on this point was taken to indicate its early date (cf. also Allen and Halliday, 111 f.).

This argument is refuted by Mylonas (*Eleusis*, 38 ff.). It is clear that the term νηός (or νεώς) was used in the classical period of the 'Telesterion' (as modern scholars call it). The *Hymn* could therefore refer to the building of the Archaic period, which Noack considered to be the first Telesterion. Recent excavation has also revealed a construction of the Mycenaean period on the same site, which the excavators believe to have been used for cult purposes, and this was apparently followed by an apsidal building of the Geometric period (Mylonas, 33 ff., 57 ff.). Despite the lack of positive evidence for the religious function of the Mycenaean building, and the rather slight evidence for a Geometric building, one evidently cannot date the νηός of the *Hymn* to any particular period, since it might refer equally to the Mycenaean, Geometric, or Archaic building (cf. Appendix I).

Arguments have also been drawn from the omission by the *Hymn* of certain features of Eleusinian cult and legend which

---

[1] Cf. Paus. 1. 38. 3 for this version. Elsewhere (1. 27. 4) Pausanias insists on the authenticity of his tradition as against others. Thucydides, however (2. 15), and Plutarch (*Thes.* 10. 3) date the political incorporation of Eleusis into Attica to the time of Theseus. Cf. also Philochorus, *FGH* 328. 107 (and Jacoby ad loc.), Andron, *FGH* 10. 14. There does not seem to have been any attempt to place the incorporation after the prehistoric period.

[2] The war in Hdt. 1. 30 is not necessarily against Eleusis, and cannot be dated. 'Laws of Solon', e.g. Andoc. *de Myst.* 111 and Sokolowski, *Lois sacrées, Supplément*, no. 10, prove nothing. Cf. MacDowell on Andocides l.c.

were later prominent. Eumolpus, the eponym of the priestly
genos Eumolpidae, is twice mentioned (153–5, 474–7), but his
counterpart in later cult, Keryx, ancestor of the Kerykes, does
not appear. The origin of this *genos* is obscure.[1] According to
Pausanias (1. 38. 3) there were two versions of their genealogy,
one making them descendants of Keryx son of Eumolpus, the
other, which was that supported by the Kerykes themselves, de-
riving them from Hermes and Aglauros, the daughter of Cecrops.
This second genealogy is the normal one, with variation of the
name of the Cecropid (cf. *IG* xiv. 1389. 32–3, Poll. 8. 103, Schol.
Hom. *Il.* 1. 334, Schol. Aeschin. 1. 20), and it has generally been
assumed that the connection with Cecrops indicates an Athenian
origin. This is supported by the fact that the *genos* played a part
in a number of Athenian cults, which had no direct connection
with Eleusis, i.e. the Dipoleia (cf. Töpffer, *Attische Genealogie*,
149 ff., *IG* i². 843A. 7, Sokolowski, *Lois sacrées, Supplément*, no. 2)
and the cults of Delian and Pythian Apollo (Ath. 234 e, Foucart,
Les Mystères, 141 ff.). The Kerykes provided not only the Keryx
of the Mysteries, but also the Dadouchos, the priest second in
importance to the Hierophant at Eleusis. Presumably he existed
before Athens took over control of the cult, and he must have
had a *genos*. Possibly there was a *genos* of Kerykes both at Eleusis
and at Athens, and the two were merged after the Athenian
take-over. But it still remains unclear why it should be the Keryx,
rather than the Dadouchos, whose name was attached to the
genos.

In any case, however, the absence of mention of a Keryx,
amongst the other Eleusinian rulers in the *Hymn*, may well be
significant, and is possibly an indication of composition before
the period of Athenian control.

The *Hymn* does not mention the procession along the Sacred
Way from Athens to Eleusis, or the eponym of this procession,
Iacchus, whose name derived from the cry (ἰαχή) of the initiates
during the journey. Herodotus (8. 65) implies that this was
already an established procedure by 480 B.C. It has been suggested that Demeter's journey from Thoricos to Eleusis, in her
'false tale' (*Dem.* 126 ff.), must have taken her via Athens and

---

[1] Cf. Dittenberger, 'Die Eleusinischen Keryken', *Hermes* 20 (1885), 1–40;
P. Roussel, *Mélanges Bidez* (Brussels, 1934), 819–34; Foucart, *Les Mystères*, 141 ff.;
J. Töpffer, *Attische Genealogie*, 80 ff.

along the Sacred Way. But if this were intended by the poet the failure to mention Athens would be still more remarkable (cf. notes on *Dem.* 126). It seems more likely that the procession was not yet in existence.

It is also noticeable that Triptolemus, who is mentioned among the Eleusinian princes in *Dem.* 153 and 474, receives no special prominence. Later, the myth of his receipt of the gifts of corn and agriculture from Demeter, and his communication of these to the rest of mankind, became very popular in Attic art and literature. This theme first appears on Attic vases of the mid sixth century, and is particularly frequent in the first half of the fifth century. The *Hymn*, however, actually excludes this story, by presupposing that agriculture was already in existence before the Rape of Persephone (305 ff.: cf. notes ad loc.). The story was very probably much older than the *Hymn*, and there may be a reflection of it in *Dem.* 450 ff. and 470 ff. (cf. notes ad loc.). But the Mission of Triptolemus plays no part in the epic poet's account.

The last point of interest is the relative position of Celeus and Eumolpus. In the *Hymn* it seems to be implied, although it is nowhere explicitly stated, that Celeus has a leading position among the Eleusinian princes (cf. *Dem.* 97, 296 ff., 475, notes ad loc.). Later, he recedes into the background, and the leading position appears to be taken by Eumolpus. It has been argued that Eumolpus' leadership is already mentioned by Pindar, and that this tradition may derive from a sixth-century epic account of the descent of Heracles to Hades. Eumolpus appears with deities of Eleusis on an Attic vase of the early fifth century showing the Mission of Triptolemus, and his prominence was presumably established by that date (cf. notes on *Dem.* 154).

The growth of Athenian interest in Triptolemus (and perhaps also Eumolpus) *c.* 550 B.C. strongly suggests that control of the Mysteries was by then in Athenian hands. Confirmation seems to be provided by the archaeological evidence, which shows that the Telesterion at Eleusis was rebuilt on a much larger scale in the time of Pisistratus, the area of the Sanctuary was surrounded by a strong peribolos wall, and the city was also fortified.

Formerly, the approach to the Telesterion had been from the south, the side turned away from Athens, but now the main entrance to the Sanctuary was placed on the other side, towards

Athens. Beside this entrance was located the Callichoron well, whose stone construction is dated to this period, although the name presumably existed earlier, whether attached to this or another well (cf. Appendix I; Mylonas, 97 ff.). At this point the Sacred Way from Athens to Eleusis ended, and the sacred dances were held in a courtyard beside the well. All these indications suggest that the Pisistratean period marks the growth of Athenian interest in, and control over the Mysteries, and that the procession from Athens to Eleusis was either instituted, or perhaps established on a more regular basis, in this period (cf. Mylonas, 77 ff., 103 ff.).

At Athens the first temple on the site identified as that of the Eleusinion dates only from the beginning of the fifth century, or later (*c.* 490 B.C. according to H. A. Thompson, *Hesperia* 29 (1960), 334 ff.), and the sacral inscriptions regulating sacrifices there are of the same period (*c.* 510–480 B.C.: L. H. Jeffery, *Hesperia* 17 (1948), 86 ff.). There are however some indications that a sanctuary may have existed previously on the site (Thompson, 338). The temple disturbs a massive retaining wall at its southern end, and this is dated by Travlos (*Pictorial Dictionary of Ancient Athens* (London, 1971), s.v. Eleusinion) to the mid sixth century B.C. A number of figurines and small votive bowls were found to the east of the temple. More important is the fact that the sacral inscriptions, which refer to the Mysteries, the Kerykes, etc., are written *boustrophedon*, and this was abnormal after *c.* 530 B.C. Miss Jeffery argues that this was due to religious conservatism, and that the inscriptions represent the codification of earlier regulations. This would indicate a date for these of at latest the mid sixth century, and possibly earlier. They must represent what was later regarded as the Solonian code (cf. Andoc. *de Myst.* 111, Sokolowski, *Lois sacrées, Supplément*, no. 10), although there are no grounds for supposing that they were drafted by Solon himself.

On balance, the view that the *Hymn* reflects a time before the growth of Athenian interest in the Mysteries seems reasonable, and we may therefore with some assurance assign a *terminus ante* of the mid sixth century. It is of course possible that this interest or control dates from the Solonian period, the time of the struggle for Salamis, and perhaps also of the building of the Archaic Telesterion. If this were the case, one would feel justified on these grounds in raising the date to *c.* 600. But there is no positive evidence.

It might be thought that a poem which shows most of the characteristics of traditional oral epic (cf. Introduction V: Language, and Appendix II) is unlikely to belong to as late a period as the sixth century.[1] Unfortunately, the boundary area between oral and literary epic is too uncertain to allow any firm conclusion on this basis. It may, however, be worth stating a subjective opinion, which is that on grounds of style and language a seventh-century date seems to me definitely preferable to one in the sixth century. In terms of style the *Hymn* seems closer to the Delian *Hymn to Apollo*, to the *Hymn to Aphrodite*, and to the poetry of Alcman, than to the second part of the Apollo hymn, for which a sixth-century date seems probable,[2] or to what survives of Stesichorus, for example. How subjective such opinions must be is obvious, especially as the dating of the other hymns is also uncertain. Perhaps one might quote the view of the *Hymn*'s first editor, Ruhnken. Commenting on the χνοῦς ἀρχαιοπινής of the poem, which led him to date it soon after Homer, he said: 'hoc a peritis sentiri potest, imperitis quid sit explicari non potest.'

The circumstances of composition must now be considered. In later times there were hymns attributed to various authors, Olen, Pamphos, Orpheus, and Musaeus, which were explicitly designed for use as an accompaniment to the ritual of certain cults, e.g. the mystery cult of the Great Goddess (or Ge) at Phlya in Attica, which was administered by the Lycomidae (Paus. 1. 22. 7, 4. 1. 5, 7. 21. 9, 9. 27. 2, 29. 8, 30. 12), and the cults of Delos (Hdt. 4. 35, Paus. 1. 18. 5, 8. 21. 3). The hymns used by the Lycomidae may have been at least partly secret. Pausanias was allowed to read those to Eros, 'after conversation with a Dadouchos' (9. 27. 2), and he refuses to say anything about their content. These hymns included ones to Demeter, by Pamphos, Orpheus, and Musaeus, whose contents Pausanias does to some extent reveal (cf. Introduction XI, c: Orphic versions). Pamphos' hymn seems to have resembled the Homeric one in some respects, but the hymns of Orpheus were of a different

---

[1] But K. Stiewe, *Der Erzählungsstil des hom. Demeterhymnus* (Diss. Göttingen, 1954), 111 n. 2, apparently dates the *Hymn* to the early sixth century on stylistic grounds.
[2] *Ap.* 540 ff. indicates this, in my opinion.

character, very brief and of no great literary merit (Paus. 9. 30. 12). Cf. also Allen and Halliday, Introduction, lxxxiii–lxxxvii.

At some period before the first century B.C. the *Homeric Hymn* was taken over and attributed to Orpheus, parts of it being quoted in a papyrus of that date as the work of Orpheus (fr. 49 Kern; cf. Introduction VIII: Manuscript and Papyri). This shows that it may well have been reused in later times for various purposes, and recited at festivals of initiation, like the hymns referred to above. There is however nothing to indicate that it was originally intended for such a use, and the analogy of other Homeric hymns, with their references to poetic contests, and the public nature of the *Hymn* itself, suggest that it was originally composed for recitation at a public festival, and perhaps for a traditional epic contest. The most natural candidate for such an occasion would be the Eleusinian Games, which were celebrated in the first, second, and third year of each Olympiad, and whose existence is first attested *c.* 500 B.C. (*IG* i². 5; cf. Deubner, *AF* 91 f.). But there is no positive evidence to indicate this. Walton (*Harv. Theol. Rev.* 45 (1952), 109 n. 16) thought that the *Hymn* might have been recited at the Βαλλητύc, the festival in honour of Demophon whose foundation is ordained by Demeter in the *Hymn* (265–7: cf. notes ad loc.). Kern (*RE* 16. 1215. 12 f.) suggested that the Βαλλητύc formed the original core of the Eleusinian Games. This is an attractive theory, but it does seem that by the time of Athenaeus (406 d; cf. Hsch. s.v. Βαλλητύc, ad *Dem.* 265–7) the Βαλλητύc was a separate festival, which had remained purely local, in contrast to the Games whose importance grew under Athenian influence.

IV. THE *HYMN* AND THE ELEUSINIAN MYSTERIES

'Uno itinere non potest perveniri ad tam grande secretum'
(Symmachus, *Rel.* 3. 10)

A. THEORIES OF ORIGINS, DEVELOPMENT, AND SIGNIFICANCE OF THE MYSTERIES

The *Homeric Hymn* is the earliest literary evidence for the cult of Demeter at Eleusis, but it appears to represent in some respects a relatively developed stage in the history of the cult, and also to have adapted some features of the myth to suit a traditional epic presentation. If we look for evidence of earlier stages of development, we must turn to archaeology, to other versions of the myth, and to the testimony of later writers concerning the ritual and its significance, and finally to comparison with similar religious phenomena in other societies.

The last method has in the past been widely used. The studies of Mannhardt, Frazer, Jane Harrison, and others did much to popularize an anthropological approach, which emphasized the analogies between Demeter and Core and the Corn-mother and Maiden who appeared in the harvest customs of many northern countries, and also the spirits or deities of crops in other societies throughout the world. A leading feature in many cases was the 'death' of the spirit of the corn, which could be identified with various points in the cycle of the crops, reaping, threshing, grinding, or sometimes the sowing of the seed, or a stage in the cycle of seasons, the disappearance of vegetation in winter, or the dry period of summer in hotter climates. The descent of Persephone to Hades was seen as analogous to those beliefs and customs. In ancient times the two goddesses were clearly recognized as deities of corn, and of vegetation in general, and the Rape and Return of Persephone were identified normally with the time of sowing in autumn and the growth of the crops in spring and early summer (cf. *Dem.* 401 ff. etc.), although Plutarch (*de Is. et Osir.* 70) mentions a double interpretation of the Rape, as the disappearance of fruit from the trees and the sowing of seed. Recently another theory has been put forward (Cornford, Nilsson), which identifies the Rape with the time of harvest, when the seed-corn is stored in underground chambers, to be taken out again in autumn, after the dry summer months, and used for sowing (the Return). There is no evidence for this interpretation in ancient times, but it shows the variety of possible meanings to which the myth may give rise.[1]

Despite the widely differing character of many of the parallels adduced, this comparative method did serve to bring out very fully the agricultural nature and significance of the cult of Demeter and Persephone. Their festivals are linked to the important stages in the farmer's year, ploughing and sowing in autumn (Greater Mysteries, Proerosia, Thesmophoria), the first

[1] See notes to *Dem.* 399 ff.

growth in January (Haloa), spring (Chloa), and harvest-time (Calamaia?, Thalysia, Κόρης Καταγωγή, the threshing-floor of Triptolemus, Skira?). The question of Demeter's own original identity, whether as Earth-mother or Corn-mother, can hardly be solved by the etymological method (cf. Nilsson, *Gesch*. i³. 461 f.). But the division into two deities, Mother and Maiden, in character originally identical, and even in the classical period hardly separable (τὼ θεώ, Δημήτερες), is closely similar to that found in other societies, where they are sometimes identified as the corn of last year and this year, or as the young and fully grown crop. This is one way in which the division may be explained, but undoubtedly it does not exhaust its possible significance, and it should be remembered that Demeter herself was in ancient times sometimes seen as equivalent to the Earth, the 'Mother of All', more often as a separate deity, the goddess of corn, and sometimes also as the corn itself (Hdt. 7. 141, Plut. *de Is. et Osir.* 66), just as Dionysus was sometimes wine itself. Core is reborn with the flowers in spring, but more widely she represents the spirit of youth and young growth, in mankind as well as plants, just as Demeter may represent the maturer stage of life (the two qualities of χάρις and cεμνότης perhaps: cf. Introduction VI: Style). Zuntz (*Persephone*, 100 f.) rightly insists that Demeter's gifts should not be restricted to corn or crops. She is the giver of all good things which the earth nourishes (cf. Call. *Hy*. 6. 136).

These considerations in fact hint at a fundamental weakness in the earlier anthropological theories, with their concentration on 'primitive origins' and 'more advanced' or 'higher' religious ideas. Undoubtedly religions develop and change, and crude and simple beliefs and customs may form the basis for more complex or refined conceptions. But in the case of the Eleusinian Mysteries we are faced with an essential problem, how far their development can be divided into two separate stages, the agricultural and the personal (or 'eschatological'). Many scholars have assumed in the past that the origins of the Mysteries were to be found in a simple agricultural ritual, whose purpose was to assist or sanctify the growth of the crops, and that they only assumed a significance for the individual person by an analogical extension at a later stage. In Frazer's words (*GB*³, vii, p. 90) 'in the long course of religious evolution high moral and spiritual conceptions were grafted on this simple original stock', and 'above all, the thought of the seed buried in the earth in order to spring up to new and higher life readily suggested a comparison with human destiny, and strengthened the hope that for man too the grave may be but the beginning of a better and happier existence in some brighter world unknown.' Frazer's fine words have been echoed many times since.[1]

We should remember here that we are dealing with speculation about a period for which there is no direct evidence. The *Homeric Hymn* quite plainly connects the two sides of the cult, linking the Return of Persephone and of life to the fields with the gift by Demeter of her ὄργια, and the two promises, of prosperity in this life, and happiness after death (471 ff., 480 ff., 486 ff.). These two aspects are always in later times inseparable, and there is nothing in ancient literature to suggest that one could exist without or before the other. If we turn to comparative evidence, we find examples of aetiological myths from other cultures which explain the origin of the fruits of the earth in terms of the death of a divine being (sometimes the first death on earth), who is also responsible for or connected with the introduction of agriculture and other arts, sacrifice, and the propagation of human life. The ceremonies associated with these myths govern not only the agricultural cycle but also the important stages in the life of the community, birth, marriage, and death, and the initiation of young men and girls into adult society.[2]

This association is not confined to so-called primitive societies, since it is seen also in the Indian mythology of the god Soma, who is god of vegetation and of life in general, and also the immortal drink of the gods, collected in the moon, and on earth the plant which men sacrifice to the gods and of which they also partake in order to gain immortality. The preparation of this drink is seen as the death of Soma. The Egyptian beliefs about Osiris and Isis also show this association between the deities of the corn and the after-life of men, who are identified with Osiris after death.

---

[1] Cf. Allen and Halliday, 118, F. Wehrli, *ARW* 31 (1934), 97 ff., Ch. Picard, *Rev. Hist.* 166 (1931), ad fin., S. Eitrem, *Symb. Osl.* 20 (1940), 133 ff., Nilsson, *Gesch.* i³. 470, H. J. Rose, *Ancient Greek Religion* (Hutchinson, 1946), 73 f.; cf. also P. Foucart, *Les Mystères*, 445 ff.; but Rohde, *Psyche*, English translation, 223 ff., denied the possibility of analogical extension; and cf. P. Roussel, *BCH* 54 (1930), 72 n. 2.

[2] Cf. E. Jensen, *Das religiöse Weltbild einer frühen Kultur* (Stuttgart, 1948).

There is no indication here of two separate stages of development. One might sum up this theory of association by saying that the famous words in St. John's Gospel (12 : 24) about the 'corn of wheat' (cf. also I Cor. 15 : 36–8) represent not simply an elevated metaphor or analogy, but something fundamental to the beliefs about death of many peoples at all times in history.

This view also makes it easier for us to understand the awe-inspiring importance that was attached to the secrecy of the Mysteries (cf. notes to *Dem.* 478 f.). If they were originally simply agricultural, it is not easy to see how they could have acquired this aspect. We must remember that the goddesses of Eleusis were from the earliest recorded times regarded as awe-inspiring, dread powers of the Underworld (*cεμναί τ' αἰδοῖαί τε, Dem.* 486), of whose rites men were deeply afraid to speak. They had power over men on earth, to give and take away the means of life, and equally over what happened after death, when their favour was essential to ensure that 'a worse fate' should be averted.

A possible argument in favour of distinguishing two separate stages in the cult depends on the view that Persephone is a non-Greek goddess in origin, who was the ruler of the Underworld, whereas Core, as her name implies, is Greek, and originally an agricultural deity (cf. e.g. Zuntz, *Persephone*, 75 ff.). It may well be true that Persephone is not of Greek origin, as far as her name goes, and it is certainly the case that in Homer she appears only as queen of the dead. But if there was a fusion of cults, as seems possible, can one be sure that the local, non-Greek cult did not have a dual significance already, both agricultural and eschatological?[1]

Comparative theories, however, such as that outlined above, have their dangers. One must be careful not to exaggerate the importance of cults of initiation in ancient Greece, under the influence of parallels from other societies. The Mysteries retained throughout antiquity their local character, as the cult of Eleusis, although they spread abroad, first to Attica, and then the Greek world, finally to the wider sphere of Graeco-Roman civilization. They do not therefore occupy the central position in

---

[1] This is a possibility which is considered by Zuntz, o.c. 76 f., together with the second possibility, that the Greek Core could have been felt to have a connection with the Underworld before her fusion with Persephone.

Greek mythology and religion which the parallels from other cultures would seem to require.[1] Demeter and Core share many of their functions and aspects with other Greek deities, and this may be explained by the fragmentary way in which Greek religion developed. The *Homeric Hymn*, which follows the common epic traditions of Homer and Hesiod, must to some extent represent a compromise between local beliefs and the rather artificial synthesis found in the epics. This perhaps explains why, for example, the existence of agriculture is presupposed in the *Hymn*, although one seems to detect traces of the more fundamental belief, which associated the foundation of the Mysteries with the institution of agriculture (*Dem.* 471 ff.).

The parallels with the initiation ceremonies of other societies have been much emphasized by some scholars.[2] But initiations can be of widely differing types.[3] In the historical period the Eleusinian Mysteries were open to both sexes and apparently to all ages and they were also, unlike some initiations, not obligatory. There is no question of restriction either to one sex[4] or to certain age groups.[5] Nor do the Mysteries belong to the 'secret society' type of initiation, although they may originally have been the property of certain families or clans, and there was a later tradition (Plut. *Thes.* 33. 2) that Heracles and the Dioscuri were adopted as Athenian citizens before initiation, implying the exclusion at one period of ξένοι from the cult. The Mysteries in the *Hymn* are apparently open to the whole community of Eleusis (cf. *Dem.* 296 ff.?), and probably already to a wider public than this (*Dem.* 480). Whatever their origins, therefore, it would be quite wrong to interpret them solely in terms of a more restricted type of initiation, of young men and girls, of women, or of members of a special group.

---

[1] Even in the case of these parallel cults one must remember that not all the elements mentioned by Jensen are found together, and it may therefore be misleading to speak of a single 'Weltbild'.

[2] e.g. Jeanmaire, *Couroi et Courètes* (Lille, 1939).

[3] For a good criticism of the work of Jeanmaire, Éliade, Thomson, and others cf. A. Brelich, 'Initiation et histoire', in *Initiation*, ed. Bleeker, Studies in the History of Religions, X (Leiden, 1965), 222 ff.

[4] Other festivals of Demeter have this character, and at some points in the Mystery ceremonies segregation perhaps occurred: cf. e.g. Ar. *Ran.* 444 ff.

[5] But the role of the ephebes was important, at least in the Roman period. Cf. Foucart, *Les Mystères*, 274 f., who concludes that initiation before becoming an ephebe was normal practice.

The emphasis in the cult of Demeter and Core on the feminine aspect, the Mother and Daughter, their chthonic character and aspects as deities of fertility, led some scholars in the past to attach them to a presumed pre-Greek stage of culture, an indigenous 'Mediterranean' religion, contrasted with the supposedly northern emphasis on Olympian deities and a god of the sky. This rather crude dichotomy is now generally discredited, and one might observe the parallels from northern cultures for the Mother and Maiden of the corn, and the reasonable assumption that Demeter's name is not pre-Greek in origin. On the other hand tentative connections with Crete have been made.[1] The presumed existence of a cult at Eleusis in the Mycenaean period does not help to decide the issue, and our knowledge of Minoan and Mycenaean religion is still too scanty to enable a clear distinction to be drawn. The celebrated ivory group from Mycenae, showing two seated women and a child, was connected by Wace with Demeter and Persephone, but of course without literary evidence all names are speculative (cf. Mylonas, *Eleusis*, 51 f.). The tradition that the Ionians took with them to Asia Minor the cult and hereditary priesthood of Eleusinian Demeter (Hdt. 9. 97, Str. 633) strongly supports the view that this cult was already widespread in Greece in the Mycenaean period. On the other hand, the later Attic legends of the introduction of the Mysteries to Attica in the reign of Pandion or Erechtheus (cf. Mylonas, *Eleusis*, 14, 41) can hardly be taken to prove that they were introduced in this period.

It may, however, be permissible to speculate about the manner in which a local cult and mythology of Demeter and Core developed at Eleusis. We find Core portrayed as leader of the nymphs, the daughters of Oceanus, who dwell in springs and grottoes, and who are connected as κουροτρόφοι with birth, growth, and marriage (cf. Nilsson, *Gesch.* i[3]. 244 ff.). Originally the worship of Core herself must have been closely associated with the spring (Callichoron, Parthenion, Anthion) and nearby cavern (Ploutonion) at Eleusis. In Syracuse she actually disappeared with Hades into the spring Cyane, and at Andania she appears to have been identified with the spring Hagne. At Agrae also we find the spring Callirhoe, and one might add the

---

[1] Cf. notes on *Dem.* 123; A. Pearson, *ARW* 21 (1922), 287 ff.: Ch. Picard, *RÉG* 40 (1927), 320 ff., *Rev. Arch.* 34 (1949), 122 ff. But see Mylonas, *Eleusis*, 16 ff.

proximity of Enneacrounos at Athens to the Eleusinion, and the sanctuary of the nymphs in Phaleron, near the River Cephisus, where a relief was found showing the Rape of Basile by Echelos, dedicated to Hermes and the nymphs, and a second dedication to nymphs, and other deities of rivers, springs, and child-birth (Nilsson, o.c. 248 f.). The myth of Hylas may also be compared. His disappearance into the spring, and the search for him, was commemorated in an annual festival. Likewise there was dancing in honour of the Charites at Orchomenus because they were thought to have been thrown into the spring while dancing round it. All these parallels suggest that the cult of Core grew up around the spring and grotto, together with the rock (Ἀγέλα-cτoc πέτρα) on which Demeter sat beside Callichoron. The importance of Callichoron is indicated by Pausanias' statement that the women first danced and sang in honour of the goddess here (1. 38. 6). The names Callichoron, Parthenion, Anthion (cf. Appendix I) remind one of the lines in the *Hymn to Ge* (30. 14 ff.) : παρθενικαί τε χοροῖc φερεcανθέcιν εὔφρονι θυμῷ | παίζουcαι cκαί-ρουcι κατ' ἄνθεα μαλθακὰ ποίηc (etc.). Anthion suggests a spring with flowers growing round it, and Callichoron and Parthenion suggest that choruses of girls (with flowers?) danced and sang around the spring in honour of Core, who was carried off from the chorus of flower-gathering nymphs, and whose Rape and Return with the spring flowers must have been celebrated here. Here too ceremonies connected with marriage and birth will have been celebrated (cf. Nilsson, o.c. 102 ff.). Above the spring an altar will have been built, and later a temple, where other, more sacred and secret rites might be celebrated (*Dem.* 270–2). The grotto was the place where Hades sprang to light, the χάcμα γῆc (cf. *Dem.* 16), or perhaps where he disappeared into the earth again, and here he was especially honoured. Another element was added in the theme of the search for Core, the grief and anger of the Mother, her withdrawal from the gods, and the famine caused by her wrath. This last motif is found also, in a similar form, in the Arcadian myth at Phigaleia (Paus. 8. 42). The theme of the famine due to the wrath of the goddess is a counterpart to the death of vegetation with the disappearance of Core, and both have their parallels in other cultures (cf. ad *Dem.* 305 ff.). Finally, the institution of the cult had to be explained, and this must have been due to Demeter herself, whose visit to Eleusis during her search was rewarded by information from the inhabitants, in return for which she gave them her rites. The story of the nursing of Demophon probably arose as the *aition* for part of the ritual of initiation (see below).

Such speculation about origins and development must of its nature be somewhat sketchy and vague, and we must now turn to consideration of the evidence from the historical period for the nature of the Mysteries, and see what light the *Hymn* can shed on them, and how far the later evidence can illuminate the *Hymn* itself.

B. THE HYMN, AND THE MYSTERIES IN THE HISTORICAL PERIOD

In the later historical period the Mysteries were divided into several stages. It is not certain how many there were, but Clement, in a passage about 'the mysteries in Greece',[1] speaks of a preliminary stage of purificatory rituals, followed by the Little (or Lesser) Mysteries, which formed a preparatory stage for what was to come, and these again followed by the Great Mysteries. The Lesser Mysteries were celebrated at Agrae, near the Ilissos in Athens in the month Anthesterion,[2] the Greater at Eleusis in Boedromion. Elsewhere initiation is divided into two grades, μύηϲιϲ and ἐποπτεία.[3] We are also told that the ἐποπτεία was only open to those who had allowed a year to elapse after attending the Greater Mysteries.[4] This indicates two stages in the Greater Mysteries themselves, and suggests that the first was the μύηϲιϲ.[5] It has, however, been argued[6] that μύηϲιϲ refers to a preliminary ceremony. An important early-fifth-century inscription (*IG* i². 6 = Sokolowski, o.c. no. 3C) has been thought to indicate that μύηϲιϲ was conducted individually, by members of the two *gene* of the Kerykes and Eumolpidae, and that it could take place either at Eleusis or at Athens. But the text is very uncertain at the crucial points, and it is possible to read it in such a way that there is no reference to individual μύηϲιϲ, or to

[1] *Strom.* 5. 70. 7 p. 373. 23 Stählin.
[2] Schol. Plat. *Gorg.* 497 c, Polyaen. 5. 17. 1, Deubner, *AF* 70.
[3] Cf. Plut. *Alc.* 22. 3, *IG* i². 6B. 4 ff. = Sokolowski, *Lois sacrées, Supplément*, no. 3B. 4 ff., *Suda* s.v. ἐπόπται, etc.
[4] Plut. *Demetr.* 26. 2.
[5] This is explicitly stated in the *Suda*, l.c.
[6] Cf. P. Roussel, *BCH* 54 (1930), 51 ff.

initiation at Athens.[1] Two fourth-century inscriptions (*IG* ii².
1672. 207 and 1673. 24) refer to μύηϲιϲ of public slaves, who were
working in the sanctuary at Eleusis. The second cannot be used as
evidence for the time and place, as it is not in chronological order.
The first lists this item in the sixth prytany, between third Game-
lion and eighth Anthesterion, and so cannot refer to the Greater
Mysteries. It might, however, refer to initiation at the Lesser
Mysteries in Anthesterion.[2] Alternatively, such μύηϲιϲ of public
slaves might constitute a special case, as an emergency measure.

In Aristophanes, *Pax* 374–5 Trygaeus asks to borrow three
drachmae to buy a piglet, as he wishes to be initiated (μυηθῆναι)
before he dies. It is not clear from this whether μύηϲιϲ could take
place at any time, nor how large a part of the whole process of
initiation is involved, although if it is a necessary precaution
before death it should involve more than a preliminary ceremony. One might note that the expenses of μύηϲιϲ of a public
slave in *IG* ii². 1672. 207 are 15 drachmae, a substantial sum.

In Ps. Dem. 59. 21 μυεῖν apparently refers, at least primarily,
to paying the cost of μύηϲιϲ for someone else, and this evidently
took place at *the* Mysteries (cf. εἰϲ τὴν ἑορτὴν καὶ τὰ μυϲτήρια). In
Andoc. *de Myst.* 132 the sense of the verb is uncertain (cf. Mac-
Dowell ad loc.), but it may refer to sponsoring non-Athenians for
initiation (cf. ἔτι δὲ ἄλλουϲ ξένουϲ ἐμαυτοῦ).

The question of these various stages is important for the reconstruction of the cult, since there is considerable uncertainty as
to the features which should be assigned to each stage. The
series of stages implied for the classical period may not have
existed when the *Hymn* was composed. The Lesser Mysteries
were a separate festival, originally a local Athenian cult, and it
became customary at some stage for mystery-goers to attend
these as a preliminary to the Greater. The other stages may have
evolved with the growth of numbers attending (cf. Nock,
Mnemosyne 5 (1952), 179). But a twofold division, into μύηϲιϲ
and ἐποπτεία, seems likely to be an older feature. The *Hymn*

---

[1] On the second point, cf. Sokolowski's text at C39 ff. On the first, M. H.
Jameson suggests that C16 ff. may refer to the expenses of initiation. At 22 it
would be possible to read (e.g.) Κέρυκαϲ δὲ μυ[ὲν τοϲοῦτο (i.e. τοϲούτου)] μύϲταϲ
ἑκαϲτον, or instead of τοϲοῦτο e.g. κατὰ δύο or ἑκατόν (making ἑκαϲτον refer to
the initiator).

[2] Cf. 1672. 204–5, referring to expenses for the Chóes, which certainly occurred
after the end of the sixth prytany, on twelfth Anthesterion.

does not shed light directly on this problem, but the ceremonies for which it provides the *aitia* in the narrative can, to some extent at least, be most plausibly assigned to the preliminary stages of initiation (i.e. fasting, running or dancing with torches, purification, drinking of the *cyceon*, *aischrologia*, and perhaps also the fire-ceremony), whereas the ὄργια whose secrecy is emphasized, and whose institution is twice referred to (273 f., 473 ff.), are never of course explicitly described, and it may be doubted whether their nature is more than hinted at in the narrative of the *Hymn*. Such parallels as may be detected with later evidence for the ceremonies in the Telesterion at Eleusis, are rather obscurely suggestive than truly enlightening.

That purification preceded initiation is indicated not only by the passage of Clement quoted above, but also by the myth of Heracles, who before initiation at Eleusis had to undergo purification from the murder of the Centaurs.[1] According to one version (Diod. 4. 14. 3) the Lesser Mysteries were instituted for this purpose. The purification of Heracles, by means of the Διὸς κῴδιον, veil, and torch or λίκνον, is shown in art,[2] and the similarity of the scenes to that described in *Dem.* 192 ff. indicates that the *Hymn* is portraying the *aition* for this ritual (cf. notes ad loc.), and therefore that it was undergone by all candidates for initiation (and not simply Heracles as a specially polluted case).

In the same passage of the *Hymn* we find references to Demeter's fasting, and silent sorrow, until she is persuaded by the jesting of Iambe to laugh, and to break her fast by drinking a *cyceon*, that is, a mixture of barley and water flavoured with pennyroyal. The three elements of fasting, jesting (*aischrologia*), and drinking the *cyceon* all form part of the preparations for the Mysteries. In the classical period fasting was probably divided into two stages, partial abstention and strict (cf. ad *Dem.* 47 ff.). The second stage may have lasted for a day only, and was concluded by drinking the *cyceon*. Both are attested by the Eleusinian cύνθημα, a 'token' by which the initiate proclaimed that he had performed the necessary preliminaries to initiation: ἐνήϲτευϲα, ἔπιον τὸν κυκεῶνα . . .[3] It is not known when this took place, but the *Hymn* seems to indicate that in the archaic period it was com-

---

[1] Apollod. 2. 5. 12, Plut. *Thes.* 30. 5, Diod. 4. 14. 3.
[2] Mylonas, *Eleusis*, Figs. 83, 84.
[3] Clem. *Protr.* 2. 21. 2 p. 16. 18 Stählin; cf. Deubner, *AF* 79 ff.

bined with the ceremony of purification (cf. ad *Dem.* 192 ff., 208 ff.). Jesting, or *aischrologia*, whose origin at Eleusis is ascribed to Iambe, certainly took place in the classical period during the Iacchus procession from Athens to Eleusis (cf. ad *Dem.* 192 ff.). It was, to some extent at least, probably in iambic verse. It may also have formed part of the παννυχίc which took place after the arrival at Eleusis, accompanied by dancing. Again, the *Hymn* connects it with drinking the *cyceon*, and this connection is brought out by other versions of the myth (cf. ad *Dem.* 192–211: 3. Iambe).

The cύνθημα continues with a reference to a ritual involving the mystic κίcτη and κάλαθοc. It is not known what these contained, and the *Hymn* makes no reference to them.[1] In one of the scenes showing the purification of Heracles (Mylonas, *Eleusis*, Fig. 84) Demeter is portrayed sitting on the κίcτη (cf. ad *Dem.* 192 ff.), and this might perhaps hint at the connection of the purification ritual with the second part of the cύνθημα.

Fasting is also mentioned earlier in the *Hymn* (*Dem.* 47 ff.). Here it is connected with Demeter's search for Core. For nine days she fasts and abstains from washing, roaming over the earth with lighted torches in her hands. These features were presumably all reflected in the cult, although it is not certain exactly how or when (cf. notes on *Dem.* 47 ff., 59–61). This problem is connected with the wider one, of the nature of the 'mystic drama' enacted at Eleusis (see below).

One portrayal of the purification of Heracles also shows a priestess holding near to the veiled figure a lighted torch, lowered towards the ground (Mylonas, o.c. Fig. 84). This has been compared with another scene, on a fifth-century B.C. Attic relief, showing two women, one of whom holds out torches towards a seated child, and the two scenes may be linked by the story in the *Hymn* of Demeter's attempt to immortalize the child Demophon by placing him in the fire at night (*Dem.* 231 ff.). It is possible that this reflects part of the preliminary ritual of purification. The other features of Demeter's divine nursing (anointing with ambrosia, breathing on the child, and holding him in her

---

[1] If the ritual involved symbols of fertility, the omission may have been due to the epic poet's avoidance of τὸ ἀπρεπέc. But other explanations have also been proposed. The whole ritual has sometimes been held to belong to the Alexandrian cult of Demeter, but the κάλαθοc is not necessarily foreign to Eleusis. Cf. Deubner, *AF* 79 n. 9; Nilsson, *Gesch.* i³. 659, and Nachträge to p. 657.

bosom) are not directly paralleled in known ritual from Eleusis, but they do have some similarities with features of later cults.[1] Demophon himself had a festival in his honour, which involved a mock battle (the Βαλλητύс), and he may even perhaps have been the original hero of the Eleusinian Games (cf. notes to *Dem.* 265–7). Demeter's attempt to immortalize him is unsuccessful, and she condemns mankind for the folly which has prevented her from helping them (cf. notes to 256 ff., also 147 f., 216 f.). But she promises to teach the Eleusinians her ὄργια, and orders them to build a temple (270–4). That is, she wished to save Demophon from death and old age, but was unable to do so because men were ignorant and blind. She could, however, give to the Eleusinians the means of obtaining a better fate after death, through her favour and that of Persephone, and the special knowledge which the Mysteries supplied. The assumption that the myth of Demophon refers primarily to part of the preliminary ritual is supported by its position in the poem. At the same time, a deeper significance has been seen in it, and Demophon has been considered as a form of the divine child whose birth was announced at the climax of the Mysteries, and as the model for the initiates, who were adopted as children by the divine nurses (κουροτρόφοι) Demeter and Persephone.

We must now consider the more general problem of the extent to which the myth related in the *Hymn*, of the rape of Persephone, Demeter's search, her visit to Eleusis, and the return of Persephone, was reflected in the ritual at Eleusis. (The Famine, an important episode in the *Hymn*, does not appear to have had any direct counterpart in ritual, and one may note its apparent exclusion from the Orphic versions.) The Christian Fathers[2] say that the rape and search, and Demeter's sorrow, were celebrated at Eleusis with torches during the night, and the ceremony closed with thanksgiving and tossing of torches. Gregory also mentions Celeus, Triptolemus, and the snakes, i.e. presumably his winged chariot, but in a general and vague way. That Demeter's visit to Eleusis was narrated at some stage in the secret ceremonies is also suggested by Isocrates (*Panegyr.* 28), who

---

[1] For a discussion of this whole episode, and its significance for the Mysteries, cf. notes to *Dem.* 231 ff.

[2] Clement, *Protr.* 2. 12. 2 p. 11. 20 St., Lactantius, *Inst. Epit.* 18. 7, Gregory of Nazianzus, *Or.* 39. 4; cf. Deubner, *AF* 84 n. 8.

speaks of Demeter as being well disposed to the people of Attica 'because of benefits of which only the initiated may hear'.[1] The scholiast on Theocritus (2. 35/36b, p. 279. 7 Wend.) quotes Apollodorus (*FGH* 244. 110) for the sounding of a kind of gong by the hierophant 'when Core is being called upon' (τῆς Κόρης ἐπικαλουμένης: this is probably the correct sense). This suggests a ceremonial invocation. We also hear of 'sacred lamentations' in mysteries of Demeter and Core (Procl. *in Plat. Remp.* I p. 125. 20 Kroll).

These *testimonia* are of very general character and mostly late, and the nature of this 'sacred drama' has been much debated.[2] Wilamowitz (*Glaube*, ii. 473 f.) went so far as to deny its real existence at Eleusis.[3] He claimed that the use of the word δρᾶμα (by Clement) was purely metaphorical. Other scholars have accepted its reality, but differ as to what form it took. Any theory which assumes a full-scale dramatic representation inside the Telesterion is almost certainly wrong. The Telesterion was not equipped for such performances, nor for any form of simulated 'underworld-journey' (cf. Noack, *Eleusis*, 236 ff.). We may also doubt whether the initiates themselves participated to any great extent in the drama, as a passage of Plutarch (περὶ ψυχῆς, Loeb ed., fr. 178) has led some to suppose (cf. Mylonas, 262, 264 ff.). Elsewhere Plutarch (*Mor.* 81 e) would rather seem to deny such participation, and one can hardly believe that vast crowds, of perhaps thousands of initiates, roamed about the Sanctuary, searching for Core (as Mylonas suggests, 262 f.). It seems more likely that any enactment of the myth was purely formal, partly perhaps by means of dancing with torches (cf. Nilsson, *Gesch.* i³. 662 f., Farnell, *Cults*, 3. 182), such as we know took place during the παννυχίς after the arrival of the Iacchus procession.[4] The use of the gong on the other hand presumably occurred at another stage, perhaps within the Telesterion. We must freely admit that we do not know what happened here, but as has sometimes been observed, the analogy of Christian church

---

[1] Cf. XI, c: Orphic Versions. One may reasonably suppose that the Orphic versions are closer in some respects than the Homeric to the form taken by the secret ceremonies themselves.

[2] Cf. P. Foucart, *Les Mystères*, 457 ff., O. Kern, *Die griech. Mysterien der class. Zeit*, 75 f., *RE* 16. 1241 ff., Farnell, *Cults*, 3. 173 ff., Wehrli, *ARW* 31 (1934), 85 f., Mylonas, *Eleusis*, 261 ff., Nilsson, *Gesch.* i³. 662 f.

[3] Cf. Kerényi, *Eleusis*, 26 f., 116 ff., who refers it to Alexandria.

[4] The *taedarum iactatio* of Lactantius is reminiscent of Ar. *Ran.* 340 ff., Statius, *Silv.* 4. 8. 50 f. Cf. ad *Dem.* 47 ff., 59–61.

ceremonies shows quite clearly that the spoken words of the priest, together with a few actions, the display of sacred objects, and something as simple as the sounding of a bell, are all that is needed to suggest to the worshipper the sense and significance of the sacred narrative. At Eleusis, likewise, the ceremony could be divided into δρώμενα, δεικνύμενα, and λεγόμενα (cf. ad *Dem.* 474–6).

These reflections have led us on to the central part of the Mysteries, the ceremonies within the hall of initiation of Eleusis. It has already been remarked that the *Hymn* itself naturally observes its own prescription of secrecy with regard to these ὄργια cεμνά.[1] It would therefore be out of place here to attempt a reconstruction of these, even were such reconstruction possible. Certain leading features may however be mentioned, since they have suggested parallels with the *Hymn*. These are:

   (i) the symbolism of light and darkness;
   (ii) the birth of a child;
   (iii) the ear of corn.

The first of these is central to the Mysteries. Their final stage, the ἐποπτεία, was essentially a vision (cf. ad *Dem.* 480), and this was evidently accompanied by a great light, which is contrasted with the darkness which preceded at earlier stages of the ceremonies.[2] The light is a feature of all divine manifestations or revelations, and we find it already emphasized in the two epiphanies of Demeter in the *Hymn* (188–90, 275 ff.), together with other features which have their parallels in the Mysteries.[3] It is closely connected by the Gnostic source quoted by the Christian writer Hippolytus (*Ref. Haer.* 5. 8 p. 96. 16 W.) with the second feature, the announcement by the hierophant at Eleusis during the night, accompanied by a great fire (ὑπὸ πολλῷ πυρί), of the birth of a divine child to the goddess, in the words ἱερὸν ἔτεκε Πότνια Κοῦρον, Βριμὼ Βριμόν (he explains the last words as ἰσχυρὰ ἰσχυρόν). The genuineness of this testimony is

   [1] Cf. ad *Dem.* 478–9, and note the contrast drawn by Libanius and others, ad loc., between the preliminary rituals and general precepts, whose secrecy was not strict, and the secret elements.

   [2] Cf. especially Hippol. l.c. below, Plut. fr. 178, Dio Chrys. 12. 33 p. 163. 24 Arn., Plut. *Mor.* 81 e, etc. Some of these do not refer specifically to Eleusis, but to mysteries in a general or vague sense. Cf. also Deubner, *AF* 87, P. Boyancé, *RÉG* 75 (1962), 460 ff.

   [3] Cf. ad *Dem.* 188–90.

supported by Eur. *Supp.* 54 ἔτεκες καὶ σύ ποτ' ὦ πότνια κοῦρον which seems to echo the words, in an Eleusinian context.[1] The 'great fire' suggests the blaze of many torches at the climax of the ceremonies. This may be connected with the third element, the revelation to the ἐπόπται, in silence (cf. ad *Dem.* 478–9), of what is described by Hippolytus in the same passage (*Ref. Haer.* 5. 8. 39 p. 96. 10 W.) as τὸ μέγα καὶ θαυμαστότατον καὶ τελειότατον ἐποπτικὸν ἐκεῖ μυστήριον, an ear of reaped corn (τεθερισμένον στάχυν). Hippolytus adds that 'this is for the Athenians the great and perfect light.'

The divine child (Κοῦρος) born to the goddess (Πότνια) at Eleusis has no name, just as the leading deities of the cult were often nameless (Θεός and Θεά, τὼ Θεώ, Πότνιαι, Σεμναὶ Θεαί, Μήτηρ and Κόρη, etc.). But he may be variously identified.[2] In Hesiodic myth the child of Demeter is Ploutos, who is mentioned in the *Hymn* (489). He represents the wealth of the earth, and he is shown as a child holding a cornucopia on Eleusinian monuments. His birth is also shown, as that of a child seated on a cornucopia, being offered by the goddess Earth to the deities of Eleusis. The scene belongs to the same type as that of the birth of Erichthonius, who is the nursling and protégé of Athena, and the myth of Erichthonius, and its corresponding ritual, in turn offer interesting parallels with the story of Demophon (cf. ad *Dem.* 231 ff.). Demophon is a form of the anonymous Θρεπτός of Eleusinian cult, later identified with Triptolemus (cf. ad *Dem.* 153, 234). We find here two separate notions, of the divine child of the goddess herself, and the child who is born of the Earth and entrusted to the care of the goddess, who is herself the κουροτρόφος. The two ideas seem to be fused, as the goddess adopts him as her own. Later we also find evidence for the identification of Iacchus, or Dionysus, with the child. This fusion is usually dated to the fourth century B.C., but it is probably considerably older.[3]

[1] Cf. also Deubner, *AF* 85 n. 4. The word-order of the formula suggests a kind of liturgical 'verse-form', such as one finds on some of the gold-leaf inscriptions. Cf. Zuntz, *Persephone*, 340 ff. for some significant parallels for such liturgical formulae.

[2] I do not discuss the question of a ἱερὸς γάμος at Eleusis, as the evidence is confused and probably impossible to disentangle. Cf. Nilsson, o.c. 661 f., who rules it out altogether; Deubner, *AF* 84 ff., who accepts it; Mylonas, *Eleusis* 310 ff., who refuses to believe anything told him by Christian writers.

[3] Cf. Schol. Ar. *Ran.* 482, Farnell, *Cults* 3. 149, and notes to *Dem.* 489.

As the personification of the earth's produce, it might be reasonable to expect that Ploutos would be identified with, or represented by, the ear of corn which was shown to the initiates in the ἐποπτεία.[1] We have no proof that this was so: it remains a very natural supposition.

If we return to the first element mentioned above, the role of light in the Mysteries, we find striking testimonies to the actual identification of the divine child with the light itself (cf. ad *Dem.* 489). The clearest indication of this is the passage of Pindar (*Ol.* 2. 53 ff.) in which he begins his great exposition of the doctrines of reincarnation and life after death. Here πλοῦτος, or Πλοῦτος, is called ἀστὴρ ἀρίζηλος, ἐτυμώτατον ἀνδρὶ φέγγος, in words whose similarity to those of St. John's Gospel (1 : 9) suggests that here also, as with the 'corn of wheat', we have to do with a very ancient symbolism.[2] The Pindaric passage may of course reflect other beliefs which are not originally the property of Eleusis, and cannot be taken as a direct reflection of the Mysteries, but the symbolism here expressed may ultimately derive from this source.

Pindar continues with the words εἰ δέ νιν ἔχων τις οἶδεν τὸ μέλλον, ὅτι θανόντων μὲν . . . (leading on to his exposition of reincarnation). The pronoun (νιν) refers to Πλοῦτος: 'if one has this, and knows the future . . .' The emphasis on knowledge is fundamental to later references to the Mysteries (cf. especially Pindar's own words, fr. 137a Sn.), and explains why one finds the philosophers adopting so readily mystic terminology, the concept of knowledge as ultimately based on vision.[3] We find elsewhere the symbolism of πλοῦτος, light, and knowledge combined (cf. ad *Dem.* 480). The Mysteries are contrasted with the normal state of men, needy, blind, and ignorant, unable to foresee the future or to avert the twin catastrophes of old age and death (*Dem.* 256 ff.; cf. ad loc.). This is the characteristic portrayal of the human lot, from Homer onwards. It is the gods who give and take away prosperity (ὄλβος, πλοῦτος) as they desire, and their condition of ageless immortality is contrasted with that of men. They live in

---

[1] Cf. Deubner, *AF* 85 f. Nilsson, *Gesch.* i³. 662, denies this, as he does not consider that Ploutos belongs to the Mysteries, at least in the earlier historical period.

[2] Later we find Iacchus/Dionysus as the 'Star of the Mysteries'; cf. ad *Dem.* 489.

[3] Cf. ad *Dem.* 147 f., 480. οἶδα is of course the perfect corresponding to εἶδον. Likewise μύστης is 'one who shuts his eyes', as opposed to ἐπόπτης, and μυέω 'make someone shut his eyes'. Cf. Frisk, *Etym. Wörterbuch*, s.v. μύω.

pure regions where the light always shines: no cloud of darkness disturbs their vision, and when they appear to men, they appear in a blaze of glorious light.

The Mysteries do not break down the barrier between gods and men: at least, in the classical period there does not seem to be any suggestion of this. Demophon does not gain immortality, but he does become the θρεπτός of the divine nurse, and men will receive the favour of the goddesses, if they will only perform the necessary sacrifices and pay them the gifts which are due (*Dem.* 273–4; cf. 367–9). How far ethical considerations enter into these requirements is not a subject on which the *Hymn* has anything to say: later we find a conflict over this question (cf. ad *Dem.* 367 ff.). The essentials are the divine favour, and the knowledge which the Mysteries conveyed.

On this last point we run against an insoluble problem. One may point to the symbolism of the ear of corn, promising rebirth for men as for the world of nature, and to the parallel of the myth of Core. (This sounds again like 'analogical extension', but it may go deeper than this.) One may, on the other hand, stress the elements of Eleusinian myth (Demophon, Iacchus?, Ploutos) which suggest the theme of adoption by the divine nurses. The words in which Sophocles refers to the Mysteries (*OC* 1050 ff.), οὗ Πότνιαι cεμνὰ τιθηνοῦνται τέλη θνατοῖcιν, with their strong Eleusinian colouring, seem to emphasize this aspect. Were the initiates adopted as children of Demeter (or Persephone)? Did the birth of Ploutos symbolize for them also a divine rebirth? Or were these ideas alien to the early stages, at least, of the cult? One must be wary of all interpretations in terms of symbolism, since these are bound to be indefinite. The essential for happiness was simply initiation. Some modern scholars go so far as to deny that there were really any secrets to be revealed behind the veil. On this theory, initiation was simply admission to membership of a club (secret society), which marked one off from other men. One may doubt whether such a 'reductionist' view will work. But early Greek religion, at least, is largely a matter of performance, and this was the basis of the Mysteries (ὄργια, δρηcμοcύνη). Whatever was revealed, one is sure that it did not resemble in any way the kind of manual or guide-book to the after-life that we find in Egypt, or apparently in some later Greek cults. The important point was not so much *how* ὄλβοc, or a better fate, was to be given, but rather *that* it was promised. Beyond this point the *Hymn*, at any rate, will not allow us to advance.[1]

V. LANGUAGE, AND RELATIONSHIP TO OTHER EARLY EPIC POETRY

A formulaic analysis of each line is given with the text, at the foot of each page. This shows the nearest equivalent words or phrases found in Homer, Hesiod, and other early epic (or elegy). An asterisk after the word indicates that it is found in the same metrical position. '(etc.)' after a word or reference indicates that other grammatical variants, of declension or conjugation, are found. 'etc.' after a reference indicates that there is more than one example of the same word or formula. ～ refers to other similar examples. The list does not claim to be complete, and where several examples of a formula exist, only one reference is normally given.[2]

The general conclusions to be drawn from such an analysis are bound to be to some extent subjective. It is clear that there are a considerable number of words and phrases which do not occur elsewhere in early epic. Equally, the great majority of expressions used do have definite parallels elsewhere. Of these, the greatest proportion are Homeric, but there are also a striking number of Hesiodic parallels. In addition, there are several parallels from other Homeric hymns, especially the longer ones, of which the

---

[1] This chapter is, of necessity, very summary, and it deals rather shortly with some important questions, e.g. as to the existence of the 'sacred birth' in the Eleusinian cult. Nor has the administrative side been covered. For the latter Foucart, *Les Mystères*, is important; cf. also Nilsson, *Gesch.* i³. 663 ff., Deubner, *AF* 70 ff., Mylonas, *Eleusis*, 229 ff., S. Dow, *HSCP* 48 (1937), 111 ff. The evidence relating to the Mysteries was first critically examined by C. A. Lobeck, in his great work *Aglaophamus* (Königsberg, 1829). Besides the works referred to, H. G. Pringsheim, *Arch. Beiträge zur Geschichte des eleus. Kults* (Diss. Bonn, 1895), is important and valuable, and Nilsson's study, 'Die eleusinischen Gottheiten', *ARW* 32 (1935), 79 ff. = *Op. Sel.* ii. 542 ff., should be read. Cf. also Kern, *Rel. d. Gr.* ii (1935), 182 ff., and *RE* 16. 1211 ff.; Wilamowitz, *Glaube d. Hell.* ii. 42 ff.; and the articles of F. Wehrli, *ARW* 31 (1934), 76 ff., S. Eitrem, *Symb. Osl.* 20 (1940), 133 ff., 37 (1961), 72 ff. The study of Mylonas, *Eleusis*, 237 ff. and 287 ff., is worth reading, but confused over the relationship between Eleusis and Orphic poetry, as also over that of the Eleusinian Mysteries with other cults. Cf. the reviews of Mylonas's book by P. Boyancé, *REG* 75 (1962), 460 ff., and D. M. Lewis, *JHS* 83 (1963), 206.

[2] A list of parallels is also given in Bücheler's edition. My own has been compiled largely independently.

Hymn to Aphrodite presents the most striking resemblances. A few significant examples from other early epic fragments, and early elegy, have also been included.

There is little in the results to indicate whether the *Hymn* is the work of a 'genuine' oral poet, or rather a good literary imitation of the traditional style.[1] Some signs of awkwardness and abrupt transition exist, but these may as easily be due to the individual character of a single oral poet as to the use of writing. In fact, a literary poet might have avoided them. A number of formulaic doublets, especially of proper-name formulae, are found, and will be discussed below. Such doublets are found also in Homer, but to a lesser degree, and their spread might be regarded as the result of a decline in the oral tradition, owing to the influence of writing, which led to a loss of the strict *economy* of traditional oral poetry.[2] When looked at individually, however, they can usually be seen either to have been created for a special purpose or to have come about through a natural development, by adaptation of existing formulae.[3] On the other hand, the unusually high frequency of 'necessary' enjambement might be considered to suggest literary composition: on this, and some other classes of evidence, see Appendix II, where the question of 'oral' versus 'literary' origin is also reviewed.

The Homeric character of the *Hymn* might be taken simply as an indication that it is 'traditional' in style. However, there are some indications that the poet may have had actual passages from the *Iliad* and *Odyssey* in mind. In the case of Hesiod, the coincidences with certain passages, especially in the *Theogony*, are still more striking.

A. HOMER

1. *Iliad*

The chief coincidences are with episodes in Books 15 and 22. The parallels are between *Dem.* 38 ff. and *Il.* 22. 401 ff., and

---

[1] That some early epic was of this second type is argued most recently by Kirk in *YCS* 20 (1966), 155–74.

[2] The whole question of doublets needs further examination: see L. E. Rossi, *Gött. gel. Anzeigen* 223 (1971), 167 f., and the useful articles of B. Alexanderson, *Eranos* 68 (1970), 1 ff. (especially p. 43), and M. W. Edwards, *HSCP* 74 (1970), 1 ff. (especially p. 35).

[3] The influence of Hesiodic material here is sometimes noticeable, but it would be unwise to speak of the 'contamination' of separate streams in the epic tradition.

Dem. 170 ff. and *Il.* 15. 263 ff. (see notes ad locc.). In the first case, a number of independent phrases from the scene in which Andromache hears of Hector's death appear to be echoed in the passage where Demeter hears her daughter's cry. In the second, a famous traditional simile comparing Hector to a stall-fed horse (applied also to Paris in *Il.* 6. 506 ff.), is followed by another describing the Greeks harrying their prey. In the *Hymn*, elements of both similes have been incorporated into one. It is of course possible that the similes were juxtaposed in other epic poetry besides the *Iliad*. The coincidence, however, remains striking.[1]

Other notable parallels are between *Il.* 5. 364 ff. and *Dem.* 377 ff.; 18. 550 ff. and *Dem.* 455–6 (cf. also Hes. *Sc.* 288 ff.); and 24. 77 ff. and *Dem.* 317 ff.[2] These passages come from scenes which were popular in the archaic period.[3] But most of these resemblances with the *Hymn* may also be explained in terms of reuse of traditional material by separate poets.

2. *Odyssey*

The most important parallels are those between the scene of Demeter's encounter with the daughters of Celeus, followed by her reception at the palace (*Dem.* 98 ff.), and the scenes of meeting between Odysseus and Nausicaa (*Od.* 6. 149 ff.), his meeting with Athena and visit to Alcinous' palace (*Od.* 7. 18 ff.), and his meeting with Athena in *Od.* 13. 96 ff. Demeter's false story (*Dem.* 118 ff.) also resembles those of Odysseus (*Od.* 13. 253 ff., 14. 192 ff., 19. 165 ff.). These parallels are listed and discussed in the notes on *Dem.* 98 ff. (with Appendix III), and 120 ff. The traditional nature of these scenes is there illustrated. There are, however, some features which suggest possible imitation of the actual episodes in the *Odyssey*. The verbal echoes of *Od.* 13. 96–392 are numerous, and are given in full in Appendix III.

---

[1] The simile of the horse has several relatively 'late' linguistic features: cf. G. P. Shipp, *Studies in the Language of Homer* (Cambridge, 1953), 27, 40, 63, 85 n. 2, 117.

[2] There are also some interesting parallels between *Iliad* 9 and the *Hymn*: *Il.* 9. 143–4 ~ *Dem.* 164–5 (141b ~ *Dem.* 450b); 9. 259–61, 496–7 ~ *Dem.* 82–3, 339b, 350–1; 9. 474 ~ *Dem.* 51; 9. 537–8 ~ *Dem.* 246+251 (see notes ad locc.). But *Iliad* 9 shows signs of remodelling (cf. Page, *History and the Homeric Iliad*, 297 ff.), and the speech containing Agamemnon's offer to Achilles may also be traditional (cf. M. D. Reeve, *CQ* 22 (1972), 1 f.).

[3] For the popularity of Books 5, 9, 18, 22, and 24 in archaic art see K. F. Johansen, *The Iliad in Early Greek Art*, 244 ff.

Those of Odysseus' Cretan tales are also striking.[1] *Od.* 20. 122–54 is similar to *Dem.* 106, 285 ff., but here a 'typical scene' structure might be responsible for the parallels.[2]

The evidence is nowhere sufficient to constitute a certain case. There does, however, remain a distinct possibility that the poet already knew the *Iliad* and *Odyssey*, and that certain of the most popular episodes, such as the Death of Hector in the *Iliad*, and Odysseus' meeting with Nausicaa and arrival in Ithaca in the *Odyssey*, influenced him in his choice of language and narrative construction.[3]

B. HESIOD[4]

1. *Mythology*

The most notable parallel is the Catalogue of Oceanids in *Dem.* 418 ff., a 'shortened version' of that in Hes. *Th.* 349 ff., with some additions. The list may be a reminiscence of Hesiod. It may, however, equally well be traditional. A similar question arises in the case of the Nereids (*Il.* 18. 39 ff. ~ *Th.* 243 ff.).

The reference to the Rape of Persephone in Hes. *Th.* 913b–14 is also closely parallel to *Dem.* 2b–3. Here again, the lines may be traditional (cf. ad loc.). *Dem.* 18–19 may also have had a parallel (traditional probably) in the Hesiodic account of Apollo and Cyrene (cf. fr. 215, Pi. *P.* 9. 5–6, and notes to *Dem.* 19).

Hecate (*Dem.* 24 ff., 52 ff., 438 ff.) first appears in Hesiod (*Th.* 411–52), and so does Ploutos (*Th.* 969–74, *Dem.* 488–9). Their presence in the *Hymn* is, however, due to their role in Eleusinian myth, rather than to Hesiodic influence. The roles of Zeus and Gaea in the *Hymn* do not necessarily reflect Hesiodic influence, as has been thought. It is true that Zeus appears more remote in the *Hymn* than in Homer. He does not, for example, ever speak directly, although he sends four separate embassies. The Hesiodic Zeus is an august god, difficult to deceive, but there

---

[1] Cf. ad *Dem.* 120, 123, 125, 127 ff., 129, 132.

[2] Cf. ad *Dem.* 106, 285, 287, 289 f.

[3] It is, of course, theoretically possible that these parallels indicate imitation *of* rather than *by* the poet of the *Hymn*. But this seems unlikely.

[4] The Hesiodic character of the *Hymn* has been discussed and illustrated by C. A. Trypanis in *Athena* 48 (1938), 199–237. See also H. Fietkau, *De carminum Hesiodeorum atque hymnorum quattuor magnorum vocabulis non Homericis* (Königsberg, 1863); K. Francke, *De hymni in Cererem Homerici compositione, dictione, aetate* (Kiel, 1881); J. R. Sterrett, *Qua in re hymni homerici quinque maiores inter se differant antiquitate vel homeritate* (Boston, 1881).

is no very obvious point of contact with the *Hymn*. Likewise, Gaea's role (*Dem.* 9) as an active participant is similar to the one she plays in the *Theogony*, but is rather to be explained by the nature of the myth of Persephone. Demeter herself is more prominent in Hesiod than in Homer. But here also subject-matter accounts for this, and we need not assume a 'Hesiodic' as opposed to a 'Homeric' portrayal of the goddess.

In general, the *Hymn*'s treatment of the gods is grave and solemn, in contrast to the lighter tone of the hymns to *Hermes* and *Aphrodite*. This has been thought to reflect the Hesiodic attitude, which is reverential towards the gods (cf. Trypanis, o.c.), in contrast to the more sceptical, irreverent attitude of the Ionic poets. It should, however, be said that humorous treatment of religion is not always a sign of irreverence. On the contrary, laughter played an important part in many Greek cults (cf. notes on *Dem.* 192 ff., (3) Iambe), and the tone of epic varied from serious to comic according to its subject, Aphrodite being traditionally a target for comedy (like her counterpart Ishtar in the *Epic of Gilgamesh*), and Hermes a god of deceit, whereas Demeter and her daughter are essentially cεμναί τ' αἰδοῖαί τε (*Dem.* 486). Moreover, the distinction between humorous Ionic and serious mainland epic breaks down if the *Hymn to Hermes* belongs to the 'Hesiodic school' (cf. Allen and Halliday, 274 f.). We should be wary of such attempts at broad classification.

Mythology alone gives no very definite grounds for assuming Hesiodic influence. But the evidence of language and formulae is more significant.

2. *Language*

(a) The *Hymn* shares with Hesiodic poetry a number of *words* not found in Homer:

Dem. 2, 77 τανίcφυροc ∼ *Th.* 364 etc.

3, 334, 441, 460 βαρύκτυποc ∼ *Th.* 388 etc.

18, 32 πολυώνυμοc ∼ *Th.* 785

38 ἠχέω ∼ *Th.* 42 etc. (περιηχέω Hom.)

83 ἄπλητοc ∼ *Th.* 153 etc.

87 μεταναιετάω(?) ∼ *Th.* 401 (μεταναιέταc)

89 τανύπτεροc ∼ *Th.* 523 (τανυπτέρυξ, τανυcίπτεροc Hom.)

103, 215, 473 θεμιcτοπόλοc ∼ fr. 10. 1 etc.

109, 425 ἐρόειc ∼ *Th.* 245 etc.

168, 223 ζηλόω ～ *Op.* 23 etc.
168, 223 θρεπτήρια ～ *Op.* 188 (θρέπτρα Hom.)
205 ὀργή ～ *Op.* 304 (but with different meaning?)
209 γληχών ～ fr. 70. 21
219 ἄελπτος ～ fr. 204. 95
240 γονεύς ～ *Op.* 235 etc.
258 νήκεςτος(?) ～ *Op.* 283
272, 298 κολωνός ～ fr. 59. 2
279 κατενήνοθε ～ *Sc.* 269 (ἐπενήνοθε Hom.)
294 εὐρυβίης ～ *Th.* 931 (～ 239)
319, 360, 374, 442 κυανόπεπλος ～ *Th.* 406
352 χαμαιγενής ～ *Th.* 879
362 δυςθυμαίνω ～ *Sc.* 262 (θυμαίνω)
367 ἀδικεῖν ～ *Op.* 260 etc. (ἄδικος)
439 ἀμφαγαπάω ～ *Op.* 58 (ἀμφαγαπάζω Hom.)
450, 451, 469 φερέςβιος ～ *Th.* 693

(*b*) There are also some Homeric words whose *form or meaning* is different in Hesiod and the *Hymn* from Homer:

Dem. 50 λουτροῖς ～ *Op.* 753 (Hom. λοετρά)
56 (etc.) Περςεφόνην ～ *Th.* 913 (Hom. Περςεφόνεια)
144 διδαςκήςαιμι (ex coni.) ～ *Op.* 64 (Hom. ἐδίδαξε etc.)
156 πορςαίνουςιν ～ fr. 43(a). 69 etc. (Hom. πορςύνω, v.l. πορςαίνω)
311 γεράων ～ *Th.* 393, 396 (Hom. only γέρας, γέρα)
327 δίδον, 437 ἔδιδον ～ *Op.* 139 (Hom. δίδοςαν)
328 (etc.) τιμάς ～ *Th.* 74 etc. (in Hom. always singular)
351 παύςειεν intrans. ～ *Sc.* 449 (in Hom. trans.; v.l. *Od.* 4. 659;
    but cf. ad loc.)
402 θάλλει pres. ～ *Op.* 173, 236 (Hom. τέθηλε etc.)
425 δρέπομεν active ～ *Th.* 31 v.l. (Hom. δρεψάμεναι)
458 κεχάρηντο ～ *Sc.* 65 (Hom. κεχάροντο)
459 'Ρέη ～ *Th.* 467 (Hom. 'Ρείη, 'Ρέα)
    Note also 406 ἐρέω with synizesis ～ *Op.* 202 (Hom. ἐρέω).

(*c*) There are numerous *phrases and formulae* which have close parallels in Hesiod, but not in Homer:

Dem. 2b–3 ～ *Th.* 913–14 (cf. above: Mythology)
3b ～ *Th.* 388, *Op.* 79, *Sc.* 318 (name formula)
10–11 (δ δόλον), 403–4 ～ *Th.* 588–9
37 (μέγαν νόον) ～ *Th.* 37*

38a ∼ *Th.* 835b

44b ∼ *Op.* 10* (This is a doublet of a Hom. formula)

49–50a ∼ *Th.* 796–7 (798a ∼ *D.* 285)

60, 75a ∼ *Th.* 625, 634 (name formula)

(85b ∼ *Op.* 74*)

85–6 ∼ *Th.* 424–5

98–100 (ἕζετο δ᾽ . . . ἐν cκίῃ) ∼ *Op.* 593

103, 215, 473b ∼ frr. 10. 1, ? 9. 1, PSI 6. 722. 1

108 ∼ fr. 26. 6

110 ∼ *Th.* 79, 361 (349–61 ∼ *D.* 418–23)

144 (ἔργα διδαcκήcαιμι) ∼ *Op.* 64

168b, 223b ∼ *Op.* 188b*

179, 292 (κυδρὴν θεόν) ∼ *Th.* 442*

182 (κατὰ κρῆθεν κεκαλυμμένη), 197b ∼ *Th.* 574–5, *Sc.* 7*

182b–3 (ῥαδινοῖcι . . . ποccίν) ∼ *Th.* 194b–5a

203 (παρὰ . . . ἐτρέψατο) ∼ *Th.* 103

(203b), 439b ∼ *Op.* 465*

204b ∼ *Op.* 340 (336–8 ∼ *D.* 368–9)

209b ∼ fr. 70. 21*

217b ∼ *Op.* 815*

224, 307, 384, 470b = *Op.* 300b (301 ∼ *D.* 374) (name formula)

258b ∼ *Op.* 283b*

269 ∼ *Th.* 871, *Op.* 822

274, 368–9 ∼ *Th.* 417, *Op.* 336–8 (340 ∼ *D.* 204b)

276b ∼ *Th.* 583b, *Sc.* 7–8

276–9 ∼ fr. 43(a). 73–4

279b = *Sc.* 269b (269a ∼ *D.* 452?)

285 (εὐcτρώτων λεχέων) ∼ *Th.* 798 (796–7 ∼ *D.* 49–50, 802 ff.
    ∼ *D.* 354–5)

303b ∼ *Th.* 813b*

310 ∼ *Op.* 180 (310b = *Op.* 180b)

311b (γεράων . . . τιμήν) ∼ *Th.* 393, 396, 426–7

315b ∼ *Th.* 908b* (cf. frr. 25. 39, 136. 2)

334b–5a ∼ *Th.* 514b–15a*

343a ∼ *Op.* 501a*

352b = *Th.* 879b (doublet of Hom. formula)

358 (Διὸc βαcιλῆοc) ∼ *Th.* 886, 923, *Op.* 668, fr. 308 (name
    formula)

360–1 . . . κυανόπεπλον, | ἤπιον . . . ∼ *Th.* 406–7 κυανόπεπλον . . . |
    ἤπιον* . . . (of Leto: cf. West ad loc.)

367–9 ~ *Op.* 334, 336–8 (cf. ad loc.)
374 (αἰδοίη Δημήτερι) ~ *Op.* 300–1 (~ *D.* 224 etc.)
403–4 (δόλῳ) ~ *Th.* 588–9 (~ *D.* 8–11), 500
414b ~ *Th.* 572 = *Op.* 71
418–23 ~ *Th.* 349 ff. (Mythology: cf. ad *D.* 417–24)
418 ~ frr. 291. 3?, 169. 1
419 Μελίτη ~ *Th.* 247; *Th.* 361 ~ *D.* 110
424a ~ *Th.* 925* (ἐγρεκυδοιμόν) (name formula)
439b ~ *Op.* 465b* (name formula)
440a (ἐκ τοῦ) ~ *Th.* 556a*
450–2 (οὖθαρ ἀρούρης | τὸ πρίν . . . ἔκευθε . . .) ~ *Th.* 505
456a ~ *Sc.* 290a* (456b ~ *Sc.* 291a, *Il.* 18. 553b*)
486b–7a ~ *Th.* 96–7

(*d*) A number of formulae and phrases have parallels in Hesiod which are themselves *adaptations* of Homeric expressions:

Dem. 7a ~ *Th.* 279 (~ *Od.* 5. 72)
11b, 403b θνητοῖς (τ') ἀνθρώποις ~ fr. 1. 7 καταθνητοῖς τ' ἀνθρώποις* (1. 7a ~ *D.* 11a). *Th.* 296 etc. θνητοῖς ἀνθρώποις at beginning of verse ~ *Il.* 14. 199 θνητοὺς ἀνθρώπους* (~ *Od.* 7. 210 etc.). ἀνθρώποις in Homer comes at the beginning of the verse (*Od.*, 3 times). Cf. *Dem.* 306, 489 ἀνθρώποις in second–third feet ~ *Th.* 296 etc.
33b = *Th.* 470b (~ *Il.* 5. 769 etc., *Il.* 14. 174 etc., 15. 371 etc.)
79b ~ *Th.* 921* etc. (frequent in Ps. Hesiod) (~ *Il.* 3. 53, 14. 268, 3. 138)
88b–9a = *Sc.* 341–2 (~ *Il.* 17. 457–8 etc.)
135b–6a ~ *Op.* 81–2 (~ *Il.* 1. 18 ff. etc.)
145a (φῆ ῥα) ~ *Th.* 550* (~ *Il.* 21. 361, 3. 355 etc.)
151b–2a ~ *Sc.* 105 (~ *Il.* 16. 100 etc., *Od.* 6. 265, *Il.* 16. 542)
152b ~ *Th.* 86a, *Op.* 36a (~ *Il.* 18. 508, 23. 579 f.)
182 (κατὰ κρῆθεν) ~ *Sc.* 7* (ἀπὸ κρῆθεν) (~ *Il.* 16. 548 etc. κατὰ κρῆθεν)
203b πότνιαν ἀγνήν ~ *Th.* 11 πότνιαν Ἥρην* (in Homer always πότνια, nominative or vocative, in fifth foot). *Dem.* 54 πότνια (at beginning of verse) ~ *Th.* 926 πότνιαν* (name formula)
276 (περί τ' ἀμφί τε) ~ *Th.* 848* (~ *Il.* 17. 760, in another position in verse)
277b ~ *Th.* 557b* (~ *Il.* 8. 48 etc.)
278b ~ *Th.* 191 (~ *Il.* 14. 177, 17. 571)

287b = *Th.* 3* (~ *Il.* 19. 92)
296b ~ *Sc.* 472 (~ *Il.* 24. 776)
311a ~ *Sc.* 43a* (~ *Il.* 13. 667)
336b ~ *Th.* 90b* (~ *Od.* 10. 70, *Il.* 24. 771)
347 ~ *Th.* 850 (~ *Il.* 15. 188, *Od.* 11. 491) (name formula)
397b ~ *Th.* 415 (~ *Il.* 24. 533), 499 (and *Hymns*)
482b ~ *Th.* 729–31a ὑπὸ ζόφῳ ἠερόεντι ... χώρῳ ἐν εὐρώεντι ~
Il. 23. 51 ὑπὸ ζόφον ἠερόεντα (~ 21. 56 etc. ὑπὸ ζόφου ἠερόεντος),
and *Od.* 10. 512, 23. 322 Ἀίδεω δόμον εὐρώεντα (the dative
formula is not found in Homer).

Particular interest attaches to those formulae in the above lists
which are for names, and these will be discussed below. Formulaic
doublets will also be considered separately. Many of the formulae listed could be traditional, and some are found elsewhere
(in the *Hymns*, *Cypria*, etc.). A few passages do however look as if
they might be definite echoes of passages in Hesiod:

(i) *Rape of Persephone*
Dem. 2b–3 ~ *Th.* 913–14 (But see above, Mythology, and on
Dem. 1–18.)

(ii) *Pandora*
Dem. 8–11 νάρκισσόν θ᾽ ὃν φῦσε δόλον ...
          θαυμαστὸν γανόωντα, cέβας τό γε πᾶcιν ἰδέcθαι
          ἀθανάτοιc τε θεοῖc ἠδὲ θνητοῖc ἀνθρώποιc
Dem. 403–4 αὖτιc ἄνει μέγα θαῦμα θεοῖc θνητοῖc τ᾽ ἀνθρώποιc.
          καὶ τίνι c᾽ ἐξαπάτηcε δόλῳ κρατερὸc πολυδέγμων;
~ *Th.* 588–9 θαῦμα δ᾽ ἔχ᾽ ἀθανάτουc τε θεοὺc θνητούc τ᾽
          ἀνθρώπουc
          ὡc εἶδον δόλον αἰπὺν ἀμήχανον ἀνθρώποιcιν.

The first and third passages refer to a 'snare' set by the gods
(δόλοc) which causes gods and men alike to wonder. But in the
second passage there is no connection between the two lines, except perhaps one of verbal association from the other passages.
(The abrupt transition led earlier editors to assume a lacuna.
But see notes ad loc.) The coincidence of language between the
three passages is notable. In the same episode (*Creation of Woman*)
in Hesiod note *Th.* 572b~*Dem.* 414b, *Th.* 574–5~*Dem.* 182, 197,
Th. 580 (χαριζόμενος Διὶ πατρί) ~ *Dem.* 9*, *Th.* 583b ~ *Dem.* 276
(and perhaps 577 ~ *Dem.* 417: West ad loc.).

Hesiod repeats the story in *Op.* 47 ff., and here too there are echoes in the *Hymn*:

Op. 58 ἀμφαγαπῶντες ~ *Dem.* 439 (ἀμφαγάπησε)

64a ἔργα διδασκῆσαι ~ *Dem.* 144? (ἔργα διδασκήσαιμι?)

74b ἀμφὶ δὲ τήν γε ~ *Dem.* 85b ἀμφὶ δὲ τιμήν*

(75b ἄνθεσιν εἰαρινοῖσι ~ *Dem.* 401 ἄνθεσι . . . ἠαρινοῖσι ~ *Il.* 2. 89, *Th.* 279, *Cypr.* 4. 2)

79 Διὸς βουλῆισι βαρυκτύπου ~ *Dem.* 3, 334, 441, 460 βαρύκτυπος . . . Ζεύς + *Dem.* 9 Διὸς βουλῆισι* (~ *Il.* 13. 254*)

81–2 πάντες Ὀλύμπια δώματ᾽ ἔχοντες | δῶρον ἐδώρησαν . . . ~ *Dem.* 135–6 πάντες Ὀλύμπια δώματ᾽ ἔχοντες | δοῖεν . . .

(Note also *Op.* 71–2 = *Th.* 572–3, *Op.* 83 δόλον.)

(iii) *Hecate* (*Th.* 404 ff.)

The prominence of Hecate in the *Hymn* might lead one to look for parallels with Hesiod's description of her. It is therefore interesting to find a probable echo at the opening of the passage, in the lines about Leto (*Th.* 406–7 ~ *Dem.* 360–1 : see above). The coincidence of the two epithets in Hesiod may have suggested the second in the *Hymn*. Possible echoes of the Hecate passage itself are (besides 409 Πέρσης ~ *Dem.* 24):

Th. 415 and 449 ~ *Dem.* 339

417 (and *Op.* 336–8) ~ *Dem.* 274, 368–9

419 (ᾧ πρόφρων γε θεὰ ὑποδέξεται εὐχάς) ~ *Dem.* 226

424–5 ~ *Dem.* 85b–6 (87 ~ *Th.* 401 μεταναιέτας)

426–7 (and 393, 396) ~ 311a

442 (κυδρὴ θεός) ~ 179, 292

(iv) *The Muses* (*Th.* 75 ff.)

Th. 79 (~ 361) ~ *Dem.* 110

86a (and *Op.* 36) ~ 152 (ἰθείηισι δίκηισιν)

90b μαλακοῖσι παραιφάμενοι ἐπέεσσιν ~ 336

92 αἰδοῖ . . . μετὰ δὲ πρέπει ~ 214 ἐπί τοι πρέπει . . . αἰδώς

96–7 ὁ δ᾽ ὄλβιος, ὅντινα Μοῦσαι | φίλωνται ~ 486–7 μέγ᾽ ὄλβιος, ὅντιν᾽ ἐκεῖναι | προφρονέως φίλωνται

103 παρέτραπε (of diverting from grief) ~ 203 παρὰ . . . ἐτρέψατο

107–10 ἁλμυρὸς . . . Πόντος | . . . καὶ γαῖα . . . καὶ πόντος οἴδματι θύων | . . . καὶ οὐρανὸς εὐρὺς ὕπερθεν (~ 839–41) ~ *Dem.* 13–14

(v) *Aphrodite's birth* (*Th.* 188 ff.)

Th. 191 ἀπ' ἀθανάτου χροός ~ *Dem.* 278 ἀπὸ χροὸς ἀθανάτοιο
194–5 ἀμφὶ δὲ ποίη | ποccὶν ὑπὸ ῥαδινοῖcιν ~ 182–3 ἀμφὶ
δὲ πέπλος . . . ῥαδινοῖcι . . . ποccίν

(vi) *Styx* (*Th.* 775 ff.)

Th. 777 νόcφιν δὲ θεῶν (~ 813 θεῶν ἔκτοcθεν ἀπάντων) ~ *Dem.* 303
μακάρων ἀπὸ νόcφιν ἀπάντων
785 πολυώνυμον ~ *Dem.* 18, 32
796–7 οὐδέ ποτ' ἀμβροcίης καὶ νέκταρος ἔρχεται ἆccον | βρώcιος . . .
~ *Dem.* 49–50 οὐδέ ποτ' ἀμβροcίης καὶ νεκταρος ἡδυπότοιο |
πάccατ' . . .
798 cτρωτοῖc ἐν λεχέεccι ~ *Dem.* 285 ἀπ' εὐcτρώτων λεχέων
(800–4 εἰνάετες δὲ θεῶν ἀπαμείρεται . . .
    οὐδέ ποτ' ἐς βουλὴν ἐπιμίcγεται . . .
    ἐννέα πάντ' ἔτεα· δεκάτῳ δ' ἐπιμίcγεται αὖτις . . .
~ *Dem.* 354–5 οὐδὲ θεοῖcι | μίcγεται, ἀλλ' ἀπάνευθε)

(vii) *Typhoeus* (*Th.* 820 ff.)

Th. 835 ὑπὸ δ' ἤχεεν οὔρεα μακρά (~ 42) ~ *Dem.* 38 ἤχηcαν δ'
ὀρέων κορυφαί
836–8 καί νύ κεν ἔπλετο ἔργον ἀμήχανον . . .
    καί κεν . . .
    εἰ μὴ ἄρ' ὀξὺ νόηcε πατὴρ ἀνδρῶν τε θεῶν τε . . .
~ *Dem.* 310–3 καί νύ κε πάμπαν ὄλεccε . . .
    καὶ . . .
    εἰ μὴ Ζεὺς ἐνόηcεν . . .
(839–41 ~ *Dem.* 13–4: cf. sup.)
848 περί τ' ἀμφί τε ~ *Dem.* 276*
850 τρέε δ' Ἀίδης ἐνεροῖcι καταφθιμένοιcιν ἀνάccων ~ *Dem.* 347
Ἀίδη . . . καταφθιμένοιcιν ἀνάccων
(867 πυρὸς μένει v.l. ~ *Dem.* 239*)
871 οἵ γε μὲν ἐκ θεόφιν . . . θνητοῖc μέγ' ὄνειαρ (~ *Op.* 822) ~
Dem. 268–9 μέγιστον | ἀθανάτοιc θνητοῖcί τ' ὄνεαρ
879 χαμαιγενέων ἀνθρώπων ~ *Dem.* 352*

It is interesting that, as in the case of Homer, all these episodes
in the *Theogony* are ones which may well have become popular
from an early date. Equally, several of them may have been traditional, and well known before Hesiod wrote his poem. This

may have been true of Aphrodite, Styx, and Typhoeus, all of whose myths are clearly very old. But it is less likely in the case of the Muses and Hecate, both of whom receive special 'hymns' from the poet. It is even possible that these were composed specially to fit the occasion of the first recitation of the *Theogony* (cf. West, Introduction, 44–5), and it is fairly certain that we have the poet himself speaking.[1] In the case of the Oceanids, and the lines summarizing the Rape of Persephone, there are some indications that the material may be traditional. But if the poet of the *Hymn* knew parts of the *Theogony*, he surely knew it all, and we should not be surprised if he knew the *Works and Days* also. The relationship with Pseudo-Hesiod, most of which in its final form seems to be of sixth-century date, is more problematical, and must remain an open question. The *Hymn* has some formulae which seem peculiar to the *Catalogue*, and common there: e.g. *Dem.* 315 πολυήρατον εἶδος ἔχουσαν ∼ *Th.* 908, and similarly frr. 25. 39, 136. 2; 79 θαλερὴν κεκλῆσθαι ἄκοιτιν ∼ *Th.* 921, etc., West, p. 398; 103 (∼215, 473) θεμιστοπόλων βασιλήων ∼ frr. 10. 1, 9. 1 (?), PSI 6. 722. 1. There are also one or two unusual expressions which coincide, notably *Dem.* 209 γληχῶνι τερείνῃ ∼ fr. 70. 21*. But it would seem impossible to establish any precedence.

3. *Style*

Finally, the style of the *Hymn* resembles that of Hesiod in certain important features, all of which concern the conventions governing epic speeches:

(*a*) Some speeches (but not all) are short: *Dem.* 54–8, 248–9, 321–3. These are rare in Homer, but normal in Hesiod (West, p. 74).

(*b*) Zeus sends four sets of messengers, without a single direct speech (314 ff., 325 ff., 334 ff., 441 ff.). This avoidance of direct speech is abnormal in Homer, but occurs in Hesiod (*Th.* 392 ff., *Op.* 60 ff.).

(*c*) After indirect speech, ὣς ἔφατο is twice used (316, 448), as if a speech had preceded. This is only used in Homer when one speech is reported inside another. Cf. *Op.* 69.

---

[1] Cf. West, p. 32 and note to *Th.* 76, suggesting that the Muses' names were invented by him, and pp. 276 ff., on Hesiod's family as devotees of Hecate.

C. HYMN TO APHRODITE

The relationship between the two hymns has been discussed most recently by E. Heitsch, *Aphroditehymnus, Aeneas und Homer* (Göttingen, 1965), 38 ff.

The parallels which I have noted are:

Dem. 5 κούρῃσι . . . βαθυκόλποις (nymphs) ~ *Aph.* 257 νύμφαι . . . βαθύκολποι. In Homer the epithet is only used of Trojan women (3 times)

8 καλυκώπιδι κούρῃ ⎫ ~ *Aph.* 284 νύμφης καλυκώπιδος (not
420 Ὠκυρόη καλυκῶπις ⎭ in Homer or Hesiod)

22–3 ⎫ ~ *Aph.* 2 ff., also *Herm.* 143–5 (but this is a parallel of
44–6 ⎭ form of expression, not of language)

83–4 οὔ τοι ἀεικὴς | γαμβρὸς . . . Ἀϊδωνεύς (~ 363) ~ *Aph.* 136 οὔ σφιν ἀεικελίη νυὸς ἔσσομαι, ἀλλ᾿ ἐϊκυῖα

145–6   παρθένος ἀδμὴς
        Καλλιδίκη . . . εἶδος ἀρίστη
~ *Aph.* 82 παρθένῳ ἀδμήτῃ μέγεθος καὶ εἶδος ὁμοίη

159b δὴ γὰρ θεοείκελός ἐσσι ~ *Aph.* 279b μάλα γὰρ θεοείκελος ἔσται

188–9   ἡ δ᾿ ἄρ᾿ ἐπ᾿ οὐδὸν ἔβη ποσί, καί ῥα μελάθρου
        κῦρε κάρη, πλῆσεν δὲ θύρας σέλαος θείοιο
~ *Aph.* 173–5 ἔστη ἄρα κλισίῃ, εὐποιήτοιο μελάθρου
        κῦρε κάρη, κάλλος δὲ παρειάων ἀπέλαμπεν
        ἄμβροτον . . .

194b = *Aph.* 156b κατ᾿ ὄμματα καλὰ βαλοῦσα

268–9 εἰμὶ δὲ Δημήτηρ τιμάοχος, ἥ τε μέγιστον
        ἀθανάτοις θνητοῖσί τ᾿ ὄνεαρ καὶ χάρμα τέτυκται
~ *Aph.* 31–2 πᾶσιν δ᾿ ἐν νηοῖσι θεῶν τιμάοχός ἐστι,
        καὶ παρὰ πᾶσι βροτοῖσι θεῶν πρέσβειρα τέτυκται

285 ἀπ᾿ εὐστρώτων λεχέων ~ *Aph.* 157 ἐς λέχος εὔστρωτον (~ Hes. *Th.* 798)

(352b = *Aph.* 108b = Hes. *Th.* 879b χαμαιγενέων ἀνθρώπων)

355 θυώδεος ἔνδοθι νηοῦ ⎫ ~ *Aph.* 58 θυώδεα νηόν
385 νηοῖο . . . θυώδεος ⎭

397 πάντεσσι τετιμ[ένη ἀθανάτοι]σιν + 403 αὖτις ἄνει μέγα θαῦμα θεοῖς θνητοῖς τ᾿ ἀνθρώποις ~ *Aph.* 205 θαῦμα ἰδεῖν, πάντεσσι τετιμένος ἀθανάτοισι (~ Hes. *Th.* 415, 449, 588).

Of these, the most important are *Dem.* 188–9, 194b, and 285, which are all paralleled in the same part of the *Hymn to Aphrodite*, and *Dem.* 268–9. These passages are discussed in the notes (188–9, 269), and it is suggested that the *Hymn to Demeter* may have been influenced by the *Hymn to Aphrodite*, although this is by no means certain. Heitsch comes to the same conclusion, but some of his stylistic arguments seem unconvincing.

The *Hymn to Aphrodite* has always been regarded as closest in style and language to Homer, and is often thought to be one of the earliest of the *Homeric Hymns*. (The second hypothesis of course does not necessarily follow from the first.) It shows several Hesiodic features, but to a lesser degree than the *Hymn to Demeter* (cf. Allen and Halliday, p. 350, and notes, Heitsch, o.c. 19 ff.).

If it were later than Homer's and Hesiod's poems, and earlier than *Demeter*, this would tend to lower the *terminus post* for the latter to some extent. But the ground seems too uncertain for building any sure theory.[1]

D. LANGUAGE PECULIAR TO THE *HYMN TO DEMETER*[2]

Many words and forms are found in the *Hymn* which do not occur in Homer, Hesiod, or other early epic (*Hymns, Cycle*, inscriptions, etc.).

(*a*) *Words*
(* before line reference indicates words not found elsewhere in Greek)

1, 478, 486 cεμνόc (Cf. *Hy.* 30. 16, which is probably influenced by *Dem.*, and of a later period; Solon etc.)

6 ῥόδον (Hom. ῥοδόεις etc.; Sappho, etc.)

7 ἀγαλλίς (late Greek)

9 πολυδέκτης (Elsewhere only Cornut. 35, perhaps quoting from *Dem.* Cf. ad loc.)

---

[1] See however Heitsch, o.c. 19–38. He considers that the *Hymn to Aphrodite* is later than Homer (main part of *Iliad*) and Hesiod, and dates it to the second half of the seventh century (p. 112). Cf. also Hoekstra, *Sub-epic Stage*, 39 ff., arguing for imitation of the *Iliad* by this *Hymn*, and supporting a similar date; and J. C. Kamerbeek, *Mnem.* 20 (1967), 385 ff., who also considers the *Hymn* later than the *Iliad*, and very probably a literary composition (p. 389). F. Solmsen, *Hermes* 88 (1960), 1 ff., considers that *Aph.* 7–44 shows Hesiodic influence.

[2] Cf. O. Zumbach, *Neuerungen*, with Forderer's review, *Gnomon* 30 (1958), 94 ff.; and see also Hoekstra, *Sub-epic Stage*, chapters I and IV, which contain many useful observations on language and formulae.

10 θαυμαστός (Archilochus, Theognis etc.)

17, 31, 404, 430 πολυδέγμων (Hellenistic and late Greek)

*31, 84, 376 πολυcημάντωρ

51 φαινόλις (Sappho, Moschus)

*54, 192, 492 ὠρηφόρος

54, 192, 492 ἀγλαόδωρος (Nonnus)

55 οὐράνιος (Pindar etc.)

85 ὁμόσπορος (Pindar etc.)

*87 μεταναιετάω (cf. Hes. *Th.* 401)

102 φιλοστέφανος (Bacchylides etc.)

*106 εὐήρυτος

*108 κουρήϊος

142 τιθηνέομαι (Theognis etc.)

142 τηρεῖν (Pindar etc.)

144 δεσπόσυνος (Tyrtaeus, Pindar etc.)

149 σαφέως (Pindar etc.)

*165 πολυεύχετος (πολύευκτος Orac. ap. Hdt. etc.)

166 ἐκτρέφειν (v.l. *Od.* 18. 130; Herodotus, Sophocles etc.)

*178 κροκήϊος

197 προκατέχομαι (later only active, Thuc. etc.)

198 ἄφθογγος (Theognis etc.)

200 ἀγέλαστος (v.l. in Homer; Heraclitus etc.)

202 χλεύη (Hellenistic and late Greek)

203 (παρα)σκώπτω (simple verb Hdt. etc.; compound Plutarch. See note ad loc.)

207 θεμιτός (Pindar etc.)

211 πολυπότνια (Aristophanes etc.)

227 κακοφραδίη (v.l. in Homer; Hellenistic and late Greek)

*228 ὑποταμνόν

229 ἀντίτομον (Pindar etc.)

230 ἐρυσμός (late Greek)

238 καταπνέω (Aeschylus etc.)

*241 προθαλής

244 ἐπιτηρεῖν (Aristophanes, Thuc. etc.)

254 ἐξαναιρέω (Eur., A.R.)

256 ἀφράδμων (ἀφράσμων Aesch., Soph.)

257 προγιγνώσκω (Eur. etc.)

273, 476 ὄργια (Aesch. etc.)

274, 369 εὐαγέως (A.R. etc., εὐαγής Soph. etc.

278 φέγγος (Pindar etc.)

296 πολυπείρων (Orphic *Argonautica*)
308 μάτην (Theognis etc.)

353 καταφθινύθω (Empedocles)
*362 δυϲθυμαίνω (θυμαίνω Ps. Hesiod)
365 δεϲπόζω (Aesch. etc.)
367 ἀδικέω (Archilochus or Hipponax, Sappho etc.)
372 κόκκος (Hdt. etc.)
399 μέρος (*Herm.* 53 f.l.; Pindar etc.)
402 παντοδαπός (Sappho etc.)
413 προϲαναγκάζω (?) (Hippocr., Thuc. etc.)
427 ῥόδεος (Ibycus etc.)
427 λείριον (Hom. λειριόειϲ; Hippocr., Thphr., A.R. etc.)
440 πρόπολος (? Ps. Hesiod; Xenophanes, etc.)
*452 πανάφυλλος (Hom. ἄφυλλος)
*476 δρηϲμοϲύνη (Hom. δρηϲτοϲύνη)

(*b*) *Forms or meanings of words*

10 ϲέβαϲ of object of reverence; 190, 479 ϲέβαϲ of reverence towards
   the gods (cf. *Hy.* 28. 6, Hom. *Epig.* 8. 3). Cf. ϲεμνός *Dem.* 1,
   478, 486
15 ἄμφω as dative (Hellenistic poetry)
16 εὐρυάγυια as epithet of earth
?19 ὄχοιϲιν (perhaps corrupt)
47 (etc.) Δηώ, Δηοῖ
118 πότνα as nominative (Callimachus)
126 κατέχω intransitive (Theognis etc.)
128 ἐπαρτύνομαι middle (Hom. ἀρτύνομαι, ἐπαρτύνω)
129 ἔραμαι imperfect (ἤρατο)
?132 τιμή = 'price' (but cf. *Il.* 3. 290, *Od.* 22. 57)
140 ἀφῆλιξ = 'aged'
149, 273 ὑποτίθεμαι = 'tell, teach'
165, 219 ὀψίγονος meaning 'late-born'
170 κυδιάουϲαι (Hom. κυδιόων etc.)
174, 401 ἦαρος, ἠαρινοῖϲι
175 ἄλλομαι present
176 ἐπέχομαι of holding up robes
176 ἑανῶν plural as noun
(? 183, 279 θεῆϲ M: read θεᾶϲ?)
205 ὀργαῖϲ plural, of single person's 'temper'?

208 ἄλφι singular (Hom. ἄλφιτον)

215 ὡς εἴ πέρ τε . . . : this combination seems to be unique

217 ζυγός (v.l. *Il.* 9. 187)

240 λάθρᾰ (λάθρῃ Hom.; not found elsewhere)

262 οὐκ ἔσθ' ὡς κεν . . . : οὐκ ἔσθ' ὡς does not occur in Homer

277 πέπλων plural, of single robe

279 κατενήνοθεν plural (not found elsewhere; perhaps corrupt)

289 ἐλούεον (not found elsewhere)

311 λιμός feminine (Hellenistic and late Greek, Doric)

312 ἀμέρδειν with double accusative (not found elsewhere)

[*312 ἐθέλοιτο? (probably corrupt)]

347 Ἄιδη

351 παύσειεν intransitive (v.l. *Od.* 4. 659, *Hy.* 33. 14)

366 σχήσησθα (not found elsewhere)

?368 θυσίαισι (perhaps corrupt)

373 νωμᾶν = 'look'

379, 413 ἄκοντε, ἄκουσαν with contraction (v.l. *Il.* 5. 366 etc.)

383 βαθύν feminine (cf. πουλύν, ἡδύς, θῆλυς Hom.) or ἀήρ masculine (cf. Hesiod)? ἀήρ = 'air' here? (See note ad loc.)

?383 τέμνον (τάμνον should perhaps be read. Cf. *Od.* 3. 175 τέμνειν, also corrupt?)

403 ἄνει (Hom. εἶσθα)

412 ἔμβαλέ μοι . . . κόκκον

424 Παλλάς alone, of Athena (Pindar etc.)

426 ἀγανός of flowers (conjecture; not found elsewhere)

429 περὶ χάρματι = 'for joy' (Pindar etc.)

437 γηθοσύνας plural (Hellenistic poetry; Hom. εὐφροσύναι etc.)

439 κόρη ([Archil.] 322 West etc.)

440 ὀπάων of woman (Hecate)

443 ὑποδέχομαι with infinitive

448 ἀπιθέω with genitive (not found elsewhere)

451 ἔκηλος of the earth (Hellenistic poetry)

455 ἦρος (cf. Hes. ἔαρι,' ἔαρος)

455 πέδῳ (cf. πέδονδε, πεδόθεν Hom., Hes.) = 'on the ground' (later 'to the ground')

481 ἀτελής = 'uninitiated'

(c) *Formulae*

In the category of proper-name formulae the *Hymn* shows some interesting developments, several being formed by adaptation or combination of Homeric and Hesiodic formulae, whilst some are doublets of formulae found elsewhere in early epic:[1]

(i) *Demeter*

Cf. *Dem.* 1 (new formula), 4 (new formula from Homeric elements), 47 (formula on Homeric pattern), 54 (adaptation of nominative formula, *Dem.* 192, to vocative, with hiatus; doublet of *Dem.* 75, 492; πότνια not in Homeric position in verse, but cf. Hesiod, *Th.* 926 πότνιαν*), 60 (adaptation of Hesiodic formula), 75 (cf. *Dem.* 60; adaptation of Hom. formula; doublet of 54, 492), 192 (new formula; cf. 54), 211 (cf. 47), 224 etc. (Hesiodic formula), 251 (new formula; cf. 224, *Il.* 14. 326), 295 (cf. 251), 297 (adaptation of *Dem.* 1 etc.), 302 (Homeric formula), 315 (cf. *Dem.* 1; adaptation and combination of Hesiodic formula), 319 (new formula; cf. 360, 374, 442), 374 (adaptation of Hesiodic and Hom. formulae; cf. *Dem.* 319 etc.), 439 (adaptation of Hesiodic formula), 453 (new formula; doublet of *Th.* 912, *Dem.* 4), 492 (doublet of *Dem.* 54; cf. 47, 75, 192).

(ii) *Zeus*

Dem. 3 etc. (combination of Hom. and Hes. formulae; doublet of *Il.* 1. 544 etc., 2. 205 etc.; also of *Dem.* 321), 21 (adaptation and combination of Hom. formulae), 27 (cf. *Dem.* 21), 78 (Hom. formula), 316 (combination of Hom. formulae), 321 (combination of Hom. formulae; doublet of *Dem.* 3 etc., *Il.* 1. 544 etc.), 396 (combination of Hom. formulae; cf. *Dem.* 316), 408 (adaptation of Hom. formula; cf. *Dem.* 21, 27; doublet of *Il.* 2. 787), 468 (Hom. formula), 485 (Hom. formula).

(iii) *Persephone*

? *Dem.* 8 (formula with new epithet, on Hom. pattern; cf. *Aph.* 284, *Dem.* 333), ? 333 (Hom. formula), 337 (adaptation of Hom. formula), 348 (adaptation of Hom. formula), 359 (formula on Hom. pattern, but using δαΐφρων, which is normally applied to men in Homer; cf. 370), 370 (formula on Hom. pattern; cf. 359), 405 (cf. *Dem.* 493), 439 (cf. *Dem.* 348), 493 (cf. *Il.* 5. 389, *Dem.* 405).

This group shows no actual doublets. A number of epithets *could* have been used in different cases, but this is not done. Cf.

[1] Cf. M. Parry, *L'Épithète traditionnelle*, 218 ff., Edwards, *Language of Hesiod*, 55 ff.

Dem. 8 καλυκώπιδι κούρῃ, 333 ἐὴν εὐώπιδα κούρην, 493 κούρῃ περικαλλὴς Περσεφόνεια; and 348 ἀγαυὴν Περσεφόνειαν, 359 δαΐφρονι Περσεφονείῃ, 370 περίφρων Περσεφόνεια, 439 κόρην Δημήτερος ἀγνῆς.

This seems to point to a genuine system.

(iv) *Hades*

Dem. 17 (cf. 430; ἄναξ in 17 violates Hermann's bridge), 18 = 32 (new formula; cf. Κρόνου υἷε/υἱέ in Hom. and Hes., πολυώνυμον* Hes.), 31 (new formula; doublet of *Dem.* 84, 376?; cf. also *Dem.* 9); 84, 376 (new formula; doublet of *Dem.* 31?), 347 (adaptation of Hom. and Hes. formula), 357 (Hom. formula; doublet of *Dem.* 430; cf. *Dem.* 18), 404 (cf. 17, 430), 430 (new formula; doublet of *Dem.* 357 etc.; cf. *Dem.* 17, 404).

(v) *Rhea*

Cf. Demeter. *Dem.* 60, 75 (adaptation of Hes. formula), 442 (cf. *Dem.* 60 etc.), 459 (new formula; cf. *Il.* 18. 382, *Dem.* 25, 438).

(vi) *Helios*

Dem. 26 (combination and adaptation of Hom. formulae; cf. *Hy.* 28. 13), 62 (new formula).

(vii) *Hermes*

Dem. 335 (adaptation of Hom. formula), 346, 377 (Hom. formula), 407 (see notes ad loc.; new formula from Hom. elements; doublet of *Il.* 21. 497 etc., *Ap.* 200 etc.).

(viii) *Aphrodite*

Dem. 102 (combination of Hom. formulae; doublet of *Il.* 20. 105, *Aph.* 1, 9).

(ix) *Hecate*

Dem. 24–5 (adaptation of Hom. formulae; cf. *Dem.* 438, 458), 438 (cf. *Dem.* 25). The poet takes an epithet used only once in Homer (λιπαροκρήδεμνος) for both Hecate and Rhea.

(x) *Athena*

Dem. 424 (new formula? Cf. *Phoronis*, oracle, inscriptions; Παλλάς always with Ἀθήνη/-αίη in Homer and Hesiod; cf. *Th.* 925).

The possible significance of doublets as evidence for the break-down of formulaic 'systems' has already been mentioned. Not all, however, of those mentioned above are necessarily strict doublets. The existence of three separate whole-line formulae for Demeter in the vocative (60, 75, 492) is notable, especially as they cannot easily be explained as due to separate traditions. More probably they are due to the fact that formulae for De-meter had not developed sufficiently to form a set system. Two of them (*Dem.* 60, 75) are apparently adapted from nominative formulae (cf. ad loc.). Moreover, Zeus in Homer has four dif-ferent whole-line forms of address (*Il.* 2. 412, 3. 276 etc., 8. 31 etc., 16. 233; these vary according to circumstances). In *Dem.* 453 the poet perhaps deliberately avoided the Hesiodic πολυ-φόρβης, as inappropriate here. χρυσαόρου (*Dem.* 4) would have been possible also. (καλλισφύρου is a general epithet.)

Zeus-formulae are more important, as Homer shows a de-veloped system here:

Dem. 3 (etc.) βαρύκτυπος εὐρύοπα Ζεύς does not appear else-where, and combines Homeric with Hesiodic elements. Homer already has two formulae for this position, Κρόνου πάις ἀγκυλο-μήτεω (*Il.* 2. 205 etc.) and πατὴρ ἀνδρῶν τε θεῶν τε (1. 544 etc.). The first of these is not used for Zeus in Hesiod. The poet of the *Hymn* may have created a new formula here, adapting the Hesiodic Ζηνὶ βαρυκτύπῳ (*Th.* 388, *Sc.* 318), Διὸς . . . βαρυκτύπου (*Op.* 79). πατὴρ ἀνδρῶν τε θεῶν τε is too general for the *Hymn*: in *Dem.* 3 he is mentioned in connection with his daughter Persephone, in 441 and 460 with his mother Rhea.

Dem. 321 πατὴρ Ζεὺς ἄφθιτα εἰδώς is again a doublet for this position. The poet perhaps had *Il.* 24. 88 (or a similar passage) in mind (cf. ad loc.).

Dem. 408 πὰρ πατέρος Κρονίδαο is a doublet of *Il.* 2. 787 πὰρ Διὸς αἰγιόχοιο (where 786 is similar to *Dem.* 407: see notes ad loc.). The Homeric formula is, however, itself an adaptation from the regular Διὸς αἰγιόχοιο at the end of the verse, and αἰγιόχοιο* Διός in the 2nd–4th feet, and it occurs nowhere else in Homer or Hesiod (cf. *Herm.* 551). It was therefore more natural for the poet to adapt a formula which he had already used (*Dem.* 21, 27 πατέρα Κρονίδην).

The absence of doublets for Persephone has been noted. In the case of Hades, *Dem.* 31b and 84b (= 376b) are not really doublets. In *Dem.* 31 alliteration and euphemism play an important role (cf. ad loc.). The use of πολυδέγμων in *Dem.* 17, 31, 404, 430 created a further doublet between the Homeric ἄναξ ἐνέρων Ἀϊδωνεύς (357) and ἄναξ κρατερὸς πολυδέγμων (430), but this is perhaps due to extension:

   17   ἄναξ πολυδέγμων
+ 404 κρατερὸς πολυδέγμων
> 430 ἄναξ κρατερὸς πολυδέγμων

The other cases of doublets are:

(*a*) *Dem.* 407 (Hermes): εὖτέ μοι ἄγγελος ἦλ[θ' ἐριούνιος Ἀργεϊφόντης. The reading is due to restoration, from papyrus 2, but ἐριούνιος in M seems to guarantee that this is right. Homer has διάκτορος Ἀργεϊφόντης (cf. especially *Od.* 24. 99), and cf. ἐύσκοπος Ἀργεϊφόντης (*Hymns*, 3 times). The *Hymn* constructs a new formula from Homeric elements.

(*b*) *Dem.* 102 φιλοστεφάνου Ἀφροδίτης. Cf. *Il.* 20. 105 Διὸς κούρης Ἀφροδίτης, from the nominative Διὸς θυγάτηρ Ἀφροδίτη (*Il.* 3. 374 etc.). This occurs only once, and is clearly an adaptation.

Cf. also Hes. *Th.* 980 πολυχρύσου Ἀφροδίτης. This is the commoner (Hesiodic) formula (6 times in Hes. and *Aph.*). *Dem.* 102 is itself perhaps a combination of

      φιλομμειδὴς Ἀφροδίτη (*Il.* 3. 424 etc.) and
      ἐϋστεφάνου Κυθερείης (*Od.* 8. 288 etc.) ∼
      ἐϋστεφάνου τ' Ἀφροδίτης (*Od.* 8. 267)

providing a variant to the latter with initial consonant. (It is notable that Aphrodite already has two equivalent nominative formulae in Homer, as quoted above.)

A few other formulae illustrate well the various possibilities for development from existing models. Some arise from combination:

Dem. 14 ἁλμυρὸν οἶδμα θαλάσσης (∼ *Od.* 12. 236 etc., *Il.* 4. 422 etc., Hes. *Th.* 107, 964, *Certamen* 131). Cf. ad loc.

34 πόντον ἀγάρροον ἰχθυόεντα (*Il.* 9. 4 etc., 2. 485). This is a doublet of *Od.* 4. 510. Cf. ad loc.

107, 180 φίλα πρὸς δώματα πατρός (*Od.* 19. 458, *Il.* 12. 221). This shows a shift of epithet. Cf. similarly 113 γρηῢ παλαιγενέων ἀνθρώπων (*Od.* 22. 395, Hes. *Th.* 879 etc.)

118 ἡ δ' ἐπέεσσιν ἀμείβετο (Il. 15. 127, Od. 4. 706 etc.).
118 πότνα θεάων (Od. 5. 215 etc., Il. 5. 381 etc.). This is a doublet
of Hom. δῖα θεάων, and shows a misuse of πότνα as nominative.
Od. 13. 391–2 (vel sim.) perhaps had some influence.

Adaptation of case, position in verse, etc. accounts for others,
e.g. Dem. 11b, 18a, 23b, 38a, 38b, 40b, 44b, 66b (εἴδεϊ κυδρήν),
71 (φίλον τέκος), 103b, 204b, 340b, 351b, 383 (βαθὺν ἠέρα), 471b.
    Dem. 119–20 τέκνα φίλ', αἵ τινές ἐστε . . . | χαίρετ', ἐγὼ δ'
ὑμῖν . . . is curiously similar to the epiphany language of Emp.
112. 1–4 (~ Od. 11. 248–52), and is perhaps derived from such
an original context.
    There are a few doublets besides those already noted:

Dem. 28 ἀπάνευθε πολυλλίστῳ ἐνὶ νηῷ ~ 355 ἀπάνευθε θυώδεος
ἔνδοθι νηοῦ.
30 Διὸς ἐννεσίῃσιν ~ Th. 572 etc. Κρονίδεω διὰ βουλάς (the poet
could not use this here, as Κρονίδεω would be ambiguous in the
context. It is also not a strict doublet, on account of the double
consonant Κρ-.).
44 ἐτήτυμα μυθήσασθαι (adapted from Hes. formula) ~ Il. 6. 382
etc. ἀληθέα μυθήσασθαι.
103 θεμιστοπόλων βασιλήων (adapted from Hes. formula) ~
Il. 1. 176 etc. διοτρεφέων βασιλήων.
352 χαμαιγενέων ἀνθρώπων (Hesiodic formula) ~ καταθνητῶν
ἀνθρώπων (Il. 6. 123 etc.). But the Hesiodic formula seems to be
used in a particular context (cf. notes ad Dem. 113, 352).

Misinterpretation of words is also a fruitful source of new
expressions (cf. M. Leumann, Hom. Wörter). Cf. the following:

Dem. 15 χερσὶν ἅμ' ἄμφω = Il. 7. 255b (~ 23. 686). In Homer
ἄμφω goes with the subject of the verb, but it was easy for
a later poet to misunderstand the words and take ἄμφω as
dative. (But cf. ad loc.)
16 χθὼν εὐρυάγυια. This seems to be due to interpretation of the
Homeric χθονὸς εὐρυοδείης as connected with ὁδός rather than
ἔδος (cf. ad loc.). The epithet εὐρυάγυια is only used of cities
in Homer.
140 γυναικὸς ἀφήλικος: παναφήλικα in Il. 22. 490 means 'without
contemporaries'. The sense 'aged' for ἀφῆλιξ is probably due
to understanding ἡλικία as 'youth'. This sense of ἀφῆλιξ, ἡλικία,

etc. is found commonly in the classical period. Cf. Zumbach, *Neuerungen*, 45 f.

279 κόμαι κατενήνοθεν ὤμουϲ (~ Hes. *Sc.* 269b). The use with a plural subject is probably due to interpretation of an obscure verb form as plural, perhaps by analogy with aorist passives in -θεν. (It would, however, be possible to emend to the singular here. Cf. ad loc.)

296 πολυπείρονα λαόν: cf. δῆμοϲ ἀπείρων (*Il.* 24. 776), λαὸϲ ἀπείρων (Hes. *Sc.* 472). The poet seems to have taken the ἀ- of ἀπείρων as an intensifying prefix (cf. Zumbach, o.c. 19).

383 βαθὺν ἠέρα τέμνον: it is possible that the poet intended ἠέρα here to mean 'air', the sense which it has in classical Greek. In Homer it means 'darkness, mist', but in *Il.* 14. 288 it was later understood as 'air'. In Hes. *Th.* 697 ἠέρα would have this sense, but one should perhaps read αἰθέρα (cf. West ad loc.). However, the sense 'air' may not have come in until much later (fifth century only), and in *Dem.* 383 the sense 'mist' might be possible. Cf. ad loc.[1]

E. ATTICISMS

Voss first argued for an Attic poet on the grounds of language, and several scholars have followed. For early views cf. Gemoll, and see also Wackernagel, *Spr. Unt.* 179, Zumbach, *Neuerungen*, 56 ff., 62 f. Francke, however, pointed out that the *Hymn* contains some distinctively non-Attic forms. Cf. especially γληχών (*Dem.* 209), λιμόϲ as feminine (*Dem.* 311). A case can only be made on the basis of words or forms which definitely occur in Attic but not epic or Ionic, and in particular those cases where an epic word or form was at hand which the poet might as easily have used. These are not very numerous. The following list is of those words and forms which have at some time been labelled 'Attic':

Words

Dem. 142, 244 (ἐπι)τηρεῖν (Voss, Gemoll, Zumbach). In the first case, the epic δῶμα φυλάϲϲειν might have been expected. The sense in *Dem.* 244 is not certain. τηρεῖν occurs in Pindar and Attic, ἐπιτηρεῖν in Attic. But τηρεῖν is used by Democritus (fr. 239), and may well be Ionic also.

---

[1] On adaptations etc. see also Hoekstra, *Sub-epic Stage*, especially 49 ff.

203 (παρα)cκώπτειν (Zumbach). This occurs in Herodotus
(2. 121 δ), and it may also be connected with cκώψ (cf. Ath.
9. 391 ab, Ael. *NA* 15. 28), which is Homeric (*Od.* 5. 66).
There is no reason to consider it exclusive to Attic.

268 τιμάοχοc (Zumbach). This also comes in *Aph.* 31, and is
hardly a normal form in Attic, any more than Ionic. The
later Attic and Ionic form was τιμοῦχοc. Cf. n. ad loc., and
Hoekstra, *Sub-epic Stage*, 56.

278 φέγγοc (Zumbach). The normal epic word is φάοc. φέγγοc
occurs in Pindar and Attic poetry. In classical Attic prose it
seems to be normally used only of moonlight (cf. Hsch. s.v.).
There is again no reason to suppose this un-Ionic.

312, 368 θυcία (Voss, Gemoll). The normal epic word is θύοc,
which could have been used here, and has been restored. If
the word is Attic, it could be due to transmission. Cf. Pl. *Rep.*
364 d, where θυcίαιcι is quoted in *Il.* 9. 499, as at *Dem.* 368.
But Herodotus uses θυcίη frequently, also θύcιμοc (1. 50), and
cf. *Titanomachia* fr. 6. It may be doubted whether in the case of
such religious terms Herodotus would choose an exclusively
Attic word. The word is not Homeric, but cannot be used as
evidence for an Attic poet.

367 ἀδικεῖν (cf. Gemoll). ἄδικοc occurs first in Hesiod, ἀδικεῖν
perhaps first here (cf. Homeric ἁμαρτάνειν, παραβαίνειν). It is
as much Ionic as Attic: cf. Hippon. fr. 115 West (or Archilochus?). It is also Aeolic and Doric.

Vocabulary, therefore, gives no grounds for assuming an Attic
composer.

Forms

Declension

11 etc., 40 etc. (cf. Gemoll): datives in -οιc, -αιc. These are not
very common in Homer, commoner in Hesiod and the *Hymns*.
Cf. C. Reichelt, *De dativis in -οιc et -ηιc (-αιc) exeuntibus* (Progr.
Breslau, 1893), 19: in Homer the proportion of short to long
forms is 1:5, in the early *Hymns* more than 1:4, in Hesiod
(*Th.* and *Op.*) more than 1:3.[1] Wackernagel (*Spr. Unt.* 53 f.)
thought -αιc was an Atticism. It is found only twice for
certain in Homer, but three times in the *Theogony* and five

---

[1] For further discussion see Appendix II, 334 f.

in this *Hymn*. It might be due to Attic transmission (for -ηc).
Neither -οιc nor -αιc is likely to be due to an Attic poet of
the archaic period, since early Attic used -οιcι, and -ηcι or
-αcι. The same argument applies to the form θυcίαιcι (*Dem.* 368),
which was never used in spoken Attic, and in tragedy perhaps
not before Sophocles (cf. ad loc.).

12 κάρᾱ (nominative plural) (cf. Voss): this form, which is only
definitely attested once in Attic (Sannyrion, fr. 3), is an
anomaly, and perhaps due to the analogy of κέρᾱ (cf. ad loc.).
It is hardly good evidence for Attic composition.

15 ἄμφω as dative (Zumbach): this, again, is not normal in
Attic (ἀμφοῖν), although it occurs in Arist. *Top.* 118ᵃ28. Cf.
ad loc.

19 ὄχοιcιν (Voss, Gemoll, Zumbach): epic only uses ὀχέεccιν,
ὄχεcφιν, and as the latter is found at *Dem.* 375, it might have
been corrupted here (cf. ad loc.). The second-declension
form, however, is used by Pindar and Herodotus, as well as
Attic.

406 cοι (Wackernagel): Hermann's conjecture τοι is confirmed
by the papyrus here. This illustrates the dangers of searching
for Attic forms.

Verb forms

383 τέμνον (Wackernagel, Zumbach): this occurs also at *Od.*
3. 175, and Hes. *Op.* 570 v.l. Cf. ὑποταμνόν in *Dem.* 228 and
note to *Dem.* 383.

403 ἄνει (Wackernagel, Zumbach): Homer uses εἶcθα, which is
a secondary form, Hesiod εἶc (*Op.* 208), Attic εἶ. Ionic evidence
seems to be lacking, but there is no reason why εἶ should not
be normal there also. εἶcθα only occurs twice in Homer (*Il.* 10.
450, *Od.* 19. 69), and this is not enough evidence even for the
normal epic form.

Usage

132 τιμή = 'price' (Voss). This sense is found in Herodotus
(7. 119), and for similar uses in Homer cf. ad loc.

242 ἀθάνατον ποιεῖν (Voss). Cf. ad loc. for epic parallels.

253 πέδονδε (Voss). One might have expected χαμᾶζε here, as in
Od. 21. 136, but πέδονδε is Homeric, and the sense is not an
unusual one.

Contraction, synizesis, crasis

55 (etc.) θεῶν (synizesis), 137 τοκῆ(ε)ς, 173 καλ(ε)εῖν, 284 ἐλ(ε)εινήν, 379 ἄκοντε, 413 ἄκουσαν(?), 406 ἐρ(έ)ω, 455 ἦρος, 494 ᾠδῆς:—none of these forms need be considered Attic. For detailed discussion cf. ad locc.

227 κοὐ (crasis; cf. Zumbach): although this particular crasis is not found in Homer, it is not un-epic. Cf. Parm. fr. 6. 9, ?Hes. fr. 62. 3.

Aspirate and contracted form

347 Ἅιδη (Wackernagel, Zumbach). Epic uses Ἀΐδης, but the contraction is not impossible in epic, and the aspirate could be due to Attic transmission. Cf. also Pindar (*P.* 4. 44) Ἀΐδᾱ.

Treatment of digamma

439 κόρην (Voss, Gemoll, Wackernagel, Zumbach). The epic form is κούρη, found in *Dem.* 8 etc. κόρη is Attic, but also found in [Archilochus], fr. 322 (West), which is probably not genuine. It occurs in some later Ionic inscriptions, as the title of Persephone, as also in Hdt. 8. 65. 4 (the context is Eleusinian). The compensatory vowel-lengthening, after loss of ϝ, is not universal in Ionic (cf. Buck, *Greek Dialects*, 49 f., 143).

In *Dem.* 439 the Attic form is probably used as a deliberate reference to Persephone's title at Eleusis (cf. ad loc.). A non-Attic poet might as easily have paid her this compliment as an Attic one. Although, therefore, this is the strongest piece of evidence pointing to Attic composition, it is by no means conclusive.[1]

Summary

There is some evidence which might suggest Attic *transmission*, (-οις, -αις, θυσίαισι, ὄχοισιν, τέμνον, Ἅιδη). But equally these may be corruptions due to generalization in the medieval tradition. The only certain Attic form in the poem which cannot be assigned to this stage is Persephone's title Κόρη, and the presence of this can be explained on other grounds. (Ἅιδη also looks

---

[1] Cf. also Forderer, *Gnomon* (1958), 98 f.: κόρη/κούρη is due to analogy with (epic) ὄρος/οὖρος etc.?

In *Dem.* 56, 405 the form Φερσεφόνη(ν) is given by papyri. This is not the form of spoken Attic but could be due to Attic influence on the composer. Equally, it may have come in during transmission.

suspicious, but is less certain.) Attic composition cannot therefore be proved by language alone. But the probability that the *Hymn* was composed for recitation at Eleusis has already been considered, and the presence of some slight Attic colouring would not disagree with this.

VI. STYLE AND NARRATIVE TECHNIQUE

The *Hymn* seems to exhibit two distinctive qualities, which one might call ϲεμνότηϲ and χάριϲ. It is grave and gay by turns, as suits its subject, the two goddesses who are ϲεμναί τ' αἰδοῖαί τε (486), whose ὄργια are ϲεμνά (478), but who are also the deities of the gay harvest (ἀγλαόκαρποϲ), and of the rich blessings of Πλοῦτοϲ.

At the opening a tone of awful grandeur is set, with the theme of the Rape, and the rapidity of the narrative here suggests the terrible suddenness with which Persephone is carried off, contrasting sharply with her youthful gaiety as she plays with her companions, the nymphs, and her amazement at the magic flower, the 'lovely plaything' (15 f.). In this amazement the whole upper world seems to share (10 f., 13 f.), and the freshness of youth seems to be emphasized by the catalogue of flowers. Persephone's cry for help is not heard by her father Zeus, who is a distant, august figure in the *Hymn*. In contrast, Hecate, who hears, is not as solemn as she later became, being described as ἀταλὰ φρονέουϲα (26), a suitable attendant for Persephone (440).

The story then turns to Demeter, and shows her anguish at her loss. Throughout the main part of the *Hymn* it is her sorrow which is the keynote, together with her anger against the gods, and later against men too. The effect of her meeting with the daughters of Celeus is heightened because she takes the disguise of a very old woman (100 ff.), whereas they are in the first freshness of youth, κουρήϊον ἄνθοϲ ἔχουϲαι (108). In the following scene their gaiety and eagerness to help are contrasted with Demeter's reticent sorrow, and this is especially poignant in the picture of them running down the road from the palace, like young deer or calves in spring-time (174 ff.), to find the reverend goddess, who then follows them, sorrowful at heart, her head veiled, her dark robe moving about her feet as she walks (179 ff.). This leads on to the first awe-inspiring epiphany of Demeter, as she enters the palace, and the solemn scene which follows, itself the *aition* for Eleusinian solemn ritual, but centred on the figure of Iambe, the eponym of the jesting and *aischrologia* of the Mysteries (188–211). This is balanced by Demeter's second epiphany, before she leaves the palace, and her command to build a temple in which her ὄργια will be celebrated (256–80).

The central episode, the nursing of Demophon (212–91) is again characterized by a mixture of solemnity and humour. Metaneira is horrified to discover Demeter's methods as a nurse and the goddess is angry and condemns mortals for their folly, which prevents the gods from helping them. But instead, Demeter promises to teach men her solemn rites. After her departure Metaneira is speechless with terror, but her daughters hear the piteous wail of the child Demophon, who has been placed on the ground by Demeter. They leap from their beds to help him, and gathering round wash him and try to console him. 'But', the poet says, 'his spirit was not appeased, for far inferior were the nurses who now were holding him.'

The *Hymn* then describes the terrible Famine, by which Demeter threatens the existence of mankind, even perhaps of the gods, and eventually forces Zeus to recall Persephone from Hades. The scene in the Underworld is again both solemn and humorous. Hades is an ambiguous figure, who smiles with his eye-brows, and consoles Persephone (357 ff.), but who also ensures that she will return to him. She herself is promised the highest honours amongst the gods, rule over all living things, and the power to exact punishment from 'those who do wrong, whoever do not propitiate her'. She is full of joy, and does not seem to see Hades' trick (370 ff.). Later, she protests that she was compelled to eat the pomegranate seeds by force (411–13), perhaps a touch of irony such as one might find several times in the poem (cf. notes on 98 ff., 113, 120 f., 147 f., 216 f., 225, 406).[1]

The return journey to the upper world is described with a slight pictorial elaboration (380 ff.), which seems characteristic of this poet (cf. *Dem.* 33 ff., 38 f., 174 ff.). The reconciliation of mother and daughter again shows a delicate mixture of anxiety and joy. At the end it is the joy which is most important (434–40), all fears for the future being set aside as the poem prepares for

[1] But *Dem.* 413 may not be genuine. See notes ad loc.

the closing episodes, the embassy of Rhea, herself a solemn figure like Demeter (441 ff.), the return of life to the fields (450 ff., 471 ff.), and the accompanying institution of the Mysteries at Eleusis, whose awesome secrecy is emphasized (473–9). The poet promises happiness to the initiates, and another fate after death to the rest of mankind, once more sounding the ominous note (480–2). The *Hymn* closes with the ascent of the goddesses to Olympus, a further promise of happiness and prosperity to their followers, and a final invocation and prayer for material welfare (483–95).

Throughout the poem the richness of nature, the realm of Demeter, receives special attention, and the result is a pictorial quality which adds great charm and grace. The catalogues of flowers, the list of nymphs, the descriptions of Celeus' daughters, the journeys over land and sea, the death and rebirth of the crops, portrayed in all their stages of growth from spring to harvest, the appearance of Persephone herself with the spring flowers, and the participation of Earth and the whole of nature in the Rape and Recovery of the goddess: these and many other touches seem to give this *Hymn* a quality of archaic χάρις, which has led some of its readers to compare its tone with that of the early Greek lyric, or the Greek art of the seventh and sixth centuries.[1] The lyrical quality of the language accounts for some words referring to nature and growth which are not found in Homer and Hesiod (e.g. 8, 420 καλυκῶπις, 54 etc. ὡρηφόρος, ἀγλαόδωρος, 102 φιλοστέφανος, 108 κουρήϊος, 178 κροκήϊος, 241 προθαλής, 452 πανάφυλλος, etc.).

In accordance with the solemnity of the style, the poet also seems to be careful to observe that *propriety* which was recognized by later scholars as a feature of Homeric epic. It is perhaps for this reason that the nature of Iambe's jesting is so delicately referred to (202–5), and she is characterized as κέδν' εἰδυῖα (195, 202; cf. ad loc.). It is also probable that the poet (or the epic tradition) has suppressed an older version of the story of Demophon, in which the child died in the fire (cf. ad *Dem.* 254).

The traditional quality of the language has already been discussed. On a larger scale, also, the *Hymn* conforms closely to epic conventions. It is possible to detect the structure of a 'typical scene' under many of the episodes. At the same time these

[1] Cf. for example H. Fränkel, *Dichtung and Philosophie*[2] (1962), 288 f.

preserve an individual character, and sometimes a traditional *schema* is used for a very particular purpose, the representation of the *aitia* for Eleusinian ritual. This reuse of traditional patterns is most skilful, and suggests a poet who was to a great extent in command of his techniques. For details see especially the notes to 180 ff., 188–211 ff., 192 ff., and also 64 ff., 82 ff. ~ 362 ff., 147 f. ~ 216 f., 98 ff. (also 119 ff., 127 ff.), 179 etc., 256 ff., 314 ff. ~ 334 ff. ~ 441 ff., 375 ff., 19 (~ 40, 44–5, 380 ff., 383).

In one respect, however, the poet does not follow the Homeric conventions, in his avoidance of direct speech by Zeus when sending out a messenger, the conclusion of indirect speech with ὡς ἔφατο, and the elaboration of a message with the speaker's own comments (cf. notes to 314 ff., etc.). It may be questioned whether this is necessarily due to clumsiness or a desire to hurry over his narrative. Another possible reason has already been suggested, in the character of Zeus. Some of the direct speeches are also unusually short, in the Hesiodic manner.

In contrast, 'epic repetition' is practised quite regularly (e.g. 5–20+340–74 ~ 405–33, 147–8+164–8 ~ 216–23, 321–3+ 327–8+443–7 ~ 460–8, 338–9 ~ 349–50 ~ 409–10, etc.). But such repetition is not rigidly observed, and there is scope for considerable variation and expansion (e.g. 416 ff. with its Catalogue of Oceanids and variant list of flowers; cf. also 15–20 ~ 429–32, where 19–20 and 431–2 are interchangeable). Sometimes repetition is used for a technical purpose, as in the device known as ring-composition, to mark off an episode and open the way for a further stage. An example of this is the opening scene, where 17b–18 are repeated at 31b–2. This opening narrative shows considerable repetition of a rather similar type, especially in 16–39 (cf. notes to 20, 22–37, 25, 27, 30, 39). The repetition has been considered awkward here, but it seems rather to convey an insistence on the important features of the narrative. The same device is noticeable elsewhere, for example where a detail is emphasized which has ritual significance, such as Demeter's black veil and robe (42, 182 f., 197, 319, 360, 374), the torches of Demeter and Hecate (48 ~ 61, 52), her fasting (49 f., 200, 206 ff.) and silence (59–60, 194, 198–9), and above all her sorrow (40 ff., and *passim*) and anger (83, 91, 251 ff., 305 ff., 330, 338–9, 349–50, 354, 467–8). Another good example of 'ritual repetition'

is 195 ~ 202, and in fact the whole structure of 192 ff. (cf. ad
loc.). The terms of Persephone's division of the year between
upper and lower worlds are also emphasized (398–403, 445–7,
463–5).

Another type of repetition, which may strike a modern reader
as a fault of style, is the apparently fortuitous recurrence of
words several times in the same passage, or within a few lines.
This is quite common in the *Hymn*. It occurs also in Homer, and
epic poets do not seem to have troubled to avoid it. (Cf. notes
to 43–4 ~ 46, 58 ~ 60, 171–2, 136–44, 407 ~ 409, 411, 426 ~
428, 434–6.)[1]

Occasionally the poet uses an elliptical construction which
seems slightly awkward, as in 126–8, where he is perhaps combining two separate formulaic sentences, and 445–7, which are
readily understandable after 398 ff. At 403 a lacuna was suspected by earlier editors. But P. Oxy. 2379 confirms the text,
at least for the third century A.D. There is also a slight com-
pression, and corresponding ambiguity, at 185, where ἔνθα must
mean 'to the place where . . .'. Sometimes also his word-order is
unusually complex, as in 71–3, 153–6, 169–70, 182b–3 (where it
is perhaps deliberate: note the chiasmus and polarization of
πέπλος . . . ποςςίν), 251–5 (also repetitive: χωςαμένη . . . θυμῷ
κοτέςαςα μάλ' αἰνῶς), 414–16 (~ 71–3). 208b–9 is also slightly
involved (and 209a looks 'unformulaic'). In general, however,
the poet's construction and word-order have the traditional clarity
and simplicity of early epic.

This does not of course mean that his narrative always proceeds
by short sentences. The most striking example of extended sentence structure is that of the opening lines, whose 'rapidity of
narrative' has already been mentioned. Here the poet proceeds
immediately from his title ('Demeter . . . and her daughter') by
way of a relative clause to a traditional summary of the Rape
myth (2–3), mentioning Hades and Zeus, and then with two
participial clauses into the opening scene. This is expanded by
the list of flowers, leading again to a relative clause describing
the origin of the narcissus, a theme which is itself then developed
for seven lines. The first 'full stop' comes at line 14, but we are

---

[1] H. N. Porter's interesting discussion of 'Repetition in the Homeric Hymn to
Aphrodite' (*AJP* 70 (1949), 249 ff.) has some good remarks on the functions of
repetition in hymnal poetry, and examples of the different types noticed here.

carried forward at once to the moment when Persephone picks the flower, the earth gapes, and Hades springs out. In a flash she is carried off, crying for help, and the following lines develop the theme of her ἰαχή (20–9), returning to her rape (30–2), and then again probably to her cry (33–9: cf. ad *Dem.* 37), which is heard by Demeter. The story continues at breathless speed (cf. 43 cεύατο ... 48 cτρωφᾶτο ... 58 ὦκα ... 60 ὦκα ... 61 ἤϊξ' ...) until Demeter learns the truth from Helios. Despite some slight imperfections (cf. above on 16–39, 43–6, and notes to 7, 17) this is a remarkably effective passage.[1]

Effects of sound are a feature of style of which the poet seems at times to have been conscious. Alliteration is quite common in epic formulae generally,[2] but the repetition and alliteration of 31–2 must be deliberate, and perhaps intended to produce what I have called an 'incantatory' effect. This may also be detected at 228–30, and 238 (cf. notes ad loc.). A truly remarkable example of vowel assonance occurs at 289–90, where there is a parallel in Homer (cf. ad loc.).

The use of three compound epithets with πολυ- in 31–2 is also an example of this poet's remarkable fondness for such compounds. Cf. 9 πολυδέκτῃ, 18, 32 πολυώνυμος, 28 πολυλλίcτῳ, 31 πολυcημάντωρ πολυδέγμων, 165 πολυεύχετος, 211 πολυπότνια, 220 πολυάρητος, 230 πολυπήμονος, 296 πολυπείρονα, 315 πολυήρατον. Six are new to epic, and occur rarely or not at all later. Of the rest, only πολυάρητος is Homeric; the rest occur in Hesiod and the *Hymns*. The frequency of these compounds might be considered a sign of later epic development, but it may have been felt more appropriate to the style of a hymn.

VII. METRE AND PROSODY

Dactyls and Spondees

Spondaic endings are more than twice as common in the *Hymn* as in Homer. Francke counted 63 (omitting 387–402, 462–71),

---

[1] Rapidity of narrative may be connected with a feature of style unusual in early epic, the high frequency of what Milman Parry called 'necessary enjambement'. On this, and its bearing on the question of composition of the poem, see Appendix II.

[2] Cf. A. Shewan, *CP* 20 (1925), 193 ff., and in the *Hymn* such phrases as καλυκώπιδι κούρῃ, δι' αἰθέρος ἀτρυγέτοιο, ἀέκουcαν ἀνάγκῃ, etc.

i.e. about 2 in 15, whereas in Homer the proportion is 1 in 18 (Maas, *Greek Metre*, § 83). In the *Theogony* there are 66 in 1,022 lines, i.e. 1 in 15 or 16, but the proportions vary in different parts of the poem (West, *Theogony*, pp. 93 f.). 14 of those in the *Hymn* also have a spondaic fourth foot (including 195, 202, 474), again more than twice as often as in Homer (*Iliad* 1:87, *Odyssey* 1:89, *Dem.* 1:33). Of these, 7 are of the type ἠδὲ θνητοῖς ἀνθρώποις (-ῶν -ων etc.) and 5 are due to proper names. *Dem.* 204 is very unusual, having a self-contained final foot and monosyllable in the fifth-foot thesis (cf. ad loc., and Meister, *Hom. Kunstsprache* 7 f.).

A spondaic fourth foot followed by word-end occurs 33 times (including 293, but not 1 or 179). The proportion of spondaic to dactylic fourth feet with word-end is about 1 to 7, in Homer 1 to 8 (Maas o.c. § 84; I have counted 28 or 29 spondaic cases in *Il.* 1. 1–495). Most examples are of a genitive in -ης (ἥβης etc.) or -ων (γυναικῶν). There is no case of lengthening by position in the fourth-foot thesis. These statistics do not include cases of καί, prepositions, etc. in fourth-foot thesis. There is no example of spondaic fourth foot followed by a stop, which occurs in Homer and Hesiod (Maas, o.c. § 84, West, *Theogony*, p. 97).

There are four lines which describe rapid movement beginning with ῥίμφα or αἶψα, which are notably dactylic (89, 171, 184, 380). All except 89 have trochaic caesurae in both second and third feet, which contributes to the effect of lightness. For similar lines in Homer cf. notes ad locc. (Cf. also 469, 471.)

Caesurae

206 lines have strong caesurae in the third foot, 279 weak (excluding *Dem.* 387–92, and 477, and counting enclitics as such). This gives a proportion of about 425 strong in 1,000, not much differing from Homer (*Iliad* 381, *Odyssey* 410: cf. H. N. Porter, *Yale Class. Studies* 12 (1951) 1 ff.).[1] 3 lines have no third-foot caesura (74, 109, 458), i.e. about 6 in 1,000 lines, compared with 14 in 1,000 in the *Iliad*, 9 in 1,000 in the *Odyssey*. Two are due to proper names, and the third (458) is unusual also in having a pyrrhic word in the second-foot thesis, with caesurae in the second and fourth feet. This is rare in Homer (1:1,120 verses), and

---

[1] Van Leeuwen, *Enchiridium*, 14 n. 2 gives different figures: *Iliad* 437, *Odyssey* 419.

occurs only *once* with a verb, as at *Dem.* 458 (*Il.* 15. 339). Cf. also Porter, o.c. 46 f., on the special effect of some lines without third-foot caesura.

Trochaic caesura in the fourth foot occurs twice, in breach of Hermann's bridge (*Dem.* 17 and 248). *Dem.* 17 ends with a four-syllable word, as in some Homeric examples (Monro, *HG*², § 367. 2). But it has some other unusual features, and is perhaps due to reshaping of an older version (cf. ad loc.). In *Dem.* 248 an enclitic monosyllable precedes, another type which is found in Homer. Porter (o.c. 48) counts *Dem.* 452, but here ἔκευθε δ' ἄρα go closely together. See also Hoekstra, *Sub-epic Stage*, 54, 62 ff., and the useful criticism of this by L. E. Rossi, *Gött. gel. Anzeigen* 223 (1971), 170 f.

The awkward τῇ scanned short in the third foot in *Dem.* 17 also reappears at 46, another metrically bumpy line.

Word-end after the trochee or end of the second foot, with a word beginning in the first, occurs 12 times (16, 92, 137, 194, 200, 254, 275, 295, 325, 339, 350, 441, cf. also 46; 194 has an illicit hiatus at this point, and should perhaps be emended). This is slightly less often than in Homer or the *Theogony* (West, p. 95), i.e. 1 in 41 or 45, as opposed to 3 in 100. In Hellenistic poetry this hardly ever occurs (cf. Maas, *Greek Metre*, § 94). Cf. also Porter, o.c. 37 ff., who notes the special effect of *Dem.* 200.

On the position of θεά (etc.) in *Dem.* 34 (etc.) see Appendix V.

Hiatus

'Illicit' hiatus occurs at:

(i) 76 μέγα ἄζομαι (in third-foot thesis). This hiatus is paral-leled by Hes. *Th.* 532 ταῦτ' ἄρα ἀζόμενος (cf. West ad loc. and pp. 92, 96).

(ii) 194 ἀλλ' ἀκέουσα ἔμιμνε (in second-foot thesis). This should perhaps be emended (cf. above).

(iii) 241 θεοῖσι δὲ ἄντα ἐῴκει is cited by Zumbach as a third example. But the hiatus at the bucolic diaeresis, though rare, is paralleled in Homer (28 times in the *Iliad*), and the hiatus in the fifth foot is paralleled by *Od.* 4. 654 πάντα ἐῴκει (on which see Chantraine, *GH* i. 479 f.).

(iv) 424 καὶ Ἄρτεμις (in third-foot thesis): the line has been suspected, but the hiatus with καί has parallels in early epic (cf. ad loc.).

Lengthening in arsis

There are three examples of lengthening of a final dative singular in -ι, followed by hiatus. Two are at the third-foot caesura, and occur within three lines (99, 101). The third is in the fifth foot, at 248. For parallels cf. notes ad loc. A short final syllable is lengthened before a vowel also at 57 (γὰρ ἤκουϲ').

Lengthening in thesis

There are only two examples which I have noted of a short final syllable ending in a consonant made long by position in any other foot than the first (where this is normal). These occur at 147 and 216, in the second thesis: θεῶν μὲν δῶρα (the phrase is the same). For such lengthening with μέν cf. Hes. *Th.* 150, 671, 762, 969. I do not count *Dem.* 157. See also below on *mute and liquid*. At 381 ὕδωρ is lengthened in the first-foot thesis. In Homer this only occurs in the final arsis, and 'metrical lengthening' in the thesis is in general rare (except between two longs, e.g. ὑπεροπλίῃϲι etc.) as the thesis is actually longer than the arsis.

Shortening of normally long vowel

At 105 Ἐλευϲῑνίδαο is shortened, presumably because it would not otherwise fit into the verse. Cf. 266 Ἐλευϲινίων, which may however be a case of synizesis (cf. ad loc.).

Mute and liquid

At 113 a short final vowel is lengthened in the second thesis (ἐϲὶ γρηῦ: cf. note ad loc.). Attic correption occurs once, at 256, καὶ ἀφράδμονεϲ (cf. ad loc.).

Digamma

Statistics for observance and neglect of the digamma are given by Allen and Halliday (Introduction, xcvi ff.). Their figures should be adjusted, to exclude cases where neglect is not certain (e.g. movable *nu*). They list 47 observances, and 35 neglects, of which not more than 21 are definite and hence significant (and I should add 35 ἤλπετο). Most of these have Homeric parallels. The ratio of observances to neglects is 2·1 : 1. This is lower than that of Homer (*c.* 6:1), or Hesiod's *Theogony* (*c.* 3:1) and

Scutum (*c.* 5 : 1), but not *Works and Days* (*c.* 2 : 1). But it is doubtful whether any conclusions can be drawn from this.[1]

Synizesis, contraction, and crasis

Synizesis of θεῶν, θεούς occurs at 55, 259, 325. It is found only twice in Homer, and once in the *Theogony* (cf. ad *Dem.* 55). At 325 the synizesis of a monosyllable before the bucolic diaeresis is also unusual. M has θεάν in the same position at 1 and 179, but θεόν should probably be read there, as at 292. Cf. Hoekstra, *Sub-epic Stage*, 49.

Other examples are: 137 τοκῆ(ε)ς (cf. *Il.* 11. 151, Hes. *Op.* 263, 607, *Herm.* 113); 210 κυκεῶ, 266 Ἐλευσινίων (or -ινίων? Cf. above), 269 ὄνεαρ, 406 ἐρέω (cf. Hes. *Op.* 202), 425 ἄνθεα (in Homer this synizesis of neuter plural nouns in -ος usually occurs at the verse-end: but cf. Chantraine, *GH* i. 56). The following may be classed as synizesis or contraction: 110 ἁπασῶν (Attic transmission? Read ἁπασέων?), 173 καλ(ε)εῖν (cf. *Il.* 3. 390 etc.), 284 ἐλ(ε)εινήν, 379 ἄκοντε, 413 ἄκουσαν (cf. ad *Dem.* 379), 455 ἧρος (cf. Hes. *Op.* 462, 492), 494 ᾠδῆς (cf. *Ap.* 20, *Hy.* 30. 18). Note also λουτροῖς (from λοϝετροῖς: cf. *Op.* 753).

Crasis: 227 κοὐ (cf. Parm. fr. 6. 9, ?Hes. fr. 62. 3). At 13 κᾦζ' is due to emendation, and is open to a number of objections (cf. ad loc.).

VIII. MANUSCRIPT AND PAPYRI

There is only one medieval manuscript of the *Hymn*, the celebrated Mosquensis (M), discovered in Moscow in 1777 by Christian Friedrich Matthaei, and now in Leiden (= Leidensis BPG 33H, f. 31 col. 1 lin. 13–f. 36 col. 2). An account of this is given by Allen and Halliday (xvii ff.). It is dated by the watermarks to the early fifteenth century.[2] Bücheler's edition reproduces the part which contains the *Hymn* in full, and there are plates of individual pages in Goodwin's edition, and a reproduction of half of it in Merkelbach and van Thiel's *Griech. Leseheft* (Göttingen, 1965), No. 1. The manuscript was found, according to Matthaei, in a stable, 'ubi per plures annos . . . inter pullos et

---

[1] Cf. West, *Theogony*, pp. 91, 99 f., and Hoekstra, *Sub-epic Stage*, 31 ff. For further discussion see Appendix II, p. 335.

[2] See *Bibliotheca Universitatis Leidensis, Codices Manuscripti*, VIII (Leiden, 1965), 49 f. Mr. N. G. Wilson confirms that the date is probably in the first quarter of the fifteenth century.

porcos latitabat'. For an excellent account of this, and of how it may have come there from its home (the Moscow Imperial Archive) see O. von Gebhardt, *Centralbl. f. Bibliothekswesen* 15 (1898), 441 ff.

The manuscript is fragmentary, the main lacunae in the *Hymns* which it preserves being *Ap.* 23–73 and *Aph.* 68–112. It was conjectured that these were due to the loss of single leaves, of 22–6 lines to a page (cf. Allen and Halliday, xx f.). This is supported by the existence of lacunae at *Dem.* 137, 211, 236, i.e. at intervals of 25 or 100 lines. It is notable that all of these occur at the foot of the page in M also. At *Dem.* 37 it is possible that an attempt has been made to fill a gap, as 37 is a suspect line (cf. ad loc.). At 236 the last word or words have been replaced by $\Delta\eta\mu\acute{\eta}\tau\eta\rho$, to give a subject to the following lines. 437 is also a doubtful line, which could have been added to fill a lacuna (cf. ad loc.). Cf. also ad *Dem.* 13, 413.

M itself was torn at some stage, resulting in a V-shaped rent in the lines 387–404 and 462–79. A sixteenth-century scribe repaired the damage roughly and added supplements which were apparently conjectural (cf. Allen and Halliday, xxi f., and for facsimiles Goodwin's edition).

M's tendency for 'restoring' unmetrical 'epicisms' may be noted at 137, 173, 269, 284. Possibly $\mathring{\alpha}\chi\acute{\epsilon}\epsilon\iota\nu$ at 479 has also replaced $\mathring{\iota}\alpha\chi\acute{\epsilon}(\epsilon)\iota\nu$ (i.e. $\mathring{\iota}\alpha\chi\epsilon\mathring{\iota}\nu$). Cf. West ad Hes. *Th.* 800.

The most complete apparatus criticus is provided by Goodwin. The deficiencies of M's text are well illustrated by a small fragment of papyrus (pap. 2), of the third century A.D., which contains 402–7 (P. Oxy. 2379). In the space of six lines (and only 14 fragmentary words) it confirms two previous conjectures (at 404 and 406) and gives the true reading of 407, which had long been suspected (and was in fact marked as corrupt in M itself). The papyrus also contradicts the suspected lacuna after 403, and provides an Attic form of the name Persephone at 405 ($\Phi\epsilon\rho\sigma\epsilon\phi\acute{o}\nu\eta$). For a discussion cf. R. Merkelbach, *Studien zur Textgeschichte und Textkritik* (Cologne and Opladen, 1959), 155 f.

There is one other papyrus which has bearing on the *Hymn* (pap. 1). This was first published by Schubart and Bücheler in *Berliner Klassikertexte*, V, 1 p. 7 (P. Berol. 13044). It is at present in East Berlin, and is probably mid-first-century B.C. (Dr. W. Müller, in a letter to me). It can conveniently be found in Kern, *Orph. Frag.* 49, pp. 119 ff. This papyrus contains an account of the Rape of Persephone and Demeter's Visit to Eleusis which differs considerably from the *Hymn*, ascribed to Orpheus (and Musaeus, as his amanuensis), together with lengthy quotations from the *Hymn*, two of which are ascribed to Orpheus and Musaeus(?) respectively. The lines quoted are 418–23 (Catalogue of Nymphs, omitting 419), 8–18+33–6, 248–9, 256–62, 268a+54b–56. The papyrus makes it clear, first, that the *Hymn*, or parts of it, were here treated as the work of Orpheus. It also appears to adapt the lines of the *Hymn* to suit a different, Orphic version (see below: Introduction XI, c). At 256–62 its text differs considerably from that of M, and between 258b and 261 it cannot be reconstructed. It omits lines (19–32: cf. ad loc.), and transfers and adapts 54–6 to follow 268a. Despite these idiosyncrasies, it provides useful testimony, especially at 418–23, where it has correct readings of all but one name (M is full of mistakes here), and agrees with Pausanias' quotation in omitting 419 (cf. ad loc.). At 8–18 it agrees closely with M (12b–16 are missing in the papyrus), but reads ἀθανάτα[ιcι at 18, which might, just possibly, point to a true reading ἀθανάτῃcι. At 33–6 it omits δέ in 35 and clearly breaks off at 36. This is interesting, as 37 had already been suspected as an interpolation (cf. above). At 248 the papyrus apparently read [πυρῇ ἔνι πο]λλῇ, but this can hardly be correct. Its text of 256–7 is significantly different, suggesting a variant version of lines which are traditional in character (cf. ad loc.). The adaptation of 54–6 may be deliberate, but the reading ἤπα]φε θυμόν in 56 suggests a variant version, and it also has Φερcεφόνην (cf. pap. 2).

The papyrus also presents a slightly different version of the names of Celeus' daughters (cf. ad *Dem.* 105). It represents Athena and Artemis as present at the Rape (Orph. fr. 49. 40 f.), and there is no reason to assume that the version of the *Hymn* which it used omitted *Dem.* 424.[1]

IX. QUOTATIONS

Direct quotations are not numerous, and all are late. Apart from the 'quotations' in the Orphic papyrus there are five definite cases, three in Pausanias. Cf. Allen and Halliday, lxxix ff.

---

[1] For other features of this version see below (Introduction XI, c: Orphic versions). Cf. also the articles referred to by Kern (l.c.), and L. Malten, *ARW* 12 (1909), 426 ff., A. Krüger, *Hermes* 73 (1938), 352 ff.

1. Philodemus περὶ εὐcεβείας 40. 5 (ed. Gomperz, *Herkulanische Studien*, ii (1866), 42, tab. 91, vv. 12 ff.) refers to *Dem.* 440.
2. Paus. 1. 38. 2 refers to *Dem.* 154, but reads ἀγήνορος (cf. 155) instead of ἀμύμονος.
3. Paus. 4. 30. 4 quotes *Dem.* 417–20, omitting 419 (cf. the Orphic papyrus).
4. Paus. 2. 14. 3 quotes *Dem.* 474–6, with variant readings (476 δρηςμοςύνην . . . πᾶςι Paus.: χρηςμοςύνην . . . καλά M). He probably did not have 477, which is not original (cf. ad loc.).
5. Schol. Nic. *Alex.* 130 (cf. Schol. Eur. *Or.* 964) paraphrases *Dem.* 202 ff.

Pausanias and Philodemus quote from 'Homer', or 'the Hymns of Homer', whereas Schol. Nic. refers to τοῖς εἰς Ὅμηρον ἀναφερομένοις ὕμνοις.

In addition there are two possible references in Philodemus to *Dem.* 2 and 269 (Allen and Halliday, lxix; cf. Philodem. o.c., Gomperz, *Sb. Akad. Wien* 123 (1890), vi, p. 29, and *Herkul. Stud.* ii. 29, col. 57a). The first is highly doubtful (καὶ τανύςφορον εἰπεῖν, with no author's name), the second at best garbled. Cornutus (35) cites πολυδέκτης, πολυδέγμων, which are probably from *Dem.* 9 and 17 (etc.). Apollodorus (ap. Schol. Genav. ad *Il.* 21. 319) quotes φερέcβιος from 'Homer': it appears at *Dem.* 450, 451, 469, and also *Ap.* 341 and *Hy.* 30. 9, but not in Homer. Paus. 1. 38. 3 quotes 'Pamphos and Homer' for the names of Celeus' daughters, but gives them as Diogeneia, Pammerope, and Saesara (cf. ad *Dem.* 105, and below, Introduction XI, A).

It appears from Pausanias' quotations that he possessed a form of the *Hymn* which differed considerably from ours, but which he accepted as Homeric. The existence of variant versions is indicated also by the Orphic papyrus (above), and there were other versions attributed to Pamphos and Musaeus, which perhaps resembled the *Homeric Hymn* to some extent (cf. below, Introduction XI, A and C).

X. INFLUENCE ON LATER LITERATURE

The influence of the *Hymn*, certain or probable, may be detected or suspected in many places in Greek literature. But its popularity was clearly greatest in the Hellenistic period. Many of the echoes of it are in passages where the subject is either Demeter or the

Eleusinian Mysteries. The *Hymn to Ge* (*Hom. Hy.* 30) is perhaps
the earliest piece which may be influenced by the *Hymn to Demeter*,
although it is always possible that the parallels are due to traditional formulae, and it is also possible that it is of a much later
period.[1]

In the fifth century both Pindar and Sophocles refer to the
Mysteries in language which probably recalls *Dem.* 480–2 (Pi. fr.
137a Snell, S. fr. 837 P.). Bacchylides may also have known the
Hymn (cf. below, Introduction XI, A).

Euripides has an ode in the *Helen* about the Rape of Persephone and Wrath of Demeter, here identified with the Mother
of the Gods (1301 ff.). It is probable that he has the *Hymn* in
mind, although his version of the myth is different.[2] Carcinus
fr. 5 is dependent on the *Helen* ode. At Ar. *Thesm.* 1155 f. the
invocation ὦ Θεσμοφόρω πολυποτνία probably belongs to the cult,
rather than recalling *Dem.* 211 (cf. A.R. 1. 1125, 1151, *Orph.
Hy.* 40. 16). See also Addenda.

In this period it is perhaps significant that Antimachus,
the precursor of learned Alexandrian poetry, apparently related
the story of Demeter's wanderings, and shows some traces of
knowledge of the *Hymn*.[3] In the third century Callimachus in his
Hymn to Demeter also seems to echo the Homeric poet's description of Demeter's wanderings.[4] Philitas also wrote an elegiac
poem called *Demeter* (Powell, *Collectanea Alexandrina*, 90 f., frr.
1–4), in which someone (Demeter?) complains of his (her?)
troubles, but not much more can be deduced about it with
certainty.

It is Apollonius Rhodius who shows most clearly the influence
of the *Hymn*. His description of Thetis' attempt to immortalize
Achilles (4. 869 ff.) is closely similar to *Dem.* 237 ff. Both passages

---

[1] Cf. *Hy.* 30. 6 ~ *Dem.* 54, 492 πότνια at beginning of verse; 7–8 ~ *Dem.* 486–7;
9 ~ *Dem.* 450–1, 456, 469; 12 ~ *Dem.* 489; 16 ~ *Dem.* 1; 18–9 ~ *Dem.* 494–5.
    For a possible link between *Dem.* 380 ff., Ibycus, and Bacchylides, *Ode* 5 see
notes to *Dem.* 383.

[2] Cf. especially 1301 ff. ~ *Dem.* 40 ff., 1306 f. ~ 201, 304; 1315 f. ~ 424;
1316a–18 ~ *Dem.* 9, 30, etc.; 1327–37 ~ 305–12; 1338–45 ~ 313–28; 1342 f. ~
77; 1349 ff. ~ 202–4. Perhaps also 1355–7 ~ *Dem.* 367–9?

[3] Fr. 32. 5 W. ~ *Dem.* 8–11; fr. 109 ~ *Dem.* 208?; cf. also frr. 67, 96, Wyss
ad loc.

[4] Call. *Hy.* 6. 12, 15–16 ~ *Dem.* 49–50, 99–100, 201–2; 6. 47 ~ *Dem.* 165, 220;
6. 57–8 ~ *Dem.* 188–9, 251 ff.; note also fr. 611 ~ *Dem.* 98 f., *Hy.* 6. 134 ~ *Hom. Hy.*
13.3 (to Demeter); fr. 63. 8 πότνα as nominative, of Demeter ~ *Dem.* 118.

might reflect an earlier epic model, but this seems unlikely on internal grounds (cf. ad loc. for discussion and parallels). There are many other parallels of expression between the two poems, some of which are probably fortuitous, but hardly all.[1]

Theocritus 25. 38 ff. was thought by Ruhnken to be an imitation of *Dem.* 213 ff., but the passages are traditional in character and he may have had other models (cf. ad loc.). Note however also 25. 163 ὡc εἴ περ (cod.) ∼ *Dem.* 215 (cf. ad loc.), and 25. 46 ∼ 151–2.

Nicander refers to the story of Demeter's reception at Eleusis (*Alex.* 128 ff.) in language which clearly recalls *Dem.* 202 ff.[2]

The choriambic *Hymn to Demeter* of Philicus[3] tells of the famine caused by Demeter, and the attempts to pacify her, culminating in the appearance of Iambe, who makes her laugh. The poet evidently has the *Homeric Hymn* in mind, although his version of the story is different.[4]

Another lyric hymn which perhaps belongs to this period (or the fourth century B.C.) is that to the Mother of the Gods.[5] This has affinities with Eur. *Hel.* 1301 ff., but also with the *Homeric Hymn.*[6]

A third hymn to Demeter of the Hellenistic period, in dactylic hexameter and tetrameter couplets, is Page, *Greek Lit. Pap.* no. 91. Here too one may detect traces of possible influence.[7] P. Harris 6,[8] of the second or third century A.D., preserves a frag-

---

[1] These are: *Dem.* 8–11, 17 a∼A.R. 2. 1209, 1214; 20b∼4. 70; 25, 52∼3. 1212–16; 67∼4. 1422; 94∼1. 834; 101∼3. 72; 107∼1. 1207 (∼Theocr. 13. 39, 46); 111, 147–8∼1. 298 ff.(?); 131b∼4. 181(?); 168∼1. 283; 176–7∼3. 874–5, 4. 940 ff. (936b∼*Dem.* 269b), 4. 45; 190∼3. 741 f.; 201, 304∼1. 286; 211∼1. 1125, 1151 (cf. sup.); 231, 254∼3. 867 (4. 1135 f.)(?); 259∼3. 714; 269∼ 4. 936; 274a∼2. 699, 3. 1204; 281∼3. 158; 282∼3. 811(?) (Mosch. *Eur.* 18); 293∼4. 752 (Mosch. *Eur.* 16 f.); 308∼1. 686 f.(?); 355∼1. 307(?); 362b∼ 1. 466; 437∼2. 878; 451∼3. 969.

[2] Cf. Schol. ad loc., and especially *Alex.* 128∼*Dem.* 208–9; 129∼207a, 210; 130∼47 ff., 200; 132∼202–4; cf. also Nic. *Ther.* 483–7.

[3] Cf. A. Körte, *Hermes* 66 (1931), 444 ff.; also D. L. Page, *Greek Lit. Papyri*, no. 90 and K. Latte, *Kl. Schr.* 539 ff.

[4] Col. i fr. 4a, 21∼*Dem.* 305 ff.; 24 ff.∼314 ff., 441 ff.; col. ii fr. 5, 33 ff.∼ 325 ff., esp. 327 f.; 36 ὥραcιν∼265; 53∼305 ff.; 54 ff.∼202 ff. Cf. Latte, o.c. 553, 559, F. R. Walton, *HTR* 45 (1952), 107 n. 7.

[5] *PMG* 935; cf. especially P. Maas, *Epidaurische Hymnen*, 134 ff., and M. L. West, *CQ* 20 (1970), 212 ff.

[6] 5 ff. ∼ *Dem.* 40 ff.; 9, 15∼313 ff.; 19∼331 f.; cf. Maas l.c.

[7] Page 91. 1∼*Dem.* 1, 18, 32; 3 ff., 9∼*Dem.* 85–7.

[8] Cf. Snell, *Gnomon* 13 (1937), 580 f., Körte, *Arch. Pap.* 13 (1938), 80 f.

ment of another hexameter poem about Demeter, in which Hermes is sent as a messenger by Zeus to entreat her and offer her honours.[1]

The last poet of this era who shows definite knowledge of the *Hymn* is Moschus, in his *Europa*. The flower-catalogue (*Europa* 63 ff.) is similar to that of *Dem.* 6 ff., 425 ff., and although both might derive from an earlier epic version of the Rape of Europa, there is no doubt that Moschus had the *Hymn* in mind (cf. notes to *Dem.* 6 ff., Bühler, *Europa*, 108 ff.). This is supported by other clear parallels.[2]

Of the many inscriptions in verse referring to the Eleusinian cult there is only one which I have noted which shows a possible reminiscence of the *Hymn*, *IG* ii². 3661. 3 (second/third century A.D.): ὄργια πᾶcιν ἔφηνε βροτοῖc φαεcίμβροτα Δηοῦc, cf. *Dem.* 474–6 δεῖξε . . . καὶ ἐπέφραδεν ὄργια πᾶcι (cf. ad loc.).

The use of the *Hymn* as a work of Orpheus has already been noted (see above, Introduction VIII). Apart from Orph. fr. 49, another well-known reference to the 'works of Musaeus and Orpheus' (Plato, *Rep.* 364 e 3 ff.) possibly indicates use of the *Hymn* as an Orphic poem (cf. ad *Dem.* 367–9). There are also some parallels between the *Homeric Hymn* and the *Orphic Hymns* and *Argonautica*.[3]

In prose the account of the Rape by Apollodorus (1. 5) appears to paraphrase the Homeric version, although he also includes features from other accounts, and differs from the *Hymn* in making Demophon die in the fire. He echoes the language of the *Hymn* at several points.[4] See also Addenda.

In Latin poetry definite reminiscences are confined to those poets who retell the myth, Ovid and (probably) Claudian. Ruhnken compared *Dem.* 101–2 with Virgil, *Aen.* 4. 33, 'nec

---

[1] Cf. *Dem.* 313 ff., and v. 5 λίccομαι ἀγλαόδω[ρε ~ *Dem.* 54 etc.; 7 Ζεὺc γάρ με πρ[οέηκε ~ *Dem.* 314, 335, 348, etc.; 9–10 δώcειν γὰρ τιμὰc [. . .] ἔν τε θεοῖc μακά-ρ[εccι ~ *Dem.* 328, 443–4, 461–2.

[2] *Eur.* 16–7 ~ *Dem.* 285, 293; *Eur.* 18 ~ *Dem.* 198, 282; *Eur.* 126 ff. ~ *Dem.* 176, *Eur.* 127b ~ *Dem.* 131b; cf. Bühler, 61 ff., 169 ff.

[3] Orphic *Hy.* prologue 6b ~ *Dem.* 4* etc.; 38a ~ 424*; 10. 18b ~ *Dem.* 291*; 18. 11b ~ 17* etc.; 24. 1b ~ *Dem.* 337a; 29. 4b ~ *Dem.* 340, 415*, 29. 12 f. ~ *Dem.* 401 ff.; 40. 16b ~ 211*; 55. 18b ~ 431*; 56. 8b ~ 66*; 79. 2b ~ 8*; *Arg.* 33b ~ *Dem.* 296*; 377b ~ 272*; 625b ~ 459*; 730–1 ~ 99, 272(?); 1191–6 ~ *Dem.* 2 ff., 1195b ~ 300*, 1196a ~ 19*; 1339b ~ 108 (?).

[4] Cf. *Dem.* 3, 22 ff., 44 ff.; 47 f.; 91 ff., 98–9, 101, 184, 191, 202–4, 233–5, 239 ff., 244, 248, 268, 334 ff., 372, 373, 399–400, 445–7; Förster, *Raub und Rückkehr*, 57.

dulcis natos Veneris nec praemia noris', and *Dem.* 176 with Cat. 64. 129, 'mollia nudatae tollentem tegmina surae'. The first of these has no closer parallel elsewhere, but need not necessarily be an echo of the *Hymn*. The second is more directly derived from Hellenistic poetry (cf. notes ad loc.).

Ovid has two versions of the Rape, *Metamorphoses*, 5. 341 ff., and *Fasti*, 4. 417 ff. There has been considerable discussion about the sources of these, and it has been thought that those passages which recall the *Hymns* to Demeter and Aphrodite depend on a Hellenistic intermediary.[1] But there is no reason to doubt that Ovid knew and imitated the *Hymns* directly, although he follows in the main the version popular later, which placed the Rape in Sicily.[2]

The last poet who concerns us here is Claudian, whose unfinished mythological epic, *De Raptu Proserpinae*, is indebted partly to Ovid and partly to other Latin and Greek sources.[3] It is debatable whether he knew the *Hymn*, or was influenced by it. There is remarkably little evidence of such knowledge, 'although it is a reasonable assumption that as an Alexandrian born he would have been familiar with it' (Hall, o.c. p. 197). His method of telling the story is full-blown and rhetorical, in complete contrast to the Homeric poet's directness and simplicity, and also to Ovid, who at times comes close to the brevity of the *Hymn* (e.g. *F.* 4. 445–6, *M.* 5. 395–6 ~ *Dem.* 16 ff.; Claudian takes 55 lines over this, 2. 151–205). Claudian's flower-catalogue (2. 128 ff.; cf. 92 ff.) is indebted mainly to Ovid rather than the *Hymn*, but he includes the narcissus, which is important in the *Hymn* but does not appear in Ovid's versions. He is closest to the *Hymn* in Pluto's speech of consolation to Proserpine.[4]

---

[1] Cf. Herter, *Rhein. Mus.* 90 (1941), 236 ff., for bibliography.

[2] Cf. Bömer, *Fasti*, l.c., and *F.* 4. 437 ff. ~ *Dem.* 6 ff., 425 ff.; 447 f. ~ *Dem.* 20 ff., etc.; 453 ~ 38, 455 ~ 39, 457 f. ~ 41 ff., 386; 498 ff. ~ 43b; 502 ff. ~ *Dem.* 96 ff., 503 f. ~ 98, 201 f.; 513 f. ~ 113 ff., 147a; 517 f. ~ 101 ff., 42, 182, 197; 540 ff. ~ 233–41; 550 ~ 231, 238; 553 ff. ~ 239 ff.; 557 ff. ~ 256 ff., 561 f. ~ 275–81; 577 ff. ~ 69 ff.; 581 ff. ~ 62 f., 69 f., 76 ff.; 584 ~ 85–7; 591 f. ~ 83–5, 363–4; 598–600 ~ 83–7, 363 ff.; 603 f., 607–8 ~ 372–4, 393 ff., etc.; 605 ~ 335; 613–14 ~ 445 ff., 463 ff.; 615 f. ~ 470 ff.; *M.* 5. 391 ff. ~ *Dem.* 6 ff., 16–20; 438 ff. ~ 43 ff., 446–7 ~ 49–50; 449 ff. ~ 202–11; 471 f. ~ 40 f., 90; 477–86 ~ 305 ff.; 506–8 ~ 83 ff., 363–9; 521 f., 526–9 ~ 83 ff., 363–4; 530–2, 564 ff. ~ 393 ff., 445–7, 463–5.

[3] Cf. J. B. Hall, *Claudian De Raptu Proserpinae* (Cambridge, 1969), 106 ff., for recent discussion and bibliography, and also A. Cameron, *Claudian* (Oxford, 1970), 310–11.

[4] 2. 276 ff.: 277–8a ~ *Dem.* 361–2; 278b–80a ~ 363–6; 294–9 ~ 364–5; 302b, 303b–4 ~ 367–9.

Ovid does not have this address to Proserpine in either version, although he echoes it (with *Dem.* 82 ff.) in speeches addressed to Ceres (*F.* 4. 598–600, *M.* 5. 506–8(?), 526–9). It is possible that Claudian is influenced here by another version which we do not possess (perhaps one ascribed to Orpheus), in which Hades consoles Persephone as he carries her off rather than when she returns to her mother (cf. ad *Dem.* 363). Consolation by an abductor is also a feature of Mosch. *Eur.* 153 ff. (cf. Bühler ad loc.).

There are a few other parallels, of which the most notable is Claud. 2. 313–14, where Pluto smiles: 'facili passus mollescere risu, dissimilisque sui' (cf. *Dem.* 357–8, notes ad loc.). This is an unusual feature (not in Ovid) and as it comes shortly after Pluto's speech of consolation it might have been suggested by Hades' smile before he addresses Persephone in the *Hymn*.

The appearance of Minerva and Diana as companions of Proserpine in Claudian is probably due to Ovid and/or another source (Orphic version?). The description of them at 2. 20–1, 'haec tristibus aspera bellis, haec metuenda feris', is close to *Dem.* 424, but this is probably simply traditional. The same applies to 3. 50–1 (∼ *Dem.* 43–4) and 149–50 (∼ *Dem.* 40–1). But note 3. 169 ff., where Electra, one of the Oceanids, is described as the nurse of Proserpine (∼ *Dem.* 418).[1]

We must therefore conclude that, whilst knowledge of the *Hymn* by Claudian is definitely possible, it cannot be demonstrated.[2]

Claudian completes this brief survey of the *Hymn*'s influence. It has often been said (e.g. Allen and Halliday, Introduction lxxviii ff.) that the *Homeric Hymns* were not widely read in antiquity, on the ground that they are seldom quoted (see above, Introduction IX). In comparison with Homer or Hesiod their influence is slight, but it can, I think, be traced throughout antiquity (this applies equally to the other major *Hymns*), although it is the learned Alexandrian poets who show the greatest interest in the *Hymn to Demeter*.[3]

[1] There is an interesting parallel between Claudian's *De Consulatu Stilichonis*, 2. 277 and *Dem.* 188–9 (∼ *Aph.* 173–4), but the motif probably occurred elsewhere.

[2] Cf. also below, Introduction XI, c.

[3] As the manuscript of the *Hymn* was not apparently known to the world in general until the end of the eighteenth century, the *Hymn* exercised no influence over Renaissance literature. A paper was once written which endeavoured to

XI. OTHER VERSIONS[1]

A. LITERARY VERSIONS

The myth was a stock subject of hymns, and popular in all literary forms throughout antiquity.[2] It is referred to in Hes. *Th.* 913–14, in a way which suggests that it was already traditional (cf. ad *Dem.* 1–18). Other epic versions besides the *Hymn* are attested. We know something of Pamphos' hymn, thanks to Pausanias, who calls him the earliest hymn-writer for the Athenians (7. 21. 9; 9. 29. 8), and earlier than Homer (8. 37. 9). Pamphos agreed with Homer in calling Demeter's daughter by her proper name Persephone (8. 37. 9), and like the Homeric poet he made the narcissus the means by which Persephone was deceived, and so carried off, in contrast to the Sicilian version later popular, in which she was picking violets (Paus. 9. 31. 9; *Dem.* 8 ff.). In this he perhaps followed local Attic legend (cf. Soph. *OC* 681 ff., Förster 30 f.). In other details, however, he differed from the *Homeric Hymn*, as he called the well by which Demeter sat Anthion (but cf. ad *Dem.* 99), and Pausanias locates this on the road to Megara, and distinguishes it from Callichoron. She was disguised as an old woman as in the Homeric version, but here she claimed to come from Argos, rather than Crete (Paus. 1. 39. 1; contrast *Dem.* 99, 123 ff.). Pamphos also named the daughters of Celeus, who greeted Demeter and took her to their mother Metaneira, differently from our version of the *Hymn*, although according to Pausanias (1. 38. 3) he agreed with Homer on this point. One of his names, Saesara, seems to belong to local Attic legend again (cf. ad *Dem.* 105). Diogeneia also is perhaps local (cf. Apollod. 3. 15. 1), but Pammerope cannot be identified.

We seem to find in Pamphos a variant epic version which both agrees and disagrees with ours, and which also preserves some traces of Attic legend that are not found in ours. In the main,

identify Milton's debts to the *Hymn*. This should serve as a warning against the perils of any such attempts to trace literary influences; that applies also to the tentative identifications which have been made in the preceding pages.

[1] On this subject see especially R. Förster, *Der Raub und die Rückkehr der Persephone* (Stuttgart, 1874); also F. Bräuninger, *RE* 19. 948 ff.

[2] Cf. Aristides, *Eleus.* i p. 416 D. εἰς μέσον ποιηταὶ καὶ λογοποιοὶ καὶ cυγγραφεῖς πάντες ὑμνοῦcι Κόρην τὴν Δήμητρος ἀφανῆ γενέcθαι; Menander, *Rhet. Gr.* 9. 144 Walz = 3 p. 338 Spengel; Nonnus *D.* 19. 80 ff., 47. 47, 27. 285 f.

however, it looks as if his version of the myth was closely similar.

Further evidence for variant 'rhapsodic' texts may perhaps be detected in the quotations of Pausanias from the *Homeric Hymn* itself (see above, Introduction IX). The evidence for various Orphic versions, which also supports this view, will be considered separately below.

The allusions by the later epic poet Panyassis may here be mentioned. He referred to Demeter's arrival at Eleusis, but replaced Celeus by Triptolemus as a son of Eleusis (fr. 24 K. ap. Apollod. 1. 5. 1). He also mentioned in passing how Demeter was in service to a mortal for a whole year, presumably as nurse to the king of Eleusis (fr. 16).[1]

Of the lyric poets, several wrote hymns to Demeter and Persephone, of which very little is known for certain. [Archilochus] fr. 322 (West) is at best of doubtful authenticity (but see on *Dem.* 192–211 : 3. Iambe). Cf. also Lasus, *PMG* 702, Pindar fr. 37 Sn. (= 18 Bowra), probably also Bacch. fr. 3 Sn. (and perhaps frr. 2, 47). Archilochus had important family connections with the cult of Demeter, and could have composed a poem following a local version which made Paros the scene of the Rape (cf. ad *Dem.* 17). It is very likely that Lasus did so for Hermione, whose claim to have been the scene was taken seriously later (cf. Apollod. 1. 5. 1, etc.). Bacchylides, somewhat surprisingly, located it in Crete (fr. 47). In the *Homeric Hymn* Demeter claims to have come to Eleusis from Crete (123 ff.), and Bacchylides perhaps followed this version, making her actually come from the place of the Rape itself (cf. Förster, 65). He also mentioned Celeus (fr. 3). The Orphic *Rhapsodies* seem to locate the Rape of Persephone by Zeus in Crete (Orph. fr. 303), but this is a separate affair (see below).

The story of how Pindar composed a hymn to Persephone, or Demeter, after a dream in which either goddess had appeared to him, may have been suggested by something in the poem itself (cf. Bowra, *Pindar*, 51). The hymn contained many epithets of Hades (Paus. 9. 23. 4) but perhaps did not tell the story of the

---

[1] R. Rapetti, *Parola del Passato* 107 (1966), 131 ff., suggests that Hyginus, *Fab.* 147 is dependent on Panyassis for the major part of his version, since Triptolemus is also son of Eleusis here (on this see Förster, 70 f., *contra*). He also conjectures that the episode came in the *Heraclea* of Panyassis, in connection with Heracles' initiation at Eleusis before his descent to Hades.

Rape (cf. Malten, *ARW* 12 (1909), 429 n. 1). In *O.* 6. 92 ff. he mentions the festival of Demeter and Persephone at Syracuse, but this would not necessarily indicate that he also located the Rape there (Malten l.c.), although *Nem.* 1. 13 does probably imply this (cf. Schol. ad loc., Zuntz, *Persephone,* 71). Another lyric poet, Melanippides, also wrote a poem called *Persephone,* in which an etymology of Acheron was given (*PMG* 759). This may have been a hymn (cf. Meleager, *Anth. Pal.* 4. 1. 7). He also made the identification of Demeter with the Mother of the gods (*PMG* 764).

It is not known if Aeschylus referred to the myth of Persephone. He was Eleusinian by birth, and was accused of revealing secrets from the Mysteries (Arist. *EN* 1111ᵃ9 f.), but whether he was initiated or not is unclear (cf. Ar. *Ran.* 886–7; Clem. Alex. *Strom.* 2. 461). His play Ἐλευcίνιοι may have contained allusions to the cult or myths of Eleusis, but there is no evidence for this. Sophocles, besides echoing the *Hymn* in his words about the Mysteries (fr. 837 P.) also made the story of Triptolemus the subject of a tragedy (frr. 596–617 P.), which evidently followed the version popular at Athens in the classical period, in which Triptolemus received from Demeter the gift of corn and became the teacher of mankind (cf. ad *Dem.* 153). Although direct influence from the *Hymn* is not perceptible, the occurrence of the word ἀφράcμων, rare enough to be quoted by Hesychius, in this play is interesting (fr. 613; cf. *Dem.* 256).

The Euripidean ode, in the *Helen,* has been mentioned above (Introduction X: Influence). Of the logographers, Pherecydes (*FGH* 3. 53) gave a genealogy of Triptolemus, and Phanodemus (*FGH* 325. 27) located the Rape in Attica, being the first attested authority for this (cf. ad *Dem.* 17). Philochorus apparently gave a rationalized account of the myth (*FGH* 328. 104), at least in so far as concerns his explanation of the winged chariot of Triptolemus.

The Parian Marble has an account of Demeter's visit to Athens and invention of corn, followed by Triptolemus' sowing of it (*Mar. P.* 12–13; see below: XI, c). Apollodorus (1. 5) gives a summary of the myth, largely based on the *Hymn,* but drawing on other versions also (cf. Frazer ad loc.).

The first explicit appearance of the Sicilian version[1] is in

[1] But cf. Pi. *N.* 1. 13 (above). The earliest coins from Henna (*c.* 450 B.C.) perhaps

Carcinus (the younger), who refers to the Rape and Famine, in language closely similar to Euripides, but locates it in Sicily (fr. 5). It is thought that the Sicilian historian Timaeus, of the late fourth and early third century, is the source (*FGH* 566. 164) for the later full accounts given by Diodorus (5. 2–5) and Cicero (*Verr.* 4. 106 ff.). It was this version which prevailed in later Greek and Roman poetry and mythographical accounts.[1]

The other versions and references of the fourth century and Hellenistic period, in Antimachus, Philitas, Callimachus, Nicander (cf. fr. 56), and Philicus, and the various papyrus fragments of poems about Demeter have been discussed above (Introduction X: Influence). There is an interesting Roman version (Virg. *G.* 1. 39, Serv. ad loc., Colum. 10. 272 ff., Lucan, *Bell. Civ.* 6. 698 f., 739 ff.) in which Proserpine is reluctant to return from Hades.[2] For other late accounts cf. Förster, Bräuninger l.c.

B. LOCAL VERSIONS

On these see notes to *Dem.* 17, 75 ff., 96, 200, 227, and Bräuninger, *RE* 19. 951. 37 ff., 954. 19 ff., 959. 43 ff.

C. ORPHIC VERSIONS[3]

Under this heading may be classed those versions of the Rape of Persephone and Wanderings of Demeter, and also those hymns to Demeter and other related deities, which are ascribed to Orpheus, Musaeus, or Eumolpus.

(a) Orpheus

The *Parian Chronicle* (*FGH* 239 A 14 = Kern, *Orph. Frag. Test.* 221) refers to poetry published by Orpheus[4] concerning the

already show Demeter looking for Persephone: cf. B. V. Head, *Brit. Mus. Cat. of Coins, Sicily,* 58, Zuntz, *Persephone,* 70 f. Demeter is represented with torches, driving her chariot. The connection with the myth is not explicit, but it is probably there in the background.

[1] Cf. Moschus, 13. 121 ff., Opp. *H.* 3. 486–96, Nonn. *D.* 6. 1 ff.; Ovid and Claudian above, Val. Fl. 5. 343 ff., Stat. *Ach.* 2. 149–51, Sil. Ital. 7. 688 ff., 14. 239 ff.; Hygin. *Fab.* 146, 147, Lact. Plac. ad *Theb.* 2. 482; Firm. Mat. *de err. prof. rel.* 7; etc.

[2] Förster traced this back to Philochorus l.c., but cf. Jacoby ad loc.

[3] Cf. especially L. Malten, *ARW* 12 (1909), 417 ff., 'Altorphische Demetersage'; and for a good general account of Orphic literature I. M. Linforth, *The Arts of Orpheus* (Univ. of California Press, 1941); cf. also L. Moulinier, *Orphée et l'orphisme* (Paris 1955). See also Preface, p. viii.

[4] The name is in a lacuna, but is probably correct. Cf. Jacoby, *Mar. Par.* ad loc.

Rape, Demeter's Search, her Discovery of Corn, and its Dissemination throughout the world. The Orphic papyrus which quotes parts of the *Homeric Hymn* (Orph. fr. 49 K.) also contains a prose paraphrase of such a version, with commentary, and tells us that Musaeus acted as Orpheus' amanuensis (49. 4 f.). Pausanias (1. 14. 3 = Kern, fr. 51) again refers to a poem of Orpheus about Demeter's Visit to Eleusis and Gift of Corn, which he distinguishes from another version, ascribed to Musaeus. The Orphic *Argonautica* (26 f. = Kern, Test. 224) includes in a catalogue of poetry by Orpheus 'Demeter's Wanderings and Grief for Persephone, and how she was Thesmophoros', and the poet also mentions a past song, addressed to Musaeus, on the Rape (1191–6; Kern, pp. 115–16). Clement claims to quote lines from a poem of Orpheus about Demeter's visit to Eleusis (Kern, fr. 52).

Mention should also be made of the Orphic *Rhapsodies*, which included references to the Marriage of Persephone with Zeus, and Rape by Plouton (cf. Orph. frr. 58, 153, 303; 151, 191–7, 360). The *Rhapsodic Theogony* seems to have been compiled *c.* 100 B.C. from a number of poems ascribed to Orpheus. The Rape of Core, with the weaving-scene, perhaps goes back to the *Peplos*, ascribed to the early-fifth-century Pythagorean Bro(n)tinus (see below).

Further direct evidence is provided by the Scholiast on Hesiod, *Th.* 914 (Kern, fr. 43), by scattered references in the Orphic *Hymns* (18. 12 ff., 29. 9 ff., 41. 3 ff., 43. 7 ff.; Kern, 115), and the quotation by Justin of the opening line of a poem on the 'Wrath of Demeter', adapted from *Il.* 1. 1 (Orph. fr. 48).

(b) Musaeus

The *Parian Chronicle* (A 15 = Diels, *Vorsokr.*[6] 2 B 8) refers to the publication of the poetry of Musaeus by his son Eumolpus,[1] after the foundation of the Mysteries. Pausanias (10. 5. 6 = Musaeus fr. 11 Diels) also speaks of poetry ascribed to Musaeus, entitled Εὐμολπία, and the *Suda* (s.v. Μουϲαῖοϲ = Diels 2 A 1) calls him a pupil of Orpheus, who wrote, amongst other poetry, Ὑποθῆκαι to his son Eumolpus, consisting of 4,000 lines.

Pausanias, who quotes 'Musaeus' for a genealogy of Triptolemus (1. 14. 3 = Orph. fr. 51 K., Diels 2 B 10), doubted the

---

[1] Again the name Eumolpus occurs in a lacuna, but is almost certainly correct.

authenticity of any of the works ascribed to Musaeus, except the *Hymn to Demeter*, which was composed for the Lycomidae (1. 22. 7 = Diels 2 A 5; cf. 4. 1. 5 = Diels 2 B 20). Part, at least, of 'Musaeus' he attributed to Onomacritus (1. 22. 7; cf. Hdt. 7. 6).

(c) Eumolpus

In addition to the *testimonia* referred to above, the *Suda* (s.v. Εὔμολπος) makes him a son of Musaeus, and ascribes to him 3,000 lines of poetry about the Rites of Demeter, her Visit to Celeus, and Institution of the Mysteries, which she communicated to Celeus' daughters (cf. ad *Dem.* 105 ff., 154).

For a discussion of the 'poetry of Musaeus and his son', and 'the hubbub of books of Musaeus and Orpheus' in Plato, *Rep.* 363 c 3 ff., 364 e 3 ff., cf. notes on *Dem.* 367–9.

It is difficult to be certain how many separate poems are indicated by this evidence, but it may be noted that Pausanias clearly distinguishes between two versions, ascribed to Musaeus and Orpheus. It is, therefore, unwise to speak of a single 'Orphic version'. Kern thought that he detected four separate poems, of varying dates (*Orph. Frag.* p. 116). But the most complete account, despite its fragmentary condition, is that of Orph. fr. 49, and it may be useful to take this as a basis, and consider how far other *testimonia* agree with or supplement it. Only where actual disagreement is discernible can one safely speak of another version.

This account begins with Persephone, the daughter of Zeus and Demeter, apparently picking flowers (as in the *Hymn*) with the Oceanids, whose names are quoted (*Dem.* 418–23). Persephone picks the narcissus, the earth opens, and Hades appears and carries her off (fr. 49. 17–38 ~ *Dem.* 4–20).

The place of the Rape is not mentioned. According to Schol. Hes. *Th.* 914 (fr. 43) Orpheus placed the Rape near Oceanus, and this is supported by *Orph. Hy.* 18. 13, *Arg.* 1196. Here too, this version probably agrees with the *Hymn*, as also in the mention of the 'Meadow' (*Hy.* 18. 13 ~ *Dem.* 7; cf. ad *Dem.* 5, 7, 17).

The papyrus commentary goes on to mention thunder and lightning in connection with Zeus, and then Artemis' archery, and Athena. In the *Hymn* Artemis and Athena are mentioned as present (*Dem.* 424), but Zeus is far away (27–9). The Orphic version can here be supplemented from Euripides (*Helen*, 1314 ff.), where Artemis and Athena pursue Hades, but Zeus looks down from heaven and brings 'another destiny to pass', together with Claudian (*RP* 2. 205 ff.), who describes how they attack Pluto, but are driven off by Jupiter, who hurls a thunderbolt. In the *Hymn to the Mother of the Gods* (*PMG* 935. 9 ff.) Zeus' thunderbolt is again referred to, but its purpose there is not clear. In this version, then, Zeus is both a witness and an active participant, and Athena and Artemis also take an active part.

The next part is fragmentary and will be discussed below. When the thread can be resumed (line 45) Demeter has heard Persephone's cry (cf. *Dem.* 39), and leaving Sicily wanders over the earth. This indicates the influence of the Sicilian version, but does not necessarily mean that the Rape itself took place there (cf. sup.). The next words,]ε πε[ρὶ] τ[ὴν] πόλιν ἀφανὴς γέγονεν, are obscure, but perhaps refer to the place where Persephone disappeared into the earth with Hades. If so, the city might be Eleusis (see below). The *Hymn* does not mention Persephone's Catabasis.

In the next section preserved Demeter is lamenting her daughter's loss (52 ff.) when she is met by the daughters of the king (of Eleusis), whose names are here different from those of the *Hymn*, and who come together with the *queen* to fetch water (cf. ad *Dem.* 105 ff.). Demeter is disguised as a woman, and they ask why she has come (reading αὐτὴ παραγέγονεν. διὸ . . . in line 57). The next section is apparently part of the commentary, leading to the quotation of *Dem.* 8–36, with the significant omission of *Dem.* 19–32. The omitted lines describe how no one heard Persephone's cry except Hecate and Helios, and how Zeus was far away. The witness of Hecate and Helios leads in the *Hymn* to Demeter's discovery of the truth about the Rape (51–90), but the Orphic version has no place for this, and probably omits it deliberately. Zeus' role has already been shown to be different from the *Hymn*'s portrayal of him.

The next legible section (81 ff.) describes how Demeter is offered the child (Demophon) to nurse and consents to this, and how she anoints him with ambrosia, puts him in the fire, and is detected by his mother (with quotation of *Dem.* 248–9 and 256 ff.). The only difference from the Hymn is in the name of the mother, who is called Baubo (lines 81, 89). But the papyrus goes on to tell how Demeter then burns and kills the child (100 f.). This does not happen in the *Hymn*, but it was quite possibly the original story, and is also found in the version of Apollodorus (cf. ad *Dem.* 254).

Demeter reveals herself (101 ff.), in words which combine her self-revelation in the *Hymn* (268a) with Hecate's question there 'who has stolen Persephone?' (54–6). Demeter, then, still does not know what happened. At this point someone, whose name is uncertain, returns from the fields. In what follows there seems to be a dialogue, in which he asks who the stranger is, and is told that she is looking for her daughter. After another few fragmentary lines the words πρὸς Τριπτ[όλ]εμον . . . occur, followed by ὅθεν κάθοδος λέγεται. The papyrus ends here, but it is by no means certain that this is the end of the commentary.

At this point it is possible to take the story further, by means of Orph. fr. 51 (Paus. 1. 14. 3), which tells us that Eubuleus and Triptolemus, sons of Dysaules, revealed to Demeter information about her daughter, and were rewarded by her with the gift of agriculture (cf. Aristid. *Panath.* 105. 11 p. 53 Dind.).

They must therefore have witnessed the Rape, and Demeter's visit to Eleusis was here motivated by her search for her daughter. This form of the legend, whereby she learns the truth from local inhabitants of the place where the Rape occurred, is common (cf. ad *Dem.* 75 ff., 96), and is more likely to be original than that of the *Hymn*, where Demeter's wanderings on earth and visit to Eleusis have no special purpose. Cf. also *Orph. Hy.* 18. 14–15, where Persephone's κατάβασις took place at Eleusis. Orph. fr. 49. 120 perhaps means 'whence the Κάθοδος is said to have taken place here' or 'the place is called Κάθοδος'.[1]

Further information comes from Clement (Orph. fr. 50), who mentions the Rape and 'the chasm in the earth, and the pigs of Eubuleus which were swallowed up in the earth for the goddesses, which are the origin of the custom by which they throw swine into pits at the Thesmophoria' (on this custom cf. notes on *Dem.* 16). He also recounts elsewhere (Orph. fr. 52) how the inhabitants of Eleusis were autochthonous, and their names were Baubo and Dysaules and Triptolemus, and also Eumolpus and Eubuleus. The last three were respectively cowherd, shepherd, and swineherd. It appears, therefore, that Eubouleus and Triptolemus

---

[1] Cf. also Claudian, *RP* 3. 48 ff.; Förster, 94.

saw their swine being swallowed in the earth with Hades' chariot, and hence were able to report it to Demeter.[1]

That this version may have been already current in the fourth century B.C. is indicated by Asclepiades of Tragilus (*FGH* 12. 4), who described Dysaules as αὐτόχθων, and mentioned his wife Baubo, and his children, whom he called Protogone and Misa.[2] Asclepiades' master Isocrates was perhaps thinking of the Orphic version when he referred to the benefits which Demeter *received from* the people of Attica, of which only the initiated may learn (*Panegyr.* 28). Once again, this suggests that the Orphic version is simply the local legend of Eleusis, and later of Attica. The story of how Demeter rewarded Triptolemus with the gift of agriculture was in the classical period the standard Athenian myth (cf. ad *Dem.* 153 and 305 ff.).[3]

Attempts have been made to find a reference to the pigs in Orph. fr. 49. 39, 41 and 117, but the text is too damaged to allow any certain readings. The words βραβευτὴς δυς[in line 42 were compared by Malten (o.c. 433) with *Orph. Hy.* 18. 16, but this last passage refers to Hades and it would therefore be unwise to restore Δυς[αύλης.

Clement, in the same passage about the γηγενεῖς of Eleusis, describes how Baubo received Demeter and gave her the κυκεών. When Demeter refused to drink it because of her sorrow, Baubo caused her to laugh and accept it, by an indecent exposure. Clement then quotes some verses of Orpheus about this.

This incident is clearly a variant of the episode in *Dem.* 192–211 (cf. ad loc.). Baubo was worshipped in Paros in association with Demeter and Persephone, and may even have belonged to local Eleusinian legend also. It is possible that the Homeric poet glosses over this version as ἀπρεπές, just as he may have omitted the death of Demophon. But it should be stressed that it is impossible to know exactly when the various features of this version were put together, and some may have been added at a much later date than others (cf. Kern, 116). See also Addenda.

In Euripides' *Helen*, another version seems to be reflected.

[1] A trace of this version appears in Ovid, *F.* 4. 465–6, and he also makes the Eleusinians poor rustics, 507 ff.

[2] The last two names are both due to emendation. Cf. Palaiphatos, *FGH* 44. 1, and Malten, o.c. 430, also Headlam on Herodas, 1. 56.

[3] Note that in this myth the gift of the Mysteries comes two generations later (*FGH* 239 A 14–15).

Here, Demeter is consoled by the sending of the Charites, Muses, and Aphrodite by Zeus (*Hel.* 1341 ff.). In *Orph. Hy.* 43. 7 ff. Persephone is brought back to earth by the Moirai and Charites, together with the Horai, her companions in dancing (cf. *Hy.* 29. 9). Malten pointed out that already on the altar of Hyacinthus at Amyclae Demeter, Core, and Pluto were portrayed with the Moirai and Horai, and also Aphrodite, Athena, and Artemis (Paus. 3. 19. 4; Malten, 424 f.).[1] Euripides' reference to the κύκλιοι χοροί of Persephone (*Hel.* 1312 f.) is also similar to *Orph. Hy.* 43. 8 κυκλίοιϲι χοροῖϲ. His equation of Demeter and the Mother of the Gods (cf. notes on *Dem.* 441 ff. and especially the Derveni papyrus) is supposed to be a feature of Orph. fr. 47 (Malten, 419 n. 2, 421), but the original is almost wholly unintelligible.[2] It should be noted that the version given by Orph. fr. 49 does not refer to this identification, but keeps to the traditional relationship of Demeter as sister of Zeus, and the alternative account is explicitly referred to other sources than Orpheus (fr. 49. 15 ff.). Equally, the sending of Charites and Moirai to cheer up Demeter can hardly belong to the same 'Orphic' version as fr. 52, and might even be a poetic invention of Euripides himself, based on an assimilation of several earlier motifs (cf. *Dem.* 192 ff., 313 ff.).

Another detail which is difficult to place is that of Orph. *Arg.* 1191 ff., where Persephone is said to have been 'deceived' by her ϲυνόμαιμοι when she was carried off. In Claudian (*RP* 1. 214 ff.) Venus is sent by Jupiter to entice Proserpine from her weaving, and Pallas and Diana are also ordered to go as her companions (229 ff.), and they are later said to have conspired against Proserpine (3. 198 f.), but wrongly so, since Pallas and Diana in fact oppose the Rape. Förster detected evidence of a version where all the goddesses assisted, on Roman sarcophagi (135, 201–10). If this is in fact the sense of Orph. *Arg.* 1191 ff. it would again suggest that more than one 'Orphic' version was current (but cf. Malten, 422 n. 4).

The reference to Sicily in Orph. fr. 49. 47 seems to indicate that the Sicilian version has contributed something to 'Orpheus'. A further link may be found in Diodorus' reference to Athena and Artemis as Persephone's helpers in weaving the πέπλος for

---

[1] But this is probably irrelevant. In fact it is doubtful how far, if at all, Euripides is following an 'Orphic' version in this ode.

[2] See Zuntz, *Persephone*, 344 ff., especially 352 f., on this inscription.

Zeus (5. 3. 4). In Claudian she is also weaving a robe, for her mother, on which the universe is portrayed (1. 246 ff.; cf. also Nonnus *D.* 6. 145 ff.), and the πέπλος of Core or Athena is a feature of the account in the Orphic *Rhapsodies* (cf. Malten, 426, Kern, Orph. frr. 192, 193, 178). This may derive from the *Peplos* of Bro(n)tinus (cf. Kern, 314). Cf. also fr. 33, and the robe of Chthonie in Pherecydes, fr. 2 Diels (Orph. fr. 192).

The Anodos of Core is caused by Zeus in the *Homeric Hymn*, and she is brought up by Hermes (334 ff.). But there are traces of a version in which Demeter herself went down to Hades in order to recover her, taking Eubouleus (or Euboulos) as her guide (*Orph. Hy.* 41. 5 ff.; cf. Ovid, *F.* 4. 611 ff., *M.* 5. 533?, Claud. *RP* 3. 107 f.). One may note in passing that the Famine, by which Demeter forces Zeus to bring Persephone back in the *Hymn*, does not seem to have a place in the Orphic accounts. In Callimachus (fr. 466 = Orph. fr. 42) Hecate, as the daughter of Demeter (cf. Orph. fr. 41), brought her back. In *Orph. Hy.* 41 Demeter is called Ἀνταία, which was a title of Hecate (cf. ad *Dem.* 52). Hecate herself is portrayed leading Persephone back on a vase-painting (cf. ad *Dem.* 24 ff., 440). It is notable that Hecate's role is here confined to the Anodos, and she is not mentioned at the Cathodos (cf. Malten, 438 f. n. 6). In the *Hymn* she appears in connection with both.

Euboulos, or Eubouleus, is a title of Zeus and other deities in Greek cults, and especially of Hades. At Eleusis he appears in inscriptions as a separate person, receiving offerings with ὁ θεός and ἡ θεά.[1] In the Orphic *Hymns* he is also equated with Plouton (18. 12), or made a son of Demeter and Dysaules (41. 6, 8), or Persephone (29. 8), and he appears on gold-leaf inscriptions (Orph. fr. 32 c–e 2, g 2) and the Gurob papyrus (fr. 31 I 18).[2]

This general survey should have shown some of the difficulties involved in reconstructing the Orphic versions of the myth. Several significant variations have been noted, and it is often difficult to assess the antiquity of any single element. What does seem to emerge is the likelihood that many features attributed to Orpheus are reflections of local Eleusinian legend.[3] Although

[1] *IG* i². 76. 39; Mylonas, *Eleusis*, 198 f.; *IG* ii/iii². 4701, 4615.
[2] Cf. also Orph. fr. 237. 4, *Hy.* 30. 6, 42. 2, 52. 4, 56. 3, 72. 3.
[3] Cf. Wehrli, *ARW* 31 (1934), 80 f.

the *Homeric Hymn* was taken over and apparently adapted as an Orphic poem it is possible that in some respects the Orphic versions may represent earlier and more genuine traditions than those of the Homeric poet, who adapts to suit the requirements of traditional epic narrative. Orpheus, in the classical period, was regarded as the founder of τελεταί in general and, with Musaeus, as the general author of poetry concerning religion and cults (e.g. Ar. *Ran.* 1032 f., [Eur.] *Rhes.* 943–7). Hence poetry relevant to this subject tended to be ascribed to these two, with whom Eumolpus was associated as the founder of the Eleusinian Mysteries, and it is hardly surprising if we find a greater degree of emphasis on the ritual elements of Demeter's cults than we do in the Homeric poem (e.g. the pigs swallowed up in the chasm, Eubouleus, Baubo and her indecency, the gift of corn to Triptolemus, associated with the ceremonies of ritual ploughing, sowing, and reaping at Eleusis, etc.).

Wilamowitz and others have warned against the misconceptions which led scholars to postulate an Orphic body of 'doctrine' and an Orphic 'sect'. As far as concerns the myth of Demeter and Persephone, nothing exists which could support such an assumption. The further general question, when such religious poetry began to be attributed to Orpheus and Musaeus, cannot here be answered with any certainty. The *testimonia* quoted above do not antedate the fourth century B.C. Plato, *Rep.* 363 c ff. (cf. ad *Dem.* 367 ff.) might perhaps suggest that the *Homeric Hymn* was already used by the purveyors of Orphic poetry in the late fifth century. This could hardly be a firm assumption, but other references of the period (especially Eur. *Hipp.* 953–4) indicate that such poetry was already a controversial matter. Herodotus' reference to Onomacritus' forgery of oracles of Musaeus (7. 6) shows that as early as the mid sixth century B.C. there was a body of poetry attributed to Musaeus, and that this was already being tampered with at this date. This is the period in which Athenian interest in the Eleusinian Mysteries is generally thought to have become dominant, and it may be true that the attribution of poetry about the Rape of Persephone and the Mysteries to Orpheus and Musaeus begins at this time. The rise to prominence of Eumolpus may also belong to the sixth century (cf. ad *Dem.* 154). Although he is not clearly related to Musaeus as his son until the end of the fifth century the association must have begun at an earlier period. But it would be dangerous to speculate further on a matter where speculation has in the past been so notably misleading.

XII. SELECT BIBLIOGRAPHY

A. EDITIONS AND TRANSLATIONS

The following is a list of the more noteworthy editions of the *Hymn*:

D. RUHNKEN, *Homeri Hymnus in Cererem*, Leiden, 1780. This edition was defective, omitting 21 lines of the *Hymn*, and was withdrawn when the error was discovered.

—— *Homeri Hymnus in Cererem*, Leiden, 1782 (actually published 1781). The first complete edition. With introduction, text, and commentary by Ruhnken (assisted by Valckenaer, Wyttenbach, Fontein, Voss, and others), and Latin tr. by Voss. For the history of these two editions see O. von Gebhardt, *Centralblatt für Bibliothekswesen* 15 (1898), 442 ff. Another edition, with additional notes by Mitscherlich, Leiden, 1808. Another edition, Leipzig, 1827.

C. G. MITSCHERLICH, *Homeri Hymnus in Cererem*, Leipzig, 1787. With text, commentary, and Latin tr. by Mitscherlich, and the emendations of N. Ignarra.

C. D. ILGEN, *Hymni Homerici cum reliquis carminibus minoribus*, Halle, 1796. Text and commentary.

A. MATTHIAE, *Homeri Hymni et Batrachomyomachia*, Leipzig, 1805. Text, commentary, and Latin tr. Matthiae had previously published *Animadversiones in hymnos Homericos*, Leipzig, 1800.

G. HERMANN, *Homeri Hymni et epigrammata*, Leipzig, 1806. Text and commentary.

C. W. F. A. WOLF, *Homeri et Homeridarum opera et reliquiae*, vol. 5, Leipzig, 1807. Text.

J. H. VOSS, *Hymne an Demeter*, Heidelberg, 1826. Text, commentary, and German translation.

F. FRANKE, *Homeri Hymni Epigrammata Fragmenta et Batrachomyomachia*, Leipzig, 1828. Text and commentary.

F. H. BOTHE, *Homeri Carmina . . . Odysseae, Batrachomyomachia, Hymni*, etc., vol. 3, Leipzig, 1835. Text and commentary.

A. BAUMEISTER, *Hymni Homerici*, Leipzig, 1860. Text and commentary.

F. BÜCHELER, *Hymnus Cereris Homericus*, Leipzig, 1869. Text and facsimile.

E. ABEL, *Homeri Hymni Epigrammata Batrachomyomachia*, Leipzig and Prague, 1886. Introduction and text.

A. GEMOLL, *Die Homerischen Hymnen*, Leipzig, 1886. Text and commentary.

A. GOODWIN, *Hymni Homerici*, Oxford, 1893. Introduction, text, very full apparatus criticus, and photographs of torn parts of M.

V. PUNTONI, *L'Inno Omerico a Demetra*, Leghorn, 1896. Lengthy introduction, text, and extensive apparatus criticus.

D. B. MONRO, *Homeri Opera*, vol. 5, Oxford, 1896. Text.

T. W. ALLEN and E. E. SIKES, *The Homeric Hymns*, Macmillan, London and New York, 1904. Text and commentary.

T. W. ALLEN, *Homeri Opera*, vol. 5, Oxford, 1912. Text. Reprinted 1930, 1946 with corrections, etc.

H. G. EVELYN-WHITE, *Hesiod, the Homeric Hymns and Homerica*, London, 1914, revised 1920, 1936 (Loeb edition). Text and Eng. tr.

T. W. ALLEN, W. R. HALLIDAY, and E. E. SIKES, *The Homeric Hymns*, Oxford, 1936. Second edition of 1904 commentary. This follows in the main the text of 1912, but not invariably (e.g. *Dem.* 1 θεάν, etc.).

J. HUMBERT, *Homère. Hymnes*, Paris, 1936 (Budé edition). Introduction, text, and French translation.

A. WEIHER, *Homerische Hymnen*, second edition, Munich, 1961 (Tusculum Bücherei). Text and German translation.

Of the early editions, those by Ruhnken, with its elegant introduction, Hermann, and Voss are perhaps the most valuable. Franke's introduction is worth reading. Baumeister is based on the unfinished edition of Schneidewin, and summarizes the work of earlier editors. Bücheler is useful for his collection of parallels, and facsimile.

Gemoll's edition was designed to replace that of Baumeister. He gives extensive bibliography, incorporating the work of many other scholars besides those already mentioned, and a detailed commentary.

The fine folio edition of Goodwin gives the fullest information on manuscript readings. Allen and Sikes are still useful, and have some good notes which are omitted from the second edition of Allen and Halliday. The latter have a good introduction, but the commentary is selective and uneven. Allen's text is also too conservative in many places. I find myself in agreement with Allen and Sikes against the second edition in twenty places on the text. Humbert's Budé edition has a good short introduction.

Translations

Besides those already mentioned, I have noted the following:

R. H. HOLE, *Hymn to Ceres, translated into English verse*, Exeter, 1781 (from the defective 1780 edition of Ruhnken). Reprinted in *A Complete Edition of the Poets of Great Britain*, vol. 12, pp. 845 ff., London, 1795.

R. LUCAS, *Homer's Hymn to Ceres, translated into English verse*, London, 1781 (also from the 1780 edition). Reprinted in *Poems on Various Subjects*, Tewkesbury, 1810, 219 ff.

J. EDGAR, *The Homeric Hymns translated into English prose*, Edinburgh, 1891.

A. LANG, *The Homeric Hymns. A new prose translation*, London, 1899.

R. BORCHARDT, *Altionische Götterlieder unter dem Namen Homers* (German verse tr.), Munich, 1924 (Bremer Press).

A. S. WAY, *The Homeric Hymns, with Hero and Leander, in English verse*, London, 1934.

B. BOOKS AND ARTICLES

In addition to those works listed under 'Abbreviations', the following selection may be noted:

1. *Text, Epic Technique, Language, and Metre*

AREND, W., *Die typischen Scenen bei Homer*, Problemata, Heft 7, Berlin, 1933.

BECHTEL, F., *Lexilogus zu Homer*, Halle, 1914.

BUTTMANN, P., *Lexilogus*, tr. by J. R. Fishlake, sixth edition, London, 1869.

COBET, C. G., 'Ad Homericum Hymnum in Cererem', *Mnemosyne* 10 (1861), 309–33.

DITTMAR, F., *Prolegomenon ad Hymnum in Cererem Specimen*, Halle, 1882.

EBERHARD, E., *Metrische Beobachtungen zu den homerischen Hymnen*, Magdeburg, 1887.

EDWARDS, G. P., *The Language of Hesiod in its Traditional Context*, Blackwell, 1971.

FIETKAU, H., *De carminum Hesiodeorum atque Hymnorum quattuor magnorum vocabulis non Homericis*, Königsberg, 1863.

FRANCKE, K., *De hymni in Cererem Homerici compositione, dictione, aetate*, Kiel, 1881.

GRONINGEN, B. A. VAN, *La Composition littéraire archaïque grecque*, Amsterdam, 1958.

HAINSWORTH, J. B., *The Flexibility of the Homeric Formula*, Oxford, 1968.

HEITSCH, E., *Aphroditehymnos, Aeneas und Homer*, Göttingen, 1965.

HOEKSTRA, A., *Homeric Modifications of Formulaic Prototypes*, Amsterdam, 1965.

—— *The Sub-epic Stage of the Formulaic Tradition*, Amsterdam, 1969.

KIRK, G. S., *The Songs of Homer*, Cambridge, 1962 (abbreviated as *Songs*).

—— 'Formular Language and Oral Quality', *Yale Classical Studies* 20 (1966), 155–74.

LEEUWEN, J. VAN, *Enchiridium dictionis epicae*, Leiden, 1892–4.

LEHRS, K., *De Aristarchi studiis homericis*, second edition, Leipzig, 1865; third edition, Leipzig, 1882.

LEUMANN, M., *Homerische Wörter*, Basel, 1950.

MAAS, P., *Greek Metre*, translated by H. Lloyd-Jones, Oxford, 1962.

MEISTER, K., *Die homerische Kunstsprache*, Leipzig, 1921.

NOTOPOULOS, J. A., 'The Homeric Hymns as Oral Poetry', *Amer. Journ. of Philology* 83 (1962), 337–68.

PAGE, D. L., *The Homeric Odyssey*, Oxford, 1955.

—— *History and the Homeric Iliad*, Berkeley, 1959.

PARRY, M., *The Making of Homeric Verse*, ed. A. Parry, Oxford, 1971.

PORTER, H. N., 'Repetition in the Homeric Hymn to Aphrodite', *Amer. Journ. of Philology* 70 (1949), 249–72.

—— 'The Early Greek Hexameter', *Yale Class. Studies* 12 (1951), 1–63.

PORZIG, W., *Die Namen für Satzinhalte im Griechischen und im Indogermanischen*, Berlin, 1942 (abbreviated as *Satzinhalte*).

RISCH, E., *Wortbildung der homerischen Sprache*, Berlin, 1937.

SOLMSEN, F., *Untersuchungen zur griechischen Laut- und Verslehre*, Strassburg, 1901.

—— *Beiträge zur griechischen Wortforschung*, vol. i, Strassburg, 1909.

STERRETT, J. R. S., *Qua in re hymni homerici quinque maiores inter se differant antiquitate vel homeritate*, Boston, 1881.

TESKE, A., *Die Homer-Mimesis in den homerischen Hymnen*, Greifswalder Beitr. zur Lit.- und Stilforschung, 15, 1936.

TRYPANIS, C. A., Περὶ τῆς ῥοπῆς τῶν Ἡσιοδείων ἐπῶν ἐπὶ τὸν ὕμνον εἰς Δήμητραν, *Athena* 48 (1938), 199–237.

WACKERNAGEL, J., *Sprachliche Untersuchungen zu Homer*, Göttingen, 1916.

—— *Vermischte Beiträge zur griechischen Sprachkunde* = *Kleine Schriften*, Göttingen, 1953, i. 764 ff.

ZUMBACH, O., *Neuerungen in der Sprache der homerischen Hymnen*, Diss. Zürich, Winterthur, 1955.

2. *Cult, Religion, and Ethics*

ADKINS, A. W. H., *Merit and Responsibility, a Study in Greek Values*, Oxford, 1960.

ARBESMANN, R., *Das Fasten bei den Griechen und Römern*, Giessen, 1929.

BLEEKER, C. J., *Initiation*, Studies in the History of Religions, vol. x, ed. by C. J. Bleeker, Leiden, 1965.

BOYANCÉ, P., 'Sur les Mystères d'Éleusis', *Revue des études grecques* 75 (1962), 460–82.

BURG, N. M. H. VAN DEN, Ἀπόρρητα, Δρώμενα, Ὄργια, Diss. Utrecht, 1939.

CASEL, O., *De philosophorum graecorum silentio mystico*, Giessen, 1919.

DEICHGRÄBER, K., 'Eleusinische Frömmigkeit und homerische Vorstellungswelt im homerischen Demeterhymnos', *Abh. d. Akad. d. Wiss. in Mainz*, 1950, Nr. 6, 501–37.

DELATTE, A., *Le Cycéon. Breuvage rituel des Mystères d'Éleusis*, Paris, 1955.

DEUBNER, L., 'Zum Weihehaus der eleusinischen Mysterien', *Abh. d. Akad. d. Wiss. zu Berlin*, Jahrg. 1945–6, Phil.-hist. Kl., Nr. 2, Berlin, 1948.

DIETERICH, A., *Nekyia. Beiträge zur Erklärung der neuentdeckten Petrusapokalypse*, Leipzig, 1893.

DODDS, E. R., *The Greeks and the Irrational*, Berkeley, 1951.

DOW, S., 'Athenian Decrees of 216–212 B.C.: The Calendar of the Eleusinian Mysteries', *Harv. Stud. in Class. Philology* 48 (1937), 111–20.

EITREM, S., *Opferritus und Voropfer der Griechen und Römer*, Kristiania, 1915.

—— 'Eleusinia—les mystères et l'agriculture', *Symbolae Osloenses* 20 (1940), 133–41.

—— 'Die eleusinischen Mysterien und das Synthema der Weihe', *Symbolae Osloenses* 37 (1961), 72–81.

FARNELL, L. R., *Cults of the Greek States*, 5 vols., Oxford, 1896–1909.

FOUCART, P., *Les Mystères d'Éleusis*, Paris, 1914.

HARRISON, J. E., *Prolegomena to the Study of Greek Religion*, 3rd edition, Cambridge, 1922.

JUDEICH, W., *Topographie von Athen*, 2nd edition, Munich, 1931.

KERÉNYI, K., *Eleusis*, New York, 1967.

KERN, O., 'Mysterien': *RE*, vol. 16, 1210 ff.

—— *Die Religion der Griechen*, 3 vols., Berlin, 1926–38 (especially vol. ii, pp. 182 ff.).

KEYSSNER, K., *Gottesvorstellung und Lebensauffassung im griechischen Hymnos*, Stuttgart, 1932.

KOUROUNIOTES, K., Κόρης ἄνοδος, *Arch. Deltion* 15 (1933–5), 1–15.

LEWIS, D. M., review of Mylonas, *Eleusis* in *Journal of Hellenic Studies* 83 (1963), 206–7.

LLOYD-JONES, H., 'Heracles at Eleusis', *Maia* 19 (1967), 206–29.

LOBECK, C. A., *Aglaophamus*, Königsberg, 1829.

MOMMSEN, A., *Feste der Stadt Athen im Altertum*, Leipzig, 1898.

MYLONAS, G. E., *The Hymn to Demeter and her Sanctuary at Eleusis*, Wash. Univ. Studies, new ser. 13, St. Louis, 1942.

—— *Eleusis and the Eleusinian Mysteries*, Princeton, 1961.

NILSSON, M. P., *Griechische Feste von religiöser Bedeutung*, Leipzig, 1906.

—— *Opuscula Selecta*, 2 vols., Lund, 1951–2; especially pp. 542–623, 'Die eleusinischen Gottheiten', and 624–7, 'Das eleusinische Relief aus der Sammlung Este'.

NOACK, F., *Eleusis, die baugeschichtliche Entwicklung des Heiligtums*, Berlin, 1927.

NOCK, A. D., 'Hellenistic Mysteries and Christian Sacraments', *Mnemosyne* 5 (1952), 177–213 (= *Essays on Religion and the Ancient World*, ed. Z. Stewart, Oxford, 1972, ii. 791–820).

NORDEN, E., *Agnostos Theos*, Leipzig, 1913.

—— *Vergilius, Aeneis VI*, ed. E. Norden, 3rd edition, Leipzig, 1926.

ONIANS, R. B., *The Origins of European Thought about the body, etc.*, 2nd edition, Cambridge, 1954.

PRELLER, L., *Demeter und Persephone*, Hamburg, 1837.

PRINGSHEIM, H. G., *Archäologische Beiträge zur Geschichte des eleusinischen Kults*, Diss. Bonn, 1895.

ROHDE, E., *Psyche*, 9th edition, Tübingen, 1925.

—— *Psyche*, translated from the 8th edition by W. B. Hillis, London, 1925.

ROUSSEL, P., 'L'initiation préalable et le symbole éleusinien', *Bull. de Corr. Hell.* 54 (1930), 51–74.

RUBENSOHN, O., 'Das Weihehaus von Eleusis und sein Allerheiligstes', *Jahrb. des Deutsch. Arch. Inst.* 70 (1955), 1–49.

RUHLAND, M., *Die Eleusinischen Gottheiten*, Strassburg, 1901.

SOKOLOWSKI, F., *Lois sacrées des cités grecques, Supplément*, Paris, 1962.

TÖPFFER, J., *Attische Genealogie*, Berlin, 1927.

WALTON, F. R., 'Athens, Eleusis, and the Homeric Hymn to Demeter', *Harv. Theol. Review* 45 (1952), 105–14.

WEHRLI, F., 'Die Mysterien von Eleusis', *Archiv für Religionswissenschaft* 31 (1934), 77–104.

WILAMOWITZ-MOELLENDORFF, U. VON, *Der Glaube der Hellenen*, 2 vols., Berlin, 1931–2.

ZIJDERVELD, C., Τελετή, Diss. Utrecht, 1934.

ZUNTZ, G., *Persephone*, Oxford, 1971.

3. *Later Literature and Art*

BÜHLER, W., *Die Europa des Moschos*, ed. W. Bühler, Hermes Einzelschr. 13, Wiesbaden, 1960.

FÖRSTER, R., *Der Raub und die Rückkehr der Persephone*, Stuttgart, 1874.

KANNICHT, R., *Euripides, Helena,* ed. R. Kannicht, 2 vols., Heidelberg, 1969.

LATTE, K., 'Der Demeterhymnos des Philikos', *Museum Helveticum* 11 (1954), 1–19, = *Kleine Schriften,* Munich, 1968, 539–61.

MAAS, P., *Epidaurische Hymnen* (Schriften der Königsberger gel. Gesellschaft, Jahrg. 9, Heft 5), Halle, 1933.

MALTEN, L., 'Altorphische Demetersage', *Archiv für Religionswissenschaft* 12 (1909), 417–46.

METZGER, H., *Les Représentations dans la céramique attique du IVe siècle,* Paris, 1951.

—— *Recherches sur l'imagerie athénienne,* Paris, 1965.

SIGLA

pap. 1	P. Berol. 13044, mid 1st c. B.C. (see Kern, Orph. fr. 49, whose line-numbering I follow)
pap. 2	P. Oxy. 2379, 3rd c. A.D.
M	('Mosquensis') = Leidensis BPG 33H, early 15th c.
m	second hand in M, 16th c.

For the system used in listing formulaic parallels see Introduction, p. 30.

ΥΜΝΟC ΕΙC ΔΗΜΗΤΡΑ

Δήμητρ' ἠΰκομον cεμνὴν θεὸν ἄρχομ' ἀείδειν,
αὐτὴν ἠδὲ θύγατρα τανίcφυρον ἣν Ἀϊδωνεὺс
ἥρπαξεν, δῶκεν δὲ βαρύκτυπος εὐρύοπα Ζεύς,
νόcφιν Δήμητρος χρυcαόρου ἀγλαοκάρπου
παίζουcαν κούρῃcι cὺν Ὠκεανοῦ βαθυκόλποιc,   5
ἄνθεά τ' αἰνυμένην ῥόδα καὶ κρόκον ἠδ' ἴα καλὰ
λειμῶν' ἄμ μαλακὸν καὶ ἀγαλλίδας ἠδ' ὑάκινθον
νάρκιccόν θ', ὃν φῦcε δόλον καλυκώπιδι κούρῃ
Γαῖα Διὸc βουλῇcι χαριζομένη πολυδέκτῃ

1 = Hy. 13. 1 : Δήμητρα Hes. Th. 454 : Δήμητρ' ἠΰκομον* Dem. 315 : ἠΰκομος*
Il. 24. 602 (alibi apud Homerum ἠϋκόμοιο ad fin., ἠΰκομος pedibus IV ac V), *Hes.
Th. 625 etc. : cεμνὴ θεά* Hy. 30. 16 : ἄρχομ' ἀείδειν* Hy. 9. 8 etc.   2a ~ 493a, Hy. 13.
2 : θύγατρα* Il. 1. 13 etc. : τανίcφυροι (etc.)* Hes. Th. 364 : Ἀϊδωνεύc* Il. 20. 61, Dem.
84 etc.   2–3 ἣν Ἀϊδωνεὺc | ἥρπαcεν ἧc παρὰ μητρός, ἔδωκε δὲ μητίετα Ζεύc Hes.
Th. 913 f.   3 δῶκέν τε* Od. 10. 237, 318 : βαρύκτυποc* Hes. Th. 818 : εὐρύοπα
Ζεύc* Il. 2. 146 etc. : βαρύκτυπος εὐρύοπα Ζεύc* Dem. 334, 441, 460   4 νόcφιν*
Il. 2. 347 etc. : Δήμητροc* Il. 14. 326, Dem. 453 : χρυcαόρου* Il. 5. 509 etc. : ἀγλαό-
καρποι* Od. 7. 115 etc.   5 παιζούcαc* Od. 7. 291 : κούρῃcιν* Od. 6. 135, 222 :
Ὠκεανῷ* Od. 10. 511 : βαθυκόλπων* Il. 18. 122 etc.   6–7 αἰνύμεναι (etc.)* Od.
22. 500 (etc.) : κρόκον ἠδ' ὑάκινθον* | πυκνὸν καὶ μαλακόν . . .* Il. 14. 348–9 (~ Hy.
19. 25) : ἠδ' ἴα* ('una') Il. 13. 354 : καλά* Il. 3. 328 etc.   7 λειμῶνι μαλακῷ*
Ap. 118 : ἐν μαλακῷ λειμῶνι, τόθι κρόκος ἠδ' ὑάκινθος* Hy. 19. 25 : ἐν μαλακῷ λειμῶνι
Hes. Th. 279 (cf. ad Dem. 401) ~ Herm. 198 : λειμῶνεc μαλακοὶ ἴου ἠδὲ cελίνου Od.
5. 72 : κρόκον ἠδ' ὑάκινθον* Il. 14. 348 (~ Cypr. 4. 3) : 7b = 426b   8 δόλον*
Il. 18. 526 etc. : καλυκώπιδος Aph. 284 : γλαυκώπιδι κούρῃ* Il. 24. 26, Od. 2. 433 :
ἑλικώπιδα κούρην* Il. 1. 98 : 8a ~ 428a   9 γαῖα* Il. 2. 171 etc. : Διὸc βουλῇcιν*
Il. 13. 254 : χαριζομένη* Il. 5. 71 etc. : πολυδέγμων* Dem. 17 etc.

1 cεμνὴν | Δημήτραν Epigr. ap. Paus. 1. 37. 2 (in sepulcro Phytali) : cεμνὴ Δήμητερ
Orph. Hy. 40. 2   8 καλυκώπιδα κούρην* Orph. Hy. 79. 2   8–11 cf.
Antim. fr. 32. 5 W. αὐτὴ Γαῖ' ἀνέδωκε, cέβας θνητοῖcιν ἰδέcθαι, A.R. 2. 1209 ὃν αὐτὴ
Γαῖ' ἀνέφυcεν

TITULUS. τοῦ αὐτοῦ ὕμνοι εἰς τὴν δήμητραν M : Δήμητρα Cobet, Mnem. 1861, 311 f.
1 Δημήτηρ' M : corr. Ruhnken   θεὰν M : θεὸν Voss, Ruhnken   2 τανύ-
cφυρον M : τανίcφυρον scripsi   4 χρυcαόρου M : χρυcοθρόνου Ruhnken, Cobet :
ὠρηφόρου Bücheler, Gemoll. Versum reiecit Hermann   7 λειμῶνα μαλακόν
M : corr. Hermann   8 ἔφυcε Ilgen (cf. Dem. 428, Aph. 265 ; sed v. West
ad Hes. Th. 381 τίκτεν)   καλικώπιδι M : corr. Ruhnken   8b–18 cit. pap.
1 (Orph. fr. 49. 63–71)

θαυμαστὸν γανόωντα, σέβας τό γε πᾶσιν ἰδέσθαι   10
ἀθανάτοις τε θεοῖς ἠδὲ θνητοῖς ἀνθρώποις·
τοῦ καὶ ἀπὸ ῥίζης ἑκατὸν κάρα ἐξεπεφύκει,
†κώδιστ᾽ ὀδμή† πᾶς δ᾽ οὐρανὸς εὐρὺς ὕπερθε
γαῖά τε πᾶσ᾽ ἐγέλασσε καὶ ἁλμυρὸν οἶδμα θαλάσσης.
ἡ δ᾽ ἄρα θαμβήσασ᾽ ὠρέξατο χερσὶν ἅμ᾽ ἄμφω   15
καλὸν ἄθυρμα λαβεῖν· χάνε δὲ χθὼν εὐρυάγυια
Νύσιον ἂμ πεδίον τῇ ὄρουσεν ἄναξ πολυδέγμων
ἵπποις ἀθανάτοισι Κρόνου πολυώνυμος υἱός.

10 θαυμασίην* Herm. 443: γανόωντες (etc.) Il. 13. 265 (etc.): σέβας* Il. 18. 178 etc.: θαῦμα ἰδέσθαι* Il. 5. 725 etc. (cf. ad Dem. 427)   10–11 cf. Hes. Th. 588 f. θαῦμα δ᾽ ἔχ᾽ ἀθανάτους τε θεοὺς θνητούς τ᾽ ἀνθρώπους, | ὡς εἶδον δόλον αἰπὺν ἀμήχανον ἀνθρώποισι (cf. ad Dem. 8, 403)   11 ἀθανάτοις τε θεοῖσι* Hes. Th. 373, 415: ἀθανάτοις τε θεοῖσι καταθνητοῖς τ᾽ ἀνθρώποισι Hes. fr. 1. 7: θνητοῖς τ᾽ ἀνθρώποις* Dem. 403 (~ Hes. Th. 296 etc., init. versus): ἀθανάτοις* Il. 23. 207 etc.: θεοῖς* Il. 5. 606 etc.: θνητοὺς ἀνθρώπους* Il. 14. 199: θνητοῖσι βροτοῖσιν* Od. 7. 210 etc.   12 τοῦ καὶ ἀπὸ γλώσσης* Il. 1. 249: ῥίζης* Od. 23. 196: ἑκατόν* Il. 2. 510 etc.: τοῦ κέρα ἐκ κεφαλῆς ἐκκαιδεκάδωρα πεφύκει Il. 4. 109: ἐκπεφυνῖαι* Il. 11. 40 13–14 Γαῖα καὶ Οὐρανὸς εὐρὺς ὕπερθε(ν)* Il. 15. 36 etc.; cf. Hes. Th. 107–10, 839 ff., 847 etc.   14 γαῖα* Dem. 9 etc.: ἐγέλασσε(ν)* Od. 18. 163, Herm. 29: γέλασσε δὲ πᾶσα περὶ χθών Il. 19. 362: θαλάσσης ἁλμυρὸν ὕδωρ Od. 12. 236 etc.: κῦμα θαλάσσης* Il. 4. 422 etc.: οἶδμα θαλάσσης* Certamen 131, Simon. fr. 80. 3 D.: ἁλμυρὸς ... Πόντος (πόντος)* Hes. Th. 107, 964: πόντος ... οἴδματι θυίων Th. 109   15 ἡ μὲν θαμβήσασα* Od. 1. 360 = 21. 354 (~ 24. 101): ὠρέξατο χερσί* Il. 23. 99: χερσὶν ἅμ᾽ ἄμφω* Il. 7. 255 (~ 23. 686)   16 καλόν* Il. 1. 473 etc.: καλὸν ἄθυρμα Herm. 32: χάνοι εὐρεῖα χθών Il. 4. 182, 8. 150: εὐρυάγυια* Od. 15. 384, 22. 230   17 ἂμ πεδίον* Il. 5. 87 etc.: ἄναξ κρατερὸς πολυδέγμων* Dem. 430 (~ 31, 404. ἄναξ numquam hoc versu loco apud Homerum, Hesiodum)   18 = 32: ἵπποις* Hy. 31. 9: ἵππων ἀθανάτων* Il. 17. 476, Dem. 382: ἵπποις ἀθανάτοισι (ad fin.) Il. 16. 154: Κρόνου Il. 2. 285 etc.: πολυώνυμος* Ap. 82 (~ Hes. Th. 785): υἱός* Il. 2. 564

13–14 cf. Theogn. 8 ff. πᾶσα μὲν ἐπλήσθη Δῆλος ἀπειρεσίη | ὀδμῆς ἀμβροσίης, ἐγέλασσε δὲ Γαῖα πελώρη, | γήθησεν δὲ βαθὺς πόντος ἁλὸς πολιῆς   14 γαῖα δὲ πᾶσα γέλασσεν* Nonn. D. 22. 7   15 ἄμφω χερσὶν ἔχων A.R. 1. 1169   17 οὔρεα καὶ πεδίον Νυσήϊον A.R. 2. 1214

10 τότε M:]ότε pap. 1: δέ τε Wyttenbach: δ᾽ ὅ γε Matthiae: τό γε Goodwin (puncto post γανόωντα interposito)   11 ἠδὲ correctum (a manu prima) ut videtur ex ἰδὲ M   12 ἀπορρίζης M   ἑκατόν γε κάρην᾽ ἐπεφύκει Voss: κάρη Cobet   13 κώδιστ᾽ ὀδμῆ πᾶς δ᾽ M: κηώδει δ᾽ ὀδμῆ πᾶς τ᾽ Ruhnken: κηώεντ᾽ ὀδμῆ· πᾶς δ᾽ (vel κηώδης τ᾽ ὀδμῆ πᾶς τ᾽) Ludwich: κῶζ᾽ ἥδιστ᾽ ὀδμὴ πᾶς δ᾽ Tyrrell: κωδείας δ᾽ ὀδμῆ πᾶς τ᾽ Humbert (Mitscherlich secutus): fortasse ante hunc versum statuenda est lacuna (cf. Praefationem p. 66)   14 ἐγέλασε M: corr. Matthiae 17 Μύσιον Malten (ARW 12 (1909), 300). Cf. Soph. Aj. 699 (μύσια Πc: νύσια LA) 18 ἀθανάτα[ισι pap. 1: versum reiecit Bücheler

ἁρπάξας δ' ἀέκουσαν ἐπὶ χρυσέοισιν ὄχοισιν
ἦγ' ὀλοφυρομένην· ἰάχησε δ' ἄρ' ὄρθια φωνῇ   20
κεκλομένη πατέρα Κρονίδην ὕπατον καὶ ἄριστον.
οὐδέ τις ἀθανάτων οὐδὲ θνητῶν ἀνθρώπων
ἤκουσεν φωνῆς, οὐδ' ἀγλαόκαρποι ἐλαῖαι,
εἰ μὴ Περσαίου θυγάτηρ ἀταλὰ φρονέουσα
ἄϊεν ἐξ ἄντρου Ἑκάτη λιπαροκρήδεμνος,   25
Ἡέλιός τε ἄναξ Ὑπερίονος ἀγλαὸς υἱός,
κούρης κεκλομένης πατέρα Κρονίδην· ὁ δὲ νόσφιν
ἧστο θεῶν ἀπάνευθε πολυλλίστῳ ἐνὶ νηῷ
δέγμενος ἱερὰ καλὰ παρὰ θνητῶν ἀνθρώπων.

19 ἁρπάξας* *Dem.* 81 : ἁρπάζων* *Il.* 22. 310 : ἀέκουσαν* *Od.* 20. 343 : ὑπὸ χρυσέοισι
νέφεσσιν* *Il.* 13. 523, *Ap.* 98 : ὑπὸ χρυσέοισιν ὄχεσφιν* *Dem.* 375 : ὄχεσφι(ν)* *Il.* 4. 297
etc.   20 ἦγ'* *Il.* 5. 614 : ὀλοφυρομένην* *Od.* 19. 543 : ἐβόησα δ' ἄρ' ὄρθια φωνῇ*
Dem. 432 : ἦυς'. . . ὄρθι' *Il.* 11. 10 : φωνῇ* *Il.* 3. 161   21 κεκλόμενος* *Il.* 15. 353,
16. 525 : πατὴρ Κρονίδης *Il.* 21. 508, 22. 60 (~ 8. 31 etc.) : πατέρα Κρονίδην *Dem.* 27
(~ 408) : ὕπατος καὶ ἄριστος* (invocatur Iuppiter) *Il.* 19. 258, 23. 43, *Od.* 19. 303 :
ὕπατον Κρονίδην *Il.* 5. 756   22 εἰ δέ (etc.) τις ἀθανάτων* *Il.* 6. 128 etc. : οὔτε
θνητῶν ἀνθρώπων* *Il.* 18. 404 etc. : ἠέ τις ἀθανάτων ἠὲ θνητῶν ἀνθρώπων *Herm.* 441
(~ 445)   23 φωνῆς γὰρ ἤκουσ' *Dem.* 57 : ἀγλαόκαρποι . . . καὶ ἐλαῖαι . . . *Od.*
7. 115–16 = 11. 589–90   24 εἰ μὴ ἄρ' ὀξὺ νόησε Διὸς θυγάτηρ *Il.* 3. 374 = 5. 312 :
θυγάτηρ* *Il.* 1. 538 etc. : ἀταλὰ φρονέοντες* *Il.* 18. 567   25 ἐξ ἄντρου* *Od.* 9. 407 :
Ἑκάτη λιπαροκρήδεμνος* *Dem.* 438 : λιπαροκρήδεμνος* *Il.* 18. 382   26 Ἡέλιός
θ'* *Il.* 3. 277 (~ *Od.* 8. 302 etc.) : Ἀτρείδης τε ἄναξ* *Il.* 1. 7 (~ 2. 104) : Ἡελίου . . .
Ὑπεριονίδαο ἄνακτος *Od.* 12. 176 : ἀγλαὸς υἱός* *Il.* 2. 736 etc. : Ὑπερίονος ἀγλαὸς υἱός*
Hy. 28. 13   27 κούρης* *Il.* 2. 689, *Od.* 18. 279 : πατέρα* *Il.* 4. 354, *Od.* 6. 36 :
Κρονίδην* *Il.* 5. 419   27a ~ *Dem.* 21   27b–8 ~ *Il.* 11. 80–1 : τῶν μὲν ἄρ' οὐκ
ἀλέγιζε πατήρ (Iuppiter)· ὁ δὲ νόσφι λιασθεὶς | τῶν ἄλλων ἀπάνευθε καθέζετο . . .
Cf. *Dem.* 302 ff., 355 ff.   28 ἧστο* *Il.* 6. 324 etc. : ἀπάνευθε θεῶν *Il.* 1. 549 :
οἰκέομεν δ' ἀπάνευθε πολυκλύστῳ ἐνὶ πόντῳ *Od.* 6. 204 : πολύλλιστον* *Od.* 5. 445 :
ἀπάνευθε θυώδεος ἔνδοθι νηοῦ | ἧσται* *Dem.* 355 f. : ἐνὶ πίονι νηῷ* *Ap.* 253 = 293
28 f. ~ *Ap.* 347 f. ἀλλ' ἥ γ' ἐν νηοῖσι πολυλλίστοισι μένουσα | τέρπετο οἷς ἱεροῖσι . . .
29 δέγμενος* *Il.* 2. 794 etc. : ἱερὰ καλά* *Od.* 11. 130 etc. : δέξεαι ἱερὰ καλὰ περι-
κτιόνων ἀνθρώπων *Ap.* 274 : θνητῶν ἀνθρώπων* *Il.* 1. 339, *Dem.* 22 etc.

19 τὰν . . . . ἅρπας', ἔνεγκέ τε χρυσέῳ παρθένον ἀγροτέραν δίφρῳ Pi. *P.* 9. 5–6
(~ Hes. fr. 215)   20 ὄρθια φωνῇ* A.R. 4. 70   23 ἀγλαόκαρπος . . . ἐλαίη*
Opp. *H.* 4. 272   25 ἡ δ' ἀΐουσα | κευθμῶν ἐξ ὑπάτων δεινὴ θεὸς ἀντεβόλησεν
(cf. ad *Dem.* 52) A.R. 3. 1212 f. (de Hecate)

19 ὄχεσφιν Voss (cf. *Dem.* 375)   21 κεκλημένη M : corr. Ruhnken
22 οὐδέ . . . οὔτε Hermann   23 ἀγλαόμορφοι Ruhnken   ἑταῖραι Ruhnken :
Ἔλειαι Ilgen : alii alia   24 οἴη pro εἰ μὴ coni. Wackernagel (*RhM* 44, 531 ; sed
cf. ad *Dem.* 22 ff.)   Περσαίη West (*Philologus* 110 (1966), 149)   26 τ' ἄναξ
ὑπερήονος M : corr. Ruhnken   28 πολυκλίστῳ M : corr. Ruhnken (cf. *Ap.* 347,
ubi idem error ; *Od.* 5. 445, 6. 204)   29 δέχμενος Cobet

τὴν δ' ἀεκαζομένην ἦγεν Διὸς ἐννεσίῃσι   30
πατροκασίγνητος πολυσημάντωρ πολυδέγμων
ἵπποις ἀθανάτοισι Κρόνου πολυώνυμος υἱός.
ὄφρα μὲν οὖν γαῖάν τε καὶ οὐρανὸν ἀστερόεντα
λεῦσσε θεὰ καὶ πόντον ἀγάρροον ἰχθυόεντα
αὐγάς τ' ἠελίου, ἔτι δ' ἤλπετο μητέρα κεδνὴν   35
ὄψεσθαι καὶ φῦλα θεῶν αἰειγενετάων,
τόφρα οἱ ἐλπὶς ἔθελγε μέγαν νόον ἀχνυμένης περ.
ἤχησαν δ' ὀρέων κορυφαὶ καὶ βένθεα πόντου
φωνῇ ὑπ' ἀθανάτῃ, τῆς δ' ἔκλυε πότνια μήτηρ.
ὀξὺ δέ μιν κραδίην ἄχος ἔλλαβεν, ἀμφὶ δὲ χαίταις   40

30 πόλλ' ἀεκαζομένη* Il. 6. 458 (~ Dem. 433): Διός* Il. 1. 395 etc.: ἐννεσίῃσιν*
(Iunonis) Il. 5. 894   31 πατροκασίγνητον* Od. 6. 330: πολυσημάντωρ* ... αὐτοκασίγνητος* Dem. 84 f.: πολυδέγμων* Dem. 17 etc.   32 = 18   33 γαίης τε
καὶ οὐρανοῦ ἀστερόεντος* Il. 5. 769 = 8. 46: γαῖάν τε καὶ οὐρανόν* Il. 14. 174 =
Od. 1. 54: οὐρανὸν ἀστερόεντα* Il. 15. 371 etc.: Γαῖάν τε καὶ Οὐρανὸν ἀστερόεντα*
Hes. Th. 470   33-7 ὄφρα μὲν οὖν ... τόφρα δὲ ... Il. 9. 550-1: ὄφρα μὲν ...
τόφρα (in tertio versu) Od. 20. 328-30   34 λεύσσει* Il. 3. 110: θεά* Il. 10.
462 etc. (voc.; Dem. 145* nom.): πόντον ... ἰχθυόεντα* Il. 9. 4, Od. 4. 381 etc.:
Ἑλλήσποντος ἀγάρροος* Il. 2. 485 (~ 12. 30)   35 αὐγάς* Herm. 361: ἠελίου ἴδεν
αὐγάς Il. 16. 188: Ἡελίου τ' αὐγή (init.) Od. 12. 176: ἔτι δ' ἔλπετο Il. 15. 539
(ἤλπετο vulg.): μητέρι κεδνῇ* Od. 10. 8   35-6 ἐπί τ' ἔλπεται* ... ὄψεσθαι*
Il. 24. 491-2   36 ὄψεσθαι* Il. 14. 343 etc. (cf. ad Dem. 35): φῦλα θεῶν* Il.
15. 54 etc.: θεῶν αἰειγενετάων* Il. 2. 400 etc.: φῦλα θεῶν αἰειγενετάων* Dem. 322
37 ἔθελγε* Od. 17. 521: θέλγε νοόν Il. 12. 255: μέγαν νόον* Hes. Th. 37 (Th. 42
ἤχεῖ: cf. ad Dem. 38) ~ Dem. 82, 171 etc.: ἀχνύμενός (etc.) περ* Il. 1. 241 etc. (Il.
22. 424: cf. ad Dem. 38 ff.)   38 οὐρεά τε σκιόεντα, θάλασσά τε ἠχήεσσα Il. 1.
157: ὀρέων κορυφάς* Il. 12. 282 (~ Od. 9. 121, Hy. 19. 7): βένθεσι λίμνης* Il. 13.
21, 32: θαλάσσης ... βένθεα Od. 1. 53 f., 4. 386 f.: ὑπὸ δ' ἤχεεν οὔρεα μακρά Hes.
Th. 835: βένθεα λίμνης* Hes. Th. 365: πόντος* Il. 2. 210 etc. (~ 14. 258 etc.)
38-9 ~ Il. 1. 357-8 τοῦ δ' ἔκλυε πότνια μήτηρ | ἡμένη ἐν βένθεσσιν ἁλός ...
39 φωνῇ δὲ βροτέῃ* Od. 19. 545: τοῦ δ' ἔκλυε* Il. 1. 43 etc. (cf. ad Dem. 38-9):
πότνια μήτηρ* Il. 1. 357 etc., Dem. 122, 185   40 ἄχος ὀξύ Il. 22. 405:
ἄχος ἔλλαβε Il. 14. 475: ἐπεί μιν ἄχος κραδίην καὶ θυμὸν ἵκανεν Il. 2. 171 (~ 19.
307, 23. 46 f.): ἀμφὶ δὲ χαίται* Il. 6. 509 = 15. 266, 22. 401, Dem. 177 (cf.
ad loc.)

———

32 versum delebat Cobet   33-6 cit. pap. 1 (c. 5. 3-6 = Orph. fr. 49. 71-5)
34 λεῦσε M: corr. Matthiae   ἀγά[ρ]ρουν pap. 1   35 ἔτι ἤλπετο pap. 1
37 om. pap. 1 (quod probat Bücheler in commentario ad loc.): prius deleverant
Mitscherlich, Franke   μέγαν γόον (cf. Dem. 82) vel νόον μέγα (cf. Ap. 204, app.
crit. ad loc.) Mitscherlich   ἀχνυμένη περ Cobet   lacunam post hunc versum
statuit Hermann   40 ἔλαβεν M: corr. Matthiae   40-1 χαίτης ἀμβροσίης
Hermann

ἀμβροσίαις κρήδεμνα δαΐζετο χερσὶ φίλῃσι,
κυάνεον δὲ κάλυμμα κατ' ἀμφοτέρων βάλετ' ὤμων,
cεύατο δ' ὥς τ' οἰωνὸς ἐπὶ τραφερήν τε καὶ ὑγρὴν
μαιομένη· τῇ δ' οὔ τις ἐτήτυμα μυθήcασθαι
ἤθελεν οὔτε θεῶν οὔτε θνητῶν ἀνθρώπων,   45
οὔτ' οἰωνῶν τις τῇ ἐτήτυμος ἄγγελος ἦλθεν.
ἐννῆμαρ μὲν ἔπειτα κατὰ χθόνα πότνια Δηὼ
cτρωφᾶτ' αἰθομένας δαΐδας μετὰ χερσὶν ἔχουσα,
οὐδέ ποτ' ἀμβροσίης καὶ νέκταρος ἡδυπότοιο
πάccατ' ἀκηχεμένη, οὐδὲ χρόα βάλλετο λουτροῖc.   50
ἀλλ' ὅτε δὴ δεκάτη οἱ ἐπήλυθε φαινόλις Ἠώc,
ἤντετό οἱ Ἑκάτη cέλας ἐν χείρεccιν ἔχουcα,
καί ῥά οἱ ἀγγελέουcα ἔπος φάτο φώνηcέν τε·

41 ἀμβρόcιαι* ... χαῖται Il. 1. 529: κρήδεμνα Il. 16. 100 etc.: χερcὶ φίλῃcιν*
Il. 23. 99 etc.: φίλῃcι δὲ χερcὶ κόμην ᾔcχυνε δαΐζων Il. 18. 27   42 κάλυμμ' ἕλε
δῖα θεάων | κυάνεον* Il. 24. 93 f.: κυάνεαι* Il. 22. 402 (cf. ad Dem. 38 ff.): cf. Dem.
183 (etc.): ἀμφοτέρουc* Il. 13. 281: ἀμφοτέροιcι βάλωμεν Il. 4. 16: περὶ cτιβαροῖc
βάλετ' ὤμοιc* Od. 14. 528 (~ 15. 61)   43 cεύατ' ἔπειτ' ἐπὶ κῦμα λάρῳ ὄρνιθι
ἐοικώc Od. 5. 52: ὥc τ' οἰωνοί Dem. 89: ἐπὶ τραφερήν τε καὶ ὑγρήν* Il. 14. 308,
Od. 20. 98   44 μαιομένη* Od. 13. 367 (cf. ad Dem. 98 ff.): ἐτήτυμα μυθηcαίμην*
Hes. Op. 10: μυθήcαcθαι* Il. 1. 74 etc.   45 ἤθελεν* Od. 4. 287, Dem. 193 etc.:
ᾔδεεν οὔτε θεῶν οὔτε θνητῶν ἀνθρώπων Il. 18. 404   46 οὐ γάρ οἵ τις ἐτήτυμος
ἄγγελος ἐλθών* Il. 22. 438 (cf. ad Dem. 38–46): οἰωνόν ... ἄγγελον Il. 24. 310
47–51 ~ Il. 24. 784–5 ἐννῆμαρ μὲν ... ἀλλ' ὅτε δὴ δεκάτη ἐφάνη φαεcίμβροτος ἠώc
(~ Il. 6. 174–5)   47 ἐπὶ χθόνα* Il. 3. 265 etc.: κατὰ χθόνα Herm. 517:
πολυπότνια Δηώ* Dem. 211 (~ 492)   48 cτρωφᾶτ'* Il. 13. 557: αἰθομένας
δαΐδας μετὰ χερcὶν ἔχοντεc* Od. 7. 101 (~ Dem. 61)   49 οὐδέ ποτ' ἀμβροcίης
καὶ νέκταρος ἔρχεται ἄccον | βρώcιος Hes. Th. 796 f. (798a ~ Dem. 285): ἀμβροcίης
καὶ νέκταρος* Od. 9. 359: ἡδυπότοιο* Od. 2. 340, 15. 507   50 ἀκηχέμεναι*
Il. 18. 29: χρόα νίζετο Od. 6. 224: χρόα* Il. 4. 237 etc.   51 cf. ad Dem. 47–51:
ἀλλ' ὅτε δὴ δεκάτη μοι ἐπήλυθε νὺξ ἐρεβεννή Il. 9. 474: ἐπερχομένη (sc. Aurora)
Od. 22. 198   52 ἤντετο* γάρ τοι Il. 16. 788: cέλας* Il. 15. 600: ἐν χείρεccι(ν)*
Od. 24. 410: δάος μετὰ χερcὶν ἔχουcαι* Od. 4. 300   53 ἀγγελέουcα* Il. 19. 120:
ἔπος φάτο φώνηcέν τε* Od. 4. 370

43 Ὄρεια ποτὲ δρομάδι κώλῳ μάτηρ θεῶν ἐcύθη ἀν' ὑλάεντα νάπη ποτάμιόν τε
χεῦμ' ὑδάτων βαρύβρομόν τε κῦμ' ἅλιον (etc.) E. Hel. 1301 ff.   44 μαιομένῳ*
A.R. 4. 1275   52 ἡ δ' ἀΐουcα | κευθμῶν ἐξ ὑπάτων δεινὴ θεὸς ἀντεβόληcεν ...
cτράπτε δ' ἀπειρέcιον δαΐδων cέλας (de Hecate) A.R. 3. 1212–16 (cf. ad Dem. 25)

41 χερcὶ φίλῃcι corr. ex χερὶ φίλη M (manus prima)   46 οὐδέ οἱ οἰωνῶν τις
vel οὔτε τις οἰωνῶν τῇ Hermann: οὐδέ τις οἰωνῶν οἱ Brunck   47 χθονία M:
corr. Ruhnken   48 cτροφᾶτ' M: corr. Ruhnken   49 ἢ δεπότοιο M: corr.
Ruhnken   50 πᾶcατ' M: corr. Ruhnken   βάλλετο M: βάπτετο Ignarra:
θάλπετο Mitscherlich: ἄταλλε λοετροῖc Ilgen   51 φαινόλη M: corr. Ruhnken
53 ἀγγέλλουcα Ruhnken: ἄγχι θέουcα Matthiae: ἐγκονέουcα Ludwich

Πότνια Δημήτηρ ὡρηφόρε ἀγλαόδωρε
τίς θεῶν οὐρανίων ἠὲ θνητῶν ἀνθρώπων   55
ἥρπασε Περσεφόνην καὶ σὸν φίλον ἤκαχε θυμόν;
φωνῆς γὰρ ἤκους᾽, ἀτὰρ οὐκ ἴδον ὀφθαλμοῖσιν
ὅς τις ἔην· σοὶ δ᾽ ὦκα λέγω νημερτέα πάντα.
῾Ως ἄρ᾽ ἔφη ῾Εκάτη· τὴν δ᾽ οὐκ ἠμείβετο μύθῳ
῾Ρείης ἠϋκόμου θυγάτηρ, ἀλλ᾽ ὦκα σὺν αὐτῇ   60
ἤϊξ᾽ αἰθομένας δαΐδας μετὰ χερσὶν ἔχουσα.
᾽Ηέλιον δ᾽ ἵκοντο θεῶν σκοπὸν ἠδὲ καὶ ἀνδρῶν,
στὰν δ᾽ ἵππων προπάροιθε καὶ εἵρετο δῖα θεάων·
᾽Ηέλι᾽ αἴδεσσαί με θεὰν θεός, εἴ ποτε δή σευ
ἢ ἔπει ἢ ἔργῳ κραδίην καὶ θυμὸν ἴηνα.   65
κούρην τὴν ἔτεκον γλυκερὸν θάλος εἴδεϊ κυδρὴν

54 πότνια* Dem. 492, Hy. 30. 6 (apud Hom. semper quinto pede) ~ Hes.
Th. 926 (πότνιαν*): Δημήτηρ ὡρηφόρος ἀγλαόδωρος* Dem. 192: cf. Dem. 492, 4
55 ἠὲ θνητῶν ἀνθρώπων* Herm. 441: cf. Dem. 45, 73 etc.   56 ἥρπασε*
Il. 13. 528: Περσεφόνην* Hes. Th. 913 (~ Dem. 360, 387, 405): φίλον ὤλεσε
θυμόν* Il. 11. 342 = 20. 413: θυμὸν ἀκηχέμεναι Il. 18. 29   57 ἤκουσεν
φωνῆς Dem. 23: φωνή* Il. 2. 490 etc.: ἤκουσα/ε (etc.)* Od. 11. 421 etc.: ἴδον
ὀφθαλμοῖσιν* Il. 3. 169 etc.: ἀτὰρ οὐκ ἴδον ὀφθαλμοῖσιν* Dem. 68: cf. Dem. 67–8
58 αἰψά κ᾽ ἐγὼ νημερτέα πάντ᾽ ἐνέποιμι Od. 17. 561: τὰ δέ τοι νημερτέα εἴρω Od. 11.
137: ταῦτα ... ἀληθέα πάντ᾽ ἀγορεύω Dem. 433: ἐρέω νημερτέα πάντα* Dem. 406
59 ὣς ἄρ᾽ ἔφη* Il. 1. 584 etc.: ῾Εκάτη* Dem. 52: ἠμείβετο μύθῳ* Od. 9. 506 etc.
59b–60a = 74b–5a   60 ῾Ρείης ἠϋκόμου θυγάτηρ* Dem. 75 (~ 442):
ἠύκομος ῾Ρείη Hes. Th. 625, 634: ἠϋκόμου Hes. Sc. 216 (~ frr. 37. 8, 25. 17): θυγάτηρ* Il. 1. 538 etc.: ὦκα* Il. 13. 671 etc.   61 ἤϊξ᾽* Dem. 386 (~ 177, Il. 21.
247, Od. 15. 183): cf. Dem. 48   62 ἠέλιον* Il. 18. 239 etc.: δ᾽ ἵκοντο* Il. 4.
383 etc.: θεῶν* Il. 1. 549 etc.: σκοπὸν (etc.) Il. 10. 526 (etc.): ἠδὲ καὶ ἀνδρῶν*
Il. 1. 334, 7. 274: ᾽Ηέλιος γάρ οἱ σκοπιὴν ἔχεν Od. 8. 302   63 στῆ δ᾽ ἵππων
προπάροιθεν* Il. 24. 286, Od. 15. 150: καὶ εἵρετο* Il. 1. 513: δῖα θεάων* Il. 5. 381 etc.
64 ᾽Ηέλι᾽* Od. 12. 385: αἴδεσσαι Il. 9. 640: θεὰν θεός* Herm. 154   64 f. εἴ ποτε
δή τι | ἢ ἔπει ὤνησας κραδίην Διὸς ἠὲ καὶ ἔργῳ Il. 1. 394 f.: εἴ ποτε δή σε μετ᾽ ἀθανά-
τοισιν ὄνησα | ἢ ἔπει ἢ ἔργῳ Il. 1. 503 f.   65 cf. ad Dem. 64 f., 117, 199: κραδίην
καὶ θυμόν* Il. 2. 171 etc.: θυμὸν ἰήνῃ* Il. 24. 119 etc. (~ 23. 600 etc.): θυμὸν ἴαινον*
Dem. 435   66 f. κούρην ἥν* ... τήν* ... Il. 16. 56 ff., 18. 444 f.: ἔτεκεν (etc.)*
Il. 24. 562 etc.: φίλον θάλος* ὃν τέκεν αὐτή Il. 20. 87 (~ Dem. 187): εἴδεϊ* Od. 17.
308: εἶδος ἀρίστην* Il. 3. 124 etc.

54 καρπὸν ᾽Ελευσινίης Δημήτερος ἀγλαοδώρου* Agallias, in versu post Il. 18. 551
addito   66 γλυκερὸν θάλος* Orph. Hy. 56. 8

54–6 cf. pap. 1 (Orph. fr. 49. 102–5)   54 Δημήτηρ M: Δήμητερ Ilgen
ὡρίφόρε M: corr. Ruhnken   εἰμὶ δὲ Δημήτηρ ὡρηφόρ[ος ἀγλαό]δωρος pap. 1
55 τίς θεὸς οὐράνιος pap. 1   56 Φερσεφ[ό]νην pap. 1   ἤπα]φε θυμόν pap. 1
57 εἶδον M: corr. Ruhnken   58 lacunam post hunc versum statuerunt Hermann, alii   64 θεᾶς ὕπερ M: θεὰν θεός Peerlkamp ap. Cobet (cf. Herm. 154):
θέης ὕπερ Hermann: θεᾶς ὕπερ Voss, Hermann senex: θεὰν σύ περ Ludwich

τῆς ἀδινὴν ὄπ' ἄκουσα δι' αἰθέρος ἀτρυγέτοιο
ὥς τε βιαζομένης, ἀτὰρ οὐκ ἴδον ὀφθαλμοῖσιν.
ἀλλὰ σὺ γὰρ δὴ πᾶσαν ἐπὶ χθόνα καὶ κατὰ πόντον
αἰθέρος ἐκ δίης καταδέρκεαι ἀκτίνεσσι, 70
νημερτέως μοι ἔνισπε φίλον τέκος εἴ που ὄπωπας
ὅς τις νόσφιν ἐμεῖο λαβὼν ἀέκουσαν ἀνάγκῃ
οἴχεται ἠὲ θεῶν ἢ καὶ θνητῶν ἀνθρώπων.
    Ὣς φάτο, τὴν δ' Ὑπεριονίδης ἠμείβετο μύθῳ·
Ῥείης ἠϋκόμου θυγάτηρ Δήμητερ ἄνασσα 75
εἰδήσεις· δὴ γὰρ μέγα ἄζομαι ἠδ' ἐλεαίρω
ἀχνυμένην περὶ παιδὶ τανισφύρῳ· οὐδέ τις ἄλλος
αἴτιος ἀθανάτων εἰ μὴ νεφεληγερέτα Ζεύς,
ὅς μιν ἔδωκ' Ἀΐδῃ θαλερὴν κεκλῆσθαι ἄκοιτιν
αὐτοκασιγνήτῳ· ὁ δ' ὑπὸ ζόφον ἠερόεντα 80

67 τῆς δ' ἀδινὸν* γόοωσα Od. 4. 721: ὄπ' ἄκουσα* Il. 7. 53: δι' αἰθέρος ἀτρυγέτοιο* Il. 17. 425 (~ Dem. 457, Hes. fr. 150. 35). Cf. P. Oxy. 2509. 1 (Hes. Cat.?) ἐσσυμένως δ' ἤϊξε (= Dem. 449a) δι' αἰθέρος ἀτρυγέτοιο (cf. ad Dem. 322)   68 ὣς τέ* μοι ὑβρίζοντες Od. 1. 227: ἀτὰρ οὐκ ἴδον ὀφθαλμοῖσιν* Dem. 57   69 ἐπὶ χθόνα* Il. 3. 265 etc.: κατὰ πόντον* Od. 5. 377: χθόνα ... πόντον Hy. 30. 3   70 αἰθέρος ἐκ δίης* Il. 16. 365: καταδέρκεται ἀκτίνεσσιν* Od. 11. 16 (ἐπι- codd. plerique: κατα- Ar. Byz., Aristarch.) ~ Hes. Th. 760   71 νημερτές μοι ἔνισπε* Od. 4. 642: νημερτέως* ... ἐνισπήσω Od. 5. 98: φίλον τέκος* Il. 3. 162 etc. (semper vocative, exc. Il. 18. 63 ὄφρα ἴδωμι φ. τ.): ἐνισπεῖν εἴ που ὄπωπας* Od. 3. 93 = 4. 323 (cf. ad Dem. 64 ff.)   72 νόσφιν ἐμεῖο* Ap. 314, Herm. 537: ἀέκουσαν ἀνάγκῃ* Dem. 124: ἀέκουσαν* Od. 2. 130 etc.: ἀνάγκῃ* Il. 14. 128 etc.   73 οἴχεται* Il. 15. 223 etc.: οὔτε θεῶν οὔτε θνητῶν ἀνθρώπων Dem. 45 (~ 55 etc.)   74 ὣς φάτο* Il. 1. 188 etc.: τὴν δ' ... ἠμείβετο μύθῳ* Dem. 59 (60a = 75a)   75 Ῥείης ἠϋκόμου θυγάτηρ* Dem. 60: Δήμητρος ... ἀνάσσης Il. 14. 326: ἄνασσα* Dem. 440, 492   76 εἰδήσεις* Od. 7. 327: μέγαν ἄζετο* Il. 5. 434: μέγα κήδεται ἠδ' ἐλεαίρει* Il. 2. 27 etc. (~ Hes. fr. 204. 114)   77 ἀχνυμένη* Od. 11. 388: περὶ παιδί* Il. 16. 568: τανίσφυρον* Dem. 2   77 f. ἀχνύμεθα* ... οὐδέ τις ἄλλος | αἴτιος* ἀλλὰ Ζεύς Od. 11. 558 f. (~ 22. 154 f., 1. 347 f.)   78 ἀθανάτων* Il. 5. 186 etc.: νεφεληγερέτα Ζεύς* Il. 1. 511 etc.   79 ἔδωκε* Il. 22. 285: Ἀΐδῃ* Od. 10. 534 = 11. 47: θαλερὴν παράκοιτιν Il. 3. 53: θαλερὴν ... ἄκοιτιν* Hes. Th. 921 etc.: δώσω ... σὴν κεκλῆσθαι ἄκοιτιν* Il. 14. 268: φίλη κεκλήσῃ ἄκοιτις* Il. 3. 138   80 αὐτοκασίγνητος* Il. 2. 706 etc. (Dem. 85, 364): ὑπὸ ζόφον ἠερόεντα* Il. 23. 51, Dem. 446, 464 (~ 402, 482)

67 ἀδινῇ ὀπί A.R. 4. 1422

67 ἀδινὴν M: ἀδινὴν Allen   68 εἶδον M: corr. Ruhnken (cf. Dem. 57) 70 καταδέρκεται M (cf. Od. 11. 16): corr. Ruhnken   71 ὄπωπεν M: corr. Ruhnken   72 ἐμοῖο M: corr. Matthiae (probante Ruhnken)   75 θύγατερ Bücheler   76 μέγα c' Ruhnken: γάρ σε μέγ' Voss   77 τανυσφύρῳ M: τανισφύρῳ scripsi (cf. Dem. 2)   οὐδέ M: οὔ νύ Gemoll

ἁρπάξας ἵπποισιν ἄγεν μεγάλα ἰάχουσαν.

ἀλλὰ θεὰ κατάπαυε μέγαν γόον· οὐδέ τί σε χρὴ
μὰψ αὔτως ἄπλητον ἔχειν χόλον· οὔ τοι ἀεικὴς
γαμβρὸς ἐν ἀθανάτοις πολυσημάντωρ Ἀϊδωνεὺς
αὐτοκασίγνητος καὶ ὁμόσπορος· ἀμφὶ δὲ τιμὴν   85
ἔλλαχεν ὡς τὰ πρῶτα διάτριχα δασμὸς ἐτύχθη·
τοῖς μεταναιετάει τῶν ἔλλαχε κοίρανος εἶναι.

῞Ως εἰπὼν ἵπποισιν ἐκέκλετο, τοὶ δ' ὑπ' ὁμοκλῆς
ῥίμφα φέρον θοὸν ἅρμα τανύπτεροι ὥς τ' οἰωνοί·
τὴν δ' ἄχος αἰνότερον καὶ κύντερον ἵκετο θυμόν.   90

81 ἁρπάξασα φέρεν Od. 10. 48: ἁρπάξας* Dem. 19: ἵπποισιν* Il. 8. 184 etc.: ἄγεν*
Il. 2. 557 etc.: μεγάλα ἰάχοντα* Od. 9. 392: cf. Dem. 18–20, 431–2   82 θεά* Il. 10.
462 etc.: κατέπαυσα θεῶν χόλον* Od. 4. 583: μέγαν νόον* Dem. 37   82–3 νῦν δ'
ἤτοι μὲν ἐγὼ παύω χόλον· οὐδέ τί με χρὴ | ἀσκελέως αἰεὶ μενεαινέμεν Il. 19. 67 f.: ἀλλ'
Ἀχιλεῦ δάμασον θυμὸν μέγαν· οὐδέ τί σε χρὴ | νηλεὲς ἦτορ ἔχειν . . . Il. 9. 496 f.; cf.
Il. 9. 260, 20. 133, Herm. 494 f.   83 μὰψ αὔτως ἀτέλεστον* Od. 16. 111: ἄπλητον
κοτέουσα Hes. Th. 315: ἔχει χόλον* Dem. 354: οὔ τοι ἀεικές* Il. 9. 70, Dem. 120
84 γαμβρός* Il. 9. 142 etc.: ἀθανάτους πολυσημάντωρ Ἀϊδωνεύς* Dem. 376 (cf. Dem.
2, 31, 357)   85 αὐτοκασίγνητος* Il. 2. 706 etc. (~ Dem. 364, 82): αὐτοκασι-
γνήτην ὁμοπάτριον* Hes. fr. 280. 18: ἀμφὶ δὲ τιμῆς* Herm. 172: ἀμφὶ δὲ τήν γε* Hes.
Op. 74   86 ἔλλαβε* Il. 5. 83 etc.: ὡς τὰ πρῶτα* Aph. 185 (~ Il. 1. 276): ἀλλ'
ἔχεν ᾗ τὰ πρῶτα* Il. 13. 679 (~ 24. 27): ὅσσοι . . . τιμὴν ἔλαχον . . . (ὅσσ' ἔλαχεν) . . .
ἀλλ' ἔχει, ὡς τὸ πρῶτον ἀπ' ἀρχῆς ἔπλετο δασμός Hes. Th. 421–5: τριχθὰ δὲ πάντα
δέδασται, ἕκαστος δ' ἔμμορε τιμῆς . . . Ἀΐδης δ' ἔλαχε ζόφον ἠερόεντα Il. 15. 189–91:
ὡς τὰ πρῶτα γένοντο, καὶ ὡς λάχε μοῖραν ἕκαστος Herm. 428: διὰ τρίχα* Il. 2. 655:
δασμός* Il. 1. 166: ἐτύχθη* Il. 2. 155 etc.   87 ναιετάουσι (etc.)* Od. 9. 23 etc.:
αἱ περιναιετάουσιν* Od. 4. 177: κοίρανος εἶναι* Od. 18. 106   88 ὡς εἰπὼν ἵπποισιν
ἐκέκλετο* Il. 8. 184 = 23. 442   88–9 ὡς εἰπὼν ἵπποισιν ἐνέπνευσεν μένος ἠΰ. | τὼ
δ' . . . ῥίμφα φέρον θοὸν ἅρμα* Il. 17. 456–8: ὀμοκλῇ (etc.)* Il. 6. 137 (etc.): τοὶ δ' ὑπ'
ὁμοκλῆς | ῥίμφ' ἔφερον θοὸν ἅρμα* Hes. Sc. 341–2   88–90 ὡς φάτο, Πηλείωνι δ'
ἄχος γένετ' . . . Il. 1. 188 etc.   89 ῥίμφ' ἔφερον θοὸν ἅρμα* Il. 11. 533 (~ 17. 458,
cf. ad Dem. 88–9): τανύπτερον* Hes. Th. 523: οἰωνοῖσι τανυπτερύγεσσι Il. 12. 237:
οἰωνόν . . . τανυσίπτερον Herm. 213   90 ἀλλὰ τόδ' αἰνὸν ἄχος κραδίην καὶ θυμὸν
ἱκάνει Il. 8. 147 etc.: αἰνότερον καὶ κύντερον* Od. 11. 427: αἰνότατον . . . καὶ κύντατον* Dem. 305 f.: ἵκετο θυμόν* Il. 11. 88

83 μαίνεται . . . ἄπλητον Semon. fr. 7. 33 f. D.³   89 θοὸν ἅρμα, de Solis curru,
Mimn. 10. 9 D.³: τανύπτερος ὡς ὅκα πορφυρίς Ibycus, PMG 317b

81 ἵπποις ἄγαγεν Cobet   82–3 γόον . . . ἔχειν reiecerunt Schneidewin,
Bücheler: οὐδέ . . . χόλον reiec. Baumeister, Flander: μέγαν χόλον Hermann
83 αὔτως M: corr. Hermann   85 τιμῆς Hermann (apud Franke): τιμῇ
Schneidewin   86 lacunam post hunc versum statuerunt Matthiae, Bücheler
(e.g. πᾶσι καταφθιμένοισιν ἀνασσέμεν εἰν Ἀΐδαο): cf. ad Dem. 87   87 μετάναιεται
M: μεταναιετάει Voss: μέτα ναιετάει Ilgen: μέτα ναιετάειν ὧν Valckenaer: versum
delebat Hermann (apud Ilgen): post 81 ponebat Brunck   89 ῥίμφα φέρον M:
ῥίμφ' ἔφερον Ruhnken

χωσαμένη δῆπειτα κελαινεφέϊ Κρονίωνι
νοσφιςθεῖςα θεῶν ἀγορὴν καὶ μακρὸν Ὄλυμπον
ὤχετ' ἐπ' ἀνθρώπων πόλιας καὶ πίονα ἔργα
εἶδος ἀμαλδύνουςα πολὺν χρόνον· οὐδέ τις ἀνδρῶν
εἰςορόων γίνωςκε βαθυζώνων τε γυναικῶν,   95
πρίν γ' ὅτε δὴ Κελεοῖο δαΐφρονος ἵκετο δῶμα,
ὃς τότ' Ἐλευςῖνος θυοέςςης κοίρανος ἦεν.
ἕζετο δ' ἐγγὺς ὁδοῖο φίλον τετιημένη ἦτορ
Παρθενίῳ φρέατι ὅθεν ὑδρεύοντο πολῖται
ἐν ςκιῇ, αὐτὰρ ὕπερθε πεφύκει θάμνος ἐλαίης,   100
γρηῒ παλαιγενέϊ ἐναλίγκιος, ἥ τε τόκοιο
εἴργηται δώρων τε φιλοστεφάνου Ἀφροδίτης,
οἷαί τε τροφοί εἰςι θεμιστοπόλων βαςιλήων

91 χωσαμένη* Il. 9. 530: κελαινεφέι Κρονίωνϊ* Il. 1. 397 etc. (Dem. 316 etc.): cf.
Dem. 468   92 νοσφιςθείς* Od. 11. 73: θεῶν ἀγορήν* Il. 8. 2: καὶ μακρὸν Ὄλυμπον* Il. 5. 398   93 ὤχετ'* Il. 2. 71 etc.: ἀνθρώπων* Il. 4. 84 etc.: πόλιας καὶ
πίονας ἀγρούς* Od. 8. 560: ἀμαλδύνων πίονα ἔργα* Il. 12. 283: ὤχετ' ἐπὶ κλυτὰ φῦλ'
ἀνθρώπων Il. 14. 361 (de deo) ~ 19. 131   94 εἶδος ἀτιμήςαςα* Dem. 158:
τεῖχος ἀμαλδῦναι* Il. 12. 18 (~ 12. 32, 7. 463): πολὺν χρόνον* Il. 12. 9: οὔτε τιν'
ἀνδρῶν* Herm. 444   95 εἰςορόων* Il. 8. 52 etc.: γίνωςκε* Il. 6. 191: βαθυζώνουc
τε γυναῖκας* Il. 9. 594, Od. 3. 154   96 πρίν γ' ὅτε δή* Od. 23. 43, Dem. 195, 202,
Ap. 49: Κελεοῖο δαΐφρονος* Dem. 233: Ἀλκινόοιο δαΐφρονος ἵκετο δῶμα* Od. 8. 13
97 Ἐλευςῖνος θυοέςςης* Dem. 490 (~ 318): κοίρανος* Il. 2. 204, Dem. 87 etc.:
κοίρανοι ἦςαν Il. 2. 487 etc.   98 ἕζετο* Il. 23. 235: ἐγγὺς ὁδοῖο* Od. 13. 268:
φίλον τετιημένη ἦτορ* Od. 4. 804, Dem. 181 (~ 198), Hes. Th. 163   99 ὅθεν
ὑδρεύοντο πολῖται* Od. 7. 131, 17. 206   100 ἐν ςκιῇ* ἑξόμενον Hes. Op. 593
(~ Dem. 98 ἕζετο): αὐτὰρ ὕπερθε* Od. 14. 476: πεφύκει* Od. 5. 63: θάμνος ἔφυ
τανίφυλλος ἐλαίης Od. 23. 190 (~ 13. 102, 122, 346, 372)   101 γρηῒ δέ μιν
ἔϊκυῖα παλαιγενέϊ* Il. 3. 386: ἐναλίγκιος* Il. 14. 290: οὐ πρὶν εἰδυῖα τόκοιο* Il. 17. 5
102 δῶρ' Ἀφροδίτης* Il. 3. 54 (~ 64): ἐϋςτεφάνου τ' Ἀφροδίτης* Od. 8. 267 (ἐϋςτ.
Κυθερείης/η Od. 8. 288 etc.)   103 θεμιστοπόλων βαςιλήων* Dem. 215 (~ 473,
Hes. frr. 10. 1, 9. 1(?), PSI 6. 722. 1): δικαςπόλοι, οἵ τε θέμιςτας | πρὸς Διὸς εἰρύαται
Il. 1. 238–9

92 νοσφιςθεῖςα* γέρα προτέρων Orac. ap. Paus. 8. 42. 6 (de Cerere)   94 ἀμαλδύνουςα* A.R. 1. 834: ἀμαλδυνθεῖςα χρόνῳ περικαλλέα μορφήν AP 6. 18 (Iulianus). Cobet
(Mnem. 10 (1861), 317) confert veterem inscriptionem apud Ruhnken γρηῒ δὲ
θήκατό μιν πάντ' ἴκελον (cf. Dem. 101) . . . κάλλος ἀμαλδύναςα καὶ ἀγλαίην ἐρατεινήν
101 γρηῒ δέ μ' εἰςαμένην (Iunonem) A.R. 3. 72 (cf. ad Dem. 93 f.)   102 Κυπρο-
γενοῦς δῶρον ἰοςτεφάνου Theognis 1304, 1332

91 δ' ἤπειτα M: δὴ ἔπειτα Hermann: δῆπειτα scripsi   95 γίνωςκε M:
γίγνωςκε Hermann   97 τότε λευςῖνος M: corr. Ruhnken   98 τετιημένος M:
corr. Ruhnken   99 lacunam post 98 statuit Hermann (exeunte versu ἐπὶ κρήνῃ
μελανύδρῳ): 99 reiecit Bücheler: πὰρ θείῳ φρέατι Wolf: θείῳ πὰρ φρέατι Hermann:
φρείατι Παρθενίῳ Porson, Cobet: πὰρ φρέατ' Ἀνθείῳ Tucker   101 παλαι-
γενέη M: corr. Ruhnken   103 'fuitne θεμιστοπόλοις βαςιλεῦςι, an 104 ab alio
adiectus?' Bücheler

EIC ΔHMHTPA

104

παίδων καὶ ταμίαι κατὰ δώματα ἠχήεντα.
τὴν δὲ ἴδον Κελεοῖο Ἐλευσινίδαο θύγατρες   105
ἐρχόμεναι μεθ᾽ ὕδωρ εὐήρυτον ὄφρα φέροιεν
κάλπιςι χαλκείῃςι φίλα πρὸς δώματα πατρός,
τέccαρεc ὥc τε θεαὶ κουρήϊον ἄνθοc ἔχουcαι,
Καλλιδίκη καὶ Κλειcιδίκη Δημώ τ᾽ ἐρόεccα
Καλλιθόη θ᾽, ἣ τῶν προγενεcτάτη ἦεν ἁπαcῶν·   110
οὐδ᾽ ἔγνων· χαλεποὶ δὲ θεοὶ θνητοῖcιν ὁρᾶcθαι.
ἀγχοῦ δ᾽ ἱcτάμεναι ἔπεα πτερόεντα προcηύδων·
Τίc πόθεν ἐccὶ γρηῦ παλαιγενέων ἀνθρώπων;
τίπτε δὲ νόcφι πόληοc ἀπέcτιχεc οὐδὲ δόμοιcι
πίλναcαι, ἔνθα γυναῖκεc ἀνὰ μέγαρα cκιόεντα   115

104 παίδων* Il. 15. 663 etc.: ταμίη* Il. 6. 390 etc.: κατὰ δώματα* Od. 7. 102,
Dem. 156 etc.: κὰδ δώματα ἠχήεντα* Od. 4. 72 (~ Hes. Th. 767)   105 τὴν δὲ
ἴδε* Il. 18. 382: Κελεοῖο* Dem. 96: θύγατρεc* Il. 6. 238 etc.   106 ἐρχομένη*
Il. 4. 445 etc.: ταὶ δὲ μεθ᾽ ὕδωρ | ἔρχεcθε κρήνηνδε Od. 20. 153–4 (cf. ad Dem. 285 ff.):
ὕδωρ προτὶ ἄcτυ φέρεcκον* Od. 10. 108: φέροιεν* Il. 5. 303 etc.   107 κάλπιν
ἐχούcῃ Od. 7. 20: φίλα οἰκία Il. 12. 221: πρὸς δώματα πατρός* Od. 4. 657, 15. 459,
Dem. 160: φίλου πρὸς δώματα πατρός* Od. 19. 458: φίλα πρὸς δώματα πατρός*
Dem. 180   108 τέccαρεc* ἠΰτε φῶτεc Herm. 195 (~ Il. 11. 698 etc.): ὥc τε θεῷ*
Od. 13. 231: τρεῖc οἷαί τε θεαί, περικαλλέα ἔργ᾽ εἰδυῖαι Hes. fr. 26. 6: ἔχει ἥβηc ἄνθοc
Il. 13. 484 (~ Herm. 375, Hy. 10. 3, Hes. Th. 988, fr. 132): κροκηΐῳ ἄνθει* Dem. 178
109 Ἁλίη τ᾽ ἐρόεccα* Hes. Th. 245   110 Καλλιόπη θ᾽· ἡ δὲ προφερεcτάτη ἐcτὶν
ἁπαcέων Hes. Th. 79 (~ 361): ἀνδρῶν προγενέcτεροc ἦεν Od. 7. 156: πάντων προφε-
ρέcτατοc ἦεν (-εροc codd. pauci) Od. 8. 128: πολὺ φιλτάτη ἔcκεν ἁπαcέων* Od. 8. 284
111 ῥεῖ᾽ ἔγνων* Il. 13. 72 (~ Od. 17. 273, 19. 475): χαλεποὶ δὲ θεοὶ* φαίνεcθαι
ἐναργεῖc Il. 20. 131: χαλεπὸν δὲ τάδε ζωοῖcιν ὁρᾶcθαι* Od. 11. 156: θεοὶ θνητοῖcιν*
Hy. 31. 19 (~ Il. 20. 41, Od. 24. 64)   112 ἀγχοῦ δ᾽ ἱcταμένη ἔπεα πτερόεντα
προcηύδα Il. 4. 92 etc.: προcηύδων* Od. 10. 418 (cf. ad Dem. 118)   113 τίc
πόθεν* εἰc ἀνδρῶν Il. 21. 150 etc.: γρηῦ* παλαιγενέc Od. 22. 395 (cf. ad Dem. 144):
χαμαιγενέων ἀνθρώπων* Dem. 352, Aph. 108, Hes. Th. 879   114 τίπτε δέ*
Od. 2. 363 etc.: τίπτε . . . ἀφέcτατε* Il. 4. 340: νόcφι πόληοc Od. 1. 185 etc. (ad fin.
versus): ἀπέcτιχε* Od. 12. 143   115 γυναῖκεc* Il. 8. 520 etc.: ἀνὰ μέγαρα
cκιόεντα* Od. 1. 365 etc.

107 χαλκείη cὺν κάλπιδι A.R. 1. 1207 (cf. Theocr. 13. 39, 46, Gow ad loc.)
108 κούριον ἄνθοc in versu post Il. 13. 433 addito (ap. Schol. T), Orph. Arg. 1339,
fr. 98 (κούριμον codd.): κούριον ἥβην Orac. ap. Paus. 9. 14. 3

107 κάλπῃcι M: corr. Ruhnken   φίλου Matthiae (cf. Od. 19. 458, Dem.
180)   109 Κλειcιδίκη nominis posteriorem partem suspectam habuit Ruhnken
110 versum reiecit Preller   προγενεcτέρη Voss   ἁπαcέων Wolf   111 ἔγνον
Cobet (cf. Dem. 327, 437); cf. H. L. Ahrens, De Graecae Linguae Dialectis, 2. 317,
Schulze, QE 426   112 δ᾽ om. M: corr. Ruhnken   113 χαμαιγενέων
Bücheler, Herwerden, Abel   115 πιλνᾶ M: πίλναcαι Voss: πιλνᾷ Hermann
(cf. Il. 14. 199 δαμνᾷ): πιλνᾶc Allen: πίλνᾳ(?) Schwyzer, Gr. Gr. i. 695

τηλίκαι ὡς cύ περ ὧδε καὶ ὁπλότεραι γεγάαcιν,
αἵ κέ cε φίλωνται ἠμὲν ἔπει ἠδὲ καὶ ἔργῳ;
Ὣς ἔφαθ', ἡ δ' ἐπέεccιν ἀμείβετο πότνα θεάων·
τέκνα φίλ' αἵ τινές ἐcτε γυναικῶν θηλυτεράων
χαίρετ', ἐγὼ δ' ὑμῖν μυθήcομαι· οὔ τοι ἀεικὲς   120
ὑμῖν εἰρομένῃcιν ἀληθέα μυθήcαcθαι.
Δωcὼ ἐμοί γ' ὄνομ' ἐcτί· τὸ γὰρ θέτο πότνια μήτηρ·
νῦν αὖτε Κρήτηθεν ἐπ' εὐρέα νῶτα θαλάccηc
ἤλυθον οὐκ ἐθέλουcα, βίῃ δ' ἀέκουcαν ἀνάγκῃ
ἄνδρεc λῃcτῆρεc ἀπήγαγον. οἱ μὲν ἔπειτα   125
νηὶ θοῇ Θορικὸν δὲ κατέcχεθον, ἔνθα γυναῖκεc

---

116 τηλίκου ὥc* περ ἐγών Il. 24. 487: γέρων δὲ δὴ ὡς cύ περ ὧδε Il. 24. 398:
ὁπλότεροι γεγάαcιν Il. 4. 325   117 φίλωνται Dem. 487: ἐπέων . . . ἠδὲ καὶ ἔργων*
Il. 11. 703 (~ Od. 17. 313): ἠ ἔπει . . . ἠὲ καὶ ἔργῳ* Il. 1. 395: cf. Dem. 199
118 ὡς ἔφαν Od. 10. 422 (418 ~ Dem. 112): ἡ δ' ἐπέεccι καθάπτετο* Il. 15. 127:
ἐπέεccιν* ἀμειβομένῳ Od. 11. 81 = 465 (~ 225 etc.): δῖα θεάων* Dem. 63 etc.:
πότνια Δηώ* Dem. 47: πότνα θεά Od. 5. 215 etc.: ἀμείβετο δῖα θεάων* Od. 4. 398:
cf. Od. 13. 391–2 cὺν coί, πότνα θεά . . . | τὸν δ' ἠμείβετ' ἔπειτα θεά . . .   119 τέκνα
φίλ'* Od. 4. 78: αἵτινές εἰcι* Herm. 311 (~ 277): γυναικῶν θηλυτεράων* Od. 11.
386, 23. 166, Dem. 167, 222   120 χαίρετ'* Il. 24. 706 etc.: ἐγὼ μυθήcομαι*
Od. 4. 240 etc.: οὔ τοι ἀεικές* Il. 9. 70 (cf. Dem. 83)   121 εἰρομένη* Od. 24.
474: ἀληθέα μυθήcαcθαι* Il. 6. 382 etc. (cf. Dem. 44)   122 αὐτὰρ ἐμοί γ' ὄνομ'
ἐcτίν* Ἐπήριτος Od. 24. 306: Ἀρναῖος δ' ὄνομ' ἔcκε· τὸ γὰρ θέτο πότνια μήτηρ Od.
18. 5: Οὖτις ἐμοί γ' ὄνομα* Od. 9. 366   123 νῦν αὖτε Il. 11. 363 etc.: Κρήτηθεν
Il. 3. 233: ἐπ' εὐρέα νῶτα θαλάccηc* Il. 2. 159   123–4 cf. Od. 13. 256–7 ἐν Κρήτῃ
εὐρείῃ, | τηλοῦ ὑπὲρ πόντου· νῦν δ' εἰλήλουθα . . . (cf. ad Dem. 98 ff.)   124 ἰλλάcιν
οὐκ ἐθέλοντα βίῃ δήcαντες ἄγουcιν Il. 13. 572: οὐκ ἐθέλουcα* Il. 18. 434: βίῃ δ'
ἀέκοντος Il. 1. 430: ἀέκουcαν ἀνάγκῃ* Dem. 72   125 λῃcτορες ἄνδρες Od. 15.
427: ἄνδρεc* δυcμενέες νηυcὶν λάβον ἠδὲ πέραccαν Od. 15. 387 (cf. ad Dem. 132):
λῃcτῆρεc Od. 3. 73 etc.: ἀπήγαγον* Od. 13. 211   125–7 ~ Od. 13. 113–14 ἡ
μὲν ἔπειτα | ἠπείρῳ ἐπέκελcεν . . .   126 νηὶ θοῇ* Il. 16. 123 etc.: νῆα* κατιcχέ-
μεναι Od. 11. 456

---

118 πότνα (nominative, de Cerere Thesmophoro) Call. fr. 63. 8

---

117 φίλονται M: φίλωνται Voss   118 ἔφαθ' M: ἔφαν Voss   ἡ δὲ ἔπεccιν
Hermann   'alibi in hoc carmine πότνια Δηώ aut δῖα θεάων' Bücheler   119 φίλα·
τίνεc M: φίλ' αἵτινεc Fontein   120 οὔτι M: οὔτοι Fontein   121 εἰρο-
μένοιcιν M: corr. Ruhnken   122 δὼc ἐμοίγ' M: Δωρὶc Ruhnken: Δωὶc
Hermann (cf. Bechtel, Nachr. Gött. Ges. 1890, 29 ff.) vel Δωὰc: Δμωὶc Mitscherlich: Δὼc μὲν Brunck: Δωcὼ Passow: Δηὼ Fontein: Δὼc ὄνομ' ἐcτὶν ἐμοί γε Ludwich
123 δ' αὖτε Ruhnken (sed cf. Od. 11. 485 etc.)   124 ἀέκουcαν ἐλόντεc
Bücheler   126 versum reiecit Lenz (cf. 133–4): 'νῆα θοὴν Homericum ut Od.
11. 456' Voss   126–7 γυναῖκεc . . . ἀολλέαc dubitanter proposuit Baumeister
(qui tamen ipse lacunam post 127 indicavit)

ἠπείρου ἐπέβηϲαν ἀολλέεϲ ἠδὲ καὶ αὐτοὶ
δεῖπνον ἐπηρτύνοντο παρὰ πρυμνήϲια νηόϲ·
ἀλλ' ἐμοὶ οὐ δόρποιο μελίφρονοϲ ἤρατο θυμόϲ,
λάθρῃ δ' ὁρμηθεῖϲα δι' ἠπείροιο μελαίνηϲ   130
φεῦγον ὑπερφιάλουϲ ϲημάντοραϲ, ὄφρα κε μή με
ἀπριάτην περάϲαντεϲ ἐμῆϲ ἀποναίατο τιμῆϲ.
οὕτω δεῦρ' ἱκόμην ἀλαλημένη, οὐδέ τι οἶδα
ἥ τιϲ δὴ γαῖ' ἐϲτὶ καὶ οἵ τινεϲ ἐγγεγάαϲιν.
ἀλλ' ὑμῖν μὲν πάντεϲ 'Ολύμπια δώματ' ἔχοντεϲ   135
δοῖεν κουριδίουϲ ἄνδραϲ καὶ τέκνα τεκέϲθαι

127 ἠπείρου ἐπιβῆναι Od. 5. 299: ἀολλέεϲ* Il. 5. 498: ἠδὲ καὶ αὐτοί* Od. 19. 429:
cf. ad Dem. 125–7   127 ff. cf. Od. 9. 85 f. (= 10. 56 f.) ἔνθα δ' ἐπ' ἠπείρου
βῆμεν ... | αἶψα δὲ δεῖπνον ἕλοντο θοῆϲ παρὰ νηυϲὶν ἑταῖροι: 9. 546 f. (= 12. 5 f. ~
9. 149 f.) νῆα μὲν ἔνθ' ἐλθόντεϲ ἐκέλϲαμεν ἐν ψαμάθοιϲιν | ἐκ δὲ καὶ αὐτοὶ βῆμεν ἐπὶ
ῥηγμῖνι θαλάϲϲηϲ: 14. 345 ff. (cf. ad Dem. 125) ἔνθ' ἐμὲ μὲν κατέδηϲαν ... αὐτοὶ
δ' ἀποβάντεϲ | ἐϲϲυμένωϲ παρὰ θῖνα θαλάϲϲηϲ δόρπον ἕλοντο· | αὐτὰρ ἐμοὶ ...
(deinde aufugit Ulixes): 15. 499 f. ἐκ δὲ καὶ αὐτοὶ βαῖνον ἐπὶ ῥηγμῖνι θαλάϲϲηϲ, |
δεῖπνόν τ' ἐντύνοντο (~ Il. 1. 437, Ap. 505–11): 11. 20 f. νῆα μὲν ἔνθ' ἐλθόντεϲ ἐκέλ-
ϲαμεν, ἐκ δὲ τὰ μῆλα | εἱλόμεθ'· αὐτοὶ δ' αὖτε ... Cf. Arend, Typische Scenen, 79 ff.
128 δεῖπνόν τ' ἐντύνοντο* Od. 15. 500 (cf. ad Dem. 127 ff.): παρὰ πρυμνήϲια νηόϲ*
Il. 1. 476, Od. 12. 32   129 ϲίτοιο μελίφρονοϲ* Od. 24. 489: θυμόϲ* Od. 8. 202,
Dem. 290, 324, 436 etc.: οὐδέ τιϲ ἡμῖν | δόρπου μνῆϲτιϲ ἔην ... | ἀλλ' αὔτωϲ ἀποβάντεϲ
ἐκείμεθα νηὸϲ ἄπαντεϲ Od. 13. 279 f.   130 λάθρῃ* Il. 7. 243 etc.: ὁρμηθείϲ*
Il. 13. 562 etc.: ἠπείροιο μελαίνηϲ* Od. 14. 97 etc.   131 φεῦγον* Il. 9. 478:
ὑπερφιάλουϲ* Od. 3. 315: ϲημάντοραϲ Il. 4. 431: ὄφρα καὶ ἤδη* Il. 24. 635
132 ἀπριάτην* Il. 1. 99 (~ Od. 14. 317): τιμῆϲ ἀπονήμενοϲ Od. 24. 30 (de honore):
κεῖθε δέ μ' ὡϲ περάϲειε καὶ ἄϲπετον ὦνον ἕλοιτο Od. 14. 297: cf. Od. 15. 387 f., 428 f.,
452 f.   133 νῦν αὖ δεῦρ' ἱκόμην* Od. 13. 303: οὐδέ τι οἶδα* Od. 3. 184
134 Κρήτη τιϲ γαῖ' ἔϲτι* Od. 19. 172: τίϲ γῆ; τίϲ δῆμοϲ; τίνεϲ ἀνέρεϲ ἐγγεγάαϲιν;
Od. 13. 233   135 ff. ὑμῖν μὲν θεοὶ δοῖεν 'Ολύμπια δώματ' ἔχοντεϲ ... παῖδα δ'
ἐμοὶ λύϲαιτε Il. 1. 18 ff.: πάντεϲ 'Ολύμπια δώματ' ἔχοντεϲ | δῶρον ἐδώρηϲαν Hes.
Op. 81 f.   136 ἀνδρὸϲ κουριδίου* Od. 24. 196: καὶ τέκνα τεκέϲθαι* Od. 22. 324
(in precatione): ἄνδρ' ὀλέϲαϲα | κουρίδιον, τῷ τέκνα τέκῃ Od. 19. 265 f.

131 ὄφρα ἑ μή τιϲ A.R. 4. 181: ὄφρα κε μή μιν Mosch. Eur. 127 (cf. ad Dem. 176):
cf. [Opp.] Cyn. 4. 92

127–8 aut deesse versum post 127 aut poetam scripsisse δεῖπνον δ' ἠρτύνοντο
putabat Hermann (qui etiam senex οἱ δὲ καὶ αὐτοὶ coniecit): δεῖπνον δ' ἐντύνοντο
Voss: δεῖπνόν τ' ἐντύνοντο Bücheler   132 ἀπονοίατο M: corr. Ruhnken
134 γαῖ (ε a manu alia) ... ἐκγεγάαϲιν M: corr. Ruhnken: ἥτιϲ γαῖ' ἤδ' ἐϲτὶ Cobet
135 ὑμῖν πάϲῃϲιν Hermann

ὡς ἐθέλουϲι τοκῆϲ· ἐμὲ δ' αὖτ' οἰκτίρατε κοῦραι

προφρονέωϲ φίλα τέκνα τέων πρὸς δώμαθ' ἵκωμαι
ἀνέροϲ ἠδὲ γυναικόϲ, ἵνα ϲφίϲιν ἐργάζωμαι
πρόφρων οἷα γυναικὸϲ ἀφήλικος ἔργα τέτυκται·   140
καί κεν παῖδα νεογνὸν ἐν ἀγκοίνῃϲιν ἔχουϲα
καλὰ τιθηνοίμην καὶ δώματα τηρήϲαιμι
καί κε λέχοϲ ϲτορέϲαιμι μυχῷ θαλάμων ἐϋπήκτων
δεϲπόϲυνον καί κ' ἔργα διδαϲκήϲαιμι γυναῖκας.

Φῆ ῥα θεά· τὴν δ' αὐτίκ' ἀμείβετο παρθένος ἀδμὴς   145
Καλλιδίκη Κελεοῖο θυγατρῶν εἶδος ἀρίϲτη·

Μαῖα θεῶν μὲν δῶρα καὶ ἀχνύμενοί περ ἀνάγκῃ
τέτλαμεν ἄνθρωποι· δὴ γὰρ πολὺ φέρτεροί εἰϲιν.

137 ἐθέλουϲι* Il. 14. 51   138 προφρονέωϲ* Il. 6. 173 etc., Dem. 487: φίλα τέκνα*
Il. 10. 192: τέων* Il. 24. 387, Od. 20. 192   138 f. πῇ γὰρ ἐγὼ φίλε τέκνον ἴω; τεῦ
δώμαθ' ἵκωμαι | ἀνδρῶν . . . Od. 15. 509 f.: ὦ μοι ἐγώ, τέων αὖτε βροτῶν ἐς γαῖαν
ἱκάνω; Od. 6. 119 = 13. 200   139 ἀνὴρ ἠδὲ γυνή* Od. 6. 184: ἀνέρες ἠδὲ γυναῖκες* Il. 15. 683, Od. 15. 163: ϲφίϲιν ἐργάζεϲθαι Od. 14. 272 = 17. 441: ἐργάζοντο*
Od. 24. 210   140 πρόφρων* Il. 1. 543 etc.: παναφήλικα* παῖδα Il. 22. 490: ἔργα
τέτυκται* Il. 22. 400, 24. 354   141–3 καί κε* . . . καί κε (tertio versu) Od. 15.
313–15: ἐν ἀγκοίνῃϲιν Il. 14. 213 etc., Dem. 264: ὧδε νεογνὸς ἐὼν καὶ νήπιος Herm. 406
142 καλά* (adverb.) Ap.202, 516, Herm. 479 (in Homero semper medio versu):
δῶμα φυλάϲϲοις Od.5. 208   143 ϲτορέϲαι πυκινὸν λέχος Il. 9. 621 etc.: μυχῷ
θαλάμων ἐϋπήκτων* Od. 23. 41   144 δυῳαί· τὰς μέν τ' ἔργα διδάξαμεν ἐργάζεϲθαι Od. 22. 422 (Eurycleia loquitur; τ' om. Allen): ἔργα διδαϲκῆϲαι Hes. Op. 64
145 φῆ* (= dixerat) Il. 21. 361: ἦ ῥα* Il. 3. 355 etc.: φῆ ῥα* Hes. Th. 550 (∼
Herm. 212, 241): θεά* Dem. 34 (∼ Il. 10. 462 etc., voc.): ἡ δ' αὐτίκ' ἀμείβετο* Od. 4.
382 etc.: παρθένος ἀδμής* Od. 6. 109, 228   145 f. παρθένῳ ἀδμήτῃ μέγεθος καὶ
εἶδος ὁμοίη Aph. 82   146 Λαοδίκην, Πριάμοιο θυγατρῶν εἶδος ἀρίϲτην Il. 3. 124
(∼ 6. 252 etc.)   147 μαῖα* Od. 19. 482 etc.: θεῶν* Il. 1. 339 etc.: θεῶν . . .
δῶρα Il. 3. 65, 20. 265: δῶρα θεῶν Od. 18. 141: καὶ ἀχνύμενοί περ ἀνάγκῃ* Il. 12. 178
(∼ 15. 133)   147 f. ϲὺ δὲ τετλάμεναι καὶ ἀνάγκῃ Od. 13. 307: cf. Dem. 216–17
148 τέτλαμεν Od. 20. 311 (cf. 6. 190): πολὺ φέρτεροί εἰϲιν* Il. 10. 557 etc.

137 οἳ' ἐθέλουϲι τοκῆεϲ· ἔμ' αὖτ' Fontein: ἐμοὶ δ' αὖτ' εἴπατε κοῦραι Cobet: τοκῆες
. . . οἰκτείρατε M: τοκῆϲ . . . οἰκτίρατε West   lacunam post 137 statuit Allen
138 πρόϲτροπον ὦ φίλα Voss   τέωϲ Ruhnken   141 αἵ κεν Matthiae   ἔχουϲα
corr. ex ἔχουϲαν M   143 ἐϋπήκτων M: εὐπήκτων Wolf   144 'potuisset
κε omittere' Hermann   διαθήϲαιμι γυναικός M: διδαϲκήϲαιμι γυναῖκας Voss:
διαντλήϲαιμι γυναικός Mitscherlich: διαθλήϲαιμι γυναικός Ignarra: διαθρήϲαιμι
γυναικῶν Bothe: διαϲκήϲαιμι γυναικός Sikes: διαθρήϲαιμι γυναικός Allen (1936)
146 θυγατεράων M: corr. Ruhnken   147 ἠχνύμενοί M: corr. Ruhnken
147 f. ἀχνυμένοιϲ περ ἀνάγκῃ τετλάμεν ἀνθρώποιϲ Brunck

ταῦτα δέ τοι cαφέωc ὑποθήcομαι ἠδ' ὀνομήνω
ἀνέραc οἷcιν ἔπεcτι μέγα κράτοc ἐνθάδε τιμῆc,   150
δήμου τε προὔχουcιν, ἰδὲ κρήδεμνα πόληοc
εἰρύαται βουλῆιcι καὶ ἰθείηιcι δίκηιcιν·
ἠμὲν Τριπτολέμου πυκιμήδεοc ἠδὲ Διόκλου
ἠδὲ Πολυξείνου καὶ ἀμύμονοc Εὐμόλποιο
καὶ Δολίχου καὶ πατρὸc ἀγήνοροc ἡμετέροιο   155
τῶν πάντων ἄλοχοι κατὰ δώματα πορcαίνουcι·
τάων οὐκ ἄν τίc cε κατὰ πρώτιcτον ὀπωπὴν
εἶδοc ἀτιμήcαcα δόμων ἀπονοcφίccειεν,
ἀλλά cε δέξονται· δὴ γὰρ θεοείκελόc ἐccι.
εἰ δ' ἐθέλειc, ἐπίμεινον, ἵνα πρὸc δώματα πατρὸc   160
ἔλθωμεν καὶ μητρὶ βαθυζώνῳ Μετανείρῃ
εἴπωμεν τάδε πάντα διαμπερέc, αἴ κέ c' ἀνώγῃ
ἡμέτερον δ' ἰέναι μηδ' ἄλλων δώματ' ἐρευνᾶν.

149 coὶ δ' αὐτῷ πυκινῶc ὑποθήcομαι* Od. 1. 279: μυθήcομαι οὐδ' ὀνομήνω* Il. 2.
488   150 μέγα κράτοc* Il. 13. 486: cf. Theogn. 171 v.l. οἷc ἐcτι μέγα κράτοc
151 δήμου* Il. 17. 577 etc.: προὔχουcιν* Od. 10. 90: Τροίηc ἱερὰ κρήδεμνα*
Il. 16. 100, Od. 13. 388   151 f. ὃc Θήβηc κρήδεμνον ἔχει ῥύεταί τε πόληα
Hes. Sc. 105   152 εἰρύαται* Od. 6. 265: βουλῆιcι(ν)* Il. 13. 524, Dem. 9: ὃc
Λυκίην εἴρυτο δίκῃcί τε καὶ cθένεϊ ᾧ Il. 16. 542: ἰθείηιcι δίκηιcιν Hes. Th. 86 ~ Op. 36
(initio versus)   153–5 ἠμὲν . . . ἠδὲ . . . ἠδὲ . . . καὶ . . .* Il. 10. 109 f.
153 Τριπτολέμῳ* Dem. 474: πυκιμήδεοc* Od. 1. 438   154 f. πατρὸc ἀμύμονοc*
Od. 7. 29: Ἀγήνοροc* Il. 20. 474, 21. 595   156 τῶν πάντων* Il. 22. 424: ἄλοχοι*
Il. 8. 155 etc.: κατὰ δώματα* Od. 7. 102, 20. 122, Dem. 104: πορcαίνουcαι* Hes.
fr. 70. 8 (~ 43 (a). 69, 217. 5)   157 τάων οὔ* τιc Od. 2. 121: οὐκ ἄν τίc cε
Od. 19. 107: πρώτιcτον* Il. 2. 702, Herm. 35: ὀπωπῆc* Od. 4. 327   158 εἶδοc*
ἀμαλδύνουcα Dem. 94: εἰ δέ μ' ἀτιμήcουcι δόμον* κάτα Od. 16. 274: δόμων ἄπο*
Od. 3. 313, 15. 10: νοcφιccαμένη τόδε δῶμα Od. 21. 77: ἀπονοcφιcθῶcι Herm. 562
159 μάλα γὰρ θεοείκελοc ἔcται* Aph. 279   160 εἰ δ' ἐθέλειc ἐπίμεινον, ἐγὼ δ' εἰμὶ
προπάροιθε Od. 17. 277: πρὸc δώματα πατρὸc* Od. 4. 657 etc. (Dem. 107, 180)
160 f. ἔνθα καθεζόμενοc μεῖναι χρόνον, εἰc ὅ κεν ἡμεῖc | ἄcτυδε ἔλθωμεν καὶ ἱκώμεθα
δώματα πατρὸc Od. 6. 295 f.   161 ἔλθωμεν* Od. 22. 77: καὶ μητρὶ* Il. 14.
502 etc.: βαθυζώνουc* Il. 9. 594, Od. 3. 154 (cf. ad Dem. 95): εὔζωνοc (-ον)
Μετάνειρα(ν)* Dem. 212 etc.   162 ἤματα πάντα διαμπερέc, εἰ κέ μ'* Il. 16. 499:
ἀνώγῃ* Il. 9. 101 etc.   163 ἡμέτερον δ' ἐλθόντεc Od. 8. 39: ἄλλων* Il. 1. 198
etc.: δώματ'* Il. 1. 18 etc.: ἐρεύνα* Od. 22. 180 (~ Il. 18. 321).

151 πόληοc corr. ex πόλιοc M   ante 153 vers. 156 collocabat Schneider
153–4 ἠ μὲν . . . ἠ δὲ . . . ἠ δὲ M: corr. Matthiae   154 f. ἀμύμονοc . . . ἀγήνοροc M:
transposuit Ruhnken: cf. Paus. 1. 38. 2 Ὁμήρῳ δὲ ἐc μὲν τὸ γένοc ἐcτὶν οὐδὲ αὐτοῦ
πεποιημένον, ἐπονομάζει δὲ ἀγήνορα ἐν τοῖc ἔπεcι τὸν Εὔμολπον   155 δολιχοῦ M:
corr. Voss   157 ὀπωπῆc Ignarra   158 ἀπονοcφίccειεν M: corr. Matthiae
159 versum interpolatum censebat Mitscherlich   160 δὲ θέλειc M: δ' ἐθέλειc
Hermann (cf. Dem. 45, 137, 193)   ἕωc πρὸc Brunck   162 ἀνώγει M: ἀνώγῃ
Fontein: ἀνώγοι Brunck

τηλύγετος δέ οἱ υἱὸς ἐνὶ μεγάρῳ εὐπήκτῳ
ὀψίγονος τρέφεται, πολυεύχετος ἀσπάσιός τε.   165
εἰ τόν γ᾽ ἐκθρέψαιο καὶ ἥβης μέτρον ἵκοιτο
ῥεῖά κέ τίς σε ἰδοῦσα γυναικῶν θηλυτεράων
ζηλώσαι· τόσα κέν τοι ἀπὸ θρεπτήρια δοίη.
Ὣς ἔφαθ᾽· ἡ δ᾽ ἐπένευσε καρήατι, ταὶ δὲ φαεινὰ
πλησάμεναι ὕδατος φέρον ἄγγεα κυδιάουσαι.   170
ῥίμφα δὲ πατρὸς ἵκοντο μέγαν δόμον, ὦκα δὲ μητρὶ
ἔννεπον ὡς εἶδόν τε καὶ ἔκλυον. ἡ δὲ μάλ᾽ ὦκα
ἐλθούσας ἐκέλευε καλεῖν ἐπ᾽ ἀπείρονι μισθῷ.
αἱ δ᾽ ὥς τ᾽ ἢ ἔλαφοι ἢ πόρτιες ἤαρος ὥρῃ
ἄλλοντ᾽ ἂν λειμῶνα κορεσσάμεναι φρένα φορβῇ,   175

164 τηλύγετος (etc.) in Hom. in secundo vel quinto pede (Il. 3. 175 etc.; cf. Dem.
283)   164 f. ὅς μοι τηλύγετος τρέφεται θαλίῃ ἔνι πολλῇ (~ Dem. 248). | τρεῖς δέ
μοί εἰσι θύγατρες ἐνὶ μεγάρῳ εὐπήκτῳ Il. 9. 143 f. ~ 285 f. (cf. Praefationem, p. 32 n. 2)
165 Cf. Dem. 219–20   166–8 Cf. Dem. 221–3   166 θρέψαιο Od. 19. 368:
καὶ ἥβης μέτρον ἵκοιτο* Hes. Op. 132 (~ Od. 11. 317, 18. 217 etc.)   167 ἰδοῦσα*
Od. 5. 78: γυναικῶν θηλυτεράων* Od. 11. 386 etc. (Dem. 119, 222)   168 ζηλώσει
Hes. Op. 312: ἀπὸ θρεπτήρια δοῖεν* Hes. Op. 188: θρέπτρα . . . ἀπέδωκε Il. 4. 478,
17. 302   169 ὡς ἔφαθ᾽* Il. 2. 807 etc.: ἀνένευε καρήατι* Il. 22. 205 (~ 19. 405,
Hy. 1. 16): ἐπένευσα κάρητι Il. 15. 75, Dem. 466: φαεινός (etc.)* Il. 10. 156 (etc.)
170 πλησάμενος* δ᾽ οἴνοιο Il. 9. 224 (~ Od. 14. 87, 17. 603): ἐμπλήσας ὕδατος
Od. 9. 209: πέσον ἄγγεα* Od. 16. 13: κυδιόωντες* Il. 21. 519   171 ῥίμφα*
Il. 6. 511 = 15. 268 etc.: αἶψα δὲ δώμαθ᾽ ἵκοντο* Dem. 184: πατρός* Il. 2. 662 etc.
(Dem. 415): ἵκοντο* δόμον Od. 16. 335: μέγαν δόμον* Herm. 178: αἶψα δ᾽ ἵκοντο
φίλου πρὸς δώματα πατρός Od. 19. 458: ὦκα δέ* Il. 13. 671 = 16. 606: μητρί*
Od. 15. 127   172 ἔννεπον* Hy. 19. 29: εἶδον* Od. 11. 298 etc.: ὡς εἶδον Il. 5. 515
etc.: ἰδόμην οὐδ᾽ ἔκλυον* Il. 10. 47: αἱ δὲ μάλ᾽ ὦκα* Od. 3. 157, 176   173 ἐλθούσας*
Od. 10. 411 (cf. ad Dem. 174 f.): ἐκέλευε* Il. 5. 199 etc.: ἤνωγον καλέειν* Ap. 105:
ἐπ᾽ ἀπείρονα γαῖαν* Il. 7. 446 etc.: μισθῷ ἐπὶ ῥητῷ Il. 21. 445   174 οἱ δ᾽ ὥς τ᾽ ἢ
ἔλαφον* Il. 15. 271: πόρτιος Il. 5. 162: ἔαρος δ᾽ ἐπιγίγνεται ὥρη* Il. 6. 148: ἐν λειμῶνι
(~ Dem. 175) . . . ὥρῃ* Il. 2. 467 f. (simile): ἐν λειμῶνι . . . εἰαρινοῖσιν Hes. Th. 279
174–5 ὡς δ᾽ ὅτ᾽ ἂν ἄγραυλοι πόριες περὶ βοῦς ἀγελαίας | ἐλθούσας (~ Dem. 173) ἐς
κόπρον, ἐπὴν βοτάνης κορέσωνται, | πᾶσαι ἅμα σκαίρουσιν ἐναντίαι . . . Od. 10. 410–12
175 ἐν λειμῶνι* Il. 2. 461, 467 etc.: ἀν᾽ . . . λειμῶνα Dem. 417: ἐπεί τ᾽ ἐκορέσσατο
φορβῆς* Il. 11. 562: κεκορημένον ἦτορ ἐδωδῆς Hes. Op. 593

164–5 ὀψιγόνοι τε καὶ ἀσπασί|οι …]ν ἐν μεγάροισιν Stesich. PMG 222. i. 2–3

164 εὐπήκτῳ M: εὐπήκτῳ Wolf (cf. ad 143)   165 versum eiciebat Matthiae
πολύευκτός τ᾽ Bücheler   166 γ᾽ ἐκθρέψαιο M: γε θρέψαιο Gemoll (cf. Dem.
221)   167 ῥεῖά M: ἦ ῥά Matthiae (cf. Dem. 222)   ῥεῖά σέ τίς κεν Brunck
168 ἀποθρεπτήρια M (cf. 223)   170 κυδιόωσαι Ruhnken   171 αἶψα δὲ
μητρὶ Mitscherlich   172 ὡς M: ὅσσ᾽ Ruhnken ('epicus poeta dicturus fuisset
ὅσσα ἴδον' Hermann)   εἶδον τε M: εἶδόν τε Hoffmann (Quaest. Hom. 2. 191)
173 καλέειν M: καλεῖν Ruhnken   174 ὥς τοι M: ὥς τ᾽ ἢ Brunck   ἤαρος M:
εἴαρος Ruhnken (cf. Dem. 401; Ap. 9)   175 ἄλλοντ᾽ M: corr. Ruhnken   φορβῇ
M: φορβῆς Voss

ὡς αἱ ἐπισχόμεναι ἑανῶν πτύχας ἱμεροέντων
ἤϊξαν κοίλην κατ' ἀμαξιτόν, ἀμφὶ δὲ χαῖται
ὤμοις ἀίσσοντο κροκηΐῳ ἄνθει ὁμοῖαι.
τέτμον δ' ἐγγὺς ὁδοῦ κυδρὴν θεὸν ἔνθα πάρος περ
κάλλιπον· αὐτὰρ ἔπειτα φίλα πρὸς δώματα πατρὸς   180
ἡγεῦνθ', ἡ δ' ἄρ' ὄπισθε φίλον τετιημένη ἦτορ
στεῖχε κατὰ κρῆθεν κεκαλυμμένη, ἀμφὶ δὲ πέπλος
κυάνεος ῥαδινοῖσι θεᾶς ἐλελίζετο ποσσίν.
αἶψα δὲ δώμαθ' ἵκοντο διοτρεφέος Κελεοῖο,
βὰν δὲ δι' αἰθούσης ἔνθα σφίσι πότνια μήτηρ   185
ἧστο παρὰ σταθμὸν τέγεος πύκα ποιητοῖο
παῖδ' ὑπὸ κόλπῳ ἔχουσα νέον θάλος· αἱ δὲ παρ' αὐτὴν
ἔδραμον, ἡ δ' ἄρ' ἐπ' οὐδὸν ἔβη ποσὶ καί ῥα μελάθρου
κῦρε κάρη, πλῆσεν δὲ θύρας σέλαος θείοιο.

176 βῆ δὲ κατασχομένη ἑανῷ ἀργῆτι φαεινῷ Il. 3. 411: πτύχας* Il. 11. 77, Od. 19.
432: ἱμερόεντος* Il. 14. 170   177 ἤϊξαν* πεδίονδε Od. 15. 183: κατ' ἀμαξιτόν*
Il. 22. 146 (~ Parm. 1. 21)   177 f. ἀμφὶ δὲ χαῖται | ὤμοις ἀίσσονται* Il. 6. 509f.
= 15. 266 f.: χαῖται δ' ἐρρώοντο μετὰ πνοιῆς ἀνέμοιο Il. 23. 367   178 ὑακινθίνῳ
ἄνθει ὁμοίας* Od. 6. 231 = 23. 158: κουρήϊον ἄνθος* Dem. 108   179 τέτμε
δέ* Dem. 342: οὐδ'... ἔτετμεν... ἔνθα πάρος περ* Od. 5. 81 f.: ἐγγὺς ὁδοῖο* Od.
13. 268, Dem. 98: κυδρὴν θεόν* Dem. 292, Hy. 28. 1: κυδρὴ θεός* Hes. Th. 442
180 κάλλιπον* Od. 22. 156: κάλλιπες, αὐτάρ* Il. 21. 414: κάλλιπεν* (ante pausam)
Od. 1. 243: αὐτὰρ ἔπειτα* Il. 3. 335 etc.: φίλα πρὸς δώματα πατρός* Dem. 107
181 ἡγεῖτ' (ante pausam) Il. 12. 28, 24. 96: ὁ δ' ὄπισθε* Il. 9. 332: φίλον τετιημένη
ἦτορ* Dem. 98 etc.   182 κατὰ κρῆθεν Il. 16. 548, Od. 11. 588, Hes. fr. 23 (a). 23:
κατὰ κρῆθεν δὲ καλύπτρην Hes. Th. 574 (cf. ad Dem. 197): ἀπὸ κρῆθεν* Hes. Sc. 7:
κεκαλυμμένος* Il. 16. 360 etc.: ἀμφὶ δὲ πέπλοι* Il. 5. 194   183 κυάνεος* Il. 11. 39
(cf. ad Dem. 42): ῥαδινήν* Il. 23. 583: θεᾶς* Il. 2. 182 etc.: ἐλελίζετ'* Hy. 28. 9:
ποσσίν* Il. 7. 212 etc.   184 αἶψα δ' ἔπειθ' ἵκοντο* Il. 5. 367, Od. 15. 193: δώμαθ'
ἵκοντο* Od. 3. 388: διοτρεφέος Κεάδαο* Il. 2. 847   185 βὰν δ'* ἴμεναι διὰ δῶμα
Od. 18. 341: βὰν δ'* ἴμεν ἔνθα Il. 13. 789: αἰθούσης* Od. 4. 297 etc.: πότνια μήτηρ*
Il. 1. 357 etc.   186 ἧστο* Il. 6. 234 etc.: στῆ ῥα παρὰ σταθμὸν τέγεος πύκα
ποιητοῖο Od. 1. 333 etc.   187 παῖδ' ἐπὶ κόλπῳ ἔχουσα* Il. 6. 400: ὑπὸ κόλπῳ
Od. 15. 469: φίλον θάλος* Il. 22. 87 (cf. Dem. 66)   188 ἔδραμον* Il. 18. 30:
προσέβαν ποσίν* Ap. 520: ὑπὲρ οὐδὸν ἐβήσετο* Od. 7. 135, 13. 63: οὐδοῦ ἐπεμβεβαώς
Il. 9. 582: αὖτις ἐπ' οὐδὸν ἰών Od. 17. 413   188 f. cf. Aph. 173 ff. ἕστη ἄρα
κλισίῃ, εὐποιήτοιο μελάθρου | κῦρε κάρη, κάλλος δὲ παρειάων ἀπέλαμπεν | ἄμβροτον
189 πλῆσεν* Il. 17. 696 etc.: θύρας* Il. 6. 89 etc.: θείοιο* Il. 2. 335 etc.

177 τρώχων εὐρεῖαν κατ' ἀμαξιτόν* A.R. 3. 874 (cf. ad Dem. 176)

176 ἀνασχόμεναι Brunck (cf. A.R. 4. 940)   ἑανῶν M: corr. Matthiae   179 θεὰν
M: θεὸν Voss (cf. Dem. 1)   180 φίλου Matthiae (cf. Dem. 107)   182 κατ'
ἄκρηθεν M: κατὰ κρῆθεν Voss   183 θεῆς M: θεᾶς Hermann (cf. Dem. 279)
187 ὑπὸ M: ἐπὶ Gemoll   188–211 a primo poeta abiudicaverunt Preller,
alii: 195–205 reiecit Bergk, 202–5 Matthiae, Hermann, K. Francke   189 πλῆσε
M: πλῆσεν Hermann: πλῆσθεν δὲ θύραι Voss (cf. Dem. 280)

τὴν δ' αἰδώς τε σέβας τε ἰδὲ χλωρὸν δέος εἷλεν·   190
εἶξε δέ οἱ κλισμοῖο καὶ ἑδριάασθαι ἄνωγεν.
ἀλλ' οὐ Δημήτηρ ὡρηφόρος ἀγλαόδωρος
ἤθελεν ἑδριάασθαι ἐπὶ κλισμοῖο φαεινοῦ,
ἀλλ' ἀκέουσα ἔμιμνε κατ' ὄμματα καλὰ βαλοῦσα,
πρίν γ' ὅτε δή οἱ ἔθηκεν Ἰάμβη κέδν' εἰδυῖα   195
πηκτὸν ἕδος, καθύπερθε δ' ἐπ' ἀργύφεον βάλε κῶας.
ἔνθα καθεζομένη προκατέσχετο χερσὶ καλύπτρην·
δηρὸν δ' ἄφθογγος τετιημένη ἧστ' ἐπὶ δίφρου,
οὐδέ τιν' οὔτ' ἔπεϊ προσπτύσσετο οὔτε τι ἔργῳ,
ἀλλ' ἀγέλαστος ἄπαστος ἐδητύος ἠδὲ ποτῆτος   200
ἧστο πόθῳ μινύθουσα βαθυζώνοιο θυγατρός,
πρίν γ' ὅτε δὴ χλεύῃς μιν Ἰάμβη κέδν' εἰδυῖα

190 τε ... τε ἰδέ* Il. 12. 311 etc.: τοὺς δὲ χλωρὸν δέος εἷλεν* Od. 24. 533 (deae
voce audita): σέβας μ' ἔχει Od. 3. 123 etc.: ἴσχε γὰρ αἰδὼς | καὶ δέος Il. 15. 657 f.
191 εἷσεν δ' ἐν κλισμοῖσι* Il. 9. 200: τῷ δ' ἕδρης ἐπιόντι πατὴρ ὑπόειξεν Ὀδυσσεύς
Od. 16. 42: εἶξε δ' Ἀθήνη Il. 24. 100: καὶ ἑδριάασθαι ἄνωγεν* Od. 3. 35 (~ Il. 11. 646
= 778)   192 cf. Dem. 54   193 ἤθελεν* Od. 4. 287 etc., Dem. 45: ἐπὶ θρόνου
ἷζε φαεινοῦ* Il. 18. 422 (~ Od. 7. 169)   194 ἀλλ' ἀκέουσα* κάθησο Il. 1. 565:
ἀλλὰ καὶ ὣς ἀνέμιμνε* Il. 16. 363: ὄμματα καλά* Od. 1. 208: κατ' ὄμματα καλὰ
βαλοῦσα* Aph. 156   195 πρίν γ' ὅτε δή* Od. 23. 43, Dem. 96, 202, Ap. 49:
ἔθηκε(ν)* Il. 6. 139 etc.: κεδνὰ ἰδυῖα* Od. 1. 428 etc.: Ἰάμβη κέδν' εἰδυῖα* Dem. 202
196 ὅθ' ἐπὶ μέγα βάλλετο κῶας* Il. 19. 58: ἐπ' αὐτῷ κῶας ἔβαλλεν Od. 19. 101:
κῶας ὕπερθεν Od. 16. 47   197 ἔνθα καθεζόμενοι* Il. 10. 202 (~ Od. 6. 295):
πρόχνυ καθεζομένη* Il. 9. 570: ἔνθα καθεζομένη* Dem. 303: ἔνθα κάθιζ' Ἑλένη
Il. 3. 426 (419 κατασχομένη): χερσί* Il. 3. 352 etc.: καλύπτρην* Il. 22. 406 etc.:
καλύπτρην ... κατέσχεθε Hes. Th. 574 f.: ἄντα παρειάων σχομένη λιπαρὰ κρήδεμνα Od.
1. 334 etc.   198 δηρὸν δ' ἄφθογγος* Dem. 282: δηρὸν* Il. 5. 120 etc.: ἧστο ...
τετιημένος Od. 1. 114 (~ Il. 9. 13, Dem. 98, Ap. 456): δὴν δ' ἄνεῳ ἧσαν τετιηότες
Il. 9. 30 = 695: ἀλλ' ἀκέων δὴν ἧστο Il. 1. 512 (~ Od. 23. 93): ἕζετ' ... ἐπὶ δίφρου*
Od. 17. 602   199 ταύτην δ' οὔτ' ἔπεϊ προτιβάλλεαι οὔτε τι ἔργῳ Il. 5. 879:
ποτιπτυσσοίμεθα μύθῳ Od. 2. 77 (~ 4. 647)   200 κεῖτ' ἄρ' ἄσιτος ἄπαστος
ἐδητύος ἠδὲ ποτῆτος Od. 4. 788   201 cf. Dem. 304: ἧστο* Il. 6. 324 etc.:
ἡνιόχοιο πόθῳ Il. 17. 439: μινύθει δέ τοι ἦτορ Od. 4. 374 (~ 467): βαθυζώνων* Dem.
95 (~ 161): θυγατρός* Od. 7. 290, 11. 421   202 cf. Dem. 195

190 τὴν δὲ μεταῦτις | αἰδώς τε στυγερόν τε δέος λάβε A.R. 3. 741 f.   198 ἑζομένη
δ' ἐπὶ δηρὸν ἀκὴν ἔχεν Mosch. Eur. 18 (cf. ad Dem. 282)   201 σεῖο πόθῳ μινύθουσα* A.R. 1. 286: πόθῳ τᾶς ἀποιχομένας ἀρρήτου κόρας E. Hel. 1306 f.: πόθῳ δὲ
μητέρ' ἠφανισμένης κόρης Carcin. fr. 5. 4 (~ 8 f.)   202 ff. cf. Nic. Alex. 128 ff.
            τῷ δὲ σὺ πολλάκι μὲν γληχώ, ποταμηῖσι νύμφαις
            ἐμπλήδην κυκεῶνα πόροις ἐν κύμβεϊ τεύξας
            νηστείρης Δηοῦς μορόεν ποτόν, ᾧ ποτε Δηὼ
            λαυκανίην ἔβρεξεν ἀν' ἄστυρον Ἱπποθόωντος,
            Θρηΐσσης ἀθύροισιν ὑπὸ ῥήτρησιν Ἰάμβης.

192 ὡραφόρος M: corr. Ruhnken   194 ἀκέουσ' ἀνέμιμνε Voss   195 κεδνὰ
ἰδυῖα Hoffmann (Quaest. Hom. 2. 191)   196 κῶα M: corr. Ruhnken   199 οὔτε
ἔπει Hermann   202 χλεύῃσιν Hermann   κεδνὰ ἰδυῖα Hoffmann (cf. 195)

πολλὰ παρὰ σκώπτους· ἐτρέψατο πότνιαν ἁγνὴν
μειδῆσαι γελάσαι τε καὶ ἵλαον σχεῖν θυμόν·
ἢ δή οἱ καὶ ἔπειτα μεθύστερον εὔαδεν ὀργαῖς.   205
τῇ δὲ δέπας Μετάνειρα δίδου μελιηδέος οἴνου
πλήσασ᾽, ἡ δ᾽ ἀνένευσ᾽· οὐ γὰρ θεμιτόν οἱ ἔφασκε
πίνειν οἶνον ἐρυθρόν, ἄνωγε δ᾽ ἄρ᾽ ἄλφι καὶ ὕδωρ
δοῦναι μίξασαν πιέμεν γληχῶνι τερείνῃ.
ἡ δὲ κυκεῶ τεύξασα θεᾷ πόρεν ὡς ἐκέλευε·   210
δεξαμένη δ᾽ ὁσίης ἕνεκεν πολυπότνια Δηὼ

τῇσι δὲ μύθων ἦρχεν ἐΰζωνος Μετάνειρα·

203 ἔτρεψεν ἀδελφείου φρένας Il. 6. 61: κραδίη τέτραπτο νέεσθαι Od. 4. 260:
παρέτραπε Hes. Th. 103 (a luctu; cf. inf.): πότνιαν* Hes. Th. 11 (cf. West, p. 79
et ad loc.): πότνια* Il. 1. 357 etc.: ἀγνή* Od. 5. 123 etc.   204 μειδή-
caca* Il. 1. 596 etc.: γελάσαι* Od. 14. 465: cὺ δ᾽ ἵλαον ἔνθεο θυμόν* Il. 9.
639 (~ 19. 178): ὣς κέ τοι ἵλαον κραδίην καὶ θυμὸν ἔχωσιν Hes. Op. 340 (Op.
338 ~ Dem. 368)   205 αἰ δή οἱ καὶ ἔπειτα* Od. 21. 24: μετέπειτα . . . καὶ
ὕστερον* Il. 14. 310, 313 (~ Od. 12. 126): ἔπειτα* . . . μετόπισθεν Hes. Th. 210:
εὔαδεν* εὐνή Il. 14. 340: τοι εὔαδε* θυμῷ Od. 16. 28: ὀργήν* Hes. Op. 304
206 δέπας μελιηδέος οἴνου* (δόcκεν, δόc) Il. 18. 545, Od. 3. 46: δέπας* Il. 11. 631
etc.: δίδου* Il. 5. 165 etc.   207 πλησάμενος* δ᾽ οἴνοιο δέπας Il. 9. 224: ἡ δ᾽
ἐπένευσε* Dem. 169: δ᾽ ἀνένευε* Il. 22. 205: τῷ δ᾽ οὐ θέμις ἐcτί Il. 14. 386 (~ Od. 10.
73 etc.): ἔφασκε* Od. 7. 256   208 πίνειν* Od. 20. 249: οἶνον ἐρυθρόν Od. 5.
165 etc. (ad fin.): οἶνον* Il. 6. 264: καὶ ὕδωρ* Od. 1. 110 etc.   209 γληχῶνα
τέρειναν* Hes. fr. 70. 21 (cf. West, Glotta 41 (1963), 284)   210 τεύξει τοι κυκεῶ
Od. 10. 290 (~ 316): τοῖcι δὲ τεῦχε κυκειῶ Il. 11. 623: τεύξαca* Od. 11. 430: θεᾷ* Aph.
167: πόρε* Il. 1. 72 etc. πόρεν δέ οἱ ὅccα κέλευca* Od. 4. 745: ὡς ἐκέλευεν* Il. 23. 539
211 δεξαμένη* Od. 19. 255 (~ Il. 18. 44, nomen proprium): κἀγὼ τῆc ὁσίηc* ἐπιβή-
coμαι Herm. 173: ἐκ πάσηc ὁσίηc* Herm. 470: ἕνεκεν* Od. 17. 310: πότνια Δηὼ* Dem. 4
212 τοῖcι δὲ μύθων ἦρχε* Il. 5. 420 etc.: ἐΰζωνοc Μετάνειρα* Dem. 234 etc.:
ἐΰζωνοc παράκοιτιc* Il. 9. 590

211 πολυπότνια* Orph. Hy. 40. 16 (de Cerere)

203 παρασκώπτουσα τρέψατο M: παρασκώπτους᾽ ἐτρέψατο Voss: παρὰ cκώπτους᾽ i.e.
παρετρέψατο Heyne   204 ἵλαον σχεῖν θυμόν librario imputavit Franke: ἴ. cχέμεν
ἦτορ (cf. Orph. Hy. 35. 6) vel ὀργήν Mitscherlich: ἡ δ᾽ ἵλαον ἔνθετο θυμόν Heyne
205 ἤδη . . . ἔβαδεν M: corr. Ruhnken   versum damnavit Heyne: μεθύστερον etc.
librario adscripsit Franke: καὶ ἔτεια . . . εὔαδ᾽ ἑορταῖc Voss: ἔπειτα μεθίcταται vel μεθ-
ίcτατο αἰὲν ἑορταῖc Voss iuvenis   ὀργῇ Bücheler: ἐν ὀργίοιc Mitscherlich   207 τοι
M: γ᾽ οἱ Ruhnken: οἱ Hermann (Orphica, p. 780), Matthiae   208 ἀμφὶ M:
corr. Ruhnken   209 γλήχωνι M: γληχῶνι scripsi   τερίνη M: corr. Ruhnken
211 δ᾽ delevit Slothouwer, non interpungens post ἐκέλευε   ἐπέβη Voss:
ἔλαχεν Schaefer   πίε πότνια Franke: post 211 lacunam statuit Allen (cf. Puntoni),
e.g. ἔκπιεν, ἡ δὲ λαβοῦσα δέπας θέτο ἔνθ᾽ ἀνάειρε (vel ἔνθεν ἄειρε)

Χαῖρε γύναι, ἐπεὶ οὔ σε κακῶν ἄπ' ἔολπα τοκήων
ἔμμεναι ἀλλ' ἀγαθῶν· ἐπί τοι πρέπει ὄμμασιν αἰδὼς
καὶ χάρις, ὡς εἴ πέρ τε θεμιστοπόλων βασιλήων. 215
ἀλλὰ θεῶν μὲν δῶρα καὶ ἀχνύμενοί περ ἀνάγκῃ
τέτλαμεν ἄνθρωποι· ἐπὶ γὰρ ζυγὸς αὐχένι κεῖται.
νῦν δ' ἐπεὶ ἵκεο δεῦρο, παρέσσεται ὅσσα τ' ἐμοί περ.
παῖδα δέ μοι τρέφε τόνδε, τὸν ὀψίγονον καὶ ἄελπτον
ὤπασαν ἀθάνατοι, πολυάρητος δέ μοί ἐστιν. 220
εἰ τόν γ' ἐκθρέψαιο καὶ ἥβης μέτρον ἵκοιτο
ἦ ῥά κέ τίς σε ἰδοῦσα γυναικῶν θηλυτεράων
ζηλώσαι· τόσα κέν τοι ἀπὸ θρεπτήρια δοίην.
Τὴν δ' αὖτε προσέειπεν ἐϋστέφανος Δημήτηρ·
καὶ σὺ γύναι μάλα χαῖρε, θεοὶ δέ τοι ἐσθλὰ πόροιεν. 225
παῖδα δέ τοι πρόφρων ὑποδέξομαι ὥς με κελεύεις·

213-15 cf. Od. 4. 60 ff. cίτου δ' ἅπτεcθον καὶ χαίρετον (cf. ad Dem. 188 ff.) . . .
οὐ γὰρ cφῶν γε γένοc ἀπόλωλε τοκήων, | ἀλλ' ἀνδρῶν γένοc ἐcτὲ διοτρεφέων
βασιλήων | cκηπτούχων, ἐπεὶ οὔ κε κακοὶ τοιούcδε τέκοιεν: cf. Il. 14. 472, Od.
24. 252 f., Aph. 132 (Hy. 7. 11 f.)   213 χαῖρε γύναι* Od. 11. 248: οὔ cε ἔολπα
κακὸν καὶ ἄναλκιν ἔcεcθαι Od. 3. 375: ἔολπα* Il. 20. 186   214 αἰδὼc . . .
μετὰ δὲ πρέπει* Od. 8. 172 (= Hes. Th. 92): αἰδώc* Il. 15. 129 etc.   214 f. οὐδέ
τί τοι δούλειον ἐπιπρέπει εἰcοράαcθαι | εἶδοc καὶ μέγεθοc· βασιλῆι γὰρ ἀνδρὶ ἔοικαc
Od. 24. 252 f.   215 θεμιστοπόλων βασιλήων* Dem. 103   216-17 cf. Dem.
147-8   216 ἀλλὰ θεοὶ* Od. 20. 195 (cf. ad Dem. 213 ff.)   217 καὶ ἐπὶ
ζυγὸν αὐχένι θεῖναι Hes. Op. 815: ἐπὶ ζυγὸν αὐχένι κεῖται* Theognis 1357 (transl.;
cf. 1023)   218 νῦν δ' ἐπεὶ* . . . ἱκάνεις Od. 6. 191 : νῦν δὲ cεῦ εἵνεκα δεῦρο* . . .
ἱκάνω Il. 14. 309: παρέσσεται* Il. 1. 213 etc.   219 παῖδα δ' ἐμοί* Il. 1. 20:
παῖδα δέ τοι* . . . θρέψω Dem. 226 f.: παῖδα δὲ ὡc ἀτίταλλε Od. 18. 323 : ἀέλπτοιc*
Aph. 91   220 ὤπαcαν* Il. 6. 157 etc.: ὤπαcαν ἀθάνατοι Solon, fr. 1. 74: πολυάρητος δέ τοί ἐστιν* Od. 19. 404 (~ Il. 24. 620)   221-3 cf. Dem. 166-8
224 τὸν δ' αὖτε προσέειπεν ἐϋστέφανος κελαδεινή Il. 21. 511: ἐϋστέφανος Δημήτηρ*
Hes. Op. 300 (v.l. ἐϋπλόκαμος), Dem. 307 etc.   225 καὶ cὺ φίλος μάλα χαῖρε, θεοὶ
δέ τοι ὄλβια δοῖεν Od. 8. 413 (~ 24. 402 = Ap. 466, Od. 18. 122-3 = 20. 199-200)
226 παῖδα δέ μοι* Dem. 219: ὁ δέ οἱ πρόφρων ὑπέδεκτο Od. 2. 387 (~ Il. 9. 480 etc.):
ᾧ πρόφρων* γε θεὰ ὑποδέξεται εὐχάς Hes. Th. 419: θεὰ πρόφρων ὑπεδέξατο* Parm.
fr. 1. 22: ὥς με κελεύεις* Od. 11. 507

213-15 Ruhnken contulit Theocr. 25. 38 ff.: ἐπεὶ οὔ cέ γέ φημι κακῶν ἐξ (~
Il. 14. 472) | ἔμμεναι οὐδὲ κακοῖcιν ἐοικότα φύμεναι αὐτόν, | οἷόν τοι μέγα εἶδος
ἐπιπρέπει (~ Od. 24. 252 f.). ἦ ῥά νυ παῖδεc | ἀθανάτων τοιοίδε μετὰ θνητοῖcιν ἔαcι

214 ἐπεί τοι M: corr. Ruhnken   εἶδοc Mitscherlich (cf. ad Dem. 213 ff.,
Theocr. 25. 40)   215 χάρις corr. ut vid. ex χάρος M   220 πολυήρατος M:
corr. Ruhnken   221 γε θρέψαιο M: γ' ἐκθρέψαιο Hermann (cf. Dem. 166)
222 ῥεῖά κε Hermann: ῥεῖά cέ τίc κεν Brunck (cf. Dem. 167)   223 ἀποθρεπτήρια
M (cf. Dem. 168)   δοίη Matthiae (cf. 168)

E

θρέψω, κού μιν ἔολπα κακοφραδίῃσι τιθήνης
οὔτ' ἄρ' ἐπηλυσίη δηλήσεται οὔθ' ὑποταμνόν·
οἶδα γὰρ ἀντίτομον μέγα φέρτερον ὑλοτόμοιο,
οἶδα δ' ἐπηλυσίης πολυπήμονος ἐσθλὸν ἐρυσμόν.   230
Ὣς ἄρα φωνήσασα θυώδεϊ δέξατο κόλπῳ
χερσίν τ' ἀθανάτῃσι· γεγήθει δὲ φρένα μήτηρ.
ὣς ἡ μὲν Κελεοῖο δαΐφρονος ἀγλαὸν υἱὸν
Δημοφόωνθ', ὃν ἔτικτεν ἐΰζωνος Μετάνειρα,
ἔτρεφεν ἐν μεγάροις· <u>ὁ δ' ἀέξετο δαίμονι ἶσος</u>   235
οὔτ' οὖν σῖτον ἔδων, οὐ θησάμενος

                                     Δημήτηρ

227 θρέψε μέν, οὐδ'* Od. 17. 293: οὔ σε ἔολπα* Od. 3. 375 (cf. ad Dem. 213):
κακορραφίῃσι* Od. 2. 236 (v.l. κακοφραδίῃσι): τιθήνης (etc.)* Il. 6. 467   228 ἔνθα
κε σὴ βουλὴ δηλήσεται* Il. 14. 102   229 οἶδα γάρ* Il. 4. 360 etc.: φέρτερος*
Il. 19. 217 etc.   230 ἦ γὰρ ἐπηλυσίης πολυπήμονος* ἔσσεαι ἔχμα Herm. 37
231 ὣς ἄρα φωνήσασα* Il. 8. 432 etc.: κηώδεϊ δέξατο κόλπῳ* Il. 6. 483: θυώδεα*
Od. 5. 264 etc.   231–5 cf. Hy. 26. 3–5 (de Baccho) ὃν τρέφον ἠΰκομοι νύμφαι
παρὰ πατρὸς ἄνακτος | δεξάμεναι κόλποισι, καὶ ἐνδυκέως ἀτίταλλον | ... ὁ δ' ἀέξατο
πατρὸς ἕκητι   232 χείρεσσ' ἀθανάτῃσι(ν)* Il. 16. 704, Dem. 253: ἀθανάτῃσιν
χερσίν* Ap. 125 (ἀθανάτοισι v.l.); cf. ad Dem. 236 ff.: γεγήθει δὲ φρένα* Il. 11. 682:
μήτηρ* Il. 1. 280 etc.   233 Κελεοῖο δαΐφρονος* Dem. 96: Πολύβοιο δαΐφρονος
ἀγλαὸν υἱόν* Od. 15. 519   234 τὸν ἔτικτε* Il. 16. 180: ἐΰζωνος Μετάνειρα*
Dem. 212 etc.: cf. Dem. 252   235 οὓς τρέφον ἐν μεγάροισι* Il. 22. 69: Τηλέ-
μαχος δὲ νέον μὲν ἀέξετο* Od. 22. 426: ὁ δ' ἀέξετο* Hy. 26. 5 (de Baccho nympharum
alumno; cf. Dem. 231, 235a): δαίμονι ἶσος* Il. 5. 438 etc.: ὁ δ' ἀέξετο δαίμονος αἴσῃ
Dem. 300   236 οὐ γὰρ σῖτον ἔδους', οὐ* πίνους' ... Il. 5. 341: γάλα θῇσθαι Od. 4. 89:
θήσατο μαζὸν Il. 24. 58: γάλα λευκόν* Il. 4. 434: ἡμετέρης γάλα μητρός* Herm. 267
236 f. cf. Ap. 123 ff.

               οὐδ' ἄρ' Ἀπόλλωνα χρυσάορα θήσατο μήτηρ,
               ἀλλὰ Θέμις νέκταρ τε καὶ ἀμβροσίην ἐρατεινὴν
               ἀθανάτῃσιν χερσὶν ἐπήρξατο ...(∼ Dem. 232)

            ─────────

231 θυώδεϊ κάτθετο μίτρῃ* A.R. 3. 867 (867a ∼ Dem. 254; 874 ∼ Dem.
176 f.); ᾧ ἐνὶ κόλπῳ | δέξατο (de nutrice Bacchi, ab igne abrepti) A.R. 4 1135 f.:
Ov. F. 4. 550 f.

                       gremio sustulit illa suo,
               terque manu permulsit eum, ter carmina dixit ...

            ─────────

227 θρέψαι· κού aut οὐδέ τί που Hermann: θρέψω τ'· οὔ aut θρέψασθ'· οὔ Voss:
lacunam post 226 statuit Bücheler   228 ἐπηλσίῃσι M: corr. Ruhnken (cf.
Dem. 230; -ιῃσι ex 227)   ὑποταμνὸν M: οὔτε τομαῖον Voss: οὔθ' ὑποτάμνων Ignarra:
ὑπόθαμνον, ὀρόδαμνος alii   229 οὐλοτόμοιο Voss, quod ipse interpretatur 'ad
perniciem succisum', Hermann 'penitus excisum'   232 χέρσι M: χερσίν Ruhnken:
χείρεσιν Ilgen: χείρεσσ' Cobet   ἀθανάτοισι M: ἀθανάτῃσι Ilgen   234 δημοφόονθ' M·
corr. Ruhnken   235 ἔτρεφ' ἐνὶ Voss   236 duos versus in unum coaluisse vidit
Mitscherlich: θησάμενος γάλα μητρός Hermann (cf. Herm. 267)   236A ἠματίη
μὲν γὰρ καλλιστέφανος Voss: ἀλλὰ γὰρ ἤματα μέν μιν ἐϋστέφανος Baumeister: ἀλλά
μιν ἠματίη μὲν ἐϋστέφανος Stoll (Fleckeisens Jahrb. 79, 231)

χρίεσκ' ἀμβροσίῃ ὡc εἰ θεοῦ ἐκγεγαῶτα,
ἡδὺ καταπνείουcα καὶ ἐν κόλποιcιν ἔχουcα·
νύκταc δὲ κρύπτεcκε πυρὸc μένει ἠῦτε δαλὸν
λάθρα φίλων γονέων· τοῖc δὲ μέγα θαῦμ' ἐτέτυκτο   240
ὡc προθαλὴc τελέθεcκε, θεοῖcι δὲ ἄντα ἐῴκει.
καί κέν μιν ποίηcεν ἀγήρων τ' ἀθάνατόν τε
εἰ μὴ ἄρ' ἀφραδίῃcιν ἐΰζωνοc Μετάνειρα
νύκτ' ἐπιτηρήcαcα θυώδεοc ἐκ θαλάμοιο
cκέψατο· κώκυcεν δὲ καὶ ἄμφω πλήξατο μηρὼ   245
δείcαc' ᾧ περὶ παιδὶ καὶ ἀάcθη μέγα θυμῷ,
καί ῥ' ὀλοφυρομένη ἔπεα πτερόεντα προcηύδα·
Τέκνον Δημοφόων ξείνη cε πυρὶ ἔνι πολλῷ
κρύπτει, ἐμοὶ δὲ γόον καὶ κήδεα λυγρὰ τίθηcιν.
Ὣc φάτ' ὀδυρομένη· τῆc δ' ἄϊε δῖα θεάων.   250

237 χρῖcέν τ' ἀμβροcίῃ* Il. 16. 680 (~ 670) : ποτάμοιό περ ἐκγεγαῶτι* Il. 21. 185
238 ἡδὺ μάλα πνείουcαν* Od. 4. 446 (de ambrosia)   239 νύκταc δ' ἀλλύεcκεν*
Od. 2. 105 : πυρὸc μένοc* Il. 23. 238 : δαλὸν . . . ἐνέκρυψε Od. 5. 488 : πυρὸc μένε[ι
pap. 12 Hes. Th. 867 (cέλαι πυρόc codd.)   240 κρύβδα* Il. 18. 168 : φίλων
τοκέων Il. 21. 587 : θαῦμα τέτυκτο* Il. 18. 549 (ἐτέτυκτο v.l.)   241 τελέθουcι*
Il. 12. 347 etc. : θεοῖcι γὰρ ἄντα ἐῴκει* Il. 24. 630   242 ποίηcεν* Il. 1. 608 etc. :
ἀγήρων ἀθανάτην τε* Il. 2. 447 (~ 12. 323, 17. 444)   243 ἀφραδίῃcιν* Il. 5. 649,
Dem. 258 : ἐΰζωνοc Μετάνειρα* Dem. 212 etc.   244 νύκτα* Il. 10. 41 etc. :
θαλάμοιο θυώδεοc* Od. 4. 121 : θυώδεοc ἐκ θαλάμοιο* Dem. 288 (~ 331, 355, 385)
245-7 ~ Il. 15. 397-8 = Od. 13. 198-9 :
    ᾤμωξέν τ' ἄρ' ἔπειτα καὶ ὣ πεπλήγετο μηρὼ
    χερcὶ καταπρηνέcc', ὀλοφυρόμενοc δ' ἔποc ηὔδα
246 δείcαc* Il. 3. 37 etc. : φίλῳ περὶ παιδί* Il. 16. 568 : καὶ μέγ' ἀάcθη Il. 16. 685
etc. : ἀάcατο δὲ μέγα θυμῷ* Il. 11. 340 : ἀάcατο δὲ μέγα θυμῷ* Il. 9. 537 (538 ~
Dem. 251) : ἀάcατ]ο μέγα θυμῷ* Hes. fr. 25. 20   247 = Il. 18. 72 etc.
248 τέκνον* Il. 1. 362 etc. : ξεῖνοι (etc.)* Il. 6. 224 (etc.) : ἐν πυρὶ πολλῷ* Od. 12.
237 : θαλίη ἔνι πολλῇ* Il. 9. 143 (~ 285 ; 143a ~ Dem. 164 f., 144b ~ Dem. 164b)
249 κρύψαι* (etc.) Il. 18. 397 (etc.) : πατέρι δὲ γόον καὶ κήδεα λυγρά Il. 5. 156 : πόνον
καὶ κήδεα θῆκεν Il. 21. 525 (~ 23. 306) : τίθηcι* Il. 4. 83 etc.   250 λίccετ'
ὀδυρομένη* Il. 9. 591 : ἄϊε* Il. 10. 532 : δῖα θεάων* Dem. 63 etc.

237 ἤματα δ' αὖτε | ἀμβροcίῃ χρίεcκε A.R. 4. 870 f.

240-1 uncis inclusit Bücheler ('adscripti olim fortasse ad 235') : 'κρύβδα φίλων
τοκέων Homerus dixisset' Voss : λάθρα ἑῶν Spitzner   θαῦμα τέτυκτο Hermann (cf.
Il. 18. 549)   241 γὰρ ἄντα Voss : δέ τ' ἄ. Gemoll   242 ἀγήρων τ' M : ἀγήραον
Voss, qui tamen καί κεν ἀγήρων μιν ποίηcατο ἀθάνατόν τε maluit   248-9 cit. pap.
1 (Orph. fr. 49. 92-4)   248 πυρῇ ἔνι πο]λλῇ pap. 1 ('nescio an recte' Allen) : cf.
Bücheler (ap. Berl. Klass. Texte, V. 1) 'p lehrt erst die richtige Verbesserung' : cε μὲν
ἐν πυρί Voss : c' ἤδ' ἐν πυρὶ Hermann : cε πυρὸc μένει οὔλῳ Schneidewin (cf. Dem. 239)

τῇ δὲ χολωσαμένη καλλιστέφανος Δημήτηρ
παῖδα φίλον, τὸν ἄελπτον ἐνὶ μεγάροισιν ἔτικτε,
χείρεcc᾽ ἀθανάτῃcιν ἀπὸ ἕο θῆκε πέδον δὲ
ἐξανελοῦcα πυρὸς θυμῷ κοτέcαcα μάλ᾽ αἰνῶc,
καί ῥ᾽ ἄμυδιc προcέειπεν ἐΰζωνον Μετάνειραν·   255

✳ Νήϊδεc ἄνθρωποι καὶ ἀφράδμονεc οὔτ᾽ ἀγαθοῖο
αἶcαν ἐπερχομένου προγνώμεναι οὔτε κακοῖο·
καὶ cὺ γὰρ ἀφραδίῃcι τεῇc νήκεcτον ἀάcθηc.
ἴcτω γὰρ θεῶν ὅρκοc ἀμείλικτον Cτυγὸc ὕδωρ
ἀθάνατόν κέν τοι καὶ ἀγήραον ἤματα πάντα   260
παῖδα φίλον ποίηcα καὶ ἄφθιτον ὤπαcα τιμήν·
νῦν δ᾽ οὐκ ἔcθ᾽ ὡc κεν θάνατον καὶ κῆραc ἀλύξαι.

251 τὴν δὲ χολωcαμένη* Il. 3. 413 etc.: ἡ δὲ χολωcαμένη* Il. 9. 538 (cf. ad Dem.
246): καλλιcτέφανοc Δημήτηρ* Dem. 295   252 παῖδα φίλον* Il. 16. 460,
Od. 24. 103, Dem. 261; ἄελπτον Dem. 219 (etc.): ἔτικτον ἐνὶ μεγάροιcι* Il. 24. 417
253 χείρεcc᾽ ἀθανάτῃcι* Il. 16. 704, Dem. 232: ἀπὸ ἕο θῆκε χαμᾶζε* Od. 21. 136:
ἀπὸ ἕθεν ἧκε χαμᾶζε Il. 12. 205: εἶcι πέδον δέ* Il. 13. 796   254 κεκοτηότι θυμῷ
Il. 21. 456: κοτέουcα* Il. 23. 391: μάλ᾽ αἰνῶc* Il. 10. 38: κοτεccαμένη . . . θυμῷ
Il. 14. 191   255 ἡ δ᾽ ἄμυδιc* Il. 20. 114: ἐΰζωνοc Μετάνειρα* Dem. 212, 243
256 νήπιοι* ἀγροιῶται ἐφημέρια φρονέοντεc Od. 21. 85: νήπια ἄνθρωποι δυcτλήμονεc*
Ap. 532: cχέτλιοί ἐcτε θεοί, δηλήμονεc* Il. 24. 33 (~ Od. 5. 118): cf. ad Dem. 256 ff.
257 αἶcαν* Dem. 482: ἐπερχόμενον* Il. 1. 535 etc.: γνώμεναι* Il. 21. 266, 609;
κακοῖο* Il. 1. 284, Od. 3. 152   258 ἀφραδίῃcιν* Dem. 243: νήκεcτον ἀάcθη*
Hes. Op. 283   259 ἴcτω* Il. 10. 329 etc.: θεῶν μέγαν ὅρκον Od. 2. 377 etc.:
ὅρκον* Il. 19. 113 etc.: ἄγρει νῦν μοι ὄμοccον ἀάατον Cτυγὸc ὕδωρ* Il. 14. 271
(~ Il. 15. 37 f. etc.): ἀμείλικτον* Il. 11. 137, 21. 98   260 θήcειν ἀθάνατον καὶ
ἀγήραον ἤματα πάντα Od. 5. 136 etc. (~ Hes. Th. 305, fr. 23(a). 12, 24): cf.
Dem. 242   261 παῖδα φίλον* Dem. 252: ὤπαcα* Il. 13. 416: τιμήν* Il. 24. 57,
Dem. 311: τιμὴ δ᾽ ἄφθιτοc Dem. 263: ἄφθιτοc* (etc.) Il. 5. 724 etc.   262 νῦν δ᾽
οὐκ ἔcθ᾽ ὅcτιc (ὅc κεν Eust.) θάνατον* φύγῃ (φύγοι al.) Il. 21. 103: οὐκέτ᾽ ἔπειτ᾽
ἔcται θάνατον καὶ κῆραc ἀλύξαι Il. 21. 565 (~ Od. 17. 547 etc.)

---

252 παῖδα φίλον* A.R. 4. 874 (cf. ad Dem. 237 ff.)   258 ἀφραδίηcιν, | εἴ τί
περ ἀαcάμην A.R. 1. 1332 f. (~ 2. 313)   262 γῆραc ἀλάλκοι A.R. 4. 872

---

251 τὸν δὲ Bücheler (cf. ad 252): 251 post 252 Ludwich (250 τῆc . . . θεάων in
parenthesi, punctum post 252)   252 seclusit Bücheler   253 ἄπω ἕο M:
corr. Matthiae: ἀπὸ ἕο γ᾽ ἧκε Mitscherlich: ἀπὸ ἕθεν Cobet   254 spurium
iudicavit Matthiae, seclusit Bücheler: 'magis Homericum fortasse esset κοτέουcα'
Hermann   256–62 cit. pap. 1 (Orph. fr. 49. 95–100)   256–7 ἄφρονε[c]
ἄνθ[ρω]ποι δυcτλήμονεc [οὔτε κακοῖο ἐπ]ερ[χομένου πρ]ογνώμενεc οὔτ᾽ ἀ[γ]α[θοῖο
pap. 1   256 καὶ deleri voluit Hermann   257 προγνώμενοι M: πρ]ογνωμενεc
pap. 1: προγνώμεναι Matthiae   258 γ]αρ ἀβραδί[ηc   ]μοc πολυπειρατι νυ-
κτοc pap. 1   μήκιcτον M: νήκεcτον Voss   261 ποίηcαca M: corr. Ruhnken
καὶ M: τῷ Ludwich (cf. ad Dem. 263)   262 ἔcθ᾽ ὅππωc vel ἔcτ᾽ ἔθ᾽ ὅπωc,
et ἀλύξει Cobet   γῆραc Huschke   ἀλύξαι Ruhnken: ἀλύξῃ Bücheler

τιμὴ δ' ἄφθιτος αἰὲν ἐπέccεται οὕνεκα γούνων
ἡμετέρων ἐπέβη καὶ ἐν ἀγκοίνῃcιν ἴαυcεν.
ὥρῃcιν δ' ἄρα τῷ γε περιπλομένων ἐνιαυτῶν   265
παῖδεc Ἐλευcινίων πόλεμον καὶ φύλοπιν αἰνὴν
αἰὲν ἐν ἀλλήλοιcι cυνάξουc' ἤματα πάντα.
εἰμὶ δὲ Δημήτηρ τιμάοχοc, ἥ τε μέγιcτον
ἀθανάτοιc θνητοῖcί τ' ὄνεαρ καὶ χάρμα τέτυκται.
ἀλλ' ἄγε μοι νηόν τε μέγαν καὶ βωμὸν ὑπ' αὐτῷ   270
τευχόντων πᾶc δῆμοc ὑπαὶ πόλιν αἰπύ τε τεῖχοc
Καλλιχόρου καθύπερθεν ἐπὶ προὔχοντι κολωνῷ·

263 τιμή* Il. 2. 197: ἄφθιτον αἰεί Il. 2. 46 etc.: ἐπέccεται* Od. 4. 756: γούνων*
Il. 1. 407 etc.   264 ἡμετέρων* Od. 21. 292: ἐπέβη* Dem. 377: ἐν ἀγκοίνῃcιν
ἰαύειc* Il. 14. 213 (~ Od. 11. 261, Dem. 141)   265 ὥρῃcιν πάcῃcι* Aph. 102 (de
sacrificiis): περιπλομένων ἐνιαυτῶν* Od. 1. 16   266 παῖδεc* δὲ Τρώων Od. 11. 547:
παῖδεc* Ἀλωῆοc Il. 5. 586: Ἐλευcινίηc* Agallias post Il. 18. 551 (cf. ad Dem. 54):
πόλεμόν τε κακὸν καὶ φύλοπιν αἰνήν* Il. 4. 15 etc.   267 αἰὲν . . . ἤματα πάντα
Od. 5. 210 (~ Od. 8. 468, Ap. 485): cύναγον κρατερὴν ὑcμίνην Il. 14. 448 (= 16. 764)
268 εἰμὶ δέ* Od. 6. 196, Ap. 480, Hy. 7. 56 (~ Od. 9. 19, 11. 252): Δημήτηρ*
Dem. 54 etc.: τιμάοχοc Aph. 31: μέγιcτον* Il. 1. 525 etc.   268 f. ~ Aph. 31 f.
πᾶcιν δ' ἐν νηοῖcι θεῶν τιμάοχόc ἐcτι, | καὶ παρὰ πᾶcι βροτοῖcι θεῶν πρέcβειρα τέτυκται
269 ἀθάνατοι θνητοῖcιν* Od. 19. 593: πᾶcί τ' ὄνειαρ Il. 22. 433: θνητοῖc μέγ' ὄνειαρ
Hes. Th. 871 (~ Op. 822): χάρμα* βροτοῖcιν Il. 14. 325 (de Baccho), Ap. 25: μοῖρα
τέτυκται* Il. 3. 101   270 ἀλλ' ἄγε μοι Il. 10. 321 etc.: νηόν τε* Ap. 221, 245:
νηόν τε μέγαν Ap. 226   271 πᾶc δῆμοc* Il. 20. 166: ὑπὸ πτόλιν αἰπύ τε τεῖχοc*
Il. 11. 181   272 καθύπερθεν* Il. 2. 754 etc.: ἐπὶ προὔχοντι κολωνῷ Dem. 298:
ἐπὶ προὔχοντι μελάθρῳ Od. 19. 544: αἰπεῖα κολώνη* Il. 2. 811, 11. 711: ἱεροὺc ναίουcα
κολωνούc* Hes. fr. 59. 2

269 χάρμα τέτυκται* A.R. 4. 936: χαῖρε πάτερ μέγα θαῦμα μέγ' ἀνθρώποιcιν
ὄνειαρ Arat. Phaen. 15: χαῖρε, βροτοῖc μέγ' ὄνειαρ . . . Maced. Paean (Powell,
Coll. Alex. p. 139) 23: μᾶζαν, ἣν φερέcβιοc | Δηὼ βροτοῖcι χάρμα δωρεῖται φίλον
Antiphan. fr. 1. 2 f.   272 cκοπιῆc προὔχοντα κολωνόν* Orph. Arg. 379

263 ἄφθιτον M (cf. Dem. 261, Il. 2. 46 etc.): corr. Ruhnken   parum haec
convenire cum 261 animadvertit Mitscherlich: 263–4 post 267 Ludwich (cf.
Weber, Klio 21 (1927), 249)   265–7 seclusit Ilgen: lacunam ante 265 et
post 267 statuit Bücheler   265 ὥρῃ· cὺν δ' ἄρα τῷγε Ludwich: ὥρηcιν West
τοῦγε (ut esset 'matura eius aetate') Fontein   περιπλωμένων M: corr. Ruhnken
267 αἰὲν Ἀθηναίοιcι Matthiae   cυναυξήcουc' M: cυνάξουc' Ignarra: cυναύξουc'
Ruhnken: ἀέξουc' Voss: ἀλύξουc' Goettling   post 267 lacunam statuit Hermann
268 εἰμὶ δὲ Δη[μ]ήτηρ ὠρηφόρ[οc ἀγλαό]δωροc pap. 1 (Orph. fr. 49. 102–3)
269 θνητοῖcιν M: θνητοῖcί τ' Ruhnken: ἀθανάτων θνητοῖcιν Stoll   ὄνειαρ M:
ὄνεαρ Ilgen: ὄνειαρ χάρματ' ἐτύχθη vel ἐτύχθην Ruhnken: θνητοῖcί τ' ὄναρ Hermann:
θνητοῖc τ' ὄνειαρ (correpta media syllaba) vel ὄνιαρ καὶ χάρμα Buttmann, Voss
τέτυγμαι commemoravit Voss: 'ὄνειαρ πᾶcι τέτυγμαι decebat poetam' Bücheler
270 ἄγ' ἐμοὶ Voss: ἄγε μὴν Matthiae   271 ὑπὸ πτόλιν Voss

ὄργια δ' αὐτὴ ἐγὼν ὑποθήσομαι ὡς ἂν ἔπειτα
εὐαγέως ἔρδοντες ἐμὸν νόον ἱλάσκοισθε.
῍Ως εἰποῦσα θεὰ μέγεθος καὶ εἶδος ἄμειψε　　　　　　275
γῆρας ἀπωσαμένη, περί τ' ἀμφί τε κάλλος ἄητο·
ὀδμὴ δ' ἱμερόεσσα θυηέντων ἀπὸ πέπλων
σκίδνατο, τῆλε δὲ φέγγος ἀπὸ χροὸς ἀθανάτοιο
λάμπε θεᾶς, ξανθαὶ δὲ κόμαι κατενήνοθεν ὤμους,
αὐγῆς δ' ἐπλήσθη πυκινὸς δόμος ἀστεροπῆς ὥς.　　　280
βῆ δὲ διὲκ μεγάρων, τῆς δ' αὐτίκα γούνατ' ἔλυντο,
δηρὸν δ' ἄφθογγος γένετο χρόνον, οὐδέ τι παιδὸς

273 ἐγὼν ὑποθήσομαι αὐτός Od. 2. 194: ὑποθήσομαι... | ὥς κε ... Od. 5. 143 f.
274 εὐαγέως ἔρδοντες* Dem. 369: τεὸν μένος ἱλάσκωνται Dem. 368: εὐφραδέως
Od. 19. 352: ἔρδων ἱερὰ καλὰ κατὰ νόμον ἱλάσκηται Hes. Th. 417　　　275 ὡς
εἰποῦσα θεά* Il. 3. 139 etc.: μέγεθος καὶ εἶδος* (τε καὶ v.l.) Aph. 82: εἰδός τε μέγεθός
τε Il. 2. 58 etc.: ἄμειβον (etc.) Il. 14. 381 (etc.)　　　276 νεῖκος ἀπωσαμένους*
Il. 12. 276: γῆρας ἀποξύσας* Il. 9. 466: περί τ' ἀμφί τε Il. 17. 760, Hes.
Th. 848*, fr. 150. 28: θυμὸς ἄητο* Il. 21. 386: χάρις δ' ἐπὶ πᾶσιν ἄητο pap.
13 Hes. Th. 583 (cf. West ad loc.)　　　276-9 cf. Hes. fr. 43(a). 73 f. τῆς καὶ
ἀπὸ χρ]οϊῆς ἠδ' εἵματος ἀργυφέοιο | λάμφ' οἷόν τε] θεοῦ χαρίεν τ' ἀπὸ εἶδος ἄητο
277 θυηέντων ἐπὶ βωμῶν* Hes. Th. 557　　　277-8 ὀδμὴ δ' ἱμερόεσσα* ...
κίδνατο* Herm. 231 f. (228b ~ Dem. 386b)　　　278 σκίδναται* Il. 11. 308, Od.
7. 130 (~ Il. 17. 375): κίδνατο* Herm. 232: ἀπὸ χροός* Il. 4. 130 etc.: χροὸς
ἀνδρομέοιο* Il. 17. 571: ἀπ' ἀθανάτου χροὸς Hes. Th. 191: ἐκ κράατος ἀθανάτοιο
(de Iunonis capillis) Il. 14. 177　　　278 ff. ὀξέα· τῆλε δὲ χαλκὸς ἀπ' αὐτόφιν
οὐρανὸν εἴσω | λάμπ' Il. 11. 44 f.: τῆλε δὲ χαλκὸς | λάμφ' ὥς τε στεροπὴ Il. 10. 153 f.
(~ 11. 65 f.)　　　279 ξανθῆς δὲ κόμης* Il. 1. 197: ἐπενήνοθε* Il. 2. 219 etc.:
κατενήνοθεν ὤμους* Hes. Sc. 269　　　280 αὐγή* Il. 13. 341 (~ Dem. 35, Herm. 361):
ἐπλήσθη* Il. 20. 15: πυκινὸν δόμον* Od. 7. 81 etc.: ἀστεροπῇ ἐναλίγκιος Il. 13. 242 (~ 14.
386)　　　281 βὰν δὲ δι' αἰθούσης* Dem. 185: διὲκ μεγάρων* Dem. 379: διὲκ μεγάροιο
βεβήκει Od. 17. 61 (~ 10. 388 etc.): γούνατ' ἔλυσεν* Il. 5. 176 etc.: γυῖα λέλυντο*
Il. 13. 85: λύντο δὲ γυῖα* Il. 7. 16 etc.　　　281 ff. ~ Od. 4. 703 ff. ὡς φάτο, τῆς
δ' αὐτοῦ λύτο γούνατα καὶ φίλον ἦτορ (~ Od. 21. 114 etc.), | δὴν δέ μιν ἀμφασίη ἐπέων
λάβε ... (etc.)　　　282 δηρὸν δ' ἄφθογγος* Dem. 198: δηρὸν χρόνον Il. 14. 206, 305

274 εὐαγέως* A.R. 2. 699, 3. 1204　　　279 ἡ δέ οἱ κόμη ὤμους κατεσκίαζε καὶ
μετάφρενα Archil. fr. 31 West ~ Anacr. PMG 347　　　281 βῆ δὲ διὲκ μεγάλοιο*
... A.R. 3. 158 (μεγάροιο codd.; cf. ad Dem. 383)　　　282 ἔσχετο δ' ἀμφασίη δηρὸν
χρόνον* A.R. 3. 811 (cf. ad Dem. 237 ff.): ἑζομένη δ' ἐπὶ δηρὸν ἀκὴν ἔχεν Mosch. Eur.
18 (cf. Bühler, pp. 60 ff., 64 f.)

273 et 274 postea inlatos iudicavit Preller　　　'fuit qui οἷς mallet' Bücheler
274 ἔρδοντες M: ἔρδοντες Wolf (cf. 369)　　　νηόν M: corr. Ruhnken: 'melius μένος
368' Bücheler　　ἱλάσκοισθε M (priore sigma eraso): ἱλάσκησθε Schaefer　　275 μέγεθός τε καὶ Ruhnken　　　279 θεῆς M: θεᾶς Hermann (cf. 183): θεᾷ Voss　　ξανθὴ
δὲ κόμη Ruhnken　　　280 αὐτῆς M: corr. Ruhnken　　　281 δι' ἐκ M: διὲκ
Baumeister　γούνα λέλυντο tentavit Voss

μνήσατο τηλυγέτοιο ἀπὸ δαπέδου ἀνελέσθαι.

τοῦ δὲ κασίγνηται φωνὴν ἐσάκουσαν ἐλεινήν,
κὰδ δ' ἄρ' ἀπ' εὐστρώτων λεχέων θόρον· ἡ μὲν ἔπειτα   285
παῖδ' ἀνὰ χερσὶν ἑλοῦσα ἑῷ ἐγκάτθετο κόλπῳ,
ἡ δ' ἄρα πῦρ ἀνέκαι', ἡ δ' ἔσσυτο πόσσ' ἁπαλοῖσι
μητέρ' ἀναστήσουσα θυώδεος ἐκ θαλάμοιο.
ἀγρόμεναι δέ μιν ἀμφὶς ἐλούεον ἀσπαίροντα
ἀμφαγαπαζόμεναι· τοῦ δ' οὐ μειλίσσετο θυμός·   290
χειρότεραι γὰρ δή μιν ἔχον τροφοὶ ἠδὲ τιθῆναι.

Αἱ μὲν παννύχιαι κυδρὴν θεὸν ἱλάσκοντο
δείματι παλλόμεναι· ἅμα δ' ἠοῖ φαινομένηφιν
εὐρυβίῃ Κελεῷ νημερτέα μυθήσαντο,

283 μνήσατο* Od. 1. 29 (~ 4. 187) : τηλυγέτην (etc.)* Il. 3. 175 (etc.) : ἀνελέσθαι*
Il. 23. 823, Od. 21. 117 : ἀνελόντες ἀπὸ χθονός Od. 3. 453   284 κασίγνηται*
Il. 18. 52 : τὸν δὲ κασιγνήτη* Il. 21. 470 : φωνήν* Od. 4. 279 : οὐδ' ἐσάκουσε Il. 8. 97 :
ἐλεεινόν* Il. 24. 309 etc.   285 κὰδ δ' ἄρ'* ἐπ' ἀκτῆς Il. 23. 125 : ἀπὸ λέκτροιο
θορούσα Od. 23. 32 : ἐς λέχος εὔστρωτον Aph. 157 : στρωτοῖς ἐν λεχέεσσι Hes. Th. 798
286 παῖδ' ἐπὶ κόλπῳ ἔχουσ'* Il. 6. 400 (~ Dem. 187) : χερσίν* Il. 9. 171 etc. : ἑλοῦσα*
Il. 3. 424 etc. : ἑῷ ἐγκάτθετο κόλπῳ* Il. 14. 223   287 ἥ οἱ πῦρ ἀνέκαιε* Od. 7. 13
(~ 9. 251) : πόσσ' ἁπαλοῖσιν* Hes. Th. 3 (~ Il. 19. 92)   287-9 ~ Od. 20. 123
ἀγρόμεναι ἀνέκαιον ἐπ' ἐσχάρῃ ἀκάματον πῦρ (cf. ad Dem. 289 f.; Od. 20. 124 εὐνῆθεν
ἀνίστατο ~ Dem. 285)   288 μητέρ'* Il. 9. 451 : ἀναστήσας* Od. 8. 7 etc. : θυώδεος ἐκ
θαλάμοιο* Dem. 244   289 ἀγρόμεναι* Il. 7. 194 etc. (cf. ad Dem. 287-9) : κασίγνητοι
δέ μιν ἀμφὶς | ἵσταντ' Od. 7. 4 : ἀσπαίροντας* Il. 3. 293 (~ Ap. 128)   290 ἀμφαγα-
παζόμενος* Il. 16. 192 : μειλισσέμεν* Il. 7. 410 : θυμός* Il. 8. 202 etc. : ἀμφαγαπαζόμεναι . . . θυμός* Dem. 436   291 χειρότερος Il. 20. 436 (~ 15. 513) : τροφός
(etc.)* Il. 2. 361 etc. : τιθήνας (etc.)* Il. 6. 132   292 παννύχιοι* Il. 8. 508 etc. :
κυδρὴν θεόν* Dem. 179 : δεινὴν θεὸν ἱλάσκονται* Il. 6. 380 : πανημέριοι μολπῇ θεὸν
ἱλάσκοντο* Il. 1. 472   293 δεῖμα* Il. 5. 682 : παλλομένη κραδίην* ἅμα δ'* . . .
Il. 22. 461 (cf. ad Dem. 38 ff.) : παλλόμενος* Il. 24. 400 : ἅμα δ' ἠοῖ φαινομένηφι(ν)*
Il. 9. 618 etc.   294 Τρίτων εὐρυβίης Hes. Th. 931 : Εὐρυβίην* Hes. Th. 239 :
νημερτέα μυθήσασθε* Il. 6. 376

285 εὔστρωτον λέχος Alc. 283. 8 : ἡ δ' ἀπὸ μὲν στρωτῶν λεχέων θόρε δειμαίνουσα,
παλλομένη κραδίην Mosch. Eur. 16 f. (~ Dem. 293)   289 παῖδα φίλον σπαίροντα
A.R. 4. 874   291 τροφὸς ἠδὲ τιθήνη* Orph. Hy. 10. 18   293 δείματι παλλό-
μενοι* Orac. ap. Hdt. 7. 140. 3 : δείματι παλλομένην* A.R. 4. 572 (cf. ad Dem.
237 ff.) : δείματι παλλομένη* Nonn. D. 1. 56 : cf. Mosch. Eur. 161 f. (ad Dem.
285)

284 κασίγνηται M : corr. Ruhnken   ἐλεεινήν M : ἐλεινήν Ruhnken   κασιγνήτη
φωνὴν ἐσάκουσ' ἐλεεινήν Hermann   287 πυρὰν ἔκαι' M (cf. Od. 7. 13, 9. 251,
Hdt. 2. 39, Vit. Hom. Suda 111, n. ad Dem. 248) : corr. Ruhnken   289 ἐλούεον
suspectum habuit Ruhnken

ὡς ἐπέτελλε θεὰ καλλιστέφανος Δημήτηρ.   295
αὐτὰρ ὅ γ᾽ εἰς ἀγορὴν καλέσας πολυπείρονα λαὸν
ἤνωγ᾽ ἠϋκόμῳ Δημήτερι πίονα νηὸν
ποιῆσαι καὶ βωμὸν ἐπὶ προὔχοντι κολωνῷ.
οἱ δὲ μάλ᾽ αἶψ᾽ ἐπίθοντο καὶ ἔκλυον αὐδήσαντος,
τεῦχον δ᾽ ὡς ἐπέτελλ᾽· ὁ δ᾽ ἀέξετο δαίμονος αἴσῃ.   300
αὐτὰρ ἐπεὶ τέλεσαν καὶ ἐρώησαν καμάτοιο,
βάν ῥ᾽ ἴμεν οἴκαδ᾽ ἕκαστος· ἀτὰρ ξανθὴ Δημήτηρ
ἔνθα καθεζομένη μακάρων ἀπὸ νόσφιν ἁπάντων
μίμνε πόθῳ μινύθουσα βαθυζώνοιο θυγατρός.
αἰνότατον δ᾽ ἐνιαυτὸν ἐπὶ χθόνα πουλυβότειραν   305
ποίης᾽ ἀνθρώποις καὶ κύντατον, οὐδέ τι γαῖα
σπέρμ᾽ ἀνίει· κρύπτεν γὰρ ἐϋστέφανος Δημήτηρ.

---

295 ὡς ἐπέτελλεν Il. 11. 768, Od. 17. 186 (~ Dem. 300): θεά* Il. 1. 1 etc.:
καλλιστέφανος Δημήτηρ* Dem. 251   296 ἀλλὰ σύγ᾽ εἰς ἀγορὴν καλέσας* Il. 19. 34
(~ Od. 1. 272): δῆμος ἀπείρων Il. 24. 776: ἐπ᾽ ἀπείρονα γαῖαν* Il. 7. 446 etc.: πολὺν
ὤλεca λαόν* Il. 2. 115: λαὸς ἀπείρων Hes. Sc. 472   297 ἤνωγον* Od. 6. 216:
Δήμητρ᾽ ἠύκομον* Dem. 1: πίονα νηόν* Od. 12. 346   298 ποιῆcαι* Od. 1. 250
etc.: βωμόν* Il. 1. 440 etc.: ἐπὶ προὔχοντι κολωνῷ* Dem. 272   299 οἱ δ᾽
ἐπίθοντο* Il. 23. 249: τὸν δὲ μάλ᾽ αἶψ᾽ ἐνόησε* Il. 17. 116: οὐδ᾽ ἔκλυον αὐδήσαντος*
Il. 10. 47 (~ 16. 76 etc.)   300 ὡς ἐπέτελλεν* Od. 17. 186 (~ Dem. 295): ὁ δ᾽
ἀέξετο δαίμονι ἶσος* Dem. 235 (~ Hy. 26. 5): Διὸς αἴσῃ* Il. 9. 608 (~ 17. 321),
Ap. 433: δαίμονος αἶσα Od. 11. 61: θεῶν . . . αἴσῃ* Aph. 166   301 αὐτὰρ ἐπεί
ῥ᾽* ἐτέλεccε Od. 11. 246: ἐρωῆcαι πολέμοιο* Il. 13. 776, 19. 170 (~ 17. 422)
301 f. ~ Od. 7. 325 f. ἄτερ καμάτοιο τέλεccαν | . . . καὶ ἀπήνυcαν οἴκαδ᾽ ὀπίccω
302 βάν ῥ᾽ ἴμεν* Il. 10. 297, Dem. 484 etc.: οἴκαδ᾽* Il. 7. 79 etc.: ἕκαστος* Il. 9. 652
etc.: ἔβαν οἴκόνδε ἕκαστος Il. 1. 606 etc.: ξανθὴ Δημήτηρ* Il. 5. 500   303 ἔνθα
καθεζομένη* Dem. 197: μακάρων* Il. 24. 377 etc.: ἀπονόσφιν* Il. 1. 541 etc.: θεῶν
ἔκτοcθεν ἁπάντων* Hes. Th. 813 (~ Th. 277): ὁ δὲ νόσφι λιαcθεὶς | τῶν ἄλλων ἀπάνευθε
καθέζετο Il. 11. 80 f.   304 cf. Dem. 201   305 αἰνότατε* Il. 1. 552 etc.:
ἐνιαυτόν* Od. 4. 595, 11. 356: ἐπὶ χθόνα πουλυβότειραν* Il. 3. 265 etc.   305 f.
~ Dem. 90 αἰνότερον καὶ κύντερον*   306 ποίης᾽* Od. 14. 274, 19. 57: ἀνθρώποις*
Dem. 489, Ap. 259, Hes. Th. 296, 564 etc.: κύντερον* Od. 11. 427 etc.: γαῖα*
Il. 2. 95 etc.   307 σπέρμ᾽* ὑπὸ γῆς κρύπτουca Dem. 353: σπέρμα* Od. 5. 490:
ἀνίεις* Il. 5. 880: ἐϋστέφανος Δημήτηρ* Dem. 224 etc.

---

296 πολυπείρονας οἴμους* Orph. Arg. 33   300 δαίμονος αἴcᾳ Stesichorus,
P. Oxy. 2617 fr. 4 ii 8 f.: δαίμονος αἴcῃ* Orph. Arg. 1195 (de Proserpina a Plutone
rapta)

---

295 ὅcc᾽ Fontein (cf. 172)   296 πολυπείρονα 'vix sanum' Bücheler: πολυπάμονα
Gemoll (cf. Orph. Arg. 1063, ex coni. Gesner)   297 ἠνώγει . . . δημήτορι . . . ναόν
M: corr. Ruhnken   299 αἶψ᾽ ἐπίθοντο corr. ex αἶψα πίθοντο M   301 ἐτέλεccαν
M: corr. Valckenaer   302 βάν δ᾽ M: corr. Wyttenbach   304 θυγατρός
ex γυναικός corr. M   306 ἀνθρώποιcι M: corr. Ruhnken: ἀνθρώποις ἰδὲ Voss

πολλὰ δὲ καμπύλ' ἄροτρα μάτην βόες εἷλκον ἀρούραις,
πολλὸν δὲ κρῖ λευκὸν ἐτώσιον ἔμπεσε γαίῃ.
καί νύ κε πάμπαν ὄλεσσε γένος μερόπων ἀνθρώπων   310
λιμοῦ ὑπ' ἀργαλέης, γεράων τ' ἐρικυδέα τιμὴν
καὶ θυσιῶν ἤμερσεν 'Ολύμπια δώματ' ἔχοντας,
εἰ μὴ Ζεὺς ἐνόησεν ἑῷ τ' ἐφράσσατο θυμῷ.
Ἶριν δὲ πρῶτον χρυσόπτερον ὦρσε καλέσσαι
Δήμητρ' ἠΰκομον πολυήρατον εἶδος ἔχουσαν.   315
ὣς ἔφαθ'· ἡ δὲ Ζηνὶ κελαινεφέϊ Κρονίωνι
πείθετο καὶ μεσσηγὺ διέδραμεν ὦκα πόδεσσιν.
ἵκετο δὲ πτολίεθρον 'Ελευσῖνος θυοέσσης,
εὗρεν δ' ἐν νηῷ Δημήτερα κυανόπεπλον,
καί μιν φωνήσασ' ἔπεα πτερόεντα προσηύδα·   320
Δήμητερ καλέει σε πατὴρ Ζεὺς ἄφθιτα εἰδὼς

308 καμπύλα* *Od.* 9. 156, 21. 362: ἄροτρα* Hes. *Op.* 432: καμπύλ' ἄροτρα Sol. 1.
48: βόες* *Od.* 12. 355, 22. 299: εἷλκε* Herm. 116: ἄρουρα (etc.)* *Il.* 3. 115 etc.:
ἑλκέμεναι νειοῖο βαθείης πηκτὸν ἄροτρον *Il.* 10. 353 (~ 13. 32)   309 κρῖ λευκόν*
Il. 5. 196 etc.: ἐτώσιον* *Il.* 3. 368 etc.: ἔμπεσε* *Il.* 4. 108 etc.: ἐτώσια πίπτει ἔραζε*
Il. 17. 633   310 καί νύ κεν ἔνθ'... ἀπὸ θυμὸν ὄλεσσεν *Il.* 8. 90: οὐδέ τι πάμπαν |
ἤθελε λαὸν ὀλέσθαι *Il.* 13. 348–9: βίοτον δ' ἀπὸ πάμπαν ὀλέσσει *Od.* 2. 49: Ζεὺς δ'
ὀλέσει καὶ τοῦτο γένος μερόπων ἀνθρώπων Hes. *Op.* 180: γενεαὶ μερόπων ἀνθρώπων*
Il. 1. 250: μερόπων γένος ἀνδρῶν Hy. 31. 18   311 λιμῷ* *Od.* 12. 342: μνηστύος
ἀργαλέης* *Od.* 2. 199: νούσῳ ὑπ' ἀργαλέῃ* *Il.* 13. 667: νούσου ὑπ' ἀργαλέης*
Hes. *Sc.* 43: γεράων* τιμὴν δέ Hes. *Th.* 393: θεῶν ἐρικυδέα δῶρα* *Il.* 3. 65, 20. 265:
τιμήν* *Il.* 24. 57, *Dem.* 261   312 ἄμερσε* *Od.* 8. 64: 'Ολύμπια δώματ' ἔχοντες*
Il. 1. 18 etc.   313 Ζεύς* *Il.* 11. 752 etc.: Ζεὺς... ἐνόησε *Il.* 19. 112: ἐνόησε(ν)*
Il. 3. 396: ἐφράσσατο* *Il.* 24. 352, *Od.* 4. 529: θυμῷ* *Il.* 1. 24 etc.   314 Ἶριν...
χρυσόπτερον* *Il.* 8. 398, 11. 185: ὦρσε* *Il.* 13. 794 etc.: καλέσσαι *Il.* 3. 117 etc.
315 Δήμητρ' ἠΰκομον* *Dem.* 1: πολυήρατον εἶδος ἔχουσα* Hes. *Th.* 908: πολυήρατον* *Od.* 15. 366, 23. 354   316 Ζηνὶ κελαινεφεῖ* *Il.* 21. 520: κελαινεφέϊ
Κρονίωνι *Il.* 1. 397* etc.: Ζηνὶ κελαινεφέϊ Κρονίδῃ *Od.* 9. 552, 13. 25   317 πείθετο
Il. 22. 224: πείθεο* Herm. 378: καὶ μεσσηγύ* *Il.* 11. 573, 15. 316: διέδραμεν*
Hy. 19. 2: ὦκα* *Il.* 13. 671 etc.: πόδεσσι* *Il.* 11. 476 etc.: βῆ ῥα θέειν, ταχέως δὲ
διήνυσε πᾶν τὸ μεσηγύ (de Iride) Ap. 108: cf. *Il.* 24. 78 μεσσηγύς (cf. ad *Dem.* 321)
318 ἵκετο δ'* *Il.* 15. 84 etc.: πτολίεθρον* *Il.* 18. 512 etc.: 'Ελευσῖνος θυοέσσης
Dem. 97, 490: 'Ελευσῖνος... πτολίεθρον *Dem.* 356   319 εὗρεν δ'* *Il.* 1. 498
(~ 24. 83 etc.): Δημήτερα κυανόπεπλον* *Dem.* 442 (ex coni.), cf. 360, 374
320 = *Il.* 15. 35 etc.   321 καλέει σε* *Od.* 17. 553, *Dem.* 460: πατὴρ Ζεύς*
Il. 4. 235 etc.: καλέει Ζεὺς ἄφθιτα μήδεα εἰδώς* *Il.* 24. 88 (Iris loquitur)
321 f. ~ *Dem.* 460 f.

308 εἷλκον M: ἕλκον Allen   309 γαῖα M: corr. Ruhnken   312 θυσιῶν M:
θυέων Hermann (cf. *Dem.* 368)   313 ἑῷ δ' ἐφράσατο M: corr. Ruhnken, Ilgen
314 ἤρην M: corr. Ruhnken (cf. Ἥρην pro Ἶριν, Bentley ad Ar. *Av.* 575)
315 δημήτηρ' M: corr. Ruhnken (cf. *Dem.* 1)   317 μεσσηγὺ M: τὸ μεσηγὺ
Ilgen

ἐλθέμεναι μετὰ φῦλα θεῶν αἰειγενετάων.
ἀλλ᾽ ἴθι, μηδ᾽ ἀτέλεστον ἐμὸν ἔπος ἐκ Διὸς ἔστω.
Ὡς φάτο λισσομένη· τῆς δ᾽ οὐκ ἐπεπείθετο θυμός.
αὖτις ἔπειτα ⟨πατὴρ⟩ μάκαρας θεοὺς αἰὲν ἐόντας　　　325
πάντας ἐπιπροΐαλλεν· ἀμοιβηδὶς δὲ κιόντες
κίκλησκον καὶ πολλὰ δίδον περικαλλέα δῶρα,
τιμάς θ᾽ ἅς κεν ἕλοιτο μετ᾽ ἀθανάτοισι θεοῖσιν·
ἀλλ᾽ οὔ τις πεῖσαι δύνατο φρένας οὐδὲ νόημα
θυμῷ χωομένης, στερεῶς δ᾽ ἠναίνετο μύθους.　　　330
οὐ μὲν γάρ ποτ᾽ ἔφασκε θυώδεος Οὐλύμποιο
πρίν γ᾽ ἐπιβήσεσθαι, οὐ πρὶν γῆς καρπὸν ἀνήσειν,
πρὶν ἴδοι ὀφθαλμοῖσιν ἑὴν εὐώπιδα κούρην.
Αὐτὰρ ἐπεὶ τό γ᾽ ἄκουσε βαρύκτυπος εὐρύοπα Ζεύς
εἰς Ἔρεβος πέμψε χρυσόρραπιν Ἀργειφόντην,　　　335
ὄφρ᾽ Ἀΐδην μαλακοῖσι παραιφάμενος ἐπέεσσιν

322 ἐλθέμεναι μετὰ φῦλα θεῶν* Dem. 461: φῦλα θεῶν αἰειγενετάων* Dem. 36:
μετὰ φῦλα θεῶν αἰειγενετάων* P. Oxy. 2509. 10, 16 (cf. ad Dem. 67, 449)
323 ἀλλ᾽ ἴθι* Il. 1. 32: ἀτέλεστον* Od. 16. 111: ἐμὸν ἔπος* Il. 8. 8, Od. 24. 262: ἐκ
Διὸς* Il. 14. 19 etc.　　　324 ὡς φάτο λισσόμενος* Il. 16. 46: ἐπεπείθετο θυμός
Od. 2. 103 etc.　　　325 ἔπειτα πατήρ Il. 1. 544, Od. 24. 280: πατήρ* Il. 1. 579
(de Iove): μάκαρες θεοὶ αἰὲν ἐόντες* Il. 24. 99 etc.　　　326 ἐπιπροΐηλε Il. 11. 628:
ἀμοιβηδὶς δέ* Il. 18. 506, Od. 18. 310: κιόντες* Il. 19. 50 etc.　　　327 κίκλησκεν*
Il. 2. 404: περικαλλέα δῶρα* Od. 8. 420　　　328 τιμή* Il. 2. 197 etc.: τιμάς*
Dem. 366: ἅς κεν ἕλοιτο* Dem. 444: μετ᾽ ἀθανάτοισι θεοῖσι* ibid., Il. 21. 500 etc.
329 ἀλλ᾽ οὔτις δύνατο* Il. 3. 451: οὔτις δύνατο* Il. 11. 120: φρένας* Il. 1. 115 etc.:
φρένας, οὐδέ* Aph. 207 (~ Il. 1. 115 etc.): φρένες . . . οὐδὲ νόημα* Od. 18. 215, 220
(~ Il. 24. 40)　　　330 θυμῷ* Il. 10. 205 etc.: χωόμενοι (etc.)* Il. 21. 457 etc.:
αὐτὰρ ὅ γ᾽ ἠρνεῖτο στερεῶς* Il. 23. 42: ἠναίνετο Il. 18. 450: μύθους* Il. 1. 545: ὃς
δέ κ᾽ ἀνήνηται, καί τε στερεῶς ἀποείπῃ Il. 9. 510　　　331 ἔφασκε* Od. 8. 565 etc.:
θυώδεος Οὐλύμποιο* Herm. 322　　　332 πρίν γ᾽ ἀποπαύσεσθαι*, πρίν γ᾽ . . . Il. 5. 288:
καρπόν* Il. 3. 246: ἀνῆκεν* Il. 2. 71 etc.: καρπὸν ἀνῆκεν Dem. 471　　　333 πρίν
γ᾽ . . . ἐν ὀφθαλμοῖσιν ἴδηαι Il. 18. 135: οὐ . . . πρίν γ᾽ εἴα . . . | πρίν γ᾽* . . . ἐν ὀφθαλ-
μοῖσιν ἴδωμαι Il. 18. 189 f. (~ Od. 10. 383 ff.): ἴδοι τ᾽ εὐώπιδα κούρην* Od. 6. 113
334 αὐτὰρ ἐπεὶ τό γ᾽ ἄκουσε* Il. 20. 318 etc.: βαρύκτυπος εὐρύοπα Ζεύς* Dem. 3 etc.
334–5 εὐρύοπα Ζεύς | εἰς Ἔρεβος κατέπεμψε Hes. Th. 514–15　　　335 εἰς Ἔρεβος*
Od. 10. 528: πέμψῃς (etc.)* Il. 16. 445 etc.: χρυσόρραπις Ἀργειφόντης* Od. 10. 331,
Aph. 117　　　336 Ἀΐδης* Il. 5. 395: μαλακοῖσι καθαπτόμενος ἐπέεσσιν* Od. 10. 70:
ἐπέεσσι παραιφάμενος* Il. 24. 771: μαλακοῖσι παραιφάμενοι ἐπέεσσιν* Hes. Th. 90:
τὴν δὴ παρφάμεναι κοῦραι μαλακοῖσι λόγοισιν | πεῖσαν Parm. fr. 1. 15 f. (cf. ad Dem.
337 f., 379, 177, 226, Burkert, Phronesis 14 (1969), 1 ff.)

325 πατὴρ om. M: add. Valckenaer (cf. 345)　　　328 θ᾽ del. West (Philologus
110 (1966) 149), cf. Hes. Th. 412–13　　　κ᾽ ἐθέλοιτο μετ᾽ ἀθανάτοισιν ἐλέσθαι M:
κεν ἕλοιτο μετ᾽ ἀθανάτοισι θεοῖσι Hermann (cf. 444): κε βόλοιτο Allen (cf. Il. 11. 319)
329 ἠδὲ νόημα Brunck　　　331 ποτε φάσκε M: corr. Hermann　　　332 ἐπιβήσεσθ᾽
M: corr Voss　　　οὐ M: ἦ Voss　　　333 πρὶν corr. ex πρίν M

ἁγνὴν Περσεφόνειαν ἀπὸ ζόφου ἠερόεντος
ἐς φάος ἐξαγάγοι μετὰ δαίμονας, ὄφρα ἑ μήτηρ
ὀφθαλμοῖσιν ἰδοῦσα μεταλλήξειε χόλοιο.
Ἑρμῆς δ' οὐκ ἀπίθησεν, ἄφαρ δ' ὑπὸ κεύθεα γαίης   340
ἐσσυμένως κατόρουσε λιπὼν ἕδος Οὐλύμποιο.
τέτμε δὲ τόν γε ἄνακτα δόμων ἔντοσθεν ἐόντα
ἥμενον ἐν λεχέεσσι σὺν αἰδοίῃ παρακοίτι
πόλλ' ἀεκαζομένῃ μητρὸς πόθῳ †ἠδ' ἐπ' ἀτλήτων
ἔργοις θεῶν μακάρων μητίσετο βουλῇ†   345
ἀγχοῦ δ' ἱστάμενος προσέφη κρατὺς Ἀργειφόντης·
Ἅιδη κυανοχαῖτα καταφθιμένοισιν ἀνάσσων
Ζεύς με πατὴρ ἤνωγεν ἀγαυὴν Περσεφόνειαν
ἐξαγαγεῖν Ἐρέβευσφι μετὰ σφέας, ὄφρα ἑ μήτηρ

---

337 ἁγνὴ Περσεφόνεια* Od. 11. 386: ἀπὸ ζόφου ἠερόεντος* Dem. 402: ὑπὸ ζόφου ἠερόεντος* Il. 21. 56, Hes. Th. 653 (~ Il. 23. 51, Od. 11. 57 etc.)   338 ἐξάγαγε πρὸ φόωσδε Il. 16. 188: ἐξαγάγοις* Il. 19. 332: ἀνήγαγον ἐς φάος Hes. Th. 626: μετὰ δαίμονας Il. 1. 222: δαίμονας ἄλλους Herm. 381 ~ Ap. 11: ὄφρ' ἐπὶ μήτηρ* Od. 11. 152 (~ 17. 6)   338b-9 ~ 349b-50 ~ 409b-10   339 ὀφθαλμοῖσιν ἰδών* Il. 3. 28 (~ 19. 174 etc.), cf. Dem. 333: μεταλλήξαντι χόλοιο* Il. 9. 157 etc.   340 Ἑρμῆς* Herm. 25 etc.: οὐδ' ἀπίθησεν* Il. 2. 166 etc.: ὑπὸ κεύθεα γαίης* Dem. 415 (~ Il. 22. 482, Od. 24. 204): cf. Il. 24. 339 = Od. 5. 43   341 ἐσσυμένως* Il. 3. 85 etc., Dem. 359: ἐσσυμένως ὦρουσεν* Hy. 28. 8: λιποῦσ' ἕδος Οὐλύμποιο* Il. 24. 144: cf. Dem. 449   342 τέτμον δ'* Dem. 179: εὗρε δὲ τόν γε ἄνακτα* Il. 5. 794: δόμων ἔντοσθεν* Od. 1. 380 = 2. 145 (~ 23. 148): ἔντοσθεν ἐοῦσα* Od. 14. 194 342 f. τὸν δ' εὗρον ... | ἥμενον Il. 1. 329 f. (~ Il. 5. 355 f. etc.)   343 ἥμενον* Il. 1. 330 etc.: ἐν λεχέεσσι* Il. 18. 233 etc.: ἥμενον ἐν* λέσχῃ Hes. Op. 501: αἰδοίῃ παρακοίτι* Od. 3. 381   344 πόλλ' ἀεκαζομένῃ* Il. 6. 458 (~ Od. 13. 277, Dem. 432): μητρός* Od. 6. 310 etc.: πόθος* Od. 4. 596: ἀποτηλοῦ* Od. 9. 117 345 ἔργοισιν* Od. 7. 52: θεῶν μακάρων* Il. 1. 339 etc. (semper hoc versus loco): βουλῇ* Il. 2. 202 etc.: βουλὴν ἥ ῥα θεοῖσιν ἐφήνδανε μητίωσιν Il. 7. 45   346 ἀγχοῦ δ' ἱστάμενος προσέφη* Il. 13. 768 etc.: κρατὺς Ἀργειφόντης* Il. 16. 181 etc. 347 κυανοχαῖτα Il. 13. 563: καταφθιμένοισιν ἀνάσσειν* Od. 11. 491: Ἀΐδης ἐνέροισι καταφθιμένοισιν ἀνάσσων* Hes. Th. 850 (~ Il. 15. 188)   348 Ζεύς με πατὴρ* προέηκε Il. 11. 201: ἄνωγεν* Il. 6. 444 etc.: ἀγαυὴν Περσεφόνεια* Od. 11. 213, 226, 635: Ζεὺς ἐμέ γ' ἠνώγει Od. 5. 99   349 ἐξάγαγε* Il. 16. 188: Ἐρέβε(υ)σφιν* Il. 9. 572, Hes. Th. 669   349b-50a = 338b-9a

---

337 ἀπὸ M: ὑπὸ Voss   339 μεταλήξειε M: μεταλλήξειε Matthiae   343 παρα-
κοίτῃ͜ M   344 f. ἡ δ' Voss: ἀποτηλοῦ Ilgen (quod probat Allen): ἐπ' ἀτλήτοις Humbert: in 345 'excidisse videtur anapaestus' Allen: ὀργισθεῖσα Ignarra: ἠδ' ἔτ' ἀτλήτοις ἔργοις ⟨οἷα⟩ θεῶν μακάρων μητίσατο βουλή Ludwich (B. ph. Woch. 39 (1919), 552): varie tentaverunt alii   346 κρατερὸς M: κρατὺς Ruhnken   347 ἄδη M: Ἅιδη Ruhnken   348 σε M: με Wyttenbach   ἄνωγεν M: corr. Ruhnken 349 ἐρέβευσφι M: ἐρέβεσφι Franke (cf. Il. 9. 572, ubi nonnulli codices ἐρέβεσφι habent)

ὀφθαλμοῖςιν ἰδοῦςα χόλου καὶ μήνιος αἰνῆς   350
ἀθανάτοις παύςειεν· ἐπεὶ μέγα μήδεται ἔργον
φθῖςαι φῦλ' ἀμενηνὰ χαμαιγενέων ἀνθρώπων
ςπέρμ' ὑπὸ γῆς κρύπτουςα, καταφθινύθουςα δὲ τιμὰς
ἀθανάτων. ἡ δ' αἰνὸν ἔχει χόλον, οὐδὲ θεοῖςι
μίςγεται, ἀλλ' ἀπάνευθε θυώδεος ἔνδοθι νηοῦ   355
ἧςται, Ἐλευςῖνος κραναὸν πτολίεθρον ἔχουςα.
Ὡς φάτο· μείδηςεν δὲ ἄναξ ἐνέρων Ἀϊδωνεὺς
ὀφρύςιν, οὐδ' ἀπίθηςε Διὸς βαςιλῆος ἐφετμῆς.
ἐςςυμένως δ' ἐκέλευςε δαΐφρονι Περςεφονείῃ·
ἔρχεο Περςεφόνη παρὰ μητέρα κυανόπεπλον   360
ἤπιον ἐν ςτήθεςςι μένος καὶ θυμὸν ἔχουςα,

---

350 = 409b+410b: οἰζύος αἰνῆς* Od. 15. 342: χόλος αἰνός Il. 22. 94 (cf. ad Dem. 38–46) ~ Dem. 354: χόλος καὶ μῆνις* Il. 15. 122   351 ἀθανάτοις* Il. 23. 207 etc.: χόλον παύςειεν* Il. 1. 192: παύθη χόλου Hes. Th. 533: παύε', ἔα δὲ χόλον Il. 9. 260 (261b ~ Dem. 339) ~ Il. 15. 72, 19. 67 (ubi 67 f. ~ Dem. 82 f.): μάλα γὰρ μέγα μήςατο ἔργον* Od. 3. 261 (cf. Il. 2. 38 etc.)   352 φθίςειν (etc.)* Il. 16. 461 (etc.): ἀμενηνά Od. 10. 521 etc.: χαμαιγενέων ἀνθρώπων* Hes. Th. 879, Aph. 108 (~ Theognis 870): φῦλ' ἀνθρώπων* Od. 3. 282 etc.   353 ςπέρμ'* ... κρύπτεν γάρ* ... Dem. 307: κρύπτεςκε* Dem. 239: φθινύθουςα* Od. 1. 250 = 16. 127: τιμάς* Dem. 443, 461, Hes. Th. 74, 885, Op. 138   354 ἀθανάτων* Il. 5. 828 etc.: χόλος αἰνός* Il. 22. 94 (~ Dem. 350): ἔχειν χόλον* Dem. 83: οὐδὲ θεοῖςι* Herm. 167 354 f. οὐδέ τις αὐτῇ | μίςγεται οὔτε θεῶν ... Od. 7. 246 f.   355 ἀπάνευθε* Il. 1. 48, Dem. 28 etc.: θυώδεος* Od. 4. 121, Dem. 244 etc.: νηοῖο ... θυώδεος* Dem. 385: θυώδεα νηόν Aph. 58: ἔνδοθι* Il. 6. 498 etc.   356 ἧςται* Il. 19. 345 etc.: πτολίεθρον* Il. 2. 228 etc.: ἔχουςα* Il. 9. 559 etc.: Ἐλευςῖνος θυοέςςης δῆμον ἔχουςαι* Dem. 490 (~ 97): πτολίεθρον Ἐλευςῖνος Dem. 318   357 ὡς φάτο· μείδηςεν δέ* Il. 1. 595 etc.: ἄναξ ἐνέρων Ἀϊδωνεύς* Il. 20. 61   358 ὀφρύςι* νευςτάζων Od. 12. 194: οὐδ' ἀπίθηςε* Il. 2. 166, Dem. 448 etc.: Διὸς ... ἐφετμάς* Il. 15. 593, 24. 570, 586: Διὶ βαςιλῆι Theb. fr. 3. 3: θεῶν βαςιλῆι' καὶ ἀνδρῶν Hes. Th. 923 359 ἐςςυμένως* Dem. 341 etc.: ἐκέλευςεν* Il. 8. 318 etc.: δαΐφρονι Βελλεροφόντῃ* Il. 6. 196 (δαΐφρων in Homero semper de viris, excepto Od. 15. 356): περίφρονι Πηνελοπείῃ* Od. 15. 41 etc. (~ Dem. 370)   360 ἔρχεο* Il. 9. 43 etc.: Περςεφόνη* (nom.) Dem. 405: μητέρα κυανόπεπλον* Dem. 442 (~ 319)   360–1 Λητὼ κυανόπεπλον ... | ἤπιον* Hes. Th. 406–7   361 ἤπιον* Od. 14. 139, 20. 327: ἐν ςτήθεςςι μένος* Il. 5. 513: μένος καὶ θυμόν* Il. 5. 470 etc.: ἄγριον ἐν ςτήθεςςι θέτο μεγαλήτορα θυμόν Il. 9. 629: (ἀπηνέα/εὔφρονα) θυμὸν ἔχουςα* Od. 23. 97, Aph. 102

---

355 ἐκ νηοῖο θυώδεος A.R. 1. 307: θυώδεας εἵςατο ναούς* Theocr. 17. 123: νηοῖο θυώδεος* ἔνδον ἐόντα Epigr. App. Anth. 4. 18 (Epidaurio templo inscriptum)

---

351 παύςειεν M: λήξειεν C. Burney, Hermann (cf. 410)   357 ἀνέρων M: corr. Ruhnken   358 ἐφετμῆς M: ἐφετμῆς Allen

μηδέ τι δυcθύμαινε λίην περιώcιον ἄλλων.
οὔ τοι ἐν ἀθανάτοιcιν ἀεικὴc ἔccομ' ἀκοίτηc
αὐτοκαcίγνητοc πατρὸc Διόc· ἔνθα δ' ἐοῦcα
δεcπόccειc πάντων ὁπόcα ζώει τε καὶ ἕρπει,   365
τιμὰc δὲ cχήcηcθα μετ' ἀθανάτοιcι μεγίcταc,
τῶν δ' ἀδικηcάντων τίcιc ἔccεται ἤματα πάντα
οἵ κεν μὴ θυcίαιcι τεὸν μένοc ἱλάcκωνται
εὐαγέωc ἔρδοντεc ἐναίcιμα δῶρα τελοῦντεc.

Ὣc φάτο· γήθηcεν δὲ περίφρων Περcεφόνεια,   370
καρπαλίμωc δ' ἀνόρουc' ὑπὸ χάρματοc· αὐτὰρ ὅ γ' αὐτὸc
ῥοιῆc κόκκον ἔδωκε φαγεῖν μελιηδέα λάθρῃ
ἀμφὶ ἓ νωμήcαc, ἵνα μὴ μένοι ἤματα πάντα
αὖθι παρ' αἰδοίῃ Δημήτερι κυανοπέπλῳ.

362 μή μοί τι λίην* ἀκαχίζεο θυμῷ *Il.* 6. 486: περιώcια* *Hy.* 19. 41: περὶ* . . .
ἄλλων* *Il.* 13. 728 etc.: cf. *Dem.* 82 f., 467 f.   363 f. cf. *Dem.* 83–5   363 οὔτοι
ἀεικήc (ad fin.) *Dem.* 83 (~ 120): ἐν ἀθανάτοιcιν* *Il.* 1. 398, *Dem.* 84, *Ap.* 325:
ἀκοίτηc* *Il.* 15. 91   364 αὐτοκαcίγνητοc* *Dem.* 85, *Il.* 2. 706 etc.: πατρὸc Διόc*
Il. 2. 146 etc.: ἐνθάδ' ἰοῦcα* *Od.* 6. 179   365 πάντων ὅcα τε γαῖαν ἔπι πνείει τε
καὶ ἕρπει *Il.* 17. 447 = *Od.* 18. 131: ζώει τε καὶ ἔcτιν* *Od.* 24. 263   366 τιμάc*
Dem. 328 etc.: μετ' ἀθανάτοιcι* *Dem.* 328 etc.: μετ' ἀθανάτοιcι μεγιcτον* *Il.* 1. 525
367 τίcιc ἔccεται* *Od.* 1. 40: ἤματα πάντα* *Il.* 8. 539 etc.   368 θυέεccι(ν)* *Il.* 9.
499 (θυcίαιcι Pl. *Rep.* 364 d 7), *Il.* 6. 270: θυέεccί τε ἱλάcκεcθαι Hes. *Op.* 338: ἐμὸν νόον
ἱλάcκοιντο* *Dem.* 274 (~ 292)   369 εὐαγέωc ἔρδοντεc* ἐναίcιμα δῶρα
διδοῦναι* *Il.* 24. 425   370 ὣc φάτο· γήθηcεν δέ* *Il.* 6. 212 etc.: περίφρων
Πηνελόπεια* *Od.* 1. 329 etc. (~ *Dem.* 359)   371 καρπαλίμωc δ'* *Il.* 1. 359:
ἀνόρουc' ὑπὸ χάρματοc* *Dem.* 411: ἀνόρουcε* *Il.* 1. 248 etc.: περὶ χάρματι* *Dem.* 429
371–2 cf. *Dem.* 411–12   372 ῥοιῆc κόκκον, μελιηδέ' ἐδωδήν *Dem.* 412: ἔδωκε*
Il. 13. 730 etc.: μελιηδέα* *Il.* 10. 579 etc.: λάθρῃ* *Il.* 2. 515   373 ἀμφὶ ἓ παπτήναc*
Il. 4. 497 = 15. 574: ἤματα πάντα* *Il.* 8. 539, *Dem.* 260 etc.   374 μητρὶ παρ'
αἰδοίῃ* *Od.* 8. 420: Δημήτερα κυανόπεπλον* *Dem.* 319: ἐυcτέφανοc Δημήτηρ | αἰδοίη
Hes. *Op.* 300–1 (cf. *Dem.* 224 etc.)

362 περιώcιον ἄλλων* A.R. 1. 466   372 ῥοιᾶc ἔδωκεν αὐτῇ φαγεῖν κόκκον
Apollod. 1. 5. 3

362 θύcθυμαινε M: corr. Ruhnken   λίην M: φίλη Wyttenbach   363 ἔcομ'
ἄκοιτιc M: corr. Ruhnken   364 ἐνθάδ' ἰοῦcα M: ἔνθα δ' ἐοῦcα Ruhnken:
ἐνθάδ' ἐούcῃ Preller (cf. ad 365–9)   365–9 interpolatos esse censebant Preller, Stoll,
367–9 Bücheler   365 δεcπόccειc M: δεcπόccεειc Voss: δεcπόζῃc Ruhnken: δεcπόccῃc
Wolf   366 cχήcηcθα M: cχήcηcθα Ruhnken: cχήcειcθα Boissonade: cχήcεcθα Bergk
(*Poet. Lyr. Gr.* 3. 96): cχήcειc θάμ' ἐν Voss: ἀμφὶ δὲ τιμὰc ἔχηcθα Hermann: τιμὰc δ'
αἰὲν ἔχηcθα Hermann   368 θυcίαιcι M: θυcίῃcι Ruhnken: θυέεccι Hermann (cf.
Dem. 312)   ἱλάcκονται M: ἱλάcκωνται Valckenaer   371 ἀνόρουcεν M: corr.
Ruhnken   371–2 αὐτὸc . . . λάθρῃ M: αὐτῇ Voss: Ἀίδηc Schneidewin:
αὔτωc Agar: αὖτιc(?) West: ὁ λάθρῃ . . . μελιηδέ' ἐδωδὴν Jacques (cf. *Dem.* 411–12):
μελιηδέα δαῖτα Ruhnken   373 ἀμφὶ ἓ M: ἀμφί ἑ Ruhnken: ἀμφὶc Santen

ἵππους δὲ προπάροιθεν ὑπὸ χρυσέοισιν ὄχεσφιν   375
ἔντυεν ἀθανάτους πολυσημάντωρ Ἀϊδωνεύς.
ἡ δ' ὀχέων ἐπέβη, παρὰ δὲ κρατὺς Ἀργειφόντης
ἡνία καὶ μάστιγα λαβὼν μετὰ χερσὶ φίλῃσι
ϲεῦε διὲκ μεγάρων· τὼ δ' οὐκ ἄκοντε πετέϲθην.
ῥίμφα δὲ μακρὰ κέλευθα διήνυϲαν, οὐδὲ θάλαϲϲα   380
οὔθ' ὕδωρ ποταμῶν οὔτ' ἄγκεα ποιήεντα
ἵππων ἀθανάτων οὔτ' ἄκριες ἔϲχεθον ὁρμήν,
ἀλλ' ὑπὲρ αὐτάων βαθὺν ἠέρα τέμνον ἰόντεϲ.
ϲτῆϲε δ' ἄγων ὅθι μίμνεν ἐϋϲτέφανοϲ Δημήτηρ
νηοῖο προπάροιθε θυώδεοϲ· ἡ δὲ ἰδοῦϲα   385
ἤϊξ' ἠΰτε μαινὰϲ ὄροϲ κάτα δάϲκιον ὕλῃ.
Περϲεφόνη δ' ἑτέρ[ωθεν

---

375 ἵππουϲ δέ* *Il.* 24. 279: προπάροιθεν* *Il.* 3. 22 etc.: ἐπὶ χρυσέοισιν ὄχοισιν* *Dem.* 19   376 ἔντυεν (ἵππουϲ) *Il.* 5. 720, 8. 382: ἀθανάτουϲ* *Il.* 14. 199 etc.: πολυϲημάντωρ Ἀϊδωνεύϲ* *Dem.* 84   377 αὐτίκα δ' ὧν ὀχέων ἐπεβήϲετο *Il.* 11. 517 (~ 5. 221 etc.): ἐπέβη* *Dem.* 264: κρατὺϲ Ἀργειφόντηϲ* *Il.* 16. 181, *Dem.* 346 etc. 378 ἡνία* *Il.* 5. 583 etc.: μάϲτιγα* *Il.* 5. 226 etc.: λαβών* *Il.* 4. 122 etc.: μάϲτιγα καὶ ἡνία λάζετο χερϲίν *Il.* 17. 482 = 24. 441 (~ 5. 840, *Od.* 6. 81): χερϲὶ φίλῃϲιν* *Il.* 23. 99, *Dem.* 41 etc.   379 ϲεῦε* *Il.* 6. 133: διὲκ μεγάρων* *Dem.* 281: τὼ δ' οὐκ ἄκοντε πετέϲθην* *Il.* 5. 366 etc.   380 ῥίμφα δέ* *Il.* 24. 799, *Dem.* 171: ἰχθυόεντα κέλευθα διέδραμον* *Od.* 3. 177: διήνυϲε(ν)* *Od.* 17. 517, *Ap.* 108: ἠδὲ θάλαϲϲα* *Od.* 12. 404 = 14. 302   381 ποταμῶν* *Il.* 20. 9 etc.: ἄγκεα ποιήεντα* *Od.* 4. 337 = 17. 128   382 ἵππων ἀθανάτων* *Il.* 17. 476: ἄκριαϲ* *Od.* 9. 400 etc.: ἔϲχεθον* *Il.* 15. 653, 19. 418: ὁρμήν* *Il.* 9. 355 etc.   383 ἠέρα* ... βαθεῖαν *Il.* 20. 446: ἰόντεϲ* *Il.* 3. 15 etc.   384 ϲτῆϲε δ' ἄγων* ἵν' ... ἵϲταντο *Il.* 2. 558: μίμνε* *Ap.* 5: ἐϋϲτέφανοϲ Δημήτηρ* *Dem.* 244 etc.   385 προπάροιθε* *Il.* 2. 92 etc.: θυώδεοϲ ... νηοῦ *Dem.* 355: οἱ δὲ ἰδόντεϲ* *Il.* 8. 76 etc.: ἡ δὲ ἰδοῦϲα* *Ap.* 255 (Hermann: ἐϲιδοῦϲα codd.), 341 (M: ἐϲιδοῦϲα cett.)   386 ἤϊξ'* *Dem.* 61: μαινάδι ἴϲη *Il.* 22. 460 (cf. ad *Dem.* 38–46): μαινομένη ἐϊκυῖα *Il.* 6. 389: ὄροϲ καταειμένον ὕλῃ* *Od.* 13. 351, *Herm.* 228 (231–2 ~ *Dem.* 277–8), *Aph.* 285 (284 ~ *Dem.* 8): δάϲκιοϲ ὕλῃ* *Il.* 15. 273, *Hy.* 27. 7 (~ *Od.* 5. 470)   387 Πάτροκλοϲ δ' ἑτέρωθεν, ἐπεὶ ἴδεν, ἔκθορε δίφρου *Il.* 16. 427: { Πάτροκλοϲ δ' ἑτέρωθεν ἀφ' ἵππων ἄλτο χαμᾶζε / Ἕκτωρ δ' αὖθ'
Il. 16. 733, 755 (cf. ad *Dem.* 389): ὡϲ δὲ ἴδεν ... ὄμματα κάλ' ... *Aph.* 181

---

383 ἀπὸ χθονὸϲ ἐϲ [....]αν βαθ|ὺν ἀ]έρα τάμνων Ibycus(?), P. Oxy. 2637 fr. 5 ii 5–7 (~ Bacch. 5. 16 f.): cf. Archil. fr. 181. 10 West [? τάμνων κέ]λευθον ὠκέωϲ δι' αἰθέροϲ

---

381 οὔτ' ἄρ' ὕδωρ Hermann: οὔτε ὕδωρ Suhle   383 ὑπὲρ ἀκράων **Agar** (*CR* 31 (1917), 120): τάμνον? West (cf. Gemoll)   384 ἀγῶν' M: ἄγων Ruhnken (cf. *Il.* 2. 558)   386 μαινὰϲ M: κεμμὰϲ Ruhnken   κατὰ M: corr. Matthiae ὕληϲ M: ὕλῃ Ruhnken: ὄρεοϲ κατὰ δαϲκίου ὕλην Voss: ὕληϲ Allen   387 ἑτέρ M: τέρω m: ἑτέρωθεν Ilgen   ἀφ' ἅρματοϲ ἀΐξαϲα Hermann: ἐπεὶ ἴδε καλὰ πρόϲωπα Voss: ἐπεὶ ἴδεν ὄμματα καλὰ Goodwin

μητρὸς ἑῆς κατ[

ἆλτο θέει[ν

τῇ δε[390

ἀ[

πα⟨υ⟩ομε[ν-

    Τέκνον μή ῥά τί μοι c[

βρώμῃς; ἐξαύδα [

ὣς μὲν γάρ κ' ἀνιοῦca π[395

καὶ παρ' ἐμοὶ καὶ πατρὶ κελ[αινεφέϊ Κρονίωνι]

ναιετάοιc πάντεccι τετιμ[ένη ἀθανάτοι]cιν.

†εἰ δὲ πτᾶca πάλιν ἰοῦc' ὑπ[ὸ

---

388 ἡ δ' ἐν γούναcι πῖπτε … | μητρὸς ἑῆς*· ἡ δ' ἀγκὰc ἐλάζετο θυγατέρα ἦν Il. 5.
370–1 (363–9 ~ Dem. 375–85): μητρὸς ἑῆς* Od. 19. 395 (402 ~ Dem. 392)
389 ἆλτο* Herm. 65   392 παυομένῳ· δόρποιο· ἔπος τ' ἔφατ' ἔκ τ' ὀνόμαζεν Od. 19.
402 (395 ~ Dem. 388): παύομαι (a luctu)* Od. 4. 103 (~ Il. 8. 295)   393 τέκνον,
μή τοι* … Il. 19. 29: τέκνον, τί κλαίεις; τί δέ cε φρέναc ἵκετο πένθος; Il. 1. 362
= 18. 73 (1. 363 ~ 18. 74 ~ Dem. 394)   394 βρώμης Od. 10. 177, 379: ἐξαύδα,
μὴ κεῦθε νόῳ, ἵνα εἴδομεν ἄμφω Il. 1. 363 = 16. 19 (~ 18. 74)   396 Διὶ πατρί*
Il. 4. 23 etc.: κελαινεφέϊ Κρονίωνι* Il. 1. 397 etc.   397 ναιετάω* Od. 9. 21:
πάντεccι τετιμένοc ἀθανάτοιcι* Aph. 205 (cf. ad Dem. 403): πολλοῖcι τετιμένον ἀνθρώποιcιν* Ap. 479 ~ 522 (~ Dem. 399): ἀθανάτοιc τε θεοῖcι τετιμένη* Hes. Th. 415
(~ Il. 24. 533): πᾶcι μετ' ἀθανάτοιcι τετίμηται γεράεccι Hes. Th. 449   398 ὑπὸ
κεύθεα γαίης* Dem. 340, 415   398–400 cf. Dem. 445–7, 463–5

---

388 μρc̄' ἑῆς κατ M: κατ m   κατόρους' ὀχέων ἀπὸ παμφανοώντων Voss: κατ'
ἄρ' ἤ γ' ὄχεα προλιποῦcα καὶ ἵππουc Goodwin   389 ἆλτο θέει M: θείν m: ἆλτο
θέειν κύcε δ' οἱ κεφαλὴν καὶ χεῖρε λαβοῦcα Ilgen: ἆλτο θέειν, δείρῃ δέ οἱ ἔμπεcεν
ἀμφιχυθεῖcα Goodwin   390 τῇδε M: ἤδε m: τῇ δὲ κατὰ βλεφάρων χαμάδιc θερμὸν
ῥέε δάκρυ Ilgen: τῇ δὲ φίλην ἔτι παῖδα ἑῆc μετὰ χερcὶν ἐχούcῃ Goodwin   391 ἀ
M et m: ἀμφαγαπαζομένη· θαλερὴ δέ οἱ ἔcχετο φωνή Ilgen: ἀμφοτέρῃcι δὲ τῇcιν ὑφ'
ἵμεροc ὦρτο γόοιο Hermann: αἶψα δόλον θυμόc τιν' ὀίcατο, τρέccε δ' ἄρ' αἰνῶc Goodwin
392 παομε M (E. M. Thompson ap. Goodwin): παυομένη φιλότητος, ἄφαρ δ'
ἐρεείνετο μύθῳ· Goodwin   393 τέκνον· μή ῥ' ἀτίμοις M: μή ῥά τί μοι ἐπάcω
τῆc εἰν ἀίδαο Voss: μή ῥά τί μοι πάccῃ ἐνέρων παρ' ἄνακτι Ilgen: cύ γε πάccαο νέρθεν
ἐοῦcα Goodwin   394 βρώμης ἐξαύδα M: βρώμη Voss   μὴ κεῦθ' ἵν' ἴδωμαι
ἀληθέc Ilgen: μ. κ. ἵνα εἴδομεν ἄμφω Hermann   395 ὣc μὲν γάρ κε νέουcα π M
(versa scheda vestigium ex codicis M scriptura impressum dispicitur: fortasse a post
π legitur: cf. Goodwin ad Dem. 402): κεν ἐοῦcα παρ' ἄλλοιc ἀθανάτοιcι Bücheler:
κ' ἀνιοῦcα plerique: κ' ἀνιοῦcα μένοιc τέκοc (ἄνω Bothe) ἤματα πάντα Voss: κ' ἀνιοῦc'
ἐκ ταρτάρου ἠερόεντοc Ilgen: παρὰ cτυγεροῦ Ἀίδαο Goodwin   396 κελ M:
                                        οι
κελενεφέϊ κρονίωνι m   397 ναιετάειc πάντεccι τετιμ[   ]cιν M: τιμημένη ἀθανάτοιcι m (~ Ap. 522, Hes. Th. 415, PMG 880)   398 εἰ δὲ πτᾶcα πάλιν ἰοῦc' ὑπ M:
ὑπὸ κεύθεcι γαίηc m: εἰ δ' ἐπάcω Wyttenbach: εἰ δέ τι πάccαο πάμπαν Goodwin: εἰ δ'
ἐπάcω, πάλιν αὖτιc Ruhnken: εἰ δ' ἐπάcω τι πάλιν μὲν ἰοῦc' ὑπὸ κεύθεα γαίηc Bücheler:
εἰ δέ, πτᾶcα πάλιν ⟨cύ γ'⟩ ἰοῦc' ὑπ[ὸ κεύθεcι γαίηc Allen (CR 15 (1901), 27): εἰ δ'
ἐπάcω, ἄψορρον ἰοῦc', ὑπὸ κεύθεcι γαίηc West

οἰκήσεις ὡρέων τρίτατον μέρ[ος
τὰς δὲ δύω παρ' ἐμοί τε καὶ [ἄλλοις ἀθανά]τοισιν.   400
ὁππότε δ' ἄνθεσι γαῖ' εὐώδε[σιν] ἠαρινο[ῖσι]
παντοδαποῖς θάλλει, τότ' ἀπὸ ζόφου ἠερόεντος
αὖτις ἄνει μέγα θαῦμα θεοῖς θνητοῖς τ' ἀνθρώποις.
καὶ τίνι σ' ἐξαπάτησε δόλῳ κρατερ[ὸς πολυδ]έγμων;
Τὴν δ' αὖ Περσεφόνη περικαλλὴς ἀντίον ηὔδα·   405
τοιγὰρ ἐγώ τοι μῆτερ ἐρέω νημερτέα πάντα·
εὖτέ μοι ἄγγελος ἦλθ' ἐριούνιος Ἀργειφόντης
πὰρ πατέρος Κρονίδαο καὶ ἄλλων οὐρανιώνων

399 οἰκήσειν* *Ap.* 522 (~ *Dem.* 397): τριτάτην . . . μοῖραν *Od.* 4. 97 (~ *Dem.* 446, 464): τριτάτη* . . . μοῖρα *Il.* 10. 253: τρὶς . . . εἰς ἐνιαυτόν* *Od.* 4. 86: εἰν Ἀίδαο* *Il.* 22. 389 (~ 22. 52 etc.)   400 τὼ δὲ δύω* *Il.* 19. 47: καὶ ἄλλοις ἀθανά-τοισιν* *Il.* 2. 49 etc.   401 ἄνθεσιν εἰαρινοῖσιν* *Il.* 2. 89, Hes. *Th.* 279 (~ *Dem.* 7), *Op.* 75, *Cypr.* 4. 2: γαῖα* *Il.* 3. 278 etc.: εὐώδεϊ* *Il.* 3. 382   402 θάλλοντα* Hes. *Op.* 173: ἀπὸ ζόφου ἠερόεντος* *Dem.* 337   403 μέγα θαῦμα* *Il.* 13. 99 etc.: θαῦμα βροτοῖσιν *Od.* 11. 287: μέγα θαῦμα μετ' ἀθανάτοισι *Herm.* 270: θαῦμα ἰδεῖν *Aph.* 205 (cf. ad *Dem.* 397): θαῦμα θνητοῖσι βροτοῖσιν Hes. *Th.* 500: θαῦμα δ' ἐχ' ἀθανάτους τε θεοὺς θνητούς τ' ἀνθρώπους Hes. *Th.* 588 (589 ~ *Dem.* 404; cf. *Dem.* 8–11): θνητοῖς ἀνθρώποις* *Dem.* 11   404 ἐξαπάτησεν* *Od.* 9. 414: δόλῳ* *Il.* 7. 412 etc.: κρατερὸς πολυδέγμων* *Dem.* 430 (~ *Dem.* 17)   405 Περσεφόνη* *Dem.* 360: περικαλλής* Περσεφόνεια *Dem.* 493: περικαλλής* *Il.* 5. 389: ἀντίον ηὔδα* *Il.* 3. 203 etc.   406 τοιγὰρ ἐγώ τοι μῆτερ ἀληθείην καταλέξω *Od.* 17. 108: λέγω νημερτέα πάντα* *Dem.* 58   407 ἐριούνιον* *Il.* 24. 679 etc.: ἄγγελον . . . ἐριούνιον *Herm.* 3 = *Hy.* 18. 3: Ἀργειφόντης* *Il.* 16. 181 etc.   407–8 Τρωσὶν δ' ἄγγελος ἦλθε ποδήνεμος ὠκέα Ἶρις | πὰρ Διὸς αἰγιόχοιο* *Il.* 2. 786–7   408 πατέρα Κρονίδην *Dem.* 21, 27: πατὴρ Κρονίδης *Il.* 21. 508, 22. 60: πάτερ . . . Κρονίδη *Il.* 8. 31 etc.: Κρονίδη . . . πατρί Hes. *Th.* 53: οὐρανιώνων* *Il.* 5. 373 etc.

___

399 οἰκήσεις ὀρέων τρίτατον μέρ M: ὀρέων τριτάτην μοῖραν εἰς ἐνιαυτὸν (cf. 446) m: ὡρέων Ilgen: ὡρῶν Ruhnken: μέγαν εἰς ἐνιαυτὸν Hermann: τριτάτην μοῖραν παρ' ἀκοίτῃ Fontein: τρίτατον μέρος εἰν ἀίδαο Bücheler   400 καὶ[   ]τοι M: ἄλλοις ἀθανάτοισι m   401 γαῖα εὐῴ M: δεσιν ηαριν in scheda et οισι ad finem appinxit m: versa scheda litterae δε ηαρινο a prisca codicis M scriptura impressae (e contrario se offerentes) apparent (cf. Goodwin)   εἰαρινοῖσι Matthiae   402–7 habet pap. 2   402 παντοδ]απ[οις pap. 2   θάλλῃ Voss   403 ἀνεῖ M: corr. Wyttenbach:]ανει με[pap. 2   post hunc versum lacunam posuit Ruhnken, sed nulla in papyro invenitur   404 καί τιν' ἐξαπάτησε M: corr. Ruhnken: τι]νι σ' εξαπα[τησε pap. 2   litteras ὸς πολυδ refecit m   405]αυ φερσεφον[η pap. 2   406]εγω τοι μητ[pap. 2: σοι M (τοι coni. Hermann)   ἐρέω M: ἐρῶ m   407 εὖτέ μοι ἑρμῆς ἦ[   ] ἐριούνιος ἄγγελος ὠκὺς M: μοι ἑρμῆς ἐρ[ι] . . . m: ἦλθ' Mitscherlich: super vocem ὠκὺς et ad dextram versus ductae sunt a manu recentiore lineae: εὖτέ μ]οι ἄγγελος ἦλ[θ' ἐριούνιος Ἀργειφόντης pap. 2 (restituit Merkelbach): varie tentaverant edd. priores (cf. Bücheler)

ἐλθεῖν ἐξ Ἐρέβευς, ἵνα μ᾽ ὀφθαλμοῖσιν ἰδοῦσα
λήξαις ἀθανάτοισι χόλου καὶ μήνιος αἰνῆς,　　　　　　　410
αὐτὰρ ἐγὼν ἀνόρους᾽ ὑπὸ χάρματος, αὐτὰρ ὁ λάθρῃ
ἔμβαλέ μοι ῥοιῆς κόκκον, μελιηδέ᾽ ἐδωδήν,
ἄκουσαν δὲ βίῃ με προσηνάγκασσε πάσασθαι.
ὡς δέ μ᾽ ἀναρπάξας Κρονίδεω πυκινὴν διὰ μῆτιν
ᾤχετο πατρὸς ἐμοῖο φέρων ὑπὸ κεύθεα γαίης　　　　　　415
ἐξερέω καὶ πάντα διίξομαι ὡς ἐρεείνεις.
ἡμεῖς μὲν μάλα πᾶσαι ἀν᾽ ἱμερτὸν λειμῶνα,
Λευκίππη Φαινώ τε καὶ Ἠλέκτρη καὶ Ἰάνθη
καὶ Μελίτη Ἰάχη τε Ῥόδειά τε Καλλιρόη τε
Μηλόβοσίς τε Τύχη τε καὶ Ὠκυρόη καλυκῶπις　　　　　420
Χρυσηΐς τ᾽ Ἰάνειρά τ᾽ Ἀκάστη τ᾽ Ἀδμήτη τε

409 ἐλθεῖν* Il. 4. 65 etc.: ὑπὲξ Ἐρέβευς* Od. 11. 37: ὀφθαλμοῖσιν ἴδωμαι (etc.)*
Il. 1. 587 etc.　　409–10 cf. Dem. 349–11, 338–9　　410 ἀθανάτοισι* Il. 2. 306
etc.: χόλου καὶ μήνιος αἰνῆς* Dem. 350　　411 αὐτὰρ ἐγών* Il. 9. 103 etc.: αὐτὰρ
ἐγὼν ἐπόρουσα* Il. 11. 747 (~ 3. 379, 21. 33): αὐτὰρ ἐγὼ δρεπόμην περὶ χάρματι*
Dem. 429　　411–12 cf. Dem. 371–2 (λάθρῃ 372)　　412 ἐμβαλέειν* Od. 9. 489
= 10. 129: μελιηδέα* Il. 10. 579 etc.: ἐδωδήν* Il. 8. 504 etc.: μενοεικέ᾽ ἐδωδήν*
Od. 6. 76: ἡδεῖαν ἐδωδήν* Herm. 562　　413 βίῃ* Il. 7. 197 etc.: πάσασθαι*
Il. 9. 483, Od. 9. 93　　414 ἀναρπάξας* Il. 16. 437: μῆτιν* Il. 7. 324 etc.: πυκινὴν
... βουλήν Il. 2. 55 = 10. 302: Κρονίδεω διὰ βουλάς Hes. Th. 572 = Op. 71
415 ᾤχετ᾽* ἀποπτάμενος (etc.) Il. 2. 71 (etc.): ᾤχετ᾽ ἐλαύνων Herm. 340: λαβὼν
... | οἴχεται* Dem. 72–3: πατρὸς ἐμοῖο* Od. 6. 308, 15. 417: ὑπὸ κεύθεα γαίης*
Dem. 340 (~ 398)　　416 ἐξείπω, καὶ πάντα διίξομαι* Il. 9. 61: οὓς ἐρεείνεις*
Il. 10. 558　　417 ἱμερτόν* Ηγ. 10. 3: λειμῶνα* Od. 11. 539 etc.: λειμῶνας ...
ἐρατεινούς Herm. 72　　418–23 cf. Hes. Th. 349 ff.　　418 Λευκοθέη* Od. 5. 334:
Ἰάνθη τ᾽ Ἠλέκτρη τε* Hes. Th. 349　　419 καὶ Μελίτη* Il. 18. 42, Hes. Th. 247:
ἰαχῆ* Od. 11. 43: Ῥόδειά τε Καλλιρόη τε* Hes. Th. 351　　420 Μηλόβοσίς τε*
Hes. Th. 354: Τύχη τε* ... Ὠκυρόη τε Hes. Th. 360: καλυκώπιδι Dem. 8 (~
Aph. 284)　　421 Χρυσηΐς τ᾽ Hes. Th. 359: Περσηΐς τ᾽ Ἰάνειρά τ᾽ Ἀκάστη τε*
Th. 356: Ἀδμήτη τε Th. 349

411 αὐτὰρ ὁ λάθρῃ Opp. H. 2. 413

409 ἐλθ῀Π M: refecit m: ἐλθεῖν μ᾽ Ilgen　　411 αὐτὰρ (1) M: εἶθαρ Ruhnken:
αὐτίκ᾽ Ilgen: ἄντ᾽ ἄρ᾽ Mitscherlich: αἶψ᾽ ἄρ᾽ Hermann: 'ἤτοι sensum redderet'
Allen　　ἀτὰρ ὁ M: corr. Ruhnken　　λάθρῃ M (λάθρη m): ὁ γ᾽ αὐτὸς Ruhnken:
ὁ γ᾽ Ἀΐδης Schneidewin　　413 προσηνάγκασε M: corr. Matthiae　　versum
suspectum habuerunt Mitscherlich, Bücheler　　416 ὡς M: ὅσσ᾽ Fontein
417–20 cit. Paus. 4. 30. 4, om. 419: 418–23 cit. pap. 1 (= Orph. fr. 49.
21 ff.), om. 419　　418 Φαινώ M, Pausanias: φανερη pap. 1　　419 om.
pap. 1, Paus.　　ρόεια τε καλλιρρόη τε M: corr. Ruhnken　　420 μηλοβόστη τε
(μηλοβοειη vel μηλοβοτη τε correctum) ... ὠκύρθη καλλικῶπις M: corr. Ruhnken:
Μηλόβοσί[ς τε Τ]ύχη τε᾽ Ὠκυρόη καλυκῶπ[ις pap. 1　　421 ἀκατάστη M: corr.
Ruhnken: Ἀκάστη pap. 1

καὶ Ῥοδόπη Πλουτώ τε καὶ ἱμερόεccα Καλυψὼ
καὶ Cτὺξ Οὐρανίη τε Γαλαξαύρη τ' ἐρατεινὴ
Παλλάc τ' ἐγρεμάχη καὶ Ἄρτεμιc ἰοχέαιρα
παίζομεν ἠδ' ἄνθεα δρέπομεν χείρεcc' ἐρόεντα,   425
μίγδα κρόκον τ' ἀγανὸν καὶ ἀγαλλίδαc ἠδ' ὑάκινθον
καὶ ῥοδέαc κάλυκαc καὶ λείρια, θαῦμα ἰδέcθαι,
νάρκιccόν θ' ὃν ἔφυc' ὣc περ κρόκον εὐρεῖα χθών.
αὐτὰρ ἐγὼ δρεπόμην περὶ χάρματι, γαῖα δ' ἔνερθε
χώρηcεν, τῇ δ' ἔκθορ' ἄναξ κρατερὸc πολυδέγμων.   430
βῆ δὲ φέρων ὑπὸ γαῖαν ἐν ἅρμαcι χρυcείοιcι
πόλλ' ἀεκαζομένην, ἐβόηcα δ' ἄρ' ὄρθια φωνῇ.
ταῦτά τοι ἀχνυμένη περ ἀληθέα πάντ' ἀγορεύω.

Ὣc τότε μὲν πρόπαν ἦμαρ ὁμόφρονα θυμὸν ἔχουcαι
πολλὰ μάλ' ἀλλήλων κραδίην καὶ θυμὸν ἴαινον   435

422 Πλουτώ τε* Hes. Th. 355: καὶ ἱμερόεccα Καλυψώ* Th. 359   423 καὶ Cτύξ* Hes. Th. 361: Οὐρανίη Th. 350: Γαλαξαύρη τ' ἐρατή τε Διώνη Th. 353: ἐρατεινήν* Il. 2. 571 etc.   424 Παλλάc* Il. 10. 475 etc.: ἐγρεκύδοιμον* Hes. Th. 925 (de Minerva): Ἄρτεμιc ἰοχέαιρα* Il. 5. 53 etc.   425 παίζομεν* Aph. 120: φύλλα δρεψάμενοι Od. 12. 357: δρεπόμην Dem. 429: χείρεccι* Il. 3. 271 etc.: ἐρόεccα* Dem. 109, Hes. Th. 245 (~ Aph. 263, Hy. 32. 20)   426 μίγδα* Od. 24. 77: καὶ ἀγαλλίδαc ἠδ' ὑάκινθον* Dem. 7   427 θαῦμα ἰδέcθαι* Il. 5. 725 etc. 428 νάρκιccόν θ' ὃν φύcε* Dem. 8: κρόκον* Il. 14. 348, Dem. 6: εὐρεῖα χθών* Il. 4. 182 etc.   429 αὐτὰρ ἐγὼν ἀνόρουc' ὑπὸ χάρματοc* Dem. 411 (~ 371): γαῖα* Il. 2. 699 etc.: ἔνερθε* Il. 11. 234 etc.   430 χώρηcεν* Il. 12. 406: ἄναξ πολυδέγμων* Dem. 17: κρατερὸc πολυδέγμων* Dem. 404   431 βῆ δὲ φέρων* Il. 11. 247, Od. 22. 112, Hes. fr. 26. 23 (de raptu puellae): γαῖαν* Il. 17. 447 etc.: ἅρμαcι κολλητοῖcι (etc.)* Il. 4. 366 etc.   432 πόλλ' ἀεκαζομένη* Il. 6. 458 ~ Dem. 344 (~ 30): ἰάχηcε δ' ἄρ' ὄρθια φωνῇ* Dem. 20.   433 ταῦτά τοι ἀχνύμενός περ ἀληθείην κατέλεξα Od. 7. 297: ἀληθέα πάντ' ἀγορεύcω* Od. 3. 254 etc.   434 ὣc τότε μὲν πρόπαν ἦμαρ* Il. 1. 601 etc.: ὁμόφρονα θυμὸν ἔχουcαι* Od. 22. 263 (cf. ad Dem. 38–46) ~ Herm. 391, Theognis 81, 765   435 πολλὰ μάλ' Il. 9. 148 etc.: ἀλλήλων* Il. 3. 115 etc.: κραδίην καὶ θυμὸν ἴηνα* Dem. 65

424 Παλλάδι τ' ἐγρεμάχῃ* Oraculum (Parke–Wormell, no. 71) ap. D.S. 8. 29 (Batto Cyrenae fundatori datum): Παλλάδι μ' ἐγρεμάχαι IG i². 573 (~ 576): cf. Phoronis, P. Oxy. 2260, col. i. 3–7   431 cὺν ἅρμαcι χρυcεοτεύκτοιc* Orph. Hy. 55. 18

423 ταλαξαύρη M: corr. Ruhnken: Γαλαξ[αύρη pap. 1   424 versum interpolatum credebant Hermann, alii   426 κροκόεντα γανὸν M: corr. Voss 427 ῥόδα ἐc M: corr. Heyne: ῥόδα ἐκ κάλυκοc Valckenaer   428 ἔφυc' ὥcπερ κρόκον M: ἔφυcεν ἐμοὶ δόλον vel περίπλοκον Mitscherlich: εὔχροον Ilgen: ὥcπερ κόνιν vel αἰπὺν δόλον Hermann: ὑπερήφανον vel ὑπείροχον Voss: ὑπέρτατον Spitzen: varie tentaverunt alii   429 δρεπομένη M: corr. Ruhnken: αὐτὰρ δρεπτομένη Matthiae   430 τῇ M: τῆc Brunck, Fontein

ἀμφαγαπαζόμεναι, ἀχέων δ' ἀπεπαύετο θυμός.
γηθοσύνας δὲ δέχοντο παρ' ἀλλήλων ἔδιδ[όν τε.]
τῇσιν δ' ἐγγύθεν ἦλθ' Ἑκάτη λιπαροκρήδεμνος,
πολλὰ δ' ἄρ' ἀμφαγάπησε κόρην Δημήτερος ἁγνῆς·
ἐκ τοῦ οἱ πρόπολος καὶ ὀπάων ἔπλετ' ἄνασσα.   440
ταῖς δὲ μετάγγελον ἧκε βαρύκτυπος εὐρύοπα Ζεὺς
Ῥείην ἠΰκομον Δημήτερα κυανόπεπλον
ἀξέμεναι μετὰ φῦλα θεῶν, ὑπέδεκτο δὲ τιμὰς
δωσέμεν, ἅς κεν ἕλοιτο μετ' ἀθανάτοισι θεοῖσι·
νεῦσε δέ οἱ κούρην ἔτεος περιτελλομένοιο   445
τὴν τριτάτην μὲν μοῖραν ὑπὸ ζόφον ἠερόεντα,
τὰς δὲ δύω παρὰ μητρὶ καὶ ἄλλοις ἀθανάτοισιν.
ὣς ἔφατ', οὐδ' ἀπίθησε θεὰ Διὸς ἀγγελιάων.
ἐσσυμένως δ' ἤϊξε κατ' Οὐλύμποιο καρήνων,

---

436 ἀμφαγαπαζόμεναι, τοῦ δ' οὐ μειλίσσετο θυμός* Dem. 290: ἀχέων* Il. 20. 298: ἀποπαύεο* Il. 1. 422   437 γηθοσύνῃ (etc.)* Il. 13. 29 (etc.): ἀλλήλων* Il. 13. 613 etc.: ἔδιδον Hes. Op. 139 (ex coni. Rzach) ∼ Dem. 327: ἀλλήλῃσι γέλω τε καὶ εὐφροσύνην παρέχουσαι Od. 20. 8: δὸς δὲ δίκην καὶ δέξο Herm. 312   438 ἐγγύθεν ἦλθε* Il. 7. 219 etc.: Ἑκάτη λιπαροκρήδεμνος* Dem. 25   439 Δημήτερος* Il. 13. 322, 21. 76: ἁγνή* Od. 5. 123 etc. (∼ Dem. 203): Δημήτερί θ' ἁγνῇ* Hes. Op. 465: Δημήτερος ἁγνῆς* IG 12. 1. 780   440 ἐκ τοῦ δ'* Hes. Th. 556: ὀπάων* Il. 7. 165 etc.: ἄνασσα* Dem. 75, 492   441 τὸν δὲ μετ'* (etc.) Il. 8. 261 etc.: ἄγγελον ἧκαν* Od. 15. 458: βαρύκτυπος εὐρύοπα Ζεύς* Dem. 3 etc.   442 Ῥείης ἠϋκόμου* Dem. 60, 75: Δημήτερα κυανόπεπλον* Dem. 319   443 ἀξέμεναι* Od. 23. 221: μετὰ φῦλα θεῶν* Il. 15. 54 etc. (cf. Dem. 322, 36): τιμάς* Dem. 353   443–7 cf. Dem. 461–5: 443b–4 ∼ 327–8   444 δωσέμεν* Il. 10. 323 etc.: ἕλοιεν* Il. 15. 71: μετ' ἀθανάτοισι θεοῖσιν* Il. 21. 500 etc.   445 νεῦσε δέ οἱ* Il. 8. 246: κούρην* Hy. 13. 2: περιτελλομένοιο ἔτεος Od. 11. 295 etc.   446 τριτάτην . . . μοῖραν Od. 4. 97: τριτάτη ἐνὶ μοίρῃ Il. 15. 195: τῶν δύο μοιράων, τριτάτη δ' ἔτι μοῖρα λέλειπται Il. 10. 253: ὑπὸ ζόφον ἠερόεντα* Il. 23. 51, Dem. 80 etc.   447 τὰς δὲ δύω παρ' ἐμοί τε καὶ [ἄλλοις ἀθανά']τοισιν Dem. 400: μητρί* Il. 5. 555 etc.   448 ὣς ἔφατ'· οὐδ' ἀπίθησε θεά* Il. 2. 166 etc.: Ζηνὸς . . . ἀγγελιάων* Od. 5. 150, Aph. 215 (cf. Dem. 357–8, 470)   449 ἐσσυμένως δ' ἤϊξεν* Herm. 215, P. Oxy. 2509. 1 (cf. ad Dem. 67): βῆ δὲ κατ' Οὐλύμποιο καρήνων ἀΐξασα Il. 2. 167 etc. (cf. Dem. 341)

---

437 γηθόσυναι δὲ δέχοντο παρ' ἀλλήλων ἐδίδ M: post quae priorem scripturam in quod solum apparet ον corrupit m et addidit in scheda το: γηθοσύνας . . . ἐδίδόν τε Ruhnken   438–40 interpolatos credebant Mitscherlich, alii   440 λέγουσι δέ τινες . . . καὶ τὴν Ἑκάτην ὀπαδὸν Ἀρτέμιδος εἶναι, Δημήτρος δὲ λάτριν Εὐριπίδης, Ὅμηρος δὲ ἐν [τοῖς ὕμ]νοις πρόπ[ολον] καὶ [ὀπ]άονα Philod. de pietate 40. 5   441 ταῖς δὲ μετ' ἄγγελον M: τῆς δὲ μετ' Hermann: τὰς δὲ μετ', vel potius τῆς δὲ κατ' Voss: μετάγγελον Allen   442 ἦν μρᾶ M: Δημήτερα Fontein   446 post hunc versum lacunam statuerunt Hermann, Bücheler   448 ἀπίθησε M: ἀμέλησε Hermann   ἀγγελιάων M: ἀγγελίῃσιν Ruhnken

εἰς δ' ἄρα 'Ράριον ἷξε, φερέcβιον οὖθαρ ἀρούρηc   450
τὸ πρίν, ἀτὰρ τότε γ' οὔ τι φερέcβιον, ἀλλὰ ἔκηλον
εἱcτήκει πανάφυλλον· ἔκευθε δ' ἄρα κρῖ λευκὸν
μήδεcι Δήμητροc καλλιcφύρου· αὐτὰρ ἔπειτα
μέλλεν ἄφαρ ταναοῖcι κομήcειν ἀcταχύεccιν
ἧροc ἀεξομένοιο, πέδῳ δ' ἄρα πίονεc ὄγμοι   455
βριcέμεν ἀcταχύων, τὰ δ' ἐν ἐλλεδανοῖcι δεδέcθαι.
ἔνθ' ἐπέβη πρώτιcτον ἀπ' αἰθέροc ἀτρυγέτοιο·
ἀcπαcίωc δ' ἴδον ἀλλήλαc, κεχάρηντο δὲ θυμῷ.
τὴν δ' ὧδε προcέειπε 'Ρέη λιπαροκρήδεμνοc·
    Δεῦρο τέκοc, καλέει cε βαρύκτυποc εὐρύοπα Ζεὺc   460
ἐλθέμεναι μετὰ φῦλα θεῶν, ὑπέδεκτο δὲ τιμὰc
[δωcέμεν, ἅc κεν ἕλοιο] μετ' ἀθανάτοιcι θεοῖcι.
[νεῦcε δέ cοι κούρην ἔτεοc π]εριτελλομένοιο
[τὴν τριτάτην μὲν μοῖραν ὑπὸ ζόφον ἠ]ερόεντα,

450 αὐτὰρ ὅ γ' ἐc 'Ρόδον ἷξεν* Il. 2. 667: φερέcβιον* Dem. 451, 469 (cf. Ap. 341, Hy. 30. 9, Hes. Th. 693): οὖθαρ ἀρούρηc* Il. 9. 141 = 283 (cf. ad Dem. 164 etc.) 451 τὸ πρίν* Il. 9. 403 etc.: ἀλλὰ ἔκηλοc* Il. 9. 376   452 ἑcτήκει* Il. 11. 599 etc. (Il. 18. 563 ~ 557: cf. ad Dem. 454–6): κρῖ λευκόν* Od. 4. 604   453 Δήμητροc* Il. 14. 326, Dem. 4, Hes. Th. 912: καλλιcφύρου* Il. 9. 557 etc.   454 μέλλεν* Od. 1. 232: ἀcταχύεccιν* Il. 2. 148: κόμην τανυφύλλου ἐλαίηc Od. 23. 195 455 ἀέξουcιν* Od. 15. 372: πίονεc ἀγροί* Il. 23. 832: ὄγμουc* Il. 18. 546 456 βριθόμενα cταχύων* Hes. Sc. 290: ἄλλα δ'... ἐν ἐλλεδανοῖcι δέοντο* Il. 18. 553 (~ Sc. 291)   457 ἐπέβην* Od. 3. 482, 11. 167: πρώτιcτον* Il. 14. 295 etc.: ἀπ' αἰθέροc* Il. 18. 258, 15. 610: δι' αἰθέροc ἀτρυγέτοιο* Il. 17. 425, Dem. 67 458 ἀcπαcίωc* Il. 11. 327 etc.: ἴδον* Il. 15. 279, Od. 3. 221: κεχάριcτο δὲ θυμῷ Od. 6. 23 (~ Il. 1. 256, 5. 243 etc.)   459 τὸν (etc.) δ' αὖτε προcέειπε* Il. 1. 206 etc.: 'Ρέην* Hes. Th. 467: λιπαροκρήδεμνοc Il. 18. 382, Dem. 25, 438   460 δεῦρο φίλη* Od. 8. 292 (~ 424): χαῖρε, τέκοc* Hy. 7. 58: καλέει cε* Dem. 321: βαρύκτυποc εὐρύοπα Ζεύc* Dem. 3 etc.   461–5 cf. Dem. 443–7   461 ἐλθέμεναι μετὰ φῦλα θεῶν* Dem. 322: ὑπέδεκτο δὲ τιμάc* Dem. 443   462 ἐθέληcθα* Od. 18. 270, 24. 511

459 'Ρέη λιπαροκρήδεμνοc* Orph. Arg. 625

450 ῥίον M: 'Ράριον Ruhnken: ἐc δ' ἄρα 'Ράριον Hermann   451 ἀλλ' ἀπέτηλον Ruhnken, alii   452 εἱcτήκει (i.e. ἱcτήκει ex εἱcτήκει) correctum videtur a manu prima (Goodwin): ἑcτήκει Hermann   454 ἀcταχύεccιν M: ἀνθερίκεccιν Ruhnken   456 βρυcέμεν M: corr. Ruhnken   δίδεcθαι Voss, Cobet (Mnem. 10 (1861), 325 ff.)   462 δωcέμεν ἅc κε θέληcθα m: ἅc κ' ἐθέληcθα, vel potius ἅc κεν ἕλοιο Ilgen   463 νεῦcε δέ cοι κούρην ἔτεοc πε m   464 τὴν... ζόφον ἠ m: ἐρόεντᾰ M (correctio a prima manu videtur facta esse)

[τὰς δὲ δύω παρὰ coί τε καὶ ἄλλοις] ἀθανάτοισιν.   465
]εcθαι· ἑῷ δ' ἐπένευσε κάρητι.
[ἀλλ' ἴθι τέκνον] ἐμὸν καὶ πείθεο, μηδέ τι λίην
ἀ[ζηχὲς μεν]έαινε κελαινεφέϊ Κρονίωνι·
α[ἶψα δὲ κα]ρπὸν ἄεξε φερέςβιον ἀνθρώποισιν.
Ὣ[ς ἔφατ', οὐ]δ' ἀπίθησεν ἐϋςτέφανος Δημήτηρ,   470
αἶψα δὲ καρπὸν ἀνῆκεν ἀρουράων ἐριβώλων.
πᾶςα δὲ φύλλοιςίν τε καὶ ἄνθεσιν εὐρεῖα χθὼν
ἔβρις'· ἡ δὲ κιοῦςα θεμιστοπόλοις βασιλεῦςι
δ[εῖξε,] Τριπτολέμῳ τε Διοκλεῖ τε πληξίππῳ,
Εὐμόλπου τε βίῃ Κελεῷ θ' ἡγήτορι λαῶν,   475
δρηςμοςύνην θ' ἱερῶν καὶ ἐπέφραδεν ὄργια πᾶςι,

466 ὡς οἱ ὑπέςτην πρῶτον, ἐμῷ δ' ἐπένευςα κάρητι Il. 15. 75: ἡ δ' ἐπένευςε
κάρητι Dem. 169: ἔςεςθαι* Od. 4. 108, 494, Ap. 54   467 ἀλλ' ἴθι* Il. 1. 32,
Dem. 323 etc.: τέκνον ἐμόν* Il. 1. 414 etc.: οὐδέ τι λίην (etc.)* Od. 13. 238 (etc.)
468 ἀζηχὲς μεμακυῖαι* Il. 4. 435: μενέαινε* Il. 16. 491: κελαινεφέϊ Κρονίωνι*
Il. 1. 397 etc.   469 αἶψα δὲ καρπὸν ἀνῆκεν* Dem. 471: φερέςβιον* Dem. 450,
451: ἀνθρώποισιν* Il. 4. 320 etc.   470 ὡς ἔφατ', οὐδ' ἀπίθηςεν* Il. 2. 441 etc.
(cf. Dem. 448): ἐϋςτέφανος Δημήτηρ* Dem. 224 etc.   471 ἐριβώλων ἄρουραν
Il. 21. 232: ἐρίβωλον* Il. 9. 329 etc.: ἀρούρης καρπόν Il. 21. 465: cf. Dem. 469
472 ἄνθεσιν* Il. 2. 89: εὐρεῖα χθών* Dem. 428 etc.   473 βριςέμεν* Dem. 456:
βρίθει* . . . ἄρουρα φερέςβιος Hy. 30. 9: βεβρίθει* Od. 16. 474, Ap. 136: θεμιςτοπόλων
βαςιλήων* Dem. 103, 215   474 δεῖξε* Od. 3. 174 etc.: Τριπτολέμου* Dem.
153: Μενεςθῆα πληξίππον* Il. 4. 327 (~ 11. 93): Πέλοπι πληξίππῳ* Il. 2. 104
475 Κύκλωπός τε βίης* Od. 10. 200: βίῃ* Il. 7. 197 etc.: πολέων ἡγήτορι λαῶν*
Il. 20. 383   476 δρηςτοςύνη* Od. 15. 321: ἱερῶν* Dem. 481: ἐπέφραδε*
Il. 11. 794 etc.: ὑπέςχετο ἱερὰ καλά Il. 23. 195 (~ 209, 11. 726 etc.)

465 ἀθανάτοισιν M qui post hunc versum 448–52 repetivit: hos versus expunxit
m, qui etiam ἀθανάτοισιν abolere voluit: de erroribus scribarum codicis M et m
vide Goodwin ad loc. (466 in editione sua Goodwin): cetera restituit Ruhnken
466 δύο δέ πὰρ coὶ ἔc m: εcθαι· ἑῷ δ' ἐπένευςε κάρητι M: ὡς τοι ὑπέςτη ἔςεςθαι
Hermann: ὡς μὲν ὑπέςχετ' ἔςεςθαι post Voss Gemoll: καὶ ἑοῖ αὐτῷ (vel ᾧ ἑνὶ οἴκῳ)
ἔςεςθαι Bücheler: ὡς ἄρ' ἔφη τελέςεςθαι Goodwin   467 ἀλλ' ἴθι τέκνον m
468 ἀ[.......]'αινε κελενεφέι κρονίωνι M: ἀζηχὲς μαινε m: μενέαινε κελαινεφέϊ Ruhnken
469 αἶψα δὲ κ m: ἀ[......]αρπὸν etc. M   470 ὡς ἔφατ' οὐ m: ω[.......]δ' etc. M
471 αἶψα δὲ καρ refecit m   474–6 cit. Paus. 2. 14. 3   474 δˊc....ιπτολεμω
τε M: εἶπε τρ m: δεῖξεν Pausanias: δεῖξε ex Paus. 2. 14, idque ipsum in M a manu
prima fuisse credebat Schneidewin (cf. Baumeister)   476 χρηςμοςύνην θ'
(repictis ab m litteris νθ) . . . ὄργια καλά M: δρηςμοςύνην . . . ὄργια πᾶςιν
Pausanias (omissa voce θ'), quem Ruhnken secutus est   477 Τριπτολέμῳ
τε Πολυξείνῳ, ἐπὶ τοῖς δὲ Διοκλεῖ M: post Πολυξείνῳ addidit τ' Ruhnken, qui
lacunam hic subesse, amissis versibus in quibus poeta Celei filias memoraret,
suspicatur (cf. Paus. 1. 38. 3): versum interpolatum credebant Mitscherlich, alii
quos secutus sum

cεμνά, τά γ' ού πως έςτι παρεξ[ίμ]εν ού[τε] πυθέςθαι,   478
ούτ' άχέειν· μέγα γάρ τι θεών cέβας ἰςχάνει αὐδήν.

ὄλβιος ὃς τάδ' ὄπωπεν ἐπιχθονίων ἀνθρώπων·   480
ὃς δ' ἀτελὴς ἱερῶν, ὅς τ' ἄμμορος, οὔ ποθ' ὁμοίων
αἶςαν ἔχει φθίμενός περ ὑπὸ ζόφῳ εὐρώεντι.

Αὐτὰρ ἐπεὶ δὴ πάνθ' ὑπεθήκατο δῖα θεάων,
βάν ῥ' ἴμεν Οὔλυμπον δὲ θεῶν μεθ' ὁμήγυριν ἄλλων.

ἔνθα δὲ ναιετάουςι παραὶ Διὶ τερπικεραύνῳ   485
cεμναί τ' αἰδοῖαί τε· μέγ' ὄλβιος ὅν τιν' ἐκεῖναι
προφρονέως φίλωνται ἐπιχθονίων ἀνθρώπων·

478 coì δ' οὔπω φίλον ἐςτὶ δαημέναι οὐδὲ πυθέςθαι *Od.* 13. 335 (cf. ad *Dem.* 98 ff.):
ἀλλὰ μάλ' οὔπως ἔςτι Διὸς νόον αἰγιόχοιο
οὔτε παρεξελθεῖν ἄλλον θεὸν οὔθ' ἁλιῶςαι
Od. 5. 103–4 (~ 137–8)
479 μέγα γάρ ῥα θεῶν* ὤτρυνεν ἐφετμή *Il.* 21. 299: δέος ἰςχάνει* *Il.* 14. 387: cέβας
μ' ἔχει *Od.* 3. 123 etc.: *Ἐρινύες* ἔςχεθον αὐδήν* *Il.* 19. 418   480 ὄλβιος·* ἦ γὰρ ...
Od. 11. 450: ὄλβιος, ὅς* Hes. *Th.* 954: ὄπωπα* *Il.* 6. 124 etc.: ἐπιχθονίων ἀνθρώπων*
Il. 4. 45 etc.: μέγ' ὄλβιος, ὄντιν' ... ἐπιχθονίων ἀνθρώπων* *Dem.* 486–7   481 ἱερῶν*
Dem. 476: ἄμμορον* *Il.* 6. 408, 24. 773; οὔποθ' ὁμοίης ἔμμορε τιμῆς *Il.* 1. 278: οὐδὲν
ὁμοῖον* *Il.* 10. 216: οὐκέθ' ὁμοῖος* *Od.* 16. 182   482 αἶςαν* *Dem.* 257: φθιμένοιο*
Od. 11. 558: ὑπὸ ζόφον ἠερόεντα* *Il.* 23. 51, *Dem.* 80 etc.: Ἀΐδεω ... δόμον εὐρώεντα*
Od. 10. 512 (~ 23. 322): ὑπὸ ζόφῳ ἠερόεντι* ... χώρῳ ἐν εὐρώεντι Hes. *Th.* 729–31
483 αὐτὰρ ἐπεὶ δὴ πάντα* *Od.* 6. 227: αὐτὰρ ... ὑποθηςόμεθ'* *Il.* 21. 293 (~ *Od.*
5. 143): δῖα θεάων* *Il.* 5. 381 etc.   484 βάν ῥ' ἴμεν* *Il.* 10. 297 etc.: ἀψ ἴμεν
Οὔλυμπον δέ, θεῶν μεθ' ὁμήγυριν ἄλλων *Il.* 20. 142 (~ *Ap.* 187)   485 ἐνθάδε
ναιετάων* *Od.* 6. 245, 15. 360: ναιετάουςι(ν)* *Od.* 9. 23, *Herm.* 555 etc.: παραὶ Διὶ
τερπικεραύνῳ* *Ap.* 5 (cf. ad *Dem.* 483–9) ~ *Il.* 1. 419 etc.   486 αἰδοίη τε φίλη
τε* *Il.* 18. 386=425: δεινός τ' αἰδοῖός τε* *Od.* 8. 22, 14. 237: κυδρή τ' αἰδοίη τε* θεοῖς
(v.l. θεῶν) Hes. *Op.* 257 (de Iustitia): ὁ δ' ὄλβιος ὅντινα Μοῦςαι | φίλωνται· γλυκερή
οἱ ἀπὸ ςτόματος ῥέει αὐδή Hes. *Th.* 96 f. (= *Hy.* 25. 4 f.): ὁ δ' ὄλβιος, ὅν κε cὺ θυμῷ |
πρόφρων τιμήςῃς *Hy.* 30. 7 f. (12 ~ *Dem.* 489, 18 ~ 494)   487 προφρονέως*
Il. 6. 173, *Dem.* 138 etc.: φίλωνται* *Dem.* 117: ἐπιχθονίων ἀνθρώπων* *Il.* 4. 45,
Dem. 480 etc.

480–2 cf. Pi. fr. 137a Sn., S. fr. 753 N. (v. commentarium ad loc.)   486 cf.
Theocr. 17. 73 ff.
Διὶ Κρονίωνι μέλοντι
αἰδοῖοι βαςιλῆες, ὁ δ' ἔξοχος ὅν κε φιλήςῃ
γεινόμενον τὰ πρῶτα· πολὺς δέ οἱ ὄλβος ὀπαδεῖ ...

478 γ' M : τ' Ilgen   παρεξέμεν Ruhnken : παρεξίμεν Matthiae   οὔ[τε] πυθέςθαι
in M stetisse ex vestigiis collegit Goodwin   479 οὔτ' ἀχέειν· μέγα γάρ τι θεῶν
(ῶν repinxit m) cέ[βα]c (quod in ἄχος effecit m) ἰςχάνει (iteravit ἰςχ supra lineam m)
αὐδὴν M   οὔτε χανεῖν Mitscherlich : χέειν Bothe : ἠχέειν Gemoll : forsitan ἰαχεῖν
scribendum sit   in codice cέβ^ac stetisse putat Goodwin : cέβας coniecerat Cobet :
ἄχος Valckenaer   481 ὁμοίην Fontein   484 θέων M : corr. Ruhnken

αἶψα δέ οἱ πέμπουσιν ἐφέστιον ἐς μέγα δῶμα
Πλοῦτον, ὃς ἀνθρώποις ἄφενος θνητοῖσι δίδωσιν.
Ἀλλ' ἄγ' Ἐλευσῖνος θυοέσσης δῆμον ἔχουσαι   490
καὶ Πάρον ἀμφιρύτην Ἄντρωνά τε πετρήεντα,
πότνια ἀγλαόδωρ' ὡρηφόρε Δηοῖ ἄνασσα
αὐτὴ καὶ κούρη περικαλλὴς Περσεφόνεια
πρόφρονες ἀντ' ᾠδῆς βίοτον θυμήρε' ὀπάζειν.
αὐτὰρ ἐγὼ καὶ σεῖο καὶ ἄλλης μνήσομ' ἀοιδῆς.   495

488 πέμπουσιν* Il. 1. 390 etc.: ἐφέστιον* Od. 7. 248: ἐς μέγα δῶμα* Od. 8. 56 etc.
488–9 αἶψά τέ οἱ δῶ | ἀφνειὸν πέλεται Od. 1. 392 f.   489 ἀνθρώποις* Dem. 306
etc.: ἄφενος* Il. 1. 171: θνητοῖσι* Il. 17. 547 etc.: ἀνθρώποισι δίδωσιν* Od. 17. 287
(~ 474): τὸν δὴ ἀφνειὸν ἔθηκε, πολὺν δέ οἱ ὤπασεν ὄλβον (sc. Plutus) Hes. Th. 974
490 ἀλλ' ἄγ' Il. 4. 100 etc.: Ἐλευσῖνος θυοέσσης* Dem. 97: δῆμον ἔχοντες* Il. 5. 710,
15. 738   491 ἀμφιρύτῃ* Od. 1. 50 etc.: Πυθῶνά τε πετρήεσσαν* Il. 2. 519 etc.:
πετρήεντα Hy. 19. 7   492 πότνια Δημήτηρ ὡρηφόρε, ἀγλαόδωρε Dem. 54: πότνια
Δηώ Dem. 47: ἄνασσα* Dem. 75, 440   493 αὐτὴν καὶ κούρην, περικαλλέα Περσεφόνειαν Hy. 13. 2: αὐτὴν ἠδὲ θύγατρα* Dem. 2: Περσεφόνη περικαλλής* Dem. 405:
περικαλλὴς Ἡρίβοια* Il. 5. 389   494 πρόφρονι* Il. 8. 40 = 22. 184: βίοτον*
Od. 1. 160 etc.: θυμαρές* Od. 17. 199: πρόφρων δ' ἀντ' ᾠδῆς βίοτον θυμήρε' ὄπαζε
Hy. 30. 18 (~ 31. 17): ὄλβον δὲ θεοὶ μέλλουσιν ὀπάζειν* Od. 18. 19: ᾧ πρόφρων γε
θεὰ ὑποδέξεται εὐχάς, | καί τέ οἱ ὄλβον ὀπάζει Hes. Th. 419–20 (cf. ad Dem. 487)
495 = Ap. 546, Herm. 580, Hy. 6. 21, 10. 6, 19. 49, 28. 18, 30. 19 (18 ~ Dem 494)

494 τέλος θυμηδὲς ὄπαζε* A.R. 4. 1600 ~ 1. 249 (in precationibus): θυμαρὴν
ὄλβον IG 14. 433. 6

488 μέγα (ex μέγαν a prima manu correctum) δόμον M: corr. Ruhnken
490 ἀλλὰ θελευσῖνος M: corr. Ruhnken   ἔχουσα Ruhnken (cf. ad Dem. 494)
492 πότνι' M: corr. Ruhnken   494 πρόφρονες ... ὄπαζε M: πρόφρων δ' ...
ὄπαζε Ruhnken (cf. Hy. 30. 18): ὀπάζειν Voss

COMMENTARY

Title. The plural ὕμνοι in M does not indicate that there was more than one hymn to Demeter, as Bücheler thought. A stop should be placed after ὕμνοι. Similar titles precede the hymns to Apollo, Hermes, and Aphrodite, and are also found at the beginning of the hymns of Callimachus, Orpheus, and Proclus.

The late Greek form Δήμητραν often occurs in manuscripts.

1–18. The poet sings of Demeter and Persephone, whom Hades carried off with the permission of Zeus, when she was playing with the Oceanids. She was picking flowers in a meadow, and one of these was a narcissus which Earth caused to grow to deceive her, a miraculous flower. When she picked it, the earth opened and Hades sprang forth with his immortal horses.

1–3. Proem

The poet states the subject of the hymn, and gives a brief summary of the story. The first word of an epic poem often formed a kind of title, giving the main subject: cf. *Il.* 1. 1, *Od.* 1. 1, *Theb.* fr. 1, *Il. parva* fr. 1, *Herm.* 1, *Hy.* 9. 1 etc., Hes. *Th.* 1 (West ad loc.). This is followed here by attributes of the deity (cf. *Herm.* 1–3, *Hy.* 6. 1, 9. 1–2, etc.), and then the traditional formula ἄρχομ᾽ ἀείδειν (cf. Hes. *Th.* 1, *Hy.* 9. 8, 11. 1, 13. 1, 16. 1, 22. 1, 26. 1, 28. 1). With the accusative this would be most naturally taken as 'I begin *to* sing of...' (so Wünsch, *RE* 9. 149 f.). But cf. *Hy.* 9. 8 f., where it must mean 'I begin *by* singing of you', and the poet announces his intention of going on to another poem. This is also the case where the genitive is used, as in Hes. *Th.* 1, where the opening hymn to the Muses is followed by the main subject of the poem, the *Theogony*. The genitive means 'I begin from': cf. the other examples in West ad loc., and also *Th.* 36, *Aph.* 293, *Hy.* 9. 8 f., 18. 11, 25. 1, 31. 18, 32. 18, Theocr. 22. 25. The hymns were, at least originally, intended as preludes to epic recitation (cf. Introduction, pp. 3 f.), and we should probably treat the formula in the same way here also (cf. R. Keyssner, *Gottesvorstellung und Lebensauffassung im griechischen Hymnos* (Stuttgart, 1932), 9 ff.).

In the second line the poet recapitulates his subject, since it is in fact a double one, Demeter and Persephone. He hesitates, as it were, in a similar way at the end of the poem (492–3 ∼ 1–2), and returns to the single subject in the traditional closing line (495).

He then passes immediately to the narrative, which is introduced by a relative, once again a traditional epic device: cf. *Il.* 1. 2, *Od.* 1. 1, Hes. *Th.* 2, West ad loc., also Hes. *Sc.* 57, fr. 1. 3. This is also a feature of prayers and hymns, where the relative introduces the cult-places, powers, birth-legend, etc. of the deity (cf. Norden, *Agnostos Theos*, 168 ff.).

Here lines 2b–3 also introduce the other two main personalities of the hymn, Hades and Zeus (cf. ad *Dem.* 9). The lines are probably traditional, as they occur in almost identical form in Hes. *Th.* 913 f. This part of the *Theogony* (which is possibly post-Hesiodic: cf. West, pp. 397 ff.) contains a series of balanced pieces referring to the wives and children of Zeus (and other deities). These show parallels with some of the other hymns: 918 ~ *Ap.* 14 f., 924 ~ *Hy.* 28. 4 f., 940 f. ~ *Hy.* 7. 56–7 (also 926 ~ *Aph.* 10 f.). This suggests that they are traditional genealogical summaries, and there is no reason to suppose that the hymn is echoing Hesiod here.

Cf. Arist. *Rhet.* 1415^{a}12 ff. (quoting *Il.* 1. 1, *Od.* 1. 1, Choerilus fr. 1a), and especially 22 : τὸ μὲν οὖν ἀναγκαιότατον ἔργον τοῦ προοιμίου καὶ ἴδιον τοῦτο, δηλῶσαι τί ἐστιν τὸ τέλος οὗ ἔνεκα ὁ λόγος. Cf. also B. A. van Groningen, *Composition littéraire archaïque*, 106 f., and *The Proems of the Iliad and the Odyssey* (Amsterdam, 1946) (*Meded. der Kon. Nederl. Akad. van Wetenschappen, afd. Letterkunde*, Nieuwe Reeks, Deel 9, No. 8); R. Böhme, *Das Prooimion* (Baden, 1937).

1. ἠΰκομον: this is used of Demeter at *Dem.* 297, 315, Hes. fr. 280. 20, Archestr. fr. 4. 1. Cf. ad *Dem.* 60.

cεμνήν: the word occurs first here in epic. Cf. Solon, fr. 3. 14 D.^{3}, etc. (Hom. cέβας, cέβομαι). It is used particularly in relation to Demeter and Persephone: cf. *Dem.* 478, 486, and notes ad locc.

θεόν: M has θεάν in this place in the verse also at *Dem.* 179 and *Hy.* 13. 1, but θεόν at 292, *Hy.* 28. 1. Other manuscripts read θεόν also at *Hy.* 13. 1. Cf. in Homer δεινὴ(ν) θεός (-όν) 10 times (8 times in this place in the verse), Hes. *Th.* 442 κυδρὴ θεός* (cf. *Dem.* 179, 292). West ad loc. argues that Hesiod uses θεός here, although he has θεά elsewhere in the *Theogony*, because θεός is regular in this formula. But cf. cεμνὴ θεά* in *Hy.* 30. 16 (*without* synizesis).

Synizesis of the masculine θεοί occurs in epic (cf. ad *Dem.* 55), but the long monosyllable in the fourth-foot thesis, not linked closely to the following word, is metrically unusual. Cf. *Dem.* 325 μάκαρας θεούς, where, however, the following αἰὲν ἐόντας goes closely with θεούς. Synizesis of fem. θεά occurs in Attic tragedy: cf. E. *El.* 1270, *Andr.* 978, *Tr.* 969. For synizesis of other words in -εᾶ, -εᾶ in early epic cf. K–B 1. 227.

M's reading is partly supported by *Hy.* 30. 16, and the metrical awkwardness may be regarded as the result of a (grammatical) formula-variation. But the testimony of the other manuscripts at *Hy.* 13. 1 is against M, which is also inconsistent at *Dem.* 179, 292.

ἄρχομ' ἀείδειν: cf. also Anon. *Hy. Cer.* 1 (Page, *GLP* 1, No. 91, p. 408) ὕ]μνον Δήμη[τρ]ος πολυωνύμου ἄρχομαι ἰcτ[ᾶν.

2. τανίcφυρον: the iota is regularly attested in papyri (cf. West ad *Th.* 364). Cf. (of Persephone) Bacch. 5. 59 (~ 3. 60).

Ἀϊδωνεύς: only twice in Homer (*Il.* 5. 190, 20. 61). Hades himself (as opposed to his 'house') rarely appears in Homer: cf. Page, *History and the Homeric Iliad*, 326 n. 8 (add *Il.* 9. 158 f., 13. 415, also 5. 654 = 11. 445 = 16. 625, *Od.* 10. 534 = 11. 47). Persephone, however, is often mentioned in *Od.* 10 and 11. It has been suggested (cf. Nilsson, *Gesch.* i³. 454 ff.) that the proper form of the name was *Ἀϊς, and that this denoted the underworld rather than its lord. But 'the house of Hades' (*Il.* 3. 322 etc.) suggests a person. For the etymology, which is uncertain, cf. Nilsson l.c., Frisk s.v.

3. Note the chiastic order: 'whom Aidoneus carried off, but the gift was that of Zeus'.

βαρύκτυποc εὐρύοπα Ζεύς: the formula first occurs here, and again three times in the *Hymn.* It is a 'combination formula' (cf. Introduction, pp. 46 ff.), fusing Homeric εὐρύοπα Ζεύc and Hesiodic βαρύκτυποc, which is used of Zeus only in oblique cases at *Th.* 388, *Op.* 79, *Sc.* 318 (but cf. βαρύκτυποc* Ἐννοcίγαιοc *Th.* 818). It is also a doublet of Homeric πατὴρ ἀνδρῶν τε θεῶν τε (and of πατὴρ Ζεὺc ἄφθιτα εἰδώc, *Dem.* 321), and Κρόνου πάιc ἀγκυλομήτεω (cf. Hoekstra, *Sub-epic Stage*, 56, and Edwards, *Language of Hesiod*, 70). Cf. also Homeric Ὀλύμπιοc εὐρύοπα Ζεύc (*Od.* 4. 173), and (for the nominative Ζεὺc . . . βαρύκτυποc) Sem. fr. 1. 1.

εὐρύοπα: originally accusative from *εὐρύοψ, and used as nominative by analogy with μητίετα Ζεύc etc. The meaning is probably 'with far-reaching voice'. Cf. Chantraine, *GH* i. 200, Frisk s.v., Leumann, *Hom. Wörter*, 24.

The active role of Zeus, not only as consenting to the Rape, but as in some sense being at the back of it, is emphasized throughout the *Hymn*: cf. *Dem.* 9 and note ad loc., 30, 77 ff. In the second part of the *Hymn* Zeus plays a more openly active part: cf. Deichgräber, *Eleusinische Frömmigkeit*, 525 ff.

His consent to the marriage as father was necessary to make it legal (cf. H. J. Rose, *A Handbook of Greek Mythology* (Methuen, 1958), 91). But the Rape is also his plan, the Διὸc βουλή, as in *Il.* 1. 5, *Cypria* fr. 1. 7, etc. His role is ambiguous: he does not hear his daughter's cry, because he is out of earshot (*Dem.* 27 ff.), but he knows what is going on. Similarly, in the *Iliad*, he may turn away from the battle for a time, but ultimately 'his will is fulfilled'.

The role of Zeus is emphasized in later accounts: E. *Hel.* 1317 ff., Apollod. 1. 5. 1, Hyg. *fab.* 146, Claud. *RP* 1. 216 ff. (where Fate and Themis are behind Zeus: cf. Orph. *Arg.* 1195).

Aphrodite is also held responsible, in Ovid *M.* 5. 346 ff., Sil. Ital. 14. 242, Sen. *Herc.* 559 f., Claud. *RP* 1. 26 f., 216 ff., Myth. Vat. 2. 95, Lact. Plac. *narr. fab.* 5. 6. She is present at the Rape with Athena and Artemis in artistic representations (Roscher, 2. 1314), as also in Hyg. *fab.* 146, Claud. *RP* 2. 11 ff. Cf. ad *Dem.* 424.

4. νόcφιν Δήμητροc: cf. *Dem.* 72. It not only indicates that Demeter was absent, but also suggests that the Rape was without her knowledge or consent (cf. LSJ s.v. II. 3).

In some later artistic versions she is present, and pursues Hades.
Cf. Curtius, *Abh. der Berl. Akad.* 1878, 288 ff.; Treu ap. Förster,
Philol. Suppl. 4 (1884), 664–79; Murray, *JHS* 22 (1902), 3; Overbeck,
Atlas, Pls. 17. 1, 18. 1–3, 5, 6, 18, 20–2, 26, 27; P. Hartwig, *AM* 21
(1896), 380 (but the figure is perhaps Aphrodite), *RE* 19. 1. 957,
and ad *Dem.* 424. Förster and Hartwig assume that Hes. *Th.* 914
indicates her presence. This reads too much into the words.

In Firm. Mat. *de err. prof. rel.* 7 she is nearby and sees Hades
vanish with her daughter.

χρυσαόρου: the α is lengthened in composition. The change to η was
perhaps avoided, as it would have obscured the connection with ἄορ
(cf. West, *Theogony*, pp. 79 n. 2, and 82 on ἔαγε).

In Homer, the epithet is used of Apollo, *Il.* 5. 509, 15. 256; cf.
Ap. 123, 395, *Hy.* 27. 3. The Homeric form is χρυσάοροc. Cf., of Apollo,
Hes. fr. 357. 3, *Ap.* 395, *Hy.* 27. 3, but χρυσάωρ Hes. *Op.* 771, *Ap.* 123,
Pi. *P.* 5. 104, A.R. 3. 1282, Orph. *Arg.* 141. It is also used of Artemis
(χρυσάοροc, Orac. ap. Hdt. 8. 77), Orpheus (χρυσάωρ, Pi. *Thren.* 3. 12
Sn.), and Perseus (Orph. *Lith.* 545). Zeus has the cult-title Χρυσαορεύc
or Χρυσαόριοc at Stratonicea in Caria (Str. 660 C = 14. 2. 25; *CIG*
2720, 2721; cf. *OGI* 234. 24).

Homer normally uses ἄορ of a sword (*Il.* 10. 484 etc.), but the Scholia
claim that it is later used of any weapon. Cf. Schol. T ad *Il.* 14. 385
and *Il.* 21. 179, quoting Philitas fr. 23 P. In accordance with this
theory, Callimachus (*Hy.* 4. 31) uses it of Poseidon's trident, and
Ps. Oppian (*C.* 2. 553) of a rhinoceros' horn. δολιχάοροc is also quoted
from the *Phoronis* (P. Oxy. 2260 col. i 5–7, on which see Merkelbach,
APF 16 (1956), 115 ff.), probably of Athena (cf. ad *Dem.* 424).
Etymologically, ἄορ has been connected with ἀείρω (LSJ, Frisk s.v.;
Solmsen, *Unters.* 292; Trümpy, *Kriegerische Fachausdrücke im griechischen
Epos*, 63), and is taken to mean 'that which hangs' (from an ἀορτήρ),
i.e. a sword (cf. English 'hanger', used of a type of short sword, originally hung from the belt: *Shorter OED* s.v. Hanger³). If this is correct,
the extension of it to any weapon must be secondary.

In the case of Apollo, the Homeric epithet is normally explained as
referring to the sword, with which he is occasionally depicted, in the
context of the Gigantomachy or his fight with Tityus (cf. *RE* 2. 12.
10 ff., 111. 34 ff.). Artemis is shown with the sword once, on the
Louvre Tityus amphora (*RE* 2. 1349. 28 ff.). The difficulty of this
was felt by ancient scholars. The Scholia (ad *Il.* 5. 509, 15. 256)
object that Apollo's weapon is the bow, and that he is ἁγνόc, so should
not use the sword. They suggest that it refers to the strap (ἀορτήρ)
by which his quiver or his lyre was hung (quoting χρυσάορα of Orpheus), or to the rays of the rising sun.

Pindar may have used it of Orpheus because of Orpheus' connections with Apollo (cf. also χρυσολύραc of both, and K. Ziegler, *RE*
18. 1251. 68 ff.). Alternatively, the rather improbable explanation
which refers it to the lyre-strap may have already been current in
Pindar's time.

In the case of Demeter, a reference to her sickle has been suggested (Preller, *Demeter*, 77; Welcker, *Gr. Götterlehre*, 1. 536). This is, however, a comparatively rare attribute: cf. A.R. 4. 984 ff., and Schol. ad loc. She does not appear to be depicted with it in art at all. (Ch. Picard, *RÉG* 40 (1927), 351, 363 compares the golden sickles found in tombs in various parts of the Greek world.)

Demeter is called Ξιφηφόρος in Lyc. *Alex.* 153. The line refers to the Boeotian Demeter-Erinys of Tilphossa, who was represented as a seated statue, holding a sword (cf. Schol. ad loc.).

One might conjecture a connection between this type and the story of Medusa, with whom Demeter-Erinys is originally identical (cf. Malten, *JDAI* 29 (1912), 181 ff., Farnell, *Cults*, 3. 59). Medusa is the mother of Pegasus and *Chrysaor* (cf. Hes. *Th.* 280 ff.), and·Perseus' ἅρπη seems to belong here also. But it is doubtful whether any of this is relevant to our *Hymn*.

ἀγλαοκάρπου: this is used of trees in Homer (*Od.* 7. 115 = 11. 589) and *Dem.* 23. Cf. ἀγλαόδωρος (*Dem.* 54, 192, 492), and for the 'gladness' of nature cf. ad *Dem.* 10 (γανόωντα), 14 (ἐγέλαςςε).

The noun–epithet formula is a doublet of Δήμητρος καλλιπλοκάμοιο ἀνάςςης (*Il.* 14. 326). Cf. also Δήμητρος καλλιςφύρου* (*Dem.* 453), and Δήμητρος πολυφόρβης* (Hes. *Th.* 912), which also emphasizes her function as goddess of fertility.

5. κούρῃςι: Persephone was playing with the nymphs, the daughters of Oceanus: i.e. the setting is probably by Oceanus (cf. ad *Dem.* 7, 17). The Oceanids are the κοῦραι *par excellence*, and Persephone is their leader, Κο(ύ)ρη, as the Κουρῆτες are led by Ζεὺς Κοῦρος. As such, they are also κουροτρόφοι of men. Cf. Hes. *Th.* 346 f. and West ad loc., also West, *JHS* 85 (1965), 155 f. For Core herself as a water-deity cf. ad *Dem.* 99.

Nymphs are mentioned as Persephone's companions by Colum. 10. 268 ff., Stat. *Ach.* 1. 824 ff., Paus. 5. 20. 3, Porph. *de antro nymph.* 7, Claud. *RP* 2. 55 f. Also Sirens (Hyg. *fab.* 141, Claud. *RP* 3. 190, 205; cf. A.R. 4. 895 ff., Ov. *M.* 5. 554 f.) and Horae (Orph. *Hy.* 29. 9, 43. 7). For nymphs in the worship of Demeter cf. Schol. Pi. *P.* 4. 106.

Girls are carried off from a chorus of nymphs in *Il.* 16. 181 ff., *Aph.* 117 ff., Hes. fr. 140. Cf. also A.R. 1. 213 ff., Plut. *Thes.* 31. 2, and K. Reinhardt, *Festschr. B. Snell* (Munich, 1956), 11.

βαθυκόλποις: in Homer this is used always of Trojan women (*Il.* 18. 122, 339, 24. 215). Cf. similarly βαθύζωνος in Homer (ad *Dem.* 95). It is a suitable epithet for κουροτρόφοι. Cf. *Aph.* 257 (νύμφαι μιν θρέψουσιν ὀρεσκῷοι βαθύκολποι); Pi. *P.* 9. 101, of the earth; and ad *Dem.* 231 ff.

6 ff. The flower catalogue

Girls were traditionally carried off while picking flowers. Cf. Moschus, *Europa*, 63 ff., and Bühler ad loc. (pp. 75, 108, 110 ff.). Moschus' catalogue contains five of the six flowers in the *Hymn*. This might suggest that he was influenced by it here (cf. Introduction).

But as the same five flowers are listed in *Cypria* fr. 4. 3 ff. the list may be a traditional epic one, occurring also in an early epic version of the Rape of Europa. The story of this is in the *Catalogue*, and the motif of gathering flowers may have occurred there: cf. Hes. frr. 140, 141.

Cf. also Hes. fr. 26. 18 ff.: Stratonice is carried off by Apollo while picking flowers. Later examples are Oreithyia (Choer. Sam. fr. 5 K.), Creusa (E. *Ion* 887 ff.), and Helen (E. *Hel.* 243 ff.).

Some of the flowers in the *Hymn* later have a special significance in relation to Demeter and Persephone. This could be the effect of the *Hymn* (see especially notes to *Dem.* 8 νάρκιccον). At Eleusis, however, flowers certainly played an important part in the cult. Cf. ad *Dem.* 99, 192 ff., Ar. *Ran.* 373 f., 445 ff., and the Niinnion tablet (Mylonas, *Eleusis*, fig. 88).[1] Clement (*Protr.* 2. 17. 1 = Orph. fr. 50 K.) may also refer to the ritual, although he does not specify the Attic Eleusis. Flower-gathering at Eleusis is suggested by the Sicilian Anthesphoria (Pollux 1. 37), and the festival at Hipponium (Str. 256), both in honour of Core. The festival at Hipponium commemorated her having gathered flowers there. At Hermione, in the festival in honour of Demeter Chthonia, children gathered and wore garlands of κοcμοcάν-δαλον, a kind of hyacinth (Paus. 2. 35. 5). At Megalopolis, Artemis and Athena were represented with baskets of flowers on their heads in the temple of Demeter and Core (Paus. 8. 31. 1), as Core's companions at the time of the Rape (cf. ad *Dem.* 424).

At Sardis, a festival was held in honour of Persephone, called Χρυcάνθινα or Χρυcάντινα (Frazer, *Golden Bough*[3], *Adonis, Attis and Osiris*, i. 187; Head, *Cat. of Greek Coins of Lydia*, cx, cxiii). Cf. Chrys-anthis, the name of the girl who gave Demeter information about the Rape at Argos (Paus. 1. 14. 2; Malten, *ARW* 12 (1909), 300).

A festival Antheia is attested in the Attic deme Paiania (Sokolowski, *Lois sacrées, Supplément*, no. 18 A 23, B 7 f., 29). Nilsson (*Op. Sel.* iii. 96) connects this with the Eleusinian goddesses. But this is doubtful: cf. Sokolowski, who attributes it to Dionysus.

Similar flower-festivals are attested elsewhere in Greece. Cf. the Ἡροcάνθεια, or Ἡροάνθεια (Hsch., Phot. s.v.), a women's festival which took place in spring in the Peloponnese. Hera had the title Ἀνθεία at Argos (Paus. 2. 22. 1) and women ἀνθεcφόροι are mentioned in this cult (Pollux 4. 78). At the Argive Heraeum, a flower growing on the bank of the river Asterion was offered to Hera, and garlands were made from it (Paus. 2. 17. 2). Aphrodite was called Ἀνθεία at Cnossos, and had ἀνθηφόροι at Aphrodisias in Caria (*CIG* 2821 f.). *Hy.* 30. 14 (χοροῖc φερεcανθέcιν) suggests a similar custom in the cult of Ge.

If the flower-gathering at Eleusis occurred at a spring festival, this will have celebrated the *Return* of Core (cf. *Dem.* 401 ff., 455). But the story of the Rape may also have been told at this, and hence the flower-gathering will have been projected back to that event. There is

[1] Cf. also Philodamus, *Paean* 29 f. (p. 166, Powell): ἔμολεc μυχοὺc [Ἐλε]υcίνοc ἀν' [ἀνθεμώ]δειc.

no need to assume (with Jeanmaire, *Couroi et Courètes*, 271 ff.) that the Rape itself was supposed to have occurred in spring or early summer: cf. K. Kourouniotes, *Arch. Delt.* 15 (1933–5), 6 ff. Where Core is, flowers naturally grow and are gathered (cf. Clearchus apud Ath. 554 b). In the Sicilian version, flowers bloom throughout the year on the plain of Henna (Diod. 5. 4. 3, Ov. *M.* 5. 391). In fact, some of the flowers in the hymn bloom in autumn (cf. below). Moschus also confuses the seasons in his flower-catalogue, and an anonymous versifier criticizes him for doing so (cf. Bühler, 114 n. 4).

For similar 'natural sympathy' cf. *Il.* 14. 346 ff., *Cypria* fr. 4, *Hy.* 19. 25 ff.

The anthology of Core is also described by Ovid (*F.* 4. 437 ff., *M.* 5. 391 ff.) and Claudian (*RP* 2. 128 ff.), and referred to by Pamphos (ap. Paus. 9. 31. 8), Nic. fr. 74. 60 f., Diod. 5. 33 f., Plut. *QN* 917 e, Ps. Arist. *Mir. Ausc.* 836ᵇ, Orph. *Arg.* 1192.

According to Schol. Soph. *OC* 681, the use of garlands was forbidden at the Thesmophoria, because they were abhorred by Demeter and Core (cf. Deubner, *AF* 56 n. 10). For similar prohibitions against following the example of Demeter cf. ad *Dem.* 42, 47 ff., 98 f. The Scholia on Sophocles say that the goddesses do not use τὰ ἄνθινα, which suggests a general prohibition at all festivals. This may mean that *crowns* were only of myrtle or smilax, rather than that no flowers were used at all.

6. ῥόδα: roses do not appear in Homer (but cf. ῥοδόεις, ῥοδο-δάκτυλος). Cf. Theognis 537, Sappho 2. 6, etc. The name is properly applied to the cultivated rose, but is here apparently used of the wild kind, unless this is simply fantasy (cf. Olck, *RE* 7. 775. 64 ff.). They were commonly used on graves, as in the Roman grave-festival of Rosaria or Rosalia. They were also symbolic of love, and in Moschus (*Eur.* 70) it is a rose that Europa picks, like Helen in E. *Hel.* 243 f. (above, p. 141). Cf. Murr, *Die Pflanzenwelt in der griech. Mythologie* (Innsbruck, 1890), 78 ff., Hehn, *Kulturpflanzen* (Berlin, 1911), 251 ff.

κρόκον: this occurs once in Homer, *Il.* 14. 348 (cf. κροκόπεπλος), and at *Hy.* 19. 25, *Cypria* 4. 3. It was associated with Demeter: cf. Soph. fr. 451 P. (Schol. S. *OC* 684). It is mentioned by Sophocles in *OC* 684 f. together with the narcissus, which he attributes to Demeter and Core. In *Dem.* 428 the narcissus is compared to it (if the reading is correct). Its golden colour, like that of the narcissus, made it a suitable symbol of underworld deities (cf. ad *Dem.* 19).

It appears in other Rape scenes: E. *Ion* 887 ff., Mosch. 2. 68. In Scholl. AB *Il.* 12. 292 (Hes. fr. 140) Zeus as the bull 'breathed saffron' when he carried off Europa. It blooms in autumn or winter (Thphr. 6. 8. 3, 6. 10; Call. *Hy.* 2. 80 ff.; Plin. *NH* 21. 34), but as it often appears with spring flowers (e.g. hyacinth) in literature, Murr (o.c. 253) concluded that there was a spring saffron also, *Crocus vernus* L.

ἠδ' ἴα: on the neglected digamma (cf. *Dem.* 418) see Appendix II, B 6. The violet occurs once in Homer, *Od.* 5. 72 (cf. ἰοειδής, ἰόεις, ἰοδνεφής). In the Sicilian version of the Rape, Persephone was picking violets when the earth opened : cf. Diod. 5. 3. 2 f. (they bloom all the year round on the plain of Henna) ; Nic. fr. 74. 60 f. ; Paus. 9. 31. 9 ; Ps. Arist. *Mir. Ausc.* 836ᵇ ; Plut. *Mor.* 917 f ; Ov. *M.* 5. 392. Cf. also Bacch. 3. 2 Δάματρα ἰοϲτέφανόν τε κούραν (in an invocation of Demeter as patron-goddess of Sicily).

They appear in spring, but can bloom throughout the year (Theophr. *HP* 6. 6. 2, 8. 2). They were used to decorate graves in later times (cf. A. B. Cook, *JHS* 20 (1900), 11 ff.).

For roses and violets together cf. the popular song *PMG* 852.

7. λειμῶν' ἄμ μαλακόν: the phrase interrupts the flower-catalogue (cf. ad *Dem.* 17, 22 f., 34, 382, Theocr. 1. 132–6), but is 'formulaic' in this context.

At Nysa in Caria, where there was a cult of Demeter and Core, there was a place called the Meadow, where the marriage of Core and Pluto was celebrated (cf. Str. 14. 1. 45, and ad *Dem.* 17). Flowery meadows also play a prominent part in underworld topography : cf. *Od.* 11. 539, 573, 24. 13, Ar. *Ran.* 373 f., 449 f., Plut. fr. 178, Orph. frr. 32 f 6, 222. 3, 293, Dieterich, *Nekyia,* 19 ff.

The meadow in Hes. *Th.* 279 is beside Oceanus, where the Hesperides live (*Th.* 274 f., 282), i.e. it is perhaps the legendary 'garden of the gods' (cf. Roscher, *Die Gorgonen,* 24 f.). Cf. also *Il.* 16. 151 βοϲκομένη λειμῶνι παρὰ ῥόον 'Ωκεανοῖο.

ἀγαλλίδαϲ: this occurs only here and in Hsch. s.v. ἀγαλλίϲ· ὑάκινθοϲ ἢ θρυαλλίϲ, ἢ ἀναγαλλίϲ; cf. Nic. fr. 74. 31 ἶριϲ δ' ἐν ῥίζῃϲιν ἀγαλλιάϲ. Agallis was however used as a name (Scholl. AT at *Il.* 18. 483, Ath. 14 d, 583 e).

According to Murr (o.c. 246) it was a kind of iris, and was also a popular grave-flower in Greece.

ὑάκινθον: once in Homer, *Il.* 14. 348 (with κρόκοϲ). On the use of κοϲμοϲάνδαλον, a type of hyacinth, at the festival of Demeter Chthonia at Hermione, cf. ad *Dem.* 6. Hyacinthus, who was killed by Apollo accidentally with a discus, is perhaps associated with Demeter, Core, and Pluto on the pedestal of the Amyclaean statue of Apollo (Paus. 3. 19. 4). His sister Polyboea was sometimes identified with Core (Hsch. s.v.).

It is not certain what flower was meant by the name: Theophr. *HP* 6. 8. 1 ff. has two types, wild and cultivated. They flower in spring and the latter is identified with the garden hyacinth (*Hyacinthus orientalis* L.) by Murr (o.c. 256 ff.). J. Sergeaunt, *Trees, Shrubs, and Plants in Virgil* (Oxford, 1920), 56 f., suggests that squill, larkspur, and modern hyacinth, perhaps also corn-flag or red lily, are all included under this name. C. Garlick, *CR* 35 (1921), 146 f., suggests that it is the fritillary. The Orchis quadripunctata has also been advocated (Gow ad Theocr. 10. 28).

8. νάρκιϲϲον: not in Homer or Hesiod. Cf. *Cypr.* fr. 4. 6. It is called 'the ancient garland of the great Goddesses' in Soph. *OC* 683 f. (cf. ad *Dem.* 6). This, however, caused the commentators some difficulty, as the Scholia observe that the narcissus is *not* used in garlands of the two goddesses. They suggest that the reference is either to the Erinyes, or else simply an allusion to the story of the Rape, the plural μεγαλᾶν θεᾶν being an extension from the use of the flower by Core. This is probably the right explanation. Cf. also Hsch. s.v. Δαμάτριον· ἄνθος ὅμοιον ναρκίccῳ. In Pamphos' version, it was also used to deceive Persephone (cf. Paus. 9. 31. 9, ad *Dem.* 6).

Murr (o.c. 246 ff.) identifies it here with the *Narcissus tazetta* L., which has a sweet scent and rich cluster of yellow flowers (cf. *Dem.* 12 f., 428), and blooms in wet, low-lying parts of Greece, from late autumn to early spring. Cf. Soph. l.c.: ὁ καλλίβοτρυc . . . νάρκιccοc, i.e. with fine clusters. For the narcissus as an autumn flower cf. Theophr. *HP* 6. 6. 9, 8. 3, also Virg. *G.* 4. 122, 'sera comantem'. There were also two spring types (Theophr. 6. 8. 1).

It is often mentioned in connection with funerals or the underworld: cf. Nic. fr. 74. 70 (cf. Gow and Scholfield ad loc.), *Anth. Plan.* App. 120 (= 2. 238), Artemid. *Oneirocr.* 1. 77, 2. 7. It is attributed to the Eumenides (Schol. Soph. *OC* 681, Euphor. fr. 94. 3 Powell, etc.), and appears as their attribute in art. Hades also has a garland of it, or holds it (cf. Roscher, 1. 1797 f.). A gold crown from a south Italian grave has a narcissus on it (Siebourg, *ARW* 8 (1905), 393 f.). Cf. J. H. Dierbach, *Flora mythologica* (Frankfurt, 1883), 146 f. As in the case of the saffron, its golden colour aptly symbolized the underworld (cf. ad *Dem.* 19).

On the mythological figure of Narcissus and his associations with mystic cults, cf. Eitrem, *RE* 16. 1721 ff. (especially 1726 ff.).

The narcissus is made to grow by Earth, to catch the girl. It is a miraculous flower (10 ff.), and when she reaches out her hands to pick it, the earth gapes and Hades leaps forth. This suggests that the flower is a kind of 'Open Sesame', a common motif in folk-stories, in which the magic flower is the key that opens the earth, revealing the underworld, and its hidden treasures. Cf. Usener, 'Italische Mythen', *RhM* 30 (1875), 215 ff. (= *Kl. Schr.* 4. 129 ff.), for an interesting discussion of such motifs.

δόλον: as a 'lure' to catch her. Cf. *Od.* 8. 276 (Hephaestus' net), 494 (Trojan horse), *Od.* 12. 252 (bait), *Od.* 19. 137 (Penelope's weaving); of Pandora, Hes. *Th.* 589 (cf. ad *Dem.* 10 f.), *Op.* 83; Aristaen. 1. 10 (the apple of Acontius).

καλυκώπιδι: the word does not occur in Homer or Hesiod. Cf. *Dem.* 420, *Aph.* 284; Bacch. fr. 20A. 17 Sn.; Orph. *Hy.* 79. 2 (κούρην). LSJ translate 'like a budding flower in face, i.e. blushing, roseate' (cf. Murr, o.c. 83: 'mit rosigem Antlitz, mit Rosenwangen'), but it perhaps means 'with eyes like buds'. Cf. κυνῶπιc (*Il.* 3. 180 etc. ∼ κυνὸc ὄμματ' ἔχων *Il.* 1. 225), Κύκλωψ, etc. On these words cf. Chantraine, *Formation des Noms*, 257 f., Leumann, *Hom. Wörter*, 147, 152. Heitsch (*Aphroditehymnos*, 25) translates 'mit einem Blick wie Blütenknospen', and calls it 'eine sehr gesuchte Neubildung'. See also Hoekstra, *Sub-epic Stage*, 13.

κούρη: cf. ad *Dem.* 5, 439, on Persephone's title Κο(ύ)ρη.

9. The line names the three agents in the Rape, Earth, Zeus, and Hades (i.e. perhaps Earth, Heaven, and Hell, the three parts of the world? Cf. ad *Dem.* 13 f., 33–5, and especially *Il.* 15. 36 ff. etc., *Ap.* 334 ff.).

Earth appears on Roman sarcophagi representing the Rape (cf. Förster, *Raub und Rückkehr*, 131 ff.). In Homer she is not portrayed as an active personality, but in Hesiod she gives advice and conspires with Zeus and other gods, as she does here (*Th.* 160 ff., 463 ff., 469 ff., 494, 626, 884, 891 ff.).

Διὸς βουλῆιϲι: cf. ad *Dem.* 3. The Διὸς βουλή is often referred to at the opening of an epic narrative, or in the summary of a myth: *Il.* 1. 5, *Od.* 11. 297, *Cypr.* fr. 1. 7 Διὸϲ δ' ἐτελείετο βουλή. Cf. Hes. *Th.* 1002, *Herm.* 10; *Od.* 8. 82, *Th.* 572, *Op.* 71, 79, 99, *Aph.* 23; *Od.* 11. 276, *Th.* 960, 993; Kirk, *Songs*, 165.

πολυδέκτῃ: the word occurs only here and Cornut. 35. Cf. δέκτηϲ (*Od.* 4. 248). For similar epithets of Hades cf. πολυδέγμων (*Dem.* 17, 31, 404, 430), πολυϲημάντωρ (31, 84, 376), πολύξενοϲ (A. *Supp.* 157, fr. 228 N.²), νεκροδέγμων (A. *PV* 152), παϲιάναξ (*Tab. Defix. Aud.* 43. 44), Ἀγηϲίλαοϲ (Kaibel, *Ep. Gr.* 195); also A. *Theb.* 860, Sen. *Herc. Oet.* 560, *Herc. fur.* 560, Roscher, 3. 2561, Rohde, *Psyche*⁹, i. 206 ff., and ad *Dem.* 18. Hades is referred to euphemistically also at *Dem.* 17 f., 31 f., 404, 430, and perhaps at 371. On the favourable presentation of him in the *Hymn* cf. ad *Dem.* 83 ff. He is the 'host of many' because his realm is thought of as a huge palace (cf. ad *Dem.* 379).

The poet of the *Hymn* is particularly fond of πολυ- compounds: cf. Introduction, p. 61.

Noun–epithet formulae for Hades are rare in the *Iliad* and *Odyssey*. The *Hymn* adds several new epithets and formulae: cf. 17, 18 = 32, 31, 84, 347, 376, 404, 430. It shares with Homer only ἄναξ ἐνέρων Ἀϊδωνεύϲ (357). For a doublet of this cf. 430.

10. θαυμαϲτόν: not in Homer or Hesiod (cf. Homeric θαῦμα; θαυμάϲιοϲ Hes. *Th.* 584, *Herm.* 443, θαυματόϲ Sc. 165, *Herm.* 80, etc.). Cf. Archil. fr. 29. 8 West, Theognis 25, etc. θαυμάϲιον would be an easy change, but unnecessary.

γανόωντα: used in Homer of the brightness of armour (*Il.* 13. 265, 19. 359), and of flowerbeds in full bloom (*Od.* 7. 128). Cf. γάνοϲ, used in later poetry of water, wine, and honey; γάνυμαι ('brighten up, be glad'). The magic flower was 'marvellously gay'. A similar transference of sense is found with ἀγλαόϲ (cf. ad *Dem.* 4), γελάω (cf. ad *Dem.* 14), and English *glad* (= smooth, shining, cf. German *glatt*).

ϲέβαϲ: in Homer, always of the sense of awe which takes hold of the viewer (ϲέβαϲ μ' ἔχει εἰϲορόωντα *Od.* 3. 123 etc.). Cf. *Dem.* 190. It is here transferred to the object for the first time. Cf. A. *Supp.* 85 (and frequently in Attic tragedy). On ϲέβαϲ see also ad *Dem.* 190, 478–9.

τό γε: τότε is supported by the papyrus, but seems no more than a stop-gap. τό γε is probably right: τό may refer to νάρκιϲϲον, being attracted to the case of ϲέβαϲ, or, more probably, generally to what

F

precedes (i.e. θαυμαστὸν γανόωντα). Cf. *Il.* 6. 167 (∼ 417) κτεῖναι μέν
ῥ᾽ ἀλέεινε, cεβάccατο γὰρ τό γε θυμῷ.

11. For this type of 'polar' expression cf. E. Kemmer, *Die polare
Ausdrucksweise in der gr. Literatur* (Würzburg, 1903). It is common in
the *Hymn.* In Homer cf. *Il.* 5. 442 (whole line) etc.

The formula represents a 'Hesiodic' variation of Homeric elements
(see formulaic parallels).

12. On the rich cluster of the *Narcissus tazetta* or polyanthus cf.
ad *Dem.* 8. It has a hundred heads here, which suggests that it is
a divine flower.

τοῦ καί: 'used in passing to a new detail not closely connected with
what has gone before' (West ad *Th.* 910). But here the καί perhaps
introduces an epexegetic sentence (cf. Leaf ad *Il.* 1. 249, 20. 165).

κάρα: the form is found only here and in Sannyrion, fr. 3. In S.
Ant. 291 κάρα is singular, and so probably also in *Il.* 10. 259, *Herm.*
211; cf. Ebeling s.v.

It may have been influenced by κέρᾱ (neut. plur. of κέραc), as in
Il. 4. 109, a line which was perhaps in the poet's mind. The analogy
καρήατα ∼ κεράατα perhaps had some effect. Cf. Schwyzer, *Gr. Gr.*
i. 583. Chantraine, *GH* i. 231, suggests that it was influenced by
neuter plurals in short alpha. This is unlikely, since the alpha is long
here. Cf. also Frisk s.v., and Hoekstra, *Sub-epic Stage*, 57 (innovation
or archaism?).

13. Tyrrell's conjecture is the most attractive that has been offered,
but is open to some strong objections. Cf. *Od.* 5. 59 f. ὀδμὴ . . . ὀδώδει,
9. 210 ὀδμὴ δ᾽ ἡδεῖα . . . ὀδώδει. Homer uses only this form of the verb.
The crasis is also un-Homeric, but cf. Hes. *Th.* 284, and ad *Dem.* 227.
ἥδιcτα is not in Homer, but cf. ἥδιcτοc, ἡδύ (adv.). The MS. reading
ὀδμῆ suggests a dative (cf. Agar, *CR* 31 (1917), 66). A lacuna after
line 12 would not be impossible (cf. Introduction, p. 66).

The *Narcissus tazetta* is sweetly-scented (cf. ad *Dem.* 8). But here
the scent is a feature of the miraculous appearance of this divine
flower (cf. ad *Dem.* 277). Heaven, earth, and sea smile at it. At the
epiphany of a deity the earth also smiles or laughs. Cf. the birth
of Apollo: *Ap.* 118, Theognis 8 ff., Limenius (p. 149 Powell), 7 ff.;
the epiphany of Bacchus: Nonn. *D.* 22. 7; the birth of Christ: *Or.
Sib.* 8. 475 f.; and in general Pfister, *RE*, Supp. 4. 319 (to his examples
add E. *Ba.* 726 f., *IT* 1242 ff., *Ion* 1078 ff., S. *Ant.* 1146, Theocr. 7. 64,
cf. Gow ad loc., 17. 64, Lucr. 1. 6–9). Similar expressions for the
earth (etc.) smiling or rejoicing occur in *Il.* 19. 362 (ad *Dem.* 14),
Hes. *Th.* 40 (also 173), A.R. 1. 880, 4. 1171, Paul. Sil. *Ecphr.* 900, Cat.
64. 46, 284 ('domus iucundo risit odore', of flowers), Hor. *Od.* 4. 11. 6,
Lucr. 1. 8, etc.

'Heaven, earth, and sea' is a way of saying 'the whole world'. This
poet is fond of such expressions: cf. *Dem.* 33–5, 380–2, and also *Dem.* 9
(Earth, Zeus, and Hades).

14. ἐγέλαccε: γελᾶν originally meant to 'shine' (West ad Hes. *Th.* 40).
Cf. ad *Dem.* 4, 10 and Hsch. s.v. γελεῖν· λάμπειν, ἀνθεῖν. For its use of the

sea ('to shine, sparkle, laugh') cf. Hes. *Th.* 256, Sem. 7. 27 f., A.
PV 90, etc. (West, l.c.). See also Verdenius, *Mnem.* 25 (1972), 243.

ἁλμυρὸν οἶδμα θαλάccηc: the formula is new, but built of Homeric
and Hesiodic elements (although οἶδμα θαλάccηc occurs first here).
οἶδμα in Homer and Hesiod is only found in the formula οἶδματι
θυίων/θυῖον (*Il.* 21. 234, 23. 230, *Th.* 109, 131). The Homeric uses
are specific, of a river in spate, and sea stirred by the winds, but in
Hesiod the phrase is used simply as a general formula of the sea (cf.
Edwards, *Language of Hesiod*, 52). Cf. also *Ap.* 417 οἶδμ' ἅλιον πολυίχθυον.

15. χερcὶν ἅμ' ἄμφω: in Homer, ἄμφω is only found in the nominative or accusative. *Herm.* 50 has ἀμφοῖν, which is normal in later
Greek. But cf. A.R. 1. 165, 1169, Theocr. 17. 26, Q.S. 1. 261, 2. 460,
5. 140, 14. 171, and in prose Arist. *Top.* 118ᵃ28.

In *Il.* 7. 255 ἄμφω goes with the subject of the verb (cf. 23. 686 f.).
This is a good example of reuse of a formula. Possibly the Homeric
passages were misunderstood, and so led to this new use, in accordance
with Leumann's theory of formulaic development. But it is also possible
that the use is parallel to that of δύο indecl. (cf. K–B 1. 633, 635).
ἀμφοῖν does not occur in Callimachus, Theocritus, Apollonius, or
Aratus. See also Introduction, p. 51.

16. καλὸν ἄθυρμα: the 'pretty plaything' deceives her, as the child
Dionysus is deceived by the Titans: cf. Orph. fr. 34 ἀπατήcαντεc
παιδαριώδεcιν ἀθύρμαcιν. Cf. also perhaps the anonymous song of the
mystae (Snell, *Hermes*, Einzelschr. 5 (1937), 106 ff.) col. i. 11 f.:
διηπάτων γιν[   ]γανθεων ποικίλτ' ἀθύρματα.

Persephone is still something of a child. In the same way, to the
child Hermes, the tortoise is a καλὸν ἄθυρμα (*Herm.* 32 ∼ 40, 52).
Cf. Ovid, *M.* 5. 400 f., where the flowers fall from Proserpine's lap
as she is being carried off:

> tantaque simplicitas puerilibus adfuit annis:
> haec quoque virgineum movit iactura dolorem.

χάνε δὲ χθὼν εὐρυάγυια: the transition from the peaceful scene of
flower-gathering is sudden and dramatic. When Persephone reaches
out for the flower the earth opens (cf. ad *Dem.* 8).

The epithet εὐρυάγυια is applied in Homer only to cities (*Il.* 2. 12
etc.). Cf. χθονὸc εὐρυοδείηc (*Il.* 16. 635 etc.), whose original meaning
is uncertain. It may have been originally εὐρυεδείηc (Schulze, *QE*
487 f., cf. Hes. *Th.* 117, Simon. *PMG* 542. 24 f.), which was then
misunderstood and hence altered: by the time of the *Hymn* it must
have been taken as equivalent to εὐρυάγυια. Cf. West ad Hes. *Th.* 119.

The χάcμα γῆc is a leading feature of many versions of the Rape.
Cf. the Sicilian version, where it is a cave (Diod. 5. 3. 3); Cic. *Verr.*
4. 107, Sil. Ital. 14. 239 f., Solinus 5. 15, Arnob. 5. 24; Pluto goes
down through the chasm in Ps. Arist. *Mir. Ausc.* 836ᵇ; cf. also Claud.
RP 2. 172 ff. (Pluto strikes the rock to open a path to the upper
world, and the earth opens 'immenso hiatu'). Clem. Al. *Protr.* 2. 17
after mentioning τὰ Φερρεφάττηc ἀνθολόγια . . . καὶ τὸν κάλαθον, goes

on with τὴν ἁρπαγὴν τὴν ὑπὸ Ἀϊδωνέως καὶ τὸ χάсμα τῆς γῆς, καὶ τὰς ὗς τὰς Εὐβουλέως τὰς сυγκαταποθείсας ταῖν θεαῖν, referring to the aition of the ritual of throwing pigs into underground *megara* at the Thesmophoria (cf. Schol. Luc. *dial. mer.* 2. 1 pp. 275 f. Rabe; Paus. 8. 9. 1). On this see Deubner, *AF* 40 ff., Ziehen, *RE* Supp. 7. 439 ff. s.v. *Μέγαρον*, A. Henrichs, *ZPE* 4 (1969), 31 ff., and Introduction, pp. 81 f.

In art, the scene is not often illustrated in the sixth and fifth centuries B.C.: cf. Metzger, *Recherches*, and the review by E. Simon, *Gnomon* 42 (1970), 706 ff. There are no black-figure examples. It was probably the subject of a pediment at Eleusis of *c*. 490–80 B.C., from which the famous figure of a fleeing girl survives: cf. Mylonas, *Eleusis*, 102 f. and fig. 34. Metzger gives two red-figure examples:

(*a*) an amphora showing Pluto pursuing Persephone (Oenocles painter, Beazley, *ARV*² 647. 21; Förster, *Raub und Rückkehr*, pl. 2; Schauenburg, *Jahrb. des d. arch. Inst.* 73 (1958), 49 fig. 1.

(*b*) Fragmentary scyphos (*c*. 430 B.C., according to Beazley, *ARV*² 647) showing a two-horse chariot, half-sunk in the earth, with Hades holding Persephone on it; also present: Eros, Hermes, Demeter(?), Hecate(?), Oceanid(?)[1] (cf. P. Hartwig, *AM* 21 (1896), 377 ff. and pl. 12; Kourouniotis, *Eleusis, A Guide*, 116 f.). On the Locrian reliefs of the fifth century showing rape-scenes see H. Prückner, *Die lokrischen Tonreliefs* (Mainz, 1968), 68 ff. E. Simon, *Opfernde Götter*, 70 and 75, explains the absence of representations as due to the wish to avoid presenting Hades, the god of the Mysteries, in an unfavourable light.

The Rape of Persephone is shown on several South Italian vases of the fourth century B.C. (cf. Schauenburg, o.c. 57–62).

The scene was portrayed in bronze by Praxiteles (Plin. *NH* 34. 69), and painted by Nicomachus (Plin. *NH* 35. 108). For other representations cf. Förster, o.c. 108 ff. It becomes very common in Roman times on sarcophagi, funerary altars, etc. Cf. Förster, o.c. 123 ff., Roscher s.v. 'Kora' 1376 ff.; sarcophagi: Robert, *Sarkophagreliefs*, 3. 3. pls. cxix–cxxx, nos. 356–415; altars: Altmann, *Die röm. Grabaltäre*, nos. 96, 98, 194, 198 ff., 208; painting at Ostia: Helbig, *Führer*, no. 1238; S. Russian tomb-paintings: Rostovtzeff, *Peinture antique du Sud de la Russie* (1914), pls. xlix. 1, lvii, lxiv. 4, lxxxix; cf. Cumont, *Symbolisme funéraire*, 95 ff. See also K. Weitzmann, *Ancient Book Illumination* (Harvard, 1959), 129 f.

17. Νύсιον ἄμ πεδίον: this mythical location of the Rape is introduced awkwardly at this point, interrupting the flow of the verse at a dramatic moment, and producing metrical and syntactical difficulties (see below). This might suggest remodelling of an earlier version. The poet apparently does not mention the place of the descent to the underworld (cf. ad *Dem.* 33 ff.). The name is connected with Dionysus: cf. *Il.* 6. 133, where Lycurgus pursues the nurses of Dionysus κατ' ἠγάθεον Νυсήϊον (Lycurgus' name suggests Thrace).

---

[1] According to Kannicht, *Euripides, Helena*, ii. 342, Athena is also shown, in full armour. See notes to *Dem.* 424.

In *Hy.* 1. 8 f. it is a mountain near the Nile, and is Dionysus' birth-place. There were various actual or supposed places called Nysa: cf. Steph. Byz., Hsch. s.v. The most important was in Caria, and had a special cult of Demeter, Core, and Pluto (cf. ad *Dem.* 7). According to tradition, it was not called Nysa until the time of Antiochus I (Steph. Byz. s.v. *Ἀντιόχεια*). But this has been questioned, and the truth remains uncertain (cf. Stein, *RE* 17. 1634. 5 ff.). As Dionysus' birthplace it was variously located, in Ethiopia (Hdt. 2. 146, 3. 97), Arabia (Diod. 3. 66. 3 etc.), Libya (Diod. 3. 66. 4), Scythia (Plin. *NH* 5. 74), etc. (cf. *RE* 17. 1640 ff.).

An Orphic version (fr. 43 K., ap. Schol. Hes. *Th.* 914) placed the Rape 'in the regions about Oceanus'. Cf. Orph. *Arg.* 1196, Artemi-dorus ap. Str. 198, Orph. *Hy.* 18. 13. The presence of the Oceanids in the *Hymn* suggests that this may have been the case here too (and cf. ad *Dem.* 7; Wilamowitz, *Glaube*, 2. 50 f.). That is of course as much as to say 'at the (mythical) ends of the earth', which may equally be the far north or south or east or west: hence the various locations of Nysa. Cf. perhaps also a papyrus text (G. A. Gerhard, *Veröff. bad. Pap.-Samml.* (Heidelberg, 1938), 20 ff. no. 176), which locates the Rape *παρὰ τὸν* 'Ω[*κεανόν*.

Malten (*ARW* 12 (1909), 300) argued for *Μύσιον*, i.e. the Argive plain (cf. Paus. 2. 18. 3: Mysia lay between Argos and Mycenae, and had a cult of Demeter Mysia), in accordance with his view of the Argive origin of the myth. This has found few supporters (cf. Wilamowitz l.c. n. 2 *contra*; but Jacoby, *FGH* IIIb (Supp.) i p. 196 favours it).

Why choose Nysa? Did the association with Dionysus influence the choice? (Cf. Bursian, *Lit. Zentralbl.* 1875, no. 6, and Wilamowitz l.c.) One should, however, beware of assuming that the Dionysus-cult was already prominent at Eleusis. Cf. on its later development Metzger, *BCH* 68–9, (1944–5), 323 ff., and *Représentations*, 248 ff.; Mylonas, *Eph. Arch.* 1960 (1965), 68–118.[1]

The name Dionysus is often taken as connected with Nysa: cf. P. Kretschmer, *Einleitung in die Gesch. d. gr. Sprache*, 241 f., H. Jean-maire, *Dionysos* (Paris, 1951), 7. The nurses of Dionysus are called *Νύσαι* (cf. inscription on archaic vase of Sophilos: *AM* 14 (1889), pl. 1; Cook, *Zeus*, ii. 273, fig. 176), and *νύση* is interpreted by Kretsch-mer as a Thraco-Phrygian word equivalent to *νύμφη*, *κόρη*. Dionysus thus = *Διὸς κοῦρος* (or *δῖος κοῦρος*). If this were correct, the *Νύσιον πεδίον* would be 'the plain of nymphs' or 'of Core', which would be appropriate. But Kretschmer's etymology is open to objections.[2] *Νύσαι* are also trees (Pherec. Ath. *FGH* 3 F 178), which fits both nymphs and Dionysus. Nysa as the name of Dionysus' nurse and also of various mountains is thus parallel to Ida ('timber-tree'), the nurse of the Cretan Zeus.

---

[1] For evidence of the cult of Dionysus in association with Demeter and Per-sephone at Corinth, cf. R. S. Stroud, *Hesperia* 37 (1968), 299 ff., esp. 325 f., and A. D. Ure, *JHS* 89 (1969), 120 f.

[2] Lesbian *Ζόννυσσος* (Alc. 129 L.–P.) points to *νυτ-ι̯* or *νυθ-ι̯* (cf. *μέσ(σ)ος*, *ὅσ(σ)ος*).

Other locations of the Rape were:

(a) Crete: Bacch. fr. 47 (cf. the Orphic *Rhapsodies*, fr. 303 K.).

(b) Sicily (the commonest later version): cf. Introduction, pp. 76 f.

(c) Eleusis: the 'Orphic' story of Eubuleus and the pigs (cf. ad *Dem.* 16) places the *descent* at Eleusis. Cf. also Orph. fr. 49. 41(?), 105 ff., Orph. *Hy.* 18. 12 ff.; Paus. 1. 14. 3, 1. 38. 5, Schol. Aristid. *Panath.* 181B, Schol. Ar. *Eq.* 698, Myth. Vat. 2. 96, Claud. *RP* 3. 51 f. This is perhaps the original local tradition. The poet substitutes a suitably vague mythical setting. Orph. *Hy.* 18. 12 ff. combines both: Core was captured from a sacred meadow, brought over the sea, and disappeared ὑπ' Ἀτθίδος . . . ἄντρον, | δήμου 'Ελευσῖνος, τόθι περ πύλαι εἰς' Ἀΐδαο. This refers presumably to the Plutonion, which one expects to have been the site of the descent of Core at Eleusis (cf. ad *Dem.* 200, and Mylonas, *Eleusis*, 99 f., 146 ff.). But in Paus. 1. 38. 5 the Rape is located at Erineos, on the banks of the Eleusinian Cephisus.

(d) Attica: Phanodemus, *FGH* 325 F 27; Schol. Soph. *OC* 1590, 1593 (Colonus). Various sites have been proposed: cf. Jacoby on Phanodemus l.c.

(e) Lerna: Paus. 2. 36. 7.

(f) Pheneos: Conon, *FGH* 26 F 15, Paus. 8 F 15. 3 f., 21. 3, Ael. *NA* 10. 40.

(g) Philippi: App. *BC* 4. 105.

(h) Hermione: Apollod. 1. 5. 1, Schol. Ar. *Eq.* 785, Zen. *Cent.* 1. 7. Cf. Paus. 2. 35. 10, Str. 373.

(i) Hipponium (Vibo) (?): Str. 256.

(j) Lebadeia(?): Paus. 9. 39. 2.

(k) Paros: Steph. Byz. s.v. (cf. Apollod. (?) *FGH* 244 F 89, and perhaps *FGH* 502: cf. Jacoby ad 325 F 27 and 502).

(l) Cyzicus: App. *Mithr.* 75; Plut. *Luc.* 10; Prop. 3. 22. 1; *Anth. Lat.* 6. 77. 11 (ii p. 550B); Steph. Byz. s.v. Βέςβικος.

(m) Taenarum(?): cf. Philicus' *Hymn* fr. 2, Latte, *Mus. Helv.* 11 (1954), 12 (cf. Apollod. 2. 5. 12 for the descent of Heracles; *RE* 19. 951 f.).

τῇ ὄρουϲεν ἄναξ πολυδέγμων: the relative ('by which way') is odd here, and ὄρουϲεν offends against 'Hermann's bridge' (cf. Maas, *Greek Metre*, § 87). Trochaic caesura in the fourth foot normally occurs in Homer only when it is preceded by an enclitic or short monosyllable (cf. *Dem.* 248), or (as here) the line ends in a 5- or 4-syllable word (Monro, *HG*² § 367. 2; for details cf. Allen and Sikes ad loc.). One would also expect a qualification of ὄρουϲεν such as ἀν-. If the line has been remodelled (see below) this might have been squeezed out.

Contrast *Dem.* 429 f. (in Persephone's narrative): γαῖα δ' ἔνερθε | χώρηϲεν, τῇ δ' ἔκθορ' ἄναξ κρατερὸς πολυδέγμων. One would expect something similar here. Cf. also Hoekstra, *Sub-epic Stage*, 54, 62 ff.

ἄναξ πολυδέγμων: cf. ad *Dem.* 9. πολυδέγμων occurs first here. Cf. Orph. *Hy.* 18. 11 (of Hades); Lyc. 700 (name of a mountain in Italy?); Cornut. 35.

18. ἵπποιϲ ἀθανάτοιϲι: the fem. form -αιϲι(pap. 1) is nowhere well attested in early epic. -ῃϲι would be possible. Homer often uses the feminine of horses, and mares were thought to be faster (Ebeling, s.v. 599. 10). But cf. *Dem.* 32, 375–6.

It is reasonable that Hades should have a chariot when he carries off Persephone. But attempts have been made to read more into his use of horses, in view of the Homeric formulaic line, εὖχοϲ ἐμοὶ δώ-ϲειν (etc.), ψυχὴν δ᾽ Ἄϊδι κλυτοπώλῳ (*Il.* 5. 654, 11. 445, 16. 625). The epithet has been much discussed: 'Wo sollte denn der Homerische Aides spazieren fahren?' asked Lehrs (*Populäre Aufsätze*[3], 277). Schol. A ad *Il.* 5. 654 suggested, amongst other explanations, that it referred to the story of the Rape. Cf. Pi. fr. 37 Sn., a hymn to Persephone, ap. Paus. 9. 23. 4 ἐν τούτῳ τῷ ᾄϲματι ἄλλαι τε ἐϲ τὸν Ἅιδην εἰϲὶν ἐπικλήϲειϲ καὶ ὁ χρυϲήνιοϲ, δῆλα ὡϲ ἐπὶ τῆϲ Κόρηϲ τῇ ἁρπαγῇ. But it has been maintained that the horse could be a symbol of death or of the earth. It is supposedly sacrificed to 'chthonic' powers, i.e. Poseidon and heroes (cf. Stengel, *ARW* 8 (1905), 203 ff. = *Opferbräuche*, 154 ff.). In the case of heroes this is readily understandable (cf. the horses sacri-ficed on the hero's pyre in Homer, *Il.* 23. 171–2). Poseidon himself, and Demeter-Erinys, take the form of horses in Arcadian and Boeotian legend, and Poseidon Hippios is a common cult-type (cf. Farnell, *Cults*, 4. 14 ff.). The connections between Poseidon and Hades are set out by Malten, 'Das Pferd im Totenglauben', *JDAI* 29 (1914), 179 ff. He sees *Il.* 5. 654 etc. as a picture of Hades carrying off the dead man's soul in his chariot, as he carries off Core: the Rape of Core is the archetype of this theme, which is represented also in an Athenian relief of the rape of Basile by Echelos (= Echelaos, i.e. Hades?), and a funeral feast relief of Zeuxippos (= Hades?) and Basileia. He also identifies as 'Hades figures' others who are associated with horses, Neleus, Admetus, Erichthonius, Erechtheus, and Lao-medon, and suggests that the appearance of a horse's head or horse on some funeral reliefs is due to its 'chthonic' significance.

The modern Greek picture of Charos as a rider has also been com-pared (Maass, *Orpheus*, 219 n. 23; Lawson, *Modern Greek Folklore*, 105 f.).

For reservations and objections to these theories cf. Farnell, *Cults*, 3. 58 ff., 283. Nilsson, *Gesch.* i[3]. 453 f., accepts Malten's theory as 'possible'. Cf. also Schachermeyr, *Poseidon*, Index s.v. 'Pferd', and Zuntz, *Persephone*, 400–2.

Κρόνου . . . υἱόϲ: Homer normally has Κρόνου πάϊϲ of Zeus, but cf. Κρόνου υἷε (*Il.* 13. 345, of Zeus and Poseidon), Κρόνου υἱέ (Hes. *Th.* 660, of Zeus).

πολυώνυμοϲ: the epithet is not Homeric. It occurs in Hes. *Th.* 785, where it is used of the water of Styx, and is taken to mean 'cele-brated'; and in *Ap.* 82, of Apollo, where it refers to the many titles under which he will be worshipped in different places. Hades was worshipped under many euphemistic names: cf. Pi. fr. 37 (sup.), Plat. *Crat.* 403 a οἱ πολλοὶ φοβούμενοι τὸ ὄνομα Πλούτωνα καλοῦϲιν αὐτόν. Similar titles are Clymenus, Periclymenus, Euclus (Eucles), etc.; cf. Rohde, *Psyche*⁹, i. 206 ff., and ad *Dem.* 9. Underworld deities especially tend to have many names: they must be propitiated with great care, and are most to be feared. Cf. (e.g.) Virgil, *A.* 7. 337–8.

Numerous attributes increased a deity's prestige: cf. Call. *Hy.* 3. 7, Gow ad Theocr. 15. 109. Repetition in prayer was considered effective, and long lists of titles are common in hymns, and more especially in magic incantations. Cf. *Dem.* 31 f. (n. ad loc.), Lyd. *de mens.* 4. 44 p. 216 R., the Orphic and Vedic hymns, and the Egyptian *Book of the Dead*. (For discussion and examples see Lobeck, *Aglaophamus*, i. 401 f., Gruppe, *Culte und Mythen*, i. 555 n. 44, Adami, *Jahrb. f. kl. Phil.* 1901, 222 f., Pfister, *Bursians Jahresb.* 1931, Supp. 229, p. 200, Norden, *Agnostos Theos*, 144 ff., Keyssner, *Gottesvorstellung*, 46 f., and other references ad loc., *RE* 9. 143, 11. 2155.)

πολυώνυμος is used of Demeter in Anon. *Hy. Cer.* 1 (cf. ad *Dem.* 1).

19–32. Hades carries off Persephone, who cries out to her father Zeus. He does not hear her, nor does anyone else except Helios and Hecate.

These lines are omitted in pap. 1, which quotes *Dem.* 8b–18 and 33–6 (Orph. fr. 49. 63–75). The omission is perhaps due to the fact that 18 = 32. The quotation of 8–18 is apparently intended to illustrate a point about the flowers, especially the narcissus. The addition of 33–6 seems pointless, as the commentator then breaks off, and probably returns to his narrative of the myth at the point where he left off (Orph. fr. 49. 57, 75 f., with app. crit. ad 75 f.). This might suggest that he is quoting from memory, and jumping unintentionally from 18 to 32. But the omission removes the reference to Helios and Hecate as the only witnesses to the Rape, which does not agree with the Orphic version, and the author of this version may have remodelled the *Hymn* to suit his own purposes (cf. ad *Dem.* 54–6, and Introduction, p. 80).

19. ἀέκουσαν: cf. *Dem.* 72, 413. Contrast the behaviour of Europa in Moschus, *Eur.* 14 (cf. Bühler ad loc.).

ἐπὶ χρυσέοιϲιν ὄχοιϲιν: Hades' chariot is golden, like his reins (Pi. fr. 37 Sn.). It is normal for the gods to have golden things. A chariot of gold does not occur in Homer, although golden fittings for a chariot do (*Il.* 5. 722 ff.). Helios, understandably, has a golden chariot: *Hy.* 31. 15 (cf. E. *El.* 739, *Phoen.* 2; Paus. 2. 3. 2; S. *Aj.* 847). Gold is also symbolic of the underworld: cf. Norden, *Aeneis VI*, 172, who refers to the golden colour of the narcissus and saffron (*Dem.* 6, 8; cf. ad 428), the Golden Bough, etc. (cf. also ad *Dem.* 335); R. A. Brooks, *AJP* 74 (1953), 260 ff.

ὄχοιϲιν: Homer has ὄχεϲφιν (cf. *Dem.* 375) or ὀχέεϲϲιν. The second-declension form occurs first here. Cf. Pi. *O.* 6. 24 (ὄκχον), Hdt. 8. 124 (ὄχῳ), and ὄχοι in Attic tragedy. It may be due to an Attic poet, but as he uses the epic form in 375 it is perhaps more likely to be a corruption attracted by χρυσέοιϲιν (cf. Introduction, p. 54).

In Pindar's *Hymn to Zeus* (fr. 30 Sn.) the Moirai carry Themis to

Olympus from the streams of Oceanus, in a golden chariot, to be Zeus' wife (cf. ad *Dem.* 5). Cf. also Pi. *P.* 9. 5–6: Apollo carries off Cyrene in a golden chariot, and makes her δέσποιναν χθονός. Pindar is following the Hesiodic *Catalogue* here (cf. Schol. Pi. ad loc. = Hes. fr. 215). Cf. also Pi. *O.* 1. 40–2 (Poseidon carries off Pelops on golden horses to heaven), 43–5 (Ganymede), E. *Tro.* 855 (Tithonus carried off on a golden car), and J. T. Kakridis, *Philol.* 85 (1930), 463 ff. n. 31. All these passages suggest that there was a 'typical' epic description for such rapes (cf. also on *Dem.* 40, 44–5, 380 ff., 383).

20. There is a nice contrast of tenses here. The imperfect of ἄγω is commonly used in epic: *Il.* 1. 367, 7. 363, 9. 664, etc. (Chantraine, *GH* ii. 192).

ἰάχησε: Homer has ἴαχε. Cf. *Hy.* 28. 11 ἰάχησεν, 27. 7 ἰαχεῖ, Call. *Hy.* 4. 146 ἰαχεῦσα. Attic tragedy (only lyric) also uses ἰαχεῖν. Cf. Hoekstra, *Sub-epic Stage*, 14 f., 55.

Persephone's cry is repeatedly mentioned (27, 39, 57, 67, 432). In Indo-European communities the cry for help is an important element of primitive justice, especially in cases of rape or abduction, where failure to set up a cry renders the plaintiff's subsequent plea invalid. Cf. E. *Tro.* 998 ff.: Hecuba rejects Helen's plea of abduction, because she did not cry out (999 f.) and hence can produce no witnesses. This custom is fully discussed by W. Schulze, *Kl. Schr.* 160 ff. Cf. E. Fraenkel on A. *Ag.* 1317, K. Latte, *Hermes* 66 (1931), 39 n. 1, F. Wieacker, *Münchener Beitr. zur Papyrusforsch.* 34 (1944), 156 f.

The cry is often addressed to gods and men (cf. *Dem.* 22): A. *Supp.* 890 ff., 905, S. *OC* 828 f., Ovid *F.* 6. 516 f., Caecilius fr. 211 R.[3], Trag. anon. 40 R.[3], Schulze, o.c. 174 ff. For the invocation of Zeus (*Dem.* 21) cf. A. *Supp.* 892, E. *El.* 1177 f., Trag. anon. 40 R.[3], Schulze, 186. The Sun is summoned as witness in similar contexts: cf. ad *Dem.* 24 ff., Schulze, 182 n. 8. Cf. also the invocation of Zeus and Helios in oaths: *Il.* 3. 276 f., 19. 258 f., etc. (cf. ad *Dem.* 21). For invocation of the elements cf. ad *Dem.* 13, 23; for the Sun and Hecate together as witnesses ad *Dem.* 24 ff. Cf. Ovid (*F.* 4. 447 f.):

> illa quidem clamabat 'io, carissima mater,
> auferor!'

Orph. fr. 47 may contain a version of Persephone's plea on her abduction. Demeter, Zeus, and Helios are all mentioned several times in it, and some at least of the elements (fire, air, perhaps also earth). Cf. Zuntz, *Persephone*, 345–54 for a re-examination of this baffling text.

21. κεκλομένη: κέλομαι in Homer usually means 'command', but cf. *Il.* 18. 391 (= 'call to'). It is first used here to mean 'invocare': cf. A. *Supp.* 591 etc.

22–37. These lines (or 21–37) have been rejected by some critics (Matthiae, Lenz, Stoll, Gemss, Preller; cf. Gemoll ad *Dem.* 21). There is a slight awkwardness in ἄιεν (25) after ἤκουσεν φωνῆς (23), in the addition of 26, and in the repetition in 27a of 21a. But these features are due to the poet's technique of composition: as he progresses, he gradually alters his construction, and at the end he returns to his starting-point. Cf. Introduction, p. 59, and ad *Dem.* 30–2.

22. οὐδέ ... οὐδέ: this is normal (Denniston, *GP* 193, 510).

22–3. Neither gods nor men nor nature heard her: for this threefold division cf. *Dem.* 44–6, *Herm.* 143–5. In all these cases the form is 'no one *either* of gods or men heard (told her, met him), *nor* did the olives hear (birds tell her, dogs bark).' For a positive sentence with similar division cf. *Aph.* 2 ff., also Archil. fr. 177 West. Hor. *AP* 372–3 perhaps parodies the form.

The word-order (two parallel phrases with a verb, followed by the third phrase) occurs also at *Dem.* 33–4. For similar orders cf. *Dem.* 7, 380–2. For the enjambement, and ἤκουϲεν (runover word with *nu* movable making position) cf. Appendix II, c, and Hoekstra, *Sub-epic Stage*, 55 (who also notes the un-Homeric use of φωνή with ἀκούειν: cf. *Dem.* 57, 284).

22–4. οὐδέ τιϲ ἀθανάτων ... (ἤκουϲεν) ... εἰ μή ...: cf. *Dem.* 77–8.

23. The olives have caused much heart-searching. But cf. ad *Dem.* 22 f. They are a typical feature of the Mediterranean landscape, and so represent the world of nature, the world of nymphs, intermediate between gods and men (cf. *Aph.* 257 ff.: the lives of the woodnymphs are linked to those of the trees). One should perhaps personify them here, as Ἐλαῖαι? Cf. the Μελίαι, and perhaps also Νῦϲαι (ad *Dem.* 17). They could still be ἀγλαόκαρποι (cf. *Dem.* 4).

Trees are not elsewhere gifted with hearing in early epic, but from the idea of their whispering in the wind or echoing (cf. *Hy.* 27. 7) came that of their listening and replying, talking, singing, or lamenting. This is common in later bucolic poetry, and in fables (cf. Call. fr. 194. 7 and Pf. ad loc., Aesop. 325 Cha. = 385 Ha., H. Diels, *Internat. Wochenschr.* 4 (1910), 993–1002).

The elements of nature are frequently invoked as witnesses (cf. ad *Dem.* 13, 20): cf. *Il.* 3. 27 ff. etc., and often in tragedy (A. *PV.* 88 ff., S. *Aj.* 856 ff., *Ant.* 844 ff., *Phil.* 936 ff., 1453 ff., *OT* 1391 ff., E. *Alc.* 244 ff., etc.). Cf. also Hes. *Th.* 963 f. (West ad loc.).

In the story of St. Demetra told to Lenormant in 1860 by an Albanian priest at Eleusis (Lenormant, *Monographie de la voie sacrée éleusinienne*, (Paris, 1864), 399 ff.; cf. Lawson, *Modern Greek Folklore*, 80 ff.), this feature is reflected in folk-tale form. Demeter began her search for her daughter, carried off by the wicked Turkish lord of Souli, by asking her neighbours, who dared not tell her anything. She then 'turned her inquiries to the tree that grew before her house; but the tree could tell her nothing'. She went on to ask the sun, moon, and stars (cf. *Dem.* 24 ff., 62 ff.), and finally learnt the truth from a stork nesting on the house top (cf. *Dem.* 46). This example shows how easily the epic narrative of the *Hymn* may be turned into 'folk-tale'. On the many folk-tale features of the *Hymn* itself cf. also Deichgräber, *Eleus. Frömmigkeit*, 510 f. For a tree as witness of a crime in folk-tales cf. Stith Thompson, *Motif Index*, D. 1393. 4.

Wilamowitz (*Aus Kydathen*, 125 n. 43) for some reason thought it 'un-Attic' to give the olives a soul, and also supposed that they were being ascribed to Demeter (cf. *Glaube*, ii. 45 n. 2).

Kerényi (*Eleusis*, 36 f.) suggests that the olives were originally those around the well Callichoron, the original site of Persephone's disappearance at Eleusis (cf. ad *Dem.* 99 f.).

24-6. Hecate and Helios

Hecate first appears in Hes. *Th.* 409-52, where she receives a special 'hymn', and is an important figure (cf. West ad *Th.* 404 ff.). There she is the daughter of Perses and Asterie (*Th.* 409 ff.). Cf. Apollod. 1. 2. 4, A.R. 3. 467, and ad *Dem.* 24. For other accounts of her parentage cf. Schol. A.R. 3. 467, 1035. She is also mentioned in the *Great Ehoiai* (fr. 262).

She seems to have come to Greece from Caria (cf. T. Kraus, *Hekate* (Heidelberg, 1960), 20). Her main cult-centre there was Lagina. It is not known when she first arrived in Greece, but evidently her cult was firmly rooted by the time of Hesiod and the *Hymn*. The oldest representation of her on the mainland is a terracotta seated statue of the late sixth century. Her presence at Eleusis as an 'attendant' of Persephone is attested at *Dem.* 440. It is generally assumed that she is to be identified here with Artemis Propylaea, who shared a temple with Poseidon Pater at the entrance to the sanctuary (Paus. 1. 38. 6; cf. Wilamowitz, *Glaube*, i. 167 f., Kraus, o.c. 63, 93). The temple is not aligned with the Greater Propylaea, and this suggests that it existed before the Propylaea were built. Remains of a cult-building of the Geometric period were found under it (cf. Kraus, 93; Mylonas, *Eleusis*, 60, 167 f.).

Hecate is represented on vase-paintings, assisting at the Anodos of Persephone (Beazley, *ARV²* 1012. 1 = Nilsson, *Op. Sel.* ii. 619, No. 14; cf. also Kourouniotes, *Arch. Delt.* 1933-5, 1 ff.), and probably also (on south Italian vases) at the Rape (Schauenburg, *Jahrb. des d. arch. Inst.* 73 (1958), 57 f.), and present at the mission of Triptolemus (Beazley, *ARV²* 1191. 1). Cf. Kraus, 92 f., Metzger, *Recherches*, 11, 16, 25. She may also be depicted on the Niinnion tablet (Mylonas, *Eleusis*, fig. 88) leading the mystae to the Sanctuary at Eleusis (Pringsheim, *Arch. Beiträge*, 66; Kern, *Rel. d. Gr.* 2. 202; E. Simon, *Ant. Kunst* 9 (1966), 89). On South Italian vases she is sometimes shown beside Persephone and Pluto in Hades (e.g. *Mon. Ant.* 16 (1906), 517, pl. III). In the fifth century she is depicted as a young woman similar to Artemis in appearance, and with nothing uncanny or unusual about her. This fits her description in the *Hymn* as ἀταλὰ φρονέουσα, and the picture of her in Hes. *Th.* 409 ff., where she is 'a healthy, independent and open-minded goddess' (West, 277). In Pindar, *Paean* 2. 49 f. she is called παρθένος εὐμενής. As κουροτρόφος (*Th.* 450-2) she is a suitable companion to Persephone.

In the *Hymn*, she is very much a 'Nebenfigur': she does not tell Demeter anything new (54 ff.), but acts as her attendant when they go to Helios (60 ff.). Her appearance is presumably due to her position in the cult (cf. Walton, *HTR* 45 (1952), 105 ff., Kraus, 63 f.), but it fits well with Hes. *Th.* 429 ᾧ δ᾽ ἐθέλει μεγάλως παραγίγνεται ἠδ᾽ ὀνίνησιν (cf. ad *Dem.* 52 ἤντετο).

In another version (Call. fr. 466 Pf.; cf. Malten, *ARW* 12 (1909), 438 n. 6), Hecate brings Persephone up from Hades (cf. the vase-painting above) : this is done by Demeter herself in *Orph. Hy.* 41. 3 ff. (cf. ad *Dem.* 305 ff.). Wehrli (*ARW* 31 (1934), 82 ff.) suggests that Hecate and Demeter are 'doubles' in these myths, but this seems unlikely.

Hecate's cave (*Dem.* 25) has been taken as her Zerinthian cave on Samothrace (Kern, *RE* 16. 1213. 11 ff., assumes that this points to Ionian composition for the *Hymn*; cf. Wilamowitz, *Glaube*, ii. 51 n. 1). There is no necessity to suppose this. Nor does the cave make her a moon-goddess (cf. Allen and Halliday ad *Dem.* 25; *contra*: Kraus, 63 f. n. 306), although her association with Helios might also suggest this. Hecate as the moon first appears with certainty in the Hellenistic period (Kraus, 87. On S. fr. 535 P. cf. Wilamowitz, *Glaube*, i. 173, Kraus, l.c.). Her cave and torches (*Dem.* 52) may both be due to her 'chthonic' associations (cf. Farnell, *Cults*, ii. 509 f., Nilsson, *Gr. Feste*, 396 f. n. 4). The Greek moon-goddess does not have torches (Kraus, 127). The cave is perhaps one of the two grottoes inside the Sanctuary, before which the later temple of Pluto was built (cf. Kern, *Rel. d. Gr.* ii. 189). The temple of Artemis Propylaea lay quite near to this.

Helios as witness and guardian of right dealing is in the epic manner (*Od.* 8. 271, 302; later in A. *Cho.* 986 f., *PV* 91, S. *Aj.* 857, E. *Med.* 1251 ff., A.R. 4. 229 etc.; cf. ad *Dem.* 20, 69 f.). But his place in the story perhaps goes back beyond its form in Greek epic. In the Ugaritic *Poem of Baal*, ʿAnat enlists the support of Shapash, the Sun-goddess, in the recovery of Baal's body (Pritchard, *ANET*² 139, 141; T. H. Gaster, *Thespis* (New York, 1950), 194 f., 202). The Sun-god's role in the Hittite myth of Telepinu has also been compared (Gaster, o.c. 195). Telepinu has withdrawn from the gods in anger, causing a general blight. The Sun-god institutes proceedings to get him back (Gaster, 361 f.). These myths show other resemblances to the *Hymn* (cf. ad *Dem.* 40 ff., 305 ff.).

The Sun, Moon, and stars are regularly approached for information in mythology and folk-tales: cf. Roscher, 1. 2019 f., Apollod. 1. 6. 1 (Sun, Moon, and Dawn forbidden to reveal whereabouts of magic herb), Grimm, *Deutsche Mythologie*⁴, 2. 590, the modern Greek version of the story of Persephone (ad *Dem.* 23), and Ov. *F.* 4. 575 ff., where Ceres consults the Plough stars, who send her to the Sun. Cf. especially Ov. *F.* 4. 581 f. :

> crimine Nox vacua est, Solem de virgine rapta
> consule, qui late facta diurna videt.

Similarly here, Hecate in her cave (as a goddess of the night? Cf. ad *Dem.* 52) only hears, and cannot tell Demeter anything, whereas

Helios both hears and sees. There is a slight awkwardness in this, since 24–6 suggest that Helios only heard. But we should not conclude from this that two separate versions are being run together (as Wegener, *Philologus* 35 (1876), 227 ff., and Wehrli, *ARW* 31 (1934), 82 ff., suggest). Hecate and Helios are invoked together by Medea (as priestess of one and granddaughter of the other) in S. fr. 535 P. (cf. above), and A.R. 4. 1019 f.

In the Orphic version, Demeter receives her information from the inhabitants of Eleusis. Cf. Introduction, pp. 81 f. and ad *Dem.* 75 ff.

Helios is portrayed together with Demeter, Hecate, and Eos on one of the Locrian *pinakes* (cf. ad *Dem.* 51–89). For representations of Helios as a witness of the Rape cf. K. Schauenburg, *Helios* (Berlin, 1955), 41 ff. These are not numerous, and one at least (Winckelmann, *Mon. Ant. Ined.* ii. 22; Schauenburg, n. 387) is highly questionable. For the Sun's importance in later mystery-cults cf. W. Burkert, *Phronesis* 14 (1969), 1 ff.

24. Περσαίου θυγάτηρ: as the daughter of Perses she is called Περσείη (Call. fr. 474(?), *Orph. Hy.* 1. 4, *Hy. mag.* 21. 2 (vol. 3, p. 42 Pr.; cf. vol. 1, pp. 142, 158, 160), *IG* 14. 1017, Val. Flacc. *Argon.* 6. 495), and Περσαίη is an attractive suggestion. But mythological names fluctuate and Περσαίου may be right. Note that Perses' brother is called Ἀστραῖος (Hes. *Th.* 376).

ἀταλὰ φρονέουσα: this is used of ἠΐθεοι in *Il.* 18. 567, and of a child in Hes. *Th.* 989. Cf. *Il.* 6. 400 παῖδ' ἀταλάφρονα, 20. 222 πώλοισιν … ἀταλῇσι, *Od.* 11. 39 παρθενικαί τ' ἀταλαί. The meaning appears to be something like 'with youthful spirit' (rather than 'with kind intent', Allen and Halliday). Cf. also ἀταλώτατα παίζει on the eighth-century Dipylon jug (*IG* i². 919; Friedländer, *Epigrammata*, no. 53), and ἀτάλλειν (= 'play, leap' in *Il.* 13. 27; but also 'bring up, nourish', *Herm.* 400 etc., or 'be brought up', Hes. *Op.* 130). It has been suggested that the original form was ἀ-ταλάφρων, meaning 'timid' (cf. M. Leumann, *Glotta* 15 (1927), 153–5, *Hom. Wörter*, 139–41). Leumann assumes that in *Il.* 6. 400 the word was misunderstood as 'childish', and ἀταλαφρονέων formed, from which with false division ἀταλός was created, and finally ἀτάλλω. For criticisms of Leumann's theory cf. Bolling, *Language* 27 (1951), 73 f., also West ad *Th.* 989, Sealey, *RÉG* 70 (1957), 334 f., Frisk s.v. (Heitsch, *Aphroditehymnos*, 46 ff., defends Leumann.)

On the youthful appearance of Hecate cf. ad *Dem.* 24 ff.

25. ἄϊεν: on the repetition after ἤκουσεν (23) cf. ad *Dem.* 22–37. The sentence is built up piece by piece: 'No one … heard her voice— nor did the olives—except (that) Persaeus' daughter heard—Hecate— and Helios—the girl as she cried out …'

ἐξ ἄντρου: cf. A.R. 3. 1212 f. (quoted on p. 97), and ad *Dem.* 24 ff.

λιπαροκρήδεμνος: also of Charis (*Il.* 18. 382), Rhea (*Dem.* 458). Cf. λιπαρὰ κρήδεμνα (*Od.* 1. 334 etc.), and on κρήδεμνον cf. ad *Dem.* 41. The adjective suggests that it was of linen: cf. *Il.* 3. 141, 14. 184 f., E. B. Abrahams, *Greek Dress* (London, 1908), 35.

26. In Homer, Hyperion is normally used as an epithet, or by itself, for the Sun (*Il.* 8. 480 etc.). In origin it is a comparative of ὕπερος (cf. Lat. *superior*). In *Od.* 12. 176 the Sun is called Ὑπεριονίδης: this is not necessarily a patronymic (cf. Merry and Riddell on *Od.* 1. 8, Usener, *Götternamen*, 20 ff.). But Hes. *Th.* 374 makes him the son of the Titan Hyperion. Cf. *Hy.* 28. 13, 31. 4, and Ὑπεριονίδης in Hes. *Th.* 1011, *Dem.* 74, and later poets. Many of these also use Hyperion for the Sun, and make Hyperionides his son. Cf. *RE* 9. 287 f.

27 ff. Zeus' absence is a matter of convenience, as one might be 'out' to callers in the past. His design is still at work (*Dem.* 30). There is no contradiction here (cf. ad *Dem.* 3).

For the absence (ἀποδημία) of a deity cf. also *Il.* 1. 423 ff., *Od.* 1. 22 ff., Theocr. 1. 66 f. (Gow ad loc.), Hermocles (p. 174, Powell), 15 ff. If he wished, a god could hear wherever he was: *Il.* 16. 514 ff. Normally, however, the deity was considered to visit the temple where he received his honours: so here, *Dem.* 302 ff., 355 f., *Ap.* 347 f., Pi. *P.* 4. 5, Call. fr. 75. 26, Cat. 64. 387 ff. (where Bährens's conjecture *residens* is supported by *Od.* 1. 26, *Dem.* 28, etc.).

28. ἧϲτο θεῶν ἀπάνευθε: on the position of θεῶν see Appendix V. πολυλλίϲτῳ: 'full of prayers'; cf. Bacch. 10. 41 (βωμός). In *Od.* 5. 445 it is used of a god (cf. later πολύλλιτος Call. *Hy.* 2. 80, 4. 316, etc.). For a doublet of the formula cf. *Dem.* 355.

29. δέγμενος: Cobet objected to taking this as an aorist form, and wanted to read δέχμενος, as an athematic present. Schol. A ad *Il.* 9. 191 (and one MS.) have this, and Herodian read δεδεχμένος at *Il.* 8. 296; cf. Hsch. s.v. δέχμενος· προϲδιαδεχόμενος.

The athematic present is attested by δέχαται (*Il.* 12. 147), but one expects *δέγμαι (etc.) with assimilation before the *mu*, and there is no reason to follow Cobet. Cf. Chantraine, *GH* i. 296, Leaf ad *Il.* 2. 794, van Leeuwen, *Enchiridium*, 384 f.

30–2. The poet returns to the main theme of the Rape, and repeats 17b–20a in the reverse order:

$$30a \sim 19a, 20a$$
$$31b \sim 17b \ (\pi o \lambda v \delta \acute{\epsilon} \gamma \mu \omega \nu)$$
$$32 = 18.$$

Cf. ad *Dem.* 22–37, and Introduction, p. 59.

30. Διὸς ἐννεϲίῃϲι: cf. *Dem.* 3, 27 f. (also 414 f.). ἐννεϲίη occurs once in Homer; cf. Hes. *Th.* 494, Call. *Hy.* 3. 108 etc. It is a metrically lengthened form of ἐνεϲίη (see W. F. Wyatt Jr., *Metrical Lengthening in Homer* (Rome, 1969), 94).

The formula is a doublet of the Hesiodic Κρονίδεω διὰ βουλάς (*Th.* 572, *Op.* 71: cf. ad *Dem.* 414), which would be unsuitable here, owing to the ambiguity of Κρονίδεω.

31. This line, composed simply of three epithets, with its threefold alliteration, is very unusual and impressive. There is also a triple repetition of πολυ- in 31–2. Three-word lines are rare in Homer: cf. Bassett, *CP* 12 (1917), 97 ff., who notes only *Il.* 2. 706, 11. 427, 15. 678,

Od. 10. 137. Three of these have αὐτοκαςίγνητος (etc.) with a genitival name+epithet formula. The fourth (*Il.* 15. 678), is a special case: δυωκαιεικοςίπηχυ need not be regarded as a single word. In the *Hymns*, cf. 27. 3 (αὐτοκαςιγνήτην . . .). The only other early epic example which I know is Hes. *Op.* 383, the first line of the 'Works' part of the poem (cf. C. Bradford Welles, *GRBS* 8 (1967), 13, who notes its impressive character, and compares *Op.* 1). Bassett collects only 8 other examples from later verse (add (?) Call. fr. 21. 4). Cf. also Bassett, *CP* 14 (1919), 216 ff., 'Versus Tetracolos'.

Verses consisting only of epithets or accumulations are also rare in epic (cf. *Od.* 15. 406, Hes. *Th.* 320, 925), but a regular feature of hymns: cf. *Herm.* 13-15, 436, *Hy.* 19. 37, 27. 2 f., also 19. 2, 23. 2; and in the later period the Orphic hymns, some of which consist almost entirely of a string of epithets, and the 'Homeric' *Hymn to Ares* (which probably belongs to the hymns of Proclus: cf. Introduction, p. 3). Cf. also Bühler, *Moschus, Europa*, pp. 212 ff.

For alliteration of names beginning with Π- cf. *Il.* 11. 490 f., *Od.* 22. 423, Lehrs, *Aristarchus*, 461; and for repetition of part of a word cf. *Il.* 2. 325 (ὄψιμον ὀψιτέλεςτον), and Lehrs, o.c. 473 f.

Here, the language perhaps recalls that of magic incantation, where repetition is normal (cf. ad *Dem.* 228-30). For marked alliteration in a prayer cf. *Il.* 10. 288-90. For alliteration in general in Homer and Hesiod cf. ad *Dem.* 289 f. (also *Dem.* 46).

πατροκαςίγνητος: Hades is Persephone's uncle. Such marriages are not uncommon in Greek mythology. Cf. Alcinous and Arete (*Od.* 7. 63-6), Iapetus and Clymene (Hes. *Th.* 507 f.), Cretheus and Tyro (Hes. fr. 38), (?) Orthos and Chimaera (Hes. *Th.* 326 f., West ad loc.), Electryon and Anaxo (Apollod. 2. 4. 5), Butes and Chthonia (3. 15. 1), Phineus and Andromeda (2. 4. 3), etc.

πολυςημάντωρ: cf. ad *Dem.* 9. The word occurs only here, and at *Dem.* 84, 376. Cf. ςημάντωρ, *Il.* 8. 127 etc.

33-50. As long as Persephone could see the upper world, she still hoped to see her mother and the other gods. The mountains and sea echoed her cry, and Demeter heard her. She was distraught with grief. She tore her head-dress, and put on a black veil. Then she rushed over the earth, looking for her daughter. No one would tell her the truth, and for nine days she roamed the earth, with torches in her hands, and would not taste of nectar and ambrosia, or wash herself.

33 ff. In Orph. *Hy.* 18. 13 Hades carries Persephone over the sea to Eleusis, where they go down to the underworld (cf. ad *Dem.* 17). There is no suggestion of this here. 'Earth, heaven, sea, and sun' is a form of expression for 'the (upper) world'. Cf. ad *Dem.* 13 f., 380 ff. (where there is also a journey over sea and land).

There is no mention in the *Hymn* of Persephone's descent with Hades. This was important in the cult (cf. ad *Dem.* 16), and one expects something about it after *Dem.* 33-6. It might have occurred in the lacuna after *Dem.* 37 (cf. ad loc.), but as the location of the Rape is mythical rather than actual, the poet may have avoided mentioning the place of the descent.

33. μὲν οὖν: in Homer this always refers back, and usually this is made explicit by an echoed word (e.g. *Il.* 9. 543–50, where cf. 550 f.). Here, and in *Herm.* 577, it is purely transitional. It is used with increasing frequency in early epic (once in the *Iliad*, five times in the *Odyssey*, and four times in the *Hymns*). Cf. Denniston, *GP* 470 f.

34. λεῦσσε θεά: for the word-order cf. ad *Dem.* 7, 22 f., 380–2. On the position of θεά, after a verb in the first trochee, with enjambement, see Appendix V.

πόντον ἀγάρροον ἰχθυόεντα: this looks like a 'combination formula' (cf. Introduction, p. 50). ἀγάρροος is used by Homer only of the Hellespont, for which it is much more suitable ('strong-flowing'). Cf. *AP* 7. 747 (of the Tigris), Q.S. 10. 174 (of a river in flood).

The opposite development has perhaps occurred in the case of Ἑλλήςποντος ἀπείρων (*Il.* 24. 545), which may derive from πόντος ἀπείρων (Hes. *Th.* 678; cf. ἀπείρονα/ι πόντον/ῳ in Homer). Cf. Edwards, *Language of Hesiod*, 50.

Cf. also *Il.* 9. 360 Ἑλλήςποντον ἐπ' ἰχθυόεντα ∼ πόντον ἐπ' ἰχθυόεντα (5 times in Hom.), J. B. Hainsworth, *The Flexibility of the Homeric Formula* (Oxford, 1968), 124.

The phrase is also a doublet of πόντον ἀπείρονα κυμαίνοντα (*Od.* 4. 510). On 'sea formulae' in Homer cf. D. H. F. Gray, *CQ* 41 (1947), 109 ff. (= Kirk, *Language and Background of Homer*, 55 ff.), Page, *History and the Homeric Iliad*, 225 ff., Edwards, *Language of Hesiod*, 45 ff.

35. ἔτι δ' ἤλπετο: the digamma in ἔλπομαι is several times neglected in Homer: cf. Chantraine, *GH* i. 133, and especially *Il.* 15. 539, 701, 24. 491, *Od.* 9. 419. The augmented form occurs in most manuscripts at *Il.* 15. 539, 701, 17. 603 (ἔλπετο Ar.), *Od.* 9. 419. The papyrus omits δ' here, and its quotation breaks off after *Dem.* 36. The omission of δ' is probably due to carelessness. The papyrus commentator is perhaps quoting from memory (cf. ad *Dem.* 19–32).

It is tempting to make ἔτι δ' ἤλπετο (etc.) the apodosis of *Dem.* 33 ff., as *Dem.* 37 is suspect (cf. ad loc.). In that case, 37 could have been added later, by someone who failed to realize this. This was the view of Mitscherlich.

36. φῦλα ... αἰειγενετάων: θεῶν φῦλον or φῦλα is used almost always in the context of someone going to join them (which is implied here). Cf. *Dem.* 322, 443, 461, etc., similarly *Dem.* 484 (etc.) and P. Oxy. 2509. 10, 16 (Hesiod, *Catalogue?*); West ad *Th.* 202.

37. This verse is omitted in the quotation in the Orphic papyrus (cf. ad *Dem.* 35). It had already been suspected, and seems very weak. It adds little, if anything, to the sense of 35–6. μέγαν νόον is more suitable in Hes. *Th.* 37, where it is used of Zeus, than here. Hermann also objected that there is a break in the narrative after *Dem.* 37, and that one expects a sentence answering 33 (ὄφρα μὲν οὖν ...) of which the sense would be 'but when she was entering the gaping earth and realized that she was being carried down to the underworld, then indeed she despaired and cried out still more vehemently than before.' 38 ff., describing the effect of her cry, then follow naturally. A reference to the descent of Persephone would also be supplied (cf. ad *Dem.* 33–6).

It is possible that *Dem.* 37 was added to supply a lacuna of some kind (cf. Introduction, p. 66). The sense of this may have been simply 'so long she continued to cry out' (*vel sim.*). But see also on *Dem.* 35.

οἳ . . . ἀχνυμένης περ: for the combination of dative and genitive cf. *Il.* 14. 25 f., 16. 531, *Od.* 6. 155, 14. 527 etc.; Chantraine, *GH* ii. 322 f.

If the line is genuine, the poet may have had *Il.* 22. 424 in mind (cf. ad *Dem.* 38–46).

38 ff. The poet was perhaps influenced here by *Il.* 22. 401 ff.:

Il. 22. 401–2	ἀμφὶ δὲ χαῖται* | κυάνεαι* ∼ *Dem.* 40, 42.
405–7	ἥ δέ νυ μήτηρ* | τίλλε κόμην, ἀπὸ δὲ λιπαρὴν ἔρριψε καλύπτρην | τηλόσε, κώκυσεν δέ . . . ∼ *Dem.* 39–42.
[424	ἀχνύμενός περ* ∼ *Dem.* 37.]
425	ἄχος ὀξὺ . . . ∼ *Dem.* 40.
438	οὐ γάρ οἵ τις ἐτήτυμος ἄγγελος ἐλθών ∼ *Dem.* 46.
447	(Andromache hears the cries) ∼ *Dem.* 39.
460–1	διέσσυτο μαινάδι ἴςη ∼ *Dem.* 43, 386. παλλομένη κραδίην· ἅμα δ᾽* ∼ *Dem.* 293.
468–70	τῆλε δ᾽ ἀπὸ κρατὸς βάλε δέσματα . . . κρήδεμνόν θ᾽ . . . ∼ *Dem.* 40–1.

Note also *Il.* 22. 87 ∼ *Dem.* 66; 94 ∼ 354; 146* ∼ 177 (∼ *Il.* 22. 401); 263* ∼ 434; 482* ∼ 340, 398, 415; 490* ∼ 140.

Cf. Introduction, pp. 31 f. (The parallel with *Il.* 22. 461 is noted by C. P. Segal, *HSCP* 75 (1971), 44 n. 22.)

38. ἤχηςαν: the simple verb is not found in Homer, but cf. περιήχη- cεν *Il.* 7. 267. Cf. Hes. *Th.* 42, 835 and for the hills echoing also *Hy.* 19. 21. The idea of the depths of the sea echoing is poetic hyper- bole: the phrase was perhaps prompted by *Il.* 1. 157, 357–8.

ὀρέων κορυφαί: a (grammatical) formula-variant: cf. formulaic parallels (p. 30), and for the nominative Alcm. *PMG* 89. 1.

βένθεα πόντου: not in Homer or Hesiod, cf. formulaic parallels.

39. This appears to contradict *Dem.* 22 ff. But probably the poet is simply telling his story progressively: '(at first) no one (except . . .) heard. But when Persephone ⟨continued to cry?⟩ her mother heard her.' Cf. ad *Dem.* 22–37.

πότνια μήτηρ: in Homer πότνια is used generally, as an epithet of a goddess, mother, nymph, etc. In the *Hymn* it is several times applied to Demeter (47, 54, 118, 203, 211, 492). Later, we find Πότνιαι used especially of Demeter and Core:

(i) at Eleusis: S. *OC* 1050. At the climax of the Mysteries the hiero- phant cried out ἱερὸν ἔτεκε Πότνια Κοῦρον, Βριμὼ Βριμόν (Hippol. *Ref. Haer.* 5. 8. 39 p. 96. 16 W.; cf. Introduction, pp. 26 ff.).

(ii) at Athens, in the Thesmophoria: Ar. *Thesm.* 1149, 1156 (cf. ad *Dem.* 211).

(iii) at Potniae in Boeotia: Paus. 9. 8. 1. The place derives its name from the two goddesses.

(iv) at Mycale: Hdt. 9. 97 (Ποτνιεῖς); Hiller von Gärtringen, *Inschr. v. Priene*, no. 196 (Kaibel, *Epigr.* 774. 3); cf. ad *Dem.* 203.

It is used of Core alone by Pi. fr. 37 Sn., and perhaps in Theocr. 15. 14 (cf. Schol. ad loc.).

40 ff. Demeter's grief and her search for her daughter are said to have formed one of the subjects of the 'mystic drama' enacted at Eleusis. Cf. Clem. *Protr.* 2. 12. 2 p. 11. 20 St.: 'Demeter and Core have come to be the subject of a mystic drama, and Eleusis celebrates with torches the abduction of the daughter and the sorrowful wanderings of the mother'; Lact. *Div. Inst. Epit.* 18 (23). 7: 'in the Mysteries of Demeter during the night with torches kindled they seek for Persephone, and when she is found the whole ritual closes with thanksgiving and tossing of torches'; and Deubner, *AF* 84 n. 8.

What form this drama took, where and how it was enacted, whether the initiates took part, and if in fact it took place in Attic Eleusis at all, are disputed questions: cf. Introduction, pp. 24 ff. It is possible that the dancing with torches, which formed part of the pannychis after the Iacchus procession, represented in a formal way Demeter's sorrow and searching, and her subsequent joy at her daughter's recovery. Cf. ad *Dem.* 47 ff., and the late Greek phrase ἐξορχεῖσθαι τὰ μυστήρια meaning 'to reveal them' (Lucian, *de Salt.* 15, *Pisc.* 33, etc.): this, however, does not necessarily refer to Eleusis. (Cf. Nilsson, *Gesch.* i³. 662 f., Farnell, *Cults*, 3. 182, Casel, *De philosophorum Graecorum silentio mystico* (Giessen, 1919), 7 f.)

One may also note that the dancing around Callichoron involved singing in honour of Demeter (Paus. 1. 38. 6). These songs perhaps included narratives of the Eleusinian myths.

Demeter's grief and wandering are described in language similar to that used of Aphrodite searching for the lost Adonis, and 'Anat mourning for Baal. Cf. Bion 1 (*Epitaphios Adonidos*). 20 ff. λυςαμένα πλοκαμῖδας ἀνὰ δρύμως ἀλάληται, | πενθαλέα νήπλεκτος ἀςάνδαλος (etc.), and Gaster, *Thespis*, 194 (Pritchard, *ANET*² 139), 199 (~ Ov. *F.* 4. 495 f.). Cf. also E. *Hel.* 1301 ff., *PMG* 935. 4 ff. (Μάτηρ θεῶν = Demeter); Plut. *de Is. et Osir.* 14 (356 d) τὴν δ' Ἶcιν αἰcθομένην κείραcθαι μὲν ἐνταῦθα τῶν πλοκάμων ἕνα καὶ πένθιμον cτολὴν ἀναλαβεῖν . . . πλανωμένην δὲ πάντη καὶ ἀποροῦcαν οὐδένα προcελθεῖν ἀπροcαύδητον . . . The rape of Ganymede provides a parallel for the parent's grief: cf. *Aph.* 207–8 Τρῶα δὲ πένθος ἄλαστον ἔχε φρέναc (etc.), and ad *Dem.* 19, 383.

40. For the double accusative cf. *Dem.* 90, *Il.* 2. 171, etc., Chantraine, *GH* ii. 42.

ἄχοc: cf. *Dem.* 90, 436. The cult title of Demeter Ἀχαιά (or Ἀχαία), which she had in Athens, the Attic tetrapolis, and Boeotia (Farnell, *Cults*, iii. 69 ff.) was sometimes explained as due to her ἄχοc for Per-

sephone: Plut. *de Is. et Osir.* 69 (378 e), Schol. Ar. *Ach.* 708, Schol.
Nic. *Ther.* 486, Hsch., *Suda, Et. Magn.* s.v.

40 f. χαίταιϲ ἀμβροϲίαιϲ: the dative in -αιϲ occurs also at *Dem.* 205
(ad fin. vers.), 308 (ad fin.), 441 (ταῖϲ init.). In Homer, it is only
found at *Il.* 12. 284 (ad fin.), *Od.* 22. 471 (ad fin.), 5. 119 (θεαῖϲ before
a vowel; v.l. θεᾶϲ), and as a variant at *Il.* 1. 238 etc. It is commoner
in Hesiod: *Th.* 61 (ad fin.), 70 (init.), 215 (αἷϲ); cf. West ad loc. Cf.
also frr. 203. 2, 305. 3, and in the *Hymns, Aph.* 249 (αἷϲ), *Herm.* 200
(ταῖϲδε), 19. 3, 24, 33. 16.

Its presence in Homer is unexplained (Chantraine, *GH* i. 202).
Wackernagel (*Spr. Unters.* 53 f.) regards it as an Atticism. In Hesiod
it might be due to the influence of the poet's own dialect (West, 177).
But in this hymn it can hardly be due to the influence of spoken
Attic upon an Attic poet, since the archaic Attic forms were -ηϲι, -αϲι
(cf. Buck, *Greek Dialects*, § 104. 7, Barrett ad E. *Hipp.* 101). Cf. ad
Dem. 368 (θυϲίαιϲι), Introduction, pp. 53 f., and Appendix II, B (4).

Here the phrase is due to adaptation of the nominative formula
ἀμφὶ δὲ χαῖται (*Il.* 6. 509 etc.). Cf. Hes. *Th.* 61 ἀκηδέα θυμὸν ἐχούϲαιϲ ∼
Op. 112, 170 ἀκηδέα θυμὸν ἔχοντεϲ.

41. Demeter tears her head-dress: cf. *Il.* 22. 405 ff., 468 ff. (ad
Dem. 38–46), where the head-dress is cast away in grief. Normally it is
the hair which is torn: *Il.* 18. 27, 22. 405 f. etc.; cf. *PMG* 935. 7 (where
West (*CQ* 1970, 213) reads ϲύρουϲα ῥυτὰν κόμαν; cf. Maas, *Epid.
Hymnen* ad loc.), Ov. *M.* 5. 472, Plut. *de Is. et Osir.* 14 (ad *Dem.* 40 ff.),
where Isis cuts her hair. Cf. Ov. *F.* 4. 457 f.:

> mentis inops rapitur, ut quas audire solemus
> Threicias fusis maenadas ire comis (∼ *Dem.* 386).

κρήδεμνα: used of a veil (or shawl). The plural is probably for
metrical convenience. After Homer, κρήδεμνον occurs in poetry, and
also in the inventory of the Samian Heraeum (cf. *AM* 68 (1953),
46 ff.). It is used figuratively at *Dem.* 151 (etc.). Cf. H. L. Lorimer,
Homer and the Monuments, 385 ff., H. Brandenburg, *Studien zur Mitra*
(Münster, 1966), 60 n. 32, 103 n. 108.

42. κυάνεον δὲ κάλυμμα: for Demeter's black mourning veil and
peplos cf. *Dem.* 182 f., 319, 360, 374. κυάνεοϲ is used especially of
the mourning dress of deities: cf. *Il.* 24. 93 f., West ad Hes. *Th.* 406.
κάλυμμα occurs only once in Homer (*Il.* 24. 93 f.), where it is used of a
mourning veil, but in later poetry it is used generally of any veil (Bacch.
16. 38 etc.). The poet perhaps chose it here because it is associated with
mourning in Homer (Lorimer, *Homer and the Monuments*, 386).

Cf. the name of the spring Κυάνη at Syracuse, into which, according
to the Sicilian legend, Hades and Persephone vanished: Diod. 5. 4. 2
(cf. Ov. *M.* 5. 409 ff., Claud. *RP* 3. 246 ff., Ziegler, *RE* 9. 2234).
Here, the name probably reflects the cult which was practised at the
spring (cf. ad *Dem.* 99; Herter, *RhM* 90 (1941), 247). Cf. also the cult
of Demeter Melaena in Arcadia (Paus. 8. 5. 8, 42, Farnell, *Cults*,
iii. 50 ff., *RE* 4. 2734).

There is no direct evidence for the wearing of special clothing at Eleusis in the early period (Pringsheim, *Arch. Beiträge*, 14 ff.), but this is suggested by Schol. Ar. *Plut.* 845, *IG* ii². 1672. 229 (cf. Mylonas, *Eleusis*, 279). In A.D. 166–9 the ephebes accompanying the procession to Eleusis were provided with white clothing instead of black (*IG* ii². 2090, Philostr. *Vit. Soph.* 2. 1 p. 59. 12). This is stated to have been the first occasion when it was done, but it may in fact have been a revival of an earlier custom (cf. Varro, *Sesculixes*, fr. 462 Bücheler; Münscher, *RE* 8. 942. 39 ff.). White was prescribed for the Mysteries at Andania (*IG* 5. 1. 1390. 16 ff.), and was also worn in the Roman festival of Ceres (Ov. *M.* 10. 432, *F.* 4. 619 f.; cf. Bömer, Frazer ad loc.). Similarly, the initiates at both Andania and Lycosura were forbidden to wear a veil or have their hair bound up (*IG* 5. 1. 1390. 20 ff., 2. 514. 9 ff.), and this was also the case at Alexandria (Call. *Hy.* 6. 5, 124; cf. Schneider, Cahen ad loc.; Legrand, *REA* 3 (1901), 290 n. 3).

In these cases, the prohibitions would be explained as preventing the initiates from following the example of Demeter in her sorrow (cf. ad *Dem.* 6 ff., 47 ff., 98 f.). For the possibility that *Dem.* 176 ff. also reflect this practice cf. ad loc. Cf. also T. Wächter, *Reinheitsvorschriften im griech. Kult* (Giessen, 1910), 16 f.; K. Mayer, *Die Bedeutung d. weissen Farbe im Kultus* (etc.) (Diss. Freiburg, 1927), 19 ff.; Radke, *Die Bedeutung d. weissen und d. schwarzen Farbe im Kult* (etc.) (Diss. Berlin, 1936), 57 ff. See Addenda.

P. G. Maxwell-Stuart, however, in *Proc. Camb. Phil. Soc.* 196 (1970), 113 ff., argues that the initiates wore *black*, in imitation of Demeter.

43. cεύατο: cf. *Il.* 22. 460 (ad *Dem.* 38–46), E. *Hel.* 1302 (see parallels, p. 99).

ὥc τ' οἰωνόc: gods flying or moving are often compared to birds in epic, *Il.* 5. 778, 15. 237, 19. 350, *Od.* 5. 52, *Ap.* 114. Sometimes they appear to take the form of birds: *Il.* 7. 58 f., 14. 289, *Od.* 1. 320, 3. 371 f., 5. 337, 22. 239 f. For the origins of this cf. Nilsson, *Minoan-Mycenaean Religion*², 491 f.; G. Weicker, *Der Seelenvogel* (Leipzig, 1902), 34. Here the comparison is of course poetic. See also Addenda.

ἐπὶ τραφερήν τε καὶ ὑγρήν: for the omission of the nouns referring to land and sea cf. West ad *Th.* 440, and *Ap.* 529, *Aph.* 123.

44. ἐτήτυμα μυθήcαcθαι: this (Hesiodic) formula is a doublet of the Homeric ἀληθέα μυθήcαcθαι (*Il.* 6. 382 etc., *Dem.* 121).

44–5. Cf. Pi. *O.* 1. 46 (after Pelops was carried off by Poseidon) οὐδὲ ματρὶ πολλὰ μαιόμενοι φῶτες ἄγαγον. Cf. ad *Dem.* 19.

45. ἤθελεν: Wegener (*Philol.* 35 (1876), 231) supposed that this implied a version in which no one wanted to tell Demeter, although they knew, for fear of Zeus' anger (cf. Claud. *RP* 3. 292 f.). But it means simply 'no one *would* tell', i.e. because they could not. Cf. Leaf ad *Il.* 21. 366 for this use of ἐθέλειν.

46. Cf. ad *Dem.* 22 f. For birds as messengers cf. Hes. fr. 123, Call. fr. 260. 27 ff., 261 (Pf. ad loc.), and perhaps *Od.* 19. 545 ff. Here the bird would probably be an omen: cf. *Herm.* 213 f. The bird as messenger is a very common motif in folk-tales. Cf. (e.g.) ad *Dem.* 23.

οἰωνῶν: perhaps placed first to contrast with θεῶν, ἀνθρώπων.

τῇ: for its position cf. *Dem.* 17, *Il.* 14. 78, Hes. *Sc.* 210. Note the (unintentional) repetition of οἰωνός, ἐτήτυμος in 43 f., 46. Cf. Introduction, p. 60.

47. Torches, fasting, and abstention from washing

Demeter's wandering over the earth with torches is supposed to have been represented in the 'mystic drama' enacted at Eleusis (cf. ad *Dem.* 40 ff.). Torches were certainly used in the Iacchus processions and the subsequent pannychis (cf. Ar. *Ran.* 340 ff., 351 ff., 448; E. *Ion* 1074 ff.; and the Niinnion tablet, Mylonas, *Eleusis*, fig. 88). This may have included some kind of running or dancing with torches: cf. Stat. *Silv.* 4. 8. 50 f. (ad *Dem.* 59–61; but it is uncertain to what festival this refers); *Dem.* 48 (cτρωφᾶτο) ∼ 61 (ἤϊξε). The shaking or tossing of torches is often mentioned: Ar. *Ran.* 340 ff., Stat. l.c., Lact. *Div. Inst.* 1. 21. 24, *Epit.* 18 (23) 7. If the 'mystic drama' did take place at Eleusis, it may have been partially enacted in this purely formal manner (cf. ad *Dem.* 40 ff., 48, and Introduction, p. 25).[1]

Demeter's nine-day fast has been taken as reflecting a similar period of abstention by the initiates at Eleusis (cf. Roscher, *Abh. d. Sächs. Ges.* 21 (1903), 14 ff., Nilsson, *Gr. Feste* 321). The *sacra Cereris* at Rome, which were Greek in origin and character, included a fast (*castus Cereris*) which probably lasted nine days (cf. H. le Bonniec, *Le Culte de Cérès à Rome* (Paris, 1958), 404 ff.). The Sicilian Thesmophoria lasted for ten days (Diod. 5. 4. 7, cf. Pl. *Epist.* 349 d) and could have included a nine-day fast. Cf. the Isis-mysteries (Apul. *M.* 11. 23, 28, 30), and those of Cybele and Attis (H. Hepding, *Attis*, 183, H. Graillot, *Le Culte de Cybèle*, 119). At Athens, however, the Thesmophoria probably included only a one-day fast (Cornut. *Theol.* c. 28, Arbesmann, *Das Fasten bei den Griechen und Römern* (Giessen, 1929), 92; Deubner, *AF* 52).

Fasting before the Mysteries is attested by the Eleusinian cύνθημα (Clem. *Protr.* 2. 21. 2), and was probably concluded by the drinking of the *cyceon* (cf. ad *Dem.* 192 ff.). Arbesmann (o.c. 75 ff.) distinguishes two grades, partial abstention from certain foods (Arbesmann, 47 ff.), and total abstinence. The latter was probably for one day only, and ended at nightfall (cf. Call. *Hy.* 6. 6 ff., Ov. *F.* 4. 535 f.). The date is uncertain: it may have corresponded with the day of the Iacchus procession. At Alexandria, the initiates fasted on the day of the procession of the κάλαθος (Call. *Hy.* 6. 6 ff.). Cf. Arbesmann, o.c. 77 ff., Deubner, o.c. 79 ff., Roussel, *BCH* 54 (1930), 73, and notes ad *Dem.* 192 ff.

S. Dow (*HSCP* 48 (1937), 119 f.) suggests that the period of limited abstention may have run for nine days, from the fifteenth to twenty-third Boedromion, the duration of the festival. If so, it did not include

---

[1] Evidence for actual torch-races in the cult is very slight. Cf. B. Ashmole, *AJA* 66 (1962), 233–4, on a relief from Rhamnus which commemorates a *lampade-dromia*, possibly in honour of Demeter and Core. The only other recorded instance is in the Demetreia on Syros (cf. Sittlington-Sterrett, *AJP* 22 (1901), 418).

abstention from wine, since Chabrias' distribution of wine on the sixteenth Boedromion, in commemoration of his victory, can hardly have contravened the Eleusinian regulations (cf. ad *Dem.* 207). Call. fr. 21. 10 (νήϲτιεϲ ἐν Δηοῦϲ ἤμαϲι 'Ραριάδοϲ) might be taken to imply fasting for more than one day, but does not necessarily refer to Attic Eleusis. Philicus' *Hymn*, 36 f., after a reference to the Iacchus procession, has τὸμ παρὰ κῦμα νήϲτην: this could refer either to the sixteenth Boedromion, the day of the ἅλαδε ἔλαϲιϲ (cf. ὥραϲιν . . . μυϲτηλαϲίαιϲ 'Ιάκχων), or to fasting during the Iacchus procession, which skirted the sea along the Bay of Eleusis near the Rheitoi lakes (see below). The second is perhaps more likely. (Latte, *Kl. Schr.* 556, seems to identify the ἅλαδε ἔλαϲιϲ with the Iacchus procession. But cf. Polyaen. 3. 11. 2.)

The nine-day period may, however, be purely poetical (cf. Allen and Halliday ad loc.; Wehrli, *ARW* 31 (1934), 78; Arbesmann, o.c. 80; Nilsson, *Gesch.* i³. 656). The conjunction ἐννῆμαρ μὲν . . . τῇ δεκάτῃ δέ (*vel sim.*) is a conventional one in early epic (cf. especially *Il.* 1. 53 f., 6. 174 f., 9. 470–4, 24. 610–12, 664 f., 784 f., *Od.* 7. 253, 9. 82 f., 10. 28 f., 12. 447, 14. 314, West ad Hes. *Th.* 636). This has been derived from division of the lunar month into three parts (Nilsson, *Op. Sel.* i. 46 f.). In *Il.* 24. 664 f., 784 f., nine days is the period of mourning for the dead, and this was common later (Halliday, *Greek Questions of Plutarch*, 121 ff.). This may be the significance here. The echo δεκάτη . . . 'Εκάτη (*Dem.* 51 f.) should also be noted (cf. ad loc.). We are not told that Demeter ended her fast after nine days, and the contrary is implied by *Dem.* 90 ff., 200 ff. (cf. Arbesmann, o.c. 80).

Similarly the mystae may have abstained from washing for a period, but this cannot have corresponded with the duration of the festival, as they bathed in the sea on the sixteenth Boedromion (cf. above, and Mylonas, *Eleusis*, 249). The Rheitoi, on the Sacred Way to Eleusis, were also used for purification (Hsch. s.v. 'Ρειτοί; Deubner, o.c. 75 n. 11). We do not know whether this occurred during the Iacchus procession (cf. Hsch. l.c.: ὅθεν τοῖϲ λουτροῖϲ ἁγνίζεϲθαι τοὺϲ θιάϲουϲ). A ritual purification with the water of the river Ilissos formed part of the Lesser Mysteries (Polyaen. 5. 17. 1, Stat. *Theb.* 8. 763 ff., Deubner, o.c. 70).

Lustral bowls stood outside the Eleusinion at Athens ([Lys.] 6. 52), and probably also the Telesterion at Eleusis (Mylonas, o.c. 202, 248, fig. 77; Deubner, o.c. 76). An official at Eleusis was called the Hydranos: he was ὁ ἁγνιϲτὴϲ τῶν 'Ελευϲινίων (Hsch. s.v.). But on the supposed representation of a goddess 'baptizing' an initiate at Eleusis, Mylonas, 194, Fig. 70, see E. Simon, *AM* 69–70 (1954–5), 45 ff. She identifies the fragmentary relief as a procession of worshippers led by a νεωκόροϲ: there is thus no question of a baptismal rite.

The significance of these various rituals has been variously interpreted. The chief use of torches or fire is for purification: cf. ad *Dem.* 192 ff., 231 ff. (and Eitrem, *Opferritus*, 178 ff.; Kern, *Die Antike* 6 (1930), 307, and *RE* 16. 1220 f., 1230; Deubner, o.c. 78; Diels,

Sibyllinische Blätter, 47 f.). They are also used to stimulate the fertility of the earth (cf. Allen and Halliday ad *Dem.* 47), and possibly a *lampadephoria* had this as its main purpose.

Similarly fasting has various actual or supposed purposes all of which are closely related. These have been defined as:

(*a*) apotropaic, i.e. to drive out the evil powers in various foods and increase one's own powers (cf. especially Plut. *Mor.* 417 c δαιμόνων δὲ φαύλων ἀποτροπῆς ἕνεκα; also 361 b).

(*b*) preparatory for initiation, mystic ritual, ecstasy, magic ceremonies etc., both by purifying one (cf. below), and by 'heightening one's sensibilities'.

(*c*) purificatory: to enable one to approach a deity (cf. above). Cf. Porph. *de philos. ex orac. haurienda* (p. 148 Wolff) ἵνα τούτων (τῶν πονηρῶν δαιμόνων) ἀπελθόντων παρουςία τοῦ θεοῦ γένηται.

(*d*) as an ascetic practice, to please the gods.

(*e*) for health (medical and gymnastic).

Cf. Arbesmann, o.c., especially 21 ff.; P. Gerlitz, 'Das Fasten als Initiationsritus' (in *Initiation, Studies in the History of Religions*, X, ed. C. J. Bleeker (Brill, 1965), 275 ff.). Fasting as an expression of grief, or a mourning custom, is explained by Arbesmann as due to fear of the dead man's ghost, which might cause harm through food and drink. But cf. K. Meuli, *Romanica Helvetica* 20 (1943), 763 ff., who regards it as a natural reaction at times of violent distress. This seems more reasonable. In Homer *Il.* 19. 203 ff., 305 ff., 319 ff., 24. 601 ff. illustrate this.

So here, the initiates imitated the sorrow of Demeter. At the same time, their fasting was purificatory, as a preliminary to initiation, such as is common in many societies (cf. Gerlitz, o.c., Arbesmann, 74 f., and references ad loc. Cf. also ad *Dem.* 197 ff., 208 ff.).

Abstention from washing is also a reaction to grief, and a sign of mourning: cf. *Il.* 23. 43 ff., 2 Sam. 12: 16 ff. Here, however, the purificatory aim is absent, since purification is rather achieved by the opposite, i.e. ritual washing. In this respect the initiates may have imitated Demeter's grief by abstention, and then purified themselves.

47. πότνια: cf. ad *Dem.* 39.

Δηώ: not in Homer or Hesiod. It is usually regarded as a hypocoristic of Δημήτηρ (*Et. Gud.* 316. 30, Bekker, *Anecd. Gr.* 857). *Et. Magn.* 263. 48 objects to this on the ground that these usually preserve the consonant of the second syllable (e.g. Ὑψώ, Εἰδώ, etc.). Cf. Δημώ (*Dem.* 109, n. ad loc.). Various alternative explanations are offered, connecting it with δήειν, δαίειν = κόπτειν or καίω, γήω, or δηαί (= κριθαί). Modern scholars prefer to treat it as a hypocoristic (*RE* 4. 2713). But it may be rather a by-form of the first element in Δη-μήτηρ. Cf. also S. fr. 743 Τειςώ, for Tisiphone, detected by Pfeiffer, *Wien. Stud.* 79 (1966), 63 f.

48. Cf. ad *Dem.* 47 ff. Torches played an important role at all stages of the Eleusinian celebrations. For their use in the preliminary purification ceremony cf. ad *Dem.* 192 ff., 231 ff., and for their importance and significance within the Telesterion itself ad *Dem.* 231 ff., and Introduction, pp. 26 ff.

The Dadouchos, the second official at Eleusis, took his title from his use of them (cf. Mylonas, *Eleusis*, 232, and for representations of him Mylonas, 208 f., fig. 78, and Kourouniotes, *Eph. Arch.* 1937, 223 ff.). Demeter and Persephone are frequently represented with one or two torches in literature and art (cf. Roscher, 2. 1339 ff.), and torches appear as emblems on Eleusinian monuments (e.g. Mylonas, 158, 167, Fig. 59; cf. 204). Cf. also A. fr. 386, S. *OC* 1049 ff. Torchlight dances formed part of the Attic Thesmophoria: Ar. *Thesm.* 101 ff., 280 f., 1150 ff., Deubner, *AF* 53 f.

In the Sicilian legend Demeter lights her torches from Aetna: Diod. 5. 4. 3, 20. 7. 1 ff., Cic. *Verr.* 2. 4. 106, Ov. *F.* 4. 491 ff., *M.* 5. 441 ff., Stat. *Theb.* 12. 270 ff., Claud. *RP* 3. 330 ff., etc.

49. On nectar and ambrosia cf. ad *Dem.* 237, and West ad *Th.* 640. ἡδυπότοιο: for the sweetness of nectar cf. *Il.* 1. 598, Theocr. 17. 82, Ov. *M.* 14. 606; Roscher, *Nektar und Ambrosia* (Leipzig, 1883), 44 ff.

49 f. Cf. Call. *Hy.* 6. 12, 16 (probably echoing the *Hymn*): οὐ πίες οὔτ᾽ ἄρ᾽ ἔδες τῆνον χρόνον οὐδὲ λοέcca and αὐcταλέα, ἄποτόc τε, καὶ οὐ φάγεc οὐδὲ λοέcca; Hdt. 3. 52. 3, Phryn. Com. ap. Phot. Berol. p. 118. 25 (ad *Dem.* 200).

50. χρόα βάλλετο λουτροῖc: cf. E. *Or.* 303 λουτρά τ᾽ ἐπὶ χροὸc βαλοῦ. βάλλειν is used of 'dashing' someone with water, blood etc.: *Il.* 11. 536, 23. 502, A. *Ag.* 1390. Here the middle is used because one poured water over oneself.

λουτροῖc: in Homer, λοετρά is used. Cf. Hes. *Op.* 753 λουτρῷ χρόα φαιδρύνεcθαι. On abstention from washing cf. ad *Dem.* 47 ff.

Cf. also E. *Hel.* 1383–4 λουτροῖc χρόα ἔδωκα (after 1301 ff., which echoes the *Hymn*).

51–89. On the tenth day Hecate meets Demeter and asks who has carried off Persephone. Demeter does not reply; and together they go off with torches in their hands, and visit the Sun. Demeter asks him for information. The Sun tells her that Hades has carried off her daughter, and consoles her.

The scene of Demeter's meeting with Hecate, and their subsequent visit to the Sun, seem to be illustrated by one of the fifth-century clay reliefs from Locri in Southern Italy, the home of a cult of Persephone. Cf. H. Prückner, *Die lokrischen Tonreliefs* (Mainz, 1968), 82 ff., Abb. 15. The relief has been identified as a portrayal of the sorrowing Demeter, seated on a hillock or piece of rising ground (cf. ad *Dem.* 200), with her foot resting on a wave (i.e. Oceanus, or the ends of the world, perhaps). She is approached by a woman carrying a torch, who stretches out her hand towards her, i.e. Hecate (*Dem.* 52). Above their heads is an arch which indicates the vault of the sky. Above this Helios is shown, in the top right-hand corner, and in the top left, a small female figure hurries away. She is probably Eos, whose appearance is mentioned in *Dem.* 51, and who crosses the sky before the Sun.

If this identification is correct, the relief must be a direct portrayal, although compressed into one scene, of *Dem.* 51–89. It is perhaps the only definite illustration of the *Hymn*, since other episodes are not so closely portrayed as to make this certain, and could reflect other versions.

51. φαινόλιϲ Ἠώϲ: not in Homer or Hesiod. Cf. Sappho, fr. 104a φαίνολιϲ . . . αὔωϲ, Moschus 4. 121 ἠὼϲ . . . φαινόλιϲ ἦλθε, Hsch. s.v. φαινόλιϲ· λαμπρά, φωϲφόροϲ. Cf. also μαινόλιϲ (Bacch. fr. 20A 43 Sn., A. *Supp.* 109 etc.) ∼ μαινόλᾳ Sappho, fr. 1. 18.

51–2. δεκάτη ⎱ There is perhaps a word-play here. Cf. *Od.* 5. 262–3
     Ἑκάτη ⎰
τέτρατον ἦμαρ ἔην, καὶ τῷ τετέλεϲτο ἅπαντα· τῷ δ' ἄρα πέμπτῳ πέμπ' . . . Days of the month have a magical significance: cf. Hes. *Op.* 765 ff.

52. ἤντετο: a reference to Hecate's title of *Antaea* has been seen here (Nilsson, *Gesch.* i³. 724). Cf. A.R. 1. 1141, 3. 1212 ff., *Orph. Hy.* 41. 1 (Quandt ad loc.). The sense of this is apparently 'to whom one makes supplication' (LSJ s.v. II; on the original sense cf. Nilsson, o.c. 184). Cf. ad *Dem.* 53 (ἀγγελέουϲα). Hecate is a helper of all men (cf. Hes. *Th.* 429 ff., esp. 441).

ϲέλαϲ ἐν χείρεϲϲιν ἔχουϲα: this perhaps implies *two* torches, with which she is normally represented later (Ar. *Ran.* 1361 f., Roscher, 1. 1900, Farnell, *Cults*, ii. 549 f.). For Hecate as torch-bearer cf. also Bacch. fr. 1 B1. (Sn.), E. *Hel.* 569, Hsch. s.v. Ὑπολάμπτειρα, and Kraus, *Hekate*, Index s.v. Fackel, δᾳδοφόροϲ, Φωϲφόροϲ. For ϲέλαϲ of a torch cf. A.R. 3. 293, 1216, 4. 808, *AP* 9. 46, etc.

53. ἀγγελέουϲα: this use of the future is found at *Il.* 19. 120 (characterized by Page, *History and the Homeric Iliad*, 333 n. 25, as 'highly abnormal'). Present and future are equally found, the future normally with verbs of motion (*Od.* 4. 258 etc.). The present seems more usual in prose (Isocr. 1. 33 etc.). They are variants at *Od.* 13. 94, 14. 123 (etc.), and used interchangeably in Triphiod. 212, 236.

Hecate (or Artemis) was called Ἄγγελοϲ at Syracuse (Hsch. s.v.; Schol. Theocr. 2. 12). Cf. Farnell, *Cults*, ii. 517 f. for the story of Ἄγγελοϲ in Sophron. He suggests that the title may be due to her role as bringer of news to Demeter. But possibly her part in the *Hymn* at this point may be due to her title, since she does not in fact tell Demeter anything that she does not already know. Cf. also Pindar, *Paean* 2. 49 ἄγγελλε (Hecate).

ἔποϲ φάτο φώνηϲέν τε: such duplication of expression is especially a feature of epic poetry (W. B. Stanford, *Greek Metaphor*, 124 f.). It is very common in this *Hymn*.

54–6. The Orphic papyrus borrows these lines and transfers them to Demeter's speech to the Eleusinians, attaching them to *Dem.* 268. This suits the Orphic version, in which Demeter learns the truth

about the Rape from the Eleusinians, and Hecate is not mentioned.
Cf. ad *Dem.* 19–32, and Introduction, pp. 80 ff.

54. Δημήτηρ: the nominative for vocative is sometimes found in
poetry, and in some cases, as here, combined with a vocative form,
e.g. *Il.* 4. 189 (with name in voc.), S. *Aj.* 923 (name in nom.), etc.
(cf. *Hy.* 30. 17 χαῖρε, θεῶν μήτηρ, ἄλοχ᾽ Οὐρανοῦ). In *Dem.* 75 the name
is in the vocative, with θυγάτηρ in the nominative. Cf. also Page,
PMG 935. 15. Metrical convenience must play some part in determining which is used (cf. Chantraine, *GH* ii. 36) and here a nominative
formula is taken over (see below), but there may be other factors
at work: cf. West ad Hes. *Th.* 964, and *Glotta* 44 (1967), 139 ff.,
R. Loewe, *Zeitschr. f. vergl. Sprachf.* 55 (1927), 52.

ὠρηφόρε ἀγλαόδωρε: the hiatus results from the adaptation of
a nominative noun–epithet formula (cf. *Dem.* 192). Cf. e.g. *Il.* 2. 8,
18. 385, West, l.c. above. It is 'legitimate' in the bucolic diaeresis:
cf. Monro, *HG*² § 382. 2. On Demeter as 'bringer of ripeness, giver of
gladness' cf. Preller–Robert 1. 767, and ad *Dem.* 4. For ἀγλαόδωρος
cf. Agallias' line quoted on p. 100, and Nonnus *D.* 7. 85, 12. 263, 19. 44.

55. θεῶν: for the synizesis of θεός cf. *Il.* 1. 18, *Od.* 14. 251, *Dem.*
259, 325, Hes. *Th.* 44. It is probable also in Hes. frr. 1. 5, 185. 7;
Archil. fr. 19. 3 West.

οὐρανίων: not in Homer or Hesiod. Cf. Pi. *O.* 11. 2 etc.; θεῶν τῶν
οὐρανίων E. *El.* 1234; also Hom. θεοὶ οὐρανίωνες *Il.* 1. 570 etc., Οὐρανιώνων *Il.* 5. 373 etc.

Cf. Hoekstra, *Sub-epic Stage*, 49, who points out that the synizesis
is due to 'declension' of θεοὶ οὐρανίωνες.

56. Περσεφόνην: the Homeric form is always Περσεφόνεια (*Il.* 9. 457
etc.; cf. *Dem.* 337, 348, 359, 370, 493). Περσεφόνη occurs in Hes. *Th.*
913, *Dem.* 360, 387, 405. The form Φερσεφόνη (cf. pap. 1) or Φερ-
σεφόνεια is also given by pap. 2 at *Dem.* 405, by papyri at Hes. fr. 185. 4,
280. 12, and as a variant at *Hy.* 13. 2; cf. Simon. 131 D.², Pi. *O.*
14. 21, *PMG* 885. 3, *IG* ii². 6551, 7873. 10 (4th c. B.C. Attic funeral
epigrams), Philicus' *Hymn* (Attic) 2, 48, and Latte, *Kl. Schr.* 542 n. 5.
These forms are poetic: Attic prose inscriptions use Φερρέφαττα. In
decrees she is called Κόρη (cf. ad *Dem.* 439). Cf. Meisterhans, *Gramm.
d. att. Inschr.*³ p. 100. 3. It might possibly be original here, under Attic
influence.

For the possible etymologies of the name cf. Bräuninger, *RE* 19.
945–8.

57. γάρ: for lengthening of γάρ before a vowel cf. (in the same
position) *Il.* 2. 39, Epic. Adesp. 4. 9, Powell (*Coll. Alex.* 79); also
Il. 19. 49.

For the chiastic expression cf. E. *Hipp.* 86 κλύων μὲν αὐδῆς, ὄμμα
δ᾽ οὐχ ὁρῶν τὸ σόν (and cf. in reverse, E. *Med.* 653 f., Page ad loc.).
ἴδον ὀφθαλμοῖσιν: cf. ad *Dem.* 53.

58. ὅς τις ἔην: this is an indirect question added to 57 (cf. *Dem.*
71–3). *Dem.* 119, *Aph.* 92, which Allen and Halliday compare, are
different ('whoever you are': cf. ad *Dem.* 119).

coὶ δ᾽ ... πάντα: 'I am telling you at once the whole truth.' This is simply a conventional way of ending a piece of news (as in *Od.* 11. 137, *Dem.* 433, and refs. ad loc.). There is no need to assume a lacuna here. ὦκα is due to the urgency of the situation: cf. ὦκα in 60, and 171–2 ὦκα δὲ μητρὶ | ἔννεπον ... ἡ δὲ μάλ᾽ ὦκα ...

Messengers are traditionally swift (ταχὺς ἄγγελος *Il.* 24. 292, *Od.* 15. 526). Cf. *Aph.* 137 etc.

59–61. Cf. Stat. *Silv.* 4. 8. 50 f.:

> tuque *Actaea Ceres cursu* cui semper *anhelo*
> votivam *taciti* quassamus *lampada* mystae.

These lines, describing the ritual of silent torch-carrying in the mysteries of Demeter, are an excellent commentary on *Dem.* 59–61. The festival referred to in Statius perhaps took place at Naples (cf. Vollmer ad loc.), but probably the Eleusinian ritual was similar. Demeter's silence is thus explained as a feature of the cult. Silence was essential to certain parts of the mystery-ritual: cf. ad *Dem.* 192 ff., 198 f., and especially 478 f.

60. Ῥείης: this is the commonest form of the name in epic (*Il.* 14. 203 vulg., *Dem.* 60, 75, 442, Hes. *Th.* 453, 625, 634, *Ap.* 93, *Aph.* 43, *Hy.* 12. 1); but also Ῥέη (*Dem.* 459, *Th.* 467), Ῥεία (*Il.* 14. 203 v.l., *Th.* 135), Ῥέα (*Il.* 15. 187), and cf. also Ῥῆ (Pherecydes Syr. 9). Cf. West ad *Th.* 135.

Ῥείης ἠϋκόμου θυγάτηρ: the epithet seems to be a feature of 'genealogy' poetry, since it occurs especially in the context of parent–child or husband–wife relationships:

Il. 1. 36 ~ 19. 413, *Od.* 11. 318, *Ap.* 178 (τὸν | ὃν ἠΰκομος τέκε Λητώ); *Il.* 3. 329 etc. (Ἑλένης πόσις ἠϋκόμοιο); *Il.* 4. 512 ~ 16. 860 (Θέτιδος πάϊς ἠϋκόμοιο); *Il.* 10. 5 (πόσις Ἥρης ἠϋκόμοιο); *Il.* 24. 466 (μητέρος ἠϋκόμοιο); Hes. *Th.* 625 ~ 634 (οὓς τέκεν ἠΰκομος Ῥείη); *Sc.* 216 (ἠϋκόμου Δανάης τέκος); Hes. *Catalogue, passim* (cf. Index s.v.). Cf. also ad *Dem.* 442.

61. ἤϊξ᾽: cf. ad *Dem.* 47 ff. For ἤϊξε(ν) after a speech cf. *Herm.* 227, *Aph.* 291, and similarly *Il.* 6. 232. In *Herm.* 227 it is also used without any indication of direction.

62. For the Sun as watcher over all things cf. *Il.* 3. 277 (~ *Od.* 11. 109, 12. 323), A. *PV* 91, *Cho.* 985 f., fr. 192. 5, Orph. *Lith.* 695, *Orph. Hy.* 8. 1, 14. This led to his invocation as a witness, and to his ethical position as guardian of right (cf. ad *Dem.* 20, 24 ff.; Roscher, 1. 2019 f.).

63. στὰν δ᾽: this represents one of the regular stages in Homeric scenes of 'Arrival': cf. Arend, *Typische Scenen*, 28 ff. and Tafel 1, 3, Teil IV.

ἵππων: the Sun's chariot (cf. *Dem.* 88 f.) does not appear in Homer. Cf. *Herm.* 69, *Hy.* 28. 14, 31. 9, 15; Mimn. fr. 10 D.³, etc. In Homer, Dawn has a chariot (*Od.* 23. 244). In art, the Sun's chariot perhaps first appears *c.* 670–660 B.C. (cf. J. N. Coldstream, *BICS* 12 (1965), 34–7: Helios with single horse on amphora from Thera?), otherwise not before the end of the black-figure period on vases (Roscher, I. 2005). The Sun has a chariot in Persian mythology (Windischmann, *Mithra* 15. 124), in the Veda (Roscher, l.c.), and in German mythology (Grimm, *Deutsche Mythol.*⁴, 615). Its absence in Homer may be due to chance.

64 ff. For this speech of entreaty, cf. *Od.* 3. 92–101 = 4. 322–31 (Telemachus asks Nestor/Menelaus for news of his father):

1. *Request for respect and pity*:
   Dem. 64 αἴδεccαί με, 76 ἄζομαι ἠδ' ἐλεαίρω ～ (negatived) *Od.* 3. 96
   μηδέ τί μ' αἰδόμενος μειλίccεο μηδ' ἐλεαίρων

2. *Precedent*:
   64b–5 εἴ ποτε δή cευ | ἢ ἔπει ἢ ἔργῳ (etc.) ～ *Od.* 3. 98–100 εἴ ποτέ τοί
   τι πατὴρ ἐμόc . . . ἢ ἔπος ἠέ τι ἔργον ὑποcτὰc ἐξετέλεccε . . .

3. *Request for information*:
   71 νημερτέωc μοι ἔνιcπε φίλον τέκοc εἴ που ὄπωπαc
   ～ *Od.* 3. 93 ἐνιcπεῖν εἴ που ὄπωπαc . . .
   97 ἀλλ' εὖ μοι κατάλεξον ὅπωc ἤντηcαc ὀπωπῆc
   101 καί μοι νημερτὲc ἔνιcπεc . . .

For a similar speech of entreaty cf. *Dem.* 135 ff. (n. ad loc.).

64 f. Demeter uses the normal formula of entreaty, by appeal to precedent: cf. *Il.* 1. 39 f., 394 f., 503 f., and ad *Dem.* 64 ff., etc. Note the position of cευ: it goes with κραδίην καὶ θυμόν despite the intervening nouns. The pronoun is regularly brought forward to the beginning of the sentence: cf. ad *Dem.* 202.

64. θεὰν θεόc: Peerlkamp's conjecture is attractive, as θεαν θεοc might have become θεαc and ὕπερ might then have been added in an attempt to make some sense. For the polyptoton cf. West, *Th.* p. 76.

Ludwich's conjecture (adopted by Allen) is unsatisfactory: the postponement of cύ περ is awkward, and περ unnecessary. Ludwich compares *Il.* 1. 508, 9. 301, 11. 796, 12. 349, but there περ means 'at least' (cf. Scholl. BT ad *Il.* 1. 508, Ebeling, II, 164 f.), and comes at the beginning of the sentence, closely associated with a conjunction: ἀλλὰ cύ περ etc. Allen and Halliday compare *Dem.* 116, but this is not a parallel in either sense or word order.

65. ἢ ἔπει ἢ ἔργῳ: regular in this context (cf. ad *Dem.* 64 ff.).

66 f. κούρην τὴν . . . τῆc . . .: the sentence begins with asyndeton, as it explains Demeter's appeal (αἴδεccαί με), and the first word states the subject of her appeal: cf. *Il.* 16. 56, 18. 444. It is attracted to the case of the relative ('attractio inversa'). Cf. *Il.* 6. 396, 10. 416, 14. 75, 371; Monro, *HG*² § 267. 4, Chantraine, *GH* ii. 237 f., Wackernagel, *Vorlesungen über Syntax*, 1. 56 f., E. Fraenkel, *Glotta* 33 (1954), 157 ff. (on Virg. *A.* 1. 573). Wackernagel explains this inverse attraction as arising when a part of the main sentence whose construction is not yet determined precedes the relative.

εἴδεϊ κυδρήν does not occur in Homer or Hesiod (cf. Hom. εἶδοc ἀρίcτην etc.). κυδρόc is used in Homer only in the formula (Διὸc) κυδρὴ(ν) παράκοιτιc/τιν : *Il.* 18. 184, *Od.* 11. 580, 15. 26 (Hes. *Th.* 328). Cf. κυδρὴ(ν) θεόc/ν : *Dem.* 179, 292 etc. (cf. ad loc.), Hes. *Op.* 257 (of Dike), *Herm.* 461 (of Hermes). Note the neglect of digamma, for which there are virtually no parallels in Homer with εἶδοc (cf. Appendix II, в (6)). Hoekstra, *Sub-epic Stage*, 53, comments that 'the expression εἴδει κυδρήν looks rather strained.' There are no exact parallels in Homer for this use of the dative, the other cases being with comparatives, and the phrase 'was almost certainly coined by the poet'.

67. ἀδινὴν ὄπ': the basic sense of the epithet is probably 'thick, crowded' (LSJ, Frisk s.v.). From this, it comes to be used of the heart ('throbbing, thronging', *Il.* 16. 481, 19. 516), and then of violent grief, sobbing or crying (*Il.* 18. 124, 314, etc.), and of throbbing, passionate voices, e.g. the Sirens (*Od.* 23. 326), and here of Persephone's cry.

The rough breathing was read by Aristarchus (Scholl. AB ad *Il.* 2. 87), as in ἁδρόc, but the correct epic form is probably ἀδινόc.

δι' αἰθέροc ἀτρυγέτοιο: the meaning of ἀτρύγετοc is not known. Frisk (s.v.) supports the ancient interpretation 'unfruitful, barren', but the connection with τρυγάω is doubtful.

The phrase suggests that Demeter was in heaven at the time (cf. *Dem.* 92).

69 f. Demeter appeals to Helios on the grounds of his all-seeing power. Cf. the traditional formula of prayers δύναcαι γάρ (*vel sim.*), e.g. *Il.* 16. 515, *Od.* 5. 25, Hes. *Th.* 420 (West ad loc.), etc.

For the use of ἀλλὰ cύ . . . in prayers cf. Denniston, *GP* 16, Bühler on Moschus, *Europa*, 27 (p. 72), *Il.* 17. 645.

70. αἰθέροc ἐκ δίηc: cf. West ad Hes. *Th.* 687.

καταδέρκεαι ἀκτίνεccι: the Sun sees with his own rays. Cf. Hes. *Th.* 451 πολυδερκέοc 'Ηοῦc (West ad loc.) ; A. *PV* 796 f., A.R. 4. 727 ff., Dieterich, *Nekyia*, 38 f. The Greeks thought of the eyes as seeing by light emanating from them, rather than that received by them.

71. ἔνιcπε: the form ἐνίcπεc is found at *Il.* 11. 186, 14. 470 (v.l. ἔνιcπε, ad fin.), and is also attested as a variant in the *Odyssey* (3. 101 = 4. 331, 3. 247, etc.; cf. Allen ad loc.). But ἔνιcπε is guaranteed by the metre at *Od.* 4. 642. It appears to have been regarded as an imperative of a present *ἐνίcπω (cf. Chantraine, *GH* i. 467).

71–3. Line 71 is complete in itself, and 72–3 are added as an indirect question (cf. ad *Dem.* 58). The word order is complex, and 71 might be derived from a formulaic passage in which φίλον τέκοc was a vocative (as it normally is : cf. formulaic parallels). For the late position of ἠὲ θεῶν (etc.) cf. West ad *Th.* 82 (etc.).

72. ἀέκουcαν ἀνάγκη: Greek stresses this notion of restricted freedom. Cf. *Dem.* 124, 413, *Od.* 4. 646, 5. 154 f., etc., and ad *Dem.* 53 (duplication of expression). The concept of Ἀνάγκη was of an inescapable, binding force (cf. ad *Dem.* 216–17).

73. ἠὲ . . . ἢ καί: one would expect ἠὲ . . . ἠέ (cf. *Dem.* 55 etc.). ἢ καί perhaps suggests that the second possibility is more remote ('or even' : Denniston, *GP* 306).

74. Ὑπεριονίδης: cf. ad *Dem.* 26. The fourth-foot caesura is rare: *c.* 300 in all Homeric poetry, of which a third have a proper name in the middle of the verse (van Leeuwen, *Enchiridium*, 17; Lehrs, *Aristarchus*², 396 ff.).

75 ff. For the Sun's role as Demeter's informant cf. ad *Dem.* 20, 24 ff. Ovid follows this version in *F.* 4. 583 f., but makes Arethusa tell Demeter in *M.* 5. 504 ff. A number of legends gave the credit to local inhabitants. In an Orphic version, Demeter is informed by the Eleusinians Eubouleus (or Celeus) and Triptolemus, and rewards them with the gift of agriculture: Orph. fr. 51 K. (= Paus. 1. 14. 3, Schol. Aristid. *Panath.* 105. 11 p. 53 Dind.), Orph. *Hy.* 41. 6 ff., fr. 49. 103 f., Claud. *RP* 3. 52, Schol. Ar. *Eq.* 698, Myth. Vat. 2. 96. Cf. Introduction, pp. 81 f.

In another legend, she learnt the truth from the people of Hermione (Apollod. 1. 5. 1, Schol. Ar. *Eq.* 782, Zenob. *Cent.* 1. 7); at Argos, from Chrysanthis, the daughter of King Pelasgus (Paus. 1. 14. 2; cf. ad *Dem.* 6 ff.). At Paros, Cabarnos informed her (Steph. Byz. s.v. *Πάρος*). At Pheneos, Demeter rewarded the inhabitants who gave her information with her support in war (Conon, *FGH* 26 F 15). Cf. also ad *Dem.* 96.

75. θυγάτηρ: cf. ad *Dem.* 54.

ἄνασσα: of Demeter *Il.* 14. 326, *Dem.* 492, E. *Phoen.* 685 f., Ar. *Ran.* 386 ff. Rubensohn, *JDAI* 70 (1955), 48 f., suggests that the name Anaktoron for the Telesterion (and apparently also for the inner 'holy-of-holies') was due to Demeter's title ἄνασσα. Thus she sits in her temple at *Dem.* 302 ff. Cf. Mylonas, *Eleusis*, 88 (*contra* Rubensohn), and for an alternative theory cf. ad *Dem.* 96.

76. μέγα ἄζομαι: for the hiatus cf. Hes. *Th.* 532 (and perhaps also Theognis, 280 κάτοπιν ἀζόμενοι: κατόπισθ' cod. A). The hiatus is 'illicit' at this place in the verse, and the pronoun might be expected with ἀχνυμένην. But c' ἄζομαι is unattractive, and the separation of the adverb from the verb undesirable. ϲε μέγ' (Voss) would be preferable. Cf. Alcm. *PMG* 70c: cὲ γὰρ ἄζομαι.

77. περὶ παιδί: for the rare dative with περί and verbs of caring cf. E. *Hel.* 1342 f. (from *Dem.* 77? Cf. Kannicht ad loc.) and Gow on Theocr. 1. 54. It is common with verbs of fearing (*Il.* 10. 240, Thuc. 1. 60 etc.).

οὐδέ: Wegener objected to this ('vielleicht mit Recht', Gemoll), but it derives from the formula in *Od.* 11. 558 f. (22. 154 f.). Cf. also the use of οὐδέ τί ϲε χρή (ad *Dem.* 82), and *Od.* 4. 400 for δέ after 'I shall tell you (what to do)'; Denniston, *GP* 170 f.

77 f. For 'it is not your (etc.) fault but the god's' cf. *Il.* 3. 164, 19. 86 f., 409 f., 21. 275 (and ad *Dem.* 147 f.).

79. θαλερὴν ... ἄκοιτιν: this phrase is notably common in the last part of the *Theogony*, and in the *Catalogue*: cf. West, *Theogony*, 398.

81. μεγάλα ἰάχουσαν: the vowel is lengthened before an original digamma (cf. Chantraine, *GH* ii. 139 f.).

82 ff. For this speech of consolation cf. *Dem.* 362 ff. (Hades to

Persephone). The form is the same: (1) Do not be so discouraged. (2) Hades is not a bad husband. (3) The τιμή of Hades/τιμαί of Persephone.

82. οὐδέ τί ϲε χρή: Hermann objected that this phrase always refers to something already mentioned (e.g. *Il.* 19. 67 f.). But cf. *Od.* 1. 296 f., 15. 393 f., 18. 17 f., *Herm.* 494 f.

83. μὰψ αὔτωϲ: for the duplication cf. *Od.* 16. 111, *Dem.* 362, 467 f., and ad *Dem.* 53, 72, etc.

ἄπλητον: not in Homer. Cf. Hes. *Th.* 153, 315, 709, *Sc.* 147, 230 (v.l.), 250, 268. The sense is not certain: LSJ consider it equivalent to ἄπλατοϲ (unapproachable, terrible, monstrous), but it may often be regarded as equivalent to ἄπλετοϲ (boundless, immense), as in later epic (cf. West ad *Th.* 153, and *Od.* 16. 111). The sense of ἄπληϲτοϲ (insatiable) would also fit here.

83 ff. Cf. *Dem.* 363–4, Ov. *F.* 4. 598 ff., *M.* 5. 526 ff., Claud. *RP* 2. 277 ff., and similarly *Aph.* 136. In later Greek οὐ μεμπτός is used of a good match: cf. E. *Phoen.* 425, *Ion* 1519, *Hel.* 1424, *IA* 712, Phoenix, 2. 10 f., Paus. 2. 28. 4, Plut. *Cato* 24, Antig. fr. 168, P. Oxy. 1083 fr. i 19, etc.

It is notable that Hades is presented in a relatively favourable light in the *Hymn*, although always with sinister undertones (cf. ad *Dem.* 357 f.). Cf. E. Simon, *Opfernde Götter*, 75, on the reluctance of artists to portray him unfavourably.

85. αὐτοκαϲίγνητοϲ καὶ ὁμόϲποροϲ: this is not pleonastic, but means 'of the same mother and father'. Cf. καϲίγνητοϲ καὶ ὄπατροϲ (*Il.* 12. 371 ~ 11. 257, Hes. fr. 280. 21), Hes. fr. 280. 18 (see app. crit.), and (a similar formation) ὁμότροφοϲ *Ap.* 199.

ἀμφὶ δὲ τιμήν: the prepositional phrase is placed at the beginning of the sentence, as a separate colon ('and as for honour'). Cf. *Il.* 7. 408, Schol. ad loc.; E. Fraenkel, *Kleine Beiträge*, 1. 100, 125, 134.

For ἀμφί with accusative meaning 'concerning' cf. perhaps *Il.* 18. 339 (ἀμφὶ . . . ϲὲ . . . κλαύϲονται). But this is a doubtful example: cf. Chantraine, *GH* ii. 88. Other examples (*Herm.* 57, *Hy.* 7. 1, 22. 1, 23. 1, Terp. *PMG* 697, Ar. *Nu.* 595) all belong to the traditional opening formula of a hymn (ἀμφιανακτίζειν). The dative is more common (*Il.* 7. 408 etc.). For the genitive cf. *Herm.* 172, *Il.* 8. 267. Pfister, *Philol.* 84 (1928), 5 n. 3, takes ἀμφί as adverbial, but this is very improbable.

85 f. τιμήν: for τιμή of a god's 'province' or 'sphere of influence' cf. *Il.* 15. 189, Hes. *Th.* 74 (West ad loc.), 112, 393, 425–6, 885, *Aph.* 37, *Hy.* 22. 4. He receives it as his μοῖρα (ἔλλαχεν, ἔμμορε, etc.): cf. *Il.* 15. 189 ff., Hes. *Th.* 203, 413 ff., 422 ff., *Aph.* 37, *Hy.* 29. 3, Orph. *Hy.* 17. 7, 18. 6, etc.; Keyssner, *Gottesvorstellung*, 62 ff.

86. This refers to the division of the world between Zeus, Poseidon, and Hades, described in *Il.* 15. 189–91. Cf. *Hy.* 22. 4 f., and Page, *GLP* no. 91. 3 ff., especially 10: Ἀγεϲίλας δ' ἔλαχεν τὸν Τά[ρταρον εὐ]ρὺν ἔπεϲθαι; Ov. *M.* 5. 529, *Am.* 3. 10. 45 f. The language recalls Hes. *Th.* 424, which, however, refers to an earlier division of τιμαί. Other divisions are referred to in Hes. *Th.* 74 (etc.), 534 (cf. West ad loc.), Pi. *O.* 7. 55 ff., Call. *Hy.* 1. 58–67, fr. 119 (Pfeiffer ad loc.).

Persephone's division of her time between Heaven and Hades perhaps reflects the division referred to here (cf. ad *Dem.* 365–9, 399 f.).

87. τοῖς μεταναιετάει: the verb is found only here. Cf. περιναιετάειν (*Od.* 2. 66 etc.), μεταναιέτης Hes. *Th.* 401. τοῖς μέτα should perhaps be preferred.

The verse is epexegetic to 85 f., and hence in asyndeton. It is euphemistic: the dead are not named (cf. ad *Dem.* 9, 481 f.). The point seems to be 'Hades does live among the dead: but he is their king.'

88. ὁμοκλῆς: the smooth breathing is supported by Hes. *Sc.* 341, Call. *Hy.* 4. 158 (ὑπ᾽ *Ψ*: ὑφ᾽ P. Oxy. 2225). In *Il.* 20. 365 κέκλεθ᾽ ὁμοκλήσας is read (with v.l. κέκλετ᾽ ὁμ-). The rough breathing is perhaps due to false association with ὁμός (LSJ s.v.; cf. Wackernagel, *Sprach. Unters.* 47 (= 207) n. 1; Jacobsohn, *Philologus* 67 (1908), 513 ff.). It is normal in Homeric manuscripts.

89. φέρον: this should probably be retained as in *Il.* 17. 458 (ἔφερον v.l.) and elsewhere. ἔφερον occurs only in *Il.* 11. 533, 23. 849, *Od.* 18. 303 (∼ 5. 461).

τανύπτεροι ὥς τ᾽ οἰωνοί: the epithet occurs first in Hes. *Th.* 523. There is no example in Homer of the word order 'epithet–ὥς τε– noun', and it might be possible to take τανύπτεροι as referring to the Sun's horses, which are winged in art from the end of the black-figure period (although the gods' horses are already winged in art by *c.* 650, e.g. Melian amphora, Arias and Hirmer, *Greek Vase Painting*, 29 Pl. 22). In literature the first definite example of this is E. *El.* 465, although their speed is emphasized in *Hy.* 28. 14, E. *Phoen.* 3 (cf. Roscher 1. 2006 ff., J. Diggle, *Euripides, Phaethon* (Cambridge, 1970), 137). For the epithet in this position cf. *Il.* 2. 764 (of mares) τὰς Εὔμηλος ἔλαυνε ποδώκεας, ὄρνιθας ὥς.

But it is preferable to take the epithet with οἰωνοί: for this order cf. Pi. *N.* 7. 62, A. *Supp.* 751, *Cho.* 421, *Ag.* 1671.

Note the dactylic rhythm of the verse: cf. *Dem.* 171 (n. ad loc.), 184, 380 (again of flying horses). The appropriateness of this rhythm for a galloping horse has long been noticed in the case of *Il.* 6. 511 (cf. Leaf ad loc.). Cf. also *Il.* 13. 29 f. (τοὶ δὲ πέτοντο | ῥίμφα μάλ᾽ . . . etc.), 20. 497 (of oxen trampling grain, compared to Achilles' horses in full career), Virg. *A.* 8. 596.

90–7. Demeter, in her grief and anger, leaves the gods and wanders over the earth in disguise, until she comes to the palace of Celeus, king of Eleusis.

In this version, the motive for Demeter's wanderings on earth is her anger with Zeus (91). In later versions, she is normally looking for her daughter (cf. ad *Dem.* 75 ff.). At first sight this has more point to it, but the theme of the withdrawal of a deity from heaven in anger is also a traditional one: cf. ad *Dem.* 305 ff. (with 302 ff.), 192–211 (3. Iambe).

In Apollodorus (1. 5. 1) she learns about the Rape from the people of Hermione, and then is angry with the gods, leaves heaven, and comes to Eleusis.

90. κύντερον: in Homer this is used of things that are shameful (in *Il.* 8. 483, *Od.* 11. 427 as a term of censure of women, in *Od.* 7. 216 of the belly, in *Od.* 20. 18 of the maids sleeping with the suitors); hence of things that are hard to endure. Cf. κύντατον *Il.* 10. 503 (of deeds of slaughter); *Dem.* 305 f. αἰνότατον ... καὶ κύντατον of the famine, which is due to her grief, and is in fact the 'physical correlative' of it (cf. ad *Dem.* 305–33).

91. δἤπειτα: this is normal in Homeric manuscripts (cf. also Hes. *Th.* 405 and 562). Editors usually write δὴ ἔπειτα (∪ ∪ – ∪). Cf. van Leeuwen, *Enchiridium*², 70, West, *Theogony*, 100.

93. This theme of a god wandering in disguise among men is common in Greek literature. Cf. especially *Od.* 17. 485–7. (For a discussion of this cf. Pl. *Rep.* 381 ff.) For the motif of an encounter with a god in disguise cf. ad *Dem.* 98 ff. In Hes. fr. 1. 6 f. the implication is different, that once gods and men lived together (West ad Hes. *Th.* 507–616, 535; cf. Cat. 64. 384 ff.). Cf. also A.R. 3. 66 ff. (where 72 ~ *Dem.* 101), Ov. *M.* 1. 211 ff., 8. 616 ff., *F.* 5. 493 ff., Paus. 8. 2. 4 ff., Pfister, *RE*, *Supp.* 5. 291 f.

Stories of hospitality to deities were often told to account for the origins of family cults. Cf. ad *Dem.* 96, also the hosts of Dionysus, Amphiction, Icarius, and Oeneus, and in general Fr. Deneken, *De Theoxeniis* (Diss. Berlin, 1881), 24 ff., Pfister, *Der Reliquienkult im Altertum* (Giessen, 1909), i. 166 f.

94. ἀμαλδύνουςα: this epic and Ionic word occurs in Homer only in the context of the destruction of the Achaean wall. It means 'soften' (cf. ἀμαλός), hence 'efface' etc. Cf. A.R. 1. 834, 4. 112 for the sense 'disguise, wipe out'.

95. γίνωςκε: this form is given by practically all Homeric manuscripts and papyri, and should be accepted. It is explicitly vouched for as the Homeric form by Eust. 1064. 2. Cf. West ad Hes. *Th.* 429.

βαθυζώνων τε γυναικῶν: in Homer this formula is used of women from captured cities (Schol. *Od.* 3. 154 βαρβάρων γυναικῶν τὸ ἐπίθετον; *Et. Magn.* 185. 33, Eust. 1462. 3; cf. A. *Pers.* 155). Cf. βαθύκολπος (ad *Dem.* 5). It is used again of Metaneira (*Dem.* 161) and Persephone (201, 304). Cf. Hes. fr. 205. 5, etc. The sense should be 'low-girt' (cf. Allen and Sikes ad loc.), but it perhaps arises from a combination of βαθύκολπος and ἐΰζωνος (*Il.* 1. 429 etc.).

96. πρίν γ' ὅτε δή ...: this is the only 'forward-reference' in the *Hymn* (excepting perhaps *Dem.* 273–4). Cf. *Ap.* 49, van Groningen, *Composition littéraire archaïque*, 108, 307.

Κελεοῖο ... δῶμα: Celeus receives Demeter also in Pamphos (ap. Paus. 1. 39. 1), Apollod. 1. 5. 1, 3. 14. 7, Nic. *Ther.* 486, Ov. *F.* 4. 507 ff., Schol. Ar. *Eq.* 695, Serv. and Philarg. ad Virg. *G.* 1. 163, Myth. Vat. 1. 18; cf. also Bacch. fr. 3 (Sn.). For his parentage cf. ad *Dem.* 105.

In the Orphic version, Dysaules and Baubo receive Demeter (Orph.
frr. 51, 52 K.), but Celeus replaces Dysaules in Schol. Aristid. *Panath.*
105. 11 p. 53 Dind. (and perhaps Orph. fr. 49. 105). In this version
they are poor herdsmen (i.e. before the discovery of agriculture), and
this may be reflected by Ovid *F.* 4. 507 ff., where Celeus is a poor
rustic (cf. Malten, *ARW* 12 (1909), 417 ff.). It is, however, possible
that Ovid is here following the popular Hellenistic tradition, which
liked to portray humble people giving hospitality to deities (cf.
A. S. Hollis, *Ovid, Metamorphoses VIII*, pp. 106 ff., Bömer ad Ov. *F.*
4. 508, and *F* 5. 493 ff.). Cf. Introduction, pp. 72, 79 ff.

As the recipient of the gift of agriculture in later Attic legend Celeus
becomes 'the farmer': Virg. *G.* 1. 165, *IG* 12. 1. 780. 1 (cf. 781, 783),
Nonn. *D.* 27. 285, 47. 50. Cf. Herter, *RhM.* 90 (1941), 251.

He is rooted in the local cult of Eleusis and Attica: he receives
sacrifices with the other heroes at the Eleusinia (Sokolowski, *Lois
sacrées, Supplément,* No. 10. 72), and his daughters and wife have a cult
at Eleusis (cf. ad *Dem.* 105, 161 and Athenag. *Libellus pro Christianis* 14,
ed. Schwartz p. 15). He was traditionally regarded as the founder
of the custom of giving free meals in the Prytaneum at Athens (Plut.
QS 4. 4. 1 = 667 d). The story of his hospitality to Demeter was a
traditional subject of Attic hymns, and a rhetorical τόπος (Menander,
Διαίρεϲιϲ τῶν ἐπιδεικτικῶν 1. 6, Rhet. Gr. 3. 338 Spengel; Nonn.
D. 19. 80 ff.).

On the view that he originated in Celeae in the Argolid, where
there was a tomb of Dysaules (Paus. 2. 14. 1 ff.) cf. Malten, o.c. 444,
Kern, *RE* 11. 138 ff., s.v. Keleos.

In art, he appears with Demeter, Phersephasa, and Hippothoon
on a vase from Agrigento (Overbeck, *Atlas*, Taf. 15, Nr. 24).

Deubner (*AF* 90 f., and *Abh. der Deutschen Akad. der Wissensch. zu
Berlin* 1945/6, Nr. 2, 16 ff.) suggested that the palace of Celeus was
the original Telesterion (hence called Anaktoron as the palace of
the ἄναξ). Cf. Mylonas, *Eleusis*, 85 ff., Rubensohn, *JDAI* 70 (1955),
1 ff., and n. ad *Dem.* 75.

For other traditions of the recipients of Demeter at Eleusis cf.:

1. Hyg. *Fab.* 147, Serv. ad Virg. *G.* 1. 19, Myth. Vat. 2. 97: Eleusinus.
2. Schol. Nic. *Alex.* 131: Hippothoon. This is a misunderstanding of
   Nic. l.c.
3. *Suda* s.v. Ῥαριάϲ: Ῥάροϲ, father of Celeus.
4. Steph. Byz. s.v. Ἐρχία (Ἐρχία?): Herchius (or rather Erchius?).
5. Paus. 1. 37. 2: Phytalus.
6. Panyassis fr. 24 K.: Triptolemus (or Eleusis?).

An Argive legend told how she was received by Atheras and Mysios,
and rejected by Colontas, against the wishes of his daughter Chthonia.
Colontas' house was burnt down, and Chthonia was taken by Demeter
to Hermione where she built her a temple, in which honours were paid
to Demeter Chthonia. Mysios also founded a temple of Demeter at
Pellene (Paus. 2. 18. 3, 35. 4, 7. 27. 9).

In the Sicyonian version, she came disguised as a γυνὴ ξένη, and nursed Orthopolis, the child of Plemnaeus, who founded a shrine to her in gratitude (Paus. 2. 5. 8, 11. 2; cf. ad *Dem.* 227). At Pheneos in Arcadia she was received by Trisaules (cf. Dysaules) and Damithales, who built a temple to Demeter Thesmia and established a τελετή (cf. Paus. 8. 15. 3, Conon, *FGH* 26. 15, Pisani, *IF* 53 (1935), 28 ff.). On Cos she was received by Eurypylus and Clytia (Schol. Theocr. 7. 5–9). On Paros, she was entertained by the king Melissos and his sixty daughters, gave them Persephone's loom, and instituted her mysteries there (Apollod. (?) *FGH* 244 F 89). For the story of Misme and Ascalabus cf. Nic. fr. 56, Ov. *M.* 5. 446 ff., Lact. *Narr. fab.* 5. 7 (cf. Nic. *Ther.* 484). Cf. also ad *Dem.* 75 ff.

97. In 153 ff. and 474 f. Celeus is listed among the other rulers of Eleusis, and called ἡγήτορι λαῶν. Does this necessarily imply that he was the chief ruler? In 296 ff. he summons the assembly and orders the people to build a temple. He does this because Demeter had come to his house, and not necessarily because he is supreme ruler. It is usually assumed that he has the same leading position as Alcinous in Phaeacia and Odysseus in Ithaca in the *Odyssey*. (Demeter's visit to Eleusis closely resembles Odyssean scenes: cf. ad *Dem.* 98 ff.) But we are not specifically told this. In later tradition Celeus recedes into the background, and Eumolpus takes prominence: see notes to *Dem.* 154, 475.

θυοέccηc: once in Homer (θυόεν νέφοc *Il.* 15. 153). Applied to Eleusis, it is formulaic, and at this point in the story strictly speaking anachronistic, since it presumably refers to the cult of Demeter. Cf. the names Παρθένιον φρέαρ, Καλλίχορον (99, 272).

98–168. Demeter sits by the well Parthenion, disguised as an old woman. The daughters of Celeus come to draw water, and ask her who she is.

Demeter tells them a false tale, that she is from Crete, but was captured by pirates and brought to Attica. She escaped, and came to Eleusis, wandering and lost. She asks if she might go as a nurse and housekeeper to a family in the city.

Callidice consoles her, and tells her the names of the rulers of Eleusis. She remarks on her godlike appearance, and offers to ask her mother Metaneira if she will take her as nurse to her baby son, promising her a rich reward.

98 ff. Scenes of meeting

The scene of Demeter's encounter with Celeus' daughters by the well Parthenion is in many respects traditional. For the meeting at (or near) a well or spring cf. *Od.* 7. 18 ff. (with 6. 281 ff.), 10. 105 ff., 17. 204 ff. In *Od.* 7. 18 ff. Odysseus meets Athena in disguise and asks for information. This motif of meeting with a deity in disguise recurs in

(*a*) *Od.* 6. 149 ff., where Odysseus addresses Nausicaa as if she were a goddess, and asks for help.

(b) *Od.* 13. 221 ff., where Odysseus again supplicates Athena 'as a god': in this case, he is double-bluffed, since she is one. (Cf. A. Lesky, *Göttliche und menschliche Motivation im hom. Epos*, Heidelberg, 1961, p. 36 n. 68.)

(c) *Ap.* 464 ff., where the Cretans remark on Apollo's resemblance to a god, and ask for information.

(d) *Aph.* 92 ff.: here again Anchises addresses Aphrodite as a goddess.

In *Dem.* 98 ff., the normal roles are reversed, since the goddess is the suppliant. Again, the girls notice her godlike appearance (*Dem.* 159). They themselves are also 'like goddesses' (108).

For another stranger-suppliant scene cf. *Od.* 15. 260 ff. (Theoclymenus and Telemachus).

The meeting in *Od.* 6 also takes place near water, here the washing-place on the sea-shore (cf. *Od.* 15. 420 f.). In *Od.* 13. 102 ff. the scene is the cave of the nymphs, in which are 'ever-flowing waters' (109), beside an olive-tree (102 etc. ~ *Dem.* 100).

The town spring usually lay outside the walls, and as the duty of collecting water fell to women, it was a common place for scenes of abduction and love: cf. Poseidon and Amymone, Achilles and Polyxena, Boreas and Oreithyia, Heracles and Auge (E. Fölzer, *Die Hydria* (Leipzig, 1906), 5 ff.). Cf. also Men. *Dysc.* 189 ff., Genesis 29: 1 ff.; W. Burkert, *Hermes* 94 (1966), 15. Scenes of women at fountains are common on Greek hydriai, and sometimes show a man molesting a woman or women. (For a catalogue of fountain-scenes cf. B. Dunkley, *BSA* 36 (1935–6), 198 ff.) But it is possible that the scene at Callichoron is also a reflection of Eleusinian ritual. Hydriai played an important role in the cult of Demeter and Persephone, as is shown by the presence at many sites of miniature votive hydriai, figurines of hydrophoroi, and actual hydriai dedicated to the goddesses. For a catalogue of these cf. E. Diehl, *Die Hydria* (Mainz, 1964), 187–93 (note especially Paus. 4. 26. 7 ff.), and for further material from the recently discovered sanctuary at Corinth cf. R. S. Stroud, *Hesp.* 37 (1968), 303–4. A procession of hydrophoroi may have formed part of the cult at some sites. Cf. also notes on *Dem.* 99, 105 ff., 169–88.

A detailed analysis of these epic scenes of meeting is given in Appendix III.

In addition to the structural parallels listed there, Demeter's 'false tale' (119 ff.) shows several close similarities to those of Odysseus in the *Odyssey* (13. 253 ff., 14. 192 ff., 19. 165 ff.). Cf. ad *Dem.* 120 ff. There are also a number of verbal parallels with the narrative of *Od.* 13. 96 ff., which suggest that the poet of the *Hymn* may have had this part of the *Odyssey* in mind (cf. Introduction, pp. 32 f.). These are also listed in Appendix III.

98. We have to supply here 'having reached Eleusis'.

ἕζετο δ' ἐγγὺς ὁδοῖο: cf. Appendix III.

98 f. Clem. Al. *Protr.* 2. 20. 1 (= 1. 15. 24 St.), says that the initiates at Eleusis were forbidden to sit by the well, lest they should seem to imitate the action of the sorrowing Demeter (cf. ad *Dem.* 6 ff., 42).

For sitting down in sorrow cf. ad *Dem.* 197 ff.

Later versions made Demeter sit down several times, or for a long time, beside the well Callichoron, either on the ground, or on the Agelastos Petra. Cf. ad *Dem.* 99, 200.

99. Παρθενίῳ φρέατι: for the local dative cf. Monro, *HG²* § 145 (4). For the metrical lengthening of the iota of the dative *in arsi*, cf. *Dem.* 101, 248. It is common in Homer, where it is often followed by hiatus, as in *Dem.* 99, 101, 248. It may reflect the original double form of the dative in -ει or -ι: cf. K–B i. 310, 367, van Leeuwen, *Enchiridium*, 80, 91 f., La Roche, *HU* i. 49. Hiatus is commoner in the post-Homeric poets than in Homer: cf. K–B i. 195 f., Hermann, *Orphica*, 725 ff.

The form φρέᾱτι (not Attic, which has φρέᾱτι) is presupposed by the Homeric φρείᾱτα (*Il.* 21. 197) with secondary lengthening *metri gratia*, after original φρῆᾱρ had become φρέᾱρ (cf. Chantraine, *GH* i. 10).

On the location of the well, and its identification with Callichoron, see Appendix I.

Parthenios is a common name of rivers in Greece (cf. *RE* 18. 1891 ff. s.v., Frazer, *Ovid, Fasti*, vol. 3, p. 286 n. 3). Springs and rivers were associated with virginity (cf. G. Glotz, *L'Ordalie dans la Grèce primitive*, (Paris, 1904), 72 ff., Frazer l.c.). The name Parthenion may also indicate that girls drew water from it at their marriage, as was the case with Callirhoe, the fountain by Demeter's temple at Agrae (Thuc. 2. 15).

The cult of Demeter and Persephone is especially connected with sacred springs: cf. in Arcadia those of Andania, Trapezus, and Phigalia (Nilsson, *Gesch.* i³. 480), and the spring Cyane at Syracuse, into which Persephone vanished with Hades (cf. ad *Dem.* 42), and where there was a festival (Diod. 4. 23. 4, 5. 4. 2). At Andania, the cult of the spring Hagne is clearly the oldest element (cf. Kern, *RE* 16. 1268. 44 ff.), and she is identified with Core (Paus. 4. 33. 4; cf. *Dem.* 337). At Cos, a sanctuary of Demeter and Core centring on a spring has been found, and a statue of Core beside the spring suggests their close connection (Herzog, *AA* 1901, 134 ff.). There was a Laconian festival of Demeter called Ἐπικρήναια (Hsch. s.v.). At Eleusis, the cult probably began with worship of a sacred well (cf. Frazer, o.c. 288 f., and Introduction, pp. 18 f.).

For the connection between springs and initiation ceremonies cf. also W. Burkert, *Hermes* 94 (1966), 15. The story of the Charites, who were thrown into a spring at Orchomenus while dancing round it, is especially relevant. At their festival there was dancing at night (*Geop.* 11. 4). The myth of Hylas, who was pulled into a spring by the nymphs while drawing water, also belongs to this type. In the local ceremonies performed in his honour a search for him was conducted, like that for Core (cf. A.R. 1. 1354 f., Str. 12. 4. 3).

In the story of Isis looking for the body of Osiris, there is a similar episode to that in the *Hymn*. Isis comes to Byblos and sits down at a spring there, in dejection and tears, and addresses no one, until the queen's handmaidens come (Plut. *de Is. et Osir.* 15). Cf. ad *Dem.* 40 ff.

Philicus' *Hymn* (verses 40 f.) apparently refers to a βασιλεία κρήνη formed from the tears of Demeter. Cf. Latte, *Kl. Schr.* 557 f.

100. Wells in Greece have always been in the shade of trees, places in which to rest and take refreshment after the dust and heat of a journey. In Homer cf. *Il.* 2. 305 ff., *Od.* 6. 291 f., 9. 140 f., 17. 204 ff., and also 13. 102 ff. (cf. ad *Dem.* 98 ff.). The olive tree presumably stood by Callichoron in later times, and was also sacred to Demeter. Cf. perhaps ad *Dem.* 23, and the sacred olive of Athena on the Acropolis, near which was the spring which Poseidon created.

101. A goddess taking the disguise of an old woman is an epic feature (e.g. *Il.* 3. 386, and A.R. 3. 72). Cf. also Aesch. fr. 279 Loeb (Appendix, ed. H. Lloyd-Jones), Ov. *M.* 3. 273 ff., Nonnus *D.* 8. 180 ff., Hyg. *Fab.* 167, 179 (Hera is disguised as a priestess in Aeschylus, an old nurse in Ovid and later sources); and Virg. *A.* 5. 618 ff., 7.416 ff. Demeter does the same thing in Pamphos' version. For the nurse of Demophon this disguise is also appropriate (cf. 103 f., 139 ff.). It is unlikely that there is a reminiscence of the portrayal of the corn-spirit or deity as the 'Old Woman' at this stage (cf. Allen and Halliday ad loc.).

παλαιγενέϊ: cf. ad *Dem.* 99, and *Il.* 3. 386. The word means 'aged' (of persons) in epic (*Il.* 3. 386, 17. 561, *Od.* 22. 395, *Dem.* 113, *Herm.* 199). For the pleonasm cf. γυναικῶν θηλυτεράων (*Dem.* 119 etc.). For a dative *in hiatu* at the caesura before ἐναλίγκιος cf. *Il.* 5. 5, 13. 242, 14. 290, 17. 583. Hoekstra, *Sub-epic Stage*, 56, comments that *Dem.* 101a 'may be older than the expression found in *Il.* 3. 386'.

101 f. Ruhnken compared Virg. *A.* 4. 33 'nec dulcis natos Veneris nec praemia noris'.

102. δώρων . . . Ἀφροδίτης: in *Il.* 3. 54, 64 this phrase is used of Paris' charms. For its use here cf. Hes. *Sc.* 47, Pi. *N.* 8. 7. Cf. also West ad *Th.* 103.

φιλοστεφάνου: this does not occur in Homer or Hesiod, and φιλοστεφάνου Ἀφροδίτης is perhaps a 'combination formula', formed from φιλομμειδὴς Ἀφροδίτη (always in the nominative) and ἐϋστεφάνου Ἀφροδίτης. It is also a doublet of πολυχρύσου Ἀφροδίτης (Hes. *Th.* 980 etc.), and Διὸς κούρης Ἀφροδίτης (*Il.* 20. 105 only: cf. Διὸς θυγάτηρ Ἀφροδίτη). Cf. in later poetry Bacch. 13. 183 f. (of Εὔκλεια), E. fr. 453. 8 (κῶμοι), Ion Lyr. 1. 13 (ἄνδρες).

103 f. Cf. *Od.* 13. 223 οἷοί τε ἀνάκτων παῖδες ἔασιν (of Athena disguised as a young man: cf. ad *Dem.* 98 ff.).

The double genitive is a little awkward here, and 103 could stand on its own (cf. Bücheler), but the phrase has probably been adapted from *Od.* 13. 223, or a similar model.

θεμιστοπόλων βασιλήων: θεμιστοπόλος is not found in Homer, and the formula is a 'doublet' of the Homeric διοτρεφέων βασιλήων (*Il.* 1. 176 etc.). Dion. Hal. (5. 74) calls the epithet Homeric, but not necessarily because of its occurrence in the *Hymn* (as Deichgräber suggests, *Eleus. Frömmigkeit*, 532 n. 1). It occurs in Hesiod (cf. p. 103

ad loc.) and is analogous to the Homeric δικασπόλος (*Il.* 1. 238). It is hardly possible to say which of the two is the earlier formation: Wilamowitz (ad Hes. *Op.* 67) gives priority to θεμιστοπόλος, but H. Vos (*Themis* (Assen, 1956), 4) considers it a poetic word formed by analogy with δικασπόλος.

The θέμιστες are individual ordinances (precedents, or 'dooms') which are 'dealt out' by the βασιλῆες, the Homeric (and Hesiodic) aristocracy. Cf. *Il.* 1. 238, etc. For the βασιλῆες as guardians of justice cf. also ad *Dem.* 151 f.

τροφοὶ . . . καὶ ταμίαι: cf. Eurycleia (*Od.* 1. 435, 2. 345 ff., 361), and *Dem.* 141 ff.

105. Ἐλευσινίδαο: the first iota is here shortened. Cf. ad *Dem.* 266. This should mean the son of Eleusinus, who appears as son of Hermes and eponymous hero of Eleusis in Harpocr. s.v. Ἐλευσίνια; in Hyg. *Fab.* 147, Serv. ad Virg. *G.* 1. 19 as recipient (with Cothonea or Cyntinia) of Demeter. Panyassis (fr. 24 K.) made Eleusis the father of Triptolemus. According to Pausanias (1. 38. 7), tradition made him the son of either Hermes and Daeira, or Ogygius. Celeus is the son of Rarus in *Suda* s.v. Ῥαριάς (cf. ad *Dem.* 96, 450).

105 ff. Here there are four daughters of Celeus (108), and their names are given (109 f.). The paraphrase of the Orphic version (Orph. fr. 49. 53 ff.) names only three, calls them Calliope, Cleisidice, and Damonassa, and says that they came to fetch water *with the queen*. These discrepancies are not great: Callidice has been dropped out, and Callithoe replaced by Calliope, through reminiscence of Hes. *Th.* 79 (cf. ad *Dem.* 110). Demo (*Dem.* 109) is a hypocoristic, and could be extended to Demonassa. *Dem.* 285 ff. has been taken as an indication that there were only three daughters in the *Homeric Hymn*, but these lines are not a complete enumeration.

Pausanias, however, says (1. 38. 3) that both Pamphos and Homer call them Diogeneia, Pammerope, and Saisara. This caused much trouble to early editors. Pausanias also says that the daughters of Celeus 'perform the sacred rites' together with Eumolpus. The *Hymn* does not mention this (cf. 473 ff.), although it perhaps assumes their participation in the priestly functions: cf. ad *Dem.* 98 ff., 109, 169–88, 176–81, 292 f. Pausanias' testimony agrees with that of the *Suda* (s.v. Εὔμολπος) which refers to a 3,000-line poem (or poems) of Eumolpus concerning τελετὰς Δήμητρος, καὶ τὴν εἰς Κελέου ἄφιξιν καὶ τὴν τῶν μυστηρίων παράδοσιν, τὴν ταῖς θυγατράσιν αὐτοῦ γενομένην. According to the Parian Marble (*FGH* 239 A 15) Eumolpus published the poetry of his father Musaeus when he founded the Mysteries. Eumolpus is the first of the Hierophants, and the daughters of Celeus may have been considered as prototypes of the Eleusinian priestesses (cf. ad *Dem.* 169–88). The Hierophantides, however, were of the Eumolpid genos, and the priestess of Demeter belonged to the Philleidae (cf. Toepffer, *Attische Genealogie*, 61 f.). The names in Pausanias probably belong to local legend. In the case of Saisara this is certain: cf. Hsch. s.v. Σαισαρία· ἡ Ἐλευσὶν πρότερον.

According to the tradition of the Attic deme Scambonidae, Saisara married Crocon, the eponymous ancestor of the Eleusinian priestly family of the Croconidae (Paus. 1. 38. 2). For Diogeneia cf. perhaps Apollod. 3. 15. 1 (mother of Praxithea, who married Erechtheus). The daughters of Celeus also had tombs and received honours at Eleusis (Clem. *Protr.* 3. 45. 2 p. 34 St.). The names in the *Hymn*, on the other hand, have the appearance of poetic invention (cf. ad *Dem.* 109 f.). It is not at all clear why the poet should not have given the local legend at this point: possibly the names were not yet fixed in his time.

Pausanias may have written Ὅμηρος by mistake for Ὀρφεύς or Μουσαῖος (cf. Allen and Halliday ad *Dem.* 109). But he refers to Homer and Pamphos again together at 8. 37. 9, and his version is not that of Orph. fr. 49 (above). More probably he is using a version ascribed to Homer by some and to Eumolpus (or Musaeus or Orpheus) by others (just as Orph. fr. 49 quotes parts of the 'Homeric' version and ascribes them to Orpheus). For other discrepancies between Pausanias' Homeric version and ours cf. ad *Dem.* 154 f., 417 ff. (where he agrees with Orph. fr. 49), 474 ff.: these, however, may be due to the fluctuations of epic transmission. Clearly there were several epic versions current, which were variously ascribed to Homer, Orpheus, Musaeus, Eumolpus, Pamphos, etc. (cf. Introduction, pp. 68, 74 f., 77 ff.).

106. εὐήρυτον: this occurs only here. Cf. κοτυλήρυτον (*Il.* 23. 34), ἀρύω Hes. *Op.* 550, *Sc.* 301 etc.

107. κάλπισι: this is found in poetry (epic, Attic, Doric, etc.) and late prose, and is also Thessalian according to Bekker, *Anecd. Gr.* 1095. The Attic word is ὑδρία. κάλπη (cf. M's reading) occurs in late Greek (Plut. *Marc.* 30, etc.).

χαλκείηισι: valuable hydriai were often made of metal in the classical period, e.g. as prizes, dedications, etc. Cf. also Call. fr. 596 (Pf. ad loc.), Gow ad Theocr. 13. 46, A.R. 1. 1207. On the significance of hydriai in Demeter cults cf. ad *Dem.* 98 ff.

φίλα: the emendation φίλου is easy. φίλα could have been due to attraction to the nearest noun. But cf. *Dem.* 180 and *Il.* 12. 221. For other similar examples of 'epithet-shift' in combination-formulae cf. ad *Dem.* 113.

108. τέσσαρες: for this reference to their number before their names are listed cf. *Il.* 7. 161, 24. 252, *Od.* 8. 118, Hes. *Th.* 76 (West ad loc.), 148, 264, 907, frr. 7. 2, 26. 6.

ὥς τε θεαί: cf. Hes. fr. 26. 6. Nausicaa is compared to a goddess in the parallel scene at *Od.* 6. 102 ff., 149 ff.

κουρήϊον ἄνθος: κουρήϊος occurs only here (cf. p. 104 ad loc. for κούριος). The original sense of ἄνθος was perhaps 'growth' (cf. ad *Dem.* 279, and J. M. Aitchison, *Glotta* 41 (1963), 271 ff.).

109–10. The repetition in Καλλιδίκη καὶ Κλεισιδίκη and in Καλλιδίκη . . . Καλλιθόη, and the alliteration, are common features in lists of names: cf. Hes. *Th.* 135 (West ad loc.), 248, 249, 251, 257, 258, 353, 1017 f., and in general West, 76, Rzach, *RE* 8. 1199 f., Lehrs,

Aristarchus[2], 454 ff., especially 461 ff. These features make it all the more probable that the poet is inventing the names (cf. ad *Dem.* 105 ff.).

For the pattern of 109, three names of which only the last has an epithet, cf. Hes. *Th.* 140 (West ad loc.), Wackernagel, *Kl. Schr.* 194; and for the pattern of 109–10, the fourth name with τε followed by a relative clause, cf. Hes. *Th.* 976–7, and similarly 376–7.

Δημώ τ' ἐρόεccα: Demo is a hypocoristic form (cf. Demonassa in Orph. fr. 49. 53 ff.), used of Demeter herself (*Et. M.* 264. 8, *Suda* s.v.; cf. ad *Dem.* 47, and Preller, *Dem. u. Pers.* 135, 368, Baunack, *RhM* 37 (1882), 478 f.), and of the Cumaean Sibyl (Paus. 10. 12. 8–9), who is called Demophile in Varro ap. Lact. *Inst.* 1. 21. 17. As such, it is probably invented as suitable for a future servant of Demeter (cf. ad *Dem.* 105 ff., and her brother's name Demophon, ad *Dem.* 234). ἐρόεccα is not found in Homer, who has ἐρατός, ἐρατεινός. Cf. Hes. *Th.* 245, 251, 357, *Dem.* 425, *Aph.* 263, *Herm.* 31, *Hy.* 32. 20.

110. The line is perhaps modelled on Hes. *Th.* 79, reminiscence of which may also have given rise to the name Calliope in Orph. fr. 49. 53.

ἀπαcῶν: this contracted form occurs in manuscripts of Homer in words in -ιῶν and pronouns, and also at *Il.* 11. 69 (simile), 18. 529 (Shield), 21. 243. Cf. Chantraine, *GH* i. 64 f., 69, 201. -έων with synizesis is the normal form in Homer: 21 times in *Iliad*, 19 in *Odyssey*. The normal Ionic form in the fifth and fourth centuries in inscriptions is -έων. The only examples in Hesiod of the contraction are in the manuscripts at *Th.* 715 (but a papyrus has cτιβαρέων, which West reads; cf. ad loc.) and *Op.* 264 (where a papyrus has cκολιέων . . . δικέων). Cf. ορχεcτον on the Dipylon jug (Athens Nat. Mus. 2074): this may be an Attic form. Here also the form may be due to an Attic poet or copyist, or alternatively to 'normalization' in the medieval tradition. On ἀπαcέων cf. Edwards, *Language of Hesiod*, 129 f.

111. ἔγνων: this form is anomalous and ἔγνον would be correct. Cf. Pi. *P.* 4. 120, where most manuscripts have ἔγνων and ἔγνον is guaranteed by the metre. Cf. also Pi. *P.* 9. 79, *I.* 2. 23. ἔγνων may be due to false analogy with ἔδρων. Similar anomalous third-plural forms occur in Homer in μιάνθην (*Il.* 4. 146), ἔφυν (*Od.* 5. 481). Cf. Chantraine, *GH* i. 471 f., Schwyzer, *Gr. Gr.* i. 664. The reading should therefore be retained here also.

χαλεποὶ . . . ὁρᾶcθαι: cf. *Dem.* 94 f., and note ad loc. The gods rarely appear to men in their own form in epic (but cf. *Il.* 1. 197 ff., 5. 123 ff., 11. 195 ff., *Od.* 7. 201 ff., etc.). In *Od.* 16. 157 ff., 20. 30 ff., Athena appears 'as a woman' to Odysseus, but he knows who she is. Cf. also *Il.* 3. 396 ff., where Helen sees through Aphrodite's disguise. For the idea that it is dangerous for men to see them openly cf. *Il.* 20. 131, and for the notion that they are difficult to recognize cf. *Od.* 10. 573 f., 13. 312, 16. 160 f. But contrast *Il.* 13. 72 ῥεῖ' ἔγνων (cf. *Dem.* 111) ἀπιόντος· ἀρίγνωτοι δὲ θεοί περ (and cf. *Il.* 22. 9 f., *Od.* 13. 299 f.).

Does χαλεποί mean 'dangerous' here (as at *Il.* 20. 131), or 'difficult'?
The context seems rather to favour the second sense, but *Il.* 20. 131
would support the former.

A god often reveals himself on his departure, sometimes also on arrival: cf. ad *Dem.* 188 ff., 268 ff.

θεοὶ θνητοῖϲιν: this juxtaposition is a common device. Cf. *Il.* 20. 41,
Od. 24. 64, *Hy.* 31. 19; also *Od.* 13. 312, and *Il.* 2. 821, 22. 9, 24. 537,
Od. 4. 397, *Aph.* 32, 167, Hes. *Th.* 871, 942, 967 f., 987, frr. 30. 27, 33,
Call. fr. 193. 37, A.R. 1. 298.

113. ἐϲϲὶ γρηῦ: this lengthening before mute and liquid in the
second thesis occurs only twenty-eight times in Homer (Fr. Isler,
Quaestiones Metricae (Diss. Gryphiswald, 1908), 22).

γρηῦ παλαιγενέων ἀνθρώπων: this is an excellent example of a
'combination-formula' with transferred epithet (cf. Introduction,
p. 50). παλαιγενής has been transferred from γρηῦ to the genitive,
probably under the influence of χαμαιγενέων ἀνθρώπων. Cf. ad *Dem.*
107, and *Il.* 5. 463 f., Hes. *Th.* 30 (∼ *Il.* 10. 467), 319, 335, 451 (West
ad loc.).

It is less probable that χαμαιγενέων is the correct reading, corrupted
by reminiscence of *Dem.* 101. Cf., however, Theognis 870, where
παλαιγενέων and χαμαιγενέων are variants. It is also notable that
χαμαιγενέων ἀνθρώπων is used of men in relation to the superior (and
destructive) powers of the gods, nature, etc. in *Dem.* 352, Hes. *Th.* 879,
Theognis 870, and in *Aph.* 108 it is used by Aphrodite (in disguise)
in addressing Anchises. In Pindar's use of ἀνθρώπων . . . χαμαιγενέων at
P. 4. 98 the tone is perhaps one of contempt (cf. Burton, *Pindar's
Pythian Odes*, 155 f.). Cf. also *Il.* 5. 440–2. There would be a neatly
ironic twist in its use here by a mortal addressing a disguised goddess:
cf. ad *Dem.* 98 ff., 120 f., 147 f., 216 f., for similar examples of irony.
The verse is paralleled by *Dem.* 119, which has a similarly pleonastic
phraseology.

114. τίπτε δὲ . . . ἀπέϲτιχεϲ: τίπτε is often used in questions of the
sort 'why have you left (the battle, etc.) and come here?' Cf. *Il.* 4. 340,
6. 254, 7. 24 f., 14. 43, 18. 385 = 424, 23. 94, *Od.* 4. 312, 810 f., 5. 87.

νόϲφι πόληοϲ: this means 'apart from', not necessarily 'far from'.
Cf. *Et. M.* 607. 5 νόϲφι ϲημαίνει χωρίϲ; Ebeling, s.v.; Mylonas, *Hymn
to Demeter*, 72 f. The well was just outside the city walls (cf. Appendix
I). Cf. Ov. *F.* 4. 514: 'quid facis in solis incomitata locis?'

114–15. The sentence is of the type '*x* and not the opposite'. Cf. *Dem.*
163, 213 f., and in general Introduction, pp. 59 f. In later poetry cf.
e.g. S. *Ant.* 443.

115. πίλναϲαι: M has πιλνᾶϲ. πιλνάω occurs elsewhere only in
Hes. *Op.* 510, where it is transitive (cf. on this Edwards, *Language of
Hesiod*, 110). Hermann's πιλνᾷ (i.e. second sing. present middle: cf.
Chantraine, *GH* i. 301 f. on *Il.* 14. 199 δαμνᾷ) would give hiatus,
which is rare after the first foot, although commoner with a pause in
sense (cf. van Leeuwen, *Enchiridium*, 74; Schulze, *QE* 8). The sigma
might have been added to remove the hiatus. But the form is in any

case anomalous, and πίλναται is probably correct. Cf. perhaps Theognis 1388: δαμνας δ' codd., δαμνᾷς Hartung, Diehl, δάμνασαι Bergk. The loss of -αι is paralleled in *Dem.* 332.

117. φίλωνται: 'welcome, treat kindly' (cf. *Od.* 1. 123, etc.). φιλεῖν requires 'not primarily emotions or intentions . . . but actions and results' (Adkins, *CQ* N.S. 13 (1963), 34).

ἠμὲν ἔπει ἠδὲ καὶ ἔργῳ: on the neglect of digamma in this formula cf. Hoekstra, *Hom. Modifications*, 45, 56, and *Mnemosyne*, Sér. 4, 10 (1957), 214 ff. He regards ἠδὲ/ἠὲ καὶ ἔργα (etc.) as modifications of the system ἠέ (οὔτε, οὐδέ) τι ἔργον (-ῳ, -α), as in *Od.* 4. 163, *Dem.* 199, etc.

118. ὣς ἔφαθ': contrast the plural in *Dem.* 112. The slip may be due to the poet himself, under the influence of the commoner formula (ὣς ἔφαν in Homer occurs only at *Od.* 10. 422). In 145 ff., Callidice alone speaks.

ἡ δ' ἐπέεσσιν ἀμείβετο: this is not a usual formula of answer. But cf. *Od.* 11. 81, etc., and *Od.* 4. 706, etc.

πότνα θεάων: this is a 'combination formula', from πότνα θεά (in Homer always in the vocative), and δῖα θεάων, perhaps influenced by πότνια Δηώ. Schulze (*Kl. Schr.* 325 ff.) conjectured that Homeric πότνα stood for *πότνι (Skt. vocative *patni*). But in Homer πότνια is also used as vocative (*Il.* 6. 264, etc.), and the manuscripts vary between πότνα and πότνια (i.e. πότνja) at *Od.* 5. 215, etc. Hence πότνα may have been written for πότνια (cf. Chantraine, *GH* i. 170). πότνα as nominative here may be due to a misunderstanding of the Homeric use, or it may also be for πότνια. The nominative use recurs in Call. fr. 63. 8, again of Demeter. Cf. also Schwyzer, *Gr. Gr.* i. 559 Zusatz 2, R. Sjölund, *Metrische Kürzung im Griechischen* (Diss. Uppsala, 1938), 9 f. πότνα θεάων is a doublet of Hom. δῖα θεάων. Cf. also E. *Ba.* 370 'Οσία, πότνα θεῶν.

119–20. τέκνα φίλ' . . . χαίρετ', ἐγὼ δ' ὑμῖν μυθήσομαι: cf. *Od.* 13. 228 ff., *Ap.* 464 ff. (~ *Od.* 24. 400 ff.). A similar address in Emp. fr. 112. 1–4 introduces an epiphany: ὦ φίλοι οἳ . . . χαίρετ', ἐγὼ δ' ὑμῖν θεὸς ἄμβροτος . . . (cf. ad *Dem.* 256–74, 397, and Zuntz, *Persephone*, 190–1). Cf. also *Od.* 11. 248–52. This suggests that the poet might have taken the phraseology from a context in which the disguised deity revealed his or her identity at this point.

119. αἵ τινές ἐστε: this replaces the name, which is normally used in address in epic. It is a common formula of address to a deity, whose identity or proper appellation is unknown or uncertain: cf. *Od.* 4. 376, 5. 445, *Aph.* 92, A. *Ag.* 160, Pl. *Crat.* 400 e, Norden, *Agnostos Theos*, 144 ff. It is used of a mortal at *Od.* 15. 28, and similarly *Herm.* 209, 277, 311.

γυναικῶν θηλυτεράων: the 'comparative' θηλύτερος shows the original disjunctive sense of the termination (cf. ἕτερος, ἀριστερός, etc.) and emphasizes the distinction from men. For the typical epic pleonasm cf. *Dem.* 101, 136 (κουριδίους ἄνδρας).

120–1. Demeter introduces her false tale with a profession of veracity. Cf. *Od.* 14. 192 (∼ 16. 61). For further parallels with Odysseus' Cretan stories cf. ad *Dem.* 123, 125, 127 ff., 129, 132. Odysseus also attempts to fool Athena with a Cretan tale in *Od.* 13. 253 ff. (cf. ad *Dem.* 98 ff.). Persephone makes a similar protestation to her mother (*Dem.* 406). Cf. also *Herm.* 368–9!

122. Δωσώ: this is the most satisfactory solution proposed for M's Δώс. Demeter is unlikely to reveal her real name (despite Gemoll's contention that she is still unknown at Eleusis): hence Δηώ is improbable. A pseudonym suggesting her true character is more likely: cf. her epithets Ἀνησιδώρα (Paus. 1. 31. 4; Plut. *QS* 745 a), ἀγλαόδωρος (*Dem.* 54, etc.), etc. (cf. Farnell, *Cults*, iii. 37). Aphrodite was also called Εὐδώсω at Syracuse (Hsch. s.v.). Cf. also δοсω on an Attic vase (Kretschmer, *Vaseninschr.* 202), and Δεξώ, Δωρώ, Δημώ (*Dem.* 109), etc. Bechtel intended Δωσίс as a short form of Δωμάτηρ which occurs rarely in North Greek for Demeter (cf. Hoffmann, *Gr. Dial.* 2. 374, Meister, *Dial.* 1. 75). But there is no reason why the poet should have chosen such a recherché form, if in fact he knew of it at all. Brunck's μέν is out of place here: cf. *Od.* 9. 19, 366. Ludwich's transposition retains Δώс, which occurs as an abstract noun (= δόсιс) at Hes. *Op.* 356 (where it is perhaps 'semi-personalized'), and is recognized together with Ζώс as a proper name in *Et. Orionis* 138. 16, *Et. M.* 247. 16. But the loss of -ω is an easier corruption, and Ludwich's word order is less satisfactory.

τὸ γὰρ θέτο πότνια μήτηρ: as in *Od.* 18. 5, the mother gives the name (cf. also Pi. *O.* 6. 56–7). Elsewhere, it is sometimes the father: e.g. E. *Phoen.* 12 f. καλοῦсι δ᾽ Ἰοκάсτην με· τοῦτο γὰρ πατὴρ ἔθετο. Cf. *Od.* 19. 401 ff. (Odysseus' maternal grandfather tells the parents to call him Odysseus).

123. Κρήτηθεν: Demeter probably comes from Crete because this is suitable for a 'false tale' (cf. *Od.* 13. 256, 14. 199, 19. 172; also *Ap.* 469 f., and ad *Dem.* 98 ff., 120 f.). A special significance has been seen in this by those who think that the Mysteries have a Minoan origin: cf. Persson, *ARW* 21 (1922), 287 ff., Picard, *RÉG* 40 (1927), 320 ff., Wilamowitz, *Glaube*, i. 99, 124, Nilsson, *Minoan-Mycenaean Religion*[2], 468 ff., 558 ff.; also Hes. *Th.* 969 ff. (West ad 971), notes to *Dem.* 126, 489, and Introduction, p. 18. But it is probably rash to read too much into the reference.

124. Cf. *Od.* 13. 277 (Appendix III). Note the fourfold repetition of the notion 'against my will, by force'. Cf. ad *Dem.* 72, 413.

125. In Odysseus' false tale to Eumaeus he is made captive by Thesprotian pirates (*Od.* 14. 334 ff.), and escapes while they are having a meal (cf. *Dem.* 127 ff.). For capture by pirates cf. also *Od.* 15. 427, *Hy.* 7. 6 ff.

126. Θορικὸν δέ: for the accentuation cf. *Dem.* 163, 253, 484, Allen and Halliday ad *Dem.* 126 and p. lxi, Allen, *Iliad, Prolegomena*, 230 f., Lehrs, *QE* 40.

Thoricos is on the north-east coast of Attica, and is a natural

landing-place for boats from Crete. The remains of an early-fifth-
century cult-building of unusual form, with thirty-eight Doric columns
and two entrances on the longer sides, have been discovered there
(Soc. of Dilettanti, *Uned. Antiquities of Athens*, 1817, ch. IX; Stais,
Praktika, 1893, 16 f.; Frazer, *Pausanias*, vol. 5, 525 f.; H. F. Mussche,
Thorikos II, 1964 (Brussels, 1967), 73 ff.). It has been conjectured
that this was dedicated to Demeter and Persephone. A ὅρος τεμένους
τοῖν θεοῖν was found somewhere near Thoricos (*IG* ii². 2600; cf. *IG*
i². 869?). More significant is the fact that some columns from the
building were re-used in the Roman period in a small temple in the
Agora at Athens, near the Eleusinion, and in this were found fragments of a late-fifth-century statue of Demeter-type, which very
probably also came from Thoricos (cf. H. A. Thompson, *Hesp.* 29
(1960), 339 f.; E. B. Harrison, *Hesp.* 29 (1960), 371 ff.).

The side-entrances of the cult-building at Thoricos suggest comparison with the temples of Lycosura, Tegea, and Bassae, where
they were perhaps used in order to display the rituals inside the
temple to spectators outside. These have been compared with the
Telesterion at Eleusis and with a 'theatrical area' recently discovered
outside the Erechtheum at Athens (cf. ad *Dem.* 231 ff.; Berve and
Gruben, *Greek Temples, Theatres and Shrines* (London, 1963), 357, 389,
399). The building at Thoricos may possibly have been used for
some kind of mystery rites, like those of Eleusis and Lycosura.

The direct route from Thoricos to Eleusis leads through Athens,
but Demeter does not mention it, and in fact says that she has been
wandering and does not know what country she is in (133 f.: this led
Lenz to reject 126, with its mention of Thoricos). This silence has
been taken as significant: cf. Walton, *HTR* 45 (1952), 114, who
considers that Athens has been pointedly ignored here, because the
Hymn is a polemic against the Athenian take-over of control of the
Mysteries (cf. Introduction, p. 6). It is also possible to conclude that
Demeter by implication has come along the Sacred Way from
Athens, which must therefore have already existed when the *Hymn*
was composed. But it is probably unwise to press the implications of
Demeter's journey too closely, especially as she is not telling the truth
(cf. ad *Dem.* 123).

νηὶ θοῇ . . . κατέσχεθον: the verb is used transitively in Homer in
this context (cf. *Od.* 11. 456). The intransitive use occurs in Theognis
262, Hdt. 7. 188, S. *Ph.* 221, 270, *Tr.* 220, etc.

126–7. Baumeister's conjecture is designed to avoid the ellipse of
127 f. (cf. ad loc.).

127–8. The sense appears to require a connecting particle in 128.
The examples of ellipse given in Allen and Halliday ad loc. are not
parallel. But it is perhaps just possible to assume an ellipse here.
Alternatively, Baumeister's conjecture (ad *Dem.* 126–7) provides an
attractive solution, for which cf. *Od.* 11. 20 f.

128. ἐπηρτύνοντο: the verb is only used in the active in Homer.
The simple verb is used in the middle (*Il.* 2. 55, etc.), and means

'arrange' (e.g. ἔεδνα, etc.). There is no need to alter it to ἐντύνοντο (Voss, Bücheler).

129. δόρποιο: contrast δεῖπνον in 128. In Homer, δεῖπνον is normally the main meal of the day, δόρπον the evening meal. The two are clearly distinguished in *Od.* 20. 390 ff. (But cf. *Od.* 4. 61 : δείπνου after sunset, 3. 497; cf. *Od.* 4. 194 f., 213. Perhaps Menelaus' feast, *Od.* 4. 3 ff., runs on into a δόρπον here. LSJ cite *Od.* 17. 176, 20. 390 f. for δεῖπνον of an evening meal, but this is wrong.) In *Ap.* 497, 511 there is a similar equation of δειπνῆcαι and δόρπον. Cf. Lehrs, *Aristarchus²*, 127 ff., Baumeister ad *Dem.* 128–9.

ἤρατο: the imperfect is not found in Homer or Hesiod. Cf. Theognis 1346, etc. (κρειῶν ἐρατίζων *Il.* 11. 551, etc., ὀcίηc κρεάων ἠράccατο *Herm.* 130; δαῖτ' ἐρατεινήν *Od.* 8. 61, etc.).

131. cημάντορας: this always means 'leader' in Homer. The sense here is presumably 'my arrogant overlords'.

131–2. ὄφρα κε μή με . . . ἀποναίατο . . . : ὄφρα κε with the optative occurs only once in Homer (*Il.* 12. 26). On the construction cf. K–G ii. 385 f., Schwyzer, *Gr. Gr.* ii. 326, Bühler ad Moschus, *Eur.* 127.

132. ἀπριάτην: 'unbought'. The word could be an adjective here and at *Il.* 1. 99. Cf. Pi. fr. 169. 8 (Sn.) ἀπριάταc (accusative plural), and the name Ἀπριάτη. At *Od.* 14. 317 it is treated as an adverb, meaning 'gratis' (Rhianus read ἀπριάδην). Leumann, *Hom. Wörter,* 167 f., considers this a misunderstanding, but it is rather a case of an accusative singular adjective used as an adverb. Cf. Risch, *Wortbildung,* 17, 303, 'Erstarrten Akkusative'.

τιμῆc: the sense 'purchase-price' is not found in Homer, but is common in Attic: cf., however, *Il.* 3. 286 ff., 459 f., where it means 'compensation', and is equivalent to ποινή (*Il.* 3. 290), and *Od.* 22. 57 τιμήν . . . ἐεικοcάβοιον (compensation); also Hom. *Epigr.* 14. 4 τιμῆc ὦνον ἀρέcθαι. (Cf. Latte, *Hermes* 66 (1931), 30 n. 1.)

133. ἀλαλημένη: in Homer ἀλαλημένοc always comes after the hephthemimeral caesura (*Od.* 13. 333, etc.).

133–4. Cf. Appendix III, and ad *Dem.* 126, 135 ff.

134. ἤ τιc δὴ γαῖ' ἐcτί: the text should not be changed. δή emphasizes Demeter's pretended uncertainty ('just where I am').

135 ff. This speech of entreaty is 'typical' in the context of such scenes of meeting (cf. ad *Dem.* 98 ff.). Cf. *Od.* 6. 175 ff., 13. 228 ff., *Ap.* 466 ff., A.R. 4. 1025 ff. :

1. *Wish for prosperity*: *Dem.* 135–7a ~ *Od.* 6. 180 ff. (13. 229a χαῖρε), *Ap.* 466, A.R. 4. 1026–8.
2. *Request for pity*: *Dem.* 137b ~ *Od.* 6. 175a (175b–7 ~ *Dem.* 133 f., etc.), 13. 229b, A.R. 4. 1025b–6a.
3. *Request for help and information*: *Dem.* 138 ff. ~ *Od.* 6. 178–9, 13. 230–5, *Ap.* 467–8. (In *Od.* 6. 175 ff., A.R. 4. 1025 ff. the order is reversed, the wish for prosperity coming at the end.)

The 'chance echo' *Dem.* 139a ~ *Od.* 6. 184a should be noted. For a similar speech of entreaty cf. *Dem.* 64 ff.

135–7. This formula for a prayer or wish accompanied by a request is expressed by a μέν . . . δέ sentence: cf. *Il.* 1. 18 ff., etc. In English we should subordinate: 'May the gods grant you . . . if you will pity me . . .' Latin also uses parataxis: 'Sic te diva . . . regat . . . reddas . . .' (Hor. *Od.* 1. 3. 1 ff.).

136. κουριδίουc ἄνδραc: 'wedded husbands'; cf. ad *Dem.* 101, 119.

136 ff. There is considerable repetition here:

136–8 τέκνα τεκέcθαι . . . τοκῆc   138–40 προφρονέωc . . . γυναικόc
(deliberate word-play?) . . .   . . . ἐργάζωμαι
κοῦραι . . . φίλα τέκνα . . .   πρόφρων . . . γυναικὸc* . . .
    ἔργα . . .
    ∼ 144 ἔργα . . . γυναῖκας

Cf. Introduction, p. 60.

137. τοκῆc: M's τοκῆεc must be scanned as a disyllable. Cf. *Il.* 11. 151 (ἱππῆc, ἱππῆεc codd.), Hes. *Op.* 263 (βαcιλῆεc v.l.; cf. 248), 607 (ἐπηετανόν), *Herm.* 113 (ἐπηετανά); West, *Theogony*, 100, K–B i. 449, 452. For contraction of -ηε- cf. Chantraine, *GH* i. 32, 43. For unmetrical *scriptio plena* of epic forms cf. Introduction, p. 66 and West ad Hes. *Th.* 800.

There is no need to alter οἰκτίρατε, which is a traditional feature (cf. ad *Dem.* 135 ff.). But a lacuna after 137 is necessary, to supply a verb asking for information (cf. e.g. *Od.* 13. 232 = *Ap.* 467). The lacuna is probably due to the same cause as that after *Dem.* 211, 236, etc. (cf. Introduction, p. 66). In this case, it is unnecessary to assume a *homoeoteleuton* (cf. Allen's supplement) or any other contributory cause.

137–8. κοῦραι . . . φίλα τέκνα: cf. perhaps *Il.* 23. 626–7 τέκος . . . φίλος (Leaf ad loc.).

138. προφρονέωc: for the use of πρόφρων (etc.) with εἰπεῖν (etc.) cf. *Il.* 1. 543, 5. 816, 8. 39 f. = 22. 183 f., *Od.* 5. 143, *Herm.* 561. It approaches the sense 'openly, truthfully' in these cases.

139. ἀνέρος ἠδὲ γυναικός: note the 'echo' of *Od.* 6. 184 (cf. ad *Dem.* 135 ff.).

140. ἀφήλικος: in *Il.* 22. 490 παναφήλικα means 'bereft of companions of his own age'. The sense 'aged' occurs first here, and later in Ionic and Attic. The comparative and superlative are normally used (cf. Phryn. *PS* 1 B.), but the positive occurs in Cratin. 369, Phryn. Com. 67. Cf. Zumbach, *Neuerungen*, 45 f., Forderer, *Gnomon* 30 (1958), 97.

οἷα γυναικὸc . . . ἔργα τέτυκται: cf. ad *Dem.* 144. For neglect of digamma before ἔργα τέτυκται see Hoekstra, *Mnem.* sér. 4, 10 (1957), 215 f., and cf. *Sub-epic Stage*, 153. The 'tasks of an old woman' are listed in 141 ff. as nurse and housekeeper (cf. *Dem.* 103 f.).

141. νεογνόν: not in Homer or Hesiod (νεογιλός *Od.* 12. 86), but also not a neologism (cf. Hoekstra, *Sub-epic Stage*, 56, Schwyzer, *Gr. Gr.* i. 357).

142. τιθηνοίμην: not in Homer (cf. τιθήνη *Il.* 6. 132, etc.). Cf. Theognis 1231, etc.

On Demeter as nurse at Eleusis cf. ad *Dem.* 231 ff. The two goddesses are the κουροτρόφοι of the initiates: cf. especially S. *OC* 1049 ff.
λαμπάϲιν ἀκταῖϲ, οὗ πότνιαι ϲεμνὰ τιθηνοῦνται τέλη θνατοῖϲιν (cf.
Introduction, p. 29, and Kern, *RE* 16. 1239. 38 ff.).

τηρήϲαιμι: not in Homer or Hesiod. Cf. *Dem.* 244 ἐπιτηρήϲαϲα,
Pi. *P.* 2. 88, etc.

143. ἐϋπήκτων: the dactylic form is preferable in the fifth foot (La
Roche, *HU* 85). Cf. *Dem.* 164.

144. δεϲπόϲυνον: not in Homer (cf. δέϲποινα *Od.* 3. 403, etc.). Cf.
Tyrt. fr. 5. 2 (as noun), Pi. *P.* 4. 267, etc.

διδαϲκήϲαιμι γυναῖκας: the conjecture of Voss is most attractive
(cf. Ruhnken: 'nihil rectius' and Hoekstra, *Sub-epic Stage*, 20 Addendum). Cf. *Od.* 22. 422, Hes. *Op.* 64. (But can γυναῖκας stand
alone for δμῳάϲ? And would a newcomer claim to fulfil this role?)
On the form διδαϲκῆϲαι (also Pi. *P.* 4. 217) cf. West, *Theogony*, 88 and
Hoekstra, o.c. 14. M's γυναικόϲ may be due to *Dem.* 140 (cf. also 139).

For Bothe's conjecture cf. *Od.* 22. 395 f. (of Eurycleia) ἥ τε γυναικῶν |
δμῳάων ϲκοπόϲ ἐϲϲι (*Od.* 22. 395 γρηῢ παλαιγενέϲ ∼ *Dem.* 101, 113).
But διαθρεῖν means 'examine' rather than 'oversee' (Ar. *Nub.* 700, etc.).
The sense of Allen's reading (in the 1936 edition) is presumably 'see
to (i.e. perform) a woman's tasks', but again it is questionable whether
διαθρεῖν could have this meaning. It is also repetitious after 140. This
applies to the other conjectures. It might be argued that the words
summarize 141–4 and round off the sentence: but the sense would be
very feeble after 140.

145. φῆ ῥα: for Homeric ἦ ῥα. For φῆ (= 'he spoke') cf. *Il.* 21. 361,
Hes. *Th.* 550, *Herm.* 212, and later Call. *Hy.* 3. 29, 6. 45, Theocr. 24.
101, A.R. 3. 382, 693, 718, Vian, *Recherches sur les Posthomerica de
Quintus de Smyrne* (Paris, 1959), 197.

θεά: on the unusual occurrence of θεά in the nominative after a verb
in the first trochee, see Appendix V (and cf. *Dem.* 34).

147 f. The sentiment is a commonplace of Greek thought. It is
a 'typical' epic reflection at the opening of an address, especially to
a stranger: cf. ad *Dem.* 213 ff., *Od.* 6. 187–90, 18. 129–42, 20. 195–6,
4. 236–7. In Homer, the most famous example is that of Achilles'
consolatio to Priam (*Il.* 24. 518 ff.), in a scene which also has several
parallels with *Dem.* 180 ff. (*Il.* 24. 480 ff. ∼ *Dem.* 190, 24. 553 ∼ 191,
24. 601 ff. ∼ 208–11). Here, Achilles wonders at Priam's endurance
of his troubles, and his courage (ἄνϲχεο . . . ἔτλης 518–19). He advises
him to let his sorrow rest, since there is no use in it (522–4; 523
ἀχνύμενοί περ), and this is the fate allotted to mortals by the gods
(525–6). He then describes the Jars of Zeus, which contain the gifts
of the gods (δώρων οἷα δίδωϲι ∼ *Dem.* 147), and speaks of Peleus
(θεοὶ δόϲαν . . . δῶρα 534) and Priam himself, closing with encouragement to endure (ἄνϲχεο 549), and a repetition of the theme of the
uselessness of sorrow (548–50).

The motif is referred to in *Il.* 24. 48–9, where it is the Μοῖραι who
give men a heart able to endure (τλητὸν θυμόν), so that they put an

end to their sorrow. In *Od.* 18. 129–42 men are advised to bear the δῶρα θεῶν (142), ἀεκαζόμενος τετληότι θυμῷ (135). Here Odysseus also observes that men do not think of the future, but are optimists as long as prosperity lasts (cf. ad *Dem.* 256 ff.). Cf. also Hom. *Epigr.* 4. 1, 13 f., where men bear the fate (κῆρα) which god has given them, τετληότι θυμῷ (13 f.).

In later archaic literature, cf. especially Theognis 441 ff., 591 ff. (van Groningen ad loc.). In Solon, fr. 1. 63 ff. D.[3] *Μοῖρα* gives men good and evil, and the δῶρα θεῶν are inescapable (ἄφυκτα) : the theme of men's inability to foresee the future follows (65 ff.). Cf. also Archil. fr. 13. 5 ff. West (cf. Pfeiffer, *Ausgew. kl. Schr.* 44), and *Ap.* 189 ff., where the Muses on Olympus sing of θεῶν δῶρ' ἄμβροτα ἠδ' ἀνθρώπων | τλημοσύνας which they suffer because of their folly and helplessness in face of death and old age (192–3 ∼ *Dem.* 256–62! Cf. ad loc.). This perhaps indicates how common the theme was in early epic.

In later poetry, cf. Pi. *P.* 3. 80 ff. (with D. C. Young, *Three Odes of Pindar* (Leiden, 1968), 50 ff.), A. *PV* 103 ff., S. *Ph.* 1316 f., E. *Phoen.* 1763, *Alc.* 1071 (χρὴ . . . καρτερεῖν θεοῦ δόcιν), also 416 ff., 616 f., 780 ff., and 984–6 (in an ode on the power of Ἀνάγκη: cf. ad *Dem.* 216 f.); A.R. 1. 298 ff. πήματα γάρ τ' ἀίδηλα θεοὶ θνητοῖcι νέμουcιν (i.e. again the theme that men cannot *foresee* the future), τῶν μοῖραν κατὰ θυμὸν ἀνιάζουcά περ ἔμπης | τλῆθι φέρειν (∼ *Od.* 6. 188–90); Rhianus fr. 1 (Powell) ἦ ἄρα δὴ μάλα πάντες ἁμαρτίνοοι πελόμεcθα | ἄνθρωποι, φέρομεν δὲ θεῶν ἑτερόρροπα δῶρα | ἀφραδέï κραδίη . . . (here also the point is that in our folly we do not know which way our fortune will go). Cf. also E. Ahrens, *Gnomen in griechischer Dichtung* (Diss. Halle, 1937), W. C. Greene, *Moira*, 27, 232 f., Nock, *HTR* 33 (1940), 309.

The reflection of *Dem.* 147 f. is thus often linked to the motif of men's inability to find a solution to their own problems, their helplessness and folly, and their incurable optimism. Here, and at *Dem.* 216 f., there is a special irony in the fact that the words are addressed by a mortal to a goddess, and that she is about to attempt to immortalize the son of Celeus.

By themselves, they form a kind of 'gospel of resignation' which places the responsibility in the hands of the gods, or of some impersonal agency, Necessity (cf. ἀνάγκη *Dem.* 147, 216, and ad *Dem.* 216 f.), or Fate (*Μοῖραι Il.* 24. 49, *Μοῖρα* Solon frr. 1. 63, 8. 2, κῆρα Hom. *Epigr.* 4. 13). But the 'answer' to this is given by Demeter herself (*Dem.* 256 ff.) : it is mortals who by their folly and ignorance of their destiny (αἶcαν 257) bring disaster (ἄτη: cf. *Dem.* 246, 258) upon themselves, and prevent the gods from assisting them. (Cf. the parallels quoted ad loc., and Eitrem, *Symb. Osl.* 20 (1940), 148 ff.) A similar 'theodicy' occurs at the opening of the Odyssey (1. 32 ff.).[1] Here, Zeus says

---

[1] On this, see W. Jaeger, *Sb. Berl. Akad.* 1926, 73 ff. (= *Kl. Schr.* 1. 321 ff.), Pfeiffer, *Deutsche Lit.-Zeit.* 1928, 2364, Nestle, *Vom Mythos zum Logos*, 24, Schadewaldt, *HSCP* 63 (1958), 18, Page, *Homeric Odyssey*, 168 f., Dodds, *Greeks and the Irrational*, 32 f., A. Lesky, *Göttliche u. menschl. Motivation im hom. Epos*, 35, Adkins, *Merit and Responsibility*, 19 f., 24 f.

that the gods give men warning of what is to come: it is their own
fault if they do not listen. Cf. later Solon frr. 3. 1 ff., 8. 1 ff., A. *PV*
1071 ff., Pl. *Rep.* 617 d 6–e 5.

In the *Hymn*, the gulf between men and gods, as it is envisaged by
'Homeric religion', is emphasized exactly at the points where an
encounter between the two takes place, and again at the point of
Demeter's departure. It is as if the two worlds were separated by
necessity (ἀνάγκη), so that even a deity's attempt to reunite them, in
the immortalization of Demophon, is bound to fail. Men cannot
become gods: they must be content with the promise of a happy
fate after death, through the Mysteries. Cf. ad *Dem.* 231 ff., and
Deichgräber, *Eleus. Frömmigkeit*, 529 ff.

148. δὴ γὰρ πολὺ φέρτεροί εἰcιν: a commonplace of the gods. Cf.
Il. 4. 56, 6. 11, 8. 144, 10. 557, 15. 165, 181, 20. 135, 21. 264, *Od.* 5. 170,
9. 276, 22. 289.

149. cαφέωc: not in Homer (cf. cάφα). Cf. cαφέc *Herm.* 208, cαφέωc
Pi. *O.* 6. 20, Hdt. 2. 31, etc.

ὑποθήcομαι: in Homer this means 'suggest, advise'. Here the meaning has developed to 'communicate'. Cf. ad *Dem.* 273.

ἠδ' ὀνομήνω: the aorist subjunctive is used for the second verb,
after future indicative. Cf. *Il.* 2. 488, *Od.* 4. 240, 6. 126, 12. 383, 13.
215, *Ap.* 1. The two are closely related and sometimes indistinguish-
able (cf. Chantraine, *GH* i. 225 f.).

150. ἔπεcτι: in Homer this is always used literally (but cf. *Od.*
4. 756 of time). Cf. *Dem.* 263.

κράτοc . . . τιμῆc: 'power consisting in authority'. Cf. E. *Hipp.*
1280 ff. cυμπάντων δὲ βαcιλήιδα τιμάν, Κύπρι, τῶνδε μόνα κρατύνειc. τιμή
is the 'criterion for the extent of one's power and might' (Keyssner,
Gottesvorstellung, 55 ff.). τιμή and cθένοc, κράτοc, δύναμιc, etc. are
often used together, sometimes interchangeably, e.g. *Od.* 24. 30,
Pi. fr. 29. 4 f. Sn., Keyssner, l.c., and cf. *Dem.* 365 f.

151. κρήδεμνα πόληοc: in Homer *Τροίηc . . . κρήδεμνα λύωμεν* may
have been suggested by the idea of a captive woman whose veil
is torn off (cf. H. L. Lorimer, *Homer and the Monuments*, 386). For
κρήδεμνα of the walls of a city cf. also *Hy.* 6. 2, and similarly *Il.* 19. 99,
Hes. *Th.* 978 (West ad loc.) εὐcτεφάνῳ ἐνὶ Θήβῃ, Anacr. *PMG* 391,
Pi. *O.* 8. 32 f., S. *Ant.* 122, E. *Hec.* 910. On κρήδεμνον cf. ad *Dem.* 41.

152. ἰθείῃcι δίκῃcιν: the phrase is Hesiodic (*Th.* 86, *Op.* 36), but
cf. also *Il.* 18. 508, 23. 579 f. δίκη perhaps originally meant a 'mark'
or 'boundary' (cf. δείκνυμι). Hence it is described as straight or
crooked. Cf. Palmer, *Trans. Phil. Soc.* 1950, 149 ff., West ad *Th.* 86.
But for other views cf. Frisk s.v., Chantraine, *Dict. Étym. de la langue
grecque* s.v.

153–6. The genitives are awkward, and have given rise to various
conjectures, but presumably they look forward to 156. Such an anti-
cipation over several lines is not Homeric.

153. Τριπτολέμου: in the *Hymn* Triptolemus is one of the βαcιλῆεc
of Eleusis, and has no special prominence, although it is noticeable

that he is mentioned first both here and in *Dem.* 474. His later importance is due to his role as an Athenian 'propaganda hero'. Athens
claimed that he received the gift of corn, and was taught the arts of
agriculture by Demeter, and then travelled over the world teaching
the other nations in turn. This legend first appears on two black-figure
vases of the third quarter of the sixth century, which show him on
a wheeled car, holding ears of corn, and surrounded by those to
whom he is teaching his arts. On these vases he is portrayed without
Demeter, on later (black- and red-figure) vases with Demeter and
Core. A recently published vase from Locri in Italy, also of the mid
sixth century, shows him accompanying Demeter, Athena, Heracles,
Hermes, and a deity named 'Ploutodotas'. On this it is Demeter who
is mounting a chariot, and holding ears of corn. Cf. Metzger, *Recherches*,
8 ff., Nilsson, *Gesch.* i³. Nachtr. 860, and notes to *Dem.* 489.

In this period Triptolemus is bearded and has a sceptre. Later,
on red-figure vases, he becomes younger, and is beardless. A similar
development occurs in the case of Theseus and other heroes in Greek
art. He is frequently portrayed at this time being sent out on his
mission by Demeter, sometimes in the presence of other deities. His
chair becomes a winged chariot, with snakes, like that of Demeter.
Finally, he becomes a boy, as on the 'Grand Relief of Eleusis' (*c.* 450–
430 B.C.: Mylonas, *Eleusis*, 192 f., Fig. 68). The period of his greatest
popularity in vase-painting is *c.* 490–440 B.C. Sophocles' play *Triptolemus*,
possibly his first victory in 468 B.C., may have contributed to this
popularity (cf. Pearson, *Fragments*, vol. ii, pp. 239 ff.).

The representations reflect the growth of Triptolemus' popularity
as an Attic cultural hero. There is no sign of this in the *Hymn*, whose
poet ignores, if in fact he knew, the version in which Demeter gives the
Eleusinians the gift of agriculture as a reward for their information
about the Rape. This was a standard Athenian version in the classical
period (cf. Introduction, pp. 81 f.). Triptolemus' emergence to popularity probably coincides with the growth of Athenian interest in the
Mysteries, in the mid sixth century B.C. (Cf. ad *Dem.* 154: Eumolpus.)

The development of his genealogy is consistent with this artistic
progress. At first, it is vague and 'primeval': in Pherecydes (*FGH* 3. 53)
and 'Musaeus' (fr. 10 Diels) he is the son of Oceanus and Ge, in
Panyassis (fr. 24 K.) of Eleusis. Choerilus the tragedian (fr. 1 N.)
makes him the son of Rarus and of a daughter of Amphiction. In
'Orpheus' (fr. 51 K.) he is the son of Dysaules. But, as he becomes
younger and emerges as the special favourite of Demeter, he comes to
supplant Demophon as her nursling. In the revision of the Athenian
State Code of 403–399 B.C., among the heroes of Eleusis who receive
offerings is one called simply Threptos, who receives a special sacrifice
(Sokolowski, *Lois Sacrées, Supplément*, No. 10. 69 f.). The context suggests
that this is Triptolemus. (Originally the child was probably nameless:
Körte, *Glotta* 25 (1936), 137 ff., Nilsson, *Op. Sel.* ii. 544 ff., and
ad *Dem.* 234.) Thus, he is the son of Celeus and Metaneira in later
literature (Nic. *Ther.* 484 f., Schol. ad loc., Ov. *F.* 4. 539, Nonn. *D.* 19.

78 ff., Paus. 1. 14. 2, etc.). Apollodorus (1. 5. 1) also gives this account, but follows the *Hymn* in making Demophon Demeter's nursling (cf. perhaps Sophocles' *Triptolemus*). The 'Argive version' (Paus. 1. 14. 2) made him the son of Trochilus of Argos and an Athenian woman. For other accounts see *RE* 7. 221 ff., and cf. Herter, *RhM* 90 (1941), 266.

On the myth of Triptolemus Athens based her claim to receive offerings of first-fruits from all the other Greek states in the fifth and fourth centuries B.C. (cf. *IG* i². 76, ii². 140, *SIG*³ 704E, Isocr. *Paneg.* 31. 38, Xen. *Hell.* 6. 3. 6, Nilsson, *Op. Sel.* ii. 550 f., Kern, *RE* 16. 1247). This claim was supported by a Delphic oracle and an appeal to 'ancestral custom'. He himself received sacrifices with Demeter and Core from the offerings (*IG* i². 76. 38, ii. 140. 20 ff.), as well as a sacrifice at the Eleusinian Games (*IG* i². 5. 4, *c.* 500 B.C.). He was also regarded as a lawgiver (Xenocrates, fr. 98 Heinze; cf. Nilsson, *Die Antike*, 1942, 220, and notes to *Dem.* 367–9), as initiator of Heracles and the Dioscuri (Xen. *Hell.* 6. 3. 6), and as one of the judges in the underworld (Pl. *Apol.* 41 a, and on two vases, *Wiener Vorlegeblätter*, Ser. E, Taf. 2, Taf. VI 3).

Ancient etymology connected his name with τρίπολος, and he is shown with a plough on two vases (Rubensohn, *AM* 24 (1899), 59 ff.). As the first ploughman he must have been connected with the sacred ploughing on the Rarian Plain, where he had a threshing-floor and altar (Paus. 1. 38. 6, Deubner, *AF* 69; cf. ad *Dem.* 450). For modern etymologies cf. Kretschmer, *Glotta* 12 (1922), 51 ff., who connected the name with πελεμίζω, and interpreted this as 'sich heftig anstrengen, bemühen', Wilamowitz, *Glaube*, ii. 51 n. 3, Nilsson, *Op. Sel.* ii. 549, Frisk, s.v.

For Triptolemus in art cf. Fehrle in Roscher, 5. 1128 ff., Cook, *Zeus*, i. 211 ff., Schwenn, *RE* 7A. 213 ff., also D. Feytmans, *Antiq. Class.* 14 (1945), 285 ff. (unconvincing), Ch. Dugas, 'La Mission de Triptolème d'après l'imagerie athénienne', *Mélanges d'arch. et d'hist.* 62 (1950), 1 ff. = *Recueil Ch. Dugas*, 123 ff. (cf. ad *Dem.* 208 ff.).

Διόκλου: in *Dem.* 474, 477, he is called Diocles. Cf. the variation between Ἴφικλος and Ἰφικλῆς, Πάτροκλος and Πατροκλῆς.

He is a Megarian hero (like Sciron who was also connected with Eleusis), and the Diocleia were celebrated in his honour at Megara. These games included a boys' kissing contest (Theocr. 12. 28 ff., Schol. ad loc.), and perhaps also gymnastic contests (cf. Schol. Pi. *O.* 13. 156, *N.* 3. 145). The Megarians said that he was a Megarian ruler of Eleusis who was driven out by Theseus (Plut. *Thes.* 10), but he is called 'Attic' in Theocritus, and the Scholia ad loc. say that he fled to Megara at the time of Eumolpus' expedition. His name is common in Megara (*IG* 7. 133, 188, 54, 132, 27, 29, 39, 41, 42, 218). The Megarian in Ar. *Ach.* 774 swears by him.

At Eleusis he receives a sacrifice with the other heroes: Sokolowski, *Lois Sacrées, Supplément*, No. 10. 71.

There was a Hierophant named Diocles in the early fifth century (Lysias, *Contra Andoc.* 54), and the name is found in the Roman period,

given to the father-in-law and son of the Dadouchos Themistocles
(cf. Plut. *Vita X Orat.* p. 1917 Didot, P. Roussel, *Mélanges Bidez*, 819 ff.).

154. Πολυξείνου: he is the most shadowy of this list, and does not
reappear in *Dem.* 473 f. (cf. ad 477). He does, however, receive a
sacrifice with the other heroes in Sokolowski, o.c. 10. 68. In Hesychius
he is one of the Attic heroes from whom the phyle names were taken
(with Meineke's emendation, *Philol.* 13 (1858), 551 nr. 628; *contra*:
Wilamowitz, *Homerische Untersuchungen*, 185 n. 28). His name is perhaps
simply taken from one of the epithets of Hades (cf. A. *Supp.* 157,
Cornut. 35, and ad *Dem.* 9, 17, 155).

ἀμύμονος Εὐμόλποιο: Ruhnken's transposition agrees with
Pausanias, and is supported by *Od.* 7. 29. But the text may have varied
(cf. ad *Dem.* 105 ff., 417 ff., 474 ff.). Was the transposition due to the
desire to give Eumolpus greater prominence? Cf. note on *Dem.* 475.

Like Triptolemus, he becomes much more prominent in the later
history of the cult. He alone, of the princes in the *Hymn*, survives as
the eponym of a priestly family, the Eumolpidae, from whom the
Hierophant was drawn. His name, the 'good singer' ·(cf. εὐμολπεῖν
Herm. 478), indicates his function: he had to have a strong, clear
voice, for it was he who enunciated (presumably either singing or
'intoning') the sacred words of the Mysteries. Cf. *IG* 3. 713 (epitaph
of a Hierophant):

> ὃς τελετὰς ἀνέφηνε καὶ ὄργια πάννυχα μύσταις,
> Εὐμόλπου προχέων ἱμερόεσσαν ὄπα.

(Cf. Hippol. *Ref. haer.* 5. 8. 40, 96. 14 W., Arrian, *Diss. Epict.* 3. 21. 16,
Philostr. *Vit. Soph.* 2. 20; also Ar. *Ran.* 370, 380, 384 f., Radermacher
ad loc.) The Hierophant himself may have had the title Εὔμολπος
(cf. Plut. *de ex.* 18, Paus. 1. 38. 3; Hiller von Gärtringen, *De Graecorum
fabulis ad Thraces pertinentibus*, 28 n. 111). The name is similar to
Musaeus, Antiphemus, Phemius, etc.

In fragments of a poem probably by Pindar, in which Heracles is
initiated by Eumolpus before his descent to Hades (cf. ad *Dem.* 192 ff.),
Eumolpus appears to be described as founder of the Mysteries for his
citizens at Eleusis, whom he rules εὐνομίᾳ λατερπέϊ, and to be called
cοφὸν ἀγητῆρα (P. Oxy. 2622. i. a and PSI 1391). It has been argued
(H. Lloyd-Jones, *Maia* 19 (1967), 206 ff.) that this poem is dependent
on an earlier, sixth-century Attic epic version of the Catabasis of
Heracles, which is supposed to have been the source of material in
Bacchylides' *Ode* 5, Aristophanes' *Frogs*, and *Aeneid* 6.

He appears again prominently in the early-fifth-century vase of
Hieron, which shows the Mission of Triptolemus (*CVA*, *Brit. Mus.*
4, Pl. 28. 2, Nilsson, *Gesch.* i³. Taf. 43. 1). He is accompanied by
a swan, to point to his connection with music. Poseidon and Amphitrite
are also shown, suggesting that he was already regarded as the son
of Poseidon, as later (Eur. fr. 349 Nauck = 39 Austin, 360. 46 ff.
Nauck = 50. 46 ff. Austin, Lycurg. *in Leocr.* 98 ff., Apollod. 3. 15. 4).
There was a cult at Eleusis of Poseidon Pater (Paus. 1. 38. 6).

In Euripides' *Erechtheus* the story of his birth was referred to (fr. 39 Austin). His mother Chione threw him into the sea after he was born, and Poseidon rescued him and took him to the Ethiopians. This is plainly an *aition* of the ritual bath in the sea taken by the Hierophant on assuming office (cf. *Eph. Arch.* 1883, 79, verses 5–6, 9 ff., Hiller von Gärtringen, o.c., 31 n. 116a, Toepffer, *Attische Genealogie*, 28 ff.). In Euripides' play he becomes ruler of Thrace, and is called in to help in the war of Eleusis against Athens. Apparently he is killed in battle, and at the end of the play Athena probably predicts that a second Eumolpus, his descendant, will found the Mysteries (cf. fr. 65. 15?, 100 ff. Austin).

This hypothesis of two Eumolpi was presumably devised to account for the legend which made him a Thracian, and connected him with the Thracian Musaeus. On a vase of the Meidias painter he is shown as a child, together with Musaeus, who is dressed as a Thracian (G. M. A. Richter, *AJA* 43 (1939), 1 ff.), and he is the *son* of Musaeus on the Parian Marble (*FGH* 239 A 15), in Andron (*FGH* 10 F 13), and perhaps also already in Pl. *Rep.* 363 c, his *father* in Philochorus (*FGH* 328 F 208). On the Meidias vase his mother is Deiope (cf. Ister, *FGH* 334 F 22, Ps. Arist. *Mir. Ausc.* 131, Phot. s.v. Εὐμολπίδαι; in Hermes. fr. 7. 16 Pow. she is Antiope). Various attempts to reconcile the two Eumolpi are given by Schol. S. *OC* 1053.

The war between Athens and Eleusis is (according to later tradition) already attested by the early-fifth-century bronze group by Myron on the Acropolis at Athens (Paus. 1. 27. 4, 9. 30. 1), but Pausanias stresses that the correct Attic version made Immaradus, Eumolpus' son (= Ismarus in Apollod. 3. 15. 4), leader of the Eleusinians. It has been suggested that Eumolpus was associated with the Thracian Orpheus and Musaeus in the sixth century because of his role as founder of the Mysteries, and was then connected with the legend of a Thracian expedition under Immaradus to help Eleusis against Athens (Toepffer, o.c. 24 ff.). It may have been Euripides who replaced Immaradus by Eumolpus, whom he represented as heir to his father Poseidon's claim to Attica (fr. 50. 46 ff. Austin).

Later authorities also make him the founder of the Mysteries (*Mar. Par.*, Andron, Ister, above). He is associated with the poetry of Musaeus: according to the Parian Marble he published this, and in the *Suda* (s.v. Μουcαῖοc) he receives from Musaeus a work called Ὑποθῆκαι τῷ υἱεῖ αὐτοῦ. A poem of Musaeus called the Εὐμολπία is also mentioned (fr. 11 Diels, ap. Paus. 10. 5. 6), and he himself is said to have written a poem on the Mysteries and Demeter's visit to Eleusis (*Suda*, s.v. Εὔμολποc; cf. ad *Dem.* 105 ff.). If he is the son of Musaeus referred to in Pl. *Rep.* 363 c the information about life in the underworld referred to there must have appeared in these poems (cf. ad *Dem.* 367–9). Cf. Introduction, pp. 77 ff.

For Eumolpus in art see also on *Dem.* 489 (pp. 318 ff.), with Addendum to p. 318 n. 2.

155. Δολίχου: another shadowy figure. He occurs with Eumolpus and Hippothoon in a hexameter verse, possibly Hesiodic (Hes. fr. 227), and he had a temple outside the sanctuary at Eleusis (*IG* ii². 1672. 23 ff.). This has been identified by Travlos (*Hesp.* 18 (1949), 143, figs. 1–2; *Praktika* 1953, 76). He places it on the north-west corner of the outer court, behind the temple of Artemis and Poseidon. Cf. Mylonas, *Eleusis*, 170 and Fig. 4, No. 9.

In *IG* i². 5. 5, recording sacrifices at the Eleusinian Games (cf. ad *Dem.* 153) the reading Πλοῦτο]νι : Δ[. . .]χοι : Θεοῖν : has suggested Δολίχοι (cf. Prott, *AM* 24 (1899), 252). But the text is very uncertain at this point. Dolichus should be the hero of the race of that name (cf. Telesidromus in the same inscription). This formed part of the Eleusinian Games (cf. *IG* ii². 3143).[1]

Later, he was regarded as a son of Triptolemus, and eponym of Dulichium (Steph. Byz. s.v. Δουλίχιον; Eust. p. 306. 2 ad *Il.* 2. 625; cf. Str. 10. 458). Hiller von Gärtringen suggests that this tradition may derive from the *Hymn* (cf. Kern, *RE* 5. 1282. 10 ff.).

156. κατὰ δώματα πορϲαίνουϲι: in Homer πορϲαίνω occurs as a variant of πορϲύνω at *Il.* 3. 411 and *Od.* 7. 347, but in *Od.* 3. 403 only πορϲύνω is read. Both forms occur in Pindar and Apollonius, only πορϲύνω in prose and probably also in tragedy. The verb is always used euphemistically in Homer, with λέχος, of a wife sharing her bed with her husband. In the Hesiodic examples, however, it means 'look after', and later also 'prepare, arrange, order'. So here 'manage (all things) in the house' (LSJ s.v. II 3) is the most probable interpretation. Ruhnken (cf. Allen) took κατὰ . . . πορϲαίνουϲιν as a tmesis, but this seems less likely. κατὰ δώματα is formulaic and comes naturally after ἄλοχοι (cf. *Dem.* 104, 115, *Od.* 20. 122).

157. κατὰ πρώτιϲτον ὀπωπήν: a curiously 'modern' idiom (not in Homer or Hesiod). For the two-termination superlative cf. *Od.* 4. 442 (for euphony? Cf. Platt, *CR* 35 (1921), 142), *Od.* 10. 279 (v.l.), 12. 11 (v.l.), Hes. *Th.* 408, Pi. fr. 152 Sn., Schwyzer, *Gr. Gr.* i. 536 n. 5, K–B i. 554 n., K. Witte, *Glotta* 3 (1912), 106 ff., Shipp, *Studies in the Language of Homer*, 68 ff.

158. ἀπονοϲφίϲϲειεν: the compound does not occur in Homer. Cf. *Herm.* 562, S. *Ph.* 979, etc. One could write δόμων ἄπο here (cf. *Od.* 3. 313, 15. 10).

The line is a 'versus tetracolos' (cf. Bassett, *CP* 14 (1919), 216 ff.), unless we make ἀπονοϲφίϲϲειεν two words.

159. δέξονται: the poet avoids using δέξαιτο.

δὴ γάρ . . . ἐϲϲι: gods in disguise often arouse mortal admiration: cf. the examples given ad *Dem.* 98 ff. and *Hy.* 7. 17 f. Cf. also ad *Dem.* 213 ff.

θεοείκελοϲ: an epithet of heroes in Homer (cf. θεοειδής).

160. εἰ δ' ἐθέλειϲ: ἐθέλω is the proper form in Homer and Hesiod (θέλω only *Il.* 1. 277 dub., *Od.* 15. 317 v.l.; also v.l. in Hes. *Th.* 446, *Op.* 209, 210, 392). In the *Hymns*, θέλοι occurs in *Ap.* 46 (where

---

[1] The reading in Sokolowski, *Lois Sacrées, Supplément*, 10. 66 is Μελίχωι, not Δολίχωι. I owe this information to Dr. Fritz Graf and Mr. D. M. Lewis.

ἐθέλω is hardly possible), εἰ δὲ θέλεις Herm. 274, εὖτε θέλοι Aph. 38
(ἐθέλη M).

Later, θέλω is used in Ionic, Attic tragedy, and late Greek, ἐθέλω
in epic, Attic prose, comedy, and inscriptions (to c. 250 B.C.). Cf. also
Sol. fr. 19. 12 D.³ (θέλει).

161. Μετανείρῃ: this is regularly the name of Celeus' wife in later
legend. The Orphic version replaces her by Baubo (Orph. fr. 49. 81, 89;
fr. 52; cf. Introduction, pp. 80 ff.), as the wife of Dysaules. Metaneira
had a ἱερόν at Eleusis (Paus. 1. 39. 2; cf. also Athenagoras, *Libellus pro
Christianis* 14), but is otherwise a relatively shadowy figure.

162. αἴ κέ c' ἀνώγῃ: αἴ κε is normally used with the subjunctive;
for the optative cf. *Il.* 7. 387, *Od.* 13. 389.

163. The verse is again of the type 'x and not the opposite'. Cf. ad
Dem. 114 f.

164. τηλύγετος: the original meaning remains uncertain. Cf.
Buttmann, *Lexilogus*, s.v., K. F. W. Schmidt, *Glotta* 19 (1931), 282,
W. B. Stanford, *CR* 51 (1937), 168, Pisani, *Rend. Ist. Lomb.* 73 (1939/40),
525, Frisk, s.v. In Homer, it is always used of a special or favourite
child, whether an only child (cf. *Il.* 9. 482, *Od.* 16. 19) or children
last-born, or born to aged parents (*Il.* 5. 153 f.; cf. perhaps *Il.* 9. 143,
285, *Od.* 4. 11?, *Dem.* 165, 219), and so much-desired and much-loved
(cf. *Dem.* 165, 220), or born unexpectedly (ἄελπτον *Dem.* 219; cf.
Hes. fr. 204. 95 of Hermione, who is τηλυγέτην in *Il.* 3. 175; she is also
an only child of Helen: *Od.* 4. 12 ff.). So it comes to be used generally
of a spoilt or weak child (*Il.* 13. 470). Later, it is also used to mean
'born far away': E. *IT* 829, Simm. 1. 1, Com. Adesp. 1315. The
prevalent ancient interpretation took it as 'latest-born', i.e. after
whom no others are born, thus including only children: Plut. *Mor.*
94 a, *Et. Gud.* 616. 37, etc., also Virg. *A.* 6. 763–5.

Demophon fulfils most of these various qualifications, since he is
ὀψίγονος, πολυεύχετος ἀσπάσιός τε, also ἄελπτος, and presumably also
an only son.

The latest-born child (usually the last of several brothers) is often
the hero of folk-tales and myths: cf. Cronos (Hes. *Th.* 137, West ad
loc.), Zeus (Hes. *Th.* 478 f.); Stith Thompson, *Motif Index*, 5. 6–8,
Frazer on Apollod. 1. 1. 3. Often the youngest child is a weakling
when he is small, but grows up to be the hero. In a later version, the
child is sick when Demeter comes, and she cures him: Ov. *F.* 4.
512 ff.

165. ὀψίγονος: in Homer (*Il.* 3. 353, etc.) always of 'men of future
ages'. For the sense 'late-born' (∼ *Dem.* 219) cf. Hdt. 7. 3. 3, A. *Supp.*
361 ('young'), Theocr. 24. 31 ('young'? Cf. Gow ad loc.). It is used
to explain τηλύγετος (cf. *Dem.* 164) by Poll. 3. 20, and coupled with
it in Plut. *Mor.* 94 a.

πολυεύχετος: only here. Cf. πολύευκτος (Orac. ap. Hdt. 1. 85, etc.),
πολυάρητος (*Dem.* 220), and Call. *Hy.* 6. 47 (Demeter speaks): τέκνον
πολύθεστε τοκεῦσι. πολύευκτος would be the 'correct' form, but cf.
Homeric εὐχετόωντο (*Il.* 8. 347, etc.).

166. ἐκθρέψαιο: the compound occurs in Homer only as v.l. in *Od.* 18. 130. Cf. Hdt. 1. 122, etc. For the middle cf. S. *El.* 13, etc.

167. ῥεῖα: the sense is obscure here, and ἦ ῥα may well be right as in *Dem.* 222.

167–8. Cf. *Od.* 15. 537–8 etc. (Appendix III). This implies a form of 'macarismos' commonly used in praise of wealth. Cf. ad *Dem.* 480, 486 ff.

168. ζηλῶσαι: the verb is not found in Homer (but cf. ζηλήμονες *Od.* 5. 118, δύςζηλοι *Od.* 7. 307). Cf. Hes. *Op.* 23, 312, and ζῆλος Hes. *Th.* 384, *Op.* 195.

τόσα . . . δοίη: if *Dem.* 223 is not corrupt, the subject is Metaneira. In Homer and Hesiod θρέπτρα, θρεπτήρια are the recompense given by children to their parents for their upbringing. Cf. later (e.g.) Theocr. *Epigr.* 20 where it is paid by the child to his nurse after her death. Hence Matthiae suggested δοίη in 223. But the text can stand (cf. e.g. E. *El.* 626 for payment by the parents). The Attic word is τροφεῖα.

169–88. Demeter consents, and the girls hurry off to tell their mother the news. She asks them to engage Demeter as nurse and summon her. They run back, like young deer or calves, their hair streaming in the wind, and lead Demeter to the palace. She walks behind sorrowfully. When they reach the palace, they run to join their mother, who is sitting by the pillar of the hall, holding the child.

In this fine passage, the youthful gaiety of the girls is emphasized, and contrasted with Demeter's gravity and sorrow. (Cf. E. Janssens, *Annales du Centre d'étude des religions*, ii (Brussels, 1962), 39 ff.) The narrative is rapid, like the events which it portrays: cf. especially ad *Dem.* 171–2, 172–3, 184. There are many pictorial details: e.g. the simile of 174 ff. (on this cf. also ad 170–8), and the contrast between the girls with lifted robes and hair flowing freely and the goddess whose head is veiled and whose robes ripple about her feet (cf. ad *Dem.* 176–8).

That the description was appreciated in later times is shown by the echoes in the Hellenistic poets of 176 f.

On 174–89 cf. H. Fränkel, *Dichtung und Philosophie*[2], 288 f.: he takes the passage as a characteristic example of the richer, fresher style of the *Hymns* in contrast to earlier epic, and compares Greek art of the sixth century.

It is possible that the scene of the girls running down the road, and leading Demeter to Eleusis, may reflect part of the ceremonies at Eleusis, i.e. a procession or ritual dance, led by the priestesses, of whom the daughters of Celeus may be the prototypes (cf. ad *Dem.* 98 ff., 105 ff.). Their flowing robes and free-flowing hair are probably features of the cult (cf. ad *Dem.* 176 ff.), and the initiates may have worn white clothing, in contrast to Demeter's black (cf. ad 42, 176 ff.).

The following scene (188–211) definitely reflects the ritual of the Mysteries (cf. ad loc.).

169–70. ταὶ δὲ . . . κυδιάουσαι: the word order is unusual, with the separation of φαεινά from ἄγγεα by a participial phrase and verb. Cf. perhaps *Il.* 16. 104 f. δεινὴν δὲ περὶ κροτάφοιcι φαεινὴ | πήληξ βαλλομένη καναχὴν ἔχε (Kirk, *YCS* 20 (1966), 110, calls this a case of 'violent enjambement'. Note the position of φαεινή). Cf. Introduction, p. 60.

170–8. These lines possibly show reminiscences of *Il.* 15. 263 ff., where Hector is compared to a horse galloping out to pasture, and immediately afterwards the Greeks are compared to dogs chasing deer or wild goats. In *Dem.* 174 ff., features of both similes have been combined into one:

Dem. 170 κυδιάουcαι ∼ *Il.* 15. 266 κυδιόων (of the horse)

171 ῥίμφα ... ∼ *Il.* 15. 268 ῥίμφα* (and cf. the dactylic rhythm of both verses)

174 αἱ δ' ὥc τ' ἢ ἔλαφοι ∼ *Il.* 15. 271 οἱ δ' ὥcτ' ἢ ἔλαφον* ...

175 ἄλλοντ' ἂν λειμῶνα ∼ *Il.* 15. 264 θείη πεδίοιο κροαίνων κορεccάμεναι φρένα φορβῇ ∼ *Il.* 15. 263 ἀκοcτήcαc ἐπὶ φάτνη

177–8 ἀμφὶ δὲ χαῖται | ∼ *Il.* 15. 266–7 ἀμφὶ δὲ χαῖται | ὤμοιc ἀΐccοντο ... ὤμοιc ἀΐccονται ...*

(Note also *Dem.* 386 δάcκιον ὕληc ∼ *Il.* 15. 273 δάcκιοc ὕλη*.) Cf. Introduction, pp. 31 f.

170. κυδιάουcαι: Homer always has κυδιόων (etc.): four times in *Iliad* (cf. *Hy.* 30. 13). For examples of the retention of original -άω, etc. in Homer and Hesiod cf. Monro, *HG*², § 55. 6 ff., Chantraine, *GH* i. 78 f., Meister, *Hom. Kunstsprache*, 61–80. In the *Hymns* cf. *Aph.* 266 τηλεθάουcαι, *Hy.* 7. 14 μειδιάων, 41 τηλεθάων. See also Shipp, *Studies in the Language of Homer*, 63.

171. The purely dactylic rhythm, with trochaic caesura in both second and third foot, emphasizes the speed and lightness of the girls (as does the repetition ῥίμφα ... ὦκα). For this rhythm cf. *Dem.* 89 (ῥίμφα ...), 184 (αἶψα ...), 380 (ῥίμφα ...), also *Il.* 24. 691 (ῥίμφα ...).

171–2. ῥίμφα ... ὦκα ... ὦκα: for the repetition cf. *Dem.* 58–60, *Hy.* 7. 6–9, Hes. *Sc.* 464–9, and Introduction, p. 60.

172. ὡc εἶδον: cf. *Dem.* 295, 416 and *Od.* 17. 344 (where Schol. B: νῦν τὸ ὡc ἀντὶ τοῦ ὅcον).

172–3. The poet of the *Hymn*, in contrast to normal epic procedure, avoids two passages of direct speech here, which would delay his narrative. Cf. ad *Dem.* 314–23, and Introduction, p. 59.

173. καλεῖν: M's καλέειν is probably due to scribal 'emendation', such as is found often in papyri of Archilochus, and manuscripts of Herodotus and the Hippocratica. Cf. Introduction, p. 66. The contracted forms καλεῖ, κάλει occur in Homer (*Il.* 3. 390, 13. 740, etc.).

ἐπ' ἀπείρονι μιcθῷ: the epithet is rather unexpected. Evidently Metaneira is already impressed by what she hears of her visitor. Cf. Hdt. 8. 4 πείθειν ἐπὶ μιcθῷ.

174. ἢ ... ἢ ...: West (ad *Th.* 6) advocates ἠ' before a vowel. Cf. also E. *Ba.* 110, P. Oxy. 2320. 8, and Maas, *Greek Metre*, § 141.

ἤαρος ὥρῃ: the Homeric forms are ἔαρ (*Il.* 6. 148, *Od.* 19. 519), εἰαρινός (*Il.* 2. 89 etc.). The spelling ἤαρος, ἠαρινός (cf. *Dem.* 401), with η for ει ('metrical lengthening' of ε), is probably influenced by the contracted ἦρος (cf. 455), ἠρινός. ἦρος and ἦρι occur in lyric, Attic, and probably Ionic (cf. LSJ, s.v. ἔαρ). Cf. also ἔαρ, Hes. *Op.* 492, ἔαρι 462, with synizesis. On the 'metrical lengthening' see W. F. Wyatt Jr., *Metrical Lengthening in Homer* (Rome, 1969), 150 f.

It is notable that in Homer, as here, ἔαρ, εἰαρινός always occur in similes, except once (*Od.* 18. 367).

174 f. Cf. E. *Ba.* 862 ff., where the bacchants wish to dance ἐν παννυχίοις χοροῖς . . . δέραν εἰς αἰθέρα δροσερὸν ῥίπτους' (cf. ad *Dem.* 176 ff.), ὡς νεβρὸς χλοεραῖς ἐμπαίζουσα λείμακος ἡδοναῖς (cf. Dodds, ad loc.). Note also the similes of leaping fawn and foals in Bacch. 13. 83 ff., Ar. *Lys.* 1306 ff., in similar ritual contexts.

175. ἄλλοντ': the present is not found in Homer or Hesiod.

κορεσσάμεναι φρένα φορβῇ: cf. *Il.* 11. 89 (~ *Ap.* 461) σίτου . . . περὶ φρένας ἵμερος αἱρεῖ, etc. For κορέννυμι with the dative cf. *Il.* 8. 379, 13. 831, A.R. 3. 897, and (passive) Theognis 751, 1269, Hdt. 3. 80.

176–81. The girls' robes would trail along the ground if they did not lift them, and their hair streams in the breeze. The trailing robe may be a Homeric feature, although the gesture has been considered 'post-Homeric' (cf. ad *Dem.* 176). Likewise, hair worn loose is characteristic of the archaic period (cf. ad *Dem.* 177 f.). Both features are thus natural in a poem of this time. But their occurrence together is suggestive, since they are often mentioned in connection with festivals and cults, especially those of Bacchus and Cybele: cf. Call. fr. 193. 35 ff. (of the cults of Cybele and Adonis) Κυβηβῆ τὴν κόμην ἀναρρίπτειν . . . ἢ ποδῆρες ἕλκοντα Ἄδωνιν αἰαῖ . . . ἰηλεμίζειν; cf. (for Adonis) Theocr. 15. 134, and Pfeiffer ad Call. loc. cit. for further examples from these cults, and also that of Bacchus (especially E. *Ba.* 150, 833, Ar. *Lys.* 1311). See also Alcman, fr. 3. 1. 8–9; and perhaps Asius, fr. 13. 3 ff. (K.) of the Ionians at the festival of Hera of Samos (cf. ἑλκεχίτωνες Ἰάονες *Ap.* 147, at the festival of Delian Apollo; Allen and Halliday ad loc.): χιονέοις τε χιτῶσι πέδον χθονὸς εὐρέος εἶχον . . . χαῖται δ' ἐρρώοντ' ἀνέμῳ χρυσέοις ἐνὶ δεσμοῖς (see Addenda).[1]

In the Mysteries of Lycosura and Andania the initiates were forbidden to have their hair bound up or their heads veiled. This suggests that here also the picture may reflect the cult. Cf. ad *Dem.* 169–88, 174 f. Similarly, the mystae were forbidden to wear black at Andania (cf. ad *Dem.* 42).

The contrast with Demeter is emphasized formally: 177 ἤϊξαν . . . ἀμφὶ δὲ χαῖται . . . ~ 182 στεῖχε . . . ἀμφὶ δὲ πέπλος . . . For the contrasting verbs cf. also 188 ἔδραμον . . . ἔβη ποσί.

There is a kind of chiasmus: 176–7a ~ 182b–3; 177b–8 ~ 182a. Note also the colour-contrast of κροκηΐῳ ἄνθει ὁμοῖαι (178) and κυάνεος (183).

---

[1] On this fragment see C. M. Bowra, *On Greek Margins* (Oxford, 1970), 122 ff.

176. ἐπιϲχόμεναι: Brunck's ἀνα- would be more natural, but ἐπι-
is possible, meaning 'holding back'.

ἑανῶν: the substantive is used in Homer only in the singular (*Il.*
3. 385, etc.), and is a synonym for πέπλοϲ according to Schol. *Il.* 14.
178, 16. 179. (It is probably related to ἕννυμι, i.e. *ϝεϲανόϲ, as ϲτέφω :
ϲτέφανοϲ, etc., the adjective ἑανόϲ being from a different root.) Cf. the
use of the plural πέπλων in *Dem.* 277.

The trailing robe (cf. *Dem.* 182 f.) is implied in Homer by ἑλ-
κεϲίπεπλοϲ (of Trojan women only: *Il.* 6. 442, 7. 297, 22. 105).
Cf. also τανύπεπλοϲ (*Il.* 3. 228, etc.: general epithet of heroines). It is
also a feature of Doric dress, as on the François Vase (cf. Fr. Studniczka,
Beiträge zur Geschichte der Altgriechischen Tracht (Wien, 1886), 95 f.).

The gesture described is often shown in art of the seventh century
and later (cf. *CVA, Louvre*, III 1d, Pl. 51, No. 5, K. Francke, *De hymni
in Cererem compositione, dictione, aetate* (Kiel, 1881), 26). It also occurs in
Hellenistic and Roman poetry. Cf. A.R. 3. 874 f. ἂν δὲ χιτῶναϲ |
λεπταλέουϲ λευκῆϲ ἐπιγουνίδοϲ ἄχριϲ ἄειρον, where 874a ∼ *Dem.* 177a
(cf. ad loc.), suggesting that this is a reminiscence of the *Hymn* (cf. also
ad *Dem.* 231, 254 and pp. 69 f.); A.R. 4. 940 ff. αὐτίκ' ἀναϲχόμεναι
λευκοῖϲ ἐπὶ γούναϲι πέζαϲ . . . ῥώοντ' (4. 936b = *Dem.* 269b); 4. 45 f.

Moschus, *Eur.* 126 ff. again probably echoes the *Hymn*: ἐν χέρι δ'
ἄλλη | εἴρυε πορφυρέαϲ †κόλπου† πτύχαϲ, ὄφρα κε μή μιν (∼ *Dem.*
131b) δεύοι . . . ὕδωρ. Cf. Bühler ad loc. (in *Eur.* 127 he conjectures
πέπλου or ἑανοῦ for κόλπου). Ruhnken noted this parallel, and also
Cat. 64. 129 :

> mollia nudatae tollentem tegmina surae.

Cf. also Theocr. 14. 35 ἀνειρύϲαϲα δὲ πέπλωϲ, 26. 17 (but see Gow,
ad loc.), Call. *Hy.* 3. 11.

177. κοίλην κατ' ἀμαξιτόν: cf. *Od.* 10. 103 f. For κοίλην cf. *Il.* 23.
419 (but this refers to a road hollowed out by a torrent).

177 f. This motif (taken from the simile of the stall-fed horse) is
un-Homeric, since women in Homer, married or unmarried, normally wore a head-dress of some kind, usually a veil or a shawl. Cf.
Lorimer, *Homer and the Monuments*, 385 ff.; E. B. Abrahams, *Greek
Dress* (London, 1908), 34 f.: (in Homer) 'no woman would think of
leaving the house without her κρήδεμνον', whereas in post-Homeric
times 'before the Persian wars women for the most part wore their
hair down, although instances occur where it is fastened up with
bands or fillets.' (Cf. ibid. fig. 45 for illustrations.)

The girls may have been wearing a simple head-band here. But cf.
ad *Dem.* 176–8.

178. κροκηΐῳ: found only here. Cf. κρόκοϲ (*Il.* 14. 348, etc.), κροκόειϲ
Sapph. fr. 92. 7, etc. For the form -ήϊοϲ cf. Schwyzer, *Gr. Gr.* i. 468,
Chantraine, *La formation des noms en grec ancien*, 52. It occurs in all
dialects except Attic, which has -εῖοϲ. κροκήϊοϲ is an analogical ex-
tension, perhaps from χαλκήϊοϲ (< χαλκεύϲ ∼ χαλκόϲ). Cf. Zumbach,
Neuerungen, 13 f.

For the comparison of hair to flowers cf. *Od.* 6. 231 = 23. 158,
Call. fr. 274, Theocr. 2. 78; Ov. *A.A.* 530 'croceas irreligata comas'.

179. τέτμον: this is a regular feature of arrival scenes. Cf. *Dem.*
319, 342, Arend, *Typische Scenen*, Taf. 1–3. It is 'neglected' at *Dem.* 63,
185, 458.

ἐγγὺς ὁδοῦ: cf. *Od.* 6. 291 (Appendix III).

κυδρὴν θεόν: M has θεάν, but θεόν is regular in this and similar
formulae. It is also metrically preferable. Cf. *Dem.* 292 where M has
θεόν, notes to *Dem.* 1, and West ad *Th.* 442. On κυδρός cf. ad *Dem.* 66.

179–82. The run of initial verbs is notable. These are common in
narrative passages, often with enjambement and pause after the
first foot. Cf. also in this passage 172, 177, 185, 186, 188, 189, 191, etc.

180 ff. This scene is based on a typical *schema* (Journey and Visit):
cf. Arend, *Typische Scenen*, Taf. 1, and see also Appendix III.

[> marks elements inserted into the normal schema.]

I. *Journey*: 180–3 (ἡγεῦνθ', ἡ δ' ἄρ' ὄπισθε . . . στεῖχε: cf. *Il.* 3. 447,
   [9. 192], 11. 472, 12. 251 = 13. 833, 13. 690, 24. 95 f., *Od.* 2.
   405 f., 413, etc.; *Ap.* 514–16, *Hy.* 26. 9–10). > 181b, 182b–3
   (Demeter's sorrow).

II. *Arrival*: 184 (αἶψα δὲ . . . ἵκοντο*: *Il.* 5. 367, *Od.* 15. 193; cf.
   Il. 2. 168, etc.). > 185a.

III. *Situation*: 185–7a (usually expressed by εὗρε: cf. ad loc.; 185–7a
   ~ *Od.* 6. 304–7). > 187b–8a: the girls join their mother.

IV. 1. *Visitor stands in doorway*: 188b (~ *Od.* 1. 103 f.; cf. ad loc.). >
      188b–9: Epiphany.
   2. *Reaction of host(ess)*: 190 (~ *Il.* 9. 193, 11. 777, 24. 480 ff.,
      Od. 16. 12; here enlarged for epiphany).
   3. *(She) rises*: 191a (~ *Il.* 9. 193, etc.).
   4. *Takes by hand*:⎫omitted.
   5. *Leads in*:   ⎭
   6. *Offers seat*: 191 (~ *Il.* 11. 646 = 778, etc.; cf. esp. *Il.* 24. 100,
      Od. 7. 169 f., 16. 42; cf. ad loc.).
      Refusal of seat: 192–3 (~ *Il.* 11. 648, 23. 205, 24. 553:
      cf. ad loc.).
      > Iambe 195–6 (196b ~ [*Il.* 9. 200b], *Od.* 1. 130, etc., 16. 47).
      > 197–205: cf. ad 192 ff. [200: (Refusal of) food and drink
      —cf. below].
   7 and 8. *Food and drink*: 206–11.
      > Refusal of wine: 206–8a.
      > *Cyceon*: 208b–11 (~ *Od.* 10. 316 ff., in Visit scene; 10. 234
      ff.; *Il.* 11. 624 ff. Cf. also *Il.* 24. 601 ff., 641 f.: Priam is
      persuaded to take food by Achilles despite his grief, in
      Visit scene).

V. *Conversation*: 212 ff.

On the interweaving of elements from Eleusinian ritual into this
schema cf. ad *Dem.* 192 ff.

181. 'He (etc.) led, they (etc.) followed': cf. ad *Dem.* 180 ff., and Appendix III.

181 ff. For the contrast between Demeter's sorrow and the girls' gaiety cf. ad *Dem.* 169 ff., 176 ff.

182. κατὰ κρῆθεν: 'down over her head', as in *Od.* 11. 588, Hes. *Th.* 574, fr. 23 (a). 23 (cf. *Sc.* 7). This sense is probably secondary, and arises from a misinterpretation of an original κατ' ἄκρηθεν (cf. M here, and v.l. *Il.* 16. 548, *Od.* 11. 588, *Th.* 574) = κατ' ἄκρης ('from the summit downwards', i.e. 'utterly'). Cf. Leumann, *Hom. Wörter*, 57 f., West ad *Th.* 574.

On Demeter's veil cf. ad *Dem.* 42.

182–3. ἀμφὶ δὲ . . . ποccίν: note the neat chiasmus. The position of θεᾶc is unusual. For the word order cf. perhaps Hermann's conjecture at Hes. *Op.* 549 ἀὴρ πυροφόροιc τέταται μακάρων ἐπὶ ἔργοιc (πυροφόρος codd.).

183. κυάνεοc: cf. ad *Dem.* 42, 319.

ῥαδινοῖcι . . . ποccίν: ῥαδινόc is used only once in Homer, of a whip (*Il.* 23. 583). The Hesiodic formula (*Th.* 195) is a 'doublet' of the Homeric ποccὶ (δ') ὑπὸ λιπαροῖcιν (*Il.* 2. 44, etc.). This is normally used of men, but cf. *Il.* 14. 186, of a goddess. Cf. also *Il.* 13. 19 ποccὶν ὑπ' ἀθανάτοιcι and Edwards, *Language of Hesiod*, 56, 69 ('ἀθανάτοιcι or λιπαροῖcι would be flat here').

Cf. Phryn. *PS* p. 106 B. ῥαδινοὺc πόδαc· τοὺc ὀρθοὺc καὶ ἀπαλοὺc καὶ εὖ πεφυκόταc. It generally means 'slender', perhaps also 'pliant' (εὐκίνητος, Schol. A ad *Il.* 23. 583). Cf. Groeneboom ad A. *PV* 401.

θεᾶc: M has θεῆc here and at 279, elsewhere in the *Hymn* θεά, etc. Homer has θεῆc, θεῆcι (*Il.* 3. 158, 8. 305, etc.), but θεή, etc. occur only in later epic poetry (Antim. fr. 186 Wyss, Call. *Hy.* 3. 119, etc.), and θεᾶc should probably be read here.

For Demeter's trailing robe cf. ad *Dem.* 176.

184. Cf. ad *Dem.* 171, 180 ff., Appendix III.

185–8. Cf. Appendix III. Here the action is divided: the girls go to their mother (185–6 ~ *Od.* 6. 304 f., 7. 139–41, 6. 50), Demeter steps on the threshold (188 ~ 7. 135).

βὰν δὲ δι' αἰθούcηc ἔνθα . . .: the αἴθουcα does not appear elsewhere in this formula. The phrase is compressed and ambiguous: ἔνθα must mean 'to the place where' (cf. *Il.* 13. 789, 24. 733), since Metaneira is sitting in the megaron.

On the αἴθουcα cf. Lorimer, *Homer and the Monuments*, 415 ff.

ἔνθα: the second syllable is lengthened *in arsi* only here and at *Od.* 3. 367.

πότνια μήτηρ: Celeus is absent from this scene. Cf. the parallel scenes *Od.* 10. 112–14, where the king is at the agora (cf. *Od.* 6. 53 ff.), and *Od.* 7. 135 ff. where Arete is the main figure, although Alcinous is also present (Appendix III).

185–6. Cf. *Od.* 17. 96 μήτηρ δ' ἀντίον ἷζε παρὰ cταθμὸν μεγάροιο. Metaneira probably sits by one of the main supporting pillars of the megaron, which stood near the hearth. Cf. Arete in *Od.*

6. 52, 305 f., Penelope in *Od.* 17. 96, 23. 89 f. The Homeric megaron, with its hearth and pillars, has been thought to correspond closely with that of Mycenaean palaces (cf. Monro, *Odyssey* XIII–XXIV, pp. 490 ff., Myres, *Homer and his Critics*, 162–70, D. H. F. Gray, *CQ* N.S. 5 (1955), 1 ff.). But this is not certain (see Addenda).

187. ὑπὸ κόλπῳ: in *Od.* 15. 649 this must mean 'under the fold of her garment' (cf. *Il.* 9. 570, 22. 80, etc.). ἐπὶ κόλπῳ means 'on her lap' and may well be right. ὑπό and ἐπί are often confused in manuscripts: cf. Allen and Halliday ad *Ap.* 18, West ad Hes. *Th.* 843, also Hes. *Op.* 162, A.R. 4. 1064 (?), Nonn. *D.* 8. 78.

187 f. The girls' eagerness is again contrasted with Demeter's deliberate action. Cf. ad *Dem.* 176 ff.

188–211. Demeter sets foot on the threshold, her head touches the rafters, and she fills the doorway with divine radiance. Metaneira is seized by reverence, awe, and fear, and rising offers Demeter her chair. The goddess refuses it and stands in silence with downcast eyes, until the good Iambe gives her a stool, and places on it a white fleece. There she sits holding her veil before her face, for a long time, in silence and sorrow, without laughter and without tasting food and drink: until Iambe with her jokes and mockery makes the holy lady smile and laugh and have a propitious spirit, Iambe who later also pleased her heart. Metaneira offers her a cup of wine, but she refuses, saying that it is not lawful for her to drink wine, and asks her to mix barley and water with pennyroyal, and give it to her to drink. She makes the *cyceon* and gives it to the goddess. The lady Deo receives it for the sake of the rite . . .

In this scene various elements that are typical in Visit scenes are used for a special purpose. These are:

1. The visitor appears in the doorway (Epiphany).
2. Amazement of the person visited.
3. She rises and offers the visitor a seat (her *own* seat).
4. The visitor refuses the offer.
5. A stool with a fleece on it is offered (Purification ceremony).
6. Offer of wine (refused as unlawful).
7. *Cyceon.*

Cf. ad *Dem.* 180 ff., 192 ff.

The passage aroused suspicion on the grounds of its aitiological character (cf. ad *Dem.* 192 ff.), amongst critics who considered the aitiological elements of the *Hymn* secondary. It has also been objected that Demeter's epiphany and subsequent behaviour interrupt the natural course of events, and are ignored by Metaneira in 212 ff., and that Metaneira's greeting should follow Demeter's arrival.

The passage is unusual, because it describes unusual behaviour. But it follows the traditional schema of scenes of this type (cf. ad *Dem.* 180 ff.). Moreover, a sudden, momentary epiphany of the type of 188–9 arouses fear and amazement in those present (190), but often leaves them baffled, and unable to appreciate its significance. Thus Aphrodite overrules Anchises' scruples (*Aph.* 82 ff., 190 ff., 153) and the forebodings of the steersman at the sight of Dionysus are ignored by the ship's captain (*Hy.* 7. 17 ff.). Metaneira, like the girls (*Dem.* 159) is aware that Demeter is unusual (213 ff.). She is also aware of Demeter's sorrow, and tactfully attempts to console her (216 ff.). But she does not refer to what she has just seen: her reactions of αἰδώς, cέβαc, and δέοc prevent her (cf. ad *Dem.* 188–90, 275 ff.).

Metaneira's χαῖρε (213) is delayed here owing to her reactions in 190. But in general conversation tends to follow a meal (cf. ad *Dem.* 180 ff.). For χαῖρε after a meal cf. *Il.* 9. 225 (∼ *Od.* 4. 60, 18. 122).

188–90. Demeter's arrival is the signal for an epiphany. A second and grander epiphany occurs at her departure (275 ff.). These are the two main points at which deities tend to reveal themselves in Homer: e.g. (Arrival) *Il.* 4. 75 ff.; (Departure) *Il.* 13. 72, 24. 460 ff., *Od.* 1. 319 ff., 3. 371 ff. (cf. Aristarchus ad *Il.* 2. 791–5).

The epiphany is characterized here by the supernatural stature of the deity, the divine radiance which she sheds abroad, and the reactions of reverence, awe, and fear which she arouses.

1. *Supernatural stature*: this is commonly a sign of the superhuman. Cf. *Il.* 4. 443, *Aph.* 173 f., both of which may be models for *Dem.* 188 f. (cf. ad loc.), *Dem.* 275; Call. *Hy.* 6. 57 f. (epiphany of Demeter, echoing *Dem.* 188 f.? Cf. ad loc.); Virg. *A.* 2. 592 (∼ *Il.* 24. 629 f.), 4. 177 = 10. 767 (∼ *Il.* 4. 443); Claud. *Cons. Stil.* 2. 276 f. (cf. ad *Dem.* 188 f.). Often supernatural stature and beauty are linked: cf. ad *Dem.* 275. For further examples cf. Pfister, *RE, Supp.* 4. s.v. Epiphanie, p. 314.

2. *Divine radiance* is also a common epiphany feature: in Homer, Athena is like a star (*Il.* 4. 75 ff.), the gods' eyes shine (3. 397, 13. 3, etc.; cf. Hes. *Sc.* 72), and Athena's lamp makes the house appear as if on fire, so that Odysseus and Telemachus recognize her presence (*Od.* 19. 33 ff.). Cf. also *Od.* 18. 353 ff., and later *Dem.* 278 ff., *Ap.* 440 ff., *Aph.* 86 ff., 174 f., Hes. *Sc.* 70 ff., Bacch. 17. 103 ff., E. *Ba.* 1083, Theocr. 24. 38 ff., A.R. 4. 1701 ff., 3. 126, and in Latin Virg. *A.* 2. 589 f., 616 (Servius ad loc.), 3. 151, 4. 358, 8. 608 f., Ov. *F.* 1. 94, etc. Cf. (in the New Testament) Luke 24: 4, Matth. 28: 3, Mark 16: 5; and Pfister, o.c. 315 f., Dieterich, *Nekyia*, 38 ff., Stephani (*Mém. de l'acad. des sciences de St Petersb.* 6 sér. ix. 361 ff.), 'Nimbus und Strahlenkranz'; and ad *Dem.* 275 ff.

3. The reactions of the onlookers are commonly *amazement* and *terror*. (Amazement is also the common reaction to an unexpected visitor: cf. ad *Dem.* 180 ff., 190.) For θάμβοc (etc.) cf. *Il.* 3. 398, 4. 79, *Od.* 1. 323, 3. 371 f., 19. 36, *Ap.* 135, *Aph.* 84, *Hy.* 7. 37, 28. 6 (cέβαc), A.R. 2. 681, 921, Luke 24: 41, etc. For fear cf. *Il.* 20. 130 f., 24. 170, *Od.* 16. 178 ff., 24. 533 ff., *Dem.* 281 ff., 293, *Ap.* 2, 447, *Aph.* 182, Bacch. 17. 102 f., A.R. 3. 1221, Virg. *A.* 4. 279 f., Matth. 16: 5 ff., etc. (cf. also ad *Dem.* 190). For fear and amazement together at a 'pseudo-epiphany' cf. *Od.* 6. 168.

Pfister (o.c. 317) observes that these reactions are 'the beginning of the cult'. The epiphany of a deity is commonly the occasion for the institution of a cult. This is the case with Demeter's visit to Eleusis. Here the following scene describes the origins of the preliminary ritual of initiation (cf. ad *Dem*. 192 ff.), just as Demeter's self-revelation at 268 ff. is followed by her command to build a temple and altar and her promise to institute her ὄργια (cf. ad *Dem*. 270 ff.), and her second epiphany (275 ff.). In 188 ff. Demeter's epiphany creates the religious atmosphere in which the following scene takes place.

The experience of an epiphany corresponds in some respects to that of the initiate during the Mysteries themselves. He has the same reactions of terror and amazement (φρίκη, τρόμος, ἱδρώς, θάμβος) during the early stages, and at the climax a great light (φῶς τι θαυμάσιον) shines out. The religious awe aroused prevents him from speaking (cf. ad *Dem*. 188–211, 275 ff. and especially 478 f.; also here 194, 198 f.). In both cases the emphasis lies on *vision*. Cf. Pfister, o.c. 319, and notes to *Dem*. 478 f., 480.

188. ἐπ' οὐδὸν ... ποcί: entry to a house is normally expressed as crossing or stepping on a threshold: cf. *Od*. 4. 680, 7. 135, etc. Visitors on arrival (cf. ad *Dem*. 180 ff.) stand on it (*Od*. 1. 103 f.), 'in the doors' (*Il*. 11. 644) or 'in the πρόθυρα' (*Il*. 11. 777). Suppliants and beggars sit on it (*Od*. 10. 62, 17. 339, 413, etc.). The barrier between the house and the world outside it had a special significance, and to cross it was a 'significant act'. Hence Demeter's epiphany takes place at this point. Cf. K. Meister, *Die Hausschwelle in Sprache und Religion der Römer* (Sb. Heidelb. 1925), especially 17 ff., E. Norden, *Aus Altrömischen Priesterbüchern*, 141 f., 144, 152 f., 158 ff., 171 f. (also for the regular conjunction of *limen* and *stare* in Latin), M. B. Ogle, *AJP* 32 (1911), 251 ff. (especially 260 f., for the threshold in connection with prophecy and epiphany). Cf. also Porph. *de antro nymph*. 27 on the sacred character of doorways.

188 f. There is parallelism in ἐπ' οὐδὸν ἔβη ποcὶ καί ῥα μελάθρου κῦρε κάρη. Cf. *Il*. 4. 443 (Eris) οὐρανῷ ἐcτήριξε κάρη καὶ ἐπὶ χθονὶ βαίνει. This passage, or a similar one, may lie behind *Dem*. 188 f. But a closer parallel is *Aph*. 173 f., in the epiphany of Aphrodite. Both *Dem*. 188 f. and *Aph*. 173 f. have oddities of expression:

(*a*) the genitive is not used with κύρειν in Homer or Hesiod (who use dative). Cf. Hom. *Epigr*. 6. 6, [Archil.] fr. 326 West, Hdt., Attic.

(*b*) μέλαθρον properly means the roof-beam or rafter (cf. Schol. T ad *Od*. 8. 297), and hence 'roof'. In *Aph*. 173 f. this sense is natural, but in *Dem*. 188 f. the goddess stands on the threshold and fills the doorway with light. μέλαθρον should therefore strictly mean 'lintel' here (cf. Gemoll). The only evidence for this sense is Hsch. s.v. μέλαθρα· οἰκίαι, ὑπέρθυρα.

(*c*) Is κάρη the subject of κῦρε, or accusative of respect? In *Aph*. 173 f. either is possible, but the asyndeton there is perhaps easier if each clause has a separate subject, and κάρη governs κῦρε. Here, either is again possible, if κάρη may also govern πλῆcεν (cf. ad 189).

H

But it is more natural for Demeter to be the subject of all three clauses. (The dative κάρῃ is a third possibility: this occurs in Theognis 1024 and later poets, and would give an exact parallel with ἔβη ποσί.)

(d) in *Aph*. l.c., the asyndeton itself is unusual (cf. Allen and Halliday ad loc.), and ἔστη ἄρα κλισίῃ is odd, as one expects a preposition, and ἄρα comes very late in the sentence. Cf., however, J. C. Kamerbeek, *Mnem.* 20 (1967), 391, who notes *Aph*. 71, 153, 267, as examples of this poet's fondness for asyndeton.

Other parallels with *Aph*. 155–75 tend to suggest that, if there *is* a direct echo, the poet of our *Hymn* is later: in this same passage *Dem*. 194b = *Aph*. 156b; and *Aph*. 157a ∼ *Dem*. 285a. All these are phrases which occur nowhere else in early epic.

Gemoll argues for the priority of the *Hymn to Aphrodite* (ad loc.). So also K. Reinhardt (*Ilias und ihre Dichter*, 519), on the ground that there is a strong and effective contrast between *Aph*. 155 ff. and 168 ff., which is lacking in our *Hymn*. This is a rather subjective criterion.

Cf. also Heitsch, *Aphroditehymnus*, 38 ff.; K. Stiewe, 'Der Erzählungstil des homerischen Demeterhymnus' (Diss. Göttingen, 1954, unprinted); and Introduction, pp. 42 f.

Virg. *A*. 4. 177 = 10. 767 echoes *Il*. 4. 443. Cf. also Claud. *Cons. Stil*. 2. 277 (epiphany of Roma): 'summae tangunt laquearia cristae.' Did Claudian have the *Homeric Hymns* in mind? It is possible that the motif occurred elsewhere.

189. κάρη: in this position in the verse only here and at *Aph*. 174.

πλῆcεν δὲ θύραc: the conjecture of Voss avoids taking κάρη either as accusative or as subject of πλῆcεν. The latter is possible: the divine radiance comes from the body (cf. *Dem*. 278 f., Hes. fr. 43 (a). 73 f., Bacch. 17. 103 ff.) and especially from the head or face (*Il*. 5. 7, 18. 206 ff., *Od*. 18. 353 ff., *Aph*. 174, in the parallel passage; *Hy*. 31. 12 ff., 32. 3 f., Matth. 17 : 2, 28 : 3, Revelation 1 : 16, etc.). But the accusative of respect gives an easier construction (cf. ad *Dem*. 188 f.).

cέλαοc θείοιο: for cέλαc of supernatural radiance cf. *Il*. 8. 76, 18. 214, *Od*. 19. 17, 366, *Ap*. 442, 445.

189b is parallel to *Aph*. 174b–5.

190. For αἰδώc and δέοc together cf. *Il*. 15. 657 f., 3. 172 (αἰδοῖος . . . δεινός τε; cf. *Od*. 8. 22, etc.), 18. 394, 1. 331 ∼ 24. 435, also *Od*. 9. 269 ∼ 274, etc., *Cypria*, fr. 23. 2 ἵνα γὰρ δέοc ἔνθα καὶ αἰδώc, Epich. fr. 221 K., S. *Aj*. 1074–6; Wilamowitz, *Glaube*, i. 353 ff., von Erffa, *Phil. Supp.*, 30. 2 (1937), "Αἰδώc und verwandte Begriffe (etc.)", 28 ff., Verdenius, *Mnem.* sér. 3, 12 (1945), 47 ff. For αἰδώc and cέβαc cf. *Il*. 4. 242 f. ∼ 5. 787, etc., 8. 178–80, von Erffa, o.c. 26 ff., A. *Eum*. 545–9 (cf. also A. *Eum*. 522 ff., 690 f., 696 ff.). αἰδώc and cέβαc are not used in Homer of reactions to the divine (but cf. αἰδεῖcθαι *Il*. 9. 504, 24. 90, 503, *Od*. 9. 269; αἰδοίη θεόc *Il*. 18. 394). Cf. for αἰδώc *Cypr*. l.c. sup., for cέβαc *Dem*. 479, *Hy*. 28. 6, Hom. *Epigr*. 8. 3; also cεμναί τ' αἰδοῖαί τε of Demeter and Persephone, *Dem*. 486 (cf. *Dem*. 1, 343, 374, Hes. *Op*. 301). The normal reaction in Homer is amazement (cf. ad *Dem*. 188–90, and B. Snell, *The Discovery of the Mind*,

tr. T. G. Rosenmayer (Harper, 1960), 33), but sometimes also fear
(cf. ad *Dem.* 188–90 and *Od.* 14. 389, 22. 39, 14. 88, θεουδής *Od.* 6. 121,
etc.).

On cέβας cf. also ad *Dem.* 10, on αἰδώς ad *Dem.* 214 f., and *Lex. des
frühgriech. Epos*, s.v. αἰδοῖος, αἰδώς.

191. This is also a typical feature of Visit scenes. For the queen to
offer the visitor her own chair is a mark of great respect. Cf. *Od.* 7.
168 ff. (Odysseus at Alcinous' court), where Alcinous offers him his
favourite son's chair, next to his own, and *Il.* 24. 100, *Od.* 16. 42.

κλισμοῖο: this is distinguished from a θρόνος by Ap. Soph. 100. 15,
Schol. *Od.* 1. 145, as having arm-rests, but the two are sometimes used
interchangeably, as here (*Il.* 11. 623 ~ 645, 24. 515 ~ 597). It was
often decorated: cf. *Dem.* 193, *Il.* 8. 436, 24. 597, *Od.* 1. 132, etc.;
Pollux 10. 47, Helbig, *Hom. Epos*, 118 ff.

192–211. This scene forms the model for several elements of Eleusinian ritual:

1. Preliminary purification: 194–201.
2. Fasting and abstention from wine: 200 f., 206–8.
3. Aischrologia: 202–5.
4. *Cyceon*: 208–11.

The keynotes of the passage are formally emphasized by repetition,
i.e. Demeter's sitting-down (193 etc.), sorrow (194, 197, 198, 200,
201), and silence (194, 198–9), and the duration of time (194, 198).
The ritual character is also brought out by parallelism and repetition:
192–7 ~ 198–204:

i.e. ⎧192–3 ἀλλ' οὐ Δημήτηρ . . . ἤθελεν ἑδριάαcθαι
⎪194 ἀλλ' ἀκέουcα ἔμιμνε . . .
⎩195 πρίν γ' ὅτε δή . . . Ἰάμβη κέδν' εἰδυῖα . . .
~ ⎧198 ἄφθογγος τετιημένη ἧcτ' . . .
⎪199 οὐδέ τιν' . . . προcπτύccετο . . .
⎪200–1 ἀλλ' ἀγέλαcτος . . . ἧcτο . . .
⎩202 πρίν γ' ὅτε δὴ . . . Ἰάμβη κέδν' εἰδυῖα.

206–11 also show the same pattern of refusal followed by acceptance.
The ritual element is explicitly referred to in 204, 207, 211.

1. *Preliminary purification*

The similarity between the events described in 194–201 and the
scene portrayed on two Roman monuments, the 'Lovatelli urn' and
'Torre Nova sarcophagus', has long been recognized. (Cf. Diels,
Sibyllinische Blätter (1890), 122 ff.; Rizzo, *Röm. Mitt.* 25 (1910),
89–167; Roussel, *BCH* 54 (1930), 58 ff.; Mylonas, *Eleusis,* 205 ff.,
Figs. 83 and 84.) These depict the purification of Heracles from the
slaughter of the centaurs, before his initiation at Eleusis and descent
to Hades. According to Apollodorus (2. 5. 12) this was performed by
Eumolpus (cf. P. Oxy. 2622 and PSI 1391, ad *Dem.* 154). According
to Diod. 4. 25. 1 he was initiated by Musaeus. (Cf. also E. *HF* 613,

Xen. *H.* 6. 3. 6, Plut. *Thes.* 30. 8, and in art, the Kertsch pelike and
Pourtalès vase, Mylonas, o.c. 210 ff., Figs. 85 and 81.) Another tradition held that the Lesser Mysteries at Agrae were instituted by Demeter for Heracles' purification (Diod. 4. 14. 3, Schol. Ar. *Plut.* 846,
1014; cf. Ps. Plat. *Axiochus* 371 e, Maas, *AM* 20 (1895), 355). The
central scene shows Heracles seated on a stool (cf. πηκτὸν ἕδος, δίφρου
Dem. 196, 198), which is covered by his lion skin. (In some other
parallel reliefs he sits on a ram's fleece, according to Pringsheim, *Arch.
Beiträge*, 9 f., who assumes that the lion skin was substituted to charac-
terize Heracles. Cf. *Dem.* 196b.) His right foot is bare, and rests on
a ram's head. His head is veiled by a cloak (cf. *Dem.* 197b). A female
figure stands behind him and purifies him, by means of a liknon (on
the urn), or a lowered torch (on the sarcophagus). To the left, Demeter
herself is shown seated on the *cista* (on the sarcophagus), or an altar-
like seat (on the urn), both of which are covered by a pelt (a ram's
fleece according to Hauser, *Röm. Mitt.* 25 (1910), 287 f.). She is
accompanied by Persephone or Iacchus. The scene to the right of
Heracles shows a purificatory sacrifice.

Heracles' purification is by means of the Διὸς κῴδιον (or δῖον κῴδιον),
the sacred fleece taken from a ram sacrificed to Zeus Meilichios. It
was used for various ceremonies of purification, amongst others by the
Dadouchos at Eleusis (cf. *Suda* s.v.; Hsch. s.v.; Harrison, *Prolegomena*,
23 ff.).

Heracles was purified from homicide, but the ceremony formed a
part of the preliminaries to initiation (cf. Plut. l.c.: τὸν πρὸ τῆς μυήσεως
καθαρμόν). The two forms of purification, for murder, and before
initiation, are closely similar: cf. Dieterich, *Nekyia*, 66 f., and ad *Dem.*
197–8.

The *Hymn* portrays the *aition* for this purification: Demeter sits on
the stool, which is covered by the fleece. (Normally the ram's head was
placed under the feet of the candidate.) Her head is veiled, and she
is silent (198 f.). For the significance of these various features in
purification ceremonies cf., for the *fleece*, Diels, o.c. 122 ff., Persson,
ARW 21 (1922), 300, Gjerstad, *ARW* 27 (1929), 206 f., J. Pley, *De lanae
in antiquorum ritibus usu* (Naumburg, 1911); for the *veil*, Diels, l.c.;
Roussel, o.c. 63, Reinach, *Cultes, Mythes et Religion*, 1. 299 ff., Deubner,
AF 78. *Silence* is prescribed for purification: A. *Eum.* 448 ff. (ad *Dem.*
198), cf. Schol. A. *Eum.* 276, A.R. 4. 693 ff., 697 f., Diels, o.c. 123.

The emphasis on *sitting down* (*Dem.* 191, 193, 196, 197, 198, 201)
is also significant: cf. the ceremonial thronismos of the initiate in the
mysteries of the Corybantes and the Great Mother (Guthrie, *Orpheus
and Greek Religion*, 213), and notes to *Dem.* 200. See Addenda.

For the possible connection of the purification ritual with the story
of Demophon cf. ad *Dem.* 231 ff. The place and time of the ceremony
in the later period are both uncertain (cf. Introduction, pp. 20 ff.).
The Διὸς κῴδιον was certainly used at Eleusis, but one tradition connects Heracles' purification with the Lesser Mysteries, and these
are described as purificatory (Clem. *Strom.* 4. 3. 1, Schol. Ar. *Plut.*

845). It has been conjectured that the scenes on the Torre Nova sarcophagus are derived from those on the temple at Agrae (cf. Rodenwaldt, *Gnomon* 1 (1925), 127; Möbius, *AM* 61 (1936), 234 ff. = *Studia varia* (1967), 108 ff.) but this seems doubtful (cf. Nilsson, *Gesch.* i³. 668 n. 10). For the use of torches for purification at Agrae cf. Stat. *Theb.* 8. 763 ff.

The ritual of purification is parodied in Ar. *Nub.* 250, 633 ff., 723 ff., where Strepsiades is 'initiated' into the Socratic 'mysteries' (cf. C. Petersen, *Der geheime Gottesdienst bei den Griechen* (Hamburg, 1848), 41; Dieterich, *RhM* 48 (1893), 275 ff.; Guthrie, *Orpheus and Greek Religion*, 210 ff.).

2. Fasting and Cyceon

These are both mentioned in the Eleusinian cύνθημα (Clem. *Protr.* 2. 21. 2): ἐνήcτευca, ἔπιον τὸν κυκεῶνα . . . (cf. Introduction, pp. 22 f., and ad *Dem.* 47). It is natural to assume that the initiates broke their fast with the *cyceon*, as Demeter does. Fasting before a sacred meal is common practice (cf. P. Gerlitz, 'Das Fasten als Initiationsritus', in *Initiation*, ed. C. J. Bleeker, 275 ff.). But the time and place when it was drunk in the later period are not certain. It is possible that it was drunk on the arrival of the procession at Eleusis, despite the supposed difficulty of making this journey on an empty stomach (cf. Arbesmann, *Das Fasten*, 77 ff.). The procession of the κάλαθος at Alexandria took place on a day of fasting (Call. *Hy.* 6. 6 ff.). The modern Greek pilgrim would not consider such feats of endurance beyond him. It would thus coincide with the αἰcχρολογία, which in the *Hymn* causes Demeter to break her fast. The two are closely linked (see below).

Cf. also Deubner, *AF* 79 ff., Eitrem, *Symb. Osl.* 20 (1940), 140 ff. On the purpose and constitution of the *cyceon* cf. Appendix IV, and on Demeter's refusal of wine ad *Dem.* 207 f.

3. Iambe

She appears without introduction in the *Hymn*. To those familiar with Eleusinian ritual she would need no introduction. Others would not penetrate below the surface narrative to the ritual underlying it. Her epithet κέδν' εἰδυῖα simply suggests a ταμίη (cf. *Od.* 1. 428, etc.). But her importance in the cult is obscurely hinted at in *Dem.* 205.

She is the eponym of the iambic rhythm (Philoch. *FGH* 328. 103, Schol. Nic. *Alex.* 130, Hsch. s.v. ᾿Ιάμβη, ἰαμβίζειν, *Et. M.* 463. 23 ff., Schol. Hephaest. 214. 9 Consbr., *et al.*). Compare Elegeis, about whom a myth is told similar to Iambe's (Crusius, *RE* 5. 2258 ff.) and Iacchus, eponym of the cry of the procession to Eleusis. The original use of the iambic rhythm was probably religious, and connected especially with the festivals of Demeter and Dionysus. Archilochus, the first iambic poet, came from Paros, home of an important Demeter-cult (cf. ad *Dem.* 491) and of Baubo, Iambe's counterpart.

He himself probably came of a priestly family (cf. Paus. 10. 28. 3; also perhaps fr. 251 West (Tarditi, pp. 6–7), for Archilochus and Dionysus, and note frr. 322–3 West; Crusius, *RE* 2. 501. 60, Kern, *RE* 4. 2723. 15 ff.). The earliest use of the word ἴαμβος (excluding *Iliu Persis*, fr. 6 Allen) comes in Archil. fr. 215 West. This suggests the sense 'jesting' (cf. Arist. *Poet.* 1448ᵇ37, Gerhard, *RE* 9. 65 ff. s.v. Iambographen). Ritual jesting (αἰςχρολογία, cκώμματα) certainly occurred at Eleusis, and probably some of it at least was in iambics. The chorus of mystae in Aristophanes' *Frogs*, after singing the Iacchus song (396 ff.) itself in iambic rhythm and scurrilous (411 ff.), go on to iambic cκώμματα against political characters. That they are not just indulging in the traditional jesting of comedy here is suggested by *Ran.* 393, where in their hymn to Demeter they ask that they may sport and jest in a way worthy of *her* festival (τῆc cῆc ἑορτῆc ἀξίωc παίcαντα καὶ cκώψαντα). Cf. also 375 f. κἀπιcκώπτων καὶ παίζων καὶ χλευάζων ~ Dem. 202–3 χλεύηc . . . παρὰ cκώπτουcα, 444 ff., 450 ff.[1]

The jesting in the *Frogs* takes place during the procession (*Ran.* 372 ff.; cf. 389 πανήμερον). It was accompanied by dancing (374, 390, 404, 409, 451 ff.). Iambe herself danced to the iambic rhythm (Eust. *Od.* 11. 277). Philicus' *Hymn to Demeter* is entirely *choriambic*, which is why it is quoted as a rarity. Iambe comes from Halimus in Philicus' version, and the Thesmophoria at Halimus, a preliminary to the three-day festival at Athens, involved dancing (παίζειν καὶ χορεύειν, Plut. *Sol.* 8. 4; cf. Polyaen. 1. 20. 2; Ar. *Ran.* 390, 409, 419, 452 f.). Apollodorus (1. 5. 1) makes Iambe's jesting the *aition* for the cκώμματα of women at the Thesmophoria, and this may refer to the Thesmophoria at Halimus. In the similar ritual of Damia and Auxesia Herodotus (5. 83) mentions χοροῖcι γυναικηίοιcι κερτόμοιcι, who were led in their abuse against local women by twenty male χορηγοί. There was dancing during the Iacchus procession to Eleusis (*IG* ii². 1078. 29; Plut. *Alc.* 34. 4; Deubner, *AF* 73 f.), and this was presumably accompanied by cκώμματα. One form of these is attested by Strabo (9. 1. 24) and Hesychius (s.v. γεφυρίc, γεφυριcταί). As the procession crossed the Athenian Cephisus (cf. Bolte, *RE* 11. 248), a man sitting on the bridge with veiled head (or according to Hesychius a woman) made jokes against those who were passing (or against well-known citizens: Hsch. s.v. γεφυρίc). The person may have been a man disguised as a woman (cf. Radermacher, *Aristophanes' Frösche*, p. 203 n. 1).

Schol. Ar. *Plut.* 1014 also mentions cκώμματα by women in carriages during the procession (cf. *Suda* s.v. τὰ τῶν ἁμαξῶν cκώμματα).[2] Ar.

---

[1] Foucart, *Les Mystères*, 332 ff., and Deubner, *AF* 73 f., deny that this refers to the Mysteries. I think that it does. See also H. Lloyd-Jones, *Maia* 19 (1967), 219 f., and n. 25, for other references.

[2] This is referred to the Anthesteria by Foucart, *Les Mystères*, 328, Deubner, *AF* 73 f. Cf. also Kerényi, *Symb. Osl.* 36 (1960), 1 ff. The bridge on the Rheitoi at Eleusis was too narrow for carriages (*IG* i². 81. 11, 421/20 B.C.): but cf. Pringsheim, *Arch. Beiträge*, 47.

Vesp. 1362 f. (ἵν' αὐτὸν τωθάcω νεανικῶc, | οἵοιc ποθ' οὗτοc ἐμὲ πρὸ τῶν μυcτηρίων) is a general reference to αἰcχρολογία as a preliminary to the Mysteries (cf. Schol. ad loc.). 1361–2 perhaps suggest a connection with the purification by torches.

The dancing continued on the arrival of the procession at Eleusis, in a παννυχίc. This is portrayed on the Niinnion pinax (Mylonas, *Eleusis*, 213 ff., 241, 257, Fig. 88), which also shows that the κερνοφορία took place at this time (cf. Appendix IV).[1] In the *Frogs*, the mystae on reaching their destination divide into separate groups of men and women. The men go off to 'the sacred circle of the goddess, to sport in her flowery precinct', while the chorus-leader (the dadouchos) joins the girls and women, 'to give them sacred light, in their παννυχίc for the goddess' (444 ff., cf. 371). In the following chorus, they speak of going 'to the flowery rose-filled meadows', τὸν ἡμέτερον τρόπον, τὸν καλλιχορώτατον, παίζοντεc (451 ff.). This surely refers to the dancing around Callichoron, which was part of the παννυχίc (cf. E. *Ion* 1074 ff., E. Pfuhl, *De Atheniensium pompis sacris* (Berlin, 1900), 40, Möbius, *AM* 61 (1936), 256). Pausanias (1. 38. 6) says that 'the *women* first danced and sang here in honour of the goddess' (cf. also ad *Dem.* 292 ff. and Appendix I).

It seems very likely that during the παννυχίc further αἰcχρολογία occurred, together with the dancing. Normally only women indulged in this: cf. the Thesmophoria (above), Stenia (Plut. s.v., Hsch. s.vv. Cτήνια, cτηνιῶcαι), Haloa (Schol. Luc. *Dial. Mer.* p. 280. 14 Rabe), and cult of Damia and Auxesia. In this cult the women were led by male χορηγοί (cf. Hdt. 5. 83. 3). Cf. perhaps for Eleusis Ar. *Ran.* 447 f., Radermacher ad loc. But for men and women together cf. e.g. Call. fr. 7 ff. (*ritus Anaphaeus*).

The drinking of the *cyceon* may also have taken place at this time (see above). Originally, *aischrologia* and *cyceon* were closely linked. In the *Hymn*, it is Iambe's jesting which persuades Demeter to break her fast. There are many parallel stories (see below). The Alexandrian myth of Ascalabus also connects the two, although in a different way. Ascalabus (or Ambas), son of Misme (or Metaneira), angered Demeter by laughing at her when she was drinking the *cyceon* (or according to another version, by behaving badly during her sacrifice). She poured the dregs of the drink over him and turned him into a gecko (ἀcκαλαβώτηc). Cf. Nic. fr. 56 (= Ant. Lib. 24), Schol. Nic. *Ther.* 483 (Ambas is probably a confusion with Iambe), Ov. *M.* 5. 446 ff., Lact. Plac. *Fab.* 5. 7.

In the 'Orphic' version, Iambe is replaced by Baubo (Orph. fr. 52 K.). By an indecent exposure she causes Demeter to laugh, and to accept the *cyceon*. The story is perhaps the *aition* for the handling of ἄρρητα, which accompanied *aischrologia* at some festivals of Demeter (e.g. Haloa, l.c. above). It has been conjectured that this is referred to in the second half of the Eleusinian cύνθημα, after the drinking of the

---

[1] E. Simon, *Ant. Kunst* 9 (1966), 86 ff., argues that the Niinnion pinax portrays the Haloa. I do not find her arguments convincing.

cyceon. But this is quite uncertain (cf. Deubner, *AF* 79 ff., Nilsson, *Gesch.* i³. 658 f., Mylonas, *Eleusis*, 294 ff.).[1]

Call. fr. 21. 8 ff. suggests a connection between *aischrologia* and fasting at a festival of Demeter, and perhaps refers also to the rest of the *synthema* (cf. Pfeiffer ad loc.). Handling of *arrheta* goes with the eating of special 'cakes' of grain at the Haloa, Stenia, etc. (Schol. Luc. l.c. above), which could suggest a link with the *cyceon* or κερνοφορία.

Aischrologia was common in festivals of Demeter. Besides the examples already quoted, it occurred at Syracuse, where the *aition* was that during her search for Core the goddess was made to laugh (Diod. 5. 4. 6: the jesting seems to have involved obscenity here). It may be significant that Ath. 181 c mentions ἰαμβισταί at Syracuse. It also took place at Pallene, in the festival of Demeter Mysia (Paus. 7. 27. 9), and in Dionysiac festivals (e.g. Lenaea and Choes: *Suda* s.v. τὰ τῶν ἁμαξῶν σκώμματα). For Rome cf. Ov. *F.* 3. 675 f., 695 (and the *Fescennini versus* at marriages: these again were in poetic form), and in general Arist. *Pol.* 7. 15, 1336ᵇ, Plut. *Def. Or.* 14 (417 c), Iamblichus, *De Myst.* 1. 11, Farnell, *Cults*, iii. 104, Frazer, *GB*³ 7. 62 f.

Stories similar to those of Iambe and Baubo, and related ritual, occur in many countries. For a study of these in relation to mourning customs cf. especially K. Meuli, *Romania Helvetica* 20 (1943), 788 ff. Professional jesters are used at funeral feasts to relieve the mourners, in many parts of the world. In Sardinia, this custom used to be explained by a story about the Virgin Mary similar to the Demeter myth. When she was mourning the death of her Son, the animals tried unsuccessfully to comfort her, until a frog made her smile by boasting that her own grief was much worse, since she had lost seven children run over by a cartwheel (cf. Usener, *Kl. Schr.* iv. 469 f.). A similar story of the Virgin being made to laugh by a frog who boasted of his latest child is quoted from Rumania by Marie Holban, *Incantations, chants de vie et de mort*, 75, 79 (cf. E. *Helena*, Budé edn. p. 106 n. 1). Here, the ugliness of the frog is emphasized. The Sardinian proverb 'non v'ha dolu senza risu' was explained by this. Cf. Philicus' *Hymn* 55 [τοῖσι δὲ] σεμνοῖς ὁ γελοῖος λόγος ἆρ' ἀκερδή[ς; (*vel sim.* Cf. Latte, *Kl. Schr.* 546). Usener compared the use of *scurrae* at Roman funerals, and conjectured that the myth of Iambe indicated a similar custom in Attica.

In Scandinavian mythology, Skadi's grief for his dead father is relieved by the obscene jesting of Loki. A closer parallel is provided by the Egyptian myth of the goddess Hathor, who made her father laugh and resume his work, by exposing herself (cf. Lévy, *Mélanges Cumont*, 832 ff.). It has been suggested that the story of Baubo derives from this (Lévy, Meuli, o.c.; cf. H. Vorwahl, *ARW* 30 (1933), 396). Hathor's gesture was used by women in the cult of Bubastis, with

---

[1] For Baubo see also Emped. fr. 153; *IG* 12. 5. 227, *Praktika* 1950, p. 280 (cult on Paros and Naxos); Nilsson, *Gesch.* i³. 657 n. 2, Pl. 45. 3 (Priene), Picard, *RHR* 95 (1927), 220 ff.; Kern, *RE* 3. 150 ff. See also Addenda to p. 82.

aischrologia and dancing (Hdt. 2. 60), and a similar practice occurred in the Apis cult (Diod. 1. 85).

There are also Egyptian stories of the Sun being made to laugh and resume work (cf. Wiedemann, *Die Amulette der Aegypter* (1934), 66 ff.). In Japan, Amaterasu, the Sun-goddess, withdrew into a hole in anger, but was appeased by Uzume, who was very ugly. She danced and exposed herself so that the gods laughed, and Amaterasu, overcome by curiosity, looked out and joined in the laughter (Braun, *Japan. Märchen und Sagen*, 108 ff.). This myth was the *aition* for the ritual dances performed annually at the winter solstice and at the burial of royalty, by Uzume's descendants. The dances were supposed to cheer the souls of the dead.

In Greece, the festival of the Daedala at Plataea was explained by a similar myth (Paus. 9. 3; Plut. ap. Euseb. *PE* 3. 1. 6; Reinach, *Cultes, Mythes et Religions*, 4. 109 ff.).

These parallels show how close such rituals of mourning are to those of festivals of fertility, and how they are explained by myths of the same type. At Eleusis, the initiates who joined in the fasting, and the *aischrologia* and dancing which ended it, were not merely participating in rituals of purification and the stimulation of fertility (cf., e.g., Allen and Halliday ad *Dem.* 48, 195). More important to them personally was the fact that they were sharing in the sorrow of Demeter, and its relief by laughter, song, and dance. At the same time, the return of life to the fields and the growth of the crops formed an essential background. Thus, in the version of Euripides (*Hel.* 1301 ff.), Demeter has already caused famine over the earth (cf. *Dem.* 305 ff.) when she is appeased by the music and gaiety of the Graces, Muses, and Aphrodite. Cf. also the version of Philicus. There the famine has already occurred when Iambe appears.

Laughter is often a symbol of rebirth, or of restoration of the dead to life. In myths and folklore, it can actually create or restore life (cf. S. Reinach, l.c. above, 'Le rire rituel'; E. Fehrle, 'Das Lachen im Glauben der Völker', *Zeitschr. f. Volksk.* N.F. 2 (1930), 1 ff.; F. Dölger, 'Lachen wider den Tod', in *Pisciculi Fr. J. Dölger zum 60. Geburtstag darg.* (Münster, 1939), 84 ff.; V. Cajkanovič, 'Das magische Lachen', *Srpski Etnografski Zbornik* 31 (1924), 25 ff.). Laughter and obscenity, together with the drinking of the *cyceon* after the period of fasting, perhaps symbolized at Eleusis the initiate's entry into a new life (cf. Reinach, o.c. 115 f.). Hence, when he uttered the words of the σύνθημα, perhaps on his entry to the Sanctuary or the Telesterion itself, he signified that he was standing on the threshold of a new and transformed existence, and was qualified for the revelations that were to follow.

A similar ritual to that of *Dem.* 192–211 probably took place in the Mysteries of Isis: cf. Apul. *Met.* 6. 19–20 (especially 19. 4–5, 20. 3, and 19. 3 'ipsum limen' ∼ 11. 23. 7 and *Dem.* 188), Plut. *de Is. et Osir.* 69 (cf. ad *Dem.* 200), R. Merkelbach, *Roman und Mysterium*, 46 f.

192. There is a solemnity about this line which makes it a suitable introduction to the ceremonies that follow. Cf. ad *Dem.* 233 f.

The refusal of a seat is an epic motif found also in Hittite poetry:
cf. the Sun-god in the tale of Ullikummi (Pritchard, *ANET*² 123).

194. ἀκέουϲα: on Demeter's silence cf. ad *Dem.* 198 f., 192 ff.
ἔμιμνε: hiatus after the second trochee is rare. It occurs especially
after ϲε (*Il.* 19. 288, *Od.* 6. 251, *Ap.* 54), but also at *Il.* 2. 8 (due to
a formula-transposition), 3. 46, 5. 118, 23. 263, *Od.* 3. 480, 19. 185.
Meyer's First Law is also broken (Maas, *Greek Metre*, § 94). The conjecture of Voss is attractive. Cf. *Il.* 16. 363. But note *Il.* 1. 565, which
also breaks Meyer's Law.

κατ' ὄμματα καλὰ βαλοῦϲα: this is here a sign of sorrow, in *Aph.*
156 of αἰδώϲ. Cf. *Il.* 3. 217 κατὰ χθονὸϲ ὄμματα πήξαϲ (in pretended
αἰδώϲ), E. *IA* 1123 ἐϲ γῆν δ' ἐρείϲαϲ' ὄμμα πρόϲθ' ἔχειϲ πέπλουϲ (in
sorrow; cf. *Dem.* 197), *Med.* 24 ff. κεῖται δ' ἄϲιτοϲ ... οὔτ' ὄμμ'
ἐπαίρουϲ' οὔτ' ἀπαλλάϲϲουϲα γῆϲ πρόϲωπον (cf. *Dem.* 200). It became
a motif of love stories (cf. *Aph.* 156): Theocr. 2. 112, Call. fr. 80. 11,
A.R. 1. 784, 3. 22, 1022 f., *AP* 5. 252, Musaeus 160, Aristaen. *Epist.*
1. 15. In Latin cf. Virg. *A.* 1. 482, 6. 156, 469, 11. 480 ('oculos deiecta
decoros': a reminiscence of *Aph.* 156?).

The motif is perfectly appropriate here. Heitsch (*Aphroditehymnus*,
39) argues that it is more suitable in *Aph.* 156, where Aphrodite
feigns modesty to win Anchises, but this is unconvincing.

195. Ἰάμβη: cf. ad *Dem.* 192 ff. Later legend made her a daughter
of Echo and Pan (Philoch., *FGH* 328. 103, *Et. M.* 463. 23 ff.,
Et. G. p. 160 Rei., Schol. Nic. *Alex.* 130), and a Thracian (Schol.
Nic. l.c., Procl. ap. Plut. *Bibl.* 319 b 17) or a βάκχη (*Et. M.* l.c.).
There was a sanctuary of Echo on the Sacred Way to Eleusis (*IG*
ii². 1011. 7; cf. Kern, *RE* 16. 1226, Jacoby, *FGH* 3b Supp., Text,
pp. 422 f.). In Philicus' *Hymn*, she comes from Halimus, on the coast
near Athens (cf. ad *Dem.* 192 ff.). Schol. Heph. 214. 12 ff. makes her
meet Hipponax in Ionia, and address him in iambic metre.

κέδν' εἰδυῖα: ἰδυῖα is the original form (cf. Schulze, *Kl. Schr.* 109 f.),
but manuscripts of Homer and Hesiod regularly have εἰδ-, and
εἰδυῖα(ν) is certain in *Il.* 17. 5, Hes. *Th.* 887 (cf. West ad *Th.* 264).

196. πηκτὸν ἔδοϲ: on the ritual significance of this stool (δίφρου
198) cf. ad *Dem.* 192 ff. πηκτόν in Homer is used only of a plough,
and ἔδοϲ normally of places (but cf. οὐχ ἔδοϲ *Il.* 11. 648, 23. 205).
This 'jointed seat' is thus something unusual.

ἐπ' ἀργύφεον βάλε κῶαϲ: on the significance of the fleece cf. ad
Dem. 192 ff. Metzger (*Recherches*, 45 ff.) identifies the seat on which
Demeter sits in some works of art with this stool (cf. Metzger, o.c.,
pp. 36 f., Nos. 15–18). This seems to me doubtful.

197–201. Demeter sits down, veiled, for a long time, in silence, in
sorrow, addressing no one, unsmiling, not tasting food or drink,
mourning for her daughter.

These elements are all typical of scenes of mourning. For sitting
down, especially on the ground, in grief, cf. *Od.* 4. 716 ff., 20. 58,
21. 55 f. (Bühler, Moschus, *Europa*, p. 65, n. 5), Pritchard, *ANET*² 123,
Psalm 137: 1, Shakespeare, *Richard II*, III. ii. 155 f. Lying or rolling on

the ground are also signs of grief: *Il.* 18. 26 f., 22. 414, 23. 58 ff., 24. 161 ff., 510. For sitting down as symbolical of death cf. L. Gernet, *Anthropologie de la Grèce antique* (Paris, 1968), 288 ff., especially 295 ff.

For the sequence 'for a long time, in silence, in sorrow, she sat, and did not speak a word to anyone' (*Dem.* 198 f.) cf. Job. 2 : 13 : (Job's friends) 'sat down with him upon the ground seven days and seven nights, and none spake a word unto him: for they saw that his grief was very great.' Cf. also 2 Sam. 12 : 16. In later Greek poetry cf. A.R. 2. 859 ff.: δὴν ἄρ' . . . ἀμηχανίῃσιν . . . πεσόντες, | ἐντυπὰς εὐκήλως εἰλυμένοι, οὔτε τι cίτου | μνώοντ' οὔτε ποτοῖο· κατήμυcαν δ' ἀχέεccι | θυμόν . . . τετιημένοι (∼ *Dem.* 198). Cf. also A.R. 4. 1294 ff.: ἐν δὲ κάρη πέπλοιcι καλυψάμενοι cφετέροιcιν | ἄκμηνοι καὶ ἄπαcτοι ἐκείατο νύκτ' ἔπι πᾶcαν | καὶ φάοc . . . Cf. also the expressive veiled silence of the seated Niobe (which lasts for three days), and of Achilles in Aeschylus (Ar. *Ran.* 911–12, A. fr. 277 Loeb, *Vita Aeschyli* s. 6).

In A. *Ag.* 412 ff. Menelaus' silence after Helen has left him (πόθῳ ὑπερποντίαc) is similarly described. Note the 'privative tricolon' there: cf. ad *Dem.* 200.

Cf. also Meuli, o.c. ad *Dem.* 192 ff. (Iambe), J. G. Frazer, *Folklore in the Old Testament* (London, 1919), iii. 71 ff., 'The Silent Widow'. On fasting and sitting on the ground (especially in the cult of Demeter) cf. ad *Dem.* 200.

197. προκατέϲχετο: not in Homer (cf. προέχειν, κατέχειν, προκαθίζω, (κατα)ϲχομένη). The middle occurs only here, the active in Thuc. 4. 105, etc.

On the significance of the veil cf. ad *Dem.* 42, 192 ff.

198. The 'long silence' is 'formulaic', but later versions also make Demeter sit in sorrow for several days: cf. Call. *Hy.* 6. 15, Ov. *F.* 4. 505 f. (ad *Dem.* 200).

ἄφθογγοc does not occur elsewhere in early epic. Cf. Theognis 549, etc., and especially A. *Eum.* 448 ff. ἄφθογγον εἶναι τὸν παλαμναῖον νόμος, ἔcτ' ἂν πρὸc ἀνδρὸc αἵματος καθαρcίου cφαγαὶ καθαιμάξωcι νεοθήλου βοτοῦ (cf. ad *Dem.* 192–211 : 1. Preliminary purification).

199. οὔτ' ἔπεϊ . . . οὔτε τι ἔργῳ: cf. ad *Dem.* 65, 117.

προcπτύccετο: this verb means 'embrace' (*Od.* 11. 451), and so 'greet, address'. Here 'she greeted no one by word or gesture' (cf. LSJ s.v.). Cf. *Dem.* 117.

200. ἀγέλαcτοc: in Homer this occurs only as a v.l. at *Od.* 8. 307 (Ap. *Lex.*, γρ. Eust., interpr. schol.: ἔργα γελαcτά codd.; cf. H. Frisk, *Kl. Schr.* 200 n. 1). Cf. Heracl. fr. 92 D.–K., A. *Ag.* 794, fr. 290, etc. (in active sense).

Zumbach, *Neuerungen*, 26, argues that it should be passive as in *Od.* 8. 307, and that this shows the line to be an imitation of *Od.* 4. 788. This is unconvincing, although *Od.* 4. 788 may have been the model.

Later legend made Demeter in her sorrow sit on the so-called Agelastos Petra, and it is possible that there is a reference to it here, or else the rock may derive its name from this line of the *Hymn.* Cf.

Apollod. 1. 5. 1: he places it by the well Callichoron, and makes
it the place where she sat when she first came to Eleusis. In Ov. *F*. 4.
503 ff.:

> hic primum sedit gelido maestissima saxo:
>   illud Cecropidae nunc quoque triste vocant.
> sub Iove duravit multis immota diebus,
>   et lunae patiens et pluvialis aquae.

Schol. Ar. *Eq*. 782 (= *Suda* s.v. *Cαλαμῖνος*) say that it was so called
either because Theseus sat on the Agelastos Petra when about to
descend to the underworld, or because Demeter sat there when
searching for Core (cf. Hsch. s.v.). Proclus ap. Phot. *Bibl*. 319b 17 ff.
(Bekker) makes the incident with Iambe occur when Demeter is
sitting on the rock.
   This tradition should be connected with the ritual of fasting and
sitting on the ground which took place at the Thesmophoria. Cf.
Plut. *de Is. et Osir*. 69 (378 e) καὶ γὰρ Ἀθήνῃσι νηστεύουσιν αἱ γυναῖκες ἐν
Θεςμοφορίαις χαμαὶ καθήμεναι (cf. Nilsson, *Gr. Feste*, 48 f.; Arbesmann,
Das Fasten, 91; Deubner, *AF* 56). Plutarch compares this with a
similar practice in the cult of Isis. Cf. Apul. *Met*. 6. 19. 5 (ad *Dem*.
192 ff.). For sitting on the ground as a purification ritual cf. also
Plut. *de Superst*. 3 (166 a). Demeter herself is shown seated on the
rocky ground and approached by worshippers on a fourth-century
B.C. Eleusinian relief: Mylonas, *Eleusis*, 200, Fig. 72.[1] Cf. Call. *Hy*.
6. 15 f.:

> τρὶς δ' ἐπὶ Καλλιχόρῳ χαμάδις ἐκαθίσσαο φρητί,
> αὐσταλέα ἄποτός τε καὶ οὐ φάγες οὐδὲ λοέσσα (cf. *Dem*. 49 f.).

Rubensohn (*AM* 24 (1899), 46 ff.) identified the rocky ground in
the relief as the Agelastos Petra.[2] He also suggested, on the strength
of Schol. Ar. *Eq*. 782 (sup.), that it was originally so called because
it was an entrance to Hades. (The Hades-entrance at Colonus was
connected both with Demeter and Core and also with Theseus:
Schol. S. *OC* 1590, 1593.) The Ἀνακλήθρα (or Ἀνακληθρίς) πέτρα at
Megara was perhaps similar. This derived its name from a ceremony
of invocation in imitation of Demeter, still performed by the women
of Megara in Pausanias' own day (Paus. 1. 43. 2, Methodius in
Et. M. 96. 2). Cornford (*Essays and Studies Presented to William Ridgeway*
(1913), 191 f.) suggested that the ἀγέλαστος πέτρα was the original
scene of the summoning-up of Core. This would agree with the supposition (cf. ad *Dem*. 99) that the well Callichoron/Parthenion was
where Core was thought to have gone down to the underworld.
   Rubensohn identified the Agelastos Petra with the rock over the
Ploutonion, just inside the Sanctuary. Here stood the cave and temple
of Pluto, and it must be this cave which is referred to in *Orph. Hy*.
18. 12 ff. (cf. ad *Dem*. 17) as the place where Pluto descended into the

---

[1] He also compares a relief in the Naples museum, Harrison, *Prolegomena*, fig. 85.
But the goddess on this is identified as Aphrodite by J. Harrison, ad loc. (p. 310).
[2] See also Metzger, *Recherches*, 46 ff.

earth with Persephone. The descent, or ascent, of Core was very probably enacted here (cf. Mylonas, *Eleusis*, 146 ff.), and it may be from this rock that Euadne jumps on to her husband Capaneus' pyre, in Euripides' *Supplices*, thus taking a quick route to Φερσεφονείας θαλάμους (1022; cf. 987 ff., 1004 f., 1016 ff.; Mylonas, *Hymn to Demeter*, 87 f.). The Ploutonion, however, is about fifty yards from Callichoron, and the rock is too high to be suitable: Demeter sits down on the ground, not up on a hill (cf. also Mylonas, *Eleusis*, 200). Mylonas identifies the Agelastos Petra with a small outcrop near the Ploutonion (o.c. 145 f.), but this is also too far from the Well.

The rock is mentioned in an inscription (*IG* ii². 1672 = *SIG*² 587. 182) referring to transport of bricks from the Sanctuary to Athens. The wording suggests a point *outside* the Sanctuary (cf. Hiller von Gärtringen, *RE Supp.* 1. 25 s.v. Agelastos Petra). It was probably not a large rock, but simply a particular spot, near the Well, and it may have been covered by the Roman Propylaeon.

Cf. also Pringsheim, *Arch. Beiträge*, 66 n. 3, *Hermes* (1902), 136 n. 3, Buttmann, *Lexilogus*, ii. 179. Aristophanes, in his topography of Hades, has τὸν Αὐαίνου λίθον, ἐπὶ ταῖς ἀναπαύλαις (*Ran.* 193–4), which must be similar to the Agelastos Petra, and is also a 'resting-place'.

ἀγέλαστος ἄπαστος ... ποτῆτος: the use of 'co-ordinated epithets with negative prefix' is common in Greek (and in all literatures), but there are a number of examples referring to fasting: cf. *Od.* 4. 788, *Il.* 19. 346 ἄκμηνος καὶ ἄπαστος (∼ 19. 207, 320; A.R. 4. 1295 ad *Dem.* 197 ff.), Hdt. 3. 52. 3 ἀλουσίῃσί τε καὶ ἀσιτίῃσι, S. *Aj.* 324 ἄσιτος ἀνήρ, ἄποτος, Phryn. Com. ap. Phot. Berol. p. 118. 25 ἄσιτος ἄποτος ἀναπόνιπτος, Xen. *Cyr.* 7. 5. 53 ἄσιτος καὶ ἄποτος, Pl. *Phaedr.* 259 c ἄσιτόν τε καὶ ἄποτον. Cf. in Latin Lucil. 599 f. Marx. For other examples of this use cf. *Dem.* 242 ἀγήρων τ' ἀθάνατόν τε (cf. 260, etc.); *Od.* 1. 242 ἄϊστος ἄπυστος, Hes. *Th.* 489, 797, 955; A. *Ag.* 412 f. (cf. ad *Dem.* 197 ff.) and Fraenkel ad loc.

The rhythm and sound of this line are unusual and striking. Cf. H. N. Porter, *YCS* 12 (1951), 39 f. (and *Il.* 2. 412 Ζεῦ κύδιστε μέγιστε . . .).

201. μινύθουσα: for 'wasting' as a result of grief cf. *Il.* 1. 491, 18. 446, etc., Onions, *Origins of European Thought*, 33, 48.

202 ff. Schol. Nic. *Alex.* 130 (cf. Schol. E. *Or.* 964) recounts the story in full, referring it to τοῖς εἰς Ὅμηρον ἀναφερομένοις ὕμνοις (cf. Introduction, p. 68). They make Demeter's host Hippothoon (a misunderstanding of *Alex.* 131: cf. Herter *RhM* 90 (1941), 251 n. 31), but paraphrase the *Hymn*.

Cf. also Philicus, *Hymn* 58 ff. (Körte, *Hermes* 1931, 447), Apollod. 1. 5. 1.

202. χλεύῃς: not elsewhere before the Hellenistic period. Cf. *AP* 7. 345. 4 (Aeschrio? Cf. Gow and Page, *Hellenistic Epigrams*), and late Greek. N.B.: Clem. Al. *Protr.* 2. 15. 1 ταῦτα οὐ χλεύη τὰ μυστήρια; χλευασία, χλευασμός, etc. are classical. On χλευάζων in Ar. *Ran.* 376 cf. ad *Dem.* 192–211: 3. Iambe.

μιν: for the position of the pronoun cf. Wackernagel, *IF* 1 (1892), 333 ff. (= *Kl. Schr.* 1. 1 ff.). He showed that in early Greek the enclitic pronoun follows immediately the first accented word of the sentence, and also demonstrated (*Kl. Schr.* 70 ff.) that this is a common phenomenon in Indo-European languages. This rule is now known to apply also in Hittite.

202 f. We are not told the nature of Iambe's jests, but they probably involved indecency, like most *aischrologia.* The poet of the *Hymn* treats the subject with the proper epic decorum. For a similar example of possible suppression of τὸ ἀπρεπές cf. ad *Dem.* 254.

203. παρὰ σκώπτουϲ' ἐτρέψατο: neither simple nor compound form of ϲκώπτειν occurs elsewhere in early epic. Cf. for ϲκώπτειν Hdt. 2. 121 δ', Ar. *Ran.* 395, etc. (cf. ad *Dem.* 192 ff.). παραϲκώπτειν does not occur before Plutarch, who uses it five times (cf. especially *Cat.* 21. 7 χλευάζων καὶ παραϲκώπτων; *Cic.* 38. 2 παραϲκώπτειν τι . . . ἀλλ' αὐτὸϲ μὲν ἀγέλαϲτοϲ . . .; cf. *Dem.* 200, 202). Word division did not yet exist, and παρά probably goes with ἐτρέψατο (cf. Heyne's conjecture, and Hes. *Th.* 103, West ad loc.).

πότνιαν ἀγνήν: cf. Kaibel, *Epigr.* 774. 3 (Priene, fourth–third c. b.c.) θεϲμοφόρουϲ ἁγνὰς ποτνίαϲ.

On πότνια cf. ad *Dem.* 39, 54. The accusative (not in Homer) occurs in Hes. *Th.* 11* (cf. West, *Theogony*, 79 and ad loc.), 926, *Aph.* 24. ἀγνή is used of Demeter in *Dem.* 439, Hes. *Op.* 465, [Archil.] fr. 322 West, Moschion, fr. 6. 24, Orph. *Hy.* 40. 11, 18, *IG* 12. 1. 780. 2 (Lindos), of Persephone in *Dem.* 337, etc. (cf. ad loc.), and of both goddesses in *IG* 14. 204. 43 (Sicily). Cf. Rohde, *Psyche*[9], 206 (Eng. trans. 159, 183 n. 5), on its euphemistic use of chthonic deities.

204. The line is progressive: first Demeter smiles, then she laughs, and finally she is in a propitious mood (cf. Voss, ad loc.). The form is that of a 'tricolon crescendo'.

ἵλᾱον: the α is long in *Il.* 1. 583, Hes. *Op.* 340, A. *Eum.* 1040, Euph. fr. 12, *Pae. Erythr.* 19, Theocr. 5. 18, verse inscription ap. Paus. 5. 24. 3 (below), *IG* 12. 2. 476. 5, Parth. fr. 4, etc., short in *Il.* 9. 639, 19. 178, *Hy.* 29. 10, and elsewhere in later poetry. The short form is rarer, according to Choerob. ad Theodos. *Can.* 252. 26.

The original forms are thought to have been ἵληϝοϲ/ἵλᾰϝοϲ, on the strength of ἱλέϝοι in a Laconian verse inscription of *c.* 490 b.c. (*IG* 5. 1. 1562 = Jeffery, *Local Scripts*, 201 nr. 49: Paus. 5. 24. 3 quotes it with ἵλᾱῳ. Cf. Meister, *Hom. Kunstsprache*, 169 n. 2). Cf. Cretan ἵλεοϲ, *SIG*[3] 527. 92, *GDI* 5039. 26. ἵλᾱοϲ would then be formed in the epic Kunstsprache, by analogy with ἵλᾰοϲ, after Ionic metathesis of ἵληοϲ to ἵλεωϲ (so Frisk, s.v. ἱλάϲκομαι, Chantraine, *GH* i. 22, Bechtel, *Lexilogus*, s.v., pp. 175 ff.). But one would expect the η to be retained in epic (cf. βαϲιλῆοϲ) and the Laconian verse inscription is very doubtful testimony (the η may be a hyper-epicism). Ionic may have had ἵλᾱοϲ, and retained the ᾱ in epic through the influence of the other form (cf. ἀθάνατος, ἐᾱγη, ἐᾱνόϲ, ἄμᾱω, τριϲϲοκέφᾱλοϲ).

The sense may be rather 'well disposed, propitious' (as she is to Iambe: cf. 205) than ἱλαρός (LSJ, s.v. ἵλαος II). Cf. *Il.* 1. 583, 9. 639, 19. 178, Hes. *Op.* 340, etc. But cf. Archil. fr. 23. 10 West θυμὸν ἵλαον τίθεο, where it means 'cheerful'.

The rhythm of the end of the line, with three spondees and a monosyllable in the second half of the fifth foot, is unusual. The triple spondee occurs usually with stereotyped formulae such as ἠδὲ θνητοῖc ἀνθρώποιc (cf. *Dem.* 11, etc.), or with names. Cf. also *Dem.* 417. In Homer it occurs about once in eighty-seven verses in the *Iliad*, once in eighty-nine in the *Odyssey*. Cf. La Roche, *Wiener Stud.* 20 (1898), 55, 62 ff., 84 f., 87 ff., Ludwich, *Aristarchs Homerische Textkritik*, ii. 331. For the word division cf. *Il.* 11. 639 (v.l. κνέε), *Od.* 12. 64. Spondaic endings with diaeresis after the fifth foot are very rare: cf. Meister, *Hom. Kunstsprache*, 7 ff. for examples (most of which can be 'resolved'). Spondaic endings are much commoner in this *Hymn* than in Homer: two in fifteen verses in the *Hymn*, one in eighteen in Homer (cf. Maas, *Gk. Metre*, § 83 B; and Introduction, pp. 61 f.). The rhythm here perhaps arises from adaptation of a formula such as *Il.* 9. 639.

205. εὔαδεν: in Homer this is always used with reference to the present, i.e. as a perfect, which does not quite fit ἔπειτα.

οἱ ... ὀργαῖc: 'was also afterwards in later times pleasing to her spirit (?)'.

The double dative is common with ἀνδάνειν: cf. *Il.* 1. 24, *Od.* 16. 28, 14. 337, 20. 327, *Ap.* 220; also *Il.* 8. 129, 13. 82, Hdt. 7. 16. 1, etc.

ὀργή is not found in Homer. Cf. Hes. *Op.* 304, Theognis 98, 214, 964, etc., Semon. 7. 11 D.³, etc. The plural occurs in Pi. *I.* 5. 34, *P.* 2. 77, etc., and is used of one person in Thuc. 8. 83, etc. Its sense in early poetry is 'disposition, character' (especially used of animals: cf. Hes. l.c., Theognis 215, Semon. l.c., Pi. *P.* 2. 77, A. *Supp.* 763). From this it comes to mean 'anger' (cf. the development of θυμός). It is perhaps used here instead of θυμῷ to avoid repetition after 204 (but cf. 434-6). It is not equivalent to θυμός in sense, as it refers not to feelings but more to one's tendencies or way of behaving, and its use here (especially in the plural) is odd. It has been referred to Iambe, who pleased Demeter 'by her ways' (e.g. A. Weiher, *Homerische Hymnen*, Tusculum-Bücherei, Munich, 1961: 'Später noch mochte sie Iambe ob ihres lebendigen Treibens'). But there is nothing to indicate that it should be taken this way. One should perhaps read ὀργῇ?

The line certainly refers, implicitly or openly, to Iambe's place in the cult. Hence the attempts of Voss and Mitscherlich to make this explicit by emendation. One might postulate a word ὀργή related to ὄργια, ἔργον, ἔρδω, etc. (cf. ad *Dem.* 273), and meaning '(sacred) rite'. The form would be normal and has been suggested (cf. Mlle Bader, *Les Composés grecs du type demiourgos* (Paris, 1965), 17 ff.), but there is no evidence for it, and one would have to read εὔαδ' ἐν ὀργαῖc (with unusual rhythm?). It is best to accept the generally held interpretation.

On the etymology, still uncertain, of ὀργή cf. Frisk, s.v., F. Specht, *Zeitschr. f. vergl. Sprachf.* 59 (1932), 91 f., O. Szemerenyi, *Syncope in Greek and Indo-European* (Naples, 1964), 219 ff.
On the termination -αιc cf. ad *Dem.* 40 f.

207. θεμιτόν: not elsewhere in early epic. Cf. Pi. *P.* 9. 42 οὐ θεμιτὸν ψευδεῖ θιγεῖν etc., and Hoekstra, *Sub-epic Stage*, 13, 19 n. 56, 20 n. 57. Wherever οὐ θέμιc occurs in Homer the context always refers explicitly to a divine sanction (*Il.* 14. 386, 16. 796, 23. 44, *Od.* 10. 73, 14. 56). The positive ἥ θέμιc ἐcτίν (etc.) is used more widely to mean 'the done thing' in any situation, but again usually with reference to institutions and customs subject to some form of divine regulation (e.g. ἀγορά and βουλή, the relations between man and woman, father and son, host and guest, oath-taking). R. Hirzel (*Themis, Dike und Verwandtes* (Leipzig, 1907), 39 ff.) interprets (οὐ) θέμιc, θεμιτόν in Homeric poetry as '(not) proper, fitting' (cf. *Et. M.*, Hsch. s.v. θέμιc). But the basic idea underlying it is of an 'order of nature' which should not be contravened. Cf. H. Vos, *Themis* (Assen, 1956), 22 ff. (and 15 f.: 'Weil θέμιc für das Handeln der Menschen den Mitmenschen und den Göttern gegenüber die Grenze zieht'). Cf. also E. Ehnmark, *The Idea of God in Homer* (Uppsala, 1935), 93 ff.

Here Schol. Nic. *Alex.* 130 (cf. ad 206 ff.) says that Demeter refused to drink wine because of her grief. A. Delatte (*Le Cycéon, Breuvage rituel d'Éleusis*, 43 f.) objects that abstention from wine is not required by Greek mourning customs. But it is part of her general abstention. In the context of the myth, the explanation is natural. Cf. *Il.* 23. 43 ff., where Achilles swears by Zeus that it is οὐ θέμιc for him to wash as long as Patroclus is unburied. It might be said that Demeter, as a goddess, creates a divine sanction by imposing it on herself. For the initiates who followed her example, it was οὐ θεμιτόν to take wine because Demeter had abstained. Cf. ad *Dem.* 211 (ὁcίηc ἕνεκεν), also 196.

The incident is commonly taken as the aition of the custom of νηφάλια (wineless offerings) which was widespread in the cult of Demeter and Core (cf. Allen and Halliday ad loc.; Wächter, *Reinheitsvorschriften*, 109, for examples, and Farnell, *Cults*, iii. 102, for exceptions). Presumably it implies also abstention from wine by the mystae (cf. Arbesmann, *Das Fasten*, 76, and perhaps Ar. *Nub.* 417). If this is the case, the prohibition is unlikely to have extended over the whole period of the Mystery celebrations, since Chabrias distributed wine on Boedromion 16 (the second day of the festival) in commemoration of his victory at Naxos (Plut. *Phoc.* 6; Polyaen. 3. 11. 2). He chose the day for the battle ὅτι ἦν μία τῶν μυcτηρίων (Polyaen. l.c.), and so is unlikely to have contravened the rules for the festival. Possibly the prohibition referred to the day of full νηcτεία (cf. ad *Dem.* 47 ff.) and what followed: the mystae might break their fast by means of the *cyceon*, but not with wine. At the Roman festival of the *sacra Cereris*, which was Greek in origin, wine was also forbidden. Cf. Ov. *Am.* 3. 10. 47 f., H. Le Bonniec, *Le Culte de Cérès à Rome* (Paris, 1958), 416 f.

οἱ: M's τοι is perhaps due to a wish to 'correct' the scansion. Ruhn-ken's γ' is unnecessary: neglect of the digamma of οἱ is very rare (cf. Maas, *Gk. Metre*, § 133, West, *Theogony*, 100).

208 ff. On the *cyceon*, its constitution and purpose, see Appendix IV.

208. ἄλφι: not elsewhere in early epic (Homeric ἄλφιτον, usually plural, but singular *Il.* 11. 631, *Od.* 14. 429). Cf. Antim. fr. 109 W. (Wyss ad loc.). It was explained as an apocope (Str. 8. 5. 3, 364; cf. *Suda* s.v., *Et. M.* 769. 39), but is probably the original form, from which ἄλφιτον was derived via the neuter plur. *ἄλφατα > ἄλφιτα (cf. Hsch. ἀλίφατα· ἄλφιτα ἢ ἄλευρα). Cf. Schwyzer, *Gr. Gr.* i. 518¹ (458⁷), Zumbach, *Neuerungen*, 5, Hoekstra, *Sub-epic Stage*, 57 (and 60 n. 62, suggesting that the phrase ἄλφι καὶ ὕδωρ might 'come from sacral Eleusinian language').

L. A. Moritz (*CQ* 42 (1948), 113 ff.) argues that originally the word was used of any type of grain, and indicated that it was prepared by a rough pounding (cf. Appendix IV), whereas ἄλευρα meant meal or flour. Later it acquired the specialized sense 'barley', and ἄλευρα that of 'wheat' (e.g. Pl. *Rep.* 372 b). He suggests that the nearest English equivalent would be 'groats'. But the Albanian *el'p*, *el'bi*, and Turco-tatar *arba* (< *arbi*), which are probably parallel forms, mean 'barley'.

209. The word order is a little involved and 'unformulaic'.

γληχῶνι τερείνῃ: this is not found in Homer. γληχών is Ionic, the Attic form being βληχών, and Doric and Boeotian γλαχώ(ν) (cf. Phryn. *PS* p. 53 B.). The phrase is formulaic (Hes. fr. 70. 21): hence there is no need to assume that the herb was fresh (cf. Delatte, *Le Cycéon*, 38 f.). Foucart (*Les Mystères*, 378), Pettazzoni (*I misteri*, 49), and others supposed that the dried herb was used. The accent is oxytone in Hes. l.c., Hippon. 84. 4. Cf. West, *Glotta* 1963, 284.

210. κυκεῶ: in Homer the accusative is κυκεῶ, κυκειῶ, later κυκεῶνα (cf. Chantraine, *GH* i. 212). Synizesis of εω is common in Homer (cf. Chantraine, *GH* i. 63 ff.). Note the inversion of the Homeric word order: cf. τεῦχε κυκειῶ, τεύξει τοι κυκεῶ, τεῦχε δέ μοι κυκεῶ, and Hoekstra, *Sub-epic Stage*, 52.

211. ὁσίης ἕνεκεν: ὁσίη occurs twice in the *Odyssey*, in the phrase οὐχ (οὐδ') ὁσίη (*Od.* 16. 423, 22. 412), and three times in the *Hymn to Hermes* (130, 173, 470). Translate here 'for the sake of the rite'. Cf. E. *IT* 1461 ὁσίας ἕκατι θεά θ' ὅπως τιμὰς ἔχῃ (of those who will in future perform the ritual which is at that moment being founded). Later ὁσίας ἕνεκα comes to mean 'for form's sake' (Eub. fr. 110. 2 K., Ephipp. 15. 4 K., Marinus, *Vit. Procl.* 19, etc.). ὁσίη means 'what may be (or is) done (according to divine regulation)', and hence 'rite'. On the development of the sense cf. J. C. Bolkestein, *"Οϲιοϲ en Εὐϲεβής* (Amsterdam, 1936); M. H. van der Valk, *Mnemosyne*, 3e sér. 10 (1942), 113 ff.; *RÉG* 64 (1951), 417 ff.; H. Jeanmaire, *RÉG* 58 (1945), 66 ff.

Allen and Halliday translate 'to save the rite', Humbert 'pour fonder la rite' (cf. Jeanmaire l.c.), van der Valk (*RÉG* 64, 417) 'à cause du rite solennel (sacré)'. There is an apparent difficulty in Demeter's doing something for the sake of a rite which she is at the same time founding. Cf. Delatte, *Le Cycéon*, 42 f., on the awkwardness of the expression. But his suggestion that the missing line(s) may have eased the situation is unconvincing. Demeter, in founding the rite, is also acting as the prototype of the initiates, and observing the prescription which she herself has created. Cf. ad *Dem.* 207 οὐ θεμιτόν.

ἕνεκεν occurs only twice in Homer (*Od.* 17. 288, 310). Cf. Hes. fr. 280. 23.

πολυπότνια: cf. Ar. *Thesm.* 1155 f. ὦ Θεσμοφόρω πολυποτνία, Orph. *Hy.* 40. 16, A.R. 1. 1125, 1151 (of Rhea/Cybele). The poet is fond of compounds with πολυ- (cf. Introduction, p. 61).

A lacuna is necessary after 211, and the conjectures designed to avoid it are unconvincing. ὁσίης ἕνεκεν and πολυπότνια should not be altered. Two lines may have been lost: (1) 'she drank it', (2) 'but when she had drunk it'. The lacuna is presumably due to the same cause as that after *Dem.* 137, 236: cf. Introduction, p. 66.

212–30. Metaneira welcomes and consoles Demeter, and asks her to look after her child, promising a rich recompense. Demeter replies, guaranteeing that she will protect him against all harm from sickness or from magic spells.

213 ff. This form of address to a stranger (greeting, compliment on his appearance, *consolatio*, and offer of assistance) is a kind of counterpart to the type of *Dem.* 135 ff. (cf. ad *Dem.* 137 f.). For a shorter form cf. *Dem.* 147 ff. (147–8 ~ 216–17: *consolatio*; 149 ff.: information and 157–9 promise of help; 159a ~ 213–15: compliment).

In the parallel scene in *Od.* 6. 148 ff. (cf. Appendix III) cf. Nausicaa's reply to Odysseus (187 ff.):

ξεῖν᾽, ἐπεὶ οὔτε κακῷ οὔτ᾽ ἄφρονι φωτὶ ἔοικας, ~ *Dem.* 213
Ζεὺς δ᾽ αὐτὸς νέμει ὄλβον Ὀλύμπιος ἀνθρώποισιν,
ἐσθλοῖς ἠδὲ κακοῖσιν, ὅπως ἐθέλησιν, ἑκάστῳ· } ~ *Dem.* 216–17
καί πού σοι τάδ᾽ ἔδωκε, σὲ δὲ χρὴ τετλάμεν ἔμπης. }
νῦν δ᾽, ἐπεὶ ἡμετέρην τε πόλιν καὶ γαῖαν ἱκάνεις, } ~ *Dem.* 218
οὔτ᾽ οὖν ἐσθῆτος δευήσεαι, οὔτε τευ ἄλλου . . . }

Cf. *Ap.* 464 ff.:

ξεῖν᾽, ἐπεὶ οὐ μὲν γάρ τι καταθνητοῖσιν ἔοικας
οὐ δέμας οὐδὲ φυήν, ἀλλ᾽ ἀθανάτοισι θεοῖσιν,
οὖλέ τε καὶ μέγα χαῖρε, θεοὶ δέ τοι ὄλβια δοῖεν. ~ *Dem.* 225

Cf. also *Od.* 18. 125 ff. (122 f. ~ *Dem.* 225):

125–8 ~ *Dem.* 213–15
129–42 ~ 216–17 (cf. ad *Dem.* 256 ff.),

and *Od.* 20. 194 ff., 199 ff.:

194 ~ *Dem.* 213–15
195–6 (ἀλλὰ θεοί 195 ~ *Dem.* 216a) ~ 216–17
199a ~ 213a (199 f. ~ *Dem.* 225)

(*Od.* 20. 227 ~ 6. 187 above).

For the form cf. also *Od.* 11. 248 ff.: χαῖρε γύναι ... ἐπεὶ οὐκ ... νῦν δ' ...

213 f. For this type of sentence ('not *x* but the opposite') cf. ad *Dem.* 114 f.

214 f. αἰδώς and χάρις were thought of as having their seat in the eyes. Cf. for αἰδώς Sappho, fr. 137. 5, Aesch. fr. 355. 21 ff. M., E. *Hec.* 970–2, fr. 457, Xen. *Resp. Lac.* 3. 5 ap. Longin. 4 § 4 (cf. Russell ad loc.), Ar. *Vesp.* 446 f., Arist. fr. 96 (Rose) ap. Ath. 564 b; also [Arist.] *Physiogn.* 807ᵇ28, Call. *Aetia* fr. ap. P. Antinoop. 3. 113. 7 (on which see A. W. Bulloch, *CQ* 20 (1970), 270 f.), 2 Peter 2: 14, etc. αἰδὼς ἐν ὀφθαλμοῖς was proverbial: Eust. *Il.* 13. 121 (923), *Od.* 14. 145 (1754). Already in Homer shamelessness is located in the eyes: *Il.* 1. 225 (cf. *Il.* 1. 159 etc.). For χάρις cf. Sappho 138. 2, E. *Ba.* 236, etc. Cf. also M. Treu, *Von Homer zu Lyrik* (Zetemata 12, Munich, 1955), 248, 62, 252, etc.

αἰδώς in Homer is normally felt by a person towards someone else, or in a situation of which he is 'ashamed'. Here it is a quality distinguishing those who are royal. This suggests that it is the reverence which they arouse in others, and which makes them 'reverend'. Cf. perhaps *Od.* 8. 172, and αἰδοῖος of a king or queen: *Il.* 4. 402, *Od.* 18. 314, Hes. *Th.* 80, 434, frr. 43 (a). 89, 361 (cf. *Il.* 10. 237 ff., *Th.* 92; West, ad *Th.* 84 ff., argues that αἰδώς is more suitably used here than in *Od.* 8. 172; cf. also Edwards, *Language of Hesiod*, 168 f.). Demeter and Persephone are αἰδοῖαι (*Dem.* 343, 374, 486), and Demeter's epiphany arouses αἰδώς in Metaneira (190). Cf. also notes to *Dem.* 190, 478 f.

The whole sentiment of 213–15 ('the dignity displayed in your look declares a royal ancestry') is perhaps paralleled by Pi. *P.* 5. 15–19 ὅτι βασιλεύς ἐσσι ... · ἔχει συγγενὴς ὀφθαλμὸς αἰδοιότατον γέρας τεᾷ τοῦτο μειγνύμενον φρενί (cf. R. W. B. Burton, *Pindar's Pythian Odes*, 141).

215. ὡς εἴ πέρ τε: not found elsewhere. Cf. Homeric ὡς εἴ τε, ὡσεί ... περ Hes. *Sc.* 189, ὡσείπερ Theocr. 25. 163 cod. (εἰ περὶ σεῦ Wilamowitz).

θεμιστοπόλων βασιλήων: cf. ad *Dem.* 103. In the parallel passages *Od.* 4. 63, *Hy.* 7. 11 (cf. ad *Dem.* 213 ff.) the Homeric doublet διοτρεφέων βασιλήων is used.

216–17. ἀνάγκη τέτλαμεν ... ἐπὶ γὰρ ζυγὸς αὐχένι κεῖται: this suggests the 'yoke of necessity'. The phrase does not occur in Homer, but cf. *Il.* 6. 458 κρατερὴ δ' ἐπικείσετ' ἀνάγκη. For examples in later literature cf. A. *Ag.* 218, Fraenkel ad loc., and also Orph. *Hy.* 61. 5 (to Nemesis), E. *Heracl.* 886, Hdt. 1. 11, 9. 16, Pl. *Menex.* 240 c, Moschion fr. 2, Lucian, *Erotes* 38. H. Schreckenberg, *Ananke* (Zetemata 36, Munich, 1964), argues that ἀνάγκη originally meant 'band, yoke'. Although his main argument is not convincing, he has a useful collection of material (esp. pp. 18 n. 16, 36 ff., 79 n. 20). Cf. reviews by Adkins, *CR* 80 (1966), 68 ff., Gottschalk, *JHS* 86 (1966), 213 f. For the idea of 216–17 cf. also Pi. *P.* 2. 93 φέρειν δ' ἐλαφρῶς ἐπαυχένιον λαβόντα ζυγὸν ἀρήγει, with the whole of 88 ff. (χρὴ δὲ πρὸς θεὸν οὐκ ἐρίζειν, ὃς . . .).

217. ἐπὶ γάρ... κεῖται: cf. Hes. *Op.* 815, Theognis 1357, Call. fr. 4 Pf., *Orph. Hy.* 61. 5, and other parallels ap. Rzach ad Hes. *Op.* 815.
ζυγός: this form is first used here, but occurs as a v.l. in *Il.* 9. 187. Cf. Pl. *Tim.* 63 b (where it means 'balance'), Theocr. 30. 29, etc. It is perhaps the original form of the singular (Schwyzer, *Gr. Gr.* i. 581⁵, ii. 37³, Zumbach, *Neuerungen*, 5. But cf. Debrunner, *Rev. ét. Indoeur.* 3 (1943), 172–4).
Ammon. *de adf. voc. diff.* 214 (Nickau) distinguishes the sense of masculine and neuter: ἀρϲενικῶϲ μὲν ἐπὶ τῶν βοῶν, οὐδετέρωϲ δὲ (θηλυκῶϲ δὲ codd.) ἐπὶ τοῦ ϲταθμοῦ.

219. ὀψίγονον: cf. ad *Dem.* 165.
ἄελπτον: not in Homer. Cf. *Ap.* 91, Hes. fr. 204. 95 (ἄελπτον). Cf. ad *Dem.* 164.

220. πολυάρητος: cf. *Dem.* 165 πολυεύχετος. Πολυάρητος is found as a name in Paros (N. Kontoleon, *Archiloque*, Fond. Hardt, vol. X (1963), 68), and Tanagra (Bechtel, *Personennamen*, 377).

221–3. These lines virtually repeat *Dem.* 166–8.
221. γ' ἐκθρέψαιο: Hermann's correction is probably right. The prefix conveys the verbal aspect, and is supported by *Dem.* 166.
223. δοίην: the first person is right, as it is Metaneira who rewards the nurse. Cf. ad *Dem.* 168.
224. ἐϋϲτέφανος: used of Artemis, Aphrodite, the heroine Mycene, and Thebes (*Il.* 19. 99 ~ *Od.* 2. 120) in Homer, of Demeter in Hesiod, *Op.* 300. Demeter has a crown of corn in later representations (cf. Bömer ad Ov. *F.* 4. 616), but the epithet is probably general.
225. The reply is traditional, but here there is an irony in its use by Demeter. Cf. ad *Dem.* 147 f.
ἐϲθλά: 'good things, gifts'. Cf. Hes. *Op.* 116, 119, Solon, fr. 23. 2, Theognis 4, etc.
226. πρόφρων: this is used especially of a favourable deity. Cf. *Dem.* 487, 494, West ad Hes. *Th.* 419 (also for its use with ὑποδέχεϲθαι), Keyssner, *Gottesvorstellung*, 89, Zuntz, *Persephone*, 317 n. 2 (on *IG* 14. 641. 2. 7).
227. θρέψω: the asyndeton is striking, but should not be removed. θρέψω resumes ὑποδέξομαι, and is also emphatically placed, in contrast with the following clause. Cf. K–G ii. 339 ff. (especially § 546. 4 and 5β), Chantraine, *GH* ii. 351. For ὑποδέξομαι . . . θρέψω cf. Hes. *Th.* 479 f., frr. 30. 30, 165. 6 f., *Hy.* 26. 3 f.
κοὐ: this crasis does not occur in Homer. Cf. perhaps Hes. fr. 62. 3 (καὶ οὐ Eust.: κοὐ Rossbach: but see West, Merkelbach ad loc.), Parm. fr. 6. 7 D.–K.
κακοφραδίηϲι: not in Homer (except as v.l. at *Od.* 2. 236). Cf. Nic. *Ther.* 348, Q.S. 12. 554. The plural occurs only here. Homer has κακοφραδέϲ (*Il.* 23. 483), ἀφραδίη (*Il.* 2. 368), κακορραφίηϲι (*Od.* 2. 236).
For Demeter as κουροτρόφος cf. ad *Dem.* 231 ff. In the Sicyonian version she nurses Orthopolis, son of Plemnaeus, king of Aegialeia

(Paus. 2. 5. 8). Cf. Demeter 'Europa', the nurse of Trophonius (Paus. 9. 39. 5). For Athens cf. Farnell, *Cults*, iii. 333 n. 109, and Triptolemus' title Θρεπτός (cf. ad *Dem.* 153).

228–30. Demeter promises to protect the child against illness and magic. The language is similar to that of magical formulae. Cf. the Phalasarna lead tablet (fourth century B.C.) in Maas, *Hesp.* 13. 1 (1944), 36 f. He emends verses 11 f. to read: οὔ με καταχρί[cτω]ι δηλή-cεται οὔτ' ἐπενίκτωι οὔτε πότωι, comparing *Dem.* 228, and suggests that both may depend on a hexameter charm similar to those of the Philinna papyrus (*JHS* 62 (1942), 33 ff.).

The 'incantatory' character is emphasized formally by repetition and balanced, chiastic arrangement. *Dem.* 229 f. takes up the subjects of 228 in reverse order, with anaphora of οἶδα (cf. West ad Hes. *Th.* 27 f. for anaphora of parts of εἰδέναι. *Th.* 27 f. and *Od.* 12. 189–91 are sung by the Muses and Sirens, and *Il.* 7. 237 f. might be part of an archaic war-chant. Cf. also Pi. fr. 137 (a) Sn., ad *Dem.* 480–2). For magic formulae with antithetical repetition cf. Sappho, fr. 1. 21–4, A. Cameron, *HTR* 32 (1939), 8.

There is also repetition in ὑποταμνόν . . . ἀντίτομον . . . ὑλοτόμοιο, and double chiasmus in 229 f.:

A   B
ἀντίτομον . . . ὑλοτόμοιο ∼
B   b   a   A
ἐπηλυcίηc πολυπήμονος ἐcθλὸν ἐρυcμόν

For a similar 'incantatory' effect due to rhyme cf. *Dem.* 238 (n. ad loc.). See also Introduction, p. 61.

For Demeter as a goddess of healing and health cf. Call. *Hy.* 6. 124 f., *Orph. Hy.* 40. 20, *AP* 9. 298, Artemid. *Oneir.* 2. 39 (p. 144 Hercher), Ov. *F.* 4. 547 ff. Ex-votos from Eleusis and elsewhere record restoration of sight: cf. Kern, *Eph. Arch.* 1892, 114 ff., *Ann. d. Inst.* 33 (1861), 380 ff., P. Roussel, *Délos, colonie athénienne*, 244. In general, cf. O. Rubensohn, *AM* 20 (1895), 360 ff., 'Demeter als Heilgottheit'. The connection of Demeter and Core with Asclepius is perhaps due to this (but Rubensohn has doubts).

Demeter's antidotes may be either herbs or spells. In Ov. *F.* 4. 547 f. she heals the sick child Triptolemus by incantation and also by giving him poppy-juice and warm milk to make him sleep. In Homer, both spells (*Il.* 19. 457 f.) and herbs (*Il.* 11. 740) are used in medicine. Cf. also *Il.* 4. 218 (etc.), *Od.* 10. 302 ff.

228. ἐπηλυcίη: not in Homer or Hesiod. Cf. *Dem.* 230, *Herm.* 37; Hsch. s.v. . . . ἐπῳδὴ φαρμάκων, ἢ ἔφοδός τινος; Poll. 4. 187 (in list of diseases, between πλευρῖτιc and cτραγγουρία); Nonn. *D.* 14. 328 (= 'attack' of a god, in battle). Cf. ἐπήλυcιc (Call. fr. 331 etc.) 'assault, attack'.

It must refer here to the 'attacks' of pain, fever, etc. suffered by children, which were ascribed to the ἐπηλυcίη of some demon. Cf. the ἔφοδοι of heroes and Hecate (Nilsson, *Gesch.*, i ³. 182 ff., 723 f.) or the Erinyes (A. *Eum.* 370), Ephialtes the nightmare demon (cf. Leumann, *Hom. Wörter*, 80 n. 45), ἐπίληψις etc.

ὑποταμνόν: on this, ἀντίτομον, and ὑλοτόμοιο cf. A. Delatte, *Herbarius*³, 10 ff., 23 ff., Pfister, *RE* 19. 1446 f., *Byz. Zeitschr.* 37 (1937), 382. They must all refer to the same thing, namely the cutting of herbs for magical purposes. ὑποτάμνω (once in Homer, *Od.* 23. 204) = *succidere*. It refers to the cutting of the root (hence ῥιζοτόμος of someone who does so for magic purposes). Cf. Luc. *Tim.* 8 τὰς ῥίζας ὑποτετμημένον, Ov. *M.* 7. 226 f. (of Medea) 'et placitas herbas partim radice revellit, partim succidit curvamine falcis aenae'; Sen. *Med.* 729 'illius alta nocte succisus frutex'; Ps. Apul. *de herbis* 92. 8, *Antidotarium Bruxellense*, 2. 157. The root was cut in order to tap the juice. Cf. Soph. *Ῥιζοτόμοι* fr. 534, and Pearson ad loc.

ὑποτάμνόν (M's reading) occurs nowhere else in Greek. There are many plant-names with a similar termination (cf. Chantraine, *La Formation des noms*, 216 on the -mn- group of nouns. Some of these may be prehellenic, e.g. δίκταμνον, but ῥάδαμνος is apparently connected with ῥάδιξ, ῥίζα, etc.). ὑποταμνόν might be influenced by these. But a specific plant is not what is wanted here. Either the action of 'undercutting' or the agent (an 'undercutter') should be referred to (cf. on ὑλοτόμοιο 229). To take ὑποτάμνον, the neuter participle, as a noun ('cutting') is difficult. (There are no examples of this in Homer: cf. Schwyzer, *Gr. Gr.* ii. 408.) Delatte (l.c.) prefers ὑποτάμνων ('cutter'), and for the participle compares Chantraine, *GH* ii. 321. But the examples quoted there are not parallel. The form of the word remains unexplained.

229. ἀντίτομον: this occurs first here. Cf. Pi. *P.* 4. 221 ἀντίτομα ὀδυνᾶν (cf. Schol.); Hsch. s.v.: φάρμακον ἀντιπαθές, ὅπερ ὁ πιὼν οὐ βλάπτεται ὑπό τινος· ἀλεξιφάρμακον. Cf. A. *Ag.* 17 ὕπνου τόδ᾽ ἀντίμολπον ἐντέμνων ἄκος (Fraenkel ad loc.), E. *Alc.* 971 φάρμακα πολυπόνοις ἀντιτεμὼν βροτοῖσιν. It means a herb or root cut to counter a disease or spell, hence any antidote or remedy. Cf. Delatte, *Herbarius*, 11.

ὑλοτόμοιο: in Homer ὑλοτόμος means 'woodcutter' (as epithet of an axe, *Il.* 23. 114; as a noun *Il.* 23. 123). LSJ suggest here ὑλότομον, meaning 'plant cut in the wood', but it is hard to see how it can have this sense. ὕλη can, however, refer to all kinds of plants: it is used of undergrowth (*Il.* 12. 148 etc.), and in Theophr. *HP* 4. 4. 5 ὑλήματα are classed between δένδρα and πόῶδη, and include (4. 5. 1) τὰ φαρμακώδη ταῖς ῥίζαις καὶ τοῖς ὀποῖς, οἷον ἐλλέβορος ἐλατήριον σκαμμωνία, σχεδὸν πάντα τὰ ῥιζοτομούμενα. A ὑλοτόμος then could be a ῥιζοτόμος (cf. Delatte, o.c. 23 ff.). For the brachylogy 'an antidote more powerful than the herb-cutter' cf. K–G ii, § 597κ ff.

230. πολυπήμονος: this does not occur in Homer or Hesiod. Cf. *Od.* 24. 305 υἱὸς Ἀφείδαντος Πολυπημονίδαο (the name may have been related to πολυπήμων by a misunderstanding. Cf. *Il.* 4. 433 πολυπάμονος ἀνδρός 'very wealthy', which fits Ἀφείδας; K. Meister, *Hom. Kunstsprache*, 168 f.). Cf. also *Herm.* 37.

In Alcm. *PMG* 5 fr. 2 i 9 πολυπήμων perhaps means 'hurtful' (cf.

Lobel ad loc.; West, *CQ* 15 (1965), 188). Cf. Pi. *P.* 3. 46 πολυπήμονας
ἰᾶcθαι νόcουc, Opp. *C.* 2. 287 φάρμακον . . . πολυπήμονοc ἄτηc.

ἐρυcμόν: not in Homer or Hesiod. Cf. ἔρυμα (*Il.* 4. 137). In Paus.
Gr. fr. 182, it is the name of a vegetable whose seed was eaten by
women to relieve them in childbirth. Cf. perhaps ἐρυθμόc (Ps. Dsc. 2.
167), the name of a plant also called ἐφιάλτιον, used against an ἐφιάλτηc
(cf. ad *Dem.* 228), and ἐρύcιμον (Ps. Dsc. 2. 158).

231-55. Demeter takes the child in her arms, and nurses him. He
grows wonderfully, being anointed by her with ambrosia. She breathes
on him and holds him in her bosom, and at night she hides him
secretly in the fire like a brand. His parents are amazed at the way
he is growing. She would have made him immortal, if Metaneira
had not watched her, and cried out in terror for her child. Demeter
was terribly angry, and taking him from the fire she placed him on the
floor, and addressed Metaneira.

Demeter's nursing of Demophon, and her attempt to make him
immortal, form the centre-piece of her visit to Eleusis. It is natural
that attempts have been made to find in the story an *aition* for part of
the ritual of the Mysteries.

1. *Demophon in the fire*

The most striking element is Demophon's 'baptism of fire'. Frazer
(*Apollodorus*, ii. 311–17, Appendix I) explained the story by reference
to the practice, common in many countries, of passing children across
or taking them round the family hearth soon after birth. Various
reasons are given for this: to protect them from evil spirits, give them
strength, or see if they are changelings. In Greece it was the custom
(called Ἀμφιδρόμια) for those who had had contact with the birth
to purify their hands, and taking the baby to run with it round the
hearth. This took place a few days after the birth (cf. *Suda* s.v. and
Schol. Pl. *Theaet.* 160 e: on the fifth day; Hsch. s.v. δρομιάμφιον ἦμαρ:
seventh day; Schol. Ar. *Lys.* 758: tenth day). One authority (Schol.
Ar. l.c.) says that the child was laid down, presumably on the ground,
and they ran round it (περιδραμόντεc κειμένουc). On the seventh or
tenth day the child was given his name (*Suda*, Hsch. ἀμφιδρόμια,
Schol. Ar. *Lys.* 758, Harpocr. s.v. ἑβδομευομένου, Arist. *HA* 7. 67,
etc.).

It is clear from the reference to this ceremony in Plato (*Theaet.*
160 e) that it was primarily an adoption-ritual, similar to that used
on the introduction of a bride to her new home, or of a new slave (cf.
E. Samter, *Familienfeste der Griechen und Römer* (Berlin, 1901), 61 f.).
The child is made a part of the new household by contact with the
hearth. There may, of course, also be an idea of purification (Preuner,
Hestia-Vesta (Tübingen, 1864), 53 ff.). Plato (l.c.) suggests that the
ritual is actually a test of the child, to see whether it is genuine (τὰ
ἀμφιδρόμια αὐτοῦ ὡc ἀληθῶc ἐν κύκλῳ περιθρεκτέον, cκοπουμένουc μὴ
λάθῃ ἡμᾶc οὐκ ἄξιον ὂν τροφῆc τὸ γιγνόμενον). This is the case in some

other similar rituals, where if the child is a changeling it disappears when placed on the fire (cf. Frazer, l.c. Cf. also Dieterich, *Mutter Erde*, 6 ff.).

That the child may have been placed *on the ground* (Schol. Ar. l.c.) is supported by the parallel Roman custom of doing this at birth (e.g. Ovid, *Tr.* 4. 3. 46 f.), and that of other countries (cf. Samter, o.c. 63 ff., and *Geburt, Hochzeit und Tod* (Leipzig, 1911), 1 ff.). Probably it was placed by the hearth (as was done with new slaves: cf. Samter, *Familienfeste*, 1 ff.). J. Heckenbach, *De nuditate sacra* (Giessen, 1911), 47, cites two examples from Roman art where a child is shown on the ground, probably in a similar context.

In the story of Demophon, the child is actually placed in the fire, and after Demeter has been discovered, she places it on the ground (*Dem.* 253). The purpose of the fire-baptism is, of course, immortalization, but the child is also adopted by Demeter, as its τροφός (see below). There are thus some similarities to the Amphidromia, but there are also differences, and one therefore hesitates to say that the Demophon story refers primarily to this custom.

Allen and Halliday (ad *Dem.* 237 ff.) follow Frazer, concluding that 'the reference is to a domestic rite of infancy, and not to any part of the ritual of the mysteries.' Halliday, however, in a general discussion of this and related stories, in *CR* 25 (1911), 8 ff., was more open-minded. He compared myths of immortalization by immersion in water, and saw the main purpose as 'union with a magical or divine power', but added that the ideas of an initiatory 'death to new life', of ordeal, and of purification might play a part.

The close similarity of domestic 'rites of passage', connected with birth, marriage, and death, to those of mystery-cults, has often been remarked (cf. e.g. Samter, *Familienfeste*, 97 ff.), and one is therefore inclined to take the similarity to the Amphidromia as indicating a reference to an actual Eleusinian ritual, rather than a domestic rite. Torches are used in the purification of Heracles (cf. ad *Dem.* 192 ff.) on the Torre Nova sarcophagus, just as they are used in marriage-ceremonies. On the Lovatelli urn, a λίκνον is used, as also in marriage- and birth-rites (Samter, *Familienfeste*, 1 ff., 98 ff.), and the use of the Διὸς κῴδιον and veiling of the head has parallels in marriage-ritual (Samter, o.c. 100 ff.). These similarities may be explained by the character of the mystic initiation as a rite of adoption, with which the idea of purification is also associated.

A link between the Demophon myth and that of Heracles is provided by the fifth-century B.C. Attic relief from the Este collection, which shows a child seated on the ground, between two women and a man. One of the women holds two torches, one raised and the other lowered and held out towards the child (cf. O. Walter, *Öst. Jahresh.* 30 (1936), 50 ff., Nilsson, *ARW* 34 (1937), 108 ff. and Pl. I = *Op. Sel.* ii. 624 ff.). The gesture of holding a raised and lowered torch occurs on Eleusinian monuments (Mylonas, *Eleusis*, Figs. 67, 88) and one can compare the priestess holding torch(es) on the Torre Nova sarcophagus. Nilsson saw the scene as a portrayal of the Demophon story, and identified the figures as Metaneira, Demeter, Demophon, and Celeus. This is obviously conjectural, but the resemblance to the Demophon and Heracles myths is notable.

A further clue may be provided by the mysterious παῖς ἀφ' ἑςτίας μυηθείς.[1] This was a child chosen from a leading Athenian family, and δημοςίᾳ μυηθείς (Bekker, *Anecd.* I, p. 204). According to Porphyry (*de Abstin.* 4. 5) ἐν τοῖς μυςτηρίοις . . . ἀντὶ πάντων τῶν μυουμένων ἀπομειλίςςεται τὸ θεῖον, ἀκριβῶς δρῶν τὰ προςτεταγμένα. This suggests some form of purification ceremony (ἀπομειλίςςεται), in which evidently the child represents the community.

The ἑςτία is normally explained as the State hearth, that of the Prytaneum. One may note that this was said to have been founded by Celeus (Plut. *Mor.* 667 d), and that Celeus' descendants, the Croconidae, had a cult of Ἑςτία (*IG* ii². 1229).

This suggests that the Demophon story may have reference to part of the preliminary ritual of purification (cf. ad *Dem.* 192 ff.). It follows directly after the ritual of the Διὸς κῴδιον and κυκεών, and precedes Demeter's promise to teach her ὄργια (273-4). The fact that it occurs in the poem at all may suggest that it is not directly related to the central part of the Mysteries, whose secrecy was absolute (*Dem.* 478-9).

A connection has, however, been seen between Demophon, hidden πυρὶ ἐνὶ πολλῷ (248), and the announcement which according to Hippolytus (*Ref. Haer.* 5. 8. 39 p. 96 W.) was made by the hierophant at the climax of the Mysteries, ὑπὸ πολλῷ πυρί, when he cried ἱερὸν ἔτεκε πότνια κοῦρον, βριμὼ βριμόν (cf. Wehrli, *ARW* 31 (1934), 91 ff., Kern, *Rel. d. Gr.* ii. 142 f.). Demeter as nurse of the child is thus compared to the mother of the κοῦρος in the mystic formula. The role of fire inside the Telesterion is stressed by several ancient authors. But ὑπὸ πολλῷ πυρί probably means 'with the accompaniment of a great fire', and refers to the sudden blaze of torches, contrasting with the former darkness (Kern, *RE* 16. 124. 3 f.). One should therefore hesitate to speak of the child as born 'in the fire'. Ingenious attempts have also been made to show a pattern of stories of 'apotheosis by fire' at Eleusis (Ch. Picard, 'Les bûchers sacrés d'Éleusis', *RHR* 107 (1933), 137-54). In Euripides' *Supplices* the pyres of the Seven against Thebes are at Eleusis, and the body of Capaneus, killed by Zeus' thunderbolt (a form of apotheosis: cf. Nilsson, *Gesch.* i³. 71 ff., Burkert, *Glotta* 39 (1960-1), 208 ff.), was burnt within the sanctuary. His wife Euadne threw herself on to the pyre (cf. ad *Dem.* 200). A historical parallel is the story of the Brahman Zarmarus, or Zarmanochegas, who was initiated with Augustus at Eleusis, and then immolated himself 'according to his ancestral custom' (Str. 15. 1. 73; Dio Cass. 54. 9. 10; cf. Kerényi, *Eleusis*, 100 f.). The parallels are interesting, but cannot be said to prove anything. Picard's theory is criticized by C. M. Edsman, *Ignis Divinus* (Lund, 1949), 227 ff.

[1] Cf. A. Mommsen, *Feste*, 273 ff., Töpffer, *Att. Genealogie*, 107 ff., G. Murray *Rise of the Greek Epic*, Appendix G, K. Kerényi, *Eleusis*, 80 ff.

A difficulty in such theories is that Demophon does not in fact become immortal, and Demeter's attempt fails. The honour promised to
Demophon is in fact associated with his mortality, since he will die
and receive a festival in his honour (*Dem.* 260–7). The initiates,
however, receive the promise of happiness after death (*Dem.* 480 ff.).

Eitrem (*Symb. Osl.* 20 (1940), 148 ff.) has a possible answer to
this. The initiates are not in fact promised immortality, and the *Hymn*
explains why: it is our fault for spoiling the gods' work (*Dem.* 256 ff.).
But they do receive the Mysteries, which promise a better fate. Man
does not become θεόc or θεῖοc, but rather ὄλβιοc, and freed from fear
of death.

This interpretation would fit the view that the myth is connected
with a preliminary ritual. At the same time one should remember that
one cannot expect the relations of myth to ritual to follow the rules
of strict logic and it may be wrong to press the details of the story too
far. Heroes in general are notably ambiguous when it comes to their
status after death. One thinks above all of Heracles' dual status, and
his apotheosis by fire on Mt. Oeta, as well as of other heroes such
as Melicertes 'immortalized in the cauldron' (cf. ad *Dem.* 265–6),
Pelops, who enjoyed the same fate, and Achilles (cf. ad *Dem.* 237 ff.).
In all such cases, myths of their death alternate with stories of immortalization, partial or complete. (Cf. also the dual position of the
Dioscuri.) One is thus reluctant to deny all possible connection between Demophon and the central part of the Mysteries, with its
message of the birth of a κοῦροc.

2. *Demophon and Erichthonius*

Demophon is the Θρεπτόc of Demeter, a title which occurs in Eleusinian cult (cf. ad *Dem.* 153). He is thus very similar above all to the
nursling of Athene, Erichthonius-Erechtheus, child of Earth, who received annual sacrifices at Athens (*Il.* 2. 547–51; cf. ad *Dem.* 265–6),
and instituted the Panathenaic Games. The birth of Erichthonius is
portrayed in art in an exactly parallel form to that of the birth of
a divine child at Eleusis, who is usually identified as Ploutos, the son
of Demeter (cf. ad *Dem.* 489). In the cult, this child is nameless: he is
simply the Κοῦροc (or Θρεπτόc).

The myth of Erichthonius is commemorated by the ritual of the
Arrephoria, and the parallels between this and Eleusinian ritual have
been studied by W. Burkert, in *Hermes* 94 (1966), 1 ff. The child was
entrusted by Athene to the daughters of Cecrops, on the Acropolis
at Athens, in a κίcτη which they were forbidden to open. Like
Metaneira, they were overcome by curiosity (*Dem.* 244), and looked
inside. The result was disastrous: two, or all of them, killed themselves, or were killed by the snake(s) which they found coiled round
the child. The ἀρρηφόροι were four girls, aged between seven and
eleven, who lived for a time on the Acropolis, of whom two were
entrusted with the weaving of the πέπλοc offered to Athene at the
Panathenaea. At the Arrephoria two of them were given some sacred

objects in κίcται by the priestess of Athene, which they took down a secret path to the περίβολος of Aphrodite under the Acropolis. Here they left them, and brought back another sacred object, wrapped up (Paus. 1. 27. 3).

The ἀρρηφόροι were chosen from noble families, and dedicatory inscriptions survive, testifying to those who performed this office, which may be compared with those commemorating the παῖδες ἀφ' ἑστίας at Eleusis (Burkert, o.c. 5 n. 3). In both cases, the children represent the whole community, and are well-born. The preliminary rites at Eleusis probably involved the κίcτη and κάλαθος (cf. ad Dem. 192 ff.). At Eleusis, Demophon was honoured with contests (Βαλλητύς: cf. ad Dem. 265 ff.), which may have developed into the Eleusinian Games, as Erichthonius is connected with the Panathenaea.

There may also be a parallel to be drawn between the Cecropids (and ἀρρηφόροι) and the daughters of Celeus, who were the first priestesses at Eleusis (cf. ad Dem. 105 ff.). It was the priestesses who carried the κίcται containing the sacred objects from Eleusis to Athens. At Eleusis the Caryatids of the Lesser Propylaea show girls carrying such κίcται (Mylonas, Eleusis, 245), and may be compared to the Caryatids of the Erechtheum. The dancing-ground of the Cecropids (Eur. Ion 495 ff.; cf. Plut. Vit. X Or. 839 c) suggests comparison with the 'well of the fair dances' where Celeus' daughters met Demeter. In both cults, the role of the ephebes was also important. In Athens they took their oath at the sanctuary of Aglauros, escorted the Panathenaic procession, and competed in the games. At Eleusis they took part in the sacrifices (cf. ad Dem. 265-7), at least in the Roman period, escorted the ἱερά to Athens (Mylonas, o.c. 246; cf. Burkert, o.c. 12), and probably were the παῖδες Ἐλευcινίων who took part in the Βαλλητύς (cf. ad Dem. 266).

To the parallels which Burkert adduces, one could add the recent discovery of a theatre court on the north side of the Erechtheum, with steps round it and an altar in the centre. Such 'theatral areas' have been found in sanctuaries of Demeter, at Lycosura (Berve and Gruben, Greek Temples, Theatres and Shrines (London, 1963), 389), and Corinth (R. S. Stroud, Hesp. 37 (1968), 299 ff.), and were presumably used for displays of secret rites, like the Telesterion at Eleusis (and perhaps the platform by the Sacred Way, next to the Ploutonion: Mylonas, o.c. 143 ff.).

The parallels with Erichthonius strengthen the supposition that Demophon is one name for the Eleusinian κοῦρος, and that the story of his nursing by Demeter may have relevance not only to the preliminary rites but also to the Mysteries proper.

3. Demophon's 'adoption'

Demophon's projected immortalization is to be brought about not only by fire, but also by (a) anointing with ambrosia, (b) breathing on him with divine breath, (c) holding him in the bosom of the goddess. These are all ways of imparting divine strength (cf. ad Dem. 237 ff.), and with the fire, they suggest comparison with later cults. The use of divine breath and fire may perhaps be compared with the Christian 'baptism in the holy Spirit and fire' (Matt. 3: 11, Luke 3: 16), and in Acts 10: 38 'the Lord *anointed* him with the holy Spirit and with strength' (cf. Pfister, *Würzb. Jahrb.* 3 (1948), 273 ff.). On the gold-leaf plates found in graves in various parts of the Graeco-Roman world (Orph. fr. 32) the dead man claims

Δεσποίνας δ' ὑπὸ κόλπον ἔδυν χθονίας βασιλείας

(cf. fr. 32 (c). 8, and also fr. 31. i 24, fr. 52 v. 3, *Orph. Hy.* 52. 11), indicating that he has come into the protection of the goddess, if not that he has actually been adopted by her.[1] At Eleusis, the announcement of the birth of the child is explained by the Gnostic source of Hippolytus as referring to a spiritual or heavenly rebirth. These testimonies are much later, and must be used with caution. But it seems reasonable to suppose that the nursing of Demophon is relevant to the promise made to the initiate in the Mysteries, not of immortality but rather of divine favour and protection after death (cf. *Dem.* 260 ff., 480 ff.).

That the initiate stands in the same relationship to the Eleusinian goddesses as Demophon to Demeter is also suggested by Soph. *OC* 1050–1 (cf. ad *Dem.* 142, and Kern, *RE* 16. 1239. 38 ff.): 'the torch-lit shores, where the Potniai are nurses (τιθηνοῦνται) of the dread rites for mortals . . .'

In conclusion, we may say that whilst we have found some indications of a connection between the Demophon myth and the preliminary ritual of purification, it is also possible to see in it a wider relevance, and to link it with the central significance of the Mysteries (cf. Introduction, pp. 26 ff.). See also notes to *Dem.* 265–7.

231. θυώδεϊ . . . κόλπῳ: this poet is fond of θυώδης: cf. 244, 288, 331, 355, 385; also θυόεις 97, 318, 490, θυήεις 277.

232. χερσίν τ' ἀθανάτῃσι: M has ἀθανάτοισι. The adjective is normally three-termination in Homer (but cf. -οις(ι) as v.l. in *Il.* 7. 32, 16. 704, *Od.* 24. 47, 55, *Ap.* 130, *Aph.* 190; cf. ἀκαμάτῃσι/-οισι Hes. *Th.* 519, 747). So also in later poetry in the sense 'undying, immortal' (cf. LSJ s.v.). The two-termination use is ancient (cf. Schwyzer, *Gr. Gr.* ii. 32), but -ῃσιν is probably to be read here. Cf. especially *Dem.* 253.

233 f. Demophon receives a stately two lines, in which both his parents are named, as an introduction to the passage describing his nursing. Cf. ad *Dem.* 192.

234. The child is named here for the first time. The name was originally Δημοφάων: cf. Kretschmer, *Gr. Vaseninschr.* 142, no. 126 ΔΕΜΟΦΑΟΝ. Priscian (*Inst. Gramm.* 1. 22, 6. 69) read ΔΗΜΟΦΑϜΩΝ 'in tripode vetustissimo Apollinis, qui stat in Xerolopho Byzantii'. Elsewhere on vases it is always Δημοφῶν. Cf. Kretschmer, l.c., Cauer,

---

[1] Cf. Dieterich, *Eine Mithrasliturgie* (Leipzig, 1910), 124, 135 ff., for comparison to adoption ritual, and Zuntz, *Persephone*, 319, for criticism of this view. See also Festugière, *Rev. Bibl.* 44 (1935), 371 n. 9, 381 ff.

Grundfragen der Homerkritik (Leipzig, 1909), 109, Wackernagel, *Spr. Unters.* 176.

His name, like that of his sister Demo, suggests comparison with Demeter (cf. ad *Dem.* 109). The name may have been given to him by the epic poet (cf. ad *Dem.* 109 f.). Körte (*Glotta* 25 (1936), 137 ff.) suggested that the child was originally nameless (cf. ad *Dem.* 153). He never appears in Eleusinian inscriptions or in art. Later his role is usurped by Triptolemus. Apollodorus (1. 5. 1) keeps Demophon as the child (he follows the *Hymn* fairly closely for the most part), but makes him die in the fire (cf. ad *Dem.* 254).

235. Cf. *Dem.* 241.

Gods, giants, and heroes grow miraculously as children. Cf. *Ap.* 127 ff. (ad *Dem.* 237), *Herm.* 17 ff., *Hy.* 26. 5, Hes. *Th.* 492 f., Call. *Hy.* 1. 55 ff., Apollod. 1. 7. 4, 3. 7. 6, Conon, *FGH* 26. 44, Q.S. 6. 205 ff. For other examples from Greek and other legends cf. Usener, *Kl. Schr.* iv. 127 ff. C. Fries, 'Zum homerischen Hermeshymnos', *PhW* 1938, 879 f., compares stories of the child Heracles, the young Buddha, and the amazement of Christ's parents at his early wisdom.

236. The sense is broken and a line is required indicating that Demeter gave the child ambrosia by day (cf. A.R. 4. 870, ad *Dem.* 237). The lacuna is probably due to loss of a line at the foot of a page (cf. Introduction, p. 66). There is therefore no need to assume a homeoteleuton (cf. Hermann's supplement to 236). After loss of 236A Δημήτηρ may have been added to give a subject to 237, replacing the original end of 236. γάλα or μαζόν presumably came here (cf. formulae, ad loc., and Call. *Hy.* 1. 48, fr. 384. 26). γάλα μητρός is out of place. γάλα λευκόν (cf. E. *Ba.* 700) would be possible, or ποτε μαζόν. In 236A either ἠματίη (cf. *Od.* 2. 104 f., etc., *Il.* 9. 72) or ἤματα (cf. *Od.* 5. 154 ff., 10. 11, 16. 365 ff., 19. 513 ff., 20. 84 f., A.R. 4. 870) is possible.

οὔτ' οὖν ... οὐ: cf. Denniston, *GP* 419: 'οὔτ' οὖν emphasizes the duality, or plurality, of the ideas negatived.' Cf. *Il.* 17. 20, 20. 7, *Od.* 17. 401.

If there was an early epic version of Achilles' childhood (cf. ad *Dem.* 237 ff.) a similar line may have occurred in it. Cf. the etymology of his name in Apollod. 3. 13. 6 ὅτι τὰ χείλη μαστοῖς οὐ προσήνεγκε; *Et. M.* 181. 27 ff. ἢ διὰ τὸ μὴ θιγεῖν χείλεσι χιλῆς, ὅ ἐστι τροφῆς· ὅλως γὰρ οὐ μετέσχε γάλακτος, ἀλλὰ μυελοῖς ἐλάφων ἐτράφη ὑπὸ Χείρωνος. Cf. Euph. fr. 57 ad loc., Schol. *Il.* 1. 1, Eust. p. 15. 9, A.R. 4. 813.

237 ff. The story resembles very closely that of Thetis' attempt to immortalize Achilles. Cf. A.R. 4. 869 ff., where the description is so close to that of the *Hymn* that either both must be following the same model (an early epic version of the childhood of Achilles), or Apollonius is imitating the *Hymn*. For the first view cf. Knaack, *RE* 5. 148, Preller–Robert ii. 67 (suggesting the *Cypria*). Schol. A ad *Il.* 18. 57, 60, 16. 222 ascribe the story to οἱ νεώτεροι, adding that it took place on the twelfth day after Achilles' birth (a detail which is not in Apollonius). A different version was told in the *Aegimius* (Hes. fr. 300). Cf. also ad *Dem.* 236.

In favour of the second view is the fact that in Apollonius' version there are features which occur also in the *Hymn*, but at a different point in the story. Thus A.R. 4. 873 ~ *Dem.* 285 (and 245). In Apollonius Peleus leaps out of bed and sees what is happening. In the *Hymn* it is the girls who do this after Demeter's departure (Moschus, *Eur.* 16 probably echoes this line: cf. ad loc.). Similarly A.R. 4. 874 ~ *Dem.* 252, 261, 289 (ἀcπαίροντα), 245, A.R. 4. 876 (κεκληγῶτα) ~ *Dem.* 284, A.R. 4. 878 ~ *Dem.* 302, 281, A.R. 4. 879 (χωϲαμένη) ~ *Dem.* 251, 91. Also A.R. 4. 880 (which refers to a quite different occasion) ~ *Dem.* 281 ff., 881 ~ 294 f.; 866a ~ *Dem.* 40, 90.

There are several other possible echoes of this episode of the *Hymn* in Apollonius: *Dem.* 231+254 ~ 3. 867 (4. 1135 f.)?; 259 ~ 3. 714*; 269 ~ 4. 936*; 274a ~ 2. 699*, 3. 1204*; 281 ~ 3. 158*; 282 ~ 3. 811? (Mosch. *Eur.* 18); 293 ~ 4. 752* (Mosch. *Eur.* 16 f.) [304 (201) ~ 1. 286*; 308 ~ 1. 686 f. ?] Cf. Introduction, pp. 69 f.

A parallel story is told of Isis and the son of the king of Byblos. Cf. Plut. *de Is. et Osir.* 15 f. (357 a ff.). There is no mention of it in the earlier Pharaonic sources and it is probably due to Greek influence. Cf. H. Frankfort, *Kingship and the Gods* (Chicago, 1948), 292; J. H. Breasted, *Development of Religion and Thought in Ancient Egypt* (New York, 1912), 25 ff.; T. Hopfner, *Plutarch über Isis und Osiris*, ad loc.; J. Gwyn Griffiths, *Plutarch, De Iside et Osiride*, pp. 319 ff.; and see on *Dem.* 40 ff., 99.

Fr. Marx (*Arch. Zeit.* 43 (1885), 169 ff.) identified the scenes on a cista from Praeneste and two Etruscan mirrors as portraying a myth of the same type. On the cista, Athena holds the infant Ares over a cauldron from which flames emerge, and which probably represents the Water of Styx. Above it Cerberus is depicted. She also touches his mouth with a pencil-like object, i.e. probably anoints him with ambrosia (cf. Pi. *P.* 9. 61, Ov. *M.* 14. 601 f.). On one of the mirrors she has her breast bare, i.e. to suckle the child.

For other parallels cf. P. Roussel, *RÉA* 22 (1920), 157 ff., Ch. Picard, *Rev. Arch.* 35 (1932), 225, N. Kontoleon, *Kret. Chronika* 15–16 (1) (1961–2), 283 ff., P. Vernant, *Mythe et pensée chez les Grecs*, 106, 132 f., L. Gernet, *Anthropologie de la Grèce antique* (Paris, 1968), 382 ff., especially 387 f.

237–41. For the accumulation of forms in -cκε cf. *Od.* 11. 586–7, 596–9, Hes. *Th.* 157, frr. 67b, 204. 125–8.

237. Ambrosia (as its name implies: cf. *amṛta* in Indian mythology) gives divine strength or immortality. Thus it is given to the infant Apollo (*Ap.* 123 ff.: cf. ad *Dem.* 236), and has an immediate effect (127 ff.; cf. ad *Dem.* 235). Cf. Pi. *P.* 9. 63: Aristaeus as a baby is to be fed on nectar and ambrosia and so made immortal. Tithonus is fed on it (*Aph.* 232), although it does not make him ageless (cf. ad *Dem.* 242). Cf. Hes. fr. 23 (a). 21 ff.: Artemis makes Iphimede (= Iphigeneia) immortal by pouring it over her head. Cf. Pi. *O.* 1. 60 ff., Theocr. 15. 106 ff., Virg. *G.* 4. 415 ff. (here it is a perfume), Ov. *M.* 14. 605 ff. (Aphrodite anoints Aeneas and also touches his lips with ambrosia and nectar, to make him immortal). For its use as an unguent, or to embalm, cf. *Il.* 16. 670, 680, 19. 38 f., 23. 186 f. In *Il.* 14. 170, *Od.* 18. 192 it is a soap. It is liquid also in *Il.* 19. 347, *Od.* 9. 359, *Aph.* 232, Sapph. 141. 1, E. *Hipp.* 748, Anaxandr. fr. 57, otherwise usually solid. Cf. Hes. *Th.* 639 ff. (West ad loc.), 793 ff., *Dem.* 49 f., Onians, *Origins of European Thought*, 292 ff., Roscher, *Nektar und Ambrosia*, 39 ff., E. Lohmeyer, 'Vom göttlichen Wohlgeruch', *Sb. Heidelb.* 1919, Ph.-hist. Klasse, Abh. 9, 12 ff.

In A.R. 4. 869 ff. the ambrosia is to make the child immortal (871 f.), and the fire burns away his mortal parts (869 f.). Cf. Ov. *M.* 14. 600 ff., where Aphrodite washes away Aeneas' mortality in the river Numicius, and then gives him ambrosia and nectar.

238. The internal rhyme could be unconscious, or alternatively it might be deliberate, as in magic. Cf. *Il.* 2. 484 (Μοῦcαι ... ἔχουcαι), *Od.* 12. 70 (μέλουcα ... πλέουcα), 13. 281 (ἀποβάντεc ... ἅπαντεc), Hes. *Th.* 276, Platt, *CR* 35 (1921), 141, Shewan, *CP* 20 (1925), 200. In *Il.* 2. 484 it may be conscious. Cf. *Il.* 2. 485-6 (elaborate rhyme and anaphora), and ad *Dem.* 228-30. Ovid couples the divine touch with a magic incantation: *F.* 4. 550 f. (ad *Dem.* 228-30). For another magic rhyme cf. Virg. *E.* 8. 80 'limus ut hic durescit, et haec ut cera liquescit'.

ἡδὺ καταπνείουcα: καταπνεῖν does not occur in Homer (but cf. ἀνα-/ἐπι-/παρα-/πνεῖν etc.).

The divine breath (ἐπίπνοια) in Homer gives strength (μένοc), e.g. *Il.* 10. 482, *Od.* 24. 520; Onians, *Origins of European Thought*, 50 ff. Cf. E. Fehrle, *Die kultische Keuschheit* (Giessen, 1910), 86: 'with the breath the divine strength of the god himself enters into men.' Eitrem, *Opferritus*, 212: 'Die Götter atmen selbst, sozusagen, die reine Göttlichkeit aus — der "Atem" ist ja die "Seele".' καταπνεῖν is later used especially of the beneficent or harmful breath of a deity: cf. A. *Ag.* 105 θεόθεν καταπνείει, where Fraenkel ad loc. suggests that the phrase belongs to epic or oracular language (cf. Pl. Com. 173. 14 K.); E. *Med.* 389, *Rhes.* 387, Ar. *Lys.* 552, Ael. *NA* 12. 2. 7.

The divine breath can also give poetic and oracular inspiration, or breathe love and desire into a person (cf. Fehrle, o.c. 85 ff., Fraenkel, l.c.). In Virg. *A.* 1. 589 ff. Venus breathes beauty over Aeneas. Cf. Claud. *Bell. Gild.* 1. 208 ff., where it rejuvenates; *Orph. Hy.* 84. 8 ὄλβον ἐπιπνείουcα καὶ ἠπιόχειρον ὑγείαν. In Ov. *F.* 4. 540 Ceres 'iungere dignata est os puerile suo'.

In the story of Isis at Byblos cf. Plut. *de Is. et Osir.* 15 (357 a-b) καὶ τῷ χρωτὶ θαυμαστὴν τὴν εὐωδίαν ἐπιπνέουcαν ἀφ' ἑαυτῆc ... ἵμερον ἐμπεcεῖν τῆc ξένηc τῶν τε τριχῶν τοῦ τε χρωτὸc ἀμβροcίαν πνέοντοc ... On the fragrance of the divine breath cf. ad *Dem.* 277.

ἐν κόλποιcιν ἔχουcα: cf. ad *Dem.* 231 ff.

239. κρύπτεcκε: cf. *Dem.* 249 κρύπτει, Apollod. 1. 5. 1 εἰc πῦρ ἐγκεκρυμμένον, 3. 13. 6 (Thetis and Achilles) κρύφα Πηλέωc εἰc τὸ πῦρ ἐγκρύβουcα τῆc νυκτόc, Paus. 2. 3. 11 (Medea and her children) τὸ δὲ ἀεὶ τικτόμενον κατακρύπτειν αὐτὸ ἐc τὸ ἱερὸν φέρουcαν τῆc Ἥραc, κατακρύπτειν δὲ ἀθανάτουc ἔcεcθαι νομίζουcαν. Cf. *Od.* 5. 488.

ἠΰτε δαλόν: cf. the similes in *Od.* 5. 488 ff., *Herm.* 237 ff., Sotades
Ἐγκλειόμεναι fr. 1. 29 K. ἐνέκρυφά θ᾽ ὥσπερ δαλὸν εἰς πολλὴν τέφραν,
Archestr. fr. 35. 9 (Brandt). In the Meleager story the fire-brand is
παιδὸς δαφοινὸν δαλὸν ἥλικα (A. *Cho.* 607 f.).

Most stories of this type speak of 'burning away or purging the
mortal parts': cf. A.R. 4. 869 f., Apollod. 1. 5. 1, Plut. *de Is. et Osir.* 16,
Ov. *F.* 4. 554. Cf. the apotheosis of Heracles: Theocr. 24. 83, Ov.
M. 9. 250 ff., 262 ff., Sen. *Herc. Oet.* 1966 ff., Plin. *NH* 35. 139, Luc.
Hermot. 7, Minuc. *Oct.* 22. 7, Housman, *CR* 32 (1918), 162 f. Fire
released the divine part in man: cf. Eust. *Il.* 1. 52 (p. 43. 1); Iamblich.
de mysteriis 5. 12. Cf. also the death of Empedocles (Hor. *AP* 465 ff.,
D.L. 8. 68), the fire-births of Dionysus and Asclepius (Pi. *P.* 3. 38 ff.),
and in general Frazer, *GB*[3] 179 ff., Edsman, *Ignis Divinus* (Lund,
1949).

240. λάθρα: not in Homer or Hesiod. Cf. κρύβδα, λάθρῃ with genitive (*Il.* 18. 168; 5. 269, 24. 72). It appears to be a *hapax legomenon*
(E. fr. 1132. 28 is spurious; in E. *Hel.* 829 λάθρᾰ does not scan). It is
perhaps by analogy with κρύβδα (Zumbach, *Neuerungen*, 27). Cf. the
alternative forms ἄμα/ἀμᾷ, κρύφα/κρυφῇ, δίχα/διχῇ, τρίχα/τριχῇ,
cῖγα/cιγῇ; K–B ii. 306.

γονέων: not in Homer. Cf. Hes. *Op.* 235, 331, etc.

241. προθαλής: this occurs only here. Cf. ἀμφιθαλής (*Il.* 22. 496
etc.), εὐθαλής (A. fr. 300. 5 etc.).

θεοῖσι δὲ ἄντα ἐῴκει: cf. ad *Dem.* 235.

For the hiatus at the bucolic diaeresis cf. Monro, *HG*[2] § 382; van
Leeuwen, *Enchiridium*, 79, § 15. The majority of examples with -ε
in hiatu at the diaeresis are with τε.

242. ποίηcεν: Voss considers this use of ποίηcεν Attic, as the Homeric
expression is ἀθάνατον (etc.) τιθέναι. Dittmar, however, compares *Od.*
1. 235, 13. 42, 23. 11 ff.

ἀγήρων τ᾽ ἀθάνατόν τε: these are normally in reverse order. Cf.
Dem. 260, etc. (for examples cf. West ad Hes. *Th.* 277). But ἀγήρως is
always in this position in the verse, except in *Od.* 5. 218 and Hes. l.c.

In *Dem.* 260 M has ἀγήραον. Cf. ἀγήραος (etc.) vulg. *Il.* 2. 447,
8. 539, *Od.* 5. 136, 7. 257, 23. 336, Hes. *Th.* 305, 955, fr. 23 (a). 24. The
contracted form is required by the metre at *Il.* 12. 323, 17. 444,
Od. 5. 218, 7. 94, *Ap.* 151, Hes. *Th.* 277, 949. Cf. Hes. fr. 25. 28
ἀγή]ροc.

Deathlessness was of little value if it was not accompanied by age-
lessness: cf. Tithonus (*Aph.* 220 ff.), and the legend of the Sibyl, Ov.
M. 14. 132 ff.

242–3. καί κεν . . . εἰ μὴ ἄρ᾽ . . .: on this pattern cf. ad *Dem.*
310–13.

244. νύκτ᾽ ἐπιτηρήcαcα: the verb does not occur in Homer or
Hesiod. Cf. *Dem.* 142 (τηρεῖν), Ar. *Ach.* 197 etc. It usually means 'look
out for'. Presumably one must take νύκτα as the object here. But one
might note Apollod. 1. 5. 1 ἐπετήρηcεν ἡ Πραξιθέα, καὶ καταλαβοῦσα
. . . ἀνεβόηcε (Praxithea is unknown elsewhere: cf. the emendations

ap. Frazer ad loc.). At 3. 13. 6 he also has Πηλεὺς δὲ ἐπιτηρήςας καὶ ςπαίροντα τὸν παῖδα ἰδών.

θυώδεος ἐκ θαλάμοιο: her bedroom adjoined the megaron. Cf. Odysseus' palace: *Il.* 1. 328, 17. 492 ff., 541 f., 20. 92 ff., 387 ff.; Lorimer, *Homer and the Monuments*, 414 f.; Bassett, *AJA* 23 (1919), 293.

In some late versions it is either the child's father, or both parents, who see Demeter. Cf. Hyg. *fab.* 147, Serv. ad Virg. *G.* 1. 19, Lact. ad Stat. *Theb.* 2. 382, Myth. Vat. 2. 97.

The original point was probably that the magic could only be worked in secret. The poet perhaps misunderstood this: he stresses only Demeter's anger at discovery (*Dem.* 251, 254). Cf. however Apollod. 3. 13. 6 Θέτις κωλυθεῖςα τὴν προαίρεςιν τελειῶςαι.

The motif of curiosity to see a forbidden sight is common in folk-tales and mythology. Cf. Cupid and Psyche: Apul. *M.* 5. 6. 6 etc., 6. 19. 7, 20. 5 f. Merkelbach (*Roman und Mysterium*, 18 ff., 47 f.) sees a connection with the Isis-mysteries here, and compares the myths of Erichthonius and the daughters of Cecrops (cf. ad *Dem.* 231 ff.), and of Orpheus and Eurydice (cf. Nilsson, *Op. Sel.* ii. 637 f.), as well as those of Thetis and Achilles, and Medea's children. His interpretation of the Demophon myth as designed to warn initiands' parents against trying to witness the initiation (o.c. 22) seems more doubtful.

One might also mention the story of Pandora, and the Hittite myth in which a mortal is killed by the goddess Inara because he breaks the prohibition against seeing his wife and children (Pritchard, *ANET*² 125; cf. G. S. Kirk, *Myth* (Cambridge, 1970), 220. Kirk, o.c. 258–9, has some good remarks on such mythical themes).

245. On this line see Hoekstra, *Sub-epic Stage*, 50 f. He points out that the sigmatic aorist middle of πλήττω occurs only once in Homer (*Il.* 16. 125 πληξάμενος), but is substituted here for the Homeric πεπλήγετο.

246. δείςας' ᾧ: elision before ὅς (etc.) is rare in Homer, and the elided word is always δέ, γε, τε, ἄρα, which can often be suppressed (cf. Chantraine, *GH* i. 147 f.).

ἀάςθη: cf. *Il.* 1. 340, *Od.* 10. 68 ἄᾱςαν. The initial α is short in *Dem.* 258, *Il.* 8. 237, etc.

248 f. Such short speeches are more a feature of Hesiodic than Homeric style (cf. West, *Theogony*, 74).

248. πυρὶ ἔνι πολλῷ: for the lengthening of dat. sing. -ι and hiatus cf. ad *Dem.* 99. Hermann's bridge is neglected here (cf. Introduction, p. 63, and *Dem.* 17). On the comparison that has been made between this and Hippol. *Ref. Haer.* 5. 8. 39 (ὑπὸ πολλῷ πυρί) cf. ad *Dem.* 231 ff. The phrase is an 'inversion' of the Homeric (ἐν) πυρὶ πολλῷ (*Od.* 12. 237, *Il.* 21. 362 ~ 18. 346 etc.). Cf. Hoekstra, *Sub-epic Stage*, 51, L. E. Rossi, *Gott. gel. Anz.* 223 (1971), 171. πυρῇ, which is assumed to be the reading of the papyrus, is always used of a funeral pyre in Homer and usually so later. It is occasionally confused with πῦρ, especially in late Greek. The same papyrus has πυράν twice (Orph. fr. 49. 85, 91). (Cf. Philo, *de confus. ling.* 157; Acts 28: 2 and 3.) The two are confused in manuscripts: cf. *Dem.* 287, also *Il.* 23. 165, 172, 216 (where πυρί is v.l. for πυρῇ). The sense requires πυρί here.

249. κρύπτει: cf. ad *Dem.* 239.

251–5. This sentence is rather involved and repetitive (251a ~ 254b). The change of subject in 252 is slightly awkward (cf. ad loc.) and there is a ὕστερον πρότερον in 253–4. But there is no need to alter the text.

251. τῇ δὲ χολωσαμένη: cf. *Il.* 1. 9 etc.

καλλιστέφανος Δημήτηρ: the epithet does not occur in Homer or Hesiod. Cf. ἐϋστέφανος (*Il.* 19. 99 etc.; of Demeter *Dem.* 224 etc.), φιλοστέφανος (*Dem.* 102), χρυσοστέφανος (Hes. *Th.* 17, 136, *Hy.* 6. 1), and καλλιπλόκαμος (of Demeter *Il.* 14. 326). καλλιστεφάνο Ἀφροδίτες is found on the 'Cup of Nestor' (*Rendic. Linc.* 10 (1955), 215–34). Cf. also Tyrt. fr. 2 (of Hera); E. *Ba.* 376 (εὐφροσύνας); Orac. ap. D.S. 8. 29 (of Libya).

252. The line, with its change of subject, is slightly awkward, and seems unnecessary at this point. Wegener, *Philol.* 35 (1876), 243, suggests that it (without ἄελπτον) derives from a version of the Achilles story, where Thetis is also the mother. But it is more probably a 'fill-line'. Cf. also ad *Dem.* 233 f.

253. θῆκε πέδον δέ: cf. *Od.* 21. 136. ἧκε would be more suitable here. Cf. A.R. 4. 876 τὸν μὲν ἄρ' ἁρπάγδην χαμάδις βάλε κεκληγῶτα. πέδον δέ in Homer is used of a storm coming down on to the earth from heaven (*Il.* 13. 796), and of a stone rolling downhill to the level ground (*Od.* 11. 598). Cf. S. *Ant.* 786 ἐσπᾶτο γὰρ πέδον δὲ καὶ μετάρσιος. In tragedy πέδῳ is normally used (A. *PV* 749 etc.). Voss calls the use of πέδον δέ here Attic, but there is no need to assume this.

254. ἐξανελοῦσα: this compound does not occur in Homer or Hesiod. Cf. Homeric ἀναιρέω, ἐξανίημι. Cf. A.R. 3. 867 τό ῥ' ἥ γ' ἐξανελοῦσα θυώδεϊ κάτθετο μίτρῃ (~ *Dem.* 231); E. *Ion* 269 (middle).

In Apollod. 1. 5. 1 and Orph. fr. 49. 100 f. the child is consumed by the fire (cf. 2 Vat. Myth. 96 f.). The two accounts are similar: Orph. fr. 49. 100 f. τὸ παι]δίον . . . καίει καὶ ἀποκτείνει [κ]αὶ ὁ[ρθ]ῶς αὐτὴν δια[καλύπτει, Apollod. l.c. τὸ μὲν βρέφος ὑπὸ τοῦ πυρὸς ἀνηλώθη, ἡ θεὰ δὲ αὐτὴν ἐξέφηνε.

This version may have been the original one, suppressed as ἀπρεπές by the Homeric poet (cf. G. Murray, *Rise of the Greek Epic*, Appendix G; Wünsch, *RE* 9. 155. 32 ff.). Demophon, like other 'agonic' heroes (cf. ad *Dem.* 265 ff.), might be expected to die young. Cf. also the stories of Thetis and Achilles, and Medea and her children. In one version of the former, Thetis kills six children before Peleus discovers her and saves Achilles (Hes. fr. 300, Schol. *Il.* 16. 37, Schol. Ar. *Nub.* 1068, Lycophr. 178 f.). In the story of Medea, most or all of the children probably died: cf. Roussel, *RÉA* 22 (1920), 161. For a similar case of probable suppression of τὸ ἀπρεπές cf. ad *Dem.* 192 ff. 3. Iambe.

256–74. Demeter reproaches mankind with their folly, and swears that she would have made the child ageless and immortal. Now he will die, but an annual festival will be held in his honour. She reveals her true identity, and commands that the people of Eleusis build her a temple and altar outside the city wall. She promises to teach them her sacred rites, so that they may propitiate her in future.

Demeter's speech is in the traditional form for the self-revelation of a deity. For examples of the derogatory address to mankind by a deity or prophet cf. ad *Dem.* 256 ff. This and the self-revelation (268 f.) also occur together in Hes. *Th.* 26 ff., where they are followed by the gift of the poetic staff and command to sing of the gods (see below; and Schwabl, *Proc. Afr. Class. Assoc.* 2 (1959), 26). Cf. Emped. frr. 112. 4, 124, 141. The references to the power of the deity and the benefits which she confers (268 f.) are features which belong to the self-revelation, and contrast with the condemnation of the helplessness of men. Cf. especially A. *PV* 436 ff., where Prometheus recounts the blessings he has brought to men, and describes their previous helpless state (447 ff. ~ Orph. fr. 233, ad *Dem.* 256 ff.). For the form of 268 f. cf. ad loc. This leads on naturally to the command to build her a temple (cf. ad *Dem.* 268 ff., 188 ff.), and the promise to institute her rites. Cf. Isis' address to Lucius in Apuleius (*M.* 11. 5, A.-J. Festugière, *Personal Religion among the Greeks* (Univ. of California Press, 1960), 159 n. 6):

1. 'En adsum . . .' ⎫
2. Isis reveals her nature ⎬ cf. *Dem.* 268 f.
3. She encourages Lucius (5. 4) : contrast *Dem.* 256 ff.?
4. She gives orders (5. 4 ff.) : cf. Dem. 270 ff.
5. She makes promises for this life and the next: cf. *Dem.* 273 f.

Cf. Festugière, *HTR* 42 (1949), 209 ff., and P. Oxy. 1380.

256 ff. 256–62 are cited by the 'Orphic' papyrus (Orph. fr. 49. 95 ff.) with a variant text, part of which is fragmentary and unintelligible but evidently differed completely from 258b–61.

The derogatory address to mankind by a deity or prophet was traditional in both Greek and Jewish literature. Cf. Hes. *Th.* 26 ff. West ad loc. compares Epimenides fr. 1, Isaiah 6 : 9, Parmen. 6. 3 ff., Emped. 2, Ar. *Av.* 685 ff., Ov. *M.* 15. 153, Orph. fr. 233, [Pythag.] *Carm. Aur.* 54 ff. Cf. also *Ap.* 532 ff., Emped. 124, 141, *Orac. Sib.* 1. 174 ff., 3. 8 ff., 14. 1 ff., fr. 1. 1 ff. Rz., Poimandres, *Corpus Hermeticum* 1. 26 ff., and for an address to one individual Hes. *Op.* 286 (~ Orac. ap. Hdt. 1. 85 vs. 1), and Pi. fr. 157 Sn. (= 143 Bo.). In general, cf. Norden, *Agnostos Theos*, 132.

The form of words is also traditional. For *Dem.* 256, cf. (cited ad loc.) *Od.* 21. 85, *Ap.* 532, Theognis 10. 39, 1069 ἄφρονες ἄνθρωποι καὶ νήπιοι, Ar. *Pax* 1063 f. (in a parody) ὦ μέλεοι θνητοὶ καὶ νήπιοι . . . οἵτινες ἀφραδίῃσι θεῶν νόον οὐκ ἀίοντες . . ., Call. fr. 318 σχέτλιαι ἀνθρώπων ἀφραστύες, Triphiod. 310 ff. (exclamation by the poet) σχέτλιον ἀφραδέων μερόπων γένος, οἷσιν ὁμίχλη | ἄσκοπος ἐσσομένων . . . and Pi. fr. 157 (Silenus to Olympus) ὦ τάλας ἐφάμερε, νήπια βάζεις . . .

For the wording of *Dem.* 256-8 cf. especially Orph. fr. 233 μηδαμὰ
μηδὲν | εἰδότες, οὔτε κακοῖο προσερχομένοιο νοῆσαι | φράδμονες, οὔτ'
ἄποθεν μάλ' ἀποστρέψαι κακότητος, | οὔτ' ἀγαθοῦ παρεόντος ἐπιστρέψαι
τε καὶ ἔρξαι, [Pythag.] *Carm. Aur.* 54-6 γνώςῃ δ' ἀνθρώπους αὐθαίρετα
πήματ' ἔχοντας, | τλήμονας, οἵ τ' ἀγαθῶν πέλας ὄντων οὔτ' ἐсορῶсιν, |
οὔτε κλύουсι, λύсιν δὲ κακῶν παῦροι сυνίαсιν.
In *Ap.* 189 ff. the Muses sing of ἀνθρώπων | τλημοсύνας, ὅс' ἔχοντες
. . . ζώους' ἀφραδέες καὶ ἀμήχανοι . . . (because they cannot find a cure
for death and old age: cf. *Dem.* 259-62, and ad *Dem.* 147 f.). Cf.
Virg. *A.* 10. 501 f. (exclamation by the poet):

nescia mens hominum fati sortisque futurae,
et servare modum rebus sublata secundis.

A similar thought is expressed in *Od.* 18. 129 ff. (and cf. Pindar,
O. 12. 1-12). Cf. also Mimn. fr. 2. 4-5 πρὸς θεῶν εἰδότες οὔτε κακὸν |
οὔτ' ἀγαθόν . . .
Dem. 256 ff. can be taken either as an address or a general statement
(cf. West, l.c., p. 160). As in Hes. *Th.* 26 ff. and probably Epimen.
fr. 1, there is an audience of one but the plural is used. Schwabl
(o.c. 27) observes that 'the plural in front of a single person strikes
a note of contempt and disapproval', and the address serves 'to drive
home the contrast between mortal and god' (o.c. 25).
The case against men rests on their folly and inability to foresee the
future. Because of this, they cannot improve their lot, and especially
find a cure for death and age (cf. *Ap.* 189 ff. above). Here, Demeter
says that she would have given this to Demophon, had not the folly
of Metaneira prevented her. Her words supply the traditional 'answer'
of the gods to the 'accusation' of *Dem.* 147 f., 216 f. (cf. ad loc.).
256. The structure of the verse is similar to that of Hes. *Th.* 26,
Epimen. fr. 1, *Ap.* 532, etc.
καὶ ἀφράδμονες: corruption before -φρ- normally occurs only where
it is metrically necessary in order for the word to fit the hexameter (cf.
Monro, *HG*² § 370, Chantraine, *GH* i. 108 f.). In the phrases parallel
to *Dem.* 256 there is normally no copula (but cf. Theognis 1039, 1069).
ἀφράδμων does not occur in Homer or Hesiod (ἀφραδής *Od.* 2. 282,
11. 476, etc.; φράδμων *Il.* 16. 638). Cf. A. *Ag.* 1401, S. fr. 613 P.
(ἀφράсμων); A. *Pers.* 417 (ἀφραсμόνως). The word is quoted from
Sophocles' *Triptolemus* (fr. 613 P.), which is interesting in view of the
subject-matter of that play.
256 f. The transposition in pap. 1 is paralleled by Orph. fr. 233
(ad *Dem.* 256 ff.).
The papyrus has προγνωμενες, probably a mistake for -μεναι (influenced by δυсτλήμονες above), rather than for -μονες (Allen and
Halliday) which would require a weak ὔμμιν (*vel sim.*) instead of
αἶсαν. προγνώμων does not exist in Greek.
ἀφράδμονες . . . προγνώμεναι is parallel to Orph. fr. 233 νοῆσαι
φράδμονες. προγιγνώσκω does not occur in Homer and Hesiod (Homeric
ἀνα-/δια-/ἐπι-/γιγνώσκω). Cf. E. *Hipp.* 1072, etc.

Men's fate or appointed share (αἶcαν) is divided into good and evil:
cf. *Il.* 24. 527 f., Solon fr. 1. 63 (ad *Dem.* 147 f.), also *Od.* 4. 236 f.,
Hes. *Th.* 904-6 (West ad loc.), *Op.* 669, Orph. fr. 233, [Pyth.] *Carm.
Aur.* 55-6.

258. νήκεcτον: this is surely right, rather than M's μήκιcτον (cf. Allen
and Halliday). It is especially appropriate here, since the disaster is
irreversible (cf. *Dem.* 262). It occurs elsewhere only in Hes. *Op.* 283.

259. On Styx as the oath of the gods cf. West ad Hes. *Th.* 400. The
ὅρκοc is that by which one swears, and is here invoked as a witness (cf.
Il. 15. 36 ff. etc.). Cf. Buttmann, *Lexilogus*, 433 ff., Leumann, *Hom.
Wörter*, 81 ff. On the etymology of ὅρκοc cf. also Frisk, s.v.; Benveniste,
RHR 134 (1949), 81 ff.; Bollack, *RÉG* 71 (1958), 1 ff., Hiersche, *RÉG*
71 (1958), 35 ff. (arguing for the ancient interpretation ὅρκοc =
ἕρκοc, as that which bounds or binds the oath-taker).

θεῶν: for the synizesis cf. ad Dem. 55, and Hoekstra, *Sub-epic Stage*,
61 n. 70, who suggests that it may be due to telescoping of *Il.* 15. 36-8
= *Od.* 5. 184-6, aided by *Od.* 2. 377 etc.

ἀμείλικτον: in Homer this is used with ὄπα (*Il.* 11. 137, 21. 98),
but with δεcμῶν in Hes. *Th.* 659 (cf. West ad loc.). It replaces ἀάατον
(*Il.* 14. 271), perhaps because of ἀάcθηc in *Dem.* 258. Cf. ἀμείλιχοc of
Hades, Erinyes (*Il.* 9. 158 etc.).

Cτυγὸc ὕδωρ: this is the proper name in Homer and sometimes later
(cf. Bölte, *RE* 4A. 460 ff., West ad *Th.* 805), and is possibly original
(Schulze, *QE* 442).

259 ff. It is odd that Styx, by which Demeter swears that she would
have made Demophon immortal, was itself called ἄφθιτοc (Hes. *Th.*
389, 397, 805; cf. *Dem.* 261, 263), probably as an elixir of life (West ad
Th. 805). A late version of the Achilles story (cf. ad *Dem.* 237 ff.)
replaces the fire as immortalizing agent by the water of Styx (Stat.
Ach. 1. 268 f., etc.; *RE* 1. 225. 30 ff.). For Styx as a river of fire in this
legend cf. Fr. Marx, *Arch. Zeit.* 43 (1886) 169 ff., Dieterich, *Nekyia*, 198.

260. ἤματα πάντα: cf. West ad Hes. *Th.* 305.

262. οὐκ ἔcθ' ὧc: this does not occur in Homer (ἔcτι with infinitive
Il. 21. 565 etc.). Cf. Pi. fr. 61 etc. οὐ γὰρ ἔcθ' ὅπωc, Pl. *Men.* 76 e etc.
οὐκ ἔcθ' ὧc.

263. τιμή . . . ἐπέccεται: Wünsch (*RE* 9. 155. 32 ff.) considers this
verse 'eine spätere Umarbeitung', because it apparently clashes with
261. Originally, the child died and there was an end of it (cf. ad *Dem.*
254). But the sense is perhaps: 'I should have given him immortality
and honour. Now he will die, but his honour will always remain
(ἐπέccεται).' 262-3 correspond to 260-1.

263 f. γούνων . . . ἐπέβη: cf. *Il.* 9. 455, 488, *Od.* 16. 443, 19. 401,
Il. 21. 506, Theocr. 13. 53 (and verse added after *Il.* 3. 40).

265-7. 'And in due season, for him, as the years revolve, the children
of the Eleusinians will always wage war and bitter strife with one
another for ever.'

The reference is to the Βαλλητύc, a ritual mock battle held in honour
of Demophon. Cf. Hsch. s.v. Βαλλητύc· ἑορτὴ Ἀθήνηcιν ἐπὶ Δημοφῶντι τῷ

Κελεοῦ ἀγομένη; Ath. 406 d Ἐλευcῖνι γὰρ τῇ ἐμῇ οἶδά τινα πανήγυριν ἀγομένην καὶ καλουμένην Βαλλητύν. Ἀθήνηcιν in Hesychius is misleading. The ceremony was at Eleusis: cf. Ath. l.c.

That the πόλεμος referred to was a ceremonial one was first recognized by F. Creuzer in *Symbolik und Mythologie der alten Völker* (Leipzig, 1842, 3rd ed.), iv. 314 ff. Cf. O. Crusius, *Beiträge zur griechischen Religionsgeschichte und Mythologie* (Leipzig, 1886), 19 ff.

It is not known when the ceremony took place. Kern (*RE* 16. 1215. 12 f.) suggested that the Eleusinian Games may have developed from it (cf. ad *Dem.* 231 ff.). But the way it is referred to in Athenaeus suggests that, in his day at least, it was a separate festival. Walton (*HTR* 45 (1952), 109 n. 16) thought that the original recital of the *Hymn* may have been at a celebration of the Βαλλητύc. This would account for Demophon's prominence and give a point to *Dem.* 263–7. The recital may have taken place at the Eleusinian Games: cf. Introduction, p. 12.

Evidently the ceremony still took place in Athenaeus' day, but was not well known outside Eleusis. The speaker in Athenaeus says that he will only describe the festival if the others pay him to do so. The context in Athenaeus is of pelting with stones, and it was probably of this type. Similar mock battles are common all over the world, and involve either stone-throwing or some other form of fighting. At Troezen there was a *lithobolia* in honour of Damia and Auxesia. This involved *aischrologia* (cf. ad *Dem.* 192 ff., 3. Iambe). The *aition* for it was a civil stasis, in which Damia and Auxesia were stoned (Paus. 2. 32. 2. Cf. perhaps Hdt. 5. 85). A historical origin for these battles was often presumed (cf. Lesky, *ARW* 24 (1926), 77 ff.). Various scholars have connected Demeter's prophecy with the traditions of wars between Athens and Eleusis. Matthiae read Ἀθηναίοιcι in 267. He was followed by Baumeister.[1] But there is no reason to alter the text.

Further examples of such contests are given in Farnell, *Cults*, iii. 93 f., Nilsson, *Gr. Feste*, 402 ff., 413 ff., Usener, *Kl. Schr.* iv. 435 ff., Lesky, o.c. 73 ff. (on a Hittite example, with parallels; cf. Gurney, *The Hittites*, 155), Frazer ad Paus. 2. 30. 4. They have been variously interpreted: as designed to promote fertility (Mannhardt, *Wald- und Feldkulte* (Berlin, 1904), i. 548 ff., Frazer, *GB*³ 7. 98 ff., 173 ff., especially 184; Allen and Halliday, ad loc.), as representing the conflict of winter and summer (Usener l.c.; cf. Lesky), or as cathartic (Eitrem, *Opferritus*, 290 ff.). Nilsson distinguishes two classes, those which served as a preliminary to real battles (o.c. 402 ff.), and those belonging to agricultural cults (413 ff.). Rose (*Folklore*, 36 (1925), 322 ff.) points out the diversity of occasions for such fights, which include funeral ceremonies, marriages, seasonal festivals, etc. It is therefore unnecessary to look for a single explanation for all of them.

[1] Cf. also Ch. Picard, *Rev. phil.*, 3ᵉ série, 4 (1930), 257–65, *Rev. hist.* 166 (1931), 1 ff.; L. Weber, *Klio* 21 (1927), 245 ff., *RhM* 80 (1931), 77 f.; Wilamowitz, *Glaube*, ii. 49. Against Weber, see Deubner, *AF* 69 n. 5.

Here, the fact that Demophon's death is foretold and that in some versions he actually dies as a baby (cf. ad *Dem.* 254) suggests that he belongs to the type of child-hero in whose honour the various Greek games were celebrated (e.g. Archemorus, Melicertes, and others). According to one version of the Melicertes legend (Apollod. 3. 4. 3), the child was boiled in a cauldron by Ino, a form of ἀπαθανατισμός enjoyed by Pelops (founder of the Olympian Games, according to one account) and Achilles ([Hes.] fr. 300, from the *Aigimios*, also attributed to the Pythagorean Cercops), and a variant on the fire-ritual. There were mysteries of Ino and her son, still popular in Libanius' time (ii p. 110, 448 R.), and a Trajanic inscription from Syria (Dittenberger, *OGI* 611) dedicated to Leucothea refers to some-one as ἀποθεωθέντος ἐν τῷ λέβητι δι' οὗ αἱ ἑορταὶ ἄγονται. Farnell (*JHS* 36 (1916), 41 ff.) conjectured a ritual of rebirth, by a kind of baptism, as the origin of this. (Cf. also Frazer, *Apollod.* ii. 359 ff.; Lesky, *RE* 15. 515; Philostr. *Imag.* 2. 16.) The parallel with Demophon is suggestive (cf. ad *Dem.* 231 ff.).

The connection of *lithobolia* and *aischrologia* at Troezen also suggests that Demophon's place was originally in the preliminaries to the main ceremonies of the Mysteries. But the time of the Βαλλητύς in the historical period is unknown and it appears to have remained a purely local affair (cf. Ath. l.c.), i.e. it was not incorporated into the enlarged form of the Mysteries which was created by Athens. Mylonas (*Eleusis*, 137 ff.) suggests that it was held in a court on the south side of the Telesterion, where a stepped platform seems to indicate some kind of show with spectators. But the court can hardly have been large enough for such a battle.

The wording of *Dem.* 265–6 is similar to that of *Il.* 2. 550–1, which refers to the Athenian custom of sacrifice to Erechtheus, Athena's protégé. *Il.* 2. 551 is quoted by Artemid. *Oneirocr.* 1. 8 in the context of bull-fighting at Eleusis and elsewhere (cf. Lobeck, *Aglaophamus*, 206). This is probably to be connected with the phrase ἤραντο τοὺς βοῦς ἐν Ἐλευσῖνι τῇ θυσίᾳ in the ephebic inscriptions (*IG* ii. 467–71; cf. Ziehen, *RE* s.v. Opfer, 18. 610. 21 ff., and s.v. Ταυροκαθάψια p. 25. 49 ff., *Hermes* 66 (1931), 227 ff., Persson, *ARW* 21 (1922), 301 f., Picard, *REG* 40 (1927), 351, 363 f.). The parallel between *Il.* 2. 550 f. and *Dem.* 265 f. is striking, since Demophon as Demeter's θρεπτός is in the same position as Erechtheus in relation to Athena, and the myth of Demophon suggests comparison with that of Erichthonius/Erechtheus (cf. ad *Dem.* 231 ff.). Cf. also the wording of Hes. fr. 146, referring to funeral games at Athens in honour of Minos' son Eurygyes: (ex coni. West) Εὐρυγύη δ' ἔτι κοῦροι Ἀθηναίων . . .

265. ὥρῃϲιν: 'in due season'. Cf. *Aph.* 102, and similarly *Od.* 11. 294 f. (= 14. 293 f., *Ap.* 349 f.), 10. 469, Hes. *Th.* 58 f. In later Greek ὥραϲιν is used (preserving the old locative plur.): cf. especially Philicus' *Hymn*, verse 36 (Körte) ὥραϲιν Ἐλευϲῖνάδε μυϲτηλαϲίαιϲ ἰάκχων. Cf. also ἐν ὥρῃ (*Od.* 17. 176 etc.), εἰϲ ὥραϲ (*Od.* 9. 135 etc., Gow ad Theocr. 15. 74). West suggests ὥρῃϲιν here. But one would rather expect -ηcιν in epic, since this was generalized in Ionic for the dative plural.

τῷ γε: 'in his honour'. Cf. *Herm.* 344 etc.

περιπλομένων ἐνιαυτῶν: strictly this means 'as the anniversaries come round'. Cf. LSJ s.v. ἐνιαυτός.

266. παῖδεc Ἐλευcινίων: cf. κοῦροι Ἀθηναίων, Ἀχαιῶν etc. It probably means here 'the young men (or boys) of Eleusis'. Cf. the mock battle at Sparta (Paus. 3. 14. 8), where it is the ephebes who fight. Ἐλευcινίων may be a case of epic shortening, as in *Dem.* 105. Alternatively it could be a synizesis (Radermacher, *Philol.* 84 (1929), 257). Cf. Agallias (see formulae, ad *Dem.* 266), Epicharm. fr. 100. 2 K., Antim. fr. 96 W., perhaps *Ap.* 496, where δελφίνιος, M's reading, should probably be kept (*contra* Allen).

πόλεμον καὶ φύλοπιν αἰνήν: such mock battles can be very fierce, and may lead to bloodshed and even death (e.g. Cic., *Tusc.* 5. 77, Augustine, *de doctr. christ.* iv. 24, iii p. 87 Maur., Libanius, i. 236 R. Cf. also *Il.* 23. 805 f., Frazer, *GB³* 9. 185). There is therefore no reason to assume that this must refer to a real war (cf. ad *Dem.* 265–7).

268 ff. Demeter's self-revelation (268 f.) is followed by her command to build a temple and altar, the promise that she will institute her cult, her epiphany, and a παννυχίc in her honour (292 f.). The appearance of a deity is traditionally the occasion for the institution of honours to him: cf. ad *Dem.* 188 ff., *Od.* 16. 181 ff., *Ap.* 480 ff., *Aph.* 100 ff., Hdt. 6. 105, A.R. 3. 876 ff., Matt. 17: 1 ff., etc.; Pfister, *RE Supp.* 4. 284 f., 288 f., 298.

268. εἰμὶ δὲ Δημήτηρ: Demeter first announces her identity, in a traditional formula (cf. *Od.* 6. 196, 9. 19), which is however especially characteristic of an epiphany: cf. *Ap.* 480, *Hy.* 7. 56, *Od.* 11. 252 (*Il.* 24. 172 ∼ 2. 26, 24. 460 f., *Od.* 19. 548, 20. 47), Emped. fr. 112. 4, A. *PV* 284. Cf. the prologues of Euripides (*Hecuba, Ion, Troades, Bacchae*), and Philem. fr. 91 K., Menand. fr. 545 K., fr. adesp. 154 K., Philyll. I p. 784 K., Plaut. *Aulul.* 2, *Trinumm.* 6; also Xen. *Mem.* 2. 7. 14, Diod. 1. 14 (cf. *IG* 12 Supp. p. 98 A 7), Moschus, *Europa*, 154 f. (Bühler ad 153–61, 155).[1]

Norden called the formula a 'soteriologischer Redetypus'. Normally the deity appears in order to help men, and announces his power, and the benefits which he confers on mankind (ἔργα or εὑρήματα). For this motif in drama cf. especially Plaut. *Amph.* 41 (Leo, *Plautinische Forschungen* (Berlin, 1912), 212, 238 ff.). So here Demeter goes on to describe herself as τιμάοχος, and as 'the greatest blessing and joy to gods and men'. The same structure is found in hymns and later aretalogies, and corresponds with the divisions laid down by the rhetoricians (cf. Alexander, p. 4. 26 ff., Spengel): φύcιc and γένοc,

---

[1] Cf. Norden, *Agnostos Theos*, 186 ff., 207 ff., A. Deissmann, *Licht vom Osten* (Tübingen, 1923), 108 ff. (tr. L. R. M. Strachan (1960), 133 ff.), W. Peek, *Der Isishymnos von Andros* (Berlin, 1930), Roussel, *RÉG* 42 (1929), 147 n. 1, O. Weinreich, *ARW* 18 (1915), 38 ff., Ed. Schwyzer, *Ego eimi* (Diss. Göttingen, 1939).

δύναμις, ἔργα, εὑρήματα. Cf. Festugière, *HTR* 42 (1949), 226 n. 54, Keyssner, *Gottesvorstellung*, 119, 121–2.

Here, Demeter's claims for herself correspond with those made later for her and Athens as originators of the greatest benefits for mankind: cf. Isocr. *Paneg.* 28 ff. Δήμητρος . . . δούςης δωρεὰς διττάς, αἵπερ μέγιςται τυγχάνουςιν οὖςαι, τούς τε καρπούς . . . καὶ τὴν τελετήν . . ., Cic. *Leg.* 2. 375, *BCH* 24 (1900), 96, etc. On this was based Athens' claim to receive ἀπαρχαί of grain from all over the Greek world (cf. ad *Dem.* 153: Triptolemus).

268–9. For the formula εἰμὶ δὲ . . . ἥ τε . . . τέτυκται cf. Diod. 1. 27. 4 (inscription on the 'tomb of Isis') ἐγώ εἰμι ἡ πρώτη καρπὸν ἀνθρώποις εὑροῦςα . . . Cf. also ad *Dem.* 256 ff.

268. τιμάοχος does not occur in Homer or Hesiod. Cf. *Aph.* 31. In later Greek the forms are τιμοῦχος, τιμῶχος (as a magistrate's title in various cities). The preservation of the ᾱ in epic is unexplained. Cf. τιμάορος (Pi. *O.* 9. 84, A. *Ag.* 514, etc.), Wackernagel, *Zeitschr. f. vergl. Sprachf.* 27 (1885), 263. Hoekstra, *Sub-epic Stage*, 56 considers it an ancient epic Aeolism, and its use here as due to the influence of the Hymn to Aphrodite.

τιμα- epithets are commonly applied to deities in hymns: cf. Keyssner, *Gottesvorstellung*, 66.

On the Orphic papyrus quotation cf. ad *Dem.* 54–6.

269. θνητοῖσί τ᾽ ὄνεαρ: this is preferable to θνητοῖς τ᾽ ὄνεᾱρ as the -οιςι form of the dative is far more common. ὄνεαρ is implied for spoken Ionic by epic ὄνειαρ (with metrical lengthening, after *ὄνηαρ > ὄνεαρ; cf. Choerob. in *An. Ox.* 2. 245). Cf. φρεῖαρ/φρέαρ, etc. (ad *Dem.* 99). For the synizesis cf. ἔαρι Hes. *Op.* 462, ἔαρ *Op.* 492, Mimn. 2. 2, Chaerem. fr. 42; ϲτέᾱτος *Od.* 21. 178, 183, Schulze, *QE* 228. For the hypermetrical epic form cf. ad *Dem.* 137, 173, 284. For the expression μέγιστον . . . θνητοῖσι . . . ὄνεαρ cf. Hes. *Th.* 871, etc., and Keyssner, *Gottesvorstellung*, 122.

Why is Demeter a joy to immortals also? Because they rely on sacrifices from men of her products? Cf. *Dem.* 311 ff., and for a Hittite parallel cf. ad 305 ff. Stoll's conjecture is an attractive way of avoiding this problem, and makes the parallel with *Aph.* 31 f. (cf. ad 268 f.) closer. The corruption would be easy. But ἀθανάτων is perhaps slightly awkward with μέγιστον ὄνεαρ καὶ χάρμα.

χάρμα: cf. *Il.* 14. 325 (of Dionysus, Demeter's counterpart), *Ap.* 25, *Hy.* 16. 4; Pi. *P.* 9. 64 (from Hesiod? Cf. frr. 216, 217); *Paean Erythraeus*, 2. 3 (Powell, *Coll. Alex.* p. 137), Orac. ap. Paus. 2. 26. 7, Orph. *Hy.* 50. 7, etc.; Keyssner, *Gottesvorstellung*, 121.

τέτυκται: for the third person with a relative after first or second person antecedent cf. *Il.* 17. 248 ff., *Hy.* 29. 3 v.l., K–G ii. 406. Here the influence of the neuter predicate is perhaps felt. Cf. also *Aph.* 32, which may have influenced these lines, and A.R. 4. 936, *Hy.* 32. 13, Keyssner, o.c. 119.

270–2. On Demeter's temple see Appendix I. The altar(s) stood in the court in front of the temple. Cf. E. *Supp.* 33, *IG* ii². 1672. 141,

Kourouniotes, *Eleusiniaka*, i. 176, 179. 16–17, Picard, *Rev. Arch.* 34 (1949), 124, Mylonas, *Eleusis*, 90 f.

271. τευχόντων πᾶς δῆμος: for the plural verb with a collective noun cf. K–G i. 53. 2.

ὑπαὶ πόλιν: in Homer ὑπὸ πτόλιν is used (*Il.* 11. 181, 18. 281). ὑπαί is normally used before single consonants (*Il.* 2. 824, 3. 217, 11. 417, 12. 149), but cf. also ὑπαὶ δείους (*Il.* 10. 376, 15. 4: ὑπό v.l.), ὑπαιδείδοικε (*Herm.* 165), ὑπαὶ νεφέων (*Il.* 15. 625, 16. 374, 23. 874: ὑπό v.l.), where ὑπό might be expected. ὑπό/ὑπαί are frequently variants in Homeric manuscripts before λ, ρ, γλ, cπ.

There is no reason to treat ὑπαὶ πόλιν as a 'neologism', as Zumbach (*Neuerungen*, 50) does. Forderer, *Gnomon* 30 (1958), 99, points out that the statistical grounds are not strong enough for this, and that standardization of the Homeric text by the Alexandrians is also possible.

Sanctuaries of Demeter tend to be situated just outside the city. This is true of the Eleusinion in Athens, which is at the foot of the Acropolis (Mylonas, *Eleusis*, 246 f., with bibliography) and of the temple at Agrae, where the Lesser Mysteries were celebrated, outside the walls of Athens (cf. Judeich, *Topographie*, 420 f.). Cf. also Corinth (R. S. Stroud, *Hesp.* 34 (1965), 1 ff., 37 (1968), 299 ff., 38 (1969), 297 ff.); Paros (Hdt. 6. 134); Thasos (Pouilloux, *BCH* 75 (1951), 90 ff., and *Rech. sur l'hist. et les cultes de Thasos* (Paris, 1954), i. 25, 330); Gela (Adamasteanu, *Not. Scavi*, Ser. 8. 10 (1956), 203, 382–92, *Rev. Arch.* 1957. 1, 29 f.); Selinus (M. Santangelo, *Selinunte* (Rome, 1952), 86 ff.); and Y. Béquignon, *Rev. Arch.* 1958. 2, 149 ff., 'Déméter, déesse acropolitaine' (to be treated with caution), Wilamowitz, *Glaube*, i. 205. The same custom was observed in Italy. Vitruvius (1. 7. 2) cites as Etruscan the view that temples of Ceres should be sited 'extra urbem, loco quo ⟨non quolibet⟩ nomine semper homines, nisi per sacrificium, necesse habeant adire'. Cf. Virg. *A.* 2. 713 f., Tac. *A.* 15. 53.

Initiation houses are commonly situated outside the bounds of the community, since initiation often involves a period of seclusion from one's society (cf. Jeanmaire, *Couroi et Courètes*, 190 ff.).

272. Καλλιχόρου καθύπερθεν: on the topography see Appendix I.

The temples of Demeter and Core, and Triptolemus, at Athens are described by Pausanias (1. 14. 1) as ὑπὲρ τὴν κρήνην (Enneacrounos). On the site of Pausanias' Enneacrounos cf. Wycherley, *Athenian Agora III* (*Testimonia*), pp. 137 ff., H. Thompson, *Hesp.* 25 (1956), 52, Gomme ad Thuc. 2. 15 (vol. ii, pp. 53 ff.), Möbius, *AM* 61 (1936), 264 ff.

The temple at Agrae, where the Lesser Mysteries were held, was near the fountain Callirhoe (cf. ad *Dem.* 419, and for its location, *RE* 10. 1669–72). For the association of the cult of Demeter and Core with sacred springs cf. also ad *Dem.* 99.

ἐπὶ προὔχοντι κολωνῷ: κολωνός does not occur in Homer (but cf. κολώνη). Cf. Hes. fr. 59. 2.

Temples of Demeter, or Ceres, were commonly built on a hill or eminence. Cf. the Eleusinion at Athens, and Demeter's temple at

Agrae (Möbius, o.c. 259 ff.); the sanctuary of Demeter εὔχλοος at Colonus (S. *OC* 1600 f.); her Parian temple (Hdt. 6. 134, Rubensohn, *AM* 26 (1901), 215; cf. ad *Dem.* 491); Apul. *M.* 6. 1 'in ardui montis vertice'; and for a general discussion and list of other examples (some rather doubtful) Y. Béquignon, o.c. ad *Dem.* 271. To his list add Corinth, Thasos, and Cnidos.

Möbius (l.c.) notes that at Eleusis, Athens, and Agrae there were also temples of Artemis nearby, and shrines of Plouton, and that all were named as sites of Heracles' initiation (cf. ad *Dem.* 192 ff., 419).

273 f. Objection has been taken to these lines on the ground that the founding of the Mysteries does not occur until after the return of Persephone. But cf. Appendix I.

273. ὄργια: the word is first used here. Cf. *Dem.* 476, *Th.* 179, etc. It is connected with ἔργον, ἔρδω, etc., and hence meant originally 'rites' in general. Cf. *Dem.* 274 ἔρδοντες, 476 δρησμοσύνην θ' ἱερῶν (n. ad loc.). It is used especially of sacrifices (e.g. S. *Ant.* 1013, *Tr.* 765). Here 275 ~ 368–9, which refers explicitly to sacrifices. Then it comes to acquire specific uses in connection with certain cults, e.g. those of Demeter, Dionysus, Cybele, Hecate, Isis and Osiris, and the Bona Dea, and is applied especially to mystery-ceremonies and purification-rituals. On this development cf. N. M. H. van den Burg, Ἀπόρρητα, δρώμενα, ὄργια (Diss. Utrecht, Amsterdam, 1939), 91 ff., C. Zijderveld, Τελετή (Diss. Utrecht, 1934).

At Eleusis, the ὄργια consist of δεικνύμενα, as well as of δρώμενα and λεγόμενα. Hence they are 'shown': cf. 474 ff. δεῖξεν . . . καὶ ἐπέφραδεν, and the later τελετὴν (κατα)δεικνύναι (Zijderveld, o.c. 64). ὑποθήσομαι here perhaps means 'teach, demonstrate' (cf. ad *Dem.* 149).

273 f. The *Hymn* suggests, here and at 368 f., that the Mysteries were still at this period largely a matter of ritual actions (ὄργια, δρώμενα) of propitiation and purification (εὐαγέως . . . ἱλάσκοισθε). Cf. ad *Dem.* 367 ff.

274. εὐαγέως: this does not occur in Homer (ἄζομαι, ἁγνός). Cf. εὐαγής S. *Ant.* 521 etc., εὐαγέως A.R. 2. 699 etc.; Dieterich, *Kl. Schr.* 95, and Zuntz, *Persephone*, 317 n. 3 (on *IG* 14. 641. 2. 7).

ἔρδοντες: M has ἔρδοντες here, ἔρδοντες at 369. The aspirated form is frequent in Homeric manuscripts (also Theognis 690, Epic. ap. Pl. *Euthyphr.* 12 a; cf. Schol. Ar. *Ach.* 329). It is not original (cf. Chantraine, *GH* i. 187 f.).

ἱλάσκοισθε: for the optative in a final clause after a future in the main clause cf. *Od.* 17. 250, Chantraine, *GH* ii. 271. For optative with ἄν in a final clause (with ὡς), cf. *Il.* 19. 328, *Od.* 15. 538, etc.

275–91. Demeter resumes her true appearance, and leaves the palace. Metaneira is terrified, and forgets even to pick up the child. His sisters hear him crying, and leaping from their beds rush to the rescue, one taking him up, another rekindling the fire, a third raising their mother up. They gather round the child, washing him and trying to comfort him. But he is not appeased, for he is in the hands of nurses of far worse quality than before.

This scene is one of the most dramatic in the *Hymn*. After the awesome terror of Demeter's transfiguration, the episode of the sisters trying unsuccessfully to cheer their baby brother has a slightly comical effect, which is perhaps deliberate.

275 ff. *Epiphany*

Cf. ad *Dem.* 188 ff. The second epiphany is on a fuller scale, and takes place at Demeter's departure. Its characteristics are:

1. Supernatural stature and appearance.
2. Loss of old age.
3. Beauty 'breathed around'.
4. Divine fragrance from the goddess's clothes.
5. Divine radiance from her body, filling the house like lightning.
6. Hair flowing down over her shoulders.
7. Fear and speechlessness of the onlooker.

Supernatural stature (cf. ad 188 ff.) and beauty are often conjoined: cf. *Il.* 24. 630 (~ Virg. *A.* 2. 591 f.), *Od.* 6. 151 f., *Aph.* 85, 173 ff., Hdt. 1. 60 (Phye), 7. 12, D.H. 6. 13, Plut. *Arat.* 32, *Sulla* 17, Polyaen. 8. 59, Longus 2. 23. 1, Philostr. *Heroic.* 685, Tac. *H.* 4. 83, Pfister, *RE, Supp.* 4. 314, Deubner, *De Incubatione* (Diss. Inaug. Giessen, 1899), 12. They go together with divine radiance in *Aph.* 85 ff., 173 ff., Virg. *A.* 2. 589 ff. (cf. Claud. *Cons. Stil.* 2. 275 ff.).

Similarly, youth and beauty (276) are often linked: cf. Tac. *H.* 4. 83, Marin. *Vit. Procl.* 7, 32, Cic. *de div.* 1. 25. 53, Philostr. *Heroic.* 673 p. 141. 25, Kenyon, *Gk. Papyri*, p. 124. 11 ff., Wessely, *Gr. Zauberpap.* p. 36. 634 ff., Plato, *Crito*, 44 a f., Deubner, o.c. 12 f.

For divine fragrance (277 f.) cf. *Herm.* 231, *Hy.* 7. 36, Hes. fr. 140, Theognis 9, A. *PV* 115, E. *Hipp.* 1391, Mosch. 2. 91, A.R. 4. 430 ff., Virg. *A.* 1. 403, Ov. *F.* 5. 375; Pfister, *RE, Supp.* 4. 316. 4 ff., *RE* 1A. 267 ff., E. Lohmeyer, 'Vom göttlichen Wohlgeruch' (*Sb. Heidelb.* 1919, Ph.-hist. Klasse, Abh. 9), W. Schmid, *Philol.* 78 (1923), 179, Eitrem, *Opferritus*, 211 f.

For divine radiance cf. ad *Dem.* 188 ff., and also Hes. fr. 43 (a). 73 f. (ad 277 ff.), Deubner, o.c. 10 f., 13. Shining robes are common in epiphanies: cf. *Aph.* 86, *Hy.* 31. 13 f., 32. 8, Pl. *Crito* 44 a f., P. Oxy. 1381. 119 f., Wessely, l.c. above, Matth. 17 : 2, Mark 9 : 3, Luke 9 : 29.

Metaneira's reactions are fear (cf. ad *Dem.* 188 ff.) and speechlessness. For stunned silence after an epiphany cf. A.R. 2. 683 ff., 4. 880 (ad *Dem.* 237 ff.), Moschus *Eur.* 18 (ad *Dem.* 282), Virg. *A.* 2. 774 = 3. 48, 4. 279 f., Ov. *M.* 9. 472, Apul. *M.* 11. 14, Luke 1 : 20 ff., Pfister, *RE, Supp.* 4. 318.

276. γῆρας ἀπωсαμένη: old age is thought of as if it were something material. Cf. *Il.* 9. 446 and *Nostoi*, fr. 6, where it is 'scraped off'. The slough of a snake was called γῆρας (Arist. *HA* 549ᵇ26, Nic. *Ther.* 31, etc.) and it is perhaps seen as a kind of wrinkled skin.

περί τ' ἀμφί τε: cf. *Il.* 17. 760, Hes. *Th.* 848, fr. 150. 28, Call. fr. 260. 13, *Hy.* 4. 300, A.R. 2. 1208, 3. 633, etc. (Theocr. 7. 142 περί ... ἀμφί).

κάλλος ἄητο: beauty is also seen here as a sort of 'physical emana-
tion'. Cf. Hes. *Th.* 583, fr. 43 (a). 74, *Sc.* 7 f. In *Od.* 23. 156 Athene
pours beauty down over Odysseus' head. Cf. *Aph.* 174 f. κάλλος δὲ
παρειάων ἀπέλαμπεν ἄμβροτον (cf. ad *Dem.* 189). In Pl. *Phaedr.* 251 c
beauty flows from the beloved in the form of desire. Cf. Virg. *A.* 1. 591
(*adflarat*); Onians, *Origins of European Thought*, 73 f.

277. θυηέντων: for θυήεις of clothes cf. *Od.* 5. 264 etc. This sense
('fragrant') may be secondary, from βωμὸς θυήεις, i.e. 'an altar on
which sacrifices are made' (cf. Eust. ad *Il.* 23. 148 (1293. 28), Stengel,
*Opferbräuche*³, 4).

πέπλων: the plural is not used for a single robe in Homer. Cf.
Dem. 176 ἑανῶν.

278. φέγγος: not in Homer or Hesiod. Cf. Pi. *P.* 8. 97 etc., and
Attic poetry. In classical Attic prose it seems to be used normally of
moonlight (cf. Hsch. s.v. and the modern Greek φεγγάρι 'moon').
Occasionally its use seems to reflect the language of the Mysteries: cf.
Pi. *O.* 2. 55 f. (ad *Dem.* 489), Ar. *Ran.* 344, 448, 456, and especially
Pl. *Phaedr.* 250 b (where the whole passage is in 'mystic' language).
See also Introduction, pp. 26 ff. For Pindar's light-imagery cf. Bowra,
Pindar 35 f. and references ad loc.; also L. W. Lyde, *Contexts in Pindar*
(Manchester, 1935).

ἀπὸ χροός: cf. ad *Dem.* 189.

279. θεᾶς: cf. ad *Dem.* 183. On the position of θεᾶς, after a verb
in the first trochee, with enjambement, see Appendix V.

ξανθαὶ δὲ κόμαι: cf. ad *Dem.* 302.

κατενήνοθεν: not in Homer, and there is no other example of
ἀνήνοθε(ν), ἐνήνοθε(ν), or their compounds with a plural subject. They
occur five times in Homer: *Il.* 2. 219, 10. 134, 11. 266, *Od.* 8. 365,
17. 270; cf. *Aph.* 62, Hes. *Sc.* 269, and later A.R. 1. 664, 4. 276, Nic.
Al. 509. The use here is treated as a σχῆμα Πινδαρικόν by K–G i. 68,
Schwyzer, *Gr. Gr.* ii. 608, Maas, *Epidaurische Hymnen*, 19. The only
examples of this in epic are Hes. *Th.* 321, 825 (cf. West ad loc.).
There ἦν is followed by a plural subject, a common type later. It is
very rare for the subject to precede the verb (cf. Pi. *O.* 11. 4 ff., fr.
70b. 9 f.). Here the plural subject is more probably due to the error
of supposing the verb to be plural (by analogy with third pl. aor. pass.
-θεν?). This mistake may have arisen during transmission rather than
in the original composition (but cf. Hoekstra, *Sub-epic Stage* 49). For
the singular noun (κόμη) cf. *Il.* 1. 197, Archil. 31 West, Anacr.
PMG 347. 1 f. Contrast E. *Ba.* 695 καθεῖσαν εἰς ὤμους κόμας. The
plural κόμαι is less frequent in Homer (singular ten times; plural
three).

The origin and meaning of the verb are uncertain. Frisk s.v. ἐνθεῖν
interprets ἐνήνοθε as reduplicated perfect and pluperfect of ἐνθεῖν
(Doric, Delph., and Arc. for ἐλθεῖν), ἀνήνοθε as either a variant form
of this, or by haplology for *ἀνενήνοθεν (cf. Schol. A.R. 1. 664).
Another explanation derives these forms from the root of ἀνθεῖν
(V. Pisani, *Rend. Ist. Lomb.* 77 (1943–4), 548; see also J. M. Aitchison,

Glotta 41 (1963), 273 f.). The original sense of ἄνθος, ἀνθεῖν may be 'growth, grow' (cf. Buttmann, *Lexilogus*, 133 f., Aitchison, l.c.). The sense 'grow on the surface' for ἐπενήνοθε suits *Il.* 2. 219, 10. 134, and that of 'spring up' suits ἀνήνοθε in *Il.* 11. 266, *Od.* 17. 270. ἐπανθέω comes to mean 'be on the surface' (cf. LSJ s.v.). Hence οἷα θεοὺς ἐπενήνοθεν in *Od.* 8. 365, *Aph.* 62 = 'such as covers gods', and similarly in *Dem.* 279, Hes. *Sc.* 269 'covered the shoulders' would suit. In *Dem.* 279 'grew down (over)' would also give a vivid sense (cf. in a similar transformation-scene *Od.* 6. 231 = 23. 158 οὔλας ἧκε κόμας). Later -ένηνοθε was commonly seen as an equivalent of the verb substantive (cf. A.R. 1. 664, *Et. M.*, Apollon. *Lex.* s.v. ἐπενήνοθε, Buttmann, *Lexilogus*, 112).[1] See also Stanford, *Gk. Metaphor*, 111–14, Onians, *Origins of Eur. Thought*, 232.

A stele of the early fifth century B.C. from Eleusis shows Demeter seated, wearing a polos, with her hair flowing down over her shoulders (cf. Mylonas, *Eleusis*, 191 f., Fig. 67). The worshippers of Demeter wore their hair unbound at Lycosura, Andania and Alexandria, but this was apparently in contrast to Demeter, who was veiled (cf. ad *Dem.* 42, 176 ff.).

280. αὐγῆς: for the corruption (αὐτῆς in M) cf. S. *Ph.* 1199, and the frequent interchange of γῆς and τῆς.

281. διέκ: M has δι' ἐκ here (*contra* Allen and Halliday) and at *Dem.* 379, διεκ at *Herm.* 158. Cf. the variants at *Ap.* 110, 428 (*teste* Goodwin), *Herm.* 547, *Aph.* 36, and Herodian περὶ 'Ιλ. προσῳδίας 1. 7 p. 248 Lehrs, La Roche, *HU* 333 ff., K–B i. 297b.

281 ff. For Metaneira's reactions cf. ad *Dem.* 188–90, 274 ff. Fear and stunned silence are also characteristic reactions to speeches in epic: cf. *Od.* 4. 703 f., Hes. *Th.* 167 f., and for silence, West ad loc., Bühler, *Moschus, Europa*, 64 f.

282. δηρὸν . . . χρόνον: cf. parallels ad loc. and *Hy.* 28. 14, Ibyc. *PMG* 283, A. *Supp.* 516 etc. (always δᾱρὸν χρόνον in tragedy). δηρόν (or δαρόν) alone, as an adverb, is more common in epic and also later.

283. τηλυγέτοιο: cf. ad *Dem.* 164.

ἀπὸ δαπέδου: in Homer there are no examples of vowel-lengthening before δάπεδον. But cf. *Od.* 11. 598, where Arist. *Rhet.* 1411ᵇ34 has ἐπὶ δάπεδον δέ (ἔπειτα δάπεδόν (δε) some *Odyssey* MSS.). The variant perhaps arose from corruption of ΕΠΕΙΤΑΠΕΔΟΝΔΕ to ΕΠΙΖΑΠΕΔΟΝΔΕ (cf. Ludwich ad Ar. *Av.* 1265). The form ζάπεδον occurs in Stesich. P. Oxy. 2617 fr. 4 i 17, Xenoph. 1. 1, *IG* 12 (5) 214 (Paros *c.* 500 B.C.: verse inscription), Hsch. s.v. Cf. also Ar. *Av.* 1265, where Ludwich reads ζάπεδον *metri causa* (the language is elevated: cf. 1263). The ζ is secondary, and is perhaps due to reverse analogy with ζα/δα- (as intensive prefix). Cf. also ζάκορος (for *δάκορος), and perhaps ζακρυόεις (for δακρυόεις?); Solmsen, *RhM* 60 (1905), 500 f., *IF* 31 (1912/13), 453 ff., Risch, *Mus. Helv.* 3 (1946), 255, Chantraine, *GH* i. 169, Schwyzer, *Gr. Gr.* i. 330, R. Sjölund, *Metrische Kürzung im*

---

[1] W. F. Wyatt Jr., *Metrical Lengthening in Homer* (Rome, 1969), 116 ff. suggests a root *eno-, meaning 'move (upwards) from within'.

Griechischen (Diss. Uppsala, 1938), 24 ff. Solmsen and Risch take the metrical lengthening to be a post-Homeric feature. But it may have occurred in earlier epic.

284. Cf. *Od.* 11. 421 οἰκτροτάτην δ᾿ ἤκουϲα ὄπα Πριάμοιο θυγατρόϲ. ἐλεινήν: M's ἐλεεινήν is hypermetric (cf. Introduction, p. 66). ἐλεινόϲ is the Attic form, but the contraction is perfectly possible in epic.

Hoekstra, *Sub-epic Stage*, 55, however, points out that both the juxtaposition of φωνή and ἀκούειν (cf. *Dem.* 23 and 57) and the contraction are new to epic, and considers the line an example of the adaptation of traditional diction.

285. κὰδ᾿ δ᾿ ἄρ᾿ ἀπ᾿ εὐϲτρώτων λεχέων θόρον: εὔϲτρωτοϲ does not occur in Homer. Cf. *Aph.* 157, also Hes. *Th.* 798 (ϲτρωτόϲ). *Aph.* 157a follows 156b = *Dem.* 194b (cf. ad loc.). Heitsch (*Aphroditehymnos*, 38) argues for the influence of the *Hymn to Aphrodite*, on the ground that the new word εὔϲτρωτοϲ is explained in *Aph.* 157b–8a. This is unconvincing. But the *Hymn to Aphrodite* may well be the model for the passage in this *Hymn* on other grounds (cf. ad *Dem.* 188 f.). The poet probably also had Hes. *Th.* 798 in mind: 796 f. ~ *Dem.* 49 f. (also 200 f. ?), 802 ff. ~ *Dem.* 354 f.

Moschus *Eur.* 16 ff. is very probably a reminiscence of this passage. Cf. Bühler ad loc., and ad *Dem.* 282, 293.

In *Dem.* 285 the girls jump *down* from their beds, and this is surely what happens in Moschus also. Europa then sits down, *Eur.* 18, and finally jumps up and goes out, 28 ff. Bühler interprets *Eur.* 16 to mean that she sits *up* in bed. It is hard to believe that ἀπό . . . θόρε can mean this.

285 ff. For the list of different activities cf. *Od.* 10. 352 ff., 20. 149 ff. (where 153 f. ~ *Dem.* 106. Cf. also ad *Dem.* 287, 289 f.).

287. πόϲϲ᾿ ἁπαλοῖϲι: for this rare elision of ποϲϲί cf. *Il.* 20. 497, Hes. *Th.* 3, K–B i. 236, La Roche, *HU* 125. The formula has more point in Hes. l.c. than here, where it is rather 'ornamental'.

289. Cf. *AP* 9. 331 αἱ Νύμφαι τὸν Βάκχον ὅτ᾿ ἐκ πυρὸς ἥλατο κοῦροϲ | νίψαν ὑπὲρ τέφρηϲ ἄρτι κυλιόμενον.

ἐλούεον: this form does not occur elsewhere, and is perhaps due to contamination of epic λοέω and the more recent λούω (Schulze, *QE* 65 n. 1). For the Homeric forms cf. Chantraine, *GH* i. 34, and in general Schwyzer, *Gr. Gr.* i. 682. See also Solmsen, *Untersuchungen*, 13, and *Zeitschr. f. vergl. Sprachf.* 29 (1888), 98; Jacobsohn, ibid. 42 (1908–9), 156 n. 1.

289 f. The sound-pattern, with assonance of α and ε, is striking. Cf. *Od.* 20. 123 (ad *Dem.* 287), which the poet may have had in mind (124 ~ *Dem.* 285; cf. also ad 285 ff.), and *Dem.* 436. α and ε are the commonest letters, and such assonance is frequent, especially in formulaic phrases (cf. *Dem.* 67, 72, 78, 90, etc. for ἀ-, 230, 284, 409 for ἐ-). Lines with predominant initial vowels are also common (*c.* 30 in the *Hymn*: cf. especially 26, 127, 264, 273 f., 289 f., 363, 382, 407, 409, 480 f.), but this is natural in Greek. Later critics express admiration for vowel-patterns: cf. Demetr. *de Eloc.* 69 f., D.H. *de Comp.*

15, 167. 27 ff. U., also Arist. *Poet.* 1458ᵇ31, and Stanford, *The Sound of Greek* (Univ. of California Press, 1967), especially chaps. 3 and 4. Dionysius considers α the most euphonious sound, η the next (o.c. 14). It is hard to say how often a vowel-pattern is intentional, or whether the poet on any particular occasion is aware of its effect. (For notable vowel sound effects cf. *Il.* 1. 52, 22. 509, *Od.* 4. 442.) In the case of *Dem.* 289 f. it seems probable that the sound effect was consciously produced, or at least that the poet realized its existence.

For a general discussion of alliteration and assonance in Homer cf. A. Shewan, *CP* 20 (1925), 193 ff. (for assonance of α and ε cf. 198 ff.). He concludes that such sound effects are often (but not always) intentional, and are especially common in formulaic phrases. Cf. also (on Hesiod) A. J. Carney, *CP* 12 (1917), 225 ff., K. J. McKay, *Symb. Osl.* 36 (1960), 17 ff.

290. Words occupying the first half of the hexameter are not common: cf. *Dem.* 31, 85, 364 (πατρο-/αὐτο-κασίγνητος) and 436.

291. Cf. Pl. *Tim.* 88 d τροφὸν καὶ τιθήνην, and *Orph. Hy.* 10. 18.

292–304. The women propitiate Demeter throughout the night. At dawn they tell Celeus what she has commanded, and he summons the people and orders them to build the temple and altar. The temple is built, and they go home. Demeter sits in it, and remains there, mourning for her daughter.

The epiphany is followed by honours to the goddess (cf. ad *Dem.* 268 ff.). 292 f. refer to a παννυχίς in which the women alone took part. This may be a reflection of the παννυχίς on Boedromion 20th, after the arrival of the Iacchus procession in later times, in which women and men were apparently separated (Ar. *Ran.* 444–8), and there was dancing around Callichoron and perhaps αἰσχρολογία (cf. ad *Dem.* 192 ff. 3. Iambe). In the *Hymn* the ceremony takes place inside the palace (cf. Mylonas, *Hymn to Demeter*, 79 f.), but this is true also of *Dem.* 192 ff., which certainly refers to ritual performed elsewhere in later times. The atmosphere of dread (*Dem.* 293) might be considered inappropriate to a παννυχίς (cf. Ziehen, *RE* 18. 3. 629 f. s.v. *Παννυχίς*), and especially to what we know of the Eleusinian ceremony. But *Dem.* 192 ff. shows a mixture or alternation of solemnity and laughter (cf. ad loc.), and parts of the Eleusinian παννυχίς were probably characterized by a more solemn atmosphere. If there is a reference to actual ritual here, it is more likely to refer to the Mysteries than to the Thesmophoria (cf. Ar. *Thesm.* 280, 655, 947 ff., 1151, Allen and Halliday ad *Dem.* 292) or the Haloa or Stenia (Alciphr. 4. 6. 3, Phot. s.v. *Στήνια*).

293. For the women's terror after the epiphany cf. ad *Dem.* 188–90, 275 ff. For fear as a reaction to the Mysteries cf. ad *Dem.* 188–90. C. P. Segal (*HSCP* 75 (1971), 44 n. 22) notes that πάλλεσθαι is used in a quasi-metaphorical sense in Homer only at *Il.* 22. 452 and 461, and he assumes that *Dem.* 293 is an imitation of this passage (see notes to *Dem.* 38 ff.).

294. εὐρυβίη: this does not occur in Homer (cf. Hom. εὐρυςθενής, ὑπέρβιος). It is especially used of sea-deities (cf. West ad *Th.* 239), and of Poseidon in particular in Pi. *O.* 6. 58, *P.* 2. 12 (∼ *P.* 4. 173-6 of Periclymenus, son of Poseidon).

295. For ὡς cf. *Dem.* 172 (n. ad loc.), 416.

296. πολυπείρονα: this occurs only here and in Orph. *Arg.* 33. It is perhaps modelled on δῆμος/λαὸς ἀπείρων (*Il.* 24. 776, Hes. *Sc.* 472); cf. also ὅμιλος ἀπείριτος *Aph.* 120. The meaning seems to be 'with many boundaries, manifold' (cf. LSJ s.v.). The poet apparently took the ἀ- of ἀπείρων as intensive. Cf. Zumbach, *Neuerungen*, 19. For this poet's fondness for πολυ- compounds cf. Introduction, p. 61.

300. ὁ δ' ἀέξετο δαίμονος αἴςῃ: the temple grows 'by the dispensation (or decree?) of the deity'. Cf. Maiistas, *Hymn to Sarapis*, 33 ff. (Powell, *Coll. Alex.* p. 70) ςέθεν δ' ἅμα βουλομένοιο ῥηιδίως καὶ νειὸς ἀέξετο καὶ θυόεντες βωμοὶ καὶ τέμενος (etc.).

The phrase is a vague one for this context, since δαίμων is normally used where one is not certain of the exact nature of the divine agency involved. In δαίμονος αἶςα the original sense of δαίμων ('distributor') is perhaps felt (cf. Scholl. AD ad *Il.* 1. 222, Wilamowitz, *Glaube*, i. 363 ff., Dodds, *Greeks and the Irrational*, 12 ff., Chantraine, *Entretiens Fondation Hardt*, i. 50 ff., 81 f.). αἶςα, like μοῖρα, is what the δαίμων dispenses. (In *Il.* 8. 166 δαίμων = μοῖρα, fate.) On αἶςα in Homer cf. B. C. Dietrich, *Death, Fate and the Gods* (Univ. of London, 1965), 249 ff., 257 f. Cf. also δαιμόνη meaning 'distribution' in Alcm. *PMG* 65, A. *Eum.* 727 (P. Maas, *Zeitschr. für vergl. Sprachf.* 60 (1932), 285 f.).

302. βάν ῥ' ἴμεν οἴκαδ' ἕκαστος: this represents an 'untraditional' combination of the Homeric βάν ῥ' ἴμεν and ἔβαν οἰκόνδε ἕκαστος (note double neglect of digamma). Cf. Hoekstra, *Sub-epic Stage*, 52, and on ἀτάρ C. J. Ruijgh, *L'Élément achéen dans la langue épique*, 43 ff.

ξανθὴ Δημήτηρ: cf. *Il.* 5. 500, Orph. fr. 268 K., *Lith.* 588, *Dem.* 279; ξανθοκόμος Nonn. *D.* 11. 395, ξανθοφυής 6. 113; 'flava Ceres', Virg. *G.* 1. 96, Ov. *F.* 4. 424 (Bömer, ad loc.); of Persephone, *AP* 7. 507. The epithet is commonly used of goddesses and heroines in poetry, but is specially suitable to Demeter as the goddess of the ripe corn. Cf. Serv. ad Virg. *G.* 1. 96 ' "flava" dicitur propter aristarum colorem in maturitate'; Ov. *M.* 6. 118 'et te flava comas frugum mitissima mater'; *Am.* 3. 10. 3 'flava Ceres, tenues spicis redimita capillos' (∼ 3. 10. 36). As goddess of the young corn she is Demeter Χλόη (Paus. 1. 22. 3; Farnell, *Cults*, iii. 33 ff., 312 f.).

In *Il.* 5. 500 the epithet is appropriate to the context of threshing. Here there is an irony, probably unconscious, in the fact that the line introduces the episode of the Famine (cf. ad *Dem.* 305 ff.). Cf. Lucan, 4. 411 f. 'non proserit ullam flava Ceres segetem.'

Parallel to ξανθὴ Δημήτηρ is the Hindu goddess of abundance Gaurī, whose name means simply 'yellow', and is emblematic of the ripened harvest. Her effigies are also painted in this colour. Cf. Frazer, *GB*[3] v. 241.

Just as Demeter's hair is golden like the corn, so the corn-ears are compared to a growth of hair in *Dem.* 454 (cf. ad loc.).
303. Cf. *Dem.* 92, 354 ff.

305–33. Demeter causes a universal famine. Mankind is threatened with extinction, and the gods with loss of their sacrifices and honours. Zeus sends Iris to ask Demeter to return to Olympus. She does not listen, and he then sends the other gods, who come in turn and promise her gifts and honours. She still refuses to return, until she has seen her daughter again.

The motif of the Famine caused by the anger or disappearance of a deity is common in Greece and elsewhere. Here it is Demeter's anger which causes it, but in another form of the myth it may have been the disappearance of Persephone which made the earth barren, just as her reappearance coincides with the new flowers in spring (*Dem.* 401 ff.), and is followed by the growth of the crops (453 ff., 471 ff.).

In the Arcadian myth of Demeter at Phigaleia, a universal famine is caused by Demeter's withdrawal into a cavern, in anger at Poseidon, with whom she had mated, and also over the rape of her daughter. The human race began to perish, but Pan found Demeter's hiding-place, and Zeus sent the Fates to persuade her to lay aside her anger (Paus. 8. 42).

In the Babylonian myth of Tammuz, when Ishtar goes down to the underworld to look for Tammuz, the forces of reproduction cease to operate and all life is threatened with extinction, until a messenger of the great god Ea is sent to bring her back (Frazer *GB*[3] 5. 8 f.; Pritchard, *ANET*[2] 52 ff., 106 ff.). In the laments for Tammuz, he is himself compared to parched or barren nature (Frazer, o.c. 9 f., S. Langdon, *Tammuz and Ishtar* (Oxford, 1914), 10 f.).

The Egyptian myth of Tefnut tells how she withdrew in anger to the desert, and became a lioness (or cat). She was persuaded to return by the magic and eloquence of Thoth (cf. S. West, *JEA* 55 (1969), 161 ff.).

In Hittite mythology, when the god Telepinu flies into a rage and disappears, all nature becomes barren and begins to perish, and the gods also starve. A search for the missing god is instituted. First, the Eagle is sent out, but cannot find him. The Storm-god then looks for him, and then all the other gods, but they are unsuccessful. The Bee is sent to sting him, but this makes him still more angry. Finally, he is pacified by the combined ritual and incantation of the goddess of magic and healing and Man, and returns home. All things are then restored to normal (Pritchard, o.c. 126 ff.).

This Hittite myth shows many similarities with the narrative of the *Hymn*, in particular the references to the gods' perishing of hunger, and to the series of unsuccessful attempts to find Telepinu and bring him back. (In the *Hymn*, it is the third attempt of Zeus which suc-ceeds, a regular motif of folk-tales: cf. Deichgräber, *Eleus. Frömmig-keit*, 510.) The Hittite story of the Sun-god's disappearance also has some similarities (cf. S. N. Kramer, *Mythologies of the Ancient World*, 148; O. Gurney, *The Hittites*, 187-8).

In the Ugaritic myth of Baal and Mot, Baal's absence in the underworld causes universal barrenness. 'Anat and Shapash (the sun-goddess) 'go down into the earth' to recover him (cf. T. H. Gaster, *Thespis* (New York, 1950), 201 f., 221; S. H. Hooke, *Middle Eastern Mythology* (Penguin Books, 1963), 84 ff.). In the Poem of Aqhat, the earth is also made barren when Aqhat is killed (Gaster, 257 ff., 295 ff.; Hooke, 89 ff.). For other examples of the disastrous withdrawal, and recovery or return, of a deity in Near-Eastern mythology see G. S. Kirk, *Myth* (Cambridge, 1970), 92, 99, 102, 106, 108 f.

It is notable that in one version of the Greek myth, Demeter also goes down to Hades to find Persephone (cf. *Orph. Hy.* 41. 5, Schol. Pi. *O.* 6. 95 (160), Ov. *M.* 5. 533, *F.* 4. 611 ff., Hyg. *fab.* 251, Lact. *Narr.* 5. 8; also Virg. *G.* 1. 39, Servius ad loc., and the story of Ascalabus, Apollod. 1. 5. 3). Cf. Malten, *ARW* 12 (1909), 440 n. 4, *Hermes* 45 (1910), 515 f., 533; Wehrli, *ARW* 31 (1934), 82 ff., Kerényi, *Eleusis*, 43, and Introduction, p. 84.

According to the version later prevalent Demeter rewarded the Eleusinians for their reception of her, and in some accounts for the information which they gave her as to the author and place of the Rape, by the gift of corn and of the arts of agriculture (*Orph. Hy.* 41. 7, Orph. frr. 49. 103 ff., 51). Isocrates (*Paneg.* 28) says that Demeter was well disposed to the people of Attica because of benefits whose nature may only be revealed to the initiated, and so gave them the Mysteries and the gift of agriculture. These benefits cannot simply be Demeter's reception at Eleusis (as Wehrli supposes, *ARW* 31 (1934), 78 n. 1, referring especially to the proceedings in *Dem.* 192 ff.), since this was not secret. More probably it refers to the Orphic version(s), and the revelations made to Demeter by the Eleusinians about the Rape (although this is also referred to by Pausanias 1. 14. 3, and others).

The *Hymn*, in contrast, plainly presupposes the presence of agriculture. This suits the Homeric epic context. But the myth of Demeter's gift of corn may go back before this, and it is notable that an Orphic version (which reflects local tradition) again preserves it. Other local legends made Demeter learn the truth about the Rape from the local inhabitants, whom she then rewards in various ways (cf. ad *Dem.* 75). It is possible that *Dem.* 471 ff. reflects this version, since Demeter makes the corn grow, and immediately afterwards teaches the princes her cult (cf. Wehrli, o.c. 87 ff., Kerényi, o.c. 120 f., 127). An account of the origin of the fruits of the earth should form some part of the original mythology of Demeter and Persephone. The prominence of Triptolemus as the first cultivator apparently dates from the sixth century B.C. (cf. ad *Dem.* 153), but reflects the importance of the agricultural element in the original cult (cf. Nilsson, *ARW* 32 (1935), 86).

The *Hymn* is evidently combining two separate stories, the account of Demeter's visit to Eleusis and gift of the Mysteries (and/or agriculture) to the inhabitants, and the Famine-motif. Her original purpose in visiting Eleusis, to find her daughter, is removed in the *Hymn*, and her visit is consequently less clearly motivated. The second theme of the Famine interrupts the progress of the first, since it postpones the communication of the Mysteries which is promised in *Dem.* 273 f. The two themes do not easily fit together, as in one the return of Persephone leads to the gift of the crops for the first time, in the other to their restoration. Hence the Famine has no place in the Orphic version(s) (cf. Wehrli, o.c. 87 ff.).

Diodorus (5. 68) presents a rationalized solution to the inconsistency. According to this account, corn grew wild, and was discovered by Demeter. After the Rape, she destroyed it, and on the Return of Persephone she restored it and gave it to Triptolemus to sow. Ovid, perhaps following a similar Hellenistic version, also combines the two stories (*F.* 4. 559 f., 617, *M.* 5. 646 f., cf. Bömer ad *Fasti* l.c., Herter, *RhM* 90 (1941), 263 ff.).

305. ἐπὶ χθόνα: for the accusative cf. *Od.* 23. 371, *Ap.* 69, Hes. *Th.* 95, 187, 531, *Op.* 11, 487, 505. The dative is commoner in Homer.

306. ἀνθρώποιc: the short form occurs nowhere in the *Iliad*, three times in the *Odyssey* (at the beginning of the verse). Cf. parallels ad loc., and ad *Dem.* 11.

κύντατον: cf. ad *Dem.* 90, and κύντερον of the belly, *Od.* 7. 216, as here of famine.

308. καμπύλ' ἄροτρα: cf. Sol. 1. 48 and εὐκαμπὲc ἄροτρον Mosch. 2. 81, Orph. fr. 280. 3 K., 'curvi . . . aratri' Lucr. 5. 933 (∼ 6. 1253, Virg. *G.* 1. 494), also Moschion fr. 6. 9 ἀρότροιc καμπύλοιc? (ex coni. Nauck).

μάτην: not in Homer or Hesiod (μάψ, αὔτωc). Cf. Theognis 523, Solon 23. 19 etc.

εἷλκον: the two forms ἕλκον and εἷλκον are frequently variants in Homeric manuscripts. The augmented form is more common, but editors usually follow Aristarchus (at *Il.* 4. 213) in reading the unaugmented form. There is however no necessity to alter the text here.

ἀρούραιc: for the local dative cf. ad *Dem.* 99. For the ending -αιc (at the end of a line) cf. ad *Dem.* 40 f.

308 f. The two lines are parallel in structure, and form an expansion of 306 f.

310–13. καί νύ κε . . . εἰ μή: this is very common in Homer (twenty-seven times) and early epic. Cf. especially Hes. *Th.* 836 ff. For καί νύ κεν . . . καί κεν . . . εἰ μὴ ἄρ' ὀξὺ νόηcε πατὴρ ἀνδρῶν τε θεῶν τε (cf. ad *Dem.* 13 f., 38) cf. *Il.* 8. 131 f., *Dem.* 242–3.

311. λιμοῦ ὑπ' ἀργαλέηc: for the feminine cf. Call. fr. 346 Pf., Callisth. ap. Ath. 10. 452 b, Doric and late Greek. It may be due to influence from the formula νούcῳ/ου ὑπ' ἀργαλέῃ/ηc (*Il.* 13. 667, Hes. *Sc.* 43). Cf. Zumbach, *Neuerungen*, 4 f.

311 f. The gods are dependent on the τιμαί and sacrifices of mortals. Cf. Pl. *Symp.* 190 c, where the gods refrain from killing the human race when they misbehave: αἱ τιμαὶ γὰρ αὐτοῖc καὶ τὰ ἱερὰ τὰ παρὰ τῶν ἀνθρώπων ἠφανίζετο. Cf. also Ar. *Av.* 183 ff., *Nub.* 618 ff. The Hittite myth of Telepinu has a similar motif (cf. ad *Dem.* 305 ff.). Cf. also the tale of Ullikummi (*ANET*² 124 f.), where the gods, deprived of sacrifices, grow dizzy and faint, and for further Near-Eastern parallels, P. Walcot, *Hesiod and the Near East* (Cardiff, 1966), 56 f.

Deprivation or absence of his τιμή is detrimental to a god. Cf. Hes. *Th.* 392 ff., *Herm.* 167 ff., E. *IT* 1267 ff., 1280, Nonn. *D.* 12. 23 ff., Keyssner, *Gottesvorstellung*, 58 ff., A. W. H. Adkins, *Merit and Responsibility*, 63.

The τιμή which men pay the gods consists in gifts, sacrifices, etc. Cf. *Dem.* 353, 366 ff., Keyssner, o.c. 60 f. γέρας and τιμή are often coupled, and used more or less synonymously: cf. Hes. *Th.* 393 (West ad loc.), 396, 426 f., *Hy.* 29. 4. The genitive of γέρας is not found in Homer (cf. *Th.* 393, 396).

312. θυϲιῶν: not in Homer or Hesiod (θύος). Cf. *Dem.* 368 (n. ad loc.), *Titanomachia* fr. 6, Pi. *P.* 5. 86, etc., Hdt., Attic.

ἤμερϲε: this is used only here with double accusative, normally with accusative and genitive (*Od.* 8. 64, where the accusative dual is a variant reading, etc.).

312. Zeus seems to be unaware at first of what is going on. Cf., for example, *Iliad* 14. 159 ff. For the ambiguity of his role cf. ad *Dem.* 3. He is not seen as all-knowing and all-powerful here: his first two attempts to persuade Demeter to relent are unsuccessful. But in the end, his will is fulfilled (cf. *Dem.* 441 ff.).

314–23. These lines show the traditional *schema* of a messenger's journey (cf. Arend, *Typische Scenen*, 54 ff., esp. 56 n. 3: Botschaft). Cf. *Dem.* 334 ff., 441 ff.

1. Zeus addresses messenger: 314–15, 335–9, 441–7.
2. Messenger obeys: 316–17a, 340a, 448.
3. Journey: 317b, 340b–1, 449.
4. Arrival: 318 (ἵκετο . . .), 450 (ἷξε . . .).
5. Situation: 319 (εὗρεν δ' . . .), 342–5 (τέτμε δὲ . . .), cf. ad *Dem.* 179.
6. Speech: 320–3, 346–56, 459–69.
7. The person visited obeys (or does not do so): 324 (οὐκ ἐπεπείθετο), 357–8 (οὐδ' ἀπίθηϲε), 470 (οὐδ' ἀπίθηϲεν).

These three cases differ from the normal epic tradition, in that the poet avoids the use of direct speech by Zeus (cf. also 325 ff., and 172–3). The only case of omission of direct speech in Homer occurs at *Il.* 7. 416, where a message is not repeated by a herald (cf. *Ap.* 110 ff., and Page, *History and the Homeric Iliad*, 340). Cf. Hes. *Th.* 392 ff. (and similarly 475–6, West ad loc.), *Op.* 60 ff., *Ap.* 102 ff., K–G ii. 542 f., L. R. Palmer in Wace–Stubbings, *Companion to Homer*, 157. In *Dem.* 316, 448 ὣς ἔφατο is used, as if a speech had preceded: cf. Hes. *Op.* 69, A.R. 4. 236, 1121. In Homer this occurs only inside another speech: *Il.* 23. 149, *Od.* 8. 570 = 13. 178. In the *Hymn* the poet is perhaps diverging from normal epic convention to avoid making his narrative too long. In contrast, however, he repeats the account of the Rape in full (414 ff.). The avoidance of direct speech also adds to the remoteness of Zeus as supreme god.

It is rare for a messenger to add his own injunction or comments to a message, as is the case in *Dem.* 323, 467 ff. Cf. *Il.* 2. 33 f. (Leaf ad loc.), 8. 423 f., *Od.* 5. 100 ff., Page l.c. above.

For Iris' journey cf. especially *Il.* 24. 77 ff. (ad *Dem.* 321).

In P. Harris 6, a fragment of a hexameter poem of uncertain date, Zeus sends Hermes to entreat Demeter and offer her honours (cf. Introduction, pp. 70 f.).

314. Ἶριν ... χρυσόπτερον: Iris has wings on her heels: cf. ποδήνεμος ... Ἶρις (*Il.* 2. 786 etc.), and the representations of flying figures in archaic art. Iris is used as messenger to Demeter on earth, Hermes for the underworld (*Dem.* 335). Cf. E. Maass, *IF* 1 (1891/2), 157 ff.

315. πολυήρατον εἶδος ἔχουσαν: this formula occurs in the 'Continuation' of the *Theogony*, which is probably of sixth-century date, and the line may itself be later than its context (cf. West ad *Th.* 881–1020, 907–11). Cf. ἐπήρατον εἶδος ἔχουσαν Hes. frr. 25. 39, 136. 2. Note the neglect of digamma with εἶδος: cf. Appendix II, B (6), and Hoekstra, *Sub-epic Stage*, 54. πολυήρατον is not found in the *Iliad*, but occurs four times in the *Odyssey*, three times in Hesiod, and twice in the *Hymn to Aphrodite*, which suggests that it is 'increasingly favoured by the poets' (Hoekstra).

316. Ζηνὶ κελαινεφέϊ Κρονίωνι: the full formula does not occur in Homer. For such 'combination-formulae' cf. ad *Dem.* 3, 321, 396, and Introduction, pp. 46 ff.

317. μεσσηγύ: Ilgen read the substantive (as in *Ap.* 108), but this is probably unnecessary.

319. κυανόπεπλον: this is used of Demeter at *Dem.* 360, 374 and probably 442. Cf. *Dem.* 42, 182–3. It is used of Leto at Hes. *Th.* 406 (cf. West ad loc.), Orph. *Hy.* 35. 1, for reasons which are less obvious. Cf. also A. Audollent, *Defixionum tabellae*, Nr. 41 b 6 (Megara, i–ii A.D.).

321. πατήρ ... εἰδώς: this is a combination of two Zeus-formulae (cf. ad *Dem.* 3, 316). Ζεὺς ἄφθιτα μήδεα εἰδώς occurs once in Homer (*Il.* 24. 88), in a passage which may have been in the poet's mind: Zeus sends Iris to summon Thetis (*Il.* 24. 78 μεσσηγύς ~ *Dem.* 317, 83 εὗρε δ' ~ 319, 93 f. κάλυμμ' ... κυάνεον ~ 319, 99b ~ 325). It also occurs three times in the Prometheus myth in the *Theogony* (545, 550, 561) and in frr. 141. 26, 234. 2, *Aph.* 43.

The formula used here is a doublet of βαρύκτυπος εὐρύοπα Ζεύς (which is used in *Dem.* 460) and πατὴρ ἀνδρῶν τε θεῶν τε (cf. ad *Dem.* 3), Κρόνου πάϊς ἀγκυλομήτεω.

321 ff. There is probably an echo of these lines in the Epidaurian *Hymn to the Mother of the Gods* (*IG* 4. 1². 131 = *PMG* 935), 15 ff. (Zeus speaks):

Μάτηρ, ἄπιθ' εἰς θεούς,   15
καὶ μὴ κατ' ὄρη πλαν[ῶ] . . .
†καὶ οὐκ ἄπειμι εἰς θεούς†   19
ἂν μὴ τὰ μέρη λάβω,   20
τὸ μὲν ἥμιςυ ὠρανῶ,
τὸ δ' ἥμιςυ γαίας,
πόντω τὸ τρίτον μέρος·
χοὔτως ἀπελεύςομαι.

Cf. Maas, *Epidaurische Hymnen*, ad loc., and West, *CQ* 20 (1970), 212 ff.

322. μετὰ φῦλα . . . αἰειγενετάων: cf. ad *Dem.* 36.

323. Cf. ad *Dem.* 314–23. The underlying idea here is that the word of Zeus must be fulfilled: cf. ad *Dem.* 466, *Il.* 1. 524 ff. (cf. 527 οὐδ' ἀτελεύτητον); Deichgräber, *Eleus. Frömmigkeit*, 528.

325 ff. In Philicus' *Hymn* the gods come to Demeter and attempt to persuade her to relent, offering gifts and honours (cf. ad *Dem.* 327 f.).

325. πατήρ: this is a satisfactory addition. It may have dropped out after ἔπειτα. For πατήρ alone of Zeus cf. *Il.* 8. 69, 11. 80, etc.

θεούς: for the synizesis cf. ad *Dem.* 55, and Hoekstra, *Sub-epic Stage*, 49, 58 n. 5.

The formula μάκαρες θεοὶ αἰὲν ἐόντες occurs once in the *Iliad* (24. 99), and four times in the *Odyssey*, always in the nominative.

326. ἐπιπροῖαλλεν: the verb is used only once in Homer (*Il.* 11. 628), of bringing up a table. One would expect rather ἐπιπροέηκε: cf. *Il.* 9. 516 ἄνδρας δὲ λίςςεςθαι ἐπιπροέηκεν ἀρίςτους. But the poet perhaps wanted an imperfect of the same metrical form.

327. δίδον: this form is not Homeric (δίδοςαν). Cf. ἔδιδον *Dem.* 437, Hes. *Op.* 139 Rz. (ἐδίδων, ἐδίδουν codd.), and ἔδον Hes. *Th.* 30 (Hom. ἔδοςαν). These forms are older than the Homeric (and Attic–Ionic) ones. ἔδιδον is used in most dialects outside Attic–Ionic (cf. Buck, *Comparative Grammar of Greek and Latin*, § 340. 4). Cf. A. Davies, *Glotta* 42 (1964), 145 ff., who concludes that it is not necessarily borrowed here from Hesiod, and Hoekstra, *Sub-epic Stage*, 57.

327 f. When the gods receive their τιμαί from other gods (usually from Zeus), the regular expressions for this are ἔδωκεν, ἔπορεν δῶρα, γέρας, etc. Cf. *Herm.* 470 ff. ἔπορεν δέ τοι ἀγλαὰ δῶρα καὶ τιμάς . . . (where Allen's punctuation, a colon after δῶρα, is surely wrong), *Dem.* 443 f., 461 f., *Aph.* 29 ff., Hes. *Th.* 399 ff., 412 f., Theognis 1386 ff., *Orph. Hy.* 57. 9 ff., etc., Keyssner, *Gottesvorstellung*, 56 ff. Here West's deletion of θ' in 328 would make 328 epexegetic to 327, as in Hes. *Th.* 412 f. The false insertion of a connecting particle is a well-known form of corruption. But *Herm.* 470 f. supports M's text. Cf. also ad *Dem.* 311 f. (γέρας and τιμή). In Philicus' *Hymn* τιμαί are offered to Demeter, and the gods also offer presents (col. ii. 33, 60 f., Körte). Philicus perhaps has the *Homeric Hymn* in mind here (cf. Latte, *Kl. Schr.* 559; Walton, *HTR* 45 (1952), 107 n. 7).

328. τιμάς: τιμή is always singular in Homer. For the plural cf. *Dem.* 353, 366, 443, 461, *Herm.* 471, Hes. *Th.* 74, 112, 452, 882, 885, *Op.* 138.

ἅc κεν ἕλοιτο μετ' ἀθανάτοιcι θεοῖcιν: M has ἐθέλοιτο . . . ἐλέcθαι. The middle of ἐθέλειν is nowhere found. The poet uses cχήcηcθα (*Dem.* 366), which is also an anomalous form. But Hermann's conjecture seems the most likely solution (cf. *Dem.* 444). ἐλέcθαι might derive from a marginal ἕλοιτο, as a correction to ἐθέλοιτο. Allen's βόλεcθαι is rare in Homer (*Il.* 11. 319, *Od.* 1. 234, 16. 387).

For the expression 'honours amongst the gods' cf. *Dem.* 366, 443 f., 461 f., *Od.* 13. 128, Hes. *Th.* 393 f. A god's τιμή is allotted to him by the gods, and held amongst them (cf. ad *Dem.* 85–6), although it is dependent also on the payment of what is due to him by men. Cf. e.g. *Od.* 13. 128 f.

Ζεῦ πάτερ, οὐκέτ' ἐγώ γε μετ' ἀθανάτοιcι θεοῖcι
τιμήειc ἔcομαι, ὅτε με βροτοὶ οὔ τι τίουcι . . .

and Keyssner, *Gottesvorstellung*, 60 f.

329. Brunck's change (cf. *Il.* 5. 484, 15. 409, 17. 42, etc. for variation of η/ου in manuscripts) is unnecessary.

331. ἔφαcκε: the augmented form is normal in Homer. φάcκε is used only at the beginning of the verse, in *Od.* 24. 75, Hes. *Th.* 209.

θυώδεοc Οὐλύμποιο: cf. ad *Dem.* 231.

334–74. Finally Zeus sends Hermes to Hades to fetch Persephone. He goes and finds them sitting together. He delivers his message. Hades smiles and orders Persephone to go, consoling her and promising her honours and rule over all things on earth. She leaps up joyfully, but Hades gives her a pomegranate-seed to eat, to make her return to him.

334 ff. Hermes is the go-between of the upper and lower worlds. Cf. especially *Herm.* 572. For his role as persuader (*Dem.* 336) cf. *Herm.* 317 f. He is shown being dispatched by Zeus to fetch Persephone on a relief from Delos of the early fourth century B.C., on which Demeter, Persephone and another goddess (Rhea or Hecate?) are also depicted (cf. Picard, *BCH* 55 (1931), 11 ff., *Manuel d'archéologie grecque*, La Sculpture III (Paris, 1948), 166, 240, fig. 79).

For other possible representations of Hermes' mission see K. Schauenburg, *Jahrb. des d. arch. Inst.* 73 (1958), 49 and 62–4. He is shown assisting at the Anodos of Core on Beazley, *ARV*[2] 1012. 1 (cf. ad *Dem.* 24–6). Cf. also Metzger, *Recherches*, 11 ff. for other vase-paintings of the scene,[1] and for sarcophagi C. Robert, *Ant. Sarkophag-reliefs*, iii. 3, p. 456, Pl. 120, Nos. 363, 365, Pl. 128, No. 409a.

On the *schema* of his journey see notes to *Dem.* 314–23.

335. Ἔρεβοc: 'the darkness', and so associated with ζόφοc (*Dem.* 337, *Od.* 12. 81, 20. 356, Hes. *Th.* 658) and opposed to light (*Dem.* 338, Hes. *Th.* 669, S. *Aj.* 394–5). LSJ s.v. suggest that Erebos and Hades are distinguished in *Il.* 8. 367 f., and that Erebos is a passage between earth and Hades. But there is no reason to assume this.

---

[1] Cf. also perhaps *ARV*[2] 205. 119, c. 490 B.C. (G. Schwarz, *Arch. Anz.* 1971, 178 ff.), and P. Zanker, *Wandel d. Hermesgestalt in d. Att. Vasenmalerei* (Bonn, 1965), 81 ff.

χρυσόρραπιν: used of Hermes in the *Odyssey* and *Hymns* (*Od.* 5. 87 etc.). The wand is described in *Herm.* 528 ff. Circe also has a magic wand (*Od.* 10. 293, 389), and compare the golden sceptre of Teiresias (11. 91) and Minos (11. 568) in the underworld, Norden, *Aeneis VI*, p. 172 n. 2, F. J. M. de Waele, *The Magic Staff or Rod in Graeco-Roman Antiquity* (Gent, 1927), 65 f.

Ἀργειφόντην: the ancient explanation 'slayer of Argos' is supported by Kretschmer (*Glotta* 10 (1919), 45 ff.; 24 (1936), 236 f.; 27 (1939), 33). Cf. also J. Chittenden, *AJA* 52 (1948), 24 ff. The phrase is adapted from the Homeric nominative formula χρυσόρραπις Ἀργειφόντης.

337. ἁγνήν: cf. ad *Dem.* 203. It is used of Persephone in *Od.* 11. 386, *Orph. Hy.* 24. 11, 43. 7, *Prol.* 6, Orac. ap. Phlegon, *FGH* 257. 36, pp. 1180–1, verses 7, 9, 35; and as her title at Andania in Messenia: Paus. 4. 33. 4, *IG* 5. 1. 1390. 84 ff. = *SIG*³ 736. Cf. also *IG* 14. 641. 2. 6 (Zuntz, *Persephone*, 317), *RE* 16. 1268. 44 ff., Malten, *ARW* 12 (1909), 421 n. 4, and ad *Dem.* 99.

337 f. ἀπὸ ζόφου ... ἐς φάος: cf. West ad *Th.* 653, and *Th.* 669, Parm. fr. 1. 9–10.

ἠερόεντος: when used of the underworld, this probably means 'dark'. ἀήρ in early epic means mist, darkness, etc. (cf. West ad Hes. *Th.* 119, 697).

338. μετὰ δαίμονας: in Homer only at *Il.* 1. 222. The plural occurs only three times in Homer: cf. Dietrich, *Death, Fate and the Gods*, 308, and in later poetry, *Herm.* 381, *Ap.* 11, Pi. *O.* 1. 35, etc.

ὄφρα ἑ μήτηρ: on the position of ἑ cf. ad *Dem.* 202.

339. μεταλλήξειε χόλοιο: this compound, and the formula, occur in Homer three times in the Embassy (*Il.* 9. 157, 261, 299), and nowhere else (cf. ad *Dem.* 82 f., etc.). There most manuscripts have -λλ-, and this was read by Aristarchus at *Il.* 9. 299 (cf. *Od.* 12. 224 ἀπολλήξειαν). The reduplication is normal after loss of a sigma (Chantraine, *GH* i. 176) and as M constantly neglects a double consonant (e.g. *Dem.* 14, 40, 158, 313) -λλ- should be read here also. For the phrase cf. also *Dem.* 410, Hes. *Th.* 221.

340. Ἑρμῆς: the normal form in Homer is Ἑρμείας, but the contracted form occurs at *Il.* 20. 72 and four times in the *Odyssey*. It is frequent in the *Hymn to Hermes*. Cf. also Hes. *Th.* 444, 938, fr. 1. 21, 170.

ὑπὸ κεύθεα γαίης: 'down into the hiding-places (hidden places) of the earth' (and so of a cavern or monster's lair in Hes. *Th.* 300, 334, 483; cf. fr. 204. 130). In Homer and Hesiod the formula is found in the dative.

342. τόν γε ἄνακτα: 'him, the lord'. The article still shows traces of its pronominal force: cf. Monro, *HG*² § 261. 3 (a), Chantraine, *GH* ii. 164, and the formulae τοῖο ἄνακτος, εὗρε δὲ τόν γε.

δόμων ἔντοσθεν: on the house of Hades cf. ad *Dem.* 379.

343. This picture of Hades sitting on the couch with Persephone makes one think of representations of the two together in art. Cf. e.g. the Lysimachides relief (Farnell, *Cults*, iii, Plate I), where a banquet-scene is shown. There the god reclines and his wife sits. Cf.

also the British Museum cylix on which Hades is shown offering Persephone a cup (Farnell, Plate VIIIa).

αἰδοίη: of Persephone also at *Dem.* 486. Cf. notes to *Dem.* 190, 214.

344–5. The lines are corrupt, and no satisfactory solution has been proposed. ἀτλήτων does not make sense, and the correption is abnormal in epic: it usually occurs only where the word would not otherwise fit the hexameter (with τλ only once in Homer, cχετλίη *Il.* 3. 414; but synizesis would be possible here also). The reference to Demeter (reading ἡ δ᾽) is not wanted here, and the emendation ἀποτηλοῦ is out of place. (In *Dem.* 355 ἀπάνευθε is contrasted with οὐδὲ θεοῖcι μίcγεται. Cf. 92, 303.) A possible line would be to take 345 as referring to the θεῶν βουλή (cf. *Il.* 7. 45, and ad *Dem.* 9), reading e.g. ἠδ᾽ ἐπ᾽ ἀτλήτοιc(?) ἔργοιc οἷα... μητίcετο βουλή (cf. Ludwich, Humbert. οἷα could have been lost after ἔργοιc). This however is still awkward after ἀεκαζομένη, and ἀτλήτοιc remains unsatisfactory. θεῶν μακάρων would also be displaced from its normal formulaic position (*Il.* 1. 339 etc.).

μητίcετο: for this form of thematic aorist with sigma cf. Monro, *HG*² § 41, Chantraine, *GH* i. 416 ff. In Homer it occurs mostly with βαίνω, δύω, and their compounds, and in imperatives and infinitives (where it is artificial, and partly *metri gratia*). It was taken as imperfect by some ancient grammarians (Schol. A ad *Il.* 1. 496), and this could fit *Od.* 10. 107, also perhaps 2. 388 etc. Cf. Wackernagel, *Verm. Beitr.* 46 ff., P. Wahrmann, *Festschr. Kretschmer*, 307. One should perhaps read μητίcατο here.

347. Ἄιδη: this is the Attic form (Homeric Ἀΐδηc). The aspirate could be due to corruption during transmission, and it is questionable whether the contraction necessarily points to Attic composition (cf. Wackernagel, *Spr. Unt.* 179). There is no parallel for it in Homer, but can one exclude the possibility that it was a natural development of the (post-Homeric?) epic *Kunstsprache*? For the contraction cf. also Pi. *P.* 4. 44 Ἄιδα (Doric Ἀΐδαc). The etymology is uncertain (cf. Frisk s.v.; also Wackernagel, *Verm. Beitr.* 44 ff. = *Kl. Schr.* i. 765 ff.; Solmsen, *Unters.* 74 ff., Schwyzer, *Gr. Gr.* i. 266).

Hermann wanted to read Ἄϊδη, and compared Βορέηc (*Il.* 9. 5, 23. 195), νέα (*Od.* 9. 283) at the beginning of the line. But the parallel does not hold (cf. Chantraine, *GH* i. 36, 103).

κυανοχαῖτα: in Homer usually of Poseidon (*Il.* 13. 563 etc.), also of Boreas as a horse (*Il.* 20. 224). Cf. Hes. *Th.* 278 (Poseidon as father of Pegasus and Chrysaor), *Thebais* fr. 4, Hes. *Sc.* 120 (the horse Areion: cf. Paus. 8. 25. 8), Antim. fr. 36 W.

Hades and Poseidon share certain characteristics, and are both associated with horses: cf. ad *Dem.* 18, and Heitsch, *Aphroditehymnos*, 87 ff.

Hades is also κυάνεοc in Kaibel, *Epigr.* 1046 b 84, and μελαγχαίταc in E. *Alc.* 439.

348. Ζεύc με πατήρ: M has cε, but με is surely right. Cf. *Il.* 11. 201 and *Dem.* 335 ff. Allen and Halliday take ἐξαγαγεῖν as 'let go', which is impossible.

The pronoun is brought forward: cf. ad *Dem.* 202.

ἤνωγεν: one would have rather expected the perfect here, but ἄνωγον, ἤνωγον (*Il.* 5. 805, 9. 578, etc.) were probably treated as past tenses of ἀνώγω (cf. Chantraine, *GH* i. 312).

ἀγαυὴν Περςεφόνειαν: this formula occurs in Homer only in the Nekyia, always in the nominative. Cf. Hes. fr. 280. 12, *Orph. Hy.* 41. 5, 44. 6, 46. 6. fr. 32 d 6 K. It is a doublet of ἐπαινὴ Περςεφόνεια (etc.), which however only occurs when coupled with Hades (*Il.* 9. 569 etc.). Cf. Leumann, *Hom. Wörter*, 72.

349. Ἐρέβευςφι: this anomalous form is well attested at *Il.* 9. 572 and Hes. *Th.* 669, with -εςφι as variant. Ἐρέβεςφι is attested by Theognostus, *An. Ox.* 2. 160. 20 Cramer (cf. West ad Hes. l.c.). As the use of -φι had become artificial by the time of Homer M's reading may be kept. Cf. Chantraine, *GH* i. 234 ff. especially 241 n. 1, where he comments on Ἐρέβευςφι and ὀχέεςφι (*Il.* 5. 722): 'on n'ose pas considérer comme homériques certaines formes singulières . . . Mais il n'est pas exclu que des aèdes aient déjà utilisé ces formes.' This leaves the question nicely balanced.

351. ἀθανάτοις παύςειεν: for the dative cf. *Il.* 14. 50, Hdt. 1. 118, etc., E. *IA* 1609 (πόςει πάρες χόλον), etc.

The intransitive use of παύω is elsewhere normally found only with the imperative (Hes. *Sc.* 449 etc.). It occurs as a v.l. in *Od.* 4. 659 (most manuscripts) and *Hy.* 33. 14. Cf. also E. *Hel.* 1319 f. (in the ode on the rape of Core): δρομαίων δ' ὅτε πολυπλανήτων μάτηρ ἔπαυςε πόνων (Maas, *Epidaurische Hymnen*, 18, and Kannicht ad loc.; cf. *Dem.* 351), *Hec.* 917 μολπᾶν δ' ἀπὸ καὶ θυςιᾶν καταπαύςας (both these examples have been variously emended). Possibly the poet here had the various Homeric parallels (see ad loc.) in mind, and also examples like *Il.* 4. 191, *Od.* 4. 35, where παύω is used transitively with genitive, and direct object understood (cf. Kannicht, l.c. above).

μήδεται ἔργον: the neglect of the digamma here is due to formula-adaptation. Cf. *Od.* 3. 261 (etc.) and μήςεαι ἔργον (*Od.* 11. 474); Hoekstra, *Mnem.* sér. 4, 10 (1957), 216.

352. φῦλ' ἀμενηνὰ χαμαιγενέων ἀνθρώπων: in Homer ἀμενηνός is used of the dead (*Od.* 10. 521, 536, 11. 29, 49), of dreams (19. 562), or of someone incapacitated (*Il.* 5. 887; cf. *Aph.* 188). For the verb cf. *Il.* 13. 562. On the non-Homeric χαμαιγενέων ἀνθρώπων cf. ad *Dem.* 113. It is a doublet of καταθνητῶν ἀνθρώπων (*Il.* 6. 123 etc.). φῦλ' ἀνθρώπων occurs in Homer only in the *Odyssey*, and is common in the *Hymns* and Hesiod (cf. φῦλα (κατα)θνητῶν ἀνθρώπων). Here, both epithets are 'active': they emphasize the helplessness of men. Cf. also Ar. *Av.* 686.

353. Cf. *Dem.* 306 f.

καταφθινύθουςα: the compound verb does not occur in Homer or Hesiod (φθινύθειν etc. *Il.* 2. 346 etc., καταφθιμένοιο etc. *Il.* 22. 288 etc.). Cf. Emp. fr. 111. 3 f. ἀνέμων μένος οἵ τ' . . . καταφθινύθουςιν* ἀρούρας (~ Hes. *Th.* 878 f.: cf. ad *Dem.* 352).

353 f. τιμὰς ἀθανάτων: cf. ad *Dem.* 311 f., 328.

354 ff.: cf. Hes. *Th.* 802 ff., *Dem.* 28, 92, 303, *Ap.* 344-8.

355 f. Cf. *Dem.* 28 ἧϲτο θεῶν ἀπάνευθε πολυλλίϲτῳ ἐνὶ νηῷ. θυώδεοϲ . . . νηοῦ: cf. also Pi. *O.* 7. 32, Plut. *Mor.* 437 c.

356. κραναὸν πτολίεθρον: in Homer the epithet is always used of Ithaca (*Il.* 3. 201 etc.). Cf. αἰπὺ πτολίεθρον (*Il.* 2. 538 etc.), αἰπεινὸν πτολίεθρον (*Il.* 15. 257), etc.

357 f. Hades smiles 'with his eyebrows', knowing what is to come, and that he will not lose Persephone altogether. Hades was normally ἀμείδητοϲ: cf. *AP* 7. 439. 3, and Claudian, *RP* 2. 313–14 'facili passus mollescere risu, dissimilisque sui' (from *Dem.* 357 f.? cf. Introduction, p. 73). Cf. E. *Alc.* 261–2 ὑπ' ὀφρύϲι κυαναυγέϲι βλέπων πτερωτὸς Ἄιδαϲ; Hermesianax fr. 7. 9 (Powell) Κώκυτόν τ' ἀθέμιϲτον ὑπ' ὀφρύϲι μειδήϲαντα (ἐπ' A: ὑπ' Ruhnken, al.; cf. Agar, *CR* 31 (1917), 120). For a more gentle smile with, or *under*, the eyebrows cf. Pi. *P.* 9. 38, A.R. 3. 1024. In *Il.* 15. 101 f. Hera laughs with her lips (χείλεϲιν ∼ *Dem.* 358 ὀφρύϲιν*) but her brow does not relax, showing that she is angry. Cf. perhaps Aphrodite's 'false smile'(?) in Theocr. 1. 95 f. (Gow ad loc., Ogilvie, *JHS* 82 (1962), 107, *CQ* 10 (1960), 37 ff.).

On the 'euphemistic' portrayal of Hades in the *Hymn* cf. ad *Dem.* 83 ff., also 360–9, 361.

358. ὀφρύϲιν: usually with ὑπό or ἐπί in Homer (*Il.* 1. 528, 13. 88, etc.) but cf. *Od.* 12. 194, also *Herm.* 279, Pi. *P.* 9. 38.

ἀπίθηϲε . . . ἐφετμῆϲ: Allen and Halliday read the genitive, because this is used at *Dem.* 448 (cf. ad loc.). In Homer ἀπιθεῖν always takes the dative (*Il.* 1. 220 etc.). Despite the variation at *Dem.* 448, the text should be retained here, as it conforms to normal use. For a similar variation cf. *Dem.* 456, 473.

Διὸϲ βαϲιλῆοϲ: Homer never uses βαϲιλεύϲ of the gods, only ἄναξ, and Zeus is never 'king of the gods', only πατὴρ ἀνδρῶν τε θεῶν τε (*Il.* 1. 544 etc.). Hesiod, on the other hand, always uses βαϲιλεύϲ of kingship in heaven (*Th.* 486, 886, 923, *Op.* 668). The phrase Ζεὺϲ (θεῶν etc.) βαϲιλεύϲ occurs first there: cf. *Th.* 886 (where it has a strong predicative sense: West ad loc.), *Op.* 668, also *Th.* 923, fr. 308, *Cypr.* fr. 7. 3, *Theb.* fr. 3. 3, West ad *Th.* 883.

Later, it occurs as a cult-title in Athens, Ionia, and elsewhere (Roscher, 6. 608 f.), and also in lyric and Attic poetry. It was probably an everyday phrase in spoken Attic. Cf. Fraenkel ad A. *Ag.* 355, Wackernagel, *Spr. Unt.* 210, Wilamowitz, *Glaube*, i. 140.

On Zeus-formulae in the *Hymn* cf. Introduction, pp. 47, 49. See also Hoekstra, *Sub-epic Stage*, 49 f. on this particular instance.

359. δαΐφρονι Περϲεφονείῃ: this is normally an epithet of men in Homer, in contrast to περίφρων of women (cf. ad *Dem.* 370). But cf. *Od.* 15. 356 κουριδίηϲ τ' ἀλόχοιο δαΐφρονοϲ, and later Pi. *P.* 9. 84 f., Bacch. 5. 122 ff. (Artemis), 137 (Althaea).

360–9. Hades' speech to Persephone contains a *consolatio* with the same pattern as that of *Dem.* 82 ff. Cf. ad loc.

Deichgräber, *Eleus. Frömmigkeit*, 534 f., observes that Hades' behaviour here is not what one would expect from the viewpoint of archaic Greek religion (cf. ad *Dem.* 357 f.). His address to Persephone aims at reconciliation, which is one of the main motifs of the Homeric poet throughout the *Hymn*.

For other examples of consolation by an abductor see Bühler on Mosch. *Eur.* 153 ff. The type is found already in Homer (*Od.* 11. 248 ff. ~ Hes. fr. 31). Cf. especially *Aph.* 193 ff.

360 f. παρὰ μητέρα κυανόπεπλον, | ἤπιον . . .: cf. Hes. *Th.* 406 f. *Λητὼ κυανόπεπλον . . . | ἤπιον . . .* The first epithet is hard to explain in the case of Leto (cf. West ad loc.). Has the reminiscence of *Th.* 406 f. suggested the second epithet to the poet of the *Hymn*? The reverse could of course also be true. Or could both be derived from a common source? The two epithets fit more easily in the *Hymn*. But this does not necessarily indicate priority.

361. ἤπιον: we find here the same euphemistic treatment of the queen of the underworld as in the case of Hades (cf. ad *Dem.* 357 f.).

362. δυσθύμαινε: this verb occurs only here. Cf. δυσθυμεῖν (Hdt. 8. 100 etc.), θυμαίνειν (Hes. *Sc.* 262, etc.).

λίην περιώσιον ἄλλων: for this duplication of expression cf. μὰψ αὔτως ἄπλητον (*Dem.* 83), λίην ἀζηχές (*Dem.* 467 f.). For περιώσιον ἄλλων cf. Pi. *I.* 5. 3, A.R. 1. 466, περιώσιον *Il.* 4. 359, *Od.* 16. 203.

363 ff. Hades' words are ambiguous, suggesting that Persephone will return to the upper world (cf. 364 ἔνθα), but that he will remain her husband. Wegener objected (*Philologus* 35 (1876), 250) that ἔνθα must refer to the underworld, since it is there that Persephone is queen (364 ff.) and therefore the words cannot have been spoken *in* the underworld. He also argued that the marriage was referred to as in the future, and that a reference to Persephone as ruler of the underworld could not be made when she was about to leave. He concluded that the speech was originally made by Hades when carrying off Persephone (cf. Claud. *RP* 2. 277 ff., Introduction, pp. 72 f.).

This perhaps fails to recognize the ambiguity and subtlety of the speech. Persephone will remain Hades' wife 'amongst the gods' (363), and she will rule in the upper world over all that lives and moves (365 f.) and will hold her honours 'amongst the gods' (366). The theme of rule in the underworld is only obscurely hinted at in 367-9 (cf. ad loc.).

It should be noted that the manuscript reading in 364 is ἐνθάδ' ἰοῦσα ('when you come *here*'). This, and the asyndeton it involves, would be just possible (ἐνθάδ' ἐοῦσα might be better). But it is unlikely that Hades would give the game away at this point, and he expressly speaks of Persephone as queen of the *living*, not of the dead.

365-9. Hades promises Persephone three things:

1. Rule over all things on earth.
2. Honours amongst the gods.
3. Vengeance for ever upon those who do wrong, and fail to propitiate her with sacrifices and gifts.

In effect these three things are united in one. Persephone's τιμαί are granted by the gods, but represent power over mortals, and this is

expressed in terms of sacrifices and gifts from men on earth (cf. ad
Dem. 150, 311 f., 328).

Hades also hints at the threefold division of Persephone's τιμαί
here, on earth (365), in heaven (366), and in the underworld (cf.
ad 367–9). This corresponds to her division of time between upper
and lower worlds (cf. ad *Dem.* 86, 399 f.).

Preller rejected these lines on the grounds that the style was verbose
and the language Attic (δεcπόccειc, ἀδικηcάντων, θυcίαιcι, εὐαγέωc),
and that 367–9 referred to the Mysteries (cf. ad *Dem.* 188–211).

365. δεcπόccειc: the verb is not found elsewhere in early epic.
Cf. A. *PV* 210 etc., Hdt. 3. 142 etc. (δέcποινα *Od.* 3. 403 etc.; δεcπόcυνοc
Dem. 144 etc.). Persephone had the title Δέcποινα, especially in Arcadia (Lycosura: *IG* 5. 2. 514; Paus. 8. 37. 9), also Βαcιλίc (*IG* 14. 450,
Kaibel, *Epigr.* 822. 9). The goddess of the underworld is called Pasi-
crateia at Selinus (*IG* 14. 268). Cf. ad *Dem.* 9, and Holm, *RhM* 27
(1872), 368, Usener, *Götternamen* (Bonn, 1896), 224 n. 15, Bruch-
mann, *Epitheta deorum quae apud Graecos leguntur* (Leipzig, 1893),
190 ff., Zuntz, *Persephone*, 103 ff.

πάντων . . . ἕρπει: cf. *Il.* 17. 447 = *Od.* 18. 131, and Genesis, 1 : 21,
26, 28, etc.

366. cχήcηcθα: this form is anomalous, as there are no examples
of the termination -cθα in a future. This occurs in Homer in the
present and aorist subjunctive of some verbs (Chantraine, *GH* i. 462,
K–B ii, § 209. 3), and in the present and imperfect indicative of -μι
verbs (Chantraine, i. 469 f.). The aorist ἔcχηcα is found only in late
Greek (cf. *Or. Sib.* 11. 91; f.l. in Nonn. *D.* 17. 177). It is better to
regard this as an anomalous future indicative form (cf. cχήcω etc.,
Il. 17. 182 etc.), on the analogy of ἔχηcθα (pres. subj. *Il.* 19. 180,
Ap. 56), and perhaps ἔχηcθα (? pres. indic.) Sapph. frr. 96. 23 (εχηcθ᾽
pap.), 129. 1 (ἐχειcθα cod. A) and φίληcθα 129. 2 (φίληcθα cod. A).
cχήcειcθα (Boissonade) is called a 'verbildete Form' by Schulze
(*Zeitschr. f. vergl. Sprachf.* 33 (1895), 317). Cf. also Zumbach, *Neuerungen*, 28 f., Schwyzer, *Gr. Gr.* i. 662. On the question of iota subscript
in these forms cf. K–B ii. § 209. 6.

367–9. Hades predicts the eternal punishment of those who fail to
propitiate Persephone.

These lines have been rejected by some critics as aetiological (cf. ad
Dem. 365–9), or because the doctrine of punishment after death is
considered to be 'Orphic', and not a part of early Eleusinian beliefs.

Allen and Halliday hold that there is *no* reference to the future life
here, since 365 refers to rule over all *living* things. But ἤματα πάντα
most naturally indicates 'eternal vengeance' for the ἄδικοι, rather
than that Persephone will always in future have this power to punish.
The reference must be to Persephone's position as ruler of the underworld (cf. ad *Dem.* 365–9). It is a covert one, as Hades does not want
to give the game away.

Punishment is in store for those who do not propitiate Persephone
with sacrifices, the proper performance of ritual acts, and the pay-

ment of due gifts (368–9). The lines are similar to *Dem.* 273–4 (274 ~ 368b–9a), which refer explicitly to the Mysteries (ὄργια). That these were still largely a matter of such ritual actions is suggested by the terms used (ὄργια, δρηϲμοϲύνην, etc.: cf. ad 273 f.).

It is thus a reasonable assumption that 368–9 also refer to the Mysteries. In *Dem.* 481–2 it is explicitly stated that the uninitiated have a less happy fate after death. How many classes are envisaged in these passages? Besides the initiates, who are ὄλβιοι (*Dem.* 480), are there some who are less happy, perhaps because for them the normal Homeric picture of a shadowy existence after death still holds good, and others who are punished because they have offended the goddess (as the 'great sinners', Tityus, Tantalus, and Sisyphus, are punished in *Od.* 11. 576–600 for their offences against the gods)? Or does punishment await all those who are not initiated? If the second interpretation is right, the words used in *Dem.* 481–2 must be a deliberate euphemism, ominously concealing a reference to punishment. Such a reference is made explicit by later writers who echo the *Hymn* (cf. ad loc.), and is probably intended there also.

The answer must depend on the sense which is given to τῶν ἀδικη-cάντων in *Dem.* 367. Does their ἀδικία consist in failure to propitiate Persephone? Failure to sacrifice alone is sufficient to incur divine wrath, whether it is intentional or not (e.g. *Il.* 9. 533–7, Hes. *Op.* 136–9),[1] and it is notable that Hesiod, after enumerating the chief offences for which the gods punish men (*Op.* 321 ff.), goes on to say that one should avoid all these things, and sacrifice to the gods as much as one can, propitiating them with libations and sacrifices daily (335–41). His words are closely similar to those of *Dem.* 367–9 (*Op.* 334 ~ *Dem.* 367: 336–8 ἔρδειν . . . ἁγνῶϲ καὶ καθαρῶϲ . . . θυέεϲϲί τε ἱλάϲκεϲθαι ~ *Dem.* 368–9. N.B.: 340 ~ *Dem.* 204b). Here, the counterpart to injustice, and the way to avoid punishment by the gods, is through sacrifice and propitiation.

On this interpretation, if *Dem.* 368–9 refer to the uninitiated, the conclusion must be that *all* who are not initiated will suffer punishment after death. This agrees with the interpretation of *Dem.* 481 as euphemistic, and is the most natural way of taking οἵ κεν . . . (i.e. as defining τῶν ἀδικηϲάντων). Probably this was the intention of the poet.

It is, however, theoretically possible that the ἀδικία here referred to might be more general, i.e. covering men's dealings with one another, and not primarily with the gods. The normal use of δίκη, δίκαιοϲ, ἄδικοϲ, etc. in Homer and Hesiod is of men's justice or injustice to one another first and foremost, 'drawing in the gods only as an afterthought' (cf. Adkins, *Merit and Responsibility*, 131). On this interpretation, οἵ κεν in 368 has a limiting or conditional sense ('if they do not . . .'), and the implication is that the consequences of ἀδικία, i.e. divine retribution, may be avoided if one propitiates Persephone. The goddess is thus elevated to the status of a universal 'arbitra

---

[1] Cf. also E. *Hel.* 1355–7 (ad *Dem.* 367–9), from the hymn to the Mother of the Gods (= Demeter).

morum', who safeguards justice by punishing wrong-doers, at least after death, and possibly also before. There are then three classes in Hades, the initiates, the uninitiated, and the ἄδικοι. Only the last of these are punished. This threefold division into the blessed, the damned, and those in between appears in some later accounts of life after death, and develops into the Christian idea of Heaven, Hell, and Purgatory (cf. Dieterich, *Nekyia*, especially 84 ff.).

The idea of punishment after death for crimes committed on earth is not a new one. Already in Homer, when an oath is sworn, Agamemnon invokes, after the powers of heaven and earth, 'those two who underneath (the earth) punish the dead, whoever swears a false oath' (*Il.* 3. 278–9). Here Hades and Persephone must be intended. (In *Il.* 19. 259 f. they are replaced by the Erinyes.) Hades and Persephone, in association with the Erinyes, also hear and answer the curses of parents in *Il.* 9. 453 ff., 568 ff. There the curse takes action on earth (cf. also *Od.* 2. 134 ff., 11. 278 ff.). But it is significant that the offences which concern the powers of Hades here are those of perjury, the chief offence against the gods (cf. Dieterich, o.c. 164), and against parents. Throughout later Greek literature the commands 'Honour thy father and mother, worship and honour the gods' form a kind of basic moral code (cf. Dieterich, o.c. 163 ff.), and in later accounts of Hades it is the ἐπίορκοι and πατραλοῖαι who are singled out for special mention among those who are punished in the underworld (Dieterich, l.c.).[1] A third commandment was normally added, that one should behave respectfully towards one's fellow men (normally expressed as ξένους cέβειν, etc.).[2] Something similar may have formed a part of Eleusinian teaching from early times, if we can judge by the three 'laws of Triptolemus' (cf. *Dem.* 153): γονεῖς τιμᾶν, θεοὺς καρποῖς ἀγάλλειν, ζῷα μὴ cίνεcθαι (Xenocrates, fr. 98 Heinze, ap. Porph. *de abstin.* 4. 22 p. 267. 22 ff. N.). Triptolemus is here called 'the oldest Athenian lawgiver' by Porphyry.[3]

Probably, then, Homer shows traces of a belief in Hades and Persephone as guardians of justice, with the implication that major offences were punishable not only on earth but also in the underworld.

The Nekyia of *Odyssey* 11 knows nothing of this, and the only punishments there mentioned are those of the three 'great sinners'. But although they are special cases, the punishments which they suffer are probably derived from popular beliefs about the underworld in general, transferred to major mythical characters whom they do not always fit very well, to suit an epic description (cf. Dieterich, o.c. 63, 75 ff.).

Likewise, evidence of the belief that it is possible by means of sacrifices and prayers to propitiate the gods when one has committed an

---

[1] Cf. especially Ar. *Ran.* 145 ff., with 273 ff., Radermacher ad loc.; also Norden on Virg. *A.* 6. 608 ff.

[2] Cf. A. *Supp.* 701 ff., *Eum.* 269 ff. and Headlam–Thomson ad loc., also Thomson, *JHS* 55 (1935), 20 ff., E. fr. 311 N.²; also νόμους κοινοὺς Ἑλλάδος τιμᾶν E. fr. 853.

[3] Rohde, *Psyche*, ch. vi n. 35, however, denies any connection of these laws with the Mysteries.

offence, and thus escape their anger, is found in Homer, in *Il.* 9. 496 ff. The doctrine put forward there is often held to be 'un-Homeric' (cf. e.g. Page, *History and the Homeric Iliad*, 300 ff.). It may rather be due, like much of that book, to Homer (or the 'monumental composer') himself.

Later, this doctrine is attacked in Plato's *Republic*, together with the notions of reward and punishment after death then current (*Rep.* 363 a–366 b; there is an excellent discussion of this in I. M. Linforth, *The Arts of Orpheus* (Univ. of California Press, 1941), 75 ff.). The promise of happiness after death is offered to the just and pious man, in the form of an eternal symposium or drinking-party, by 'Musaeus and his son' (i.e. Eumolpus? Or should one read 'Orpheus and his son', assuming Musaeus to be a gloss on ὁ υἱὸς αὐτοῦ, which has then replaced Orpheus? Cf. ad *Dem.* 154). The unjust and impious will be plunged into a kind of mud in Hades. (It is not clear to whom this second notion is attributed. Cf. Dodds, *Greeks and the Irrational*, 172 n. 102.) Here, we find reward and punishment being offered for justice and injustice. But a second class of doctrine is then criticized. This holds that the gods can be persuaded, by means of sacrifices and incantations, not to punish men for their own or their ancestors' misdeeds. 'Pleasures and festivals' are also mentioned as devices to procure the gods' favour. Those who preach this are called ἀγύρται καὶ μάντεις. They go about 'to rich men's doors', quoting Hesiod and Homer to support their claims (*Op.* 287-9 and *Il.* 9. 497-501 are cited), and produce a 'babble of books' (βίβλων ὅμαδον) of Musaeus and Orpheus, which they use to persuade both individuals and cities 'that there are means of purification for wrongs done (λύσεις τε καὶ καθαρμοὶ ἀδικημάτων), by sacrifices and pleasures of play (διὰ θυσιῶν καὶ παιδιᾶς ἡδονῶν), for them when they are living and also after death (εἰσι μὲν ἔτι ζῶσιν, εἰσι δὲ καὶ τελευτήσασιν), which they call initiation-rites (τελετάς). These free us from the evils awaiting us below, but if we do not sacrifice, terrors await us (μὴ θύσαντας δέ, δεινὰ περιμένει).'

Here, ἀδικήματα are normally punishable by the gods, but certain rituals of purification and sacrifice, called τελεταί, can deliver men from punishment both before and after death (on 365 a 1–2 see Linforth, o.c. 80 ff.). Failure to perform these rituals results in suffering in Hades.

The wording of this last passage, and especially the last clause, is strikingly reminiscent of *Dem.* 367-9. As the *Hymn* was at some stage probably taken over and adapted to suit a version ascribed to Orpheus and Musaeus (Orph. fr. 49 K.; cf. Introduction, pp. 66 f., 77 f.), it is possible that such an adaptation may have been amongst the βίβλων ὅμαδος referred to here, and used by those who circulated these books to support their teachings. In this case, the words of Plato might be a direct echo of the *Hymn*.

It is, in any case, interesting to note that there is an ambiguity in this passage exactly like that of *Dem.* 367-9. The general theme of the passage is that wrongdoing brings punishment unless one is purified from it. The consequence of this should be that the just man does

K

not suffer in Hades, and this is the theme of the first class of doctrine. But the closing words suggest that a failure to secure initiation of itself leads to suffering after death. This might imply a doctrine of universal wrongdoing, or 'original sin'. But as Linforth shows (o.c. 83 ff.) this is very unlikely here. More probably, as he suggests, there is a confusion between the natural fear men have of death and of the life after death, and their fear of punishment for wrongdoing. The result, at any rate, must be that men desire initiation as a safeguard. There is also a suggestion that the initiated and the just (ὅcιoι, δίκαιοι) are identified, and that the uninitiated are classed as, or together with, the ἄδικοι (cf. Adkins, o.c. 147 f.).

In the *Homeric Hymn*, as has been shown, the same ambiguity exists. Either a failure to honour Persephone is classed as ἀδικία, or the consequences of ἀδικία could be avoided by honouring Persephone. Both notions have precedents in Homer and Hesiod. The first interpretation is more in agreement with the general trend of thought in early epic, and is probably right. But later the words may have been read in the other sense. The connection between initiation and the need for εὐcέβεια is surely suggested by the μύcται of Aristophanes' *Frogs* (455 ff.; cf. Aeschylus' prayer, 886–7; cf. also perhaps Andoc. *de Myst.* 31),[1] and at some stage the πρόρρηcιc before the Mysteries excluded not merely those tainted with bloodshed, but also those in any way polluted or ἐν αἰτίᾳ (cf. Poll. 8. 90, and perhaps Celsus ap. Orig. 3. 59, Ar. *Ran.* 354 ff., Schol. ad 369 f.; Mylonas, *Eleusis*, 247 f.). The importance of purification-rituals as a preparation for the Mysteries (cf. ad *Dem.* 192 ff.) suggests that from earliest times any form of pollution had to be removed. This, at least originally, does not necessarily indicate any ethical element as we should now understand it, since pollution might be incurred unintentionally and from a variety of causes. But it does imply that those who were conscious of having committed any offence liable to incur the anger of the gods, in any of the traditional categories, must have felt the need for purification. The proper conclusion will have been that one should behave justly if one had been initiated, not that initiation could free one from the consequences of injustice.

At the same time, the simple view which made initiation the universal passport to bliss, without regard for the conditions which it required, remained sufficiently prominent in the later period to produce the celebrated criticism of Diogenes: 'Is Pataecion the thief to have a better fate after death than Epaminondas because he has been initiated?' (Plut. *Mor.* 21 f, D.L. 6. 39, Jul. *Orat.* 7. 238 a). A Pataecion might reflect that the Mysteries provided him with a release from his fear of punishment for his misdeeds. This is exactly the criticism made by Plato against the followers of Orpheus and Musaeus. As they quoted 'Scripture' for their purpose, so might Pataecion use the lines of the *Homeric Hymn* to support his case.

[1] Rohde's arguments against using these passages, o.c. ch. vi n. 34, are not entirely convincing.

On the development of views of punishment and reward after death
cf. Dieterich, *Nekyia*, Rohde, *Psyche*, Radermacher, *RhM* 63 (1908),
531 ff., Page, *Homeric Odyssey*, 48 n. 6, Dodds, o.c. 135 ff.

367-9. Cf. E. *Hel.* 1355-7 (see Introduction, p. 69) μῆνιν δ᾽ ἔχεις
μεγάλας ματρός, ὦ παῖ, θυσίας οὐ σεβίζουσα θεᾶς (followed by instructions for propitiation by the appropriate τελεταί).

367. τῶν δ᾽ ἀδικησάντων: the verb occurs first here in epic (Homeric
ἁμαρτάνειν, ὑπερβαίνειν, etc.). Cf. Archil.(?) 79. 13 D.³ (= Hipponax
fr. 115 West), Sapph. 1. 20, Herodotus, and Attic. ἄδικος occurs in
Hes. *Op.* 260, 272, 334 (cf. ad *Dem.* 367-9).

τίσις ἔσσεται: for this threat cf. *Od.* 1. 40, 2. 76, 13. 144, Hes. *Th.* 210.

ἤματα πάντα: cf. ad *Dem.* 260.

368. Cf. Hdt. 1. 50, 6. 105 (θυσίῃσι τὸν θεὸν ἱλάσκετο, etc.).

θυσίαισι: cf. ad *Dem.* 312. In the parallel passages, *Il.* 9. 496 ff.,
Hes. *Op.* 336 ff. θυέεσσι is used, but Plato has θυσίαισι in his citation
of *Il.* 9. 499 (cf. Agar, *CR* 31 (1917), 66). Hermann read θυέεσσι at
Dem. 368 also (and θυέων at 312), but it is unlikely that both forms are
due to corruption. Although not the epic word, θυσία is not necessarily a sign of Attic composition (cf. Hdt. above).

The dative in -αισι is also not well attested elsewhere in early epic.
It occurs in choral lyric, including that of tragedy, but never in
spoken Attic or in Attic inscriptions. These have -ῃσι/-ᾱσι in early
Attic, -αις from the late fifth century onwards (cf. Wade-Gery,
JHS 51 (1931), 78 ff.). In tragic dialogue it may not have been used
before Sophocles (cf. Barrett ad E. *Hipp.* 101). It is also found in
some dialects (Lesbian, etc.: Buck, *Greek Dialects*, § 104. 7).

Probably, therefore, -αισι came in during the period of transmission.
If the poet was using an Attic form, this will have been θυσίᾱσι. More
probably θυσίῃσι is the original reading. But I have refrained from
altering the text, in view of some residual uncertainty as to the
proper reading.

370. περίφρων Περσεφόνεια: cf. *Dem.* 359 δαΐφρονι Περσεφονείῃ
(note ad loc.). περίφρων is not used of a goddess in Homer. Cf. Hes.
Th. 894, *Sc.* 297, 313.

371-2. ὅ γ᾽ αὐτός... λάθρῃ: Gemoll compares *Ap.* 140 for the use of
αὐτός. There it may be resumptive, but is probably also 'formulaic'
when used of Apollo: cf. *Ap.* 181 (αὐτὸς δ᾽...: perhaps 'and in
person'?), *Aph.* 151 (there emphatic) ~ *Herm.* 234 (with no special
force), Mosch. 4. 13 (again emphatic), also *Il.* 1. 47 (cf. Leaf ad loc.).
This use, of Apollo, might suggest that it was applied to a god to
emphasize his dignity (i.e. 'Himself'). Cf. Zeus' self-revelation
(Mosch. *Eur.* 155), and similarly perhaps αὐτὸς ἔφα of Pythagoras
(cf. Dover on Ar. *Nub.* 219), and the use of the definite article with
ἄναξ, ἥρως, γέρων (Monro, *HG²* § 261. 3(*a*)), especially αὐτὰρ ὅ γ᾽
ἥρως (*Il.* 5. 308 etc.), and τόν γε ἄνακτα (*Dem.* 342) of Hades. This
would be most appropriate in the case of Hades, where one might
compare the use of euphemisms for his name (cf. ad *Dem.* 9). There is
a similar use of *ipse* in Latin (cf. Fordyce on Catull. 3. 6 f.).

In 372, the position of λάθρῃ is less natural than in 411, where it clearly goes with ἔμβαλε. If emendation is needed, the suggestion of Jacques is very attractive. West suggests αὖτιc, meaning 'as a counter-measure'.

372. ῥοιῆc κόκκον: ῥοιαί are mentioned in *Od.* 7. 115 = 11. 589. κόκκοc occurs first here. Cf. Hdt. 4. 143, etc.

In Ov. *M.* 5. 534 ff. Persephone picks the fruit herself and eats seven seeds. In Ov. *F.* 4. 607 f. she is said to have eaten three (cf. Bömer ad loc.). For the story of Ascalaphus cf. ad *Dem.* 411 ff.

On the belief, common in many countries, that if one eats the food of the dead one must remain with them, cf. Allen and Halliday ad loc., Frazer, *Apollodorus*, i. 39 ff., Radermacher, 'Die Erzählungen der Odyssee' (*SB Wien*, 1915), 10 ff. In general, eating and drinking ratify one's membership of a community (cf. e.g. Hes. *Th.* 639 ff., West ad loc.). In particular, a meal concludes a marriage-ceremony in many countries (cf. C. Bonner, *CR* 53 (1939), 3 f., E. S. McCartney, *TAPA* 56 (1925), 70 ff.).

The significance of the pomegranate has been variously interpreted. It was symbolical of blood and death, but also of fertility and marriage. Thus it aptly signified the marriage of Persephone and Hades. The mystae at Eleusis, and the celebrants of the Haloa, were forbidden to eat it (Porph. *de abst.* 4. 16, Schol. Luc. *Dial. mer.* 7. 4). For similar prohibitions cf. ad *Dem.* 6 ff., 42, 99. At the Thesmophoria, it was forbidden to eat pomegranate-seeds that had fallen on the ground (Clem. Al. *Protr.* 2. 19. 3, p. 15. 9 Stähl.; cf. Deubner, *AF* 58). For further references see Allen and Halliday ad loc., Arbesmann, *Das Fasten*, 60, Gaster, *Thespis*, 191, Kerényi, *Eleusis*, 137 ff.

The pomegranate is frequently an attribute of Persephone and Hades in art. Cf. Preller–Robert 1. 763 n. 2, K. Bötticher, *Der Baumkultus der Hellenen* (Berlin, 1856), ch. 38, A. B. Cook, *Zeus*, 3. 1. 813 ff. A third-century B.C. Hellenistic tomb-painting from Kazanlak in Bulgaria (A. Frova, *Arti figurativi* i (1945), 105 ff., C. Verdiani, *AJA* 49 (1945), 402 ff., Ch. Picard, *RHR* 134 (1948), 113 ff.) has been thought to depict the scene of Persephone's departure. It shows a man offering a meal to a woman, which includes three pomegranate-seeds (cf. Ov. *F.* 4. 607) and also what may be eggs (or grapes?). On each side is a procession of attendants, including a man with a chariot (i.e. Hermes?), also two trumpeters (less suitable in Hades!) and a woman holding a κίcτη and miniature temple. The woman who receives the food draws her himation over her head like a veil, and appears sorrowful. But the attribution to the myth of Persephone seems rather doubtful.

λάθρῃ: this should go with ἔδωκε rather than νωμήcαc. Cf. *Dem.* 411–12.

373. ἀμφὶ ἓ νωμήcαc: νωμᾶν in Homer means 'to distribute or direct', 'handle, wield', and metaphorically 'turn over (in one's mind)'. Hence Hermann, reading ἀμφί ἕ, took it as 'dividing it in two' (i.e. Hades shared it). This, however, he did not need to do, and it is nowhere mentioned. Ilgen translated 'turning it over in his mind', Voss 'dum eam [Persephone] prope se traheret'(!). Matthiae however took it as 'peering round him' (cf. *Il.* 4. 497, 15. 574, 241). The sense 'observe, look' occurs in later Greek: Hdt. 4. 128, Pl. *Crat.* 411 d (τὸ νωμᾶν καὶ τὸ σκοπεῖν ταὐτόν), Theognostus, Περὶ Ὀρθογραφίας 62. 30 (Kl. Alpers (Diss. Hamburg, 1964), 105) νωμῆcαι· τηρῆcαι. It is thus used especially of soothsayers: S. *OT* 300, E. *Ph.* 1255 f., A. *Sept.* 25. This is an attractive explanation. Hades acts furtively (λάθρη), not wishing to be observed, presumably by Hermes: in *Dem.* 413 Persephone claims to have acted under compulsion. But it could be objected that such a phrase is rather too graphic for this context, and that λάθρη conveys the sense sufficiently on its own.

Other interpretations are:

(*a*) Hermann, reading ἀμφίc, first translated as 'seorsum tribuens', i.e. apart from Hermes (cf. Gemoll).

(*b*) Eitrem (*Opferritus*, 23): 'Es ist jedenfalls ganz deutlich, dass Hades den Granatapfelkern um sich (das heisst wohl um den Kopf) herumführt, damit der Kern, auf diese Weise selbst an Hades gebunden, auch die Gemählin selbst an den Hades binde und ihm zurückführe.' That is, he passes it round himself to unite it magically, and hence Persephone, to himself.

Similar notions of magic are advocated by:

(*c*) Agar (*CR* 31 (1917), 120): 'after making passes over it privily'.

(*d*) Myres (*CR* 52 (1938), 51 f.): 'moving it to and fro about himself', to make it a love-charm.

(*e*) Bonner, (*CR* 53 (1939), 3 f.): 'passing it round his body.'

Both Agar and Myres take λάθρη with νωμήcαc. On the development of νωμᾶν cf. E. Laroche, *Histoire de la racine NEM- en grec ancien* (Paris, 1949), 69 ff.

374. αἰδοίη Δημήτερι: cf. *Dem.* 486, also 343 and notes to 190, 214.

375–86. Hades yokes the horses to the chariot, and Persephone and Hermes mount. They leave Hades' palace and traverse sea and land, flying over the mountain-tops, until they come to where Demeter waits, in front of the temple. She rushes to greet her daughter.

The description of the Journey (cf. Arend, *Typische Scenen* 86 ff.), is elaborated pictorially in a way characteristic of the *Hymn*. Cf. ad *Dem.* 380 ff., and Introduction, p. 58.

375 f. Hades lends them his own chariot (cf. *Dem.* 19).

377–9. Cf. *Il.* 5. 364–6 (~ *Od.* 3. 481–4):

> ἣ δ᾽ ἐc δίφρον ἔβαινεν ...
> πὰρ δέ οἱ Ἶρις ἔβαινε καὶ ἡνία λάζετο χερcί,
> μάcτιξεν δ᾽ ἐλάαν, τὼ δ᾽ οὐκ ἀέκοντε πετέcθην.

(368 ~ *Dem.* 384, 371 ~ *Dem.* 388*). The situation in *Il.* 5. 364 ff. is similar (journey, and meeting of mother and daughter).

379. διὲκ μεγάρων: normally the horses leave through the πρόθυρον and αἴθουcα of the palace (*Od.* 3. 493 etc.). Here, the whole of Hades' realm is thought of as his palace: cf. *Il.* 3. 322 (etc.) δῦναι δόμον Ἄϊδος εἴσω, and especially *Il.* 23. 74, *Od.* 11. 571 εὐρυπυλὲς Ἄϊδος δῶ, and note on Dem. 9 (πολυδέκτῃ). Cf. also Parm. fr. 1, Burkert, *Phronesis* 14 (1969), 1 ff.

ἄκοντε: the contracted form occurs also at *Dem.* 413, where it is required by the metre (but the line may not be genuine). In Homer, the majority of manuscripts have the contracted form at *Il.* 5. 366, 768, etc. In every case the uncontracted form may be restored, and the contraction is not found in the non-Attic derivatives ἀεκαζόμενος, ἀέκητι (cf. Chantraine, *GH* i. 28). It may therefore be due in Homer to Attic transmission (cf. Wackernagel, *Spr. Unters.* 7; cf. 179). But some examples of the contraction α(ϝ)ε > ᾱ, which cannot be resolved, occur in Homer (Chantraine, *GH* i. 32). These are found mostly in relatively 'late' passages, but can hardly all be due to an Attic poet (e.g. ἀθλοφόρους *Il.* 9. 124 = 266, ἄθλων *Od.* 8. 160 ~ 164, ἄκαμεν *Od.* 16. 367). Moreover, the contraction is normal in Ionic. The use of ἄκοντε, ἄκουσαν (if genuine) in the *Hymn* is therefore not evidence of Attic composition.

In the revised form of the Draconian homicide law (*IG* i². 115, 409/8 B.C.) both *AKON* and *AEKON* occur (lines 17 and 34). This could mean that the contracted form was in use in spoken Attic of the late seventh century B.C., whereas legal language preserved the more archaic form. Alternatively, *AKON* may be due to the fifth-century revision. In this case, *AEKON* belongs to the seventh century, but again may be an archaizing form at this date. The law cannot therefore be used to date the introduction of ἄκων into Attic.[1]

380–3. The journey is over land and sea. Cf. *Dem.* 33–5, and similarly *Aph.* 122–5, both divine journeys and both rapes, the second of which and probably the first are also through the air (*Aph.* 125). For this way of saying 'the whole world' cf. also ad *Dem.* 13 f. Mountains and sea echo Persephone's cry at *Dem.* 38 (cf. ad loc.).

Such pictorial elaboration of a journey already occurs in Homer (e.g. *Il.* 13. 27–31). For its 'lyric' character cf. Kirk, *Songs*, 172, and notes to *Dem.* 383.

380. On the rhythm of this line cf. ad *Dem.* 171.

381. ὕδωρ: the upsilon is always short *in thesi* in early epic. Cf. Xenoph. fr. 4. 2 D.³, and A.R. 4. 290, *Batr.* 97 (both in this position in the verse), etc.

382. Gemoll found the position of ἄκριες unusual. But ἄκριας always occupies the fourth foot in Homer and the *Hymns* (five times), and ἄκριες is here emphatic (cf. ὑπὲρ αὐτάων 383). The genitive ἵππων ἀθανάτων interrupts the enumeration, as in *Dem.* 7, 22 f., 34. For its separation from ὁρμήν cf. Dem. 71 ff.

383. ὑπὲρ αὐτάων: the simple anaphoric use of αὐτός is rare in Homer (Chantraine, *GH* ii. 157). Here it is probably emphatic: 'over the very mountains'.

---

[1] [R. S. Stroud, *Drakon's Law of Homicide* (Berkeley, 1968), however, shows that the correct reading of line 34 should be *ADIKON*.—N.J.R., 1978.]

βαθὺν ἠέρα: in Homer ἀήρ is feminine, and it may be here also. Cf. ἠέρα πουλύν (*Il.* 5. 776, 8. 50) with πουλύν as a feminine (cf. *Il.* 10. 27), and the use of feminine ἡδύς (*Od.* 12. 369), θῆλυς (*Il.* 10. 216 etc.). βαθύς is feminine at Call. *Hy.* 4. 37, Eratosth. 8.

The first certain instance of ἀήρ masculine is at Hes. *Op.* 548–50. Cf. however Hes. *Th.* 9 (ἠέρι πολλῷ: v.l. πολλῇ; cf. West ad loc.), and αἰθήρ, which is feminine in Homer (except *Od.* 19. 540 v.l.), but masculine in Hes. *Th.* 124, and fr. 400.

In Homer ἀήρ means 'mist, darkness, the stuff of invisibility'. This is also the sense in Hesiod. (At *Th.* 697 the manuscripts have ἠέρα δῖαν but West reads αἰθέρα.) The Alexandrians, however, took it to mean 'the lower atmosphere', as opposed to αἰθήρ (Schol. A ad *Il.* 14. 288, Eust. p. 986. 20, Hsch. s.v.). This may be based on the interpretation of *Il.* 14. 288 (cf. Leaf ad loc., and Appendix H), where a pine-tree on Mount Ida reaches through the ἀήρ to the αἰθήρ. Leaf prefers to take this as referring to the *mist* clothing the mountain-top. In the present passage the same interpretation would be possible. In *Il.* 20. 446 (ἠέρα τύψε βαθεῖαν) this is clearly the sense (cf. 20. 444), and the mountain-tops have just been mentioned (*Dem.* 383). But in later parallels to *Dem.* 383b (see below) ἀήρ and αἰθήρ are used interchangeably, and the sense 'air' may perhaps already be intended here also. βαθύν would then refer to depth, or height. Cf. Emp. B 17. 18 ἠέρος ἄπλετον ὕψος (v.l. αἰθέρος), E. *Med.* 1297 ἐς αἰθέρος βάθος (Page ad loc.). The difficulty of this interpretation is that the Greeks are generally thought not to have realized that clear air has substance until the time of Empedocles and his κλεψύδρα experiment (fr. 100; in *Dem.* 383 τέμνον suggests substance: see below). But the translation 'air' seems the natural one here. See also P. Louis, *Rev. Phil.* 74 (1948), 63 ff., on the varying senses of the word in Homer.

τέμνον: the Attic form (with -ε-) is found only once in Homer (*Od.* 3. 175), and as a v.l. at Hes. *Op.* 570. Wackernagel (*Spr. Unters.* 14) considered this due to Attic transmission (cf. Chantraine, *GH* i. 314). Here it might be due to an Attic poet, but could equally well have come in during transmission (cf. *Dem.* 228 ὑποταμνόν). Cf. B. Forssman (*Glotta* 44 (1966), 5–14, especially p. 8), who considers that τέμνον may be right, but that the possibility of corruption cannot be excluded.

For the whole phrase cf. P. Oxy. 2637 fr. 5 ii 7 (quoted on p. 126) which is probably by Ibycus (cf. D. L. Page, *Proc. Camb. Phil. Soc.* 196 (1970), 93 f.). The lines might possibly refer to Pegasus, as another part of the same fragment clearly does (cf. Lobel ad loc.). Alternatively, they could be from Ibycus' poem on the Rape of Ganymede (*PMG* 289; cf. J. P. Barron, *BICS* 16 (1969), 140, 149 n. 92). ἀέρα looks probable here, rather than αἰθέρα, but it is not entirely clear how much space there is in the lacuna.

Cf. also Bacch. 5. 15–16 (on the eagle of Zeus: cf. the Rape of Ganymede?) βαθὺν δ' αἰθέρα . . . τάμνων.

Bacchylides' description of the eagle's flight is similar to *Dem.* 380 ff. :

Bacch. 5. 24–7   οὗ νιν κορυφαὶ μεγάλας ἴσχουσι γαίας, οὐδ᾽ ἁλὸς ἀκαμάτας δυσπαίπαλα κύματα· νωμᾶ|ται δ᾽ . . .

~ *Dem.* 380–3   οὐδὲ θάλασσα οὖθ᾽ ὕδωρ ποταμῶν . . . οὖτ᾽ ἄκριες ἔσχεθον ὁρμήν, ἀλλ᾽ ὑπὲρ αὐτάων . . .

(This has also been noted by H. Mähler, *Bacchylides: Lieder und Fragmente* (Berlin, 1968), 13. Cf. M. Lefkowitz, *HSCP* 73 (1969), 95 f.)

Ibycus' poem about Ganymede may have contained something similar. Schol. A.R. 3. 158 says that the lines describing Eros' journey from Olympus in Apollonius are an imitation of Ibycus' poem on the Rape of Ganymede (l.c. above).[1] Apollonius' description again shows similarities to *Dem.* 380–3 :

A.R. 3. 164–6   νειόθι δ᾽ ἄλλοτε γαῖα φερέσβιος ἄστεά τ᾽ ἀνδρῶν (~ *Dem.* 450 etc.) φαίνετο καὶ ποταμῶν ἱεροὶ ῥόοι, ἄλλοτε δ᾽ αὖτε ἄκριες, ἀμφὶ δὲ πόντος, ἀν᾽ αἰθέρα πολλὸν ἰόντι

(A.R. 3. 158   βῆ δὲ διὲκ μεγάλοιο . . . ἀλωήν
~ *Dem.* 379   ϲεῦε διὲκ μεγάρων) not traditional formulae:
Dem. 281   βῆ δὲ διὲκ μεγάρων)   cf. ad loc.).

A final piece of evidence which might suggest a link between the Bacchylides passage and Ibycus' poem is the similarity of Bacch. 5. 26–7 νωμᾶται δ᾽ ἐν ἀτρύτῳ χάει to Ibyc. fr. 28 Bergk[4] ποτᾶται δ᾽ ἐν ἀλλοτρίῳ χάει. This is quoted by Schol. Ar. *Av.* 192 (on the line διὰ τῆς πόλεως τῆς ἀλλοτρίας καὶ τοῦ χάους = 1218), as by *Ibycus*. Both wording and attribution have been questioned (cf. Jebb, Snell on Bacch. 5. 26), and Diehl and Page do not give the fragment under Ibycus. But there is no real ground for supposing that the Scholiast was mistaken over the author. (On this use of χάος cf. West ad *Th.* 116.)

These parallels seem to suggest that both Ibycus and Bacchylides may be following an epic description of a divine journey similar to *Dem.* 380 ff. (For other examples of this 'typical scene' see notes ad loc.) It is also possible that Bacchylides may be imitating Ibycus directly (cf. Bowra, *Gk. Lyric Poetry*[2], 258–9), but this cannot be established. Both Ibycus and Bacchylides are highly imitative of epic (cf. D. L. Page, *Aegyptus* 31 (1951), 165, Barron, o.c. 490 ff., on

---

[1] Wilamowitz wished to transfer this Scholion to A.R. 3. 114–17, and refer it to the scene with Eros and Ganymede together. But there is no reason to suppose that he was right. Ibycus *must* have described the eagle's journey. He *may* also have described Ganymede with Eros on Olympus, but not necessarily so. The scene looks Hellenistic, and Apollonius might have got the idea of Eros and Ganymede together from reading Ibycus' account of the Rape, but not the substance.

Ibycus fr. 1; and M. Lefkowitz, o.c. 45 ff. on Bacch. 5). Bacchylides also, notoriously, uses conventional lyric language and themes.

The expression ἠέρα/αἰθέρα τέμνειν (τάμνειν) is parallel to the epic use of τάμνειν of travelling through the sea (cf. *Od.* 3. 174–5 πέλαγος μέςον . . . τέμνειν, *Od.* 13. 88, and Forssman, o.c. 13), and the analogy of air to sea was, it seems, strongly felt by the Greeks. Homer uses the same epithet ἀτρύγετος of both sea and αἰθήρ (*Il.* 1. 316, 17. 425, etc.), and in later poetry birds use their wings as oars to row through the air (e.g. A. *Ag.* 52 etc.). Cf. also Ar. *Av.* 1400 αἰθέρος αὔλακα τέμνων (in a lyric parody) ~ [Arion], *PMG* 939. 16–17 ἄλοκα Νηρεΐας πλακὸς τέμνοντες, ἀςτιβῆ πόρον (here a metaphor taken originally from the land); E. *Phoen.* fr. 124. 2 f., Epigr. 2. 1 (Diehl, i³. p. 90), A.R. 4. 770–1, Orph. *Arg.* 303 ('Ἥλιος τὸν ἀπείριτον αἰθέρα τέμνων ~ πόντος ἀπείριτος *Od.* 10. 195 etc.); and especially Pl. *Phd.* 111 ab, for ἀήρ as a kind of sea.

384. στῆςε δ' ἄγων: the only other example of this phrase occurs in *Il.* 2. 558, the controversial line said to have been inserted by Solon or Pisistratus into the Catalogue of Ships. But it may be a formulaic phrase (cf. εἷςεν ἄγων* *Il.* 1. 311, *Od.* 1. 130, δεῖξε δ' ἄγων* *Ap.* 523, στῆςεν/αν* of a chariot *Il.* 24. 350, *Od.* 4. 22, 7. 4, ἔνθ' ἵππους ἔςτηςε *Il.* 5. 368).

385. Demeter stands in front of her temple, waiting to receive them.

386. ἠΰτε μαινάς: cf. also Ov. *F.* 4. 457–8 (of Ceres):

> mentis inops rapitur, ut quas audire solemus
> Threicias fusis maenadas ire comis

E. *Hel.* 543 ὡς δρομαία πῶλος ἢ βάκχη θεοῦ (cf. also E. *Hel.* 1321 ἀπόνους of Demeter, *ex emendatione*), *Hipp.* 550 δρομάδα ναΐδ' ὅπως τε βάκχαν, *Tro.* 349, Timotheus, *PMG* 778b, Xen. *Eph.* 5. 13. 2, *Or. Sib.* 5. 484, Cat. 64. 61, Virg. *A.* 4. 300–3, 7. 385 ff. In Homer the sense may be simply 'a mad woman' in *Il.* 22. 460 (~ 6. 389). Maenadism may however be referred to in *Il.* 6. 132 ff. ὅς ποτε μαινομένοιο Διωνύςοιο τιθήνας ςεῦε κατ' ἠγάθεον Νυςήϊον . . . In the *Hymn*, ὄρος κάτα etc. must surely belong to the simile, and not refer to the hill on which Demeter's temple stood (Allen and Halliday), which could hardly be described as a mountain. This implies that μαινάς is here a maenad, and the mountain is perhaps Nysa (cf. *Il.* 6. 133, and *Hy.* 1. 8 Νύςῃ ὕπατον ὄρος ἀνθέον ὕλῃ) or Cithaeron (cf. E. *Ba.* 218 f. ἐν δὲ δαςκίοις ὄρεςι θοάζειν, Virg. *A.* 4. 303).

δάςκιον ὕλη: M has ὕλης, and the dative plural ὕλης is read by Allen, who compares Anacr. *PMG* 408. 2, where Schol. Pi. *O.* 3. 52 has ὕλαις, other authors ὕλη (read by Page), Hecat., *FGH* 1. 291 οὔρεα δαςέα ὕληςι, Mosch. 3. 89 (ὕλαι), Nonnus, *D.* 10. 175 δάςκιον ὕλης, and other examples from late Greek (*CR* 20 (1906), 290 f.; cf. Zachariae, *Zeitschr. f. vergl. Sprachf.*, 34 (1895–7), 453 f.). Cf. however *Od.* 13. 351 etc., and especially *Hy.* 1. 8 (above). It seems better to adopt the singular ὕλῃ. See also Pfeiffer, *Herm.* 87 (1959), 3 f., *Hist. Class. Schol.* i. 118 n. 6.

387–404. Persephone also . . . runs [to greet her mother . . .]. Demeter asks her if she has eaten anything in Hades. If she has not, she may remain in heaven. If she has, she must return to Hades for a third of the year, and spend two-thirds in heaven, and when the earth is covered with flowers in spring, she will return from the underworld, for all to wonder at. Demeter then asks her how Hades deceived her.

The lacunae in these lines and in 462–79 are due to a tear in M. On this, and the sixteenth-century supplements of m, see Allen and Halliday, pp. xxi–ii, and Introduction, p. 66. The supplements in Allen's text, which are mainly due to Goodwin, were proposed by him 'cum magna diffidentia'.

The reunion of Demeter and Persephone was thought by Nilsson to be depicted on the upper half of the Niinnion tablet (*ARW* 32 (1935), 93 ff. = *Op. Sel.* ii. 559 ff.). This is very unlikely: cf. Mylonas, *Eleusis*, 215, *Eph. Arch.* 1960 (1965), 87. Picard (*BCH* 55 (1931), 11 ff. and pl. 1) identifies a relief in the Delos Museum as a portrayal of the scene. Cf. ad *Dem.* 334 ff.

The reunion was supposed to be represented in the cult, according to Lact. *Div. Inst. Epit.* 18 (23). 7. It is not known how this was done. Cf. ad *Dem.* 40 ff., 434–40, and Introduction, pp. 24 ff.

387. Goodwin's supplement is more suitable to a recognition-scene, such as *Aph.* 181 (~ *Il.* 3. 396–7).

389. ἆλτο θέειν: ἆλτο χαμᾶζε is used of dismounting from a chariot twelve times in Homer (cf. ad *Dem.* 387). It is not used with an infinitive in Homer or Hesiod. Cf. *Ap.* 448 ἆλτο πέτεσθαι, and βῆ δὲ θέειν in Homer (*Il.* 2. 183 etc.).

392. πα⟨υ⟩ομε[ν-: if Goodwin's reading of M is correct, the word must be corrupt (πάομαι is not found in the present, and in other tenses first in Solon 1. 7 D.³). The confusion of α and αυ in manuscripts is common (cf. Allen and Halliday, West ad *Th.* 655). But φιλότητος can hardly be right. More probable is κλαυθμοῖο: cf. *Od.* 4. 801 (παύσειε κλαυθμοῖο γόοιό τε δακρυόεντος) ~ *Od.* 21. 228, 4. 102 f. ~ 19. 268, 8. 540, 4. 35, *Dem.* 436. For weeping at a reunion in epic cf. *Od.* 16. 213 ff., 23. 207.

394. ἐξαύδα . . .: *Il.* 1. 362–3 ~ 18. 73–4 (cf. ad *Dem.* 393) are spoken by Thetis to Achilles. At *Il.* 16. 19 Achilles also asks Patroclus why he is crying.

395. κ᾽ ἀνιοῦσα: M's reading κε νέουσα is defended by van Groningen (*Mnem.* 4. 2 (1949), 42 f.). νέοντες ('going') is a variant reading at *Od.* 8. 108. Cf. perhaps Pi. fr. 124(a). 7 Sn., Hdt. 5. 59 (in an epigram; ἀνέθηκεν ἐών codd.), Sophr. fr. 101 (Kaibel). The active is thus only dubiously attested. Bücheler's supplement would be preferable, as giving point to καὶ . . . καί in 396, which (with the sense 'both . . . and') is otherwise 'ab omni sermone epicorum alienam' (Ebeling, p. 618; but cf. Denniston, *GP* 324: 'in the Hymns καὶ . . . καί is beginning to establish itself'; cf. ad *Dem.* 495). 'Both . . . and' is unnecessary here (cf. *Dem.* 447 ~ 465), and καὶ παρ᾽ . . . καί . . . awkward. But ἄλλοις would normally follow ἐμοὶ . . . καὶ πατρί, and

LINES 387–99 283

ἀθανάτοιςι here gives a triple repetition (397, 400). One might read
ἀνθρώποιςι in 397 (cf. ad loc.), and κεν ἐοῦςα παρ' ἀθανάτοιςι θεοῖςι in
395, but this is still rather weak. Alternatively, a verb may have occurred at the end of 395 (cf. Voss, Bothe), e.g. κ' ἀνιοῦςα π[άλιν
οἴκονδε νέοιο. (We do not know for certain that 'home' for Persephone
was Olympus, but presumably it was.) This removes the difficulty
of καὶ . . . καί in 396.

For the interchange of ἰοῦςα/ἐοῦςα cf. *Dem.* 364.

396. πατρὶ . . . Κρονίωνι: this full formula does not occur elsewhere.
Cf. Ζηνὶ κελαινεφέϊ Κρονίωνι (*Dem.* 316), and Introduction, p. 47.

396–7. Cf. *Dem.* 485.

397. πάντεςςι . . . ἀθανάτοιςιν: cf. *Dem.* 366. ἀνθρώποιςι (*Ap.* 479,
522 ~ *Dem.* 399) is also possible, but less likely (cf. ad *Dem.* 328).
Persephone's honour in *heaven* will be primarily from the gods. Cf. also
PMG 880 (Schol. T) ὦ Λίνε, πᾶςι θεοῖςι τετιμένε, *Orph. Hy.* 45. 5 ~
54. 2 τετιμένε πᾶςι θεοῖςι, Emped. fr. 112. 5 (cf. ad *Dem.* 119 f., 256–74)
πωλεῦμαι μετὰ πᾶςι τετιμένος, Keyssner, *Gottesvorstellung*, 65 f.

On *Aph.* 205(~ *Dem.* 397) see Heitsch, *Aphroditehymnos*, 38.

398. †πτᾶςα πάλιν ἰοῦς'†: πτᾶςα, which Allen retains, is inappropriate, unnecessary with ἰοῦςα, and un-Homeric (ἐξέπτη Hes. *Op.* 98
etc., πτᾶςα Herodian Gr. 1. 532; cf. Choerob. *in Theod.* 2. 79 etc.).
The ellipse of the verb in the conditional clause is also very abrupt
for early epic (on *Il.* 9. 46, 262, cf. Leaf ad loc.). ⟨ςύ γ'⟩ is unattractive
and πάλιν never occurs before the third-foot caesura in Homer or
Hesiod.

In the context, the correction ἐπάςω (τι) or τι πάςςαο is hard to resist.
Ruhnken's αὖτις is a possible supplement (cf. *Il.* 2. 276 etc.), and cf.
also West's conjecture.[1] For the omission of the object with πατέομαι
cf. *Il.* 24. 642 (understood from 641 f.). Goodwin's εἰ δέ τι πάςςαο is
palaeographically a simple change, but πάμπαν is unconvincing. (It
would be more natural with a negative, as *Il.* 9. 435, 21. 338 οὐδέ τι
πάμπαν.) Bucheler's εἰ δ' ἐπάςω τι is also possible palaeographically, but
his μέν after πάλιν is misplaced.

ὑπ[ὸ κεύθεα ^{ςι}⟩γαίης: (cf. m's supplement): Bücheler's accusative
(with ἰοῦςα) is an alternative to the dative if one reads εἰν Ἀΐδαο in
399. Cf. ad *Dem.* 399, 446.

399. μέρος: not in Homer or Hesiod (cf. μοῖρα). At *Herm.* 53 it is
probably a false reading for μέλος (cf. Allen and Halliday ad loc.).
Cf. Pi. *O.* 8. 77, Hdt. 1. 145, etc.

[εἰς ἐνιαυτόν]: cf. m's supplement. 'Within a year' (cf. *Od.* 4. 86,
Alc. 42. 12)? It is less suitable here than at *Od.* l.c., where the dis-
tributive sense is more natural ('three times a year'). Bucheler's εἰν
Ἀΐδαο is also attractive: this supplies a locative to οἰκήςεις (cf. ad
Dem. 398). m's supplement may very well be his own conjecture: cf.
Allen and Halliday, p. xxi (in their note on *Dem.* 399 they contradict
themselves).

[1] For the intrusion of a gloss into the text see on *Dem.* 407.

399 ff. Persephone's time of absence in the underworld is a third of the year according to Apollod. 1. 5. 3. Other versions, Alexandrian and later, divide the year equally: Ov. *F.* 4. 613 f., *M.* 5. 564 ff., Cornut. 28, Hyg. *fab.* 146, Serv. in *Georg.* 1. 39, Mythogr. Vat. 2. 100 (*Scr. rer. myth. Lat.*, ed. Bode, i. 108). Similar variant traditions are recorded about the absence of Adonis (Apollod. 3. 14. 4; cf. Frazer ad loc.), and Apollo (Preller–Robert, i². 763 n. 3). Cf. the division between Castor and Polydeuces (especially Pi. *N.* 10. 80 ff., and 87 f. ἥμιcυ μέν κε πνέοιc γαίαc ὑπένερθεν ἐών, ἥμιcυ δ' οὐρανοῦ ἐν χρυcέοιc δόμοιcιν).

The oldest division of the year is into two parts, winter and summer (Nilsson, *Die Entstehung und relig. Bedeutung d. griech. Kalenders* (Lund, 1962), 24). The division into three seasons is said to be normal in Homer and Hesiod (cf. LSJ s.v. ὥρα A. I. 1), and it occurs also in A. *PV* 454 ff., Ar. *Av.* 709, Lyr. Adesp. 37. 5 (Powell, *Coll. Alex.*, p. 199). But ὀπώρα is distinguished from θέροc in *Od.* 12. 76, 14. 384 (~ 11. 192), making a fourth season. The first clear mention of four seasons is in Alcm. *PMG* 20. Tac. *Germ.* 26 attests three seasons for the ancient Germans. Hippocr. περὶ ἑβδομάδων lists seven divisions: ch. 4 p. 8 Roscher. Cf. M. L. West, *CQ* 21 (1971), 369, 376. The division into a third and two-thirds perhaps reflects Hades' share in the world (cf. ad *Dem.* 85 f., 365–9).

In later antiquity the prevalent (Stoic) interpretation of Persephone's absence in Hades identified her with the corn and referred it to the time of winter, after the corn was sown (Cornut. 28, Cic. *ND* 2. 66, Schol. Hes. *Th.* 912, Tzetzes in Hes. *Op.* 32, Cleanthes fr. 547 ap. Plut. *Mor.* 377 d, Varro ap. Aug. *CD* 7. 20, Schol. Ar. *Vesp.* 1429). This interpretation placed the Rape of Persephone in autumn (*Orph. Hy.* 29. 14, fr. 196 K., Euseb. *PE* 3. 11. 15, Sallustius, *De diis et mundo* 4, pp. 8 f. Nock).

This agrees with the explicit assertion of the *Hymn* (401 ff.), that Persephone's return will occur in spring (on *Dem.* 6 ff. cf. ad loc.), and there can be little doubt that the *Hymn* here represents what was from very early times felt to be the significance of the myth: the absence of Core corresponds to the winter, when corn and other plants are under the earth, her return to the spring-time when the earth is again covered in flowers, and the corn is growing. Her return is also followed closely by the growth of crops and plants in *Dem.* 453 ff., 471 ff.

A modern explanation, proposed by Cornford (in *Essays and Studies presented to Wm. Ridgeway* (Cambridge, 1913), 153 ff.) and upheld by Nilsson (*ARW* 32 (1935), 105 ff. = *Op. Sel.* ii. 576 ff.; cf. *Gesch.* i³. 472 ff.) identifies the descent of Persephone with the storing of seed-corn in underground granaries after harvest. Her absence then corresponds to the dry period of summer, and her return to the removal of the seed-corn for sowing. The chief ancient evidence for this is Diod. 5. 4, which dates the festival of Κόρηc Καταγωγή in Sicily to the time of harvesting. But this is most naturally taken as referring to the 'bringing-in' of the corn: cf. the Καταγωγή of Dionysus at the Anthesteria (in springtime), Deubner, *AF* 103 f. (so originally

Nilsson, *Gr. Feste*, 356 f.). Although other ancient deities of fertility were thought to die in summer, under the sickles of the reapers or the flails of the harvesters, or in the parching of vegetation by the summer heat (cf. Introduction, p. 13, and ad *Dem.* 305 ff.), this explanation does not at all suit Persephone, and there is no ancient testimony to support it.

Cf. also (*contra* Nilsson) Kourouniotes, *Arch. Delt.* 15 (1933–5), 1 ff., Malten, *Gnomon* 20 (1944), 120 ff. W. C. Greene, *CP* 41 (1946), 105–7, attempts by a remarkable piece of special pleading to explain away *Dem.* 401 ff.

An alternative interpretation, popular in late antiquity, identified Persephone with the moon (Porph. *antr. nymph.* 18, Serv. in *Ecl.* 3. 26, *Aen.* 6. 118), whose disappearance gave rise to the story of Persephone's absence in the underworld (Ennius, *Varia* 59 V.² ap. Varr. *LL* 5. 68 = 'Epicharmus' fr. 54 Diels, Plut. *Mor.* 942 d, Mythogr. Vat. 2. 100, Fulgentius, *Myth.* 2. 16). If 'Epicharmus' fr. 54 D. goes back to the fourth or late fifth century B.C. (cf. Susemihl, *Philologus* 53 (1894), 564 ff., Pickard-Cambridge, *Dithyramb, Tragedy, and Comedy*² (Oxford, 1962), 242 f.), this view is surprisingly early in origin. But this is quite uncertain.

On the vase-paintings representing the Anodos of a female deity (Core, Aphrodite, or Pandora) see Nilsson, *Op. Sel.* ii. 611 ff., Metzger, *Représentations*, 232 f., *Recherches*, 11 ff. (especially 13 f.).

401–2. ὁππότε ... θάλλει: for the present indic. with ὁππότε cf. *Il.* 11. 492, *Od.* 18. 409, Lucian, *Toxaris* 46.

ἠαρινοῖϲι: this form occurs only here and in P. Petr. 3, p. 152 (third century B.C.). Cf. epic εἰαρινόϲ, later (poetic) ἠρινόϲ. Cf. ad *Dem.* 174.

401–3. Cf. *Orph. Hy.* 29. 12 f. (Persephone):

> εἰαρινή, λειμωνιάϲιν χαίρουϲα πνοῇϲιν,
> ἱερὸν ἐκφαίνουϲα δέμαϲ βλαϲτοῖϲ χλοοκάρποιϲ.

402. παντοδαποῖϲ: this is not found elsewhere in early epic. Cf. Sapph. 152, A. *Th.* 357, etc. (cf. παντοῖοϲ, ἀλλοδαπόϲ Homer).

θάλλει: in Homer only forms of the perfect occur. Cf. Hes. *Op.* 173 (θάλλοντα), 236 (θάλλουϲιν).

403. ἄνει: the Homeric form is εἶϲθα. Cf. εἶϲ Hes. *Op.* 208 (Edwards, *Language of Hesiod*, 114), and εἶ in Attic. Wackernagel considers this evidence for Attic composition (*Spr. Unt.* 179). Cf. Introduction, p. 54.

403 f. If there was a lacuna after 403, as suggested by Ruhnken, it existed already when the papyrus was written. But more probably the text is sound, and there is an abrupt break in the sense. Demeter's question in 404 refers to the rape, not to Persephone's having eaten in Hades, and Persephone answers her in *Dem.* 414 ff. Attempts to attach 404 more closely to the preceding lines (e.g. by reading ἢ τίνι or ἤ τινι) are therefore unnecessary. 404 looks rather like an afterthought on the poet's part, leading him to add 414 ff. (although for 403–4 cf. Hes. *Th.* 588–9. See Introduction, p. 38.

404. Ruhnken's conjecture is confirmed by the papyrus.

405–33. Persephone relates how she ate the pomegranate seed, and how Hades carried her off.

Persephone's speech contains a recapitulation (417–32) of the narratives of *Dem.* 340–74 and 5–20, expanded by a catalogue of her companions at the Rape (418–24). Such repetition and expansion is a normal feature of epic. In general, the *Hymn* avoids such lengthy repetitions (cf. ad *Dem.* 172, 314–23) but cf. 216–23 (~ 147–8, 164–8), 335–9 (~ 347–51 ~ 407–10), 442–7 (~ 460–5). Cf. also van Groningen, *Composition littéraire archaïque*, 108, and Introduction, p. 59.

405. Περσεφόνη: the Φ- of pap. 2 is Attic. Cf. ad *Dem.* 56.

406: τοι: the papyrus confirms Hermann's conjecture (cf. *Od.* 17. 108, *Il.* 10. 413, *Od.* 1. 179, etc.).

ἐρέω: for the synizesis cf. Hes. *Op.* 202. ἐξερέω without synizesis occurs at *Dem.* 416. The digamma in ἐρέω is regularly observed in Homer, and neglected only three times (Chantraine, *GH* i. 136). Cf. Hoekstra, *Sub-epic Stage*, 52.

Does Persephone, like Demeter at *Dem.* 120 f. (cf. ad loc.) protest too much? Cf. ad *Dem.* 413. For protestations of truthfulness in a speech cf. also *Dem.* 58, 433.

407. The papyrus gives the correct reading of this line, which was marked as corrupt in M and suspected by earlier editors. ὠκύς (also obelized in M) might have come in as a gloss on ἐριούνιος, which could have been interpreted by some (rightly) as 'fast runner' (cf. *Hy.* 19. 28 f., Hsch. s.vv. οὖνει (οὖνης), οὖνιος, οὖνον, Latte, *Kl. Schr.* 690 ff., Frisk s.v., Leumann, *Hom. Wörter*, 123). But there is no evidence of this interpretation in ancient times. Ἑρμῆς, however, is very probably a gloss on Ἀργειφόντης, and ὠκύς could then have been added to fill the line. ἐριούνιος Ἀργειφόντης is not found elsewhere as a formula in early epic, and in this context is replaceable by διάκτορος Ἀργειφόντης (*Il.* 21. 497 etc.; ἦλθε διάκτορος Ἀργειφόντης* *Od.* 24. 99) or ἐΰσκοπος Ἀργειφόντης (*Ap.* 200, *Herm.* 73, *Aph.* 262), but M's reading seems to guarantee it. On the development of formulae for Hermes cf. Hainsworth, quoted by Hoekstra, *Hom. Modifications*, 49 n. 1, observing the tendency for Ἀργειφόντης/ν to be replaced by κύδιμος/ν Ἑρμῆς/ν in epic (*Hy. Herm.*), once this formula became available. But (*a*) they are not genuine doublets, unlike ἀγλαὸς Ἑρμῆς and Ἀργειφόντης; (*b*) Ἀργειφόντης is almost always used with an epithet.

408. πατέρος Κρονίδαο: again a variant (here grammatical) on traditional Zeus-formulae. Cf. ad *Dem.* 407–8 (Διὸς αἰγιόχοιο is a doublet), and Introduction, pp. 47, 49.

409. ἐλθεῖν: for the infinitive after ἄγγελος ἦλθε cf. *Il.* 11. 715, 24. 194 f. For the repetition see Introduction, p. 60.

411. αὐτὰρ ... αὐτάρ: this repetition has been suspected. A second αὐτάρ occurs as a v.l. at *Il.* 18. 203. Ilgen's αὐτίκ' is the most attractive emendation. But in this *Hymn* such repetition is perhaps not impossible (cf. Introduction, p. 60). For the phrase cf. *Il.* 11. 747 (etc.), *Dem.* 429.

411 ff. Here Persephone herself reveals that she has eaten in the underworld. In a later version she is detected by Ascalaphus, who informs against her, and has a rock placed on him in Hades by Demeter (Apollod. 1. 5. 3). Heracles, in his visit to Hades, rolls away the stone, but Demeter turns him into an owl (Apollod. 2. 5. 12, Ov. M. 5. 538 ff., Serv. in *Georg.* 1. 39, in *Aen.* 4. 462, Lact. Plac. in Stat. *Theb.* 3. 511, Mythogr. Vat. 2. 100 = *Scr. rer. myth. Lat.* ed. Bode, i. 108). In Virg. *G.* 1. 39 Persephone does not care to return to her mother. In Lucan 6. 741 f., Ceres does not want her back, because she is 'contagia passam' (cf. also 699 'caelum matremque perosa'). On these versions, see Zuntz, *Persephone*, 400 ff.

412. ἔμβαλε: the use of ἔμβαλέ μοι without further specification (e.g. cτόματι) is unusual for early epic. Cf. e.g. *Od.* 2. 37 cκῆπτρον δέ οἱ ἔμβαλε χειρί. But Eitrem, *Symb. Osl.* 20 (1940), 146, is surely wrong in speaking of 'throwing' here (comparing Clem. *Protr.* 2. 17. 1).

413. In *Dem.* 371–2 no mention of compulsion is made. Persephone presumably means that she did not want to eat, but could not help it. Does she perhaps 'protest too much' in self-defence (cf. ad *Dem.* 406)? For the pleonasm cf. ad *Dem.* 72, 124. The word-order is 'untraditional' (for βίῃ ἀέκουcαν). Note the un-Homeric contraction of ἄκουcαν (cf. ad *Dem.* 379), and see Hoekstra, *Sub-epic Stage*, 51.

προcηνάγκαccε: this occurs first here. Cf. Th. 5. 42, Hippocrates (frequent), etc. (ἀναγκάζω Hdt. 1. 11 etc.). The compound seems otiose and 'unepic', and the whole line could well be removed. One wonders whether it might not be another 'fill-line', added to supply a lacuna (see app. crit., and cf. Introduction, p. 66).

414. Cf. *Dem.* 3, 30.

Κρονίδεω … μῆτιν: this phrase is perhaps modelled on the Hesiodic Κρονίδεω διὰ βουλάc (*Th.* 572 = *Op.* 71), influenced possibly by Κρόνου πάϊc ἀγκυλομήτεω, μητίετα Ζεύc. The form Κρονίδεω does not occur in Homer.

414–15. The word order is complex. Cf. *Dem.* 72–3 (λαβὼν … οἴχεται …), 169–70, 182–3, and Introduction, p. 60.

415. ᾤχετο … φέρων: cf. Ar. *Lys.* 976 etc., *Dem.* 431.

416. ὡc ἐρεείνειc: cf. ad *Dem.* 172.

417–24. The list of Oceanids is a 'shortened version' of that in Hes. *Th.* 349 ff., with some additions (Leucippe, Phaeno, Iache, Rhodope; Melite is a Nereid in *Il.* 18. 42, Hes. *Th.* 247). Sixteen of the forty-one names in Hesiod are used. The catalogue may be borrowed directly from Hesiod (cf. West, *Theogony*, p. 260), but it may equally well be a traditional feature. Cf. the catalogue of Nereids, *Il.* 18. 39–49 ~ Hes. *Th.* 243–62. On the Oceanids in general cf. ad *Dem.* 5, West, o.c. 263 ff.

There is much rhyme, alliteration, and assonance in both lists. Cf. Lehrs, *Aristarchus*[2], 463. He suggests that the greater frequency of internal rhyme in Hesiod than in the *Hymn* is due to the difference of context: Hesiod is giving a catalogue, Persephone a narrative. Cf. also West, *Theogony*, 203, 236, Rzach, *RE* 8. 1199 f., Dornseiff, *Antike und alter Orient* (Leipzig, 1959), 42, and n. ad *Dem.* 109 f.

Pausanias (4. 30. 4) quotes *Dem.* 417–24, and says that Homer in the *Hymn* was the first to mention Tyche. He therefore places Homer before Hesiod. Both he and the papyrus omit 419. The papyrus does not quote 424, but it is only listing the Oceanids (and cf. ad loc.). The catalogue is inserted into the middle of a sentence (417, 424 ~ 5–7). The verb is thus postponed.

417. Cf. *Dem.* 7a.

ἱμερτόν: this occurs once in Homer (*Il.* 2. 751). Cf. *Herm.* 510, *Hy.* 10. 3, Hes. *Th.* 577 (Pandora's crown: the line may be interpolated, West ad loc. But cf. *Op.* 75).

418. Leucippe and Phaeno are not in Hesiod. Leucippe is like Hippo in Hes. *Th.* 351 (cf. West ad loc.). 'White horses' is still the name given to foam-flecked wave-crests. For the association of water and horses (especially white) cf. Schachermeyr, *Poseidon* (Index, s.v. Pferd). Note also *Il.* 20. 228–9.

Φαινώ: cf. perhaps Hes. fr. 291. 3, where Φαιώ as one of the Hyades occurs with Εὐδώρη (an Oceanid in Hes. *Th.* 360). The Hyades are here nymphs (and in later legend they were nurses of Dionysus: *RE* 8. 1260 f. Cf. ad *Dem.* 17 Νύσιον ἂμ πεδίον).

Ἠλέκτρη: cf. West ad *Th.* 349. Like Phaeno/Phaeo, the name is also used for a star in Hes. fr. 169. 1 (one of the Pleiades). In Claudian's version of the story, she becomes the nurse of Proserpine (*RP* 3. 169 ff.). Cf. Introduction, p. 73.

καὶ 'Ιάνθη: the digamma, attested for Ϝιανθεμίς (Alcm. *PMG* 1. 76), is observed in Hesiod, ignored here. Cf. West ad loc., and the similar neglect in *Dem.* 6 (cf. Appendix II, p. 335).

419. The omission of the line in both the papyrus and Pausanias is ascribed to 'homoeomeson' by Allen (*CR* 21 (1907), 100). But it suggests that variant (rhapsodic) versions existed. Cf. Introduction, pp. 68, 74 f.

Μελίτη: a Nereid in *Il.* 18. 42, Hes. *Th.* 247. The name was also given to the heroine of the Attic deme Melite (cf. Hes. fr. 225, Philoch. *FGH* 328. 27, Musaeus, fr. 2 B 9 D.–K., Harpocr., *Suda*, Phot. s.v.). She was loved by Heracles, who was initiated into the Lesser Mysteries in her deme and there honoured as ἀλεξίκακος (Schol. Ar. *Ran.* 501, *RE* 15. 540 ff.). The Thesmophoreion must have been in her deme, and near to the Herakleion (cf. Judeich, *Topographie*, 397 n. 1). This perhaps gives a point of connection with Eleusinian legend. There was also a spring of this name in Lycia (Anton. Lib. 35). Persephone herself was called Melitodes, and the priestesses of Demeter and Persephone Melissae (Schol. Theocr. 15. 94, Porph. *de antro* 18, Call. *Hy.* 2. 110 ff.), as were those of some other deities (cf. *RE* 15. 525 ff.).

'Ιάχη: not in Hesiod. But cf. *Th.* 351 (with Rhodeia and Callirhoe) Κλυμένη τε. The name might perhaps refer to the sound of the water. But it does not occur elsewhere. If the name Iacchus is derived from the cry of the Eleusinian procession, could 'Ιάχη here also be derived from this? Cf. Nilsson, *Gesch.* i³. 664: 'Aus dem Ruf ἰαχή ist der Gott

Iakchos entstanden.' The procession from Athens is assumed to be a later feature (cf. Introduction, pp. 8 f.), but some kind of procession probably existed from early times.

Ῥόδεια: M has 'Ῥόεια. For the variant 'Ῥόδια in Hesiod cf. West ad loc. Rhodeia and Rhodope (422) probably both derive their names from ῥόδον. Cf. 'Ῥόδη, 'Ῥόδυλλα, 'Ῥόδον, 'Ῥόδιον (RE IA. 954 s.v. 'Ῥόδη 3, Hehn, Kulturpflanzen⁸ (Berlin, 1911), 252).

Καλλιρόη: this was a common name of springs, but was applied especially to the spring by the Ilissos, near the temple ἐν Ἄγραις, where the Lesser Mysteries were held (cf. ad Dem. 270-2).

This line thus unexpectedly supplies three names which could have connections with the Mysteries. But in the middle of a catalogue of this kind, it is hard to believe that this is deliberate.

420. Μηλόβοσις: protectress of flocks and herds (cf. West, ad Th. 354).

Τύχη: cf. Paus. l.c. (ad Dem. 417-24). The word (which means originally 'hitting the mark') does not occur in Homer, the common noun first(?) in Hy. 11. 5, where it means 'fortune, success' (cf. Archil.(?) fr. 16 West; Alcm. PMG 64). As such she is made an Oceanid (cf. Plouto, Dem. 422, Doris, Polydore, Eudore, Th. 350, 354, 360). Cf. West ad Th. 360. Later representations of Tyche showed her with the child Ploutos (Paus. 9. 16. 2, IG 12. 3. 1098, Wolters, AM 15 (1890), 246 ff.; cf. ad Dem. 489).

Ὠκυρόη καλυκῶπις: 'swift-flowing', perhaps like her father Oceanus (cf. West ad Th. 360). On καλυκῶπις cf. ad Dem. 8, 427.

421. Χρυσηΐς: at Th. 359 the manuscripts have χρυσηΐς, Κρυσηΐς, Κρυσίη (Χρυσηΐς Hermann: cf. West ad loc.). In Homer, Chryseis is the daughter of the priest Chryses (Il. 1. 111 etc.). Here, the name may be included because of its association with χρυσός (cf. Πλουτώ etc.).

Ἰάνειρα: also a Nereid at Il. 18. 47, with Ianassa. These are shortened forms of names such as Calli-/Iphianeira/-anassa (feminines of ἀνήρ, ἄναξ): cf. Il. 18. 44, 46. Eustathius (Il. 1130. 47, Od. 1506. 51) derives Ianeira from ἰαίνω (cf. Jessen, RE 9. 690).

Ἀκάστη τ' Ἀδμήτη τε: cf. perhaps Acastus and his brother-in-law, Admetus. Admete is a suitable name for a nymph (cf. West ad Th. 349). Acaste may be associated with her, through reminiscence of a formula such as Ἄκαστός τ' Ἀδμητός τε. ἄκαστος is also the name of a tree, σφένδαμνος, Olympian maple: i.e. a tree-nymph?

422. Ῥοδόπη: not in Hesiod. Probably 'rosy-faced' (cf. Καλλιόπη, Παρθενόπη, Λειριόπη etc.), like 'Ῥόδεια (419).

Πλουτώ: cf. Τύχη (420), and the association of Ploutos with Demeter and Persephone (489).

καὶ ἱμερόεσσα Καλυψώ: cf. West ad Th. 359. The name perhaps has no special original significance, but may be derived from the veil which women wore (cf. Od. 5. 232, and Καλύπτρη as a woman's name: Lamer, RE 10. 1777).

423. Στύξ: cf. ad Dem. 259. In Hesiod she is named last, as being προφερεστάτη . . . ἁπασέων (cf. Dem. 110).

Οὐρανίη: also the name of a Muse (Hes. *Th.* 78).
Γαλαξαύρη: cf. West ad *Th.* 353.
ἐρατεινή: usually of places in Homer (also of a feast, ambrosia, etc.). But cf. *Il.* 3. 175, *Od.* 4. 13, Hes. *Th.* 136, 909.

424. This line has been suspected by various critics, on the grounds that Athena and Artemis do not belong to the original version, which mentions only the Oceanids (cf. *Dem.* 5). The Orphic papyrus does not quote the line, but it is only listing the Oceanids, and it mentions Athena and Artemis in the paraphrase (Orph. fr. 49. 40 f.: Ἀρτέμιδος τοξεί[α] Ἀθηνᾶς . . .). They appear in E. *Hel.* 1314 ff. (cf. Maas, *Epidaurische Hymnen*, 142 ff.):

> μετὰ δ᾽ ⟨ἦιξαν?⟩ ἀελλοπόδες
> ἁ μὲν τόξοις Ἄρτεμις, ἁ
> δ᾽ ἔγχει Γοργῶ⟨πις⟩ πάνοπλος
> (West suggests ἀΐξαν *metri gratia*).

The language recalls *Dem.* 424. Claudian (*RP* 2. 204 ff.) fills in the picture: the goddesses pursue Hades and attempt to fight, but are prevented by Zeus, who hurls a thunderbolt. This last feature is referred to in Orph. fr. 49. 38 f., and *PMG* 935. 9 ff., and probably also reflected in E. *Hel.* 1317. In the 'Orphic' version the thunderbolt serves to open the earth for Hades (cf. Maas, o.c. 146.). In Euripides and the *Epidaurian Hymn* Meter (= Demeter) is apparently aided in her search or pursuit of Hades by Athena and Artemis, and in the latter Zeus throws a thunderbolt and splits the rocks when she is already searching: this perhaps points to a version in which Demeter is present at the Rape, which is attested by some late representations (cf. ad *Dem.* 4). But the lyric versions confuse the narrative order (Maas, o.c. 147, A. M. Dale, *Euripides, Helena*, pp. 150 f., Kannicht, *Eur. Helena*, ii. 338. Cf. also Walton, *HTR* 45 (1952), 107 n. 7).[1]

Diodorus (5. 3. 4) also mentions Athena and Artemis as present. Cf. Paus. 8. 31. 2, Stat. *Ach.* 2. 150 ff. (= 1. 824 ff. ed. Garrod), Val. Fl. 5. 343 ff. They are portrayed on Roman sarcophagi of the Rape, sometimes with Aphrodite (cf. Claud. *RP* 1. 229 ff.), on others with Demeter (cf. Förster, *Raub und Rückkehr*, 131 ff.). One class of sarcophagi represents them as favourable to the Rape (Förster, 201 ff., 217 f.). This agrees with Orph. *Arg.* 1191 f., according to which Persephone was deceived by her companions. In Claudian (*RP* 1. 220 ff.) Venus is sent by Zeus to lure her out to the meadow, and a hint of a version in which the two other goddesses collaborate is perhaps given by Claud. *RP* 3. 198 f. (cf. Förster, 280 ff. But see Malten, *ARW* 12 (1909), 422 n. 4, *contra* Förster).

It is possible that the presence of Athena and Artemis was already a traditional feature before the *Homeric Hymn* (cf. Walton, l.c.). The version in which they pursue Hades but are stopped by Zeus' thunder-

---

[1] According to Kannicht (o.c. 342 with n. 31), Athena already appears on the mid-fifth-century B.C. vase-painting of the Rape, first published by Hartwig, *AM* 21 (1896), Pl. 12 (cf. ad *Dem.* 16).

bolt (which also, or alternatively, opens the way for Hades) is apparently 'Orphic' (but cf. Kannicht, o.c. ii. 342 ff.) and various 'Orphic' features may belong to early local tradition at Eleusis (cf. Introduction, pp. 79 ff.). The *Hymn*, in the opening narrative, is concerned to remove all divine or human witnesses to the Rape, except Hecate and Helios (22 ff.). Zeus is also far away (27 ff.). The Orphic version has human witnesses, Athena and Artemis, and the thunderbolt of Zeus. All these features may have been omitted in the epic narrative of the Rape, leaving however a trace at this point. The line is not in itself objectionable (see below), and as Persephone does not explicitly say that her companions were all Oceanids, it is not out of place in its context. The two goddesses are placed last, as being most important (cf. Styx in Hes. *Th.* 361, West ad loc.).

Παλλάς: first here without Ἀθήνη/-αίη. Cf. Pi. *O.* 26 etc.

ἐγρεμάχη: the epithet occurs first here. Cf. ad loc. and *Orph. Hy. Prol.* 38. A fragment of the *Phoronis* (P. Oxy. 2260, col. i. 3–7) has ἐγρεμάχη* of Athena. Cf. S. *OC* 1054 f. ἔνθ' οἶμαι τὸν ἐγρεμάχαν Θησέα... (at Eleusis: cf. 1049 ff.); also ἐγρεκύδοιμος of Athena in Hes. *Th.* 925, Lamprocles, *PMG* 735b; θεᾷ... ἐγερσιμάχᾳ *AP* 6. 122. 2.

καί: before a vowel καί is unshortened in the third thesis at *Il.* 13. 316 (omitted by some MSS. and papyri), *Od.* 19. 174 (s.v.l.), *Aph.* 13 (~ *Il.* 10. 322 τε καί, 4. 226, 10. 393), 113 (but cf. 116), *Hy.* 27. 22, 33. 19 (τε καί 25. 7, 29. 14), Hes. *Th.* 250, ? 148 (cf. West ad loc.), fr. 193. 20, and in later poetry Arat. 534, P. Oxy. 1794. 12 (Powell, *Coll. Alex.*, p. 79), *Orph. Hy. Prol.* 32, 10. 14, and fr. 32 f 6; in the fourth thesis *Il.* 24. 641; in the second Hes. fr. 266 (a). 10 (cf. Merkelbach and West, *RhM* 108 (1965) 312 n. 38). Cf. also Christian epigrams (in third thesis): *AP* 1. 8. 5, 10. 52, 38. 1, 40. 1, 53. 1, 91. 1. In some of these cases the text may be altered (e.g. by addition of τε), but not in all. Examples such as *Dem.* 275, *Ap.* 198, *Aph.* 82 (τε καί v.l.) are due to the original digamma, but after its effect was no longer felt such cases may have influenced poets to use the device more freely. Cf. also Allen, *JHS* 18 (1898), 23 f.
Here one could read ἠδ', which is sometimes replaced by καί in manuscripts.

425. παίζομεν... δρέπομεν: presumably imperfects, as the historic present is not used in epic. Cf. *Dem.* 429.

δρέπομεν: the active occurs at Hes. *Th.* 31 (s.v.l.). Cf. Pi. *O.* 1. 13 etc.

ἐρόεντα: cf. ad *Dem.* 109.

426–8. The catalogue of flowers differs from that of *Dem.* 6 ff. only in the replacement of ἴα by λείρια. Cf. ad *Dem.* 427.

426. κρόκον τ' ἀγανόν: this correction of Voss is most probable, although ἀγανός is not elsewhere used of flowers. Cf. τέρην (*Dem.* 209, τέρεν' ἄνθεα ποίης *Od.* 9. 449).

427. ῥοδέας κάλυκας: ῥόδεος occurs first here (cf. ῥόδα *Dem.* 6; Hom. ῥοδόεις, etc.). ῥοδέοισιν ἐν ἄνθεσι Ibyc. *PMG* 288. 4 (3 ἀγανοβλέφαρος ~ *Dem.* 426). κάλυκες is used in *Il.* 18. 401, *Aph.* 87 for a

woman's ornaments, apparently ear-rings in the shape of flower-
buds. Cf. *Cypr.* fr. 4. 5, and ad *Dem.* 8.

λείρια: these occur first here. Cf. in Homer ὄπα λειριόεccαν (*Il.*
3. 152 ~ Hes. *Th.* 41), χρόα λειριόεντα (*Il.* 13. 830), Ποδαλείριοc (*Il.* 2.
732, 11. 832), and later λειρίων ὀμμάτων (Bacch. 17. 95), ὄπα λείριον
(A.R. 4. 903 ~ Orph. *Arg.* 253); cf. Q.S. 2. 418, *GVI* 2027. 10.
λείρια are mentioned by Cratinus in his flower-catalogue (fr. 98. 2).
Examples of the word, outside botanists and lexica, are confined to
poetry (A.R. 1. 879, Nic. *Ther.* 543, fr. 74. 27, 70; *AP* 7. 219. 2; cf.
Pi. *N.* 7. 79, Nic. *Alex.* 407), and there was no certainty as to its
meaning. It is identified by some with κρίνον, the 'lilium candidum'
(Philinus ap. Ath. 681 b; Nic. fr. 74. 27, where its use by poets is
specifically mentioned; Diosc. 3. 106, Erotian. 94. 2), by others with
νάρκιccoc (Theophr. *HP* 6. 6. 9, Diosc. 4. 158). Pollux (6. 107) says
that Homer called all flowers λείρια. This is probably derived from
explanations of *Il.* 3. 152 etc. (cf. Eust. ad loc.). It can hardly be
a reference to *Dem.* 427. Nic. *Ther.* l.c. apparently uses λείρια generally
(cf. also Hsch. s.v. and Schneider, ad Nic. fr. 74. 70). The word was
probably not in everyday use in the later classical period (cf. Olck,
RE 7. 795 f.).

Murr (*Die Pflanzenwelt in der griech. Mythologie*, 249 ff.), considers
that λείρια here replace the νάρκιccoc of *Dem.* 8, and that 428 is interpolated (θαῦμα ἰδέcθαι ~ *Dem.* 10). But the miraculous narcissus is
too important not to be named explicitly.

On the etymology see Frisk s.v., van Leeuwen, *Mnem.* 21 (1903),
114 ff., Leumann, *Hom. Wörter*, 27 f., Bechtel, *Lexilogus*, s.v. λειριόειc.

428. ὃν ἔφυc᾽: cf. *Dem.* 8 ὃν φύcε, West ad *Th.* 381.

ὥc περ κρόκον: this is unexpected, especially after *Dem.* 426. The
Narcissus tazetta (cf. ad *Dem.* 8) was sometimes compared to the κρόκοc
(Ov. *M.* 3. 509 'croceum florem'; Diosc. 4. 161 (158): it has a κοῖλον
κροκοειδέc). If the reading is genuine it may refer *either* to the colour,
on the symbolism of which see notes ad *Dem.* 6, 8, 19 (cf. Ov. l.c.;
A.R. 3. 855 χροιῇ Κωρυκίῳ ἴκελον κρόκῳ, of Medea's magic flower;
κροκόειc of colour Pi. *P.* 4. 232, Theocr. 1. 31 etc.; κροκηΐῳ ἄνθει
ὁμοῖαι *Dem.* 178), *or* to the scent (cf. *Dem.* 13 f.; Hes. fr. 140: Zeus
when he carried off Europa κρόκον ἔπνει; Theophr. *HP* 6. 6. 5).[1]
Crocus and narcissus as sacred to Demeter and Persephone are mentioned together in S. *OC* 681 ff. For the repetition after *Dem.* 426 cf.
Introduction, p. 60.

429-30. Cf. *Dem.* 15-17.

αὐτάρ: Ilgen and Gemoll object to the use of this here. But the con-
tinuative sense is common (Denniston, *GP* p. 55 (2)). For αὐτὰρ ἐγώ
cf. *Dem.* 411 (cf. ad loc.), Ruijgh, *L'Élément achéen dans la langue épique*
(Assen, 1957), 38 f., 50.

περὶ χάρματι: this use of περί is not found in Homer. Cf. περί

---

[1] In Hippon. fr. 41 B. = 104. 21-2 Masson, cited by Allen and Halliday, the
correct reading is Κροῖcoc.

δείματι (Pi. *P.* 5. 58), περὶ τιμᾷ (Pi. *P.* 2. 59), περὶ τάρβει, φόβῳ (A. *Pers.* 696, *Cho.* 35), ὀδύνῃ πέρι (A.R. 3. 866).

430. τῇ δ' ἔκθορ': cf. ad *Dem.* 17.

ἄναξ κρατερὸς πολυδέγμων: cf. ad *Dem.* 17. Hoekstra, *Sub-epic Stage*, 54 f., comments on the awkward juxtaposition of ἄναξ κρατερός, never found in Homer, and on the elision before ἄναξ in this position, which is also un-Homeric. He also considers the use of χώρησεν as runover word with *nu* movable making position a sign of modernizing tendencies, and concludes that '*Dem.* 17 and 404 show a composition which is typical of post-Homeric development.' See also Appendix II, c.

431-2. Cf. *Dem.* 19-20. Note the variation:

ἁρπάξας . . . ἦγε ~ βῆ δὲ φέρων ὑπὸ γαῖαν
ἀέκουσαν . . . ὀλοφυρομένην ~ πόλλ' ἀεκαζομένην (~ *Dem.* 30)
ἐπὶ χρυσέοισιν ὄχοισιν ~ ἐν ἅρμασι χρυσείοισι*
ἰάχησε δ' ἄρ' ὄρθια φωνῇ ~ ἐβόησα δ' ἄρ' ὄρθια φωνῇ*.

The two versions are interchangeable.

ἐν ἅρμασι χρυσείοισι: the short scansion of a vowel *in thesi* at the end of a word before mute and liquid is regular in epic (cf. West, *Theogony*, 97). For examples with χρ- cf. *Il.* 23. 186, 24. 795 (γε χρυσείην), *Od.* 8. 353, *Ap.* 293, *Herm.* 332, *Hy.* 8. 1, *Orph. Hy.* 55. 18; within a word *Ap.* 439 (Agar, *CR* 15 (1901), 145 ff.).

432. πόλλ' ἀεκαζομένην: for the rhythm cf. also *Dem.* 20a.

433. Cf. *Dem.* 406. The closing formula of the speech recalls the opening.

434-40. Demeter and Persephone spend the day in happy reunion. They are joined by Hecate, who becomes the attendant of Persephone.

438-40 are aetiological (cf. ad loc.); possibly 434 ff. may be also. The day following the main events of the Mysteries in the Telesterion was perhaps spent in festivities (cf. Plut. *Mor.* 635 a ἐν 'Ελευσῖνι μετὰ τὰ μυστήρια τῆς πανηγύρεως ἀκμαζούσης εἰστιώμεθα . . .; Mylonas, *Eleusis*, 279; Foucart, *Les Mystères*, 358). For thanksgiving at the end of the ritual search for Core cf. Lact. *Div. Inst. Epit.* 18 (23). 7 (ad *Dem.* 40 ff.). The emphasis on the restoration of the goddesses' spirits (434-6: θυμός repeated) might perhaps recall the mystic formulae εὐθυμεῖν, etc. (cf. Merkelbach, *Roman und Mysterium*, Index s.v. εὐθυμέω etc.).

434. πρόπαν ἦμαρ: cf. ad *Dem.* 434-40, and similarly 292 παννύχιαι.

434-6. The triple repetition of θυμός is unattractive, but need not be suspected. Cf. πόλλ' . . . πολλά . . . πολλά (432, 435, 439), ἀλλήλων . . . ἀλλήλων (435, 437), ἀμφαγαπαζόμεναι . . . ἀμφαγάπησε (436, 439) (and see Introduction, p. 60).

On the expression ὁμόφρονα θυμὸν ἔχουσαι cf. B. Snell, *Gnomon* 7 (1931), 84 f.

436. Note the alliteration of this line. Cf. ad *Dem.* 289 f.

ἀχέων δ' ἀπεπαύετο θυμός: cf. ad *Dem.* 392.

437. γηθοςύναϲ: the plural does not occur elsewhere before A.R. 2. 878. But cf. similar examples in Homer: ἀφροςύναι, εὐφροςύναι (θυμὸϲ | αἰὲν ἐυφροςύνῃϲιν ἰαίνεται Od. 6. 155–6), etc.

ἔδιδόν τε: cf. ad Dem. 327 (δίδον). Ruhnken's emendation is supported by Od. 20. 8, Herm. 312. The verse is a weak one after 434–6, and might have been added to supply a lacuna (cf. Introduction, p. 66).

438–40. Hecate's role in the cult of Eleusis is here explicitly accounted for. The language is that of the cult: cf. ad Dem. 439, 440.

439. ἀμφαγάπηϲε: this form of the verb (ἀμφαγαπᾶν) also occurs in Hes. Op. 58 (cf. Hom. ἀμφαγαπάζω: Dem. 290, 436).

κόρην Δημήτεροϲ ἁγνῆϲ: the Attic form κόρη is here used, perhaps deliberately. Elsewhere in the *Hymn* κούρη, the epic–Ionic form, is used (*Dem.* 8, etc.). Persephone is almost always referred to in cult inscriptions as Κόρη or Δήμητροϲ Κόρη (Doric Κόρα, Κώρα, Aeolic Κόρα, Arc. Κόρϝα): cf. Farnell, *Cults*, iii. 118, Bräuninger, *RE* 19. 954. In literature, cf. Lasus *PMG* 702 Δάματρα μέλπω Κόραν τε Κλυμένοι' ἄλοχον, and later E. *Alc.* 369, Carcin. fr. 5, Ar. *Ran.* 337, Antiph. 52. 9, Eub. 75. 10, Isocr. 10. 22, Aristid. 1. 416, Paus. 2. 22. 3, 4. 33. 4. On Δημήτηρ ἁγνή see notes to Dem. 203. The form Κόρη is also found in [Archilochus] fr. 322 West: Δήμητροϲ ἁγνῆϲ καὶ Κόρηϲ . . . The Attic form is very surprising here and the fragment was doubtfully attributed already in antiquity (cf. Hephaest. ad loc.). Κόρη (v.l. Κούρη) in Hdt. 8. 65. 4 occurs in the story of the Athenian Dicaeus. It is also found in some later Ionic inscriptions, e.g. from Paros, *IG* 12. 5. 134. 10, 227. 2 f. In the *Hymn*, it has been taken as evidence of an Attic composer (cf. Wackernagel, *Spr. Unters.* 179). But an Ionic poet might possibly have used it as the title of Persephone in Attica. Cf. Introduction, p. 55, and see also Hoekstra, *Sub-epic Stage*, 54, on the use of the whole phrase here.

Δημήτεροϲ: this form occurs in epic at *Il.* 13. 322, 21. 76, Hes. *Op.* 32, 393, 466, 597, 805, *Sc.* 290. Elsewhere Δήμητροϲ is used, *Il.* 2. 696, 14. 326, *Dem.* 4, 453, Hes. *Th.* 912, and later.

440. ἐκ τοῦ: in Hes. *Th.* 556 this is also used aetiologically.

πρόπολοϲ καὶ ὀπάων: this is quoted by Philodemus. πρόπολοϲ does not occur in Homer (cf. ἀμφίπολοϲ). Cf. perhaps Hes. fr. 23(a). 26 Ἄρτεμιν εἰνοδί[ην πρόπολον κλυ]τοῦ ἰ[ο]χ[ε]αίρ[ηϲ (of Iphimede, ex coni. Lloyd-Jones); E. *Hel.* 570 νυκτίφαντον πρόπολον Ἐνοδίαϲ (i.e. Hecate); Wycherley, *Athenian Agora*, III (*Testimonia*), p. 82, No. 226

> [Ἄ]ρρήτο τελετῆϲ πρόπολοϲ ϲῆϲ, πότνια Δηοῖ,
> καὶ θυγατρὸϲ προθύρο κόϲμον ἄγαλμα τόδε
> ἔϲτηϲεν ϲτεφανὼ Λυϲιϲτράτη . . .

(probably from the Eleusinion, c. 455 B.C.); S. *OC* 1053 προϲπόλων Εὐμολπιδᾶν (cf. ad Dem. 478–9, 39, etc.); see also Ar. *Nub.* 436 (N.B.: θαρρῶν is a 'verbum mysticum'). In S. fr. 535. 3 Pearson conjectured ⟨προπολοῦϲα⟩ (of Hecate, carrying her torch through the sky: cf. ad loc.). πρόπολοι is a variant at Hes. *Op.* 253, and the word occurs later in Xenoph. 1. 18, Pi. *O.* 13. 54, etc.

ὀπάων is only used of men in Homer ('squire'), and so also later, except *IG* 14. 1389. i. 52 (of an attendant of Faustina/Demeter): ἀμφίπολον γεράων ἔμεναι καὶ ὀπάονα νύμφην (the poem goes on to compare Iphigeneia as πρόπολος of Artemis. Cf. Hes. fr. 23 (a). 26, above).[1]

It is most natural to take οἱ as referring to Persephone. Philodemus apparently referred it to Demeter, and this is also done by Kern, *RE* 16. 1213. 29.

Strictly, πρόπολος means that Hecate goes before Persephone, and ὀπάων perhaps that she follows her (cf. Chantraine, *GH* i. 185, Frisk s.v.). Thus, she is represented leading Persephone up from Hades on the red-figure bell krater of the Persephone painter in New York (ARV² 1012. 1). Hermes and Demeter are also present. Hecate holds two torches, and turns her head back towards Persephone, who is rising from the earth.[2] She is probably also depicted leading Hades and Persephone down to the underworld on several south-Italian vases, and perhaps on the Niinnion tablet as leading the mystae to the Sanctuary (cf. ad *Dem.* 24 ff.). She has the title Hegemone (*Orph. Hy.* 1. 8), like Artemis, with whom she was apparently identified at Eleusis, where the position of her temple at the entrance to the Sanctuary (Artemis Propylaea) is appropriate to the deity who is here an attendant of the Great Goddesses and intermediary between them and mankind.

According to one tradition, she was actually sent down to Hades to look for Persephone (? Call. fr. 466 ap. Schol. Theocr. 2. 12). She is a daughter of Demeter in Orph. fr. 41, and Call. l.c., and sometimes identified with Persephone (perhaps in E. *Ion* 1048, S. *Ant.* 1199 f., and explicitly later, Schol. Theocr. l.c. and Roscher, 1. 1898).

ἄνασσα: this is used as a title of Hecate in A.R. 3. 862 (Βριμὼ . . . ἐνέροισιν ἄνασσαν), 4. 147, *Orph. Hy.* 1. 7.

441–69. Zeus sends Rhea to bring Demeter and Persephone back to heaven, promising honours to Demeter and granting that Persephone should remain in the underworld for a third of the year, and in heaven for the rest. Rhea comes to the Rarian plain, and gives her message.

On Rhea's journey see notes to *Dem.* 314–23.

It would be unwise to draw any conclusions from Rhea's employment here as to her role at Eleusis, or partial identity with Demeter. Cf. Kerényi (*Eleusis*, 132 ff.), who refers to later identifications of Demeter and the Μήτηρ θεῶν attested from the fifth century B.C. onwards.[3] But in the Homeric poem her use as an agent of reconciliation

---

[1] In A. *Supp.* 954 there is no justification for reading the feminine.

[2] For another, similar representation see Kourouniotes, *Arch. Delt.* 1933–5, 1 ff., Fig. 1. Cf. also ARV² 205. 119 (?), *Arch. Anz.* 1971, 178 ff.

[3] Cf. Maas, *Epidaurische Hymnen*, 138, Kannicht, *Euripides, Helena*, ii. 329 ff., Zuntz, *Persephone*, 352 f. Cf. also Orph. fr. 145, 153. Already on a black-figure vase (Beazley, *ABV* p. 705/29 quater) Demeter and Core are shown accompanied by a lion. Cf. Metzger, *Recherches*, 22 (No. 43), 25, and Pl. VIII.

between Zeus and Demeter is due simply to the fact that she is the mother of both.[1]

In Philicus' *Hymn*, 22 ff. (Körte), the speech by Rhea's sister (? Tethys: cf. Latte, *Kl. Schr.* 539 ff.) to Demeter is probably inspired by this episode in the *Homeric Hymn* (Latte, o.c. 553).

441. ταῖς δὲ μετάγγελον ἧκε: with M's reading, μετ᾽ ... ἧκε may be taken as a tmesis. But μεθίημι is not used in the sense 'send' (only 'let go, dismiss', etc.).

Hermann conjectured τῆς δὲ μέτ᾽,[2] but μετά is not found after its noun with the dative in Homer unless an adjective follows (*Il.* 12. 315, 321, *Od.* 12. 370), and only rarely with verbs of motion (βάλλεσθαι *Il.* 9. 434, τιθέναι 11. 413, etc., cτῆν 11. 744, εἴcαν ἄγοντεc 23. 698; cf. v.l. 24. 82). τὰc δὲ μέτ᾽ (Voss, *dubitanter*) would be better, but, as he observes, is ambiguous, and τὸν δὲ μέτ᾽ (etc.) always means 'after him' in Homer. The dative is normal after ἄγγελος ἦλθε, ἄγγελον ἧκε (cf. *Il.* 2. 786, 18. 182, etc.), but cf. *Il.* 13. 252, *Aph.* 137 for μετά with accusative.

μετάγγελοc occurs doubtfully at *Il.* 15. 144 (of Iris), ἥ τε θεοῖcι μετάγγελοc ἀθανάτοιcι (codd. aliqui: μετ᾽ cet.). It is more certain at *Il.* 23. 199 (of Iris) μετάγγελοc ἦλθ᾽ ἀνέμοιcιν (μετ᾽ v.l.), where μετ᾽ ... ἦλθε is unlikely. It probably arose from cases where μετά was originally intended as a preposition, but was thought of as a single word in *Il.* 23. 199 (cf. Leumann, *Hom. Wörter*, 69, and for other similar cases 92 ff.). Thus μετάγγελον is perhaps the simplest correction, although not altogether satisfactory.

442. Δημήτερα κυανόπεπλον: M has ἦν μητέρα. The object of ἀξέμεναι may be supplied from ταῖc (441), but this is more awkward in the case of the subject of ἕλοιτο (444). κυανόπεπλοc is a standard epithet of Demeter in the *Hymn*, but it is also used of Leto (cf. ad *Dem.* 319), and the poet might have been influenced by *Dem.* 360 in his choice of epithet. He uses ἠύκομοc of both Demeter (*Dem.* 1, 297, 315) and Rhea (60, 75, 442; it is also used of Leto, *Il.* 1. 36, etc.), and λιπαροκρήδεμνοc of both Hecate (*Dem.* 25, 438) and Rhea (459).

M's text is therefore defensible (cf. Allen and Halliday), but Δημήτερα greatly improves the construction, and is probably right. For the corruption cf. the title of *Hy.* 13, Hdt. 4. 53. 6, and perhaps Xanthus, *FGH* 765. 28 ('Ορείαc Δήμητρος cod.: 'Ορείαc Μητρός Wendel: 'Ρέαc Μητρός Hecker).

443-4. ὑπέδεκτο ... δωσέμεν: for ὑποδέχομαι meaning 'promise' in Homer cf. *Il.* 7. 93, *Od.* 2. 387. It is first used here with the infinitive. Cf. Hdt. 3. 69, etc.

We are not told what τιμαί Demeter chose. Cf. ad *Dem.* 327 f.

445-7. Cf. *Dem.* 398-400 (and notes to 399 ff.). In *Il.* 8. 246 νεῦcε δέ οἱ is followed by an accusative and infinitive. Here, the construction is highly elliptical: an infinitive must be understood with κούρην, and

---

[1] E. Simon (*Ant. Kunst* 9 (1966), 72 ff.) suggests that the episode is portrayed on the Kertsch pelike. This seems to me unlikely.

[2] Strictly τῆc δὲ μετ᾽, as the accent is not retracted when there is elision (LSJ s.v. D).

a verb of motion is required with ὑπὸ ζόφον (but cf. ad loc.). Cf. *Dem.*
398 f. ἰοῦσ' ὑπ[ὸ . . .] οἰκήσεις.
Hermann and Bücheler assume a lacuna after 446 (cf. ad loc.).
Emendation is hardly possible. The sense is clear and the com-
pression is assisted by the fact that the times of Persephone's return
have already been described.

446. ὑπὸ ζόφον ἠερόεντα: in 464 M has]ερόεντα$\overset{\ddot{\iota}}{\big)}$. But the accusative is probably right, as the *lectio difficilior*. Cf. ad *Dem.* 398, 445–7.
448. ὣς ἔφατ': cf. ad *Dem.* 314–23.
ἀπίθησε . . . ἀγγελιάων: ἀπιθεῖν takes the dative in Homer and
later (see note to *Dem.* 358). But πείθεσθαι is used with the genitive
(vulg. lect. *Il.* 10. 57, Hdt. 1. 126, etc.). Cf. ἄπιστος φίλων A. *Th.* 876.
οὐδ' ἀπίθησε is the equivalent of ἐπέκλυεν, which has the genitive (cf.
Od. 5. 150, *Aph.* 215). For ἀπειθεῖν with genitive in later Greek cf. *GDI*
3705. 111 (Cos, third century B.C., Doric dialect), LXX Josh. 5 : 6,
Ecclesiasticus 2 : 15, 16 : 28. The line has been modelled on the type of
Il. 2. 166 etc.: cf. Hoekstra, *Sub-epic Stage*, 59 n. 27. ἀγγελιάων is
normally used of several dispatches (*Od.* 1. 414, etc.), but of a single
one at *Od.* 5. 150, *Aph.* 215 (cf. West ad Hes. *Th.* 781).
450. Ῥάριον: sc. πεδίον. For the psilosis cf. Pfeiffer ad Call. fr. 21.
10. Ῥαριάς is a cult-title of Demeter: Call. fr. 21. 10, *Suda* s.v., Steph.
Byz. s.v. Ῥάριον πεδίον, Choerob. (*Gramm. Graeci* iv. 2, ed. Hilgard)
43. 28, Kaibel, *Epigr. Gr.* 931. 6. Cf. perhaps Hermes. fr. 7. 19 f.
(Powell) Ῥάριον . . . Δήμητρα (or Ῥάριον ὀργειῶνα?).
The original meaning is suggested by *Suda* s.v. Ῥάρος· ἡ γαστήρ.
It may be from the cult-name that the place name Ῥάριον πεδίον
or Ῥαρία γῆ, and (by a 'back formation') the eponymous hero, Ῥάρ
or Ῥᾶρος derive (Pfister, *RE* IA. 252. 13 ff.). The first is mentioned
by Pausanias (1. 38. 6) : τὸ δὲ πεδίον τὸ Ῥάριον σπαρῆναι πρῶτον λέγουσι
καὶ πρῶτον αὐξῆσαι καρπούς, καὶ διὰ τοῦτο οὐλαῖς ἐξ αὐτοῦ χρῆσθαί
σφισι, καὶ ποιεῖσθαι πέμματα ἐς τὰς θυσίας καθέστηκεν. ἐνταῦθα ἅλως
καλουμένη Τριπτολέμου καὶ βωμὸς δείκνυται. Cf. *Marm. Par.* 13 ἀφ'
οὗ Τριπτό[λεμος ἐθέρισε τὸν καρπόν, ὃν] ἔσπειρεν ἐν τῇ Ῥαρίᾳ καλουμένῃ
Ἐλευσῖνι . . . ; E. *Supp.* 28 ff. :

> τυγχάνω δ' ὑπὲρ χθονὸς
> ἀρότου προθύους', ἐκ δόμων ἐλθοῦσ' ἐμῶν
> πρὸς τόνδε σηκόν, ἔνθα πρῶτα φαίνεται
> φρίξας ὑπὲρ γῆς τῆσδε κάρπιμος στάχυς.

According to Plut. *Coni. praec.* 42 (144 a) one of the three Attic
sacred ploughings took place here. This was the festival called Προ-
ηρόσια, on fifth or sixth Pyanopsion, before the Pyanopsia, and shortly
before the Thesmophoria on tenth–thirteenth Pyanopsion. (On the
date see Dow and Healey, *Harv. Theol. Studies* 21 (1965), 15 f., Sokolowski, *Lois sacrées des cités grecques* (Paris, 1969), 7.)
At the Eleusinian Games, the prizes were of grain from the Rarian
Plain (*SIG*² 587. 259 ff., Schol. Pi. *O.* 9. 150, Aristid. *Eleusin.* vol. i,

p. 417 Dind.), and from this grain were made the cakes for sacrifice (Paus. l.c.).

The *Hymn* probably reflects these ritual uses in its description of the various stages of growth of the corn (*Dem.* 453–6). There may be a reflection here of the version in which Demeter gives men the gift of corn in gratitude for the return of her daughter (cf. ad *Dem.* 305 ff., 471 ff.). The poet, however, conceals this (cf. 451 f.).

Cf. also Hipp. *Ref. haer.* 5. 7. 4 'Ραρίας οἰκήτορα Δυσαύλην (Wilamowitz, *Hermes* 37 (1902), 331). Rarus is father of Triptolemus and brother of Cercyon in Choerilus fr. 1 N.² (cf. Hsch. s.v.), or father of Celeus, grandfather of Triptolemus and host of Demeter (*Suda* s.v.). Cf. Photius s.v. 'Ράρ.

For sacred fields, and the games held on them in various parts of the world cf. Frazer, *GB*³ v. 1. 70 ff., 92 ff., 107 ff., 2. 14 f., Foucart, *Les Mystères*, 73. The location of the Rarian Plain is not known, but it must have lain very close to the Sanctuary (cf. Leake, *Topography of Athens*, ii. 159).

φερέσβιον: this does not occur in Homer (cf. φυσίζοος αἶα, ζείδωρος/ν ἄρουρα(ν), πίειραν ἄρουραν, ἐρίβωλον ἄρουραν). Cf. Hes. *Th.* 693, *Ap.* 341 γαῖα φερέσβιος, *Hy.* 30. 9 ἄρουρα φερέσβιος. It is quoted by Apollodorus (ap. Schol. Genav. ad *Il.* 21. 319) as παρ᾽ 'Ομήρῳ (cf. Introduction, p. 68). It also occurs in a list of poetic compound epithets in P. Hibeh 172, line 123, in the form φερέσβιον, which only occurs in this *Hymn*. Turner (ad loc.) suggests *Dem.* 450 as a source, but this list itself shows how much epic has been lost (cf. L. E. Rossi, *Gött. gel. Anz.* 223 (1971), 169 f.). It is modified from φερέβιος (metrically impossible), by analogy with ὀρέσβιος, etc. (Solmsen, *Unters.* 20 ff.). Cf. A. fr. 300. 7 φερεσβίου Δήμητρος στάχυν, Antiph. fr. 1. 2 f. φερέσβιος Δηώ (cf. ad *Dem.* 269).

οὖθαρ ἀρούρης: this occurs only at *Il.* 9. 141 = 283, Cratin. fr. 220. Cf. Ar. fr. 110. 2 οὖθαρ ἀγαθῆς χθονός.

450–1. The second line qualifies the first to suit the particular context. For this device cf. e.g. *Il.* 2. 698–9 τῶν αὖ Πρωτεσίλαος ἀρήιος ἡγεμόνευε | ζωὸς ἐών· τότε δ᾽ ἤδη ἔχεν κάτα γαῖα μέλαινα, and similarly *Il.* 2. 768–70.

451. ἔκηλον: 'idle'. In Homer the word is used only of persons, and so later until the Alexandrians. Cf. A.R. 3. 969 (of trees), and εὔκηλος (A.R. 2. 935, Mooney ad loc., Theocr. 2. 166, etc.).

452. εἱστήκει: ἑστήκει is the normal form in epic and Attic. εἱστήκει is found as a variant in Homeric manuscripts, but also without variant at Hes. *Sc.* 264, 269. The forms with augment later occur in E. *HF* 925, Ar. *Av.* 513, Th. 1. 89, etc. εἱστήκει may be the original reading here.

πανάφυλλον: this occurs only here. Cf. ἀφύλλοισιν (*Il.* 2. 425), πανάποτμος (*Il.* 24. 255, etc.), etc. On παν- compounds cf. Leumann, *Hom. Wörter*, 101 ff.

ἔκευθε: the subject is οὖθαρ ἀρούρης. Cf. *Il.* 23. 83a, *Od.* 3. 16, Hes. *Th.* 505 (τὸ πρὶν δὲ πελώρη Γαῖα κεκεύθει ∼ *Dem.* 451), West ad loc.

The rhythm is unusual: ἔκευθε δ' ἄρα is a breach of Hermann's bridge (cf. ad *Dem.* 17), but mitigated by the close connection of the words. The monosyllabic fifth-foot thesis is also rare (cf. ad *Dem.* 204). Cf. H. N. Porter, *TCS* 12 (1951), 48.

453. Δήμητρος καλλισφύρου: a doublet of Δήμητρος χρυσαόρου (*Dem.* 4, cf. ad loc.), Δήμητρος πολυφόρβης (Hes. *Th.* 912). The latter epithet would perhaps have been out of place here.

454-6. The growth of the corn is described pictorially, and spring and harvest-time are portrayed successively. In the first part the standing corn is described. The second is divided into two pictures, of the furrows laden with ears of (reaped) corn, and of others that have been bound into sheaves.

455b-6 are similar to *Il.* 18. 550 ff. (563 ∼ *Dem.* 452), and Hes. *Sc.* 288 ff., where reaping and binding are described. Cf. *Il.* 18. 552-3:

> δράγματα δ' ἄλλα μετ' ὄγμον ἐπήτριμα πῖπτον ἔραζε,
> ἄλλα δ' ἀμαλλοδετῆρες ἐν ἐλλεδανοῖσι δέοντο.

Sc. 288–91 :
>   οἵ γε μὲν ἥμων ...
> αἰχμῆς ὀξείῃσι κορωνιόωντα πέτηλα,
> βριθόμενα σταχύων, ὡσεὶ Δημήτερος ἀκτήν,
> οἱ δ' ἄρ' ἐν ἐλλεδανοῖσι δέον ...

In these two passages, the processes are portrayed, in the *Hymn* their results. Thus βριθόμενα σταχύων in *Sc.* 290 refers to the standing corn laden with ears of grain (cf. *Il.* 18. 561 σταφυλῇσι ... βρίθουσαν ἀλωήν).

454. ταναοῖσι: the word occurs once in Homer (αἰγανέης ... ταναοῖο *Il.* 16. 589). Cf. τανύφυλλος (*Od.* 13. 102, etc.).

κομήσειν: the verb is first used metaphorically here, but cf. *Od.* 23. 195. κομᾶν of plants, trees, etc. is common in Hellenistic and later literature: Theocr. 1. 133, 4. 57 (Gow ad loc.), 7. 9, A.R. 3. 928, etc. For its use of the ground, with dative of the plant, cf. Call. *Hy.* 3. 41 ὄρος κεκομημένον ὕλῃ, [Arist.] *Mu.* 397ᵃ24 ἡ γῆ φυτοῖς κομῶσα; also Plut. *Eumen.* 6, Ael. fr. 75, Procop. Gaz. *Ep.* 23.

As the corn is compared to hair, so Demeter's golden locks represent the corn: cf. Orph. *Lith.* 240 Δημήτηρ σταχυοπλόκαμος, and note to *Dem.* 302 (ξανθὴ Δημήτηρ). Cf. also Ov. *Am.* 3. 10. 11 :

> prima Ceres docuit turgescere semen in agris,
> falce coloratas subsecuitque comas.

455. ἦρος: the contracted form is found in lyric (Alcm. *PMG* 20. 3, Sapph. 136, Alc. 115(a). 10, 367, Stes. *PMG* 211, 212. 3, Ibycus, 286. 1), elegiac (Solon 1. 19 D.³), perhaps Ionic (cf. Hdt. 1. 77, but ἔαρος 5. 31, 7. 162, al.), and Attic. Cf. ἤαρος, ἠαρινοῖσι (*Dem.* 174, 401, notes ad locc.). Note also Hes. *Op.* 462 ἔαρι, 492 ἔαρ, hardly different from the contracted forms.

When Persephone returns it is spring again (cf. ad *Dem.* 399 ff.).

πέδῳ: πέδον as a separate noun first occurs here. Cf. πέδον δέ (*Il.* 13. 796, *Od.* 11. 598, *Dem.* 253), πεδόθεν *Od.* 13. 295 and Hes. *Th.* 680).

πέδον is frequent in later poetry (Pi. *O*. 10. 46, etc.). πέδῳ later means 'to earth, on to the ground' (A. *Ch*. 48, etc., always of motion, πίπτειν, etc.: unless πέδοι should be read, cf. LSJ s.v. πέδον 4). Cf. in *Il*. 18. 552 πῖπτον ἔραζε. But πέδῳ must mean here 'on the ground'.

456. βρισέμεν ἀσταχύων: the genitive is also used at Hes. *Sc*. 290, *Od*. 9. 219, 15. 334, otherwise the dative in early epic (*Dem*. 473, etc.). For the variation cf. ad *Dem*. 358.

ἐλλεδανοῖσι: this occurs only here and *Il*. 18. 553, Hes. *Sc*. 291. Cf. Hsch., *Suda* s.v. ἐλεδανοί, ἐλεδανός. It is usually connected with Aeolic *ἐλλέω (< *ϝελνέω, Homeric εἰλέω = 'wind, bind'; cf. Solmsen, *Unters*. 244, Schwyzer, *Gr. Gr*. i. 530). But there is no trace of a digamma, which might be expected in this rare word (cf. Chantraine, *GH* i. 131).

δεδέσθαι: the present δίδεσθαι (Voss; cf. *Il*. 11. 105, *Od*. 12. 54) is in some ways attractive. It is closer to *Il*. 18. 553 and Hes. *Sc*. 291, and also more vivid: 'while others were being bound'. But after κομήσειν ... βρισέμεν, a perfect is slightly easier. μέλλειν with perfect infinitive does not occur in early epic, but here τὰ δ' ... δεδέσθαι is similar to a subordinate clause. (μέλλειν with present followed by future infinitive occurs at *Od*. 9. 475–7: but cf. Chantraine, *GH* i. 309, Szemerényi, *AJP* 72 (1951), 351.)

457. This picks up the narrative after the pictorial digression (450–6).

458. The rhythm is unusual, with caesura in the second and fourth foot and a break after the second. This occurs only about twenty-five times in Homer (*c*. one in 1,120 verses), and usually the pyrrhic word is a conjunction or similar word which goes closely with what follows. In four cases the word is a noun: δόρυ θηξάσθω *Il*. 2. 382, φρένα τερπόμενον 9. 186, ἅλα μαρμαρέην 14. 273, ξίφος ἄμφηκες *Od*. 16. 80. The sole case with a verb involves a proper name: ἕλε Πουλυδάμας (*Il*. 15. 339). The fourth-foot caesura occurs about once in every 100 verses in Homer, a third of these being in order to accommodate a proper name (Lehrs, *Aristarchus*² 394 ff., van Leeuwen, *Enchiridium*, 17 f., Maas, *Greek Metre*, § 85). In (genuine) Hesiod it occurs about once in forty-seven verses. Cf. ad *Dem*. 74.

κεχάρηντο: in Homer κεχάροντο (reduplicated aorist) is used (*Il*. 16. 600; cf. κεχαροίατο *Il*. 1. 256, -οιτο *Od*. 2. 249). The pluperfect is also found at Hes. *Sc*. 65 κεχάρητο. Cf. *Hy*. 7. 10 κεχαρημένοι, active κεχαρηότα (*Il*. 7. 312), and Hoekstra, *Sub-epic Stage*, 14.

459. Ῥέη: this form is used at Hes. *Th*. 467, Call. *Hy*. 1. 21, A.R. 1. 506, Orph. *Arg*. 625. Cf. ad *Dem*. 60.

λιπαροκρήδεμνος: used of Rhea at Orph. *Arg*. 625. Cf. ad *Dem*. 25.

460–9. Rhea's speech is a repetition (with variations) of that of Iris (321–3), and Zeus' message (443–5). Cf. also 327–8 with 461–2. 467–8 and 469 are additions to her message. Cf. ad *Dem*. 314–23, 323.

The repetition of 443–7 is important, as this contains the terms of reconciliation between Zeus and Demeter, and those on which Persephone is to return, which are stated here for the third time (cf. 399–402). On the repetition in cult-poetry of verses important to the cult (e.g. *Ap.* 490-2 ∼ 508-10), see F. Jacoby, *Der homerische Apollon-hymnos* (Berlin, 1933), 69 [748], D. Kolk, *Der pythische Apollonhymnos als aitiologische Dichtung* (Meisenheim am Glan, 1963), 32 n. 17.

460. Cf. *Dem.* 321. Note the doublet (cf. ad loc.). Rhea, for ob-vious reasons, does not use πατήρ. Cf. also Pi. *O.* 6. 62 f. Ὄρϲο, τέκοϲ, δεῦρο . . .

462-79. On the lacunae see notes to *Dem.* 387-404.

462. ἅϲ κεν ἕλοιο: m's supplement ἅϲ κε θέληϲθα is probably drawn from ἐθέλοιτο in *Dem.* 328. ἐθέληϲθα is a genuine epic form (*Od.* 3. 92, etc.; on ἐθέλειν/θέλειν cf. ad *Dem.* 160), but Ilgen's supplement is nearer to *Dem.* 444 (and the original reading in 328?), and should probably be preferred.

464. ὑπὸ ζόφον ἠερόεντα: M alters ἠ]ερόεντα to ἠ]ερόεντι, perhaps from *Dem.* 482. See note to *Dem.* 446.

465. After this verse the writer of M repeated 448-52 (wrongly reported as 449-53 in the Oxford text). m, in his zeal for correction, also expunged 465, which did not suit his version of 466. Cf. Bücheler and Goodwin ad loc.

466. Bücheler's supplements are designed to ease the construction of 463-5 (assuming a lacuna after 447 : cf. ad 445-7). For Hermann's conjecture cf. *Il.* 15. 75. Goodwin's supplement is shorter: the space suggests about ten to twelve letters, but the line may have begun further to the left than the others (cf. 468-70 = 474-6 in Goodwin's photograph). τελέεϲθαι (Goodwin) does not occur in this metrical position in Homer.

The nod of Zeus represents an irrevocable decision. Cf. *Il.* 1. 524 ff., 15. 75, also 8. 246, 17. 209, *Dem.* 323, 446 = 463, A. *Supp.* 91 f., E. *Alc.* 968 f., Call. *Hy.* 5. 131-6.

κάρητι: on this form cf. Chantraine, *GH* i. 231.

467-8. Cf. *Dem.* 323, 82, 362.

470-82. Demeter restores crops and plants, and teaches her rites to the princes of Eleusis, rites which may not be divulged. He who has seen them is blessed: he who has not been initiated, does not have a share in the same things after death, in the underworld.

This passage draws together the two themes of the *Hymn*, the foundation of the Mysteries, foreshadowed in *Dem.* 273 f., and the restoration of vegetation after the famine (the subject of the second half). It is significant that the return of life to the fields is followed here by Demeter's instruction of men in her Mysteries. This suggests a reflection of the version, current later and perhaps suppressed in the *Hymn*, in which men were given agriculture together with, or shortly before, the Mysteries (cf. ad *Dem.* 305 ff., 450). Kretschmer (*Glotta* 12 (1923), 53) suggested that the ἱερά of *Dem.* 476 included the ἱερὸϲ ἄροτοϲ, performed according to tradition by Triptolemus. The ὄργια themselves may have originally centred around the ritual perfor-mance of basic agricultural actions (cf. Eitrem, *Symb. Osl.* 20 (1940), 133 ff.).

The role of the princes as the first priests, and perhaps also as receivers of the gifts of crops and the arts of agriculture, is suggestive of the religious outlook according to which a country's material prosperity is dependent on its rulers. This is perhaps reflected in early epic: cf. *Od.* 19. 109 ff., Hes. *Op.* 225 ff. (Mazon ad loc.), and also perhaps *Il.* 18. 556 f., where the βασιλεύς is depicted standing in the middle of his harvest-field.

471–3. Cf. Ov. *F.* 4. 615–18:

> tum demum voltumque Ceres animumque recepit,
> imposuitque suae spicea serta comae;
> largaque provenit cessatis messis in arvis,
> et vix congestas area cepit opes.

472–3. Cf. *Dem.* 401–2. The sudden flowering is like that of *Il.* 14. 347 ff., at the union of Zeus and Hera. Cf. also *Ap.* 135–9 (at the birth of Apollo): χρύςῳ δ' ἄρα Δῆλος ἅπαςα | βεβρίθει*. . . (139 ἤνθης' . . . ἄνθεςιν ὕλης). Ilgen assumed that *Dem.* 472–3 was influenced by *Ap.* 136–8 (cf. Jacoby, *Der homerische Apollonhymnos*, 14 [693] n. 4, P. S. Breuning, *De hymnorum Homericorum memoria* (Diss. Utrecht, 1929), 65). See Addenda.

473. ἔβρις': cf. ad *Dem.* 456.

θεμιστοπόλοις βασιλεῦςι: cf. ad *Dem.* 103.

474–5. Cf. *Dem.* 153–5.

474–6. δεῖξε . . . δρηςμοςύνην θ' ἱερῶν καὶ ἐπέφραδεν ὄργια πᾶςι: either δεῖξε or δεῖξεν is possible: cf. La Roche, *HU* i. 36. Demeter 'demonstrated the performance of her rites, and showed her ὄργια to the princes'. The Mysteries themselves consisted of τὰ δρώμενα (cf. δρηςμοςύνην, ὄργια), i.e. certain ritual actions, τὰ δεικνύμενα (cf. δεῖξε, ἐπέφραδεν), sacred objects which were shown, and τὰ λεγόμενα, probably brief ritual sayings (cf. Mylonas, *Eleusis*, 261 ff.). Thus the language reflects the cult terminology. δεῖξε and ἐπέφραδεν here refer primarily to the revelation or institution of the cult, as in the later τελετὴν (etc.) καταδεικνύναι (-νυςθαι): cf. Andron, *FGH* 10. 13 Εὔμολπον τὸν καταδείξαντα τὴν μύηςιν καὶ ἱεροφάντην γεγονότα (cf. below); Ar. *Ran.* 1032 Ὀρφεὺς . . . τελετάς θ' ἡμῖν κατέδειξε . . .; [E.] *Rhes.* 943–4 μυςτηρίων τε τῶν ἀπορρήτων φανὰς | ἔδειξεν Ὀρφεύς; Ps. D. 25. 11 ὁ τὰς ἁγιωτάτας ἡμῖν τελετὰς καταδείξας Ὀρφεύς (Orph. fr. 23); Xen. *Hell.* 6. 3. 6 λέγεται Τριπτόλεμος τὰ Δήμητρος καὶ Κόρης ἄρρητα ἱερὰ πρώτοις ξένοις δεῖξαι . . .; Paus. 4. 2. 6 τὰ ὄργια ἐπέδειξε τῶν μεγάλων Θεῶν . . .; Diod. 5. 48. 4 τὸν δὲ Δία . . . παραδεῖξαι αὐτῷ τὴν τῶν μυςτηρίων τελετήν; Lobeck, *Aglaophamus* 48 ff., 205 f.; C. Zijderveld, *Τελετή* (Diss. Utrecht, 1934), 64; N. M. H. van den Burg, *Ἀπόρρητα Δρώμενα, Ὄργια* (Diss. Utrecht, 1939), 95 n. 1.

It was from his role as the priest who revealed the Mysteries, by showing the sacred objects and uttering the sacred sayings (cf. ad *Dem.* 154 Εὐμόλποιο), that the ἱεροφάντης at Eleusis received his title. Cf. Hsch. s.v.: ἱερεὺς ὁ τὰ μυςτήρια δεικνύων; Plut. *Alc.* 22 ςτολὴν οἵανπερ ἱεροφάντης ἔχων δεικνύει τὰ ἱερά; *IG* ii². 3661. 3 ὄργια πᾶςιν

ἔφαινε βροτοῖϲ φαεϲίμβροτα Δηοῦϲ (cf. *Dem.* 476) ; *Marm. Par.* 15
ἀφ' οὗ Εὔμολποϲ . . . τὰ μυϲτήρια ἀνέφηνεν ἐν 'Ελευϲῖνι ; *IG* ii/iii².3639. 3 f.
ὃϲ τελετὰϲ ἀνέφηνε καὶ ὄργια πάννυχα μύϲταιϲ, | Εὐμόλπου προχέων
ἱμερόεϲϲαν ὄπα (cf. ad *Dem.* 154).

It is not known what the sacred objects were. On the δρώμενα
cf. ad *Dem.* 476.

The list of princes in 474–5 omits Polyxenus (cf. 154, 477) and
Dolichus (155). They are the most obscure ones in the earlier list.
If these lines were especially subject to rhapsodic variation, a version
may have existed in which they occurred in a separate line. But complete enumeration need not be expected (cf. ad *Dem.* 105 ff.).

Διοκλεῖ τε πληξίππῳ: for the variation Dioclus/Diocles cf. ad
Dem. 153.

The games in honour of Diocles at Megara perhaps included
chariot races. The epithet is applied in Homer to Pelops (*Il.* 2. 104),
whose charioteering exploits were legendary, and Oileus (*Il.* 11. 93),
the ἑταῖροϲ and perhaps charioteer of Bianor (11. 92 f.), but also to
Menestheus (*Il.* 4. 327; cf. 2. 553 f.?) and an unknown Orestes
(*Il.* 5. 705). Cf. Hes. *Sc.* 24 Βοιωτοὶ πλήξιπποι.

475. Εὐμόλπου τε . . . ἡγήτορι λαῶν: cf. perhaps (Pindar), P. Oxy.
2622 fr. 1 (a) 2–3, PSI 1391 fr. B col. i 6, 13 ff. (H. Lloyd-Jones,
Maia 19 (1967), 206 ff.) : ϲοφὸν ἀγητῆρα . . . εὐνομίᾳ λατέρπει, probably
of *Eumolpus*. A similar transfer of epithet from Celeus to Eumolpus
has occurred in Pausanias' version of *Dem.* 154–5 (see notes ad loc.).
ἡγήτορι λαῶν possibly suggests that Celeus was the chief βαϲιλεύϲ
(cf. ad *Dem.* 97). The phrase occurs only once in Homer (*Il.* 20. 383).
Cf. ποιμένα/ι λαῶν* (*Il.* 1. 263, etc.), κοϲμήτορε/ι λαῶν* (*Il.* 1. 16, etc.,
Od. 18. 152), κοίρανε λαῶν* (*Il.* 7. 234, etc.), ἡγήϲατο λαῶν* (*Il.* 15.
311), ἡγήτορι Θρῃκῶν/Μέντῃ*, etc. (*Il.* 5. 462, 17. 73, etc.).

476. δρηϲμοϲύνην: M's χρηϲμοϲύνην is just possible. It normally
means 'need, want, poverty' (Theognis 389, Tyrt. 6–7. 8 D.³ etc.), but
also 'service, aid' (A.R. 1. 837). But the latter is a special use, and
there is no doubt that δρηϲμοϲύνην is the original reading. It occurs
only in Hsch., *Et. M.* 287. 1 s.v.: θεραπεία, ὑπηρεϲία (and Maximus,
Astrol. 351 p. 28 Ludwich, where it = δραϲμόϲ). But cf. δρηϲτοϲύνη
(*Od.* 15. 321) = 'service', and δραμοϲύνη, which is used in a religious
sense in *IG* ii². 1358. ii. 34, 40 (cf. S. Dow, *Historia* 9 (1960), 282 f.).

The simple verb δρᾶν occurs once in Homer (*Od.* 15. 317). Cf. also
δρήϲτηρ, -ειρα, παρα-/ὑπο-δρᾶν, δραίνειν, ὀλιγοδρανέων. On the form of
δρηϲμοϲύνη (from *δρήϲμων?) cf. Chantraine, *Formation des Noms*, 174,
Porzig, *Satzinhalte*, 224. It is tempting to connect δρηϲμοϲύνη here
with the later δρώμενα (cf. Zijderveld, Τελετή, 64, who considers it
synonymous). The evidence for the use of δρᾶν in a religious sense (cf.
ἔρδειν, etc.) before the Hellenistic period is scanty but definite. (The
uses of δρᾶν, δρώμενα are studied in detail by van den Burg, Ἀπόρρητα, Δρώμενα, Ὄργια, 52 ff., with German summary 128 f., and cf.
also H. Schreckenberg, ΔΡΑΜΑ (Würzburg, 1960), 49 ff., 122 ff.)
Cf. *IG* i². 188. 48, 55 (= Ziehen, *LGS* ii. 9 C 11 = Sokolowski, *Lois*

sacrées des cités grecques, No. 10; before 460 B.C.), where it apparently means 'sacrifice'; Ath. 14. 660 a οἱ παλαιοὶ τὸ θύειν δρᾶν ὠνόμαζον. ἔδρων δ' οἱ Κήρυκες ἄχρι πολλοῦ βουθυτοῦντες, φησί (Cleidemus, fourth century B.C.) . . . (etc.); Hsch. s.v. δρᾶν· πράccειν, θύειν. No other definite example of this sense is known,[1] but in later authors ἱερὰ δρᾶν is used to mean 'perform the rites', and δρώμενα is used of rites, and especially of mystery rites (cf. similarly ὄργια, ad *Dem.* 273). These uses are common in Plutarch, and in Pausanias, who is the only writer to use δρώμενα exclusively in a religious sense. For δρώμενα of the Eleusinian Mysteries cf. Paus. 2. 14. 1, 5. 10. 1, 8. 15. 1, 31. 7, 10. 31. 11; Plut. *Alc.* 34, Ael. Arist. 22 K. § 2, Sopater 8. 1 W.; of the cult of Demeter and Core: Paus. 2. 22. 3, 37. 3, 3. 20. 5. Cf. Plut. *de prof. in vert.* 10 (81 e), of οἱ τελούμενοι.

δρηcμοcύνην ἱερῶν provides the earliest example of δρᾶν (etc.) in the sense of 'performance of ritual'. On the nature of the Eleusinian δρώμενα cf. Introduction, pp. 20 ff. At no period does the use of the word suggest any form of dramatic representation, such as has often been assumed to have occurred at Eleusis (cf. van den Burg, o.c. 53 f., 128 f., Schreckenberg, o.c. 126–7, Wilamowitz, *Glaube*, ii. 57, 481). Schreckenberg (o.c. 122 ff.) gives examples of the common conjunction of δρώμενα with εἰδέναι, ἰδεῖν. Cf. especially S. *OC* 1640–4 (Oedipus' death is a 'mystery').

θ': Pausanias omits the copula (cf. Ruhnken). For this type of postponed τε, where a synonymous verb is added in the second clause, cf. Denniston, *GP* 519 f.

ἐπέφραδεν: cf. ad *Dem.* 474–6.

ὄργια: cf. ad *Dem.* 273.

πᾶcι: if 477 is out of place here, καλά directly before cεμνά is awkward. It may be due to reminiscence of ἱερὰ καλά (*Il.* 11. 726, etc.). For a possible echo of 476b cf. *IG* ii². 3661. 3: ὄργια πᾶcιν ἔφαινε βροτοῖc . . .

477. The repetition of Triptolemus and Diocles is hardly acceptable. The verse probably belongs to a variant version. Alternatively, it may have been added in order to introduce Polyxenus. But in this case one would expect Dolichus also to appear in it.

Ruhnken thought that the daughters of Celeus were mentioned here, since Pausanias (1. 38. 3) says that they perform the ritual with Eumolpus (cf. ad *Dem.* 105 ff.). But the names which he quotes, from 'Homer', are different from those of *Dem.* 109–10, and must belong to a separate version.

478–9. Secrecy of the Mysteries

On this subject see especially O. Casel, *De philosophorum Graecorum silentio mystico* (Giessen, 1919), chap. i.

That the Mysteries were secret was one of their most essential features. The words μυcτήρια, μύcτηc, μυεῖν (etc.) were connected with μύω ('to close', of one's eyes, mouth, etc.). Secrecy was enjoined

[1] But see Snell, *Philol. Supp.* 20 (1928), 7 n. 18, Schreckenberg, o.c. 49 ff.

by 'the laws and customs of the priesthoods of Eleusis' (Plut. *Alc.* 22 :
cf. Sopater, *Rhet. gr.* 8. 110 W.: Νόμος· τὸν ἐξειπόντα τὰ μυστήρια
τεθνάναι), and was commanded by the ἱεροκῆρυξ in his proclamation
at the beginning of the Mysteries (Sopater, *Rhet. gr.* 8. 118. 13 ff. W.).
Any breach of this law by revelation of the secrets, or profanation of
the Mysteries either by unlicensed entry to the Sanctuary or by
imitation or parody of the ceremonies, was punishable by death (for
examples cf. Mylonas, *Eleusis,* 224 ff., Casel, o.c. 9 ff., 17 f.).

This secrecy covered all the main ritual of the Mysteries, i.e. that
which took place within the Sanctuary, and above all, within the
Telesterion itself. Pausanias (1. 38. 7) was forbidden in a dream to
describe anything within the walls of the Sanctuary (τὸ δὲ ἐντὸς
τοῦ τείχους τοῦ ἱεροῦ τό τε ὄνειρον ἀπεῖπε γράφειν . . .). Similarly, he was
forbidden to describe the Eleusinion at Athens (1. 14. 3). Cf. Arrian,
Anab. 3. 16. 8, Procl. *in Alcib.* 1 (p. 5 ed. Creuzer), p. 288 Cousin;
Lex Andaniensis, Ziehen, *LGS* ii. 58 § 7.

To break the secret was ἀσεβεῖν, ἁμαρτάνειν (etc.) περὶ τὰ μυστήρια,
τὼ θεώ (etc.) (cf. ad *Dem.* 478, παρεξίμεν). Since the Mysteries con-
sisted of δρώμενα, δεικνύμενα, and λεγόμενα, one could do this by performing the ὄργια, or showing them, or by revealing the words which
should not be spoken. Cf. Plut. *Alc.* 25 Ἀλκιβιάδην . . . ἀπομιμούμενον
τὰ μυστήρια καὶ δεικνύοντα τοῖς αὐτοῦ ἑταίροις (etc.) ; Andoc. *de myst.* 11
Ἀλκιβιάδην . . . ἀποδείξω ὑμῖν τὰ μυστήρια ποιοῦντα (cf. 12. 16, etc.) ;
Ps. Lys. *adv. Andoc.* 51 μιμούμενος τὰ ἱερὰ ἐπεδείκνυε τοῖς ἀμυήτοις καὶ
εἶπε τῇ φωνῇ τὰ ἀπόρρητα.

Similarly, those to whom the Mysteries were revealed were said
either to *see* them (cf. ad *Dem.* 480) or to *hear* (learn of) them (cf. ad
478 πυθέσθαι). They are commonly described as ἄρρητα, ἀπόρρητα,
ἐν ἀπορρήτῳ, etc. (cf. van den Burg, Ἀπόρρητα *(etc.),* Casel, o.c. 6) : e.g.
Hdt. 6. 135 (Paros), Ar. *Nub.* 302, Xen. *Hell.* 6. 3. 6, [E.] *Rhes.* 943, etc.

Also apparently secret was the σύνθημα, by which the candidate for
initiation declared that he had fulfilled the preliminary rituals. Cf.
Clem. Al. *Prot.* 2. 22. 4 δεῖ γὰρ ἀπογυμνῶσαι τὰ ἄγια αὐτῶν καὶ τὰ
ἄρρητα ἐξειπεῖν (cf. 21. 2, and ad *Dem.* 192 ff.). But it seems that
certain of the preliminary rituals of purification and abstinence were
not secret. Thus we find them portrayed in the *Hymn* (*Dem.* 192 ff.,
perhaps also 231 ff.), and in works of art (cf. ad loc.). The precepts
which commanded purity and abstinence were not secret, and are
expressly contrasted by Libanius (*Or. Corinth.* 19) with τὰ ἀπόρρητα.
They are perhaps referred to also by Seneca (*Ep.* 95. 64; cf. Lobeck,
Aglaophamus 191) : 'Sicut sanctiora sacrorum tantum initiati sciunt,
ita in philosophia arcana illa admissis receptisque in sacra ostendun-
tur, at praecepta et alia eiusmodi profanis quoque nota sunt.' Aelian
also (fr. 44 Hercher) distinguishes between τῶν μὲν ἀπορρήτων καὶ
ἃ μὴ ἰδεῖν λῷον ἦν and τῶν δὲ πρώτων καὶ ἐξ ὧν οὔτε τοῖς θεασαμένοις οὔτε
τοῖς δείξασιν ἔμελλέ τι ἀπαντήσεσθαι δεινόν. Pausanias allows himself to
describe ἃ . . . ἐς πάντας ὅσιον γράφειν (1. 14. 3), i.e. what lay outside
the Eleusinion at Athens and the Sanctuary at Eleusis. We have

L

a good deal of information also about the other preparations for the main ceremonies, the procession, dancing, etc. But the reasons for the various forms of ritual were secret and known only to the mystae (Clem. Al. *Strom.* 2. 106; cf. Paus. 1. 37. 4; Th. Wächter, *Reinheitsvorschriften in gr. Kult*, 96, 103).

More problematical is the question of the myths. The story of the Rape of Persephone was not secret, but we are told that it formed the subject of a 'mystic drama' at Eleusis (Clem. Al. *Protr.* § 12. 2, Greg. Naz. *Or.* 39, *PG* 36. 337), and certain myths about the gods could not be told (cf. Isocr. *paneg.* 28, and notes to *Dem.* 305 ff., 478 πυθέcθαι; Call. fr. 75. 4–7, where note ἱcτορίην; Ael. fr. 43 Hercher; Casel, o.c. 15 n. 3). It seems that the form which the myths took in the Mysteries themselves must have differed considerably from their presentation in literature (cf. Introduction, pp. 24 ff.).

The original cause of this secrecy has been variously identified. Lobeck (*Aglaophamus*, 270–82) thought that it derived from the time when the Mysteries were the property of certain families, who did not wish the benefits which they conferred to fall into the hands of outsiders. For other theories see Allen and Halliday, p. 180. Such explanations may have an element of truth in them, but are not sufficient in themselves to account for the unique position held by the Eleusinian Mysteries in this respect (although other cults of Demeter and Persephone and of certain other deities were secret, or had secret elements). The *Hymn* gives its own reason for their secrecy: the ὄργια are cεμνά (478), like the deities to whom they belong (cf. ad *Dem.* 1, 486), and may not be revealed, since 'a great reverence (cέβας) of the gods restrains utterance' (479). It is the awe and terror which the great deities of the underworld inspire, by their governance of men's lives both on earth and after death, which lead their worshippers to shrink from speaking of their rites, especially those which concern the afterlife, shrouded as it is in darkness, hidden from men's eyes (cf. Farnell, *Cults*, iii. 129 f.; Deichgräber, *Eleus. Frömmigkeit*, 521). This reticence may reach even to the pronouncing of the names of such deities (cf. ad *Dem.* 9, etc., 439; and on the Erinyes, the Cεμναὶ Θεαί, S. *OC* 125 ff.).

In the same way, Metaneira, when confronted by the epiphany of Demeter, is unable to speak. Reverence, awe, and fear (αἰδώς, cέβας, and δέος) prevent her, just as they prevent the initiate from describing his experiences (cf. ad *Dem.* 188–211, 188–90, 275 ff.). These reactions, and the silence to which they lead, are regularly mentioned together by authors who refer to the Mysteries. Cf. especially Plut. *de prof. in virt.* 10, 81 e οἱ τελούμενοι . . . δρωμένων δὲ καὶ δεικνυμένων τῶν ἱερῶν προcέχουcιν ἤδη μετὰ φόβου καὶ cιωπῆc . . . ἕτερον λαβὼν cχῆμα καὶ cιωπὴν καὶ θάμβος; Plut. fr. 178 (Stob. 4. 52. 49 p. 1089 H.) τὰ δεινὰ πάντα, φρίκη καὶ τρόμος καὶ ἱδρὼς καὶ θάμβος affect the initiate; Themist. *Or.* 20. 235 (p. 287 Dind.) ὁ μὲν ἄρτι προcιὼν τοῖc ἀδύτοιc φρίκηc τε ἐνεπίμπλατο καὶ ἰλίγγου . . . ; Ael. Arist. 22. 2 (Keil): Eleusis is πάντων, ὅcα θεῖ' ἀνθρώποιc, ταὐτὸν φρικωδέcτατόν τε καὶ φαιδρότατον

... (nowhere else) τὰ δρώμενα μεῖζον' ἔσχε τὴν ἔκπληξιν; playing on the language of the Mysteries Plut. *Caesar* 66, 739 c ἔκπληξις καὶ φρίκη πρὸς τὰ δρώμενα (death of Caesar); *Cicero* 22, 871 c τοῦ δὲ δήμου φρίττοντος τὰ δρώμενα καὶ παριόντος σιωπῇ ... ὥσπερ ἱεροῖς τισι πατρίοις ... τελεῖσθαι μετὰ φόβου καὶ θάμβους δοκούντων. Demeter herself is called θεὰ φρικτή with reference to her ἱερά (Call. fr. 75. 6), and Miltiades is overcome by φρίκη when attempting to enter her Parian temple (Hdt. 6. 134. 2; cf. ad *Dem.* 491). Cf. Procl. *in remp.* 2. 108. 18 ff. (Kroll) αὗται αἱ τελεταὶ χρώμεναι τοῖς μύθοις, ἵνα τὴν περὶ θεῶν ἀλήθειαν ἄρρητον κατακλείωσιν, συμπαθείας εἰσὶν αἴτιαι ταῖς ψυχαῖς περὶ τὰ δρώμενα τρόπον ἄγνωστον ἡμῖν καὶ θεῖον· ὡς τοὺς μὲν τῶν τελουμένων καταπλήττεσθαι δειμάτων θείων πλήρεις γιγνομένους, τοὺς δὲ ... (etc.); cf. *in Alcib.* p. 142 (Creuzer). σέβας is also associated with silence and secrecy: cf. Ar. *Nub.* 302 οὗ σέβας ἀρρήτων ἱερῶν, ἵνα μυστοδόκος δόμος ἐν τελεταῖς ἁγίαις ἀναδείκνυται; Iulian. *Or.* 5. 173 a τὰ σεμνὰ καὶ ἀπόρρητα μυστήρια; Ps. Dem. *in Neaer.* 74 (τὰς θυσίας) τὰς σεμνοτάτας καὶ ἀπορρήτους; Str. 10. 467 C ἥ τε κρύψις ἡ μυστικὴ τῶν ἱερῶν σεμνοποιεῖ τὸ θεῖον; Basil, *de Spir. sancto*, § 66 (Migne, *PG* 32. 189A) τῶν μυστηρίων τὸ σεμνὸν σιωπῇ διασώζεσθαι; Hippol. *Ref. Haer.* 1 p. 1. 19 f. Wendl. οἱ διὰ τὸ σιωπᾶν ἀποκρύπτειν τε τὰ ἄρρητα ἑαυτῶν μυστήρια ἐνομίσθησαν πολλοῖς θεὸν σέβειν (cf. θεῶν σέβας, *Dem.* 479). Cf. especially S. *OC* 1050 ff. οὗ πότνιαι σεμνὰ τιθηνοῦνται τέλη θνατοῖσιν, ὧν καὶ χρυσέα κλὴς ἐπὶ γλώσσᾳ βέβακε προσπόλων Εὐμολπιδᾶν (on such formulae cf. ad *Dem.* 479).

For αἰδώς and silence together cf. Liban. *Or.* 10. 6 (1. 403. 4 ff. Förster) μυστηρίων τε τιμὴν εἶχε τὰ ἐν τούτῳ τῷ Πλέθρῳ· τοσαύτη μὲν αἰδὼς ἦν ... τοσαύτη δὲ ἡσυχία, τοσαύτη δὲ σιωπή.

Silence is regularly required in religious ceremonies in general (cf. the expressions εὐφημία ἔστω, εὐφήμει, etc., before religious ritual), as in magic (cf. Gow ad Theocr. 2. 38, Sophron in Page, *Gk. Lit. Pap.* i. 330. 14 f. εὐκαμίαν νυν παρέχεσθε; G. Mensching, *Das heilige Schweigen* (Giessen, 1926), 102 ff.), and it is also a concomitant of divine epiphanies (cf. ad *Dem.* 275 ff., and Dodds ad E. *Ba.* 1084). In the ritual of the Mysteries it played a special part: cf. the passages quoted above, and also Hippol. *Ref. Haer.* 5. 8. 39 : Ἀθηναῖοι μυοῦντες Ἐλευσίνια, καὶ ἐπιδεικνύντες τοῖς ἐποπτεύουσι τὸ μέγα καὶ θαυμαστὸν καὶ τελειότατον ἐποπτικὸν ἐκεῖ μυστήριον ἐν σιωπῇ τεθερισμένον στάχυν (cf. Introduction, p. 27). There is dispute here as to whether ἐν σιωπῇ should be taken with τεθερισμένον (cf. Deubner, *AF* 83 n. 5) or with ἐπιδεικνύντες (etc.). Despite the awkwardness of the word order, the second interpretation seems definitely preferable. Hippolytus' sentence is climactic, and ἐν σιωπῇ is postponed for effect, to increase the impression that a great and wonderful mystery is to be revealed, before the deliberate anticlimax of the last two words. This testimony thus agrees with those passages referring to silence as a concomitant of the ritual in the Telesterion (especially Plut. *de prof. in virt.* 10 sup. Cf. also Casel, o.c. 26 n. 1). Silence was perhaps also a feature of the torch-carrying ceremony at Eleusis (cf. ad *Dem.* 59-61), and is stressed in the preliminary purification ritual (cf. ad *Dem.* 192 ff., 194, 198–9). Cf. a similar emphasis in the mysteries of Andania, Ziehen, *LGS* ii. 58 § 9.

This silence should be distinguished from the 'reticentia mystica', which prevented the initiates from revealing their experiences to other people. But the underlying cause in both cases is the same, the 'great reverence for the gods' which seals the lips of those who are admitted to their rites.

On silence in the Mysteries cf. also Mensching, o.c. 86, 130 ff.

478. cεμνά: this is regularly used of the rites of Demeter. Cf. Ar. *Thesm.* 948, 1151 ὄργια cεμνὰ θεοῖν; E. *Hipp.* 25 cεμνῶν ἐc ὄψιν καὶ τέλη μυcτηρίων; S. *OC* 1050 οὗ πότνιαι cεμνὰ τιθηνοῦνται τέλη (cf. ad *Dem.* 39, etc.); hymn ap. Ath. 6. 253 d cεμνὰ τῆc Κόρηc μυcτήρια; *Orph. Hy.* 18. 18 cεμνοῖc μυcτιπόλοιc (cf. 24. 10 f.). Cf. also A. fr. 57 N. cεμνὰ Κοτυτοῦc ὄργι' ἔχοντεc; S. *Tr.* 765 cεμνῶν ὀργίων (of sacrifice; cf. *Ant.* 1013, cεμνῶν coni. Nauck); E. *Supp.* 470 (at Eleusis) cεμνὰ cτεμμάτων μυcτήρια (cf. 290 cεμναῖcι Δηοῦc ἐcχάραιc παρημένη; 359–60); and see notes to *Dem.* 1, 478–9, 486.

τά γ': Allen reads τά τ' (cf. Ilgen), but γε does not seem impossible. Cf. *Od.* 8. 280 for τά γε as a relative (*variae lectiones* τά κε, τε). There do not appear to be any other Homeric examples, but it is questionable whether alteration is justified. As in *Od.* 8. 280, γε serves to draw attention to what follows (cf. the repetition in *Dem.* 478–9 οὔ πωc . . . οὔτε . . . οὔτ' . . . and 280 f. οὔ κέ τιc οὐδὲ . . . οὐδὲ . . .).

παρεξ[ίμ]εν: Goodwin concludes that this was the reading of M. The traces would also allow παρεξέμεν. παρεξιέναι could mean 'transgress, overstep' (cf. A. *PV* 551, S. *Ant.* 60), or 'disregard, neglect' (cf. Socr. *Ep.* 6. 11 κακῶc πράττοντά τινα). παρεξελθεῖν is used in a similar formula in *Od.* 5. 103 f., 137 f., apparently with the meaning 'get by, elude', or 'overreach' (cf. παρελθεῖν in Hes. *Th.* 613). For the sense 'transgress' cf. Isocr. *de iugo*, 6 εἴ τιc εἰc τὰ μυcτήρια φαίνοιτ' ἐξαμαρτάνων; D.L. 2. 101 τίνεc εἰcὶν οἱ ἀcεβοῦντεc περὶ τὰ μυcτήρια; . . . οἱ τοῖc ἀμυήτοιc αὐτὰ ἐκφέροντεc.

Secrecy was enjoined by law, and a breach of this was a transgression: cf. Sopater, *Rhet. gr.* 8. 112. 7 f. W. τοῖc τῶν μυcτηρίων νόμον παραβῆναι τολμήcαcιν (cf. 13 f.: the accused has transgressed περὶ τὰc θεὰc καὶ τὰ μυcτήρια); Andoc. *de myst.* 29 ἑτέρων ἁμαρτόντων καὶ ἀcεβηcάντων περὶ τὼ θεώ; Plut. *Alc.* 25 ἀδικεῖν περὶ τὼ θεὼ ἀπομιμούμενον τὰ μυcτήρια. In all these cases, either a preposition is used with μυcτήρια (etc.), or the object is νόμον. The expression 'to transgress the Mysteries (etc.)' is never found, and it is much more difficult to accept. It is possible that the *Hymn* is here echoing the actual words of a ritual prohibition (cf. above, and notes on πυθέcθαι, ἀχέειν), which may have forbidden one 'either to divulge the Mysteries, or to (see or) hear them, or in any way to commit a transgression (ἀcεβεῖν, ἁμαρτάνειν) with regard to them'. In that case, there is a kind of syllepsis, since παρεξίμεν goes more loosely with ὄργια than the other verbs.

The sense 'neglect' would also be possible. Cf. Paus. 10. 31. 11
τῶν τὰ δρώμενα τὰ Ἐλευcῖνι ἐν οὐδενὶ θεμένων λόγῳ. In this case,
the reference would most naturally be to those who were not initiated
(cf. Paus. 10. 31. 9 τῶν οὐ μεμνημένων). But this does not go so well
with οὔτε πυθέcθαι οὔτ' ἀχέειν, which refers to revelation to the
uninitiated. The pejorative sense 'disregard, slight' (cf. LSJ s.v.
παρέρχομαι IV) would be more suitable. Cf. Schol. Ar. Av. 1072
οὗτος (Diagoras) . . . τὰ μυcτήρια ηὐτέλιζεν . . . ἐπεὶ τὰ μυcτήρια πᾶcι
διηγεῖτο κοινοποιῶν αὐτὰ καὶ μικρὰ ποιῶν . . . But it is doubtful whether
παρεξιέναι can have this meaning.

παρεξέμεν (from παρεξίημι) could mean 'let pass'. It is rarely used:
cf. D.C. 40. 2 (ἅρματα), 50. 31, in a literal sense; otherwise only as
a variant at Hdt. 7. 210. 1 (τέccερας . . . παρεξῆκε ἡμέρας aP: παρῆκε
cett., OCT). It was taken as meaning 'neglect' here by Ruhnken
(cf. also LSJ s.v. παρίημι II 2: 'pass unnoticed, disregard'). Agar
(CR 10 (1896), 388) supported the sense 'divulge'. But this is probably
supplied by ἀχέειν (479). In Il. 12. 213, Od. 4. 348, etc. παρὲξ ἀγορευέ-
μεν (etc.) are used, meaning 'to speak out of turn, wrongly', but it is
very doubtful whether παρεξίημι would be taken in this sense.

Both the reading and interpretation of the word remain difficult,
but the least unsatisfactory solution appears to be παρεξίμεν with the
sense 'transgress'.

οὔτε πυθέcθαι: cf. Paus. 1. 38. 7 (of Eleusis) τοῖς οὐ τελεcθεῖcιν,
ὁπόcων θέας εἴργονται, δῆλα δήπου μηδὲ πυθέcθαι μετεῖναί cφιcιν;
Theocr. 3. 51 (of Iasion: cf. ad Dem. 489) ὃς τόccων ἐκύρηcεν, ὃc' οὐ
πευcεῖcθε, βέβαλοι (Gow ad loc.); E. Ba. 471 ff.:

> Πε. τὰ δ' ὄργι' ἐcτὶ τίν' ἰδέαν ἔχοντά cοι;
> Δι. ἄρρητ' ἀβακχεύτοιcιν εἰδέναι βροτῶν.
> Πε. ἔχει δ' ὄνηcιν τοῖcι θύουcιν τίνα;
> Δι. οὐ θέμιc ἀκοῦcαί c', ἔcτι δ' ἄξι' εἰδέναι.

Cat. 64. 260:

> orgia quae frustra cupiunt audire profani

Orph. fr. 245:

> φθέγξομαι οἷc θέμιc ἐcτί. θύρας δ' ἐπίθεcθε βέβηλοι

(cf. Orph. fr. 13, 334); Orac. ap. Macr. Sat. 1. 18. 19:

> ὄργια μὲν δεδαῶτας ἐχρῆν νηπευθέα κεύθειν.

Isocr. paneg. 28 (cf. ad Dem. 305 ff.) Δήμητρος . . . πρὸς τοὺς προ-
γόνους τοὺς ἡμετέρους εὐμενῶς διατεθείcης ἐκ τῶν εὐεργεcιῶν, ἃc οὐχ
οἷόν τ' ἄλλοιc ἢ τοῖc μεμυημένοιc ἀκούειν; Diod. 5. 48. 4 τὴν τῶν
μυcτηρίων τελετὴν . . . ὧν οὐ θέμιc ἀκοῦcαι πλὴν τῶν μεμυημένων. Cf.
also Soph. OC 1640-4.

479. ἀχέειν: the word is very doubtfully attested in early epic:
cf. Il. 18. 160 ἀχέων (v.l., read by Zenodotus: ἰάχων codd.); Hes. Sc.
93 (ὀχέων Ωa: ἀχέων codd. cett., Stob.; but ὀχέων is supported by

Il. 21. 302); *Hy.* 19. 18 (ἐπιπροχέουϲα χέει codd.: ἀχέει Ilgen, ἰαχει Ruhnken, ἠχέει Gemoll; but cf. *Od.* 19. 520 f.). ἀχέων is also conjectured in Ion *Trag.* fr. 39 (ὕμνον ἀχαιῶν codd.). The middle is attested in Moschion fr. 187 ἀχήϲεται; cf. Hsch. s.v. μέγ' ἀχήϲεται· μέγα βοήϲει.

Cf. Buttmann, *Lexilogus*, 178 f., defending ἀχέειν here and conjecturing ϲτόμ' ἀχήϲεται at *Aph.* 252; but see Schulze, *Zeitschr. f. vergl. Sprachf.* 29 (1888), 247 f., against him. A verb meaning 'to tell, speak out' is needed. ἰαχεῖν or ἠχεῖν would be possible. The former seems more likely: the *scriptio plena* -έει(ν) is common in M (cf. *Dem.* 173, 284), and if ἰαχέειν was written, the iota might easily have been dropped to restore the metre, or simply by chance. For ἰαχεῖν cf. *Dem.* 20. It takes a cognate accusative sometimes in tragedy, rarely an external one. But cf. E. *Ph.* 1295 (= 'bewail'), and passive E. *Hel.* 1147 (ex coni., = 'proclaim'); also ἰαχεῖν χρηϲμόν (*IG* 7. 4240 b 2), etc.

Various terms were later used of revealing the Mysteries in words (cf. ad *Dem.* 478 f.): λέγειν (Hdt. 2. 61, cf. 46, 47; Sopator, *Rhet. gr.* 8. 117 W.); ἐκλέγειν (Sopator o.c. 110 ff., quoting the law); ἐξηγέεϲθαι (Hdt. 2. 3); ἐξαγορεύειν (Hdt. 1. 170, Luc. *de Salt.* 15); ἐκφαίνειν (Hdt. 6. 135, Iamb. *V. Pyth.* § 246); ἐξερεύγειν (Call. fr. 75. 7); ἐκφέρειν (D.L. 2. 101, etc.); ἐξορχεῖϲθαι (Luc. *de Salt.* 15, *Pisc.* 33, Clem. Al. *Protr.* 2 § 12. 1, Synes. *de Provid.* 2. 6. 125 D.), etc. For a full list cf. Casel (o.c. ad *Dem.* 478–9), 6 ff.

μέγα γάρ τι θεῶν ϲέβαϲ ἰϲχάνει αὐδήν: the initiate's lips are sealed by his 'great reverence of the gods' ('die Scheu vor der Gottheit', Rohde, *Psyche*[9], i. 280; cf. W. Otto, *ARW* 12 (1909), 537, 'Religio und superstitio'). On ϲέβαϲ cf. ad *Dem.* 10, 190, 478–9, 478 (ϲεμνά). For θεῶν ϲέβαϲ meaning 'reverence for the gods' cf. A. *Cho.* 645 Διὸϲ ϲέβαϲ, *Supp.* 396 ϲέβαϲ τὸ πρὸϲ θεῶν. In *Supp.* 85 (δαιμόνων ϲέβαϲ), 755 (θεῶν ϲέβη), etc., it refers to the object of reverence (cf. *Dem.* 10).

The language here is similar to later 'formulae of silence'. Cf. especially S. *OC* 1051 ff. (quoted ad *Dem.* 478–9), and other proverbial expressions (A. fr. 316 N., *Ag.* 36 f., Strattis fr. 67 (1. 731 Kock), Theognis 815 f.). Cf. also *AP* 10. 42 ἀρρήτων ἐπέων γλώϲϲῃ ϲφρηγὶϲ ἐπικείϲθω (and for similar phrases Lobeck, *Aglaophamus* i. 36, Casel, o.c. 5 n. 1). Fraenkel (ad *Ag.* 36 f.) concludes that the words βοῦϲ μέγαϲ (ἐπὶ γλώϲϲῃ) βέβηκε belong to the original proverb, and tentatively suggests, following Schneidewin, that the phrase belonged to the ritual of Eleusis, κλήϲ (as in S. *OC* 1051 ff., A. fr. 316 N.) being substituted for βοῦϲ 'to tone down its violence'. If some such expression belonged to Eleusinian ritual, *Dem.* 479 might be a reflection of it (cf. μέγα ϲέβαϲ ἰϲχάνει αὐδήν, as in βοῦϲ μέγαϲ etc.).

480–2. The poet proclaims the blessed state of those who have seen the Mysteries, and the unhappy fate after death of the uninitiated. These lines form, as it were, the climax of the *Hymn* (cf. Deichgräber, *Eleus. Frömmigkeit*, 521 f., Nilsson, *Gesch.* i³. 661). The emphasis is upon seeing the ὄργια, i.e. above all the ἐποπτεία, which was the climax of the Mysteries. It is this which makes the initiates ὄλβιοι, that is both prosperous in the worldly sense (cf. ad loc., and *Dem.* 486–9) and

happy. It is natural to assume that this refers both to the present life
and also to the life after death (cf. 481–2).

The emphasis here, however, is more on the second, as 481–2
show. There is no hint of an ethical viewpoint here, no suggestion
that initiation requires good conduct, or that evil deeds will be
punished (cf. ad *Dem.* 367–9). But the implication of 481–2 is surely
that those who are not initiated will actually suffer after death.
Later writers made this more explicit.

The wording ὅς . . . ἐπιχθονίων ἀνθρώπων does not indicate whether
the Mysteries were already at this stage open to the Greek world in
general, but it does at least *suggest* universality: there are no 'exclusion
clauses'. Possibly the development was rather in the opposite direction, i.e. βάρβαροι were later excluded because of anti-Persian feeling
in the fifth century (cf. Isocr. *Paneg.* 157, Kern, *Rel. d. Gr.* ii. 197 f. n. 1).

There is no reason to assume (with Kern, *RE* 16. 1216. 65 ff.) that
the gradation ὄλβιος . . . μέγ' ὄλβιος (486) implies two separate grades
of initiation at this period. If 480 refers particularly to the ἐποπτεία,
this is not possible. The distinction between μύστης and ἐπόπτης may
well, however, have already been current: cf. Introduction, pp. 20 f.

The words of the *Hymn* are echoed by later writers. Cf. especially
Pi. fr. 137a Sn. (= 121 Bo.):[1]

> ὄλβιος ὅστις ἰδὼν κεῖν' εἶς' ὑπὸ χθόν'·
> οἶδε μὲν βίου τελευτάν,
> οἶδεν δὲ διόσδοτον ἀρχάν.

S. fr. 753 N. (= 837 P.):

> ὡς τρισόλβιοι
> κεῖνοι βροτῶν οἳ ταῦτα δερχθέντες τέλη
> μόλως' ἐς Ἅιδου· τοῖσδε γὰρ μόνοις ἐκεῖ
> ζῆν ἔστι, τοῖς δ' ἄλλοισι πάντ' ἔχει κακά.

In these passages the reference to happiness in a future life is explicit. In Sophocles, it is also clearly stated that 'the rest' will have
'nothing but evil things' after death. For this cf. also Pi. *O.* 2. 67
(after the portrayal of the life of the blessed after death) τοὶ δ' ἀπρος-
όρατον ὀκχέοντι πόνον; Pl. *Rep.* 365 a 3 μὴ θύσαντας δὲ δεινὰ περιμένει.
Note the brevity and reticence of these expressions. Cf. also E. *HF* 613
τὰ μυστῶν δ' ὄργι' ηὐτύχησ' ἰδών (i.e. Heracles was able to bring back
Cerberus from Hades because he had been initiated at Eleusis); Ar.
Ran. 154–8 (a picture of the initiates as the blessed in Hades), 455 ff.
(the chorus of mystae in Hades):

> μόνοις γὰρ ἡμῖν ἥλιος
> καὶ φέγγος ἱλαρόν ἐστιν,
> ὅσοι μεμυνήμεθ' εὐ-
> σεβῆ τε διήγομεν
> τρόπον περὶ τοὺς ξένους
> καὶ τοὺς ἰδιώτας.

---

[1] Cf. Wilamowitz, *Pindaros*, 155, Kern, *ARW* 19 (1916–19), 433 f. With this
should be compared Pi. *O.* 2. 53–80, frr. 129–31, 133, 143 Sn.

Isocr. *Paneg.* 28 (speaking of Demeter's gifts to men of crops and the Mysteries) οἱ μετέχοντες περί τε τῆς τοῦ βίου τελευτῆς καὶ τοῦ σύμπαντος αἰῶνος ἡδίους τὰς ἐλπίδας ἔχουσι (ἐλπὶς ἀγαθή, etc. is a formula, used especially in connection with the Mysteries: cf. Lobeck, *Aglaophamus* i. 69 ff., Cumont, *Lux Perpetua*, 401 ff.). This perhaps refers to life on earth as well as after death. Later writers make this explicit. Cf. Crinagoras, *AP* 11. 42, especially

> τῶν ἄπο κἢν ζωοῖσιν ἀκηδέα, κεῦτ' ἂν ἵκηαι
> ἐς πλεόνων, ἕξεις θυμὸν ἐλαφρότερον.

Cic. *Leg.* 2. 14 (the Mysteries are Athens' greatest gift to men): 'quibus ex agresti immanique vita exculti ad humanitatem et mitigati sumus, initiaque ut appellantur ita revera principia vitae cognovimus, neque solum cum laetitia vivendi rationem accepimus sed etiam cum spe meliore moriendi' (cf. Isocrates, above); Aristid. *Eleus.* 2. 30 K. (1. 421 D.) ἀλλὰ μὴν τό γε κέρδος τῆς πανηγύρεως οὐχ ὅσον ἡ παροῦσα εὐθυμία ... ἀλλὰ καὶ περὶ τῆς τελευτῆς ἡδίους ἔχειν τὰς ἐλπίδας; cf. *Panath.* 1. 302 D.[1]

Other writers refer to the 'privileged position' of the initiates in Hades (προεδρία): cf. [Pl.] *Axioch.* 371 d, D.L. 6. 39. Cf. also Pl. *Rep.* 363 c–d, 365 a, *Phaedo*, 69 c (also 63 c 5–7, where note εὐελπὶς εἰμι), *Gorg.* 493 b (cf. Dodds ad loc.), Proclus *in Remp. Plat.* 616 a–b, 2. 185. 10 ff. Kroll. It is not certain how far these passages of Plato are influenced by Eleusinian beliefs (cf. Dodds, *Gks. and Irrational*, 172 n. 102). The punishment in Hades of the uninitiated, and of those who 'held of no account the rites of Eleusis' is said by Pausanias to have been depicted by Polygnotus in the Delphic *lesche* (Paus. 10. 31. 9, 11). Cf. also, more generally, *IG* ii². 3661. 5 f. (on the statue of the hierophant Glaucus, second century A.D.):

> ἢ καλὸν ἐκ μακάρων μυστήριον, οὐ μόνον εἶναι
> τὸν θάνατον θνητοῖς οὐ κακόν, ἀλλ' ἀγαθόν.

The elaboration of the notions expressed in *Dem.* 480–2 seems to have begun after the period of the *Hymn*. The development of an ethical attitude to the question of rewards and punishment after death probably led to the growth of a literature on this subject. The beginnings of this are generally considered to belong to the sixth century B.C.

On *Dem.* 480–2 see also Lobeck, *Aglaophamus* i. 69 ff., Rohde, *Psyche*, i. 289 ff. (Eng. trans. 223, 233 n. 22), Foucart, *Les Mystères*, 362 ff., Casel (o.c. ad *Dem.* 478–9), 12 f., Nilsson, *Op. Sel.* ii. 588 ff., *Gesch.* i³. 661 f., 672 ff., Deichgräber, *Eleus. Frömmigkeit*, 521 ff., Mylonas, *Eleusis*, 267, Boyancé, *RÉG* 75 (1962), 460 ff., Kern, *Rel. d. Gr.* ii. 187, *RE* 16. 1216. 65 ff.

---

[1] The use of the comparative in these passages, e.g. ἡδίους τὰς ἐλπίδας etc., should be noted. Cf. Pi. *O.* 2. 62 ἀπονέστερον ἐσλοὶ δέκονται βίοτον; Orph. fr. 222. 2 μαλακώτερον οἶτον. Cf. R. Merkelbach, *Roman und Mysterium*, 93 n. 1 on ἀρείονα πότμον.

480. ὄλβιος, ὅς . . .: this is a traditional formula of μακαρισμός. Cf. *Od.* 5. 306:

τρὶς μάκαρες Δαναοὶ καὶ τετράκις, οἳ τότ' ὄλοντο . . .

(~ 6. 153 ff.), Hes. *Th.* 96 f. ὁ δ' ὄλβιος, ὅντινα Μοῦσαι φίλωνται . . . (cf. ad *Dem.* 486 ff.), 954 (where the relative has a causal sense), *Op.* 826 ff., fr. 33(a). 13, 211. 7, *Hy.* 30. 7 ff., etc. It is, however, especially used in proclaiming the happiness of those initiated into the Eleusinian or other mystery-cults. Cf. Pi. fr. 137(a), Soph. fr. 837 P. (ad *Dem.* 480–2), whose language is so close to that of the *Hymn* that imitation seems likely (but cf. G. L. Dirichlet, *De veterum macarismis* (Giessen, 1914), 63 *contra*). Cf. similarly, of the Bacchants, E. *Ba.* 72 ff. ὦ μάκαρ, ὅστις εὐδαίμων τελετὰς θεῶν εἰδὼς βιοτὰν ἁγιστεύει καὶ θιασεύεται ψυχάν . . . (etc.; cf. Dodds, ad loc.); of the initiate into the Isis-mysteries, Apul. *M.* 11. 16. 2 ff., where Lucius is acclaimed by the crowd as 'felix hercules et ter beatus, qui . . . meruerit tam praeclarum de caelo patrocinium' (etc.); 22. 5, where the priest addresses him: 'O', inquit, 'Luci te felicem, te beatum, quem propitia voluntate numen augustum tantopere dignatur'; cf. 29. 4 (Merkelbach, *Roman und Mysterium*, 14 f.). Cf. perhaps also Theocr. 3. 49 ff. ζαλωτὸς μέν . . . ζαλῶ δὲ . . . Ἰασίωνα, ὅς . . . (cf. ad *Dem.* 478), and 15. 146 (at the Adonia) ὀλβία ὅσσα ἴcατι, πανολβία ὡς γλυκὺ φωνεῖ. On the gold plates the dead man says (Orph. fr. 32 (c). 3, etc.) καὶ γὰρ ἐγὼν ὑμῶν γένος ὄλβιον εὔχομαι εἶμεν, and is addressed with the words ὄλβιε καὶ μακάριστε, θεὸς δ' ἔςῃ ἀντὶ βροτοῖο (ibid., verse 10. See also Zuntz, *Persephone*, 322 f. n. 3). This perhaps also reflects a similar address to the initiate in the cult. That such an acclamation may have occurred in the mysteries of Sabazius is suggested by Dem. *de Cor.* 260 ἔξαρχος (etc.) . . . προcαγορευόμενος μίcθον λαμβάνων . . . ἐφ' οἷc τίc οὐκ ἂν ὡc ἀληθῶc αὐτὸν εὐδαιμονίcειε καὶ τὴν αὐτοῦ τύχην; Theon of Smyrna, in his comparison of philosophy to initiation, describes the final stage of μύηcιc as ἡ ἐξ αὐτῶν περιγενομένη κατὰ τὸ θεοφιλὲc καὶ θεοῖc cυνδίαιτον εὐδαιμονία (p. 15, Hiller).

Possibly the ritual of the Eleusinian Mysteries also closed with a μακαρισμός, which is echoed by the words of the *Hymn* (cf. Dirichlet, o.c. 63). One might compare the blessing at the end of a Christian service, although this takes the form of a benediction, that is a prayer rather than a proclamation.

Later the μακαρισμός of the mysteries is taken over by the philosophers, who proclaim the blessed happiness of those who have gained enlightenment by contemplation, and who understand the nature of the world in the same way that the initiate has insight or knowledge of the nature and purpose of his existence (cf. Pi. fr. 137 (a) above). Thus Empedocles echoes the *Hymn*'s contrast between initiate and profane (fr. 132 D.): ὄλβιος ὃς θείων πραπίδων ἐκτήσατο πλοῦτον (cf. ad *Dem.* 489), δειλὸς δ' ᾧ cκοτόεccα θεῶν πέρι δόξα μέμηλεν. Here the symbolism of light and darkness, and the reference to πλοῦτος, echo the language of the Mysteries. Cf. similarly Anaxagoras, *Vors.* 59 A 30

(Arist. *EE* 1. 4. 1215ᵇ7, 1. 5. 1216ᵃ11), E. fr. 910 N. (~ Ar. *Ran.*
1482 ff.), Pl. *Phaedr.* 250 b, Men. fr. 156, Virg. *G.* 2. 490 ff., Ov.
F. 1. 297 ff., *Ex P.* 2. 8. 57 f.
The same symbolism of πλοῦτος, light, and knowledge underlies
Bacch. 3. 10 ff. (in a hymn to Demeter and Core) ᾇ τρισευδαίμων
ἀνήρ, ὃς . . . οἶδε πυργωθέντα πλοῦτον μὴ μελαμφαρεῒ κρύπτειν σκότῳ.
Cf. perhaps Pi. *P.* 5. 1 ff. (5, 12, 20, 46, 55 ff.) ; *O.* 2. 53 ff. (cf. Norden,
Aeneis VI, pp. 37 ff.).
    On the motif of μακαρισμός in general cf. Norden, *Agnostos Theos*,
99 ff., Dirichlet, o.c., especially 62 ff., O. Regenbogen, *Das Humanist.*
Gymnasium 41 (1930), 11 (= *Kl. Schr.* 113), Snell, *Hermes* 66 (1931),
75 n. 4 (= *Ges. Schr.* 85 n. 4), Festugière, *Eranos* 54 (1956), 78 ff.
    The μακαρισμός to the initiate is perhaps parodied in the 'Socratic
mysteries', Ar. *Nub.* 463 ff. (Dieterich, *RhM* 48 (1893), 277). It is
also perhaps not due to chance that the formula is used in the context
of the games in honour of the Eleusinian hero Diocles, in Theocr.
12. 28 f., 34 (cf. ad *Dem.* 153).
    ὄλβιος usually has a strong material connotation. Cf. *Il.* 24. 543 ff.,
Od. 17. 420, 18. 138, etc., ὄλβια (sc. δῶρα) *Od.* 7. 138, 8. 413, 13. 42,
etc. (and for Herodotus, Radermacher, *Gnomon* 14 (1938), 296). So
here, the prosperity which the Mysteries bring comes in this life as
well as after death. Cf. ad *Dem.* 486–9 (Ploutos). But the Greeks
were always aware that ὄλβος and πλοῦτος were gifts of the gods.
Hence these words acquired religious overtones. Cf. ὀλβιοδαίμων in
Il. 3. 182, ὄλβιοι ἥρωες in the islands of the blest, Hes. *Op.* 172,
Regenbogen, l.c., etc.
    τάδ' ὄπωπεν: the verb stresses that the Mysteries are essentially
a 'spectacle' for the initiates, that is, their climax is the ἐποπτεία,
and not any form of ritual actions (although these were also included :
cf. ad *Dem.* 474–6), or doctrines. Cf. especially Arist. fr. 15 R. τοὺς
τετελεσμένους οὐ μαθεῖν τι δεῖ, ἀλλὰ παθεῖν καὶ διατεθῆναι, γενομένους
δηλονότι ἐπιτηδείους. Cf. also Introduction, pp. 26 ff.
    481. ἀτελὴς ἱερῶν: in Homer ἀτελής occurs only once, meaning 'un-
accomplished' (*Od.* 17. 546). The sense 'uninitiated' is found also at
Pl. *Phdr.* 248 (τῆς τοῦ ὄντος θέας). Cf. τέλος, τέλη of initiation ceremonies, especially the Eleusinian Mysteries: A. fr. 387, S. *OC* 1050,
fr. 837 P. (ad *Dem.* 480–2), E. *Hipp.* 25, Pl. *Rep.* 560 e (and already in
Homer of marriage, *Od.* 20. 74) ; also PSI 1391 fr. B col. i 24 ~ P. Oxy.
2622 fr. 1 (a) 5 (cf. Lloyd-Jones, *Maia* 19 (1967), 211). Cf. τελεῖν,
τελετή, τελεστήριον, etc. Like ὄργια, δρᾶν, etc., τέλος and τελεῖν are
also used of religious services in general (cf. LSJ s.v. τελεῖν III 3,
τέλος I 6), and here also the more general sense perhaps precedes
the specialized one (cf. ad *Dem.* 273, 476).
    ἄμμορος: if one 'has no share in the rites' one 'does not have a share
(αἶσαν) of the same things after death'. But one may note that ἄμμορος
can also mean 'ill-fated' (*Il.* 6. 408, 24. 773; cf. *Od.* 20. 76?), like
δυσάμμορος, κάμμορος, (παν)άποτμος, etc. Cf. *IG* 14. 1942. 11 f. ἄμ-
μορος ἐσθλῆς | ἐλπίδος ἄνθρωποι (cf. ad *Dem.* 480–2).

481–2. οὗ ποθ' ὁμοίων ... εὐρώεντι: the language used here is indefinite, and probably deliberately so. The vague threat suggests more than it expresses. Later writers, although more explicit, sometimes use very general expressions: cf. Pi. *O*. 2. 67 τοὶ δ' ἀπροσόρατον ὀκχέοντι πόνον; S. fr. 837. 4 P. πάντ' ἔχει κακά; Pl. *Rep*. 365 a 3 δεινὰ περιμένει. Cf. also the euphemism of A. *Eum*. 339 f. θανὼν δ' οὐκ ἄγαν ἐλεύθερος (where the language is similar to that of *Dem*. 481–2: cf. 338 f. ὄφρ' ἂν γᾶν ὑπέλθῃ ∼ ὑπὸ ζόφῳ εὐρώεντι, 339 θανὼν δ' ∼ φθίμενός περ).

For the view that the language here too is euphemistic cf. also Boyancé, *RÉG* 75 (1962), 474–5; Kern, *RE* 16. 1216. 50.

482. ὑπὸ ζόφῳ εὐρώεντι: the dative ζοφῳ is not used in Homer, and the substitution of εὐρώεντι for the formulaic ἠερόεντι is perhaps due to a reminiscence of Hes. *Th*. 729–31. It also enhances the menacing tone of these lines. The underworld is seen as a place of physical decay, probably through its association with the grave (cf. Soph. *Aj*. 1167 τάφον εὐρώεντα), and the confusion between ghost and corpse. From this perhaps developed the idea of the 'hell of mud or slime' into which sinners, or the uninitiated, are plunged in later accounts of Hades. (εὐρώεις is used of mud and slime, ἰλύς and πηλός, in Opp. *H*. 1. 781, 2. 89.) Cf. Dodds, *Greeks and the Irrational*, 172 f. n. 102, West ad *Th*. 731, Dieterich, *Nekyia*, 46 ff.

483–9. After Demeter has given men her Mysteries, the two goddesses go up to Olympus, where they live beside Zeus. Greatly blessed is the man whom they love, for they send him Ploutos, who brings men wealth.

The narrative closes with a transposition to the present tense (485 ff.) thus taking the poem out of historical narrative, and returning to the timeless context of a hymn (as in *Dem*. 478–82), in preparation for the final invocation (490 ff.). For similar transitions at the end of a hymn cf. *Herm*. 574 ff. (576–8 ∼ *Dem*. 485–9, 579 ∼ *Dem*. 490–4, 580 = *Dem*. 495), *Hy*. 15. 6 ff. (7–8 νῦν δ' ἤδη κατὰ ... 'Ολύμπου ναίει ... ∼ *Dem*. 484–5, 9 ∼ *Dem*. 490–4). In these cases also the poet refers to where the deity is now to be found (*Herm*. 576, *Hy*. 15. 7–8), and in the case of Hermes to his benefits to men. A similar formula is found in *Hy*. 20. 5 ff. νῦν δὲ δι' "Ηφαιστον ... εὔκηλοι διάγουσιν ... For an epic example cf. *Il*. 24. 614 ff. νῦν δέ που ἐν πέτρῃσιν ... ἔνθα ... κήδεα πέσσει. Cf. also Hes. frr. 25. 26, 229. 6 (both on the apotheosis of Heracles), 23 (a). 25 (Iphimede immortalized), 91. 3 (apotheosis of Ino?), and in Pindar *P*. 9. 69–70 (return from myth to present context).

The same device is used in reverse at the beginning of a hymn: cf. *Ap*. 1 ff., Hes. *Th*. 1 ff., where, however, one may speak of a 'timeless' past tense (cf. West ad *Th*. 7). In the *Hymn to Apollo*, the poet returns again to the present at *Ap*. 12 ἔνθα καθίζουσιν (cf. *Dem*. 485), in preparation for the invocation of Leto: *Ap*. 14 χαῖρε ... Cf. also similarly *Hy*. 31. 15 ff. ἔνθ' ἄρ' ὅ γε στήσας ..., 17 χαῖρε, ἄναξ ...

On this device, see also van Groningen, *Composition littéraire archaïque*, 258 n. 4, 305 n. 2, Jacoby, *Der hom. Apollonhymnos*, 49 f. [728 f.].

483. ὑπεθήκατο: cf. ad *Dem.* 149, 273.

484. Cf. ad *Dem.* 36.

486. cεμναί τ' αἰδοῖαί τε: the epithets are used especially of Demeter and Persephone (cf. notes to *Dem.* 1, 190, 214 f., 478 f.). For cεμνή of Persephone alone cf. *Orph. Hy.* 29. 10, 71. 2 f.

In this context the words suggest the honours which men (and gods) pay them as deities on Olympus and πάρεδροι of Zeus. Cf. the description of Δίκη, the daughter and πάρεδρος of Zeus, in Hes. *Op.* 256 ff. (257a ∼ *Dem.* 486a above); Keyssner, *Gottesvorstellung*, 67 f.

μέγ' ὄλβιος: cf. Hdt. 6. 24. 2, E. *Hec.* 493, and μέγα πλούcιοc Hdt. 1. 32. 5, 7. 190.

486–9. The μακαρισμός of 480 is repeated with increased emphasis. But here it is those whom the goddesses love who are 'greatly blessed', and their reward is prosperity in this life, rather than happiness after death. αἶψα δέ (etc.) gives the reason why they are ὄλβιοι. Cf. Hes. *Th.* 97, *Hy.* 30. 9 ff., where this is expressed by asyndeton. The wording here is similar to that of both these passages, and the *Hymn to Ge* enlarges on the theme of god-given prosperity. Cf. also Hes. *Op.* 170–3, where the heroes in the islands of the blest are ὄλβιοι, and the earth bears crops for them three times a year.

Initiation was thought to bring one not only prosperity but also the protection of the gods in times of danger. The gods appear to those whom they love, and assist them in their difficulties. This is perhaps why Heracles as an initiate at Eleusis was able to carry off Cerberus (E. *HF* 613). This was particularly the case with initiation into the Samothracian mysteries, which gave one protection especially from the perils of the sea. Thus Orpheus can calm storms and summon up Glaucus (Diod. 4. 43. 1 f., 48. 6). Cf. also A.R. 1. 916 ff., Schol. ad loc., Diod. 5. 49. 5 f., Schol. Ar. *Pax* 277 f., Pfister, *RE Supp.* 4. 305 f., 320, Eitrem, *Symb. Osl.* 20 (1940), 150 f.

487. προφρονέωc φίλωνται: for πρόφρων of a favourable deity see notes to *Dem.* 226, and cf. especially Hes. *Th.* 419 f. ᾧ πρόφρων γε θεὰ ὑποδέξεται εὐχάς, καί τέ οἱ ὄλβον ὀπάζει . . ., *Hy.* 30. 7 f. (ad *Dem.* 486–7), 18 (∼ *Dem.* 494). On the active nature of φιλεῖν (488 f.) cf. ad *Dem.* 117.

488 f. Wealth (and Poverty) were regarded as entering men's houses and living with them. Cf. West ad *Th.* 593, and *Vit. Hom. Herod.* 469 (= Hom. *Epigr.* 15. 3), S. fr. 273 P., Chaeremon, fr. 36 N., Plut. *Mor.* 693 f, Phoenix, fr. 2. 8 (ad *Dem.* 489).

ἐφέςτιον: cf. the θεοὶ ἐφέςτιοι (Hierocles, *Berl. Klass. Texte*, iv. p. 54. 20 f.), the gods of the hearth and home. Ploutos receives an altar together with Hestia and other deities in *SIG*³ 985 (*c.* 100 B.C.).

489. Ploutos, the personification of wealth, is the son of Demeter and Iasius (Iasion) in Hes. *Th.* 969 ff. (cf. West ad loc.). The union is located in Crete, and the story is referred to in *Od.* 5. 125 ff. (cf.

also Zwicker, *RE* 21. 1033, 1037, and the vases described in Metzger, *Recherches*, 7 f., E. Simon, *Ant. Kunst* 9 (1966), 77). Demeter appears again as mother of Ploutos in *PMG* 885, with Persephone, and both goddesses are invoked and asked to preserve the city (cf. *Dem.* 490–5) :

> Πλούτου μητέρ' 'Ολυμπίαν ἀείδω (∼ Dem. 484–9),
> Δήμητρα ϲτεφανηφόροιϲ ἐν ὥραιϲ (∼ *Dem.* 492),
> cέ τε παῖ Διὸϲ Φερϲεφόνη (∼ 493)·
> χαίρετον, εὖ δὲ τάνδ' ἀμφέπετον πόλιν (∼ 494).

In Ar. *Thesm.* 295 ff., Ploutos follows Demeter and Core in a prayer to the deities of the Thesmophoria. Demeter herself is addressed as κουροτρόφε, ὀλβιοδῶτι, πλουτοδότειρα θεά, ϲταχυοτρόφε, παντοδότειρα in *Orph. Hy.* 40. 2 f. (cf. fr. 302, Diod. 1. 12. 4, Luc. *Dial. Meretr.* 7. 1).

Ploutos is especially the personification of agricultural prosperity, on which above all wealth depended. Cf. Hsch. s.v. πλοῦτοϲ· ἡ τῶν cπερμάτων ἐπικαρπία καὶ πανϲπερμία, and s.v. εὔπλουτον κανοῦν. . . . πλοῦτον γὰρ ἔλεγον τὴν ἐκ τῶν κριθῶν καὶ τῶν πυρῶν περιουϲίαν. As such, he does not appear very much in the higher literary tradition, but is an important figure in popular cult and poetry, e.g. in the Eiresione song, *Vit. Hom. Herod.* 469 ff. :

> αὐταὶ ἀνακλίνεϲθε θύραι· πλοῦτοϲ γὰρ ἔϲειϲι
> πολλόϲ, ϲὺν πλούτῳ δὲ καὶ εὐφροϲύνη τεθαλυῖα,
> εἰρήνη τ' ἀγαθὴ . . .

and in the similar song of the Κορωνιϲταί (Phoenix, fr. 2. 8 Powell). Cf. the ritual of 'Expulsion of Famine' at Chaeronea (Plut. *Mor.* 693 f.), performed by the archon at the state hearth, and by the citizens in their homes, in which they used to beat a slave and send him out of doors, crying ἔξω Βούλιμον, ἔϲω δὲ Πλοῦτον καὶ Ὑγίειαν. Schol. Hes. *Th.* 971 quotes the proverb πυρῶν καὶ κριθῶν, ὦ νήπιε, πλοῦτοϲ ἄριϲτοϲ.

The union of Demeter and Iasion is said to have taken place νειῷ ἐνὶ τριπόλῳ (*Od.* 5. 127, Hes. *Th.* 971), and this suggests the basic agricultural nature of the myth, ploughing and sowing being seen as counterparts of sexual intercourse (cf. West ad *Th.* l.c.). The myth has also been thought to reflect a mystery ritual of ἱερὸϲ γάμοϲ. This seems to be indicated by Theocritus 3. 50 f. (cf. Gow ad 3. 51, and notes to *Dem.* 478, 480). Iasion is connected with the mysteries of Samothrace (Diod. 5. 48 f.), and is said to have introduced the mysteries of Demeter to Sicily and other places (Arrian ap. Eust. 1528. 14). Cf. Gundel, *RE* 9. 752 ff.

At Eleusis, the announcement of the birth of a divine child to a goddess formed part of the secret ceremonies (cf. Introduction, pp. 26 ff.). The deities are not identified, and their anonymity is probably original, like that of the Μήτηρ and Κόρη, Θεόϲ and Θεά, and also the nursling Θρεπτόϲ (cf. ad *Dem.* 153). But it is natural to see in the child of the 'Mighty Queen' the personification of the fruits of the earth, symbolized in the ear of corn which Hippolytus in the same passage says was shown to the initiates at the climax of the Mysteries. As such, he may be identified with Ploutos. The announcement, ὑπὸ πολλῷ πυρί, of the birth of the Κοῦροϲ at Eleusis is perhaps parallel to the light which flashed forth annually from the cave in Crete in which Zeus, the Cretan Κοῦροϲ, or deity of vegetation, was born (Ant. Lib. 19. 1–2; cf. Lobeck, *Aglaophamus*, 59, 123 n. ii), and the Cretan origin of the myth of Iasion and Demeter suggests that it may be another form of the Cretan story of the birth of Zeus. (For theories of other Cretan links with the Mysteries cf. ad *Dem.* 123, 491, and Harrison, *Prolegomena*, 565 ff.)

For the initiates, who were 'spectators' of this event, the announcement of the divine birth must have served as a guarantee that they too would participate in the prosperity which it symbolized. Ploutos was the ground of their hopes for a good life, and hence Pindar (*O. 2.* 53 ff.) speaks of πλοῦτοϲ ἀρεταῖϲ δεδαιδαλμένοϲ (cf. Sapph. 148 ap. Schol. Pi. l.c.) as ἀϲτὴρ ἀρίζηλοϲ, ἐτυμώτατον ἀνδρὶ φέγγοϲ at the opening of his exposition of the mystic doctrine of life after death. Here, as Maass perceived (*Orpheus*, 273; cf. Norden, *Aeneis VI*, pp. 39 f.), one may see the influence of mystery-terminology. Iacchus, in Aristophanes' *Frogs* (342 ff.) is νυκτέρου τελετῆϲ φωϲφόροϲ ἀϲτήρ, and that this is an echo of mystic 'doctrine' is indicated by S. *Ant.* 1146 ff., where Iacchus (Dionysus) is invoked as πῦρ πνειόντων χοράγ' ἄϲτρων (cf. Schol. ad loc. κατὰ γάρ τινα μυϲτικὸν λόγον, τῶν ἀϲτέρων ἐϲτὶ χοραγόϲ. Cf. also E. *Ion* 1074 ff., especially 1078 ff.). In the same way Pindar calls Ploutos 'the truest light for men'.[1]

In art, Ploutos is normally portrayed as a child, with other deities (e.g. with Eirene in Cephisodotus' famous group). He appears on a number of vases of the fourth century B.C., in association with the Eleusinian circle of deities. A hydria from Rhodes[2] shows a female deity (Ge) rising out of the ground and holding out a cornucopia, on which a child sits, towards a goddess with a sceptre, probably Demeter. Core, Triptolemus, and Eumolpus are also present. The same child appears on a Kertsch pelike.[3] On one side the child stands, holding his cornucopia, between Demeter, who is seated, and the standing Core. Heracles, Triptolemus, Dionysus, Eumolpus, Aphrodite, and another female figure (whose identity is disputed) complete the picture. On the other side appears the same scene of a deity rising from the ground and holding the child, as on the Rhodes hydria. Here, the

---

[1] On the similarity of these words to those used later by Christian and Gnostic writers cf. Norden, *Agnostos Theos*, 395 f. With Pi. *O. 2.* 53 ff. *O. 1.* 1 ff. may perhaps be compared.

[2] S. Reinach, *Rev. Arch.* 1 (1900), 93 ff. = *Cultes, mythes et religions*, ii. 262 ff.; Metzger, *Représentations*, 244 ff., Pl. 32; Nilsson, *Op. Sel.* ii. 563 ff., *Gesch.* i³. 317 f., Taf. 44. 1. See Addenda.

[3] Nilsson, *Gesch.* i³. 318, Taf. 46. 1 and 2. Cf. E. Simon, *Ant. Kunst* 9 (1966), 72 ff.; but her identification of the second side of the pelike as the birth of Zagreus does not seem to me convincing.

goddess has an ivy crown, and the child wears a fawn-skin and ivy crown, and is received by Hermes, behind whom stands Athena. Demeter and Core (?) are shown above, and on the other side another god and goddess (Zeus and Hera?). A seated female figure with a tympanum is also shown.

The child with the cornucopia appears again on a fragmentary vase-lid in Tübingen,[1] standing between Demeter and Core, and on a late-fourth-century relief from the Agora at Athens,[2] showing Demeter seated and Core standing, accompanied by a male deity who holds the child on his left arm and a cornucopia in his left hand. They are approached by a group of worshippers.[3] He is also shown between the seated Demeter and standing Core on the Sandford–Graham pelike.[4] Dionysus and Eumolpus are also present.

Ploutos, the child with the cornucopia, is thus shown in immediate association with the traditional cult-group of the seated Demeter and standing Core (cf. Kern, *AM* 17 (1892), 125 ff.), in a way which illustrates well the verses of the *Hymn*. On the Rhodes hydria his birth from the earth is also portrayed. The representation is parallel to those of the birth of Erichthonius,[5] and to that of a British Museum hydria,[6] which portrays a deity rising from the earth and giving a child to Athena, in the presence of Zeus, Nike, and 'Oinanthe', whose name suggests that the child may here be Dionysus. On the Kertsch pelike there appears to be a fusion of the two figures of Ploutos and Dionysus, since Ploutos is shown on one side with the Eleusinian deities, whilst on the other the child is characterized by his attributes as Dionysus.[7]

The fusion of Dionysus with Ploutos is also suggested by a fourth-century hydria from Al Mina.[8] This shows the usual group of Core and Demeter, but here Demeter has a young boy on her knees. His dress (embroidered tunic and short boots) is that of Eumolpus, but he also wears a fawn-skin, which characterizes him as Dionysus. His position, however, is that normally taken by the child Ploutos.

This fusion is perhaps not as late as the fourth century, as has been suggested (Metzger, *Représentations*, l.c.). At the Lenaea, we are told (Schol. Ar. *Ran.* 482), the Dadouchos said καλεῖτε θεόν, and the people cried Cεμελήι' "Ιακχε πλουτοδότα. Here Dionysus is both Iacchus and πλουτοδότης. See Addenda.

A deity named Πλουτοδότας appears on one of the earliest representations relating to Eleusis, a vase from Locri of the mid sixth century showing Demeter mounting a chariot and holding ears of corn,

---

[1] Nilsson, *Gesch.* i³. 318, Taf. 45. 1.

[2] H. A. Thompson, *Hesp.* 17 (1948), 177, Pl. 54. 2 ; Nilsson, *Gesch.* i³. 318 f.

[3] A second relief of the same type, with a kneeling worshipper, is published by K. Schauenberg, *Jahrb. des d. arch. Inst.* 68 (1953), p. 57 Abb. 14, and p. 59.

[4] Metzger, *Recherches*, 34, Pl. 14. 1, Nilsson, *Gesch.* i³. Nachtr. 855 f., Taf. 53. 2.

[5] Cf. Cook, *Zeus*, iii. 181 ff., and notes to *Dem.* 231 ff.

[6] Cook o.c. Pl. 22.

[7] Cf. Metzger, *Représentations*, 253 ff., Nilsson, *Op. Sel.* ii. 563 ff., *Gesch.*, i³. 318.

[8] Metzger, *Recherches*, 52 f., Pl. 25. 2, Nilsson, *Gesch.* i³. Nachtr. 855 f., Taf. 53. 1.

accompanied by Triptolemus, Athena, Heracles, Hermes, and 'Ploutodotas'.[1] Nilsson sees this as an illustration of *Dem.* 486 ff., showing
Demeter about to spread her gift of corn abroad, Ploutodotas sym-
bolizing the prosperity which she brings.

The partial identity of Ploutos and Iacchus is suggested by the comparison of Pi. *O.* 2. 53 ff. with Ar. *Ran.* 342 ff. and S. *Ant.* 1146 ff.
(above). Iacchus and Dionysus are identified by Sophocles, *Ant.*
1115 ff. Cf. also S. fr. 959 P., *Trag. Gr. Frag. Adesp.* 140, Philodamus,
Paean, 32 ff. Later Iacchus is explicitly made the child of Demeter
(Lucr. 4. 1160, *Suda* s.v. "Ιακχος· Διόνυϲοϲ ἐπὶ τῷ μαϲτῷ, Kern, *RE* 9.
621). The question of Dionysus' place at Eleusis is very much in
dispute (see references ad *Dem.* 17).

The iconography of Iacchus on vases is a matter of dispute (see
Addenda to p. 318 n. 2), but certainly Ploutos and Dionysus are portrayed together on some vases, and they were evidently regarded
normally as separate personalities. Ploutos usually appears as a baby
or a young boy. There are, however, representations of an older deity
with a cornucopia. On one side of the Pourtalès vase he is shown as
a young man, reclining on a couch with Dionysus (Kerényi, *Eleusis*,
158, Fig. 46). More often, the deity is a venerable old man with a beard
(e.g. Nilsson, *Gesch.* i³. 319, Taf. 42. 1). He has sometimes been called
Ploutos, and Ploutos is in fact once called πρεϲβύτηϲ, in Ar. *Pl.* 265.[2]

Plouton may appear in the inscription of *c.* 500 B.C. recording
sacrifices at the Eleusinian Games (*IG* i². 5. 5; cf. ad *Dem.* 155). In
literature the first occurrence of the name is in A. *PV* 806, where it
is used of a fabulous river with gold in it. Ploutos is called Πλούτων
in S. frr. 273, 283 (Pearson: cf. ad loc.) and Ar. *Pl.* 727 (cf. Pl. *Crat.*
403 a, Str. 147, Luc. *Tim.* 21, *Orph. Hy.* 18. 4). The name is first used
of the god of the underworld in literature in S. *Ant.* 1200. The two figures
became distinguished, Ploutos as deity of wealth, and Plouton as
Hades, and the latter is usually shown as an older man, with a beard.[3]

Ploutos is thus later partly identified with other Eleusinian deities,
but his chief role is as the young child of Demeter, the guarantor and
bringer of prosperity, and so of men's hopes for happiness in the
present life, balancing their expectations of a better fate after death.

ἄφενοϲ: the neuter form is normally found in early epic, but the
masculine always occurs as a variant in Homer and Hesiod (*Il.* 1. 171,
23. 299, *Od.* 14. 99, Hes. *Th.* 112, *Op.* 24, 637), and later certainly
at Call. *Hy.* 1. 96, Crinagoras, *AP* 9. 234. 3, and as a variant at

---

[1] Metzger, *Recherches*, 8 ff., Nilsson, *Gesch.* i³. Nachtr. 860; cf. ad *Dem.* 153.

[2] It has been argued that Ploutos is only portrayed as a child, and that therefore
the older figure must be Plouton (K. Schauenberg, *JDAI* 68 (1953), 38 ff.). There
is, however, nothing to prove whether Ploutos or Plouton is meant. In fact, the
two personalities are in origin identical, Πλούτων being simply a variation of
Πλοῦτος (cf. 'Ιαϲίων/-ος, etc., Solmsen, *Beitr.* 46 ff., 53 ff.; *RE* 21. 1028).

[3] On the Locrian reliefs representing a young, beardless god or hero carrying
off a girl, see H. Prückner, *Die Lokrischen Tonreliefs* (Mainz, 1968), 70–4. Prückner
suggests that he is rather a local hero than Hades himself.

Call. *Hy.* 1. 94. Cf. West ad *Th.* 112, Fehrle, *Phil. Woch.* 1926, cols. 700-1.

490-5. The poet closes with an invocation to Demeter and Persephone, as goddesses of Eleusis, Paros, and Antron, asking them to grant him 'a pleasant livelihood' in return for his song. The last line is the traditional closing formula, announcing his intention to pass to another song.

The prayer to the deity is traditional at the end of a hymn. The poet prays for prosperity here, since this is especially the gift of Demeter and Persephone. Thus the same prayer is made to Ge (*Hy.* 30. 18), and Dionysus is asked to grant 'happiness in future seasons (i.e. years)' in *Hy.* 26. 12 f. Heracles and Hephaestus are also both asked to give ἀρετήν τε καὶ ὄλβον (15. 9, 20. 8), and Athena τύχην εὐδαιμονίην τε (11. 5). In a later hymn in the Homeric collection, to Helios, the poet again prays πρόφρων δὲ βίον θυμηρέ' ὀπάζειν (31. 17). Elsewhere he asks for victory in the poetic contest (6. 19 f.; cf. 10. 5, 24. 5, 25. 6). This is presumably implied also by *Dem.* 494. Poseidon is asked to help sailors (22. 7). The shorter *Hymn to Demeter* ends with a prayer that she should save the city (13. 3). Cf. *PMG* 885, Call. *Hy.* 6. 134 (to Demeter). Callimachus' hymn closes with a prayer for prosperity in the fields and peace in the city (134 ff.). Such a prayer for prosperity and peace or safety is common in classical hymns. Cf. Aristid. *Or.* 14. 228 κράτιστον οὖν ὥσπερ οἱ τῶν διθυράμβων τε καὶ παιάνων ποιηταὶ εὐχήν τινα προσθέντα οὕτω κατακλεῖσαι τὸν λόγον; K. Ziegler, *De precationum apud Graecos formis* (Diss. Breslau, 1905), 59 ff.

Prayers to a deity traditionally refer to his cult-place(s), and this is usually done either by means of a relative clause (e.g. *Il.* 1. 37 ff.) or, as here, a participial phrase. The two constructions are used interchangeably. Cf. *Hy.* 10. 4 f. (and similarly *Herm.* 2) for a participle, 29. 1 ff. (and similarly 6. 2 f., etc.) for a relative. For later examples cf. Norden, *Agnostos Theos*, 166 ff.

490. ἀλλ' ἄγε: for this expression used in passing to a final invocation cf. *Ap.* 165 (where a manuscript error also occurs, as here and in *Il.* 7. 299, 14. 314). Cf. similarly *Hy.* 20. 8 (ἀλλ' ἵληθ' . . .), and the citharoedic closing formula ἀλλὰ ἄναξ μάλα χαῖρε (Zenob. 599, *Paroem. Gr.* i, ed. Leutsch and Schneidewin; Hsch. s.v. ἀλλ' ἄναξ) which is like the more common formula of Homeric hymns καὶ σὺ μὲν οὕτω χαῖρε (*Hy.* 1. 20, etc.). ἀλλ' ἄγε can be used equally with a plural or singular verb. But it looks as if the poet originally intended to invoke Demeter, and then had second thoughts and added Persephone. Cf. ad *Dem.* 494.

491. Πάρον: Paros was one of the most important centres of Demeter's cult. The island was called Δημητριάς after her (Steph. Byz. s.v. Πάρος). According to one tradition (Steph. Byz. ibid.), Demeter received her information about the Rape at Paros from Cabarnos, who was the ancestor of the Cabarnoi, the priesthood of Demeter on

Paros (Hsch. s.v. *Κάβαρνοι· οἱ τῆc Δήμητροc ἱερεῖc, ὡc Πάριοι*; cf. *IG* 12. 5. 292), who may be compared with the Eumolpidae at Eleusis. Another tradition related that Demeter was received on Paros by King Melissos, and that she revealed her *πάθη* and *μυcτήρια* to his sixty daughters, who became nymphs, and gave them the *κάλαθοc* and loom of Persephone (Apollod. *FGH* 244 F 89). The name is derived from the title *μέλιccαι* which was given to the priestesses of Demeter and other deities (cf. Hsch. s.v. *μέλιccαι*, Schol. Pi. *P.* 4. 60, Porph. *de antro* 18). A connection with Crete has been deduced from this, on account of the role played by bee-nymphs in the myth of Zeus' birth (cf. Neustadt, *De Iove Cretico* (Diss. Berlin, 1906), 44 ff.). The island was colonized from Crete, and the cult of Demeter may have reached it from there.

From Paros the cult was taken to Thasos, according to tradition by Cleoboea, who was portrayed with Tellis, the grandfather of Archilochus, in Polygnotus' painting of Hades at Delphi (Paus. 10. 28. 3). Archilochus himself is said to have written a hymn to Demeter, and his poetry was probably influenced by the cult (cf. ad *Dem.* 192 ff., 3. Iambe). Later, the story of Miltiades' attempt to enter the Parian Megaron of Demeter, told by Herodotus (6. 134 f.), gives a clue to the site of the sanctuary. Like the Eleusinian one, it was situated on 'the hill outside the city' (6. 134. 2; cf. ad *Dem.* 271, 272). But despite exploration, the temple has not yet been found. Inscriptions attesting the cult exist (*IG* 12. 5. 225–8). One (227) is dedicated to Demeter Thesmophoros, Core, Zeus Eubouleus, and Babo (i.e. Baubo: cf. ad *Dem.* 192 ff., 3. Iambe). Another appears to indicate a temple of Persephone inside the city (*IG* 12. 5. 225; but the reading is not certain: cf. perhaps *IG* ii². 1363, col. i. 22, *Gnomon* 39 (1967), 280). Cf. also Rubensohn, *AM* 26 (1901), 206 ff., *JDAI* 70 (1955), 28, *RE* 18. 1842 ff., Wilamowitz, *Glaube*, ii. 42 n. 2, 418 n. 2.

Ἄντρωνα: Antron in Thessaly is not elsewhere mentioned for the cult of Demeter, but in the Homeric Catalogue it is named just after Pyrasus, which is called *Δήμητροc τέμενοc* (*Il.* 2. 695–7). According to Strabo(435) Pyrasus was also called Demetrion, and it had a grove and temple of Demeter. The town and cult both appear to have been incorporated with Thebai Phthiotides in the fourth century B.C. The worship of Demeter was evidently widespread in Thessaly in early times. There was also a shrine at Anthela, the centre of the Amphictionic League (Hdt. 7. 200), and in the Dotian plain tradition told of a grove dedicated to her by the Pelasgians (Call. *Hy.* 6. 24 ff.). Cf. also Kern, *RE* 4. 2714 f.

492. This is a variant of the vocative formula in *Dem.* 54 (cf. ad loc.). Here again, as at 54, there is hiatus. On *πότνια* see notes to *Dem.* 39, on *Δηοῖ* notes to *Dem.* 47.

493. Cf. *Dem.* 2, *Hy.* 13. 2. Persephone here receives her title of *Κούρη*, as Demeter is called *Πότνια* in 492.

494. πρόφρονεc ... ὀπάζειν: in this closing invocation the poet hesitates between singular and plural, returning to the singular in

Dem. 495, just as at the beginning he announced the subject as Demeter and then added her daughter (cf. ad *Dem.* 1–3). Ruhnken, following M's ὅπαζε, wished to write ἔχουσα in 490 and πρόφρων δ᾽ here. But this involves making ἀλλ᾽ ἄγε stand on its own, whereas it is normally followed by a verb without a connecting particle. If δέ is omitted the singular is very difficult after 493. ὀπάζειν is also an easier change. For the variation cf. *Il.* 16. 92, 21. 217, 22. 259 (all at the end of the verse), Hes. *Op.* 611. The infinitive for imperative is commonly used in prayers, e.g. *PMG* 871, S. *Ant.* 1144, etc., Adami, *Jahrb. f. Class. Phil.* Supp. 26 (1901), 243. (Cf. also *Il.* 2. 412–13, 3. 282–6, 7. 179, *Od.* 17. 354, where it is used for the third person imperative.) The use is probably archaic, and hence tends to be preserved in religious language. There may also be a reluctance to address a direct command to a deity: the infinitive perhaps implies a verb on which it depends (*sc.* 'I ask you'). In Homer, the infinitive for imperative is often found after an imperative or future, or similar preliminary verb (cf. Monro, *HG*² § 241). The origin of this use, however, is not ellipse, but it is rather due to the nature of the infinitive as the nominal form of the verb. Cf. Chantraine, *GH* ii. 316 ff., Schwyzer, *Gr. Gr.* ii. 380.

πρόφρονες: cf. ad *Dem.* 226, 487.

ἀντ᾽ ᾠδῆς: the contracted form does not occur in Homer. Cf. *Ap.* 20, *Hy.* 30. 18, and Attic (but Aeschylus uses only ἀοιδή). In Hes. *Th.* 48 the manuscripts have λήγουσαί τ᾽ ἀοιδῆς (*v.l.* λήγουσί τ᾽) which is unmetrical. ἀοιδῆς, with synizesis, (or ᾠδῆς) has been proposed, but the line is probably spurious (West ad loc.). Cf. also Pi. *N.* 11. 18, where μελίζεμεν ἀοιδαῖς is unmetrical and has been variously emended.

The alternation ᾠδῆς/ἀοιδῆς in 494–5 is paralleled by *Aph.* 97–8 νυμφάων/νυμφῶν. Cf. also *Aph.* 62–3 ἀμβρότῳ/ἀμβροσίῳ, 197–8 οὕνεκα/ἕνεκα. See Addenda.

βίοτον θυμήρε᾽ ὀπάζειν: the form θυμήρης is only found once in Homer (*Od.* 10. 362), as a neuter adverb. Elsewhere, θυμαρής is used (*Il.* 9. 336, *v.l.* θυμηρέα; *Od.* 17. 199, 23. 232), although the tradition hesitated between the two forms (cf. Schol. A ad *Il.* 9. 336). θυμήρης is found in *Hy.* 30. 18, 31. 17, and in Hellenistic poetry, A.R. 1. 705 (but θυμηδές Fränkel), 714 (θυμηδές vulg., Fränkel), Mosch. 2. 29 (cf. Bühler ad loc.), and late prose. The difference of accent should be noted (cf. Hdn. Gr. 2. 65). Bechtel (*Lexilogus*, s.v. θυμήρης) argued that θυμήρης was the correct form in Homer also, on the analogy of εὐήρης, χαλκήρης (all being derived from the root of ἀραρίσκω). But θυμαρής seems to be a genuine form in Homer. The survival of the long alpha may be due to a consciousness of the derivation. Later θυμήρης perhaps prevailed because it was regarded as the proper Ionic form.

ὀπάζειν is used especially in contexts such as this. Cf. *Od.* 18. 19, Hes. *Th.* 420, *Hy.* 30. 18, 31. 17, A.R. 1. 249, 4. 1600; also *Hy.* 24. 5 χάριν δ᾽ ἅμ᾽ ὅπασσον ἀοιδῇ, Bacch. 17. 130 ff. (end of poem) Δάλιε, χόροισι Κηΐων | φρένα ἰανθεὶς | ὅπαζε θεόπομπον ἐσθλῶν τύχαν; Ar.

Thesm. 972 f. χαῖρ' ὦ ἑκάεργε, | ὅπαζε δὲ νίκην. It is particularly used of deities and in later poetry almost exclusively so.

495. The poet closes with a traditional formula of passage to another song. The *Homeric Hymns* were, at least in origin, preludes to epic recitation (cf. Introduction, pp. 3 f. and notes to *Dem.* 1–3). This is made clear by *Aph.* 293 (= *Hy.* 9. 9, 18. 11)

ϲεῦ δ' ἐγὼ ἀρξάμενοϲ μεταβήϲομαι ἄλλον ἐϲ ὕμνον.

Having sung of the deity in his proemium, the poet goes on to the subject of his main recitation. There is no reason to suppose that the formulae of *Dem.* 495, etc. were added at a later date to the larger hymns (cf. R. Böhme, *Das Prooimion*, 76 n. 78). Cf. also the hymns to Helios and Selene (*Hy.* 31. 18 f., 32. 18 ff.). There the poet announces his intention of going on to sing of the deeds of heroes. The lines, although late, presumably reflect genuine earlier epic tradition.

In *Dem.* 495 (etc.) the intention seems to be the same, although the sense is less clear. 'I shall mention (i.e. sing of) both you and another song also' seems to mean 'As of you (now) so of another song I will bethink me (next).' Elsewhere, however, the poet proclaims his intention of singing of the deity (or hero) *again* on a *future* occasion. Cf. perhaps *Ap.* 177 f. αὐτὰρ ἐγὼν οὐ λήξω ἑκηβόλον Ἀπόλλωνα | ὑμνέων . . . There, however, the lines lead on directly to another hymn to Apollo (179 ff.), and may have been added to make the link. Theocritus 1. 145 is clearer:

χαίρετ', ἐγὼ δ' ὕμμιν καὶ ἐϲ ὕϲτερον ἅδιον ᾀϲῶ.

(In 17. 135 f. it is not clear whether the reference is to past or future.) This might suggest the sense for *Dem.* 495 (etc.): 'I shall sing of you again *later*, and another song *now*.' But the first interpretation is better suited to the other formula of *Aph.* 293 (etc.).

It might be possible to connect the formula with those by which the poet announces his intention of singing of the deity 'at the beginning and end' of his song, or 'first and last' (cf. West ad *Th.* 34, Gow ad Theocr. 17. 1 f.). This probably means strictly that he will return to the deity of his proemium at the end of his recitation, although, as West points out, this practice is by no means always observed. The line would then mean 'I will return to you later, and sing another song now.'

Alternatively, this use might apply to the beginning and end of the proemium (cf. Schwabl, *Proc. Afr. Class. Assoc.* 2 (1959), 27). In that case, *Dem.* 495 might mean: 'I shall mention you (again) now, and then go on to another song.' But this seems a less natural interpretation (and cf. West, l.c., *contra* Schwabl).

It is in any case probable that the formula had long ago become so stereotyped that its original sense was no longer known or remembered. In the case of *Dem.* 495, the use of the singular ϲεῖο after the plurals in 490–4 (unless ὅπαζε is right in 494) might suggest this (cf. van Groningen, *Composition littéraire archaïque*, 73 f.). In *Hy.* 25. 7, 27. 22, 29. 14,

33. 19, the plural ὑμέων is used. But the use of the singular here is perhaps due to the fact that the poet is really singing a 'hymn to Demeter' (cf. ad *Dem.* 1–3).

καὶ . . . καὶ . . .: the sense 'both . . . and' is very rare in early epic and is probably not found at all in Homer (cf. Ebeling, 618 f.). In the *Hymns*, however, it is 'beginning to establish itself' (Denniston, *GP* 324, with reference to this formula). Cf. notes to *Dem.* 395.

μνήcομ' ἀοιδῆc: μνήcομαι is probably a subjunctive expressing resolve: cf. *Ap.* 1, Hes. *Th.* 1, West ad loc. The verb is used virtually as a synonym of ἀείδειν. Cf. *Hy.* 1. 19, *Ap.* 1, 160, *Hy.* 7. 1 f., etc. The Muses were the daughters of Μνημοcύνη, and they brought songs to one's mind. Cf. *Il.* 2. 491–2: the poet could not tell of the greater number of the Greeks,

εἰ μὴ 'Ολυμπιάδες Μοῦcαι, Διὸc αἰγιόχοιο
θυγατέρες, μνηcαίαθ' ὅcοι ὑπὸ "Ιλιον ἦλθον.

APPENDIX I

ELEUSINIAN TOPOGRAPHY (*Dem.* 99, 270–2)

A. *Parthenion and Callichoron*

In *Dem.* 99 Demeter, on arrival at Eleusis, sits down by the Παρθένιον φρέαρ. Here she meets the daughters of King Celeus, who have come to draw water, and who escort her from here to the palace. In *Dem.* 272, Demeter mentions (the well) Καλλίχορον (or Καλλίχορος), as a landmark: her temple is to be built above it, beneath the wall of the acropolis.

Demeter pretends to have come from Thoricos (*Dem.* 126), so that she is presumably on the road from Athens. Parthenion, therefore, is unlikely to be identical with Anthion, the name of the well in Pamphos' epic version (Paus. 1. 39. 1), since this was on the road to Megara, and Demeter pretended there to be an Argive woman (cf. Malten, *ARW* 12 (1909), 306). Anthion and Callichoron are also separately located by Pausanias (see below).

Later, the well at which Demeter sat was called Callichoron (Call. *Hy.* 6. 15, fr. 611 Pf., Nic. *Ther.* 486, Apollod. 1. 5. 1). Pausanias (1. 38. 6) mentions Callichoron as the place where 'the women of the Eleusinians first set up a dance and sang in honour of the goddess'. It was near the temple of Artemis Propylaea and Poseidon Pater, at the entrance to the Sanctuary. It can still be seen to-day, in the south-east corner of the outer court, next to the Greater Propylaea (Mylonas, *Eleusis*, Fig. 4 No. 10 and Fig. 33). Its stone construction is dated by the archaeologists to the Pisistratean period (Mylonas, o.c. 97 ff.).

It would be natural for the girls to fetch water from the well nearest to the city wall (cf. ad *Dem.* 98 ff.), and it is reasonable to suppose that Parthenion and Callichoron are two names for the same well. Later tradition implies this, and if there were χοροί of παρθένοι around it this would explain the two names.[1] Originally, perhaps, Anthion was also another name for this well, later transferred elsewhere (cf. *Hy.* 30. 14 ff., and Introduction, pp. 18 ff.[2]

---

[1] Cf. also Nilsson, *Gesch.* i³. 656 n. 7, Förster, *Raub und Rückkehr*, 12, Flander, *De Interpolationibus hymni in Cererem* (Parchim, 1879), 12; and notes to *Dem.* 6 ff.

[2] Curtius (*Götting. Abh.* 8 (1859), 3) wished to identify Anthion and Callichoron. Cf. also Allen and Halliday ad *Dem.* 99, Kerényi, *Eleusis*, 36 f. But see below for doubts about a similar transference.

For the identification of Callichoron and Parthenion cf. Orph. *Arg.* 729 ff., where a river in Asia Minor has both names.[1]

Callichoron originally stood in a relatively free space, outside the peribolos of the Sanctuary, and dances may have been held *round* it. But after the Persian Wars a new peribolos was built, passing close to the well on the south side, and its area was further restricted in the late fourth century, when a square tower was added, to the south-east. At this time the court of the well was paved, and a parapet wall erected round it, with two doors (Mylonas, o.c. 98, 110). In the Roman period it was completely enclosed through the building of the Greater Propylaea and the Roman outer court, which stopped at the well on the north-east side. Access remained via a door opening on to the bottom step of the Greater Propylaea (Mylonas, 98).

It thus remained as a landmark throughout the history of the Sanctuary, and was respected by the post-Pisistratean builders. Euripides (*Ion* 1074) seems to refer to dances *beside* it (παρὰ Καλλι-χόροιϲι παγαῖϲ). Whether dances continued to be held by it after the building of the parapet wall in the fourth century B.C. is uncertain. Pausanias refers only to its use in the past for this purpose.

The date of the well's stone construction, in the second half of the sixth century, does not necessarily preclude its existence in some form before this period, and if it is to be identified with either the Parthenion or Callichoron of the *Hymn*, this must be assumed. An earlier well, however, was found by the excavators directly next to, and below, the Telesterion, at the foot of the north-east corner of the retaining wall of the Stoa of Philon (Mylonas, 44 ff., and W in Figs. 6 and 18). This existed before the Archaic period, and is associated in the seventh century with a broad court, an altar, and a stepped podium. The court became unusable in the Pisistratean period, when a peribolos wall was built over it. Mylonas holds that this was the original Callichoron, and that the name was transferred in the sixth century to the well in the outer court of the Sanctuary. The court was the site of the sacred dances, and the podium was used by spectators (o.c. 44 ff., 70 ff.). Mylonas also thinks that the name Parthenion was originally given to the well in the outer court.[2]

The attraction of this hypothesis is that it fits well with Demeter's instructions to build her temple Καλλιχόρου καθύπερθεν (*Dem.* 272). The temple should be identical with the later Telesterion, but this is

[1] In A.R. 2. 904 ff. Callichoros is the name of a river by which mystic rites of Dionysus are held (907–8 ὀργιάϲαι, ϲτῆϲαί τε χορούϲ . . . ἀμειδήτουϲ νύκταϲ: cf. *Dem.* 200), and the next landmark is a river Parthenios (936 ff.).

[2] For a full discussion see Mylonas, *The Hymn to Demeter and her Sanctuary at Eleusis* (St. Louis, 1942).

about a hundred metres from the later Callichoron, and so not *directly* above it.[1]

One might accept Mylonas's identification of the original Callichoron, and at the same time assume that Parthenion and Callichoron are two names for the same well, as argued above. But it seems rather unlikely that such an important landmark of the cult should have been moved. If one accepts the ancient identification of Callichoron as the right one the topographical difficulty is not, I think, insuperable.[2] On balance, therefore, I am inclined to prefer to regard the traditional location of Callichoron as the original one.[3]

B. *The temple of Demeter*

In *Dem.* 270–2, Demeter commands the Eleusinians to build her 'a great temple, and an altar under it . . . below the citadel and high wall, over and above Callichoron, upon a jutting hill'.

The site of the Telesterion (as modern scholars call it) of classical times lies on an artificially terraced slope at the foot of the acropolis of Eleusis. The recent excavators, led by Kourouniotes (cf. Mylonas, *Eleusis*, 33 ff., 175 ff.), argue that the Telesterion is Demeter's temple. In the fifth century B.C. and later it is referred to as a νεώς (or *templum*).[4]

They also revealed the existence, below the later Telesterion, of a megaron-type building of the Mycenaean period, which they considered to have been used for a religious purpose. No cult-objects were found, but their absence could be attributed to their removal by earlier excavators, and on the strength of 'continuity of cult' a religious use for the building was presumed.

On the strength of the Mycenaean remains it was also argued that there must have been a covered building in the Geometric period, and not merely a terrace, as Noack thought. A small elliptical piece of wall is all that survives.[5] This was followed by a building of the Early Archaic period.[6] In the Pisistratean period the Sanctuary was de-

---

[1] This was regarded by Noack as an argument *against* identifying temple and Telesterion. See below.

[2] A similar difficulty arises in the case of the spring referred to in *Ap.* 300 as *near to* the temple of Apollo (cf. Allen and Halliday ad loc., Frazer ad Paus. 10. 8. 9, 12. 1).

[3] In that case, it must be admitted, Mylonas's well, with his altar, court, and podium, remains unexplained.

[4] *IG* i². 81. 8; 313. 103; Schol. Aristid. p. 308. 27 Dind.; *AP* 9. 298. 1; cf. Livy 31. 14. 7, 30. 9; Vitruv. 7, praef. 16 f.; Noack, *Eleusis*, 59 f., Mylonas, *Eleusis*, 40, Rubensohn, *JDAI* 70 (1955), 34.

[5] Mylonas, o.c. 57 ff.; but L. Deubner, *Abh. Berl. Akad.* 1945/6 Nr. 2, 17–19, argues that it belongs to a peribolos.

[6] Oblong, rather than square, as Noack supposed, and tentatively dated by Mylonas to the time of Solon (o.c. 63 ff.).

veloped considerably, and a larger, square Telesterion was built (Mylonas, o.c. 78 ff.).

If the Archaic building belongs to the late seventh or early sixth century, one might argue that it was not the first Telesterion, since the *Hymn* could hardly assign so recent a construction to the mythical period. But that is perhaps debatable. Another possible argument for the existence of an earlier temple is that the site is unsuitable for the large buildings of the classical period, and already in the Geometric period it was necessary to build an artificial terrace on the slope. The choice could have been due to a pre-existing tradition, dating from the Mycenaean period (cf. Mylonas, 43 f.). But a tradition of continuing worship does not necessarily indicate a cult-building, and a free-standing temple would be a rarity at that time.[1] This might, however, be explained as due to the special nature of the rites of Demeter. In classical times, at least, her temples were often situated outside the city (cf. notes on *Dem.* 271).

Noack's arguments against the identification of Telesterion and temple are well answered by Mylonas (o.c. 38 ff.). Noack held that the Telesterion's square plan made the name 'temple' inappropriate, that it does not lie 'above Callichoron', and that the ground is not exactly a 'jutting hill' (*Dem.* 272). He believed that the Mysteries were celebrated in the open air before the Archaic Telesterion was built, and he argued that the Telesterion had no place for the monumental statue-group of Demeter and Core postulated by O. Kern,[2] which must therefore have been kept in a separate temple. He was followed by Allen and Halliday, who also argued that as Demeter occupies her temple *before* the institution of her rites (*Dem.* 302 ff., 473 ff.), these must belong to a separate site. Noack found his temple on the rocky spur above the Telesterion, near the modern Panagia chapel, where traces exist of a building dated by him to the period before the Persian Wars.

Noack's temple has now been shown to be of Roman date, and there is no evidence for an earlier one on the site.[3] The question of the Telesterion's name and shape has been discussed above, as has that of its relation to Callichoron. The site of the Telesterion was originally a steeply inclined slope, and 'jutting hill' is not impossible. The cult-statues could have been set in the bases noted by Travlos in the Telesterion.[4]

---

[1] The prehistoric sanctuary on Ceos could perhaps be adduced as some sort of parallel. Cf. Caskey, *Hesp.* 31 (1962), 263 ff., 33 (1964), 314 ff., 35 (1966), 363 ff.

[2] *AM* 17 (1892), 125 ff. But see Rizzo, *RM* 25 (1910), 109 ff.; Metzger, *Recherches*, 42 ff.; also M. Ruhland, *Die eleusinischen Gottheiten* (Strassburg, 1901), 104 f.

[3] Travlos (*Arch. Delt.* 16 (1960 (1962)), Chronika, 55 ff.), argues that it was in fact a treasury.

[4] Mylonas, 189. Other solutions have been proposed: see above (n. 2).

Finally, Allen and Halliday's argument is worthless. Demeter's command to build a temple is followed immediately by her promise to institute her rites (273–4), and the two naturally go together. The delay is due to the necessary incorporation of the themes of the Famine and Return of Persephone (see notes to *Dem.* 305 ff.).

There is, therefore, no reason to doubt the identification of the 'great temple' with the Telesterion. One may well feel some doubts about the religious purpose claimed for the Mycenaean building, in the absence of positive evidence; and there is certainly no need to accept Mylonas's view (33 ff.), that the *Hymn* must refer specifically to the building of a temple in the Mycenaean period. But one's judgement on these issues is not of material importance for the interpretation of the *Hymn*.

APPENDIX II

ENJAMBEMENT, AND THE LANGUAGE OF THE *HYMN*

A. *Enjambement (cf. Introduction, pp. 60 f.)*

A notable stylistic feature, in which the *Hymn* stands apart from most other early epic poetry, is its frequent use of what Milman Parry called 'necessary' enjambement.[1] A comparative table, setting out the percentage of lines with no enjambement (I), 'unperiodic' enjambement (II), and 'necessary' enjambement (III), will make this clear:

	I	II	III
Iliad	48·5	24·8	26·6[2]
Odyssey	44·8	26·6	28·5[2]
Theogony	33·0	39·1	27·9[3]
Works and Days	43·0	27·2	29·7[3]
Shield	34·3	29·5	36·2[3]
Demeter	39·6	17·5	42·9[4]
Delian Apollo (1–178)	c. 33	36	31
Pythian Apollo (179–546)	c. 38	29	33
Hermes	c. 38	34	28
Aphrodite	38·6	33·4	27·6

In Homer the frequency of necessary enjambement per 100 lines varies between 21 and 33, in the *Theogony* and *Works and Days* between 14 and 38, whereas in the *Hymn to Demeter* the variation is between 37 and 44. Only the *Shield*, with a range of 29 to 42, approaches closer to the *Hymn*, but still shows a considerably lower frequency.[5]

Parry used his analysis of enjambement to illustrate the 'oral' character of Homer, in contrast to Apollonius and Virgil, whose epics

---

[1] Cf. *TAPA* 60 (1929), 200 ff. = *The Making of Homeric Verse*, ed. A. Parry (Oxford, 1971), 251 ff.

[2] Using Parry's statistics.

[3] Using Edwards's statistics, in *Language of Hesiod*, p. 96.

[4] Figures for *Demeter* are based on Parry's criteria, for the sake of comparison. For further discussion of the subject see Edwards o.c. 93 ff., and Kirk, *YCS* 20 (1966), 105 ff.

[5] Cf. Edwards, 98 f.

show a much greater use of necessary enjambement (*Argonautica*, 49·1, *Aeneid* 49·2). The *Hymn* appears to be closer to later literary epic than any other early epic piece of comparable length. Does this indicate that it is a literary composition?

If this is so, it is strange that the *Hymn to Hermes*, which has often been considered later than the other major hymns, should be closer in this respect to Homer and Hesiod.[1] The Pythian part of the *Hymn to Apollo* also belongs to the sixth century, if the reference in *Ap.* 540 ff. is to the removal of the Crisaeans from control of Delphi in the First Sacred War. In that case, it could hardly be much earlier than the latest possible date for the *Hymn to Demeter*, but it also shows a more 'traditional' use of enjambement.[2]

If we take one type of enjambement, discussed by Parry, where an adjective in one verse agrees with a noun in the next, it is notable that this occurs five times in the *Hymn*, i.e. about once in a hundred lines. Parry noted that the frequency in Homer is about one in 200 lines (o.c. 264), most examples being with πᾶς, πολύς, or ἄλλος. Two examples in the *Hymn* are of this type (10, 77). Of the other three, one has several parallels in Homer (268–9 ἥ τε μέγιστον | . . . ὄνεαρ καὶ χάρμα . . . cf. *Il.* 15. 37–8, *Od.* 5. 185–6; *Ap.* 85–6 ὅς τε μέγιστος | ὅρκος, *Il.* 17. 21–2 οὔ τε μέγιστος | θυμός), although in none of these cases is the adjective separated from the noun by other words. Another is a case of formulaic adaptation (83–4 οὔ τοι ἀεικὴς | γαμβρός: cf. *Il.* 9. 70, *Dem.* 120 οὔ τοι ἀεικές; cf. Parry, l.c.). The third is more unusual (169–70 ταὶ δὲ φαεινὰ | . . . ἄγγεα: cf. ad loc.). The word order is more complex than anything in Homer, and the noun is considerably postponed. Curiously enough there is a partial parallel for this case, in *Il.* 16. 104–5 φαεινὴ | πήληξ, although here the noun follows directly. Kirk (*TCS* 20 (1966), 110) discusses this, and suggests that it 'might reflect literate intervention'.[3]

Dem. 169 is certainly abnormal by early epic standards, and does go a step beyond anything in Homer. Yet the frequency of such adjective–noun enjambement in the *Hymn* is in no way comparable to that of Apollonius (one in twenty lines) or Virgil (one in ten lines: cf. Parry, o.c. 265). Admittedly, however, one cannot use these epics, which are so much later, as a proper standard of comparison.

The higher frequency of necessary enjambement, taken together

---

[1] Cf. Porter, *TCS* 12 (1951), 33 f. for its metrical differences from other early epic; Hoekstra, *Sub-epic Stage*, 10; Allen and Halliday, civ–cvi; Humbert, *Homère, Hymnes*, pp. 114–15.

[2] *Ap.* 540 ff. might of course be an addition: cf. Parke and Wormell, *The Delphic Oracle* i. 107 f. But I do not myself consider that this is at all likely.

[3] Cf. Leaf ad loc., who comments that 'the position of the epithet . . . is hardly Homeric', and can find no other comparable example except *Il.* 13. 611.

with other evidence for greater complexity of word order (cf. Introduction, p. 60, and see also Appendix V), might suggest a later stage
of development in epic technique than that of Homer. But in view of
the *Hymn*'s other traditional characteristics, I am very doubtful
whether these features alone can be taken as evidence for a 'literary'
poet.

B. *The language of Hesiod, and the* Homeric Hymns (*cf. Introduction,*
pp. 33 ff.)

The general similarity of the *Hymn*'s language to that of Hesiod
may be further illustrated by applying a number of tests recently used
by Edwards, in his book *The Language of Hesiod*, to illustrate the relationship of Hesiod to Homer.

1. A very rough statistical test applied by Edwards is an analysis
of 'the proportion of word-forms used by Hesiod which are identical
with forms found in the *Iliad*'.[1] In the *Theogony* the percentage of
word-forms which also occur in the *Iliad* is 78·9, in the *Works and
Days* 75·6, and in the *Shield* 81·0. *Dem.* 1–50 shows *c.* 250 Iliadic
word-forms in a total of 320, i.e. 78 per cent, which is very close to
the *Theogony*. The average of non-Iliadic forms per line in *Dem.* 1–50
is 1·4, and this is exactly the same as the average for the *Theogony*.
Dem. 187–211 is a scene which forms the *aition* for part of the Eleusinian ritual, and might therefore be expected to show a higher
frequency of non-Iliadic forms. In fact it has only 1·76 per line, which
is comparable to *Th.* 1–50 and 251–401, and to the average for the
whole of the *Works and Days* (1·7).

It is doubtful whether much significance can be attributed to such
figures (cf. Edwards, 29). The *Shield* emerges as closest to Homer, but
this is clearly due to its subject-matter, and to the imitative nature of
the poem, since it is certainly later than the *Theogony* or *Works and
Days*. The *Shield* in fact is a useful defence with which to parry
attempts to establish by such methods alone a relative chronology of
early epic poetry.[2] But at least one can say that a rough test of this
kind brings out the traditional nature of the language of these poems.

2. Edwards also discusses Parry's 'principle of economy' (55 ff.),
and shows how apparent breaches of this in Hesiod either have
parallels in Homer, or may be explained by reference to their contexts, or by the operation of analogy.[3] Similar cases in the *Hymn* have
been discussed (Introduction, pp. 46 ff.), and most of them can also
be explained in these ways.

---

[1] o.c. 28 ff.; for a definition of 'word-form' cf. Edwards, 28 n. 6.

[2] Cf. M. L. West, *Gnomon* 35 (1963), 11, *CR* 15 (1965), 159.

[3] Cf. Parry, *L'Épithète traditionelle*, 218 ff. = *Making of Homeric Verse*, 173 ff.

3. Edwards analyses the proportions in Hesiod of alternative genitive forms in -αο/-εω and -άων/-έῳν/-ῶν, and shows that the older endings tend to be preserved mainly in traditional phrases whereas the use of the newer ones is extended (122 ff.). The number of these in the *Hymn* is too small to allow any comparison with Hesiod and Homer.[1]

4. More significant are the proportions of -οισι/-οις and -ῃσι/-ῃς(-αις) datives (cf. Introduction, pp. 53 f.). If one includes cases where the short form precedes a vowel, the proportions of short to long are: *Iliad* and *Odyssey* 1:5, *Theogony* 1:2·5, *Works and Days* 1:2, *Demeter* 1:2. But one must distinguish cases of short forms before a vowel, which may conceal -οις(ι)/-ῃς(ι). The numbers are as follows:[2]

	-οις/-ῃς(-αις) before consonant	-οις/-ῃς before vowel	-οισι/-ῃσι
Iliad	79	214	1,534
Odyssey	105	149	1,270
Theogony	29	28	139
Works and Days	28	18	94
Demeter	22	10	66
Apollo 1–178	3	2	16
Apollo 179–546	4	5	59
Hermes	2	10	80
Aphrodite	4	9	57

The remarkable fact which emerges here is that whereas *Demeter* is close to Hesiod in its proportion of short forms before a consonant, the other hymns show a very infrequent use of these and are nearer to Homer. This is particularly notable in the case of *Hermes*, with only two certain short forms out of ninety-two! Once again, one may doubt whether this can be used as a dating criterion. But it is noticeable that the poet of *Demeter* clearly adopts Hesiodic short forms where he could have used long ones (e.g. *Dem.* 11 ἀθανάτοις τε θεοῖς ἠδὲ θνητοῖς ἀνθρώποις cf. *Th.* 373, 415, fr. 1. 7, where ἀθανάτοισι θεοῖς ἠδὲ θνητοῖσι βροτοῖσιν would have been possible).[3] Other examples are due to adaptation of Homeric or Hesiodic formulae (*Dem.* 5, 40–1, 269, 403,

---

[1] Κρονίδεω *Dem.* 414∼ *Th.* 572, *Op.* 71; ὡρέων 399; ἀπαςῶν 110, θυςιῶν 312. ἀπαςῶν has no parallels in Homer or Hesiod, but could be due to corruption: cf. note ad loc.

[2] Using Reichelt's figures for Homer and Hesiod, but my own counts for the *Hymns*. H. Troxler, *Sprache und Wortschatz Hesiods* (Zürich, 1964), 68, gives the figures for short forms before consonant as *Iliad* 39, *Odyssey* 75, *Theogony* 28, *Works* 30.

[3] Cf. F. Krafft, *Vergleichende Untersuchungen zu Homer und Hesiod* (Göttingen, 1963), 46 n. 4, Troxler, o.c. 67 f. Note also *Ap.* 81 ∼ 259, 288, Wilamowitz, *Ilias und Homer*, 446 n. 2!

473), illustrating the way in which such 'recent' forms would tend to come in.

5. Troxler (o.c. (p. 334 n. 2), 52 ff.) and Edwards (o.c. 122) also discuss the alternative forms of genitives in -ου/-οιο. The proportions of forms with certain -ου (i.e. *in arsi* before a consonant, and in the final thesis), as a percentage of all o-stem genitive singular forms, are: *Iliad* 20 per cent, *Odyssey* 24 per cent, *Theogony* 33 per cent, *Works and Days* 50 per cent, *Shield* 35 per cent, *Demeter* 32 per cent (23 out of 72), *Delian Apollo* (1–178) 17 per cent, *Pythian Apollo* (179–546) 27 per cent, *Hermes* 19 per cent, *Aphrodite* 33 per cent. Once again, *Demeter* is close to the *Theogony*. The low figure for *Hermes* is again striking, and the percentage of -οιο forms in this hymn (58 per cent) is higher than that of Homer (52 per cent) or Hesiod (38·5 per cent). *Demeter* has 51·3 per cent in -οιο.

6. Neglect of digamma is also discussed by Edwards (132 ff.). He shows that it tends, naturally, to occur in the context of formulaic innovations. For the *Hymn* see Introduction, pp. 64 f. The only examples which lack Homeric parallels are:

Dem. 6, 418 ἠδ' ἴα, καὶ 'Ιάνθη (no neglects in Homer or Hesiod in ten examples; but ἴον occurs only once in Homer, and cf. *Il.* 13. 354 ἠδ' ἴα = 'one').

66, 315 θάλος εἴδεϊ, πολυήρατον εἶδος. *Il.* 3. 224 shows neglect before εἶδος, but the line has been suspected; in *Od.* 8. 169 the manuscripts have γάρ τ' εἶδος, and Bentley removed τε. *Od.* 8. 174 is a similar case. Elsewhere in Homer (forty-two times) the digamma is observed. In *Dem.* 66 the neglect may be due to a junction of formulae at the bucolic diaeresis (but cf. Hoekstra, *Sub-epic Stage*, 53, and notes to *Dem.* 66). *Dem.* 315 is using a Hesiodic 'Catalogue' formula (*Th.* 908, frr. 25. 39, 136. 2; cf. also *Hy.* 12. 2, 32. 16, *Op.* 63, *Th.* 619, *Op.* 714).

One might also mention *Dem.* 37 τόφρα οἱ ἐλπίς. There are no parallels in Homer for neglect with ἐλπίς, but several with ἔλπομαι (cf. ad *Dem.* 35). *Dem.* 37 is, however, a suspect line.

The use of the digamma is therefore demonstrably traditional, and shows no significant difference from that of Hesiod.

There is, however, a noticeable frequency of contraction after the loss of internal digamma, although again several examples have parallels in Hesiod:

Dem. 50 λουτροῖς (cf. *Op.* 753), 137 τοκῆ(ε)ς (cf. *Il.* 11. 151, *Op.* 248, etc.), 413 ἄκουσαν(?) (cf. 379), and perhaps 347 Ἅιδη (cf. ad loc.). For Hesiod cf. Edwards, 139 n. 53.

One might also note that κόρην (*Dem.* 439; cf. Introduction, p. 55) is partly paralleled by Hesiod's κᾱλόν (*Th.* 585, *Op.* 63), ἴσον (*Op.* 752).

c. *Hoekstra and* nu *movable*

A. Hoekstra's books, *Homeric Modifications of Formulaic Prototypes* and *The Sub-epic Stage of the Formulaic Tradition*, contain many observations of value to students of the *Hymns*. He illustrates the various ways by which the poets have adapted traditional material, and departed from the normal practice of early epic. He concludes his discussion of the *Hymn to Demeter* (*Sub-epic Stage*, 57) by noting the poet's closeness to Hesiod rather than Homer, but adds that he 'treats epic diction as a living organism' (o.c. 57). This is a guarded statement, but it definitely suggests that the *Hymn*, although it represents a later stage of epic development than Homer (cf. *Sub-epic Stage*, chap. I), belongs still to a genuinely creative epic tradition, rather than one that is purely imitative. On the question whether or not the poets of the *Hymns* used the aid of writing in composition he is wisely cautious, regarding it as 'not impossible' (o.c. 17 n. 17), but incapable of proof.

In his earlier book, Hoekstra discusses *inter alia* the use of *nu* movable (*Homeric Modifications*, 71 ff.; cf. Fr. Isler, *Quaestiones Metricae* (Diss. Greifswald, 1908)). Isler's figures show that whereas the frequency of *nu* used to avoid hiatus is approximately the same in later poetry as in Homer, its use to lengthen the preceding syllable before a consonant becomes increasingly *less* common in Alexandrian and later hexameter poetry, until finally with Nonnus it virtually disappears (one example only in 4,514 verses). In this latter respect the *Hymn to Demeter* is closer to Homer than to either Hesiod or the *Hymns* to Apollo and Hermes,[1] but obviously no chronological significance can be attached to this fact (cf. Hoekstra, 76 f.). Lengthening in the first thesis with *nu* movable occurs seven times in the *Hymn to Demeter*, three of these with κεν. The first five hundred lines of the *Odyssey* show the same proportions, although lengthening in this position is commoner in the *Hymn* than the *Odyssey* as a whole, and commoner in the *Odyssey* than the *Iliad*.[2] Hesiod, on the other hand, has only 3 examples in 1850 lines.

Hoekstra also considers that cases of enjambement where the runover word has movable *nu* may be indicative of 'evolutionary' tendencies (*Homeric Modifications*, 85 ff., 101 ff.). He notes that *Demeter* has several examples, all with verbs (*Sub-epic Stage*, 27 n. 17, 55). These include seven where *nu* avoids hiatus (25, 45, 86, 193, 235, 376, 454),

---

[1] Cf. Hoekstra, o.c. 76, and Isler, o.c. The proportions are: Homer 1 in 21·8 lines, Hesiod 1 in 30, *Demeter* 1 in 20·7, *Apollo* 1 in 26·6, *Hermes* 1 in 41·4, *Aphrodite* 1 in 18·5.

[2] *Iliad* 1 in 224, *Odyssey* 1 in 127, *Demeter* 1 in 69 (but *Od.* 1. 1–2. 56: 7 times, 3 with κεν).

as well as three where it lengthens the syllable (3, 23, 430). Although we have already noticed the unusual frequency of necessary enjambement in the *Hymn*, it seems to me doubtful whether the use of *nu movable* here is really significant.

D. *Oral poetry and the use of writing*

This survey should suffice to demonstrate that one cannot rely on such tests alone to establish a chronology of early epic. The *Hymn to Hermes*, in particular, shows clearly that the evidence is contradictory if treated in this sense. I should myself prefer to regard this *Hymn*'s peculiarities as due partly to its very different subject-matter, but probably also to its belonging to a different branch of the epic tradition (cf. also Hoekstra, *Sub-epic Stage*, 18 n. 23). One is tempted to go further and speak of the poet's own personal style and use of his tradition, and there is no doubt that the four major hymns do have noticeable differences of style, as well as similarities. This might at least partially account for the poet's fondness for enjambement in the *Hymn to Demeter*, a feature which accords with the rapidity of narrative which we have noticed in parts of the poem (cf. Introduction, pp. 60 f.).

Kirk has recently (*YCS* 20 (1966), 155 ff.) criticized the use of quantitative analysis of formulae by itself as a means for determining whether a composer used writing or not, and also the naïve assumption that there are only *two* simple alternatives here (cf. especially 173 f.). As he says, one must take into account other criteria, 'signs such as the observation of formular economy, the naturalness of formular extension and articulation, and the preservation of traditional details of rhythm and enjambement'. The first of these has been discussed in the Introduction (pp. 46 ff.), and the second also, more briefly. It is my own personal view that the *Hymn* does not go much beyond the freedom of Hesiod in these respects, just as it shows remarkable similarities to Hesiod in the various classes of linguistic features discussed above. In its use of typical scenes also, the *Hymn* is remarkably traditional in view of its novelty of subject (cf. Introduction, pp. 58 f.).

Against this one may set the possibility that the poet is aware of, and echoes, particular passages in the poems of Homer and Hesiod, rather than simply drawing from a common tradition of formulae (cf. Introduction, pp. 31 ff.). Does this necessarily imply that he is no longer an 'oral poet', or that he uses writing as an aid to composition? I do not think that one can frame the question in such simple terms.

The real problem, as Kirk points out (o.c. 174), is that 'literate composition has come to stand as the only alternative to oral poetry.

M

Yet "oral poetry" itself is far too imprecise an expression . . .' He suggests an alternative distinction, 'between natural composition in a formular tradition . . . and deliberate, self-conscious composition in a formular style, whether with the aid of writing or not'. I am not sure that this makes the problem much clearer. But there is no doubt that far too much emphasis has recently been placed on the question of the use of writing, and there are too many possible ambiguities here. It is, for example, sometimes assumed that an 'oral poet' always extemporizes, i.e. composes as he recites: but that is nonsense. In fact, 'oral composition' is a misleading expression: no one *composes* orally. Conversely, a literate author does not necessarily require pen and paper in order to compose. Both literate and illiterate poets premeditate, although the technique of the latter does assist them at the time of recitation. Equally, a literate author may compose primarily for recitation, rather than to be read. Here, the really significant change did not come until the fifth century B.C.,[1] and this is reflected in the difference of style between, say, Herodotus and Thucydides.

There is no doubt that the longer hymns, at least, were composed for recitation, and it is equally clear that their authors were using the traditional techniques of earlier epic composition. Whether any of them could himself write or not is probably of secondary importance.[2]

[1] Cf. R. Pfeiffer, *A History of Classical Scholarship* (Oxford, 1968), 25 ff.; E. A. Havelock, *Prologue to Greek Literacy* (University of Cincinnati, 1971), especially 58 ff.
[2] The blind singer of *Ap.* 146 ff. was presumably an 'oral poet', although he may have dictated his songs.

APPENDIX III

SCENES OF MEETING
(Cf. notes to Dem. 98 ff.)

A. *Structural parallels*

1. *Encounter*

Dem. 98 ἕζετο δ' ἐγγὺς ὁδοῖο   ~ *Od.* 6. 295a ἔνθα καθεζόμενος
                                      291b ἄγχι κελεύθου

[177 κοίλην κατ' ἀμαξιτόν]   10. 103–4 λείην ὁδόν, ᾗ περ
                                        ἄμαξαι . . . καταγίνεον ὕλην (~
                                        17. 204–5)

99b ὅθεν ὑδρεύοντο πολῖται   = 17. 206b (7. 131) ~ 10. 108
                                        ἔνθεν γὰρ ὕδωρ προτὶ ἄστυ
                                        φέρεσκον

100 ἐν σκιῇ, αὐτὰρ ὕπερθε πεφύκει ~ 13. 102 τανίφυλλος ἐλαίη ~ 372
θάμνος ἐλαίης   (6. 291 ἀγλαὸν ἄλσος, 17. 208
                                        αἰγείρων . . . ἄλσος)

101 γρηῒ παλαιγενέϊ ἐναλίγκιος . . . ~ 7. 20a παρθενικῇ εἰκυῖα νεήνιδι . . .
                                        13. 222 ἀνδρὶ δέμας εἰκυῖα νέῳ . . .
                                        (*Ap.* 449–50, *Aph.* 82)

103–4 οἷαί τε τροφοί εἰσι θεμιστο- ~ 13. 223 οἷοί τε ἀνάκτων παῖδες
πόλων βασιλήων | παίδων . . .   ἔασι
(~ *Dem.* 214–15)

105 τὴν δὲ ἴδον . . . θύγατρες   ~ 7. 19a ἔνθα οἱ ἀντεβόλησε θεὰ . . .

106 ἐρχόμεναι μεθ' ὕδωρ . . . ὄφρα ~ 10. 105 κούρῃ δὲ ξύμβλητο πρὸ
φέροιεν   ἄστεος ὑδρευούσῃ
    107b φίλα πρὸς δώματα πατρός   (10. 108 above)

107a κάλπισι χαλκείῃσι   ~ 7. 20b κάλπιν ἐχούσῃ

108 (τέσσαρες) ὥς τε θεαὶ κουρήϊον ~ 7. 19–20 (above)
ἄνθος ἔχουσαι

111 οὐδ' ἔγνων· χαλεποὶ δὲ θεοὶ ~ 13. 312 ἀργαλέον σε, θεά, γνῶναι
θνητοῖσιν ὁρᾶσθαι   βροτῷ ἀντιάσαντι

112 ἀγχοῦ δ' ἱστάμεναι   ~ 7. 21 στῆ δὲ πρόσθ' αὐτοῦ
                                  10. 107 οἱ δὲ παριστάμενοι (13.
                                    221, 226)

      ἔπεα πτερόεντα προσηύδων   ~13. 228b etc.

2. *Speech of Celeus' daughters*

113 τίς πόθεν ἐccὶ . . .   ~ *Ap.* 452 ὦ ξεῖνοι τίνες ἐcτέ; πόθεν
                                  πλεῖθ᾽ ὑγρὰ κέλευθα;
114 τίπτε δὲ . . .   ~ *Ap.* 456 τίφθ᾽ οὕτως . . .

Normally the suppliant is the first to speak. (On *Od.* 15. 264 cf.
Page, *Homeric Odyssey*, 84, Merkelbach, *Untersuchungen zur Odyssee*, 69 f.)

3. *Reply of Demeter*

118 On this unusual answer-formula cf. ad loc.

119 ⎱ τέκνα φίλ᾽ . . .   ~ 7. 22 ὦ τέκος . . .
138 ⎰ φίλα τέκνα   13. 228 ὦ φίλ᾽ . . .

119 αἵ τινές ἐcτε . . . (cf. ad loc.) ~ *Aph.* 92 χαῖρε, ἄναςς᾽, ἥ τις . . .
120 χαίρετ᾽ . . .   ἱκάνεις
                                Ap. 464–6 ξεῖν᾽ . . . οὐλέ τε καὶ
                                μέγα χαῖρε . . .
                                13. 229 χαῖρέ τε . . .

120 ff. Demeter tells a 'false tale': cf. ad loc.·

123 Κρήτηθεν   ~ 13. 256, *Ap.* 470

133 οὕτω δεῦρ᾽ ἱκόμην ἀλαλη- ~ (13. 303 νῦν αὖ δεῦρ᾽ ἱκόμην)
μένη . . .   6. 175–6 cὲ γὰρ κακὰ πολλὰ
                                μογήςας | ἐς πρώτην ἱκόμην
                                7. 24–5 καὶ γὰρ ἐγὼ ξεῖνος
                                ταλαπείριος ἐνθάδ᾽ ἱκάνω |
                                τηλόθεν ἐξ ἀπίης γαίης (~ *Ap.*
                                469 ff.)

133b οὐδέ τι οἶδα   ~ 6. 176–7 τῶν δ᾽ ἄλλων οὔ τινα
134 ἥ τις δὴ γαῖ᾽ ἐcτὶ καὶ οἵ τινες   οἶδα | ἀνθρώπων οἳ τήνδε πόλιν
ἐγγεγάαςιν   καὶ γαῖαν ἔχουcιν.
                                7. 25–6 (13. 233, *Ap.* 468)

135 ἀλλ᾽ ὑμῖν μὲν πάντες Ὀλύμπια ~ 6. 180 ff. coὶ δὲ θεοὶ τόca δοῖεν ὅca
δώματ᾽ ἔχοντες   φρεcὶ cῇcι μενοινᾷς, | ἄνδρα τε καὶ
136 δοῖεν κουριδίους ἄνδρας καὶ   οἶκον καὶ ὁμοφροσύνην ὀπάςειαν |
τέκνα τεκέςθαι   ἐcθλὴν . . . (*Ap.* 466)
137a ὡς ἐθέλουcι τοκῆς

137b ἐμὲ δ᾽ αὖτ᾽ οἰκτείρατε κοῦραι ~ 6. 175 ἀλλά, ἄναςς᾽, ἐλέαιρε
                              (13. 229 ff.)

(Lacuna)

138 προφονέως φίλα τέκνα τέων ~ 7. 22–3 ὦ τέκος, οὐκ ἄν
πρὸς δώμαθ᾽ ἵκωμαι   μοι δόμον ἀνέρος ἡγήcαιο |
                                Ἀλκινόου

139 ἀνέρος ἠδὲ γυναικὸς . . .　　　∼ 6. 184 ἀνὴρ ἠδὲ γυνή
　　(cf. ad loc.)　　　　　　　　　　15. 509–10 πῇ γὰρ ἐγώ, φίλε
　　　　　　　　　　　　　　　　　　τέκνον, ἴω; τεῦ δώμαθ' ἵκωμαι |
Dem. 150–2 ∼　　　　　　　　　　ἀνδρῶν οἳ κραναὴν 'Ιθάκην κάτα
　　　　　　　　　　　　　　　　　κοιρανέουσιν; (6. 119 = 13. 200,
　　　　　　　　　　　　　　　　　10. 109–10)

4. Reply of Callidice

145 φῆ ῥα θεά· τὴν δ' αὐτίκ' ἀμεί-　∼ 6. 109*, 228* (Nausicaa)
βετο παρθένος ἀδμής　　　　　　　Aph. 82 παρθένῳ ἀδμήτῃ . . .
　　(cf. ad loc.)　　　　　　　　　ὁμοίη (7. 20 παρθενικῇ . . .
　　　　　　　　　　　　　　　　　νεήνιδι)

147 Μαῖα (∼ 113 γρηΰ) θεῶν μὲν　∼ 7. 28 ξεῖνε πάτερ . . .
δῶρα καὶ ἀχνύμενοί περ ἀνάγκῃ　　(6. 187 ξεῖν')
148 τέτλαμεν ἄνθρωποι· δὴ γὰρ　　6. 188–90 Ζεὺς δ' αὐτὸς νέμει
πολὺ φέρτεροί εἰσιν　　　　　　　ὄλβον . . .
　　　　　　　　　　　　　　　　　σὲ δὲ χρὴ τετλάμεν ἔμπης

149 ταῦτα δέ τοι σαφέως ὑποθή-　　6. 190 ff. νῦν δ' . . . ἄστυ δέ τοι
σομαι ἠδ' ὀνομήνω　　　　　　　δείξω, ἐρέω δέ τοι οὔνομα
150 ἀνέρας οἷσιν ἔπεστι μέγα　　　λαῶν . . .
κράτος ἐνθάδε τιμῆς (cf. above)　　6. 197 τοῦ δ' ἐκ Φαιήκων ἔχεται
　　　　　　　　　　　　　　　　　κάρτος τε βίη τε (15. 510 above,
　　　　　　　　　　　　　　　　　7. 22–3, 28–9, 10. 110–11)

159 δὴ γὰρ θεοείκελός ἐσσι　　　∼ Ap. 464–5, 6. 149 ff., 13. 230–1,
　　　　　　　　　　　　　　　　　Aph. 92 ff.

160 εἰ δ' ἐθέλεις, ἐπίμεινον, ἵνα　∼ 6. 295–6 μεῖναι χρόνον, εἰς ὅ κεν
πρὸς δώματα πατρὸς　　　　　　ἡμεῖς | ἄστυδε ἔλθωμεν καὶ ἱκώ-
161 ἔλθωμεν . . .　　　　　　　　μεθα δώματα πατρός

167 ῥεῖά(?) κέ τίς σε ἰδοῦσα . . .　∼ 15. 537–8 = 17. 164–5 (Theo-
168 ζηλώσαι· τόσα κέν τοι ἀπὸ　　clymenus) = 19. 310–11 (Odys-
θρεπτήρια δοίη　　　　　　　　　seus) τῷ κε τάχα γνοίης φιλότητά
　　　　　　　　　　　　　　　　τε πολλά τε δῶρα | ἐξ ἐμεῦ, ὡς ἄν
　　　　　　　　　　　　　　　　τίς σε συναντόμενος μακαρίζοι

5. The girls go to the palace, while Demeter waits (169–78 ∼ Od. 7. 2 ff.)

[177 κοίλην κατ' ἀμαξιτόν . . .　　∼ 10. 103–4 above]

6. They lead her to the palace (cf. also ad 180 ff.)

179 τέτμον δ' ἐγγὺς ὁδοῦ κυδρὴν
θεὸν . . . Cf. ad 98, 105

180–1 αὐτὰρ ἔπειτα φίλα πρὸς
δώματα πατρὸς | ἡγεῦνθ', ἡ δ' ~ 7. 37–8 ἡγήσατο Παλλὰς Ἀθήνη |
ἄρ' ὄπισθε . . .   καρπαλίμως· ὁ δ' ἔπειτα μετ'
182 στεῖχε . . .   ἴχνια βαῖνε θεοῖο (~ Ap. 514 ff.)

184 αἶψα δὲ δώμαθ' ἵκοντο διο- ~ 7. 46 ἀλλ' ὅτε δὴ βασιλῆος ἀγα-
τρεφέος Κελεοῖο   κλυτὰ δώμαθ' ἵκοντο . . .

185 βὰν δὲ δι' αἰθούσης ἔνθα σφίσι ~ 6. 304–5 ὦκα μάλα μεγάροιο
πότνια μήτηρ   διελθέμεν, ὄφρ' ἂν ἵκηαι | μητέρ'
                                    ἐμὴν . . .
                                    7. 139–41 αὐτὰρ ὁ βῆ διὰ δῶμα . . .
                                    ὄφρ' ἵκετ' Ἀρήτην . . . (~ 6. 50,
                                    10. 112–13)

186 ἧστο παρὰ σταθμὸν τέγεος ~ 6. 305 ἡ δ' ἧσται ἐπ' ἐσχάρῃ ἐν
πύκα ποιητοῖο . . .   πυρὸς αὐγῇ (~ 6. 52)

188 ἡ δ' ἄρ' ἐπ' οὐδὸν ἔβη ποσὶ . . . ~ 7. 135 καρπαλίμως δ' ὑπὲρ οὐδὸν
                                    ἐβήσετο . . .

On 188–211 cf. ad loc. (188 ff., 192 ff.) ; on 213 ff. (~ Od. 6. 187 ff.,
Ap. 464 ff.) cf. ad loc.

B. *Parallels with Od. 13. 96 ff.*

Od. 13. 102 τανίφυλλος ἐλαίη   ~ Dem. 100 (cf. ad loc.)
~ 346 (122, 372)

113–14 ἡ μὲν ἔπειτα | ἠπείρῳ ~ 125 ff. οἱ μὲν ἔπειτα . . . ἠπείρου
ἐπέκελσεν   ἐπέβησαν

198–9   ~ Dem. 245, 247

200 . . . τέων αὖτε βροτῶν ἐς ~ 138 τέων πρὸς δώμαθ' ἵκωμαι (cf.
γαῖαν ἱκάνω;   ad loc.)

211 οἵ μ' εἰς ἄλλην γαῖαν ἀπήγαγον ~ 125 ἄνδρες ληϊστῆρες ἀπήγαγον

223 οἷοί τε ἀνάκτων παῖδες ἔασι ~ 103–4 οἷαί τε τροφοί εἰσι . . .
                                βασιλήων | παίδων (cf. above)

228–9   ~ 119–20 (cf. above)

229–33   ~ 135–8 (cf. ad Dem. 137)

231 ὥς τε θεῷ*   ~ 108 ὥς τε θεαί (cf. above)

233 τίς γῆ, . . . τίνες ἀνέρες ἐγγε- ~ 134 (cf. above)
γάασιν;

254–5   cf. ad Dem. 120–1

256–7 ἐν Κρήτῃ εὐρείῃ | τηλοῦ ~ 123–4 νῦν αὖτε Κρήτηθεν ἐπ'
ὑπὲρ πόντου· νῦν δ' εἰλήλουθα καὶ εὐρέα νῶτα θαλάσσης | ἤλυθον . . .
αὐτός

268 ἐγγὺς ὁδοῖο   ~ *Dem.* 98

277 πόλλ' ἀεκαζομένους, οὐδ' ~ 124 οὐκ ἐθέλουσα, βίῃ δ' ἀέκουσαν
ἤθελον . . .   ἀνάγκῃ

279–80 οὐδέ τις ἡμῖν | δόρπου ~ 129 ἀλλ' ἐμοὶ οὐ δόρποιο . . . ἤρατο
μνῆςτις ἔην   θυμός

303 (Athena) νῦν αὖ δεῦρ' ἱκόμην* ~ 133 οὕτω δεῦρ' ἱκόμην

307 cὺ δὲ τετλάμεναι καὶ ἀνάγκῃ ~ 147–8 καὶ ἀχνύμενοί περ ἀνάγκῃ |
                                         τέτλαμεν

309 (~ 333) ἦλθες ἀλώμενος ~ 133 ἀλαλημένη

312 ἀργαλέον cε, θεά, γνῶναι ~ 111 χαλεποὶ δὲ θεοὶ θνητοῖcιν
βροτῷ . . .   ὁρᾶcθαι

351 ὄρος καταειμένον ὕλῃ   ~ 386 ὄρος κάτα δάcκιον ὕλῃ

367 μαιομένη*   ~ 44 μαιομένη

391–2 cὺν coί, πότνα θεά, . . . τὸν ~ 118b ἀμείβετο πότνα θεάων (cf.
δ' ἠμείβετ' ἔπειτα θεὰ . . .   ad loc.)

APPENDIX IV

THE CYCEON (*Dem.* 208 ff.)

Cf. A. Delatte, *Le Cycéon. Breuvage rituel des Mysterès d'Éleusis* (Paris, 1955)

A κυκεών was any form of mixture of grain (ἄλφι) and liquid (water, wine, milk, honey, oil), often seasoned with herbs (pennyroyal, thyme, mint, etc.). It belongs to an intermediate stage between that of eating the grains (or offering them to the gods) whole, and the introduction of fine milling and baking. At this stage they were lightly pounded and then sprinkled on the liquid (cf. *Il.* 11. 640 and ad *Dem.* 208). Its religious use suggests its antiquity, and one may compare the related, more solid forms of offering, πελανός, ψαιστά, θυ(α)λήματα, etc. (Ziehen, *RE* 19. 246 ff.). In Homer it is used as a means of refreshment, and as a simple form of hospitality (cf. ad *Dem.* 180 ff.). Thus it is prepared for Nestor and the wounded Machaon to revive them after the battle (*Il.* 11. 624–41), and Circe welcomes Odysseus and his companions with a drugged κυκεών (*Od.* 10. 234 ff., 316 f.). Cf. also the possible, but disputed example in the Shield, *Il.* 18. 560, where the women prepare a meal for the labourers, sprinkling λεύκ' ἄλφιτα πολλά.

In later times its use becomes restricted to the poorer classes, and to certain medicinal purposes, and it becomes a symbol of frugality (as when Heraclitus drinks one to show the need for economy: Plut. *de garrul.* 17=*Mor.* 511 b, Themist. *de virt.* p. 40, Scholl. BT ad *Il.* 10. 149, Diels–Kranz, *Vorsokr.* i. 144), or of the rustic life (Ar. *Pax* 1169, Thphr. *Char.* 4. 1; cf. Hipponax fr. 39 West. Cf. also Call. fr. 260. 46, with H. Lloyd-Jones and J. Rea, *HSCP* 72 (1967), 132 and 141–2). Hence Delatte (34 f.) suggested that it belongs to the Orphic version of the myth, in which Demeter's hosts are poor rustics. But the Homeric parallels make this unlikely.

For its medicinal uses cf. Delatte 28 f. The *Corpus Hippocraticum* mentions many different types, not all of which have herbs added. The type given to Demeter is recommended in Ar. *Pax* 712 to Trygaeus as a cure for the harm that his wife Opora may cause him. In Hipponax (l.c. above) the cyceon is a φάρμακον for the poet's πονηρίη ('poverty', but with a play on the physical sense: cf. LSJ Supplement s.v.). γλήχων (pennyroyal) was in fact believed to cure a wide range of ailments in ancient times (burning thirst, fainting, headaches, coughs, indigestion, fevers, nervous troubles, etc.) and was called *omnimorbia* in Latin (cf. Dioscor. *MM* 3. 31, Plin. *NH* 20. 152, 156, Ps. Apul. *Herbarius* 93, *Carmen graecum de virtut. herb.* 12). Cf. Delatte o.c. 38–40, H. Leclerc, 'Les vieilles panacées: le pouliot', in *Bull. des sciences pharmacologiques* 39 (1932), 184–90; and *Précis de phytothérapie*[3] (1935), 148.

Modern scholars have attempted to find an ulterior motive for its use at Eleusis. Thus cf. Baumeister, p. 306: 'fortasse autem in hac herba inesse credebatur vis quaedam genitalis vel aphrodisiaca'; R. Pettazzoni, *I misteri*, § 49: 'boisson excitante et peut-être légèrement enivrante pour celui qui était à jeun'. Other scholars confuse it with opium (cf. Ov. *F.* 4. 531, where Ceres takes poppy-juice): O. E. Briem, *Les Sociétés secrètes à mystères*, 223, 259; M. J. Lagrange, *Rev. Bibl.* 38 (1929), 73; V. Magnien, *Les Mystères d'Éleusis*[2], 86. More recently Kerényi in *Initiation* (Studies in the History of Religions, X, ed. C. J. Bleeker (Brill, 1965)), 62 ff., and *Eleusis*, Appendix I, put forward the theory that the barley-grains were fermented,[1] and that the γληχών may have also had a special effect, perhaps narcotic. He quotes pharmacological support for its use today to make a soothing drink, or as a mild stimulant. In large doses it can induce delirium, loss of consciousness, and spasms. He argues that the combination of the two ingredients might lead to hallucinations in persons whose sensibility was heightened by fasting. They would thus be 'prepared' in a physical sense for receiving the visions of the Telesterion.

There is however nothing to suggest that the Cyceon was ever fermented, and the amount of pennyroyal used cannot have had any very pronounced effects. After a period of fasting, it probably soothed and refreshed the initiates, and sustained them for what was to come. (It has been compared to peppermint tea, which is still used today for such purposes!) Cf. Schol. B ad *Il.* 11. 624 (discussing whether the cyceon was intended here as a medicine or merely for refreshment): ἔστι δὲ δίψους ἴαμα ὁ κυκεών . . . τοῖς κακοπαθοῦσι γὰρ ἐπιτήδειος ὁ κυκεὼν τροφὴν ἅμα καὶ πότον ἔχων . . . [Πορφυρίου] . . . τὸ τοῖς κεκμηκόσι σκευαζόμενον πότον.[2]

The period of fasting, especially if it was combined with the exertions of the Iacchus procession, and the dancing and other ceremonies of the pannychis which followed, might well put the initiates in a very excited and receptive condition (cf. P. Gerlitz, in *Initiation*, 279). The Cyceon, on the other hand, may have calmed them and thus

---

[1] Suggested by Skias, *Eph. Arch.* 1901, 19 ff., who was criticized by Svoronos *JIAN* 4 (1901), 179, and Leonard, *RE* 11. 323 s.v. Kernos.

[2] The Latin equivalent *polenta* (cf. Ov. *M.* 5. 449 f., 454, where Ceres drinks it) was, however, accorded magical and apotropaic powers (cf. Maass, *ARW* 21 (1922), 261 f., Wünsch, *Glotta* 2 (1910), 219 ff., 398).

helped to put them in the right frame of mind for the Mystery revelations.

A number of other theories have been put forward as to the significance of the Cyceon at Eleusis (cf. Delatte, 45 ff., for a survey of these). The simplest, favoured by Delatte himself, is that it was originally merely the means of ending the fast, and only later acquired any religious significance. Others see in it a symbol of the initiate's attachment to Demeter. In following her example, he became her protégé and disciple (cf. Foucart, *Les Mystères*, 377 ff.; W. F. Otto, 'Der Sinn der eleusinischen Mysterien', *Eranos-Jahrb.* 1939, 108; M. Brillant, *Les Mystères d'Éleusis*, 89 ff.). A more widely held view regards it as a form of communion with the goddess, originally by absorption of the 'corn-spirit' (cf. Jevons, *Introduction to the History of Religion* (1896), 365 ff., Frazer, *GB*³ vii. 37 ff., 161). This primitive 'agricultural' ritual developed a deeper eschatological significance in the course of time (cf. Wehrli, *ARW* 31 (1934), 89 ff.; Loisy, *Les Mystères païens et le mystère chrétien*, 69). Thus Diels (*Neues Jahrb. f. klass. Alt.* 1 (1922), 244) regarded it as a sacrament taken in the Telesterion. Cf. also Dieterich, *Mithrasliturgie*, 102 ff., 170.

These theories are criticized by Farnell, *Cults*, iii. 195 ff., Foucart, o.c. 380 ff., Allen and Halliday ad *Dem.* 208, Delatte, o.c. 47 ff., Eitrem, *Symb. Osl.* 20 (1940), 139, 141. Certainly, any view which accords a central significance to the Cyceon in the Mysteries must be false, since it formed part of the preliminary ritual. There is also no evidence that the initiates regarded themselves as participating in the substance of the deity. Its constitution rather suggests comparison on the one hand with the various forms of offering made from barley or other types of grain, ψαιcτά, πελανόc, ὑγίεια, etc. (cf. above, also Maass l.c., and especially the πελανόc of wheat and barley offered to the Goddesses at Eleusis, Ziehen, *RE* 19. 246 ff.). On the other hand, consumption by the worshipper makes it resemble the various types of πανcπερμία (cf. Nilsson, *Gesch.* i³. 127 ff.), e.g. the πεντάπλοα given to the victor at the Oschophoria (described as a cyceon by Delatte, 35; cf. Deubner, *AF* 142 ff.), and especially the contents of the κέρνος, which was used at Eleusis and is probably to be identified with the vessels carried on the Niinnion tablet (cf. Mylonas, *Eleusis*, 213 ff., Fig. 88), portrayed on Eleusinian monuments and coins, and found in some quantity at Eleusis (cf. Mylonas, o.c. 221 f., Leonard, *RE* 11. 271 ff.). One type of these contained many small cups (κοτυλίcκοι) holding different kinds of grain, seeds, and other things.[1] After they

---

[1] Polemon has 2 lists. The longer one contains beans and wine, and presumably was not used at Eleusis, since beans were forbidden to the initiates (cf. Paus. 1. 37. 4, 8. 15. 3 f.), and for abstention from wine cf. ad *Dem.* 207. However, some of the

had been carried round (in a dance? cf. Poll. 4. 103) their contents
were tasted (cf. Polemon ap. Ath. 11. 476 ef, 478 cd). This probably
took place at Eleusis during the pannychis after the Iacchus procession (cf. the Niinnion tablet).[1]

Such a πανσπερμία represented the grain which had been sown or
harvested, and its purpose is described by Nilsson (*Gesch.* i³. 129) as
'fruchtbarkeitfördernd und segenbringend'. Maass (l.c. above) described the effect of the Cyceon as 'heilsam'. Delatte compared the
cakes eaten at Christian festivals (cf. M. Höfler, *ARW* 12 (1909),
342 ff.). On this interpretation, drinking the Cyceon was basically
an 'agricultural' ritual, but the significance of this extended beyond
the life of the fields to that of the individual worshipper, promising
him happiness and prosperity (as the *aischrologia* which accompanied
it may have symbolized his hopes of a new life). At the same time,
the initiate will have felt that he was following the example of the
goddess, sharing her food as well as her fast, and performing an act
that had been 'consecrated' by her (cf. ad *Dem.* 211 ὁσίης ἕνεκεν).

On the relationship between the agricultural and deeper religious significance of the Mysteries in general see also Introduction,
pp. 14 ff.

In art, the drinking of the Cyceon has been thought to be portrayed
on the black-figure vase in the Naples Museum (Beazley, *ABV*,
p. 338/3 = Metzger, *Recherches*, p. 28, No. 64, Pl. IX 3), which shows
a man and a woman seated on a *kline*, with a table in front piled with
food, and underneath a basket of loaves. They wear crowns of myrtle
(cf. Delatte, o.c. 58) and are designated *MYCTA*. A third person,
presumably a priest, holding a bundle of twigs in his left hand and
standing by a little shrine, offers them a cylix.

The circumstances, however, especially the table piled with food,
do not suit the little we know about the Cyceon. More probably it
represents a 'private' mystery-cult of the type referred to in Pl. *Rep.*
364 b ff.[2]

κέρνοι found at Eleusis have many very small cups, far too shallow to contain
anything, around a large central one, which perhaps held the κυκεών. See below.

[1] It is possible that the cyceon was actually contained in the κέρνος. Cf. Kerényi,
Eleusis, 182, 185; also Skias, *Eph. Arch.* 1901, 15 f., 20 f. But see Leonard, o.c.
Nilsson, *Op. Sel.* ii. 560, thought the cyceon was contained in the vessel held by
the goddess in the lowest scene of the Niinnion pinax. But see Delatte, 59.

[2] Cf. Petersen, *Arch. Epigr. Mitt. Öst. Ung.* 6 (1882), 58, F. de Waele, *The Magic
Staff* (Gent, 1927), 149. Cf. also, in favour of identification with the Cyceon, Harrison,
Prolegomena, 156 f. ('some ceremony like the drinking of the *kykeon*'), Farnell, *Cults*,
iii. 240, Pl. 15. 6, Brillant, *Les Mystères*, 89, Roussel, *BCH* 54 (1930), 73, Allen
and Halliday ad loc., Delatte, 58. *Contra*: Noack, *Eleusis*, 231 n. 3, Deubner, *AF*
80 n. 8. Metzger, *Recherches*, 29 f., identifies the scene with an Eleusinian ritual, but
considers that the priest must be offering wine to the couple.

On the other possible representations cf. Delatte, 56 ff. He argues against Dugas's identification of the ritual of the Cyceon on vases portraying the departure of Triptolemus on his mission.

It is by no means certain that the cyceon in Eupolis' *Demoi* (Page, *GLP* i, p. 212) is that of the Mysteries. (The supplement μυcτηρικ]ῶν in v. 67 is very improbable.) Cf. Delatte, 36 f.

On Herondas, 9. 13 (quoted by Allen and Halliday with Crusius's reading) cf. Headlam–Knox ad loc.

APPENDIX V

THE POSITION OF θεά (ETC.) IN THE VERSE
(Cf. Dem. 28, 34, 82, 145, etc.)

In the course of an illuminating discussion of Hermann Fränkel's theory of colon structure of the hexameter,[1] L. E. Rossi notes the preference of disyllabic forms of θεός and θεά for a position after the third trochee, or less commonly the second trochee. He points out that θεά normally forms a separate colon in these positions, and so carries more emphasis. The *Hymn to Demeter* is unusual in this respect, as it has several examples of such forms after the first trochee. It is striking that θεά occurs three times in this position (*Dem.* 34, 82, 145). In two of these (34 and 145) it is nominative. There are no other instances in Homer or the *Hymns*, out of 117 examples of this form. In the vocative it occurs five times in the *Iliad* (10. 462, 15. 93, 206, 18. 182, 23. 770), once in the *Odyssey* (5. 215, in 49 examples), and four times in the other *Hymns*, always χαῖρε θεά (*Aph.* 292, 10. 4, 11. 5, 13. 3).

The nominative examples follow a verb, and this is also unusual. Disyllabic forms of θεός and θεά, when they occur in this position, usually follow a conjunction or pronoun, rarely a noun, preposition, adverb, or verb (excluding χαῖρε, κλῦθι θεά).[2] This use with a verb occurs again at *Dem.* 28 (ἧϲτο θεῶν) and 279 (λάμπε θεᾶς). It should be noted that *Dem.* 28, 34, 279 all involve necessary enjambement, which is unusually common in this hymn.

It is interesting to tabulate the frequency of instances of such forms of θεός and θεά after the first trochee in Homer and the *Hymns*, as a proportion of the total number of disyllabic forms:

> *Iliad* 23 in 431 (*c.* 1 in 19)
> *Odyssey* 21 in 361 (*c.* 1 in 17)
> *Hymn to Demeter* 7 in 36 (*c.* 1 in 5)[3]
> Other hymns 15 in 88 (*c.* 1 in 6).

The *Hymns* as a whole thus show a marked increase in such instances.

Rossi also discusses the use of monosyllabic aorist and imperfect verb forms in Homer, showing that they normally form a separate

---

[1] *Studi Urbinati* 39 (1965), 239 ff. See especially pp. 249 ff.
[2] With a noun *Il.* 8. 2, 16. 120, *Hy.* 23. 1; with preposition *Il.* 1. 339, 12. 466; with adverb *Il.* 10. 556, *Od.* 4. 755; with verb *Il.* 1. 310, 13. 154.
[3] i.e. *Dem.* 28, 34, 82, 145, 147, 216, 279.

colon.[1] Thus *Dem.* 145 φῇ ῥα θεά is also unusual in this respect. In fact φῇ ῥα with a noun as a single colon occurs only here! The nearest parallel is *Il.* 22. 77 ἦ ῥ' ὁ γέρων, which is also a unique use of ἦ ῥα.

[1] O.c. 260 ff.

ADDENDA

p. 69
The revision of the Athenian Sacred Code in 403–399 B.C. (Sokolowski, *Lois sacrées, Supplément*, No. 10) has a list of sacrifices to Eleusinian heroes which corresponds closely to *Dem.* 153–5 (see notes ad locc.). It is highly likely that there is direct influence from the *Hymn* at work here (cf. Körte, *Glotta* 25 (1936), 137 ff.). But Dolichus appears to be missing (see on *Dem.* 155).

p. 71
Plutarch's account of the myth of Isis, in *De Iside et Osiride*, shows obvious Greek influences, and seems to echo the *Hymn* in several places (see notes on *Dem.* 40 ff., 99, 237 ff., 238).

p. 82
Baubo is associated with Demeter Thesmophoros, and her myth may well reflect the ritual of the Thesmophoria, as Dr. Graf suggests in his work on Orphic poetry and the Eleusinian Mysteries.

p. 164 (*Dem.* 42)
For white worn by initiates see also Nilsson, *HTR* 40 (1947), 170.

p. 164 (*Dem.* 43)
Fr. Dirlmeier (*Sb. Heidelb. Akad.* 1967, 2. Abhandlung) argues that there are no genuine examples in Homer of the belief that gods appear in the form of birds, and that all the supposed instances are really similes.

p. 203 (*Dem.* 176–81)
Asius fr. 13 may not be relevant here, as the reference is perhaps simply to the traditional Ionian ἁβρότης.
For hair worn free in dancing see also E. *IT* 1143 ff., *Phoen.* 1485 ff., Men. *Dysc.* 950 ff.

p. 207 (*Dem.* 185–6)
H. Drerup, in *Griechische Baukunst in geometrischer Zeit* (Göttingen, 1969), 128 ff., argues that there is evidence from the Geometric period for houses on the same plan as the Homeric palaces. See also M. O. Knox, *CQ* 67 (1973) 1 ff.; especially 5 f.

p. 212 (*Dem.* 192–211)
Small votive stools were found in the sanctuaries of Demeter and Core in Cnidus and on the Acrocorinth. Cf. C. T. Newton, *A History of*

Discoveries at Halicarnassus, Cnidus and Branchidae (London, 1863), 392, and R. S. Stroud, *Hesperia* 34 (1965), 19 and Pl. 9c.

p. 302 (*Dem.* 472–3)

There is no need to assume that *Ap.* 136–8 influenced *Dem.* 472–3, or vice versa. But *Dem.* 472–3 does add support to the view that one should transpose *Ap.* 139 to follow 135, reading Δῆλος ἅπαca | ἤνθηc' ὡς ὅτε τε . . . ἄνθεcιν ὕλης | βεβρίθη . . . (cf. Gemoll).

p. 318 n. 2

There is considerable doubt as to the identity of the young man who wears a knee-length chiton and high boots, and carries a torch or torches, on this and other vases. I follow E. Simon, who argues (in *Ant. Kunst* 9 (1966), 89 f.), that he is not Iacchus but Eumolpus.

p. 319 (*Dem.* 489)

For other links between the Lenaea and Eleusis see Deubner, *AF* 125 f. It does not seem necessary to suppose that all these connections are a late development, as is often assumed (e.g. Wilamowitz, *Glaube*, ii. 76 n. 2).

p. 323 (*Dem.* 494)

For a defence of ἀοιδῆc in Hes. *Th.* 48 see Verdenius, *Mnem.* 25 (1972), 244.

INDEXES

[References in all indexes are to page numbers. Figures in bold type refer to the main discussion of the topic.]

I. NAMES AND SUBJECTS

Acaste, 289
Achilles, attempted immortalization, 237 f., 241, 242, 245, 247
Admete, 289
Adonis, 162
Aeschylus and Eleusis, 76
Agelastos Petra, 19, 181, 219 ff.
Agrae, 18, 20, 181, 212 f., 250 f., 289
agriculture and the Mysteries, 13 ff., 301 f.
— and Ploutos, 317
— taught by Demeter to men, 81 f., 195 f., 259 f., 298, 301 f., 346 f.
aischrologia, 22 f., 57, 211, 213 ff., 222, 246 f., 256, 347
Alexandria, cult of Demeter, 23 n. 1, 254
alliteration and assonance, 61, 159, 255 f., 287, 293
Amaterasu, 217
ambrosia, 231, 235, 237 ff.
amphidromia, 231 f.
Ananke, 173, 193 f., 227 f.
Andania, mysteries, 18, 164, 181, 203, 254, 308
— title of Core, 265
Anodos of Core, 84, 141, 155, 221, 264, 285, 295
Anthion, 18 f., 74, 326
Antimachus and the *Hymn*, 69
Antron, 321 f.
Aphrodite, 34, 40 f., 83, 285, 318
— and Adonis, 162
— formulae for, 48 f.
— on altar of Hyacinthus, 83
— plays part in Rape, 138 f., 290
Aqhat, Poem of, 259
Archilochus and cult of Demeter, 75, 213 f., 322
Argos, Demeter claims to come from, 74, 326
— version of Rape at, 174, 178, 196
arrephoria, 234 f.

Artemis, on altar of Hyacinthus, 83
— present at Rape, 67, 73, 79 f., 83, 138, 141, 290 f.
— Propylaea, 155 f., 295, 326
— temples of, 251
Ascalabus, 215, 259
Ascalaphus, 286 f.
Athena, and Erechtheus, 247
— and Erichthonius, 234 f.
— formula for, 48
— on altar of Hyacinthus, 83
— present at Rape, 67, 73, 79 f., 83, 138, 141, 290 f.
— with Eleusinian deities in art, 195, 319 f.
Athens, control of Mysteries, 6 f., 9 f., 85, 189
— knowledge of Homer, 6
— not mentioned in *Hymn*, 6, 189
— use of Eleusinian myths, 195 f., 249
— war with Eleusis, 198, 246
Atticisms, **52 ff.**, 66, 185, 266, 278, 279, 285, 294
attraction of antecedent to case of relative, 172

Baal, myths of, 156, 162, 259
Balletys, 12, 24, 235, **245 ff.**
battles, ritual, 245 ff., 248
Baubo, **80 ff.**, 85, 178, 200, 213, **215 f.**, 322
birds, as messengers, 164
— gods compared to, 164
black clothing worn by Demeter, 59, 163 f., 201
breath, divine, 231, 235 f., 239

calathos, 23
Callichoron, 10, 18 f., 74, 162, 181 f., 215, 220 f., 250, 256, **326 ff.**
Callidice, 179, 183
Calliope, 183, 185
Callirhoe, 18, 181, 250, 289

II. Greek Words and Phrases Discussed

III. SELECT LIST OF PASSAGES DISCUSSED